Readings in Microeconomic Theory

Readings in Microeconomic Theory

Edited by
Manfredi M. A. La Manna
Department of Economics
University of St Andrews
Scotland

The Dryden Press
Harcourt Brace & Company Limited
London   Fort Worth   New York   Orlando
Philadelphia   San Diego   Toronto   Sydney   Tokyo

The Dryden Press
24/28 Oval Road,
London NW1 7DX

This book is printed on acid-free paper.

Copyright © 1997 by The Dryden Press, Harcourt Brace & Company, Limited

A catalogue record for this book is available from the British Library
ISBN 0-03-099059-9

Typeset by Mackreth Media Services, Hemel Hempstead, Herts
Printed in Great Britain by WBC, Bridgend, Mid Glamorgan

Contents

PART VII: OLIGOPOLY: THEORY AND AN APPLICATION

PART VIII: SOCIAL CHOICE

Acknowledgements

This book would have not seen the light of day had it not been for the help, encouragement, and genuine cooperation by an embarrassingly large number of people. In chronological order, I should like to thank Malcolm Sawyer for suggesting that I should edit a reader in Microeconomics, Maggie Smith of Dryden Press for commissioning it and helping out in many subtle ways, current and former colleagues for their many suggestions, various vintages of undergraduate students for providing the acid test of whether an article was as stimulating and rewarding as I thought it was. Last and foremost, all the authors, who not only graciously granted that all-important permission to reprint, but also congratulated me for my good taste in classic articles in microeconomics.

Finally, my special thanks go to the American Economic Association, whose socially optimal policy for the dissemination of knowledge should be an example to other, less enlightened, institutions, which either for carelessness or misplaced greed manage to succeed in harming both authors and the academic community by restricting access to their copyright material.

Introduction

Manfredi M. A. La Manna

HOW TO USE THIS BOOK

Were this a traditional selection of readings there would be no point in burdening the reader with any advice on how to use the book, in so far as the conventional purpose of a selection of articles is to supplement a textbook, by providing examples and applications of the theoretical approaches examined there. And indeed students and lecturers are more than welcome to avail themselves of this volume for this purpose.

In selecting material for this book, however, I have proceeded from the opposite viewpoint, namely the idea that a better, and certainly more interesting, way of teaching and learning microeconomics is by putting the "original article" centre stage, relegating textbooks to a subsidiary role. Article-based teaching, of course, is nothing new—indeed it is the standard mode for *postgraduate* courses. The novelty of the approach is that my selection of readings, while being of interest to more advanced readers, is aimed especially at *undergraduate* courses in microeconomics, where textbook-based learning is the norm both in the USA and in Great Britain.

My justification is simple and can be summarised in one word: *stimulation.* I cannot think of a better way of killing any potential interest in post-introductory microeconomics in the mind of undergraduates than by inflicting a textbook on them. Even the authors of the better microeconomics textbooks would admit that by definition their work cannot compete with the articles on which it is based in terms of intellectual excitement and originality. The intention in writing a microeconomics textbook is inevitably paternalistic and the experience of reading it akin to an initiation: "you, the inexperienced undergraduate, shall not be given direct access to academic journals unless you undergo the pain and the frustration of having to absorb unadorned theory and carefully abridged versions of the relevant literature". I take the different view that the inexperienced microeconomics student can only digest the necessary theoretical apparatus if he or she is stimulated into expending the required

All articles and chapters are reproduced in their entirety; misprints have been removed and references updated.

effort by direct exposure to the original research. I believe that the increasingly desperate attempts by textbook authors to make the text more interesting by the insertion of ever more colourful diagrams, tables and boxes, peppered with summaries of articles and even potted biographies of eminent economists, simply miss the point: however spiced-up, no textbook can reproduce the intellectual excitement of a classic article.

Article-based teaching has another advantage in addition to intellectual stimulation, namely, *flexibility*. Especially with well-subscribed courses, as microeconomics core courses tend to be, the variance of students' abilities and inclination towards rigorous theorising is usually large: building course material around a common set of articles and allowing students to choose the supplementary textbook(s) best suited to their interests, backgrounds and academic aims ensures the right balance between achieving a common set of knowledge and competence on the one hand and fostering individual learning on the other.

The eight sections in which the volume is divided correspond to some of the chapter headings of a traditional microeconomics textbook, with some important omissions and additions. As to the omissions, there are no articles covering the general areas of "externalities and public goods" and "general equilibrium". The reason for leaving out these areas is two-fold: firstly and more importantly, there are no articles with the required mix of originality, accessibility, and relevance suitable for the target readership of this volume. Secondly, the student interested in these fields will find in Herve Moulin's excellent if eccentric *Cooperative microeconomics* (1995) both a problem-based approach and a wide-ranging treatment catering for all tastes, from the mathematically innocent to the very sophisticated. Mainly because of a binding space constraint, in the volume there are no articles providing a systematic treatment of principal-agent theory, even though agency theory and its applications do appear in many contributions (see especially Chapters 6, 15, 18, 20).

As to the additions with respect to a typical micro textbook, an entire section is devoted to *price discrimination* (including the often neglected but interesting example of "commodity bundling") with a seminal article on *product differentiation*. Even the "traditional" sections contain articles that rarely find their way into conventional collections of reading in microeconomics, because their approach and content make them *substitutes* rather than complements of the standard micro textbooks.

PART I: RESOURCE ALLOCATION

Twenty years since its publication, the article by Armen Alchian and Harold Demsetz on "Production, Information Costs, and Economic Organization" has lost none of its ability to inspire and infuriate in almost equal measure and it repays handsomely the investment of analysing it with the benefit of hindsight, i.e., in the light of two decades of principal-agent theory. As befits any classic, it can be read at various levels.

Consider first the starting point of the textbook analysis of the theory of the firm: profit maximisation implies that Marginal Revenue equals Marginal Cost. But *who* works out both MR and MC, let alone equating them? Of course, in the case of a one-person business the question is irrelevant. In the case where productive activity is carried out by more than one person, Alchian and Demsetz advance the proposition that different types of economic organisation would be observed, depending on whether production is a *team* effort or not. More specifically, they argue that when the production function is not made up by the sum of functions of individual inputs[1]—this is what they mean by "team production"—then the resulting economic organisation is more likely to be a "firm" rather than a series of market transactions where no one agent is in charge of all the contracts with the joint inputs. A cornerstone of their argument is that when the production function is *not* additively separable, i.e., when people work as part of a team, then "each input owner will have more incentive to shirk". With the benefit of two decades of principal-agent theory, we now know that the really relevant factor is not the non-separability of the production function, but the non-verifiability of inputs.[2] To see this let π, e_1, and e_2 be respectively gross profit, worker 1's and worker 2's effort levels (measured in effort cost units), where $\pi = f(e_1, e_2)$. The *cooperative* outcome, $\{e_1^*, e_2^*\}$, is the solution of the maximisation problem:

$$\max_{e_1, e_2}[f(e_1, e_2) - e_1 - e_2], \quad \text{where} \quad \frac{\partial f(e_1^*, e_2^*)}{\partial e_i} = 1, \ i = 1, 2.$$

Because of the non-verifiability of inputs, rewards must be based only on the joint outcome π. If we let $\sigma_1(\pi)$ and $\sigma_2(\pi) \equiv 1 - \sigma_1(\pi)$ be the sharing rules, the resulting *non-cooperative* outcome $\{\tilde{e}_1, \tilde{e}_2\}$ is the solution of the maximisation problem:

$$\max_{e_i}[\sigma_i(f(e_i, e_j)) - e_i], \ i \neq j = 1, 2.$$

Thus, since

$$\frac{d\sigma_i}{df} \frac{\partial f}{\partial e_i} = 1, \quad \text{and} \quad \frac{d\sigma_i}{df} + \frac{d\sigma_j}{df} = 1$$

the non-cooperative outcome, as compared to the cooperative solution, will involve "shirking" (i.e., $\tilde{e}_i < e_i^* = 1,2$). Notice that no assumption on the additive separability of $f(.)$ is required.

The logic, if not the details, of Alchian and Demsetz's rationale for one economic actor to be at the centre of all the contracts that make up a "firm" does not depend on their definition of "team" production. To see this, let us proceed with the two-worker model sketched above. As pointed out by Holmstrom[3], it would be in the interest of the two players to realize that, if left to their own devices, mutual free-riding would occur and hence remedial action is required. Suppose, for example, that the two workers agreed on the following reward package:[4]

$$\text{if} \ f(e_1, e_2) = f(e_1^*, e_2^*) \quad \text{then} \quad \sigma_i = \frac{e_1^*}{e_1^*, e_2^*} f(e_1^*, e_2^*); \tag{1}$$

$$\text{if} \ f(e_1, e_2) < f(e_1^*, e_2^*) \quad \text{then} \quad \sigma_i = 0. \tag{2}$$

This incentive scheme does not violate the non-verifiability of effort levels and yet achieves the first best, *without the need for an external supervisor/monitor*. The reason why

Alchian and Demsetz's reasoning may still apply is that part (2) of this incentive scheme is not *renegotiation-proof*: Should either partner renege on the (implicit) agreement to supply the first-best level of effort, it would be in the interest of *both* players to consider the contract void, thereby destroying the desirable properties of the whole incentive package and re-introducing the need for independent monitoring, as conjectured by Alchian and Demsetz.

In a historical perspective, their thought-provoking theory of the firm marked a clear improvement on Coase's celebrated but almost undisprovable contention that firms are created when doing so is cheaper than relying on costly market transactions. Some features of their theory, however, have not stood the test of time; of these I shall mention two: (i) their claims that "[T]he relationship of each team member to the *owner* of the firm . . . is simply a 'quid pro quo' contract" (p. 8) and that "[L]ong-term contracts between employer and employee are not the essence of the organisation we call a firm" (p. 9) ignore the possibilities and the difficulties due to *investment* undertaken by either side of the employment relationship (e.g., training, career, etc.). (ii) the modifications of the theory so as to make it applicable to the corporation (as opposed to the owner-managed enterprise) tend to neglect the problems created by asymmetric information for the proper working of the market for corporate control.[5]

The article by Scarf is a vivid example of how producer theory (usually treated in such a tedious way in most textbooks to render catatonic the most willing of readers) can be made interesting, relevant, and revealing—and all this with no derivatives in sight! Firstly, Scarf describes the almost magical role of prices in a competitive system under constant returns to scale and the remarkable analogy between competitive markets and the simplex method as solutions respectively to economic optimality and maximisation problems. Almost in passing, he states in stark terms "one of the major theorems of microeconomic theory", namely that under constant return to scale, if a new technique of production is introduced, all that is required to assess whether its use can lead to a potential welfare gain is to compute its profitability under *current* (i.e., pre-innovation) prices. Secondly, Scarf makes the observation that "[I]f production really does obey constant returns to scale, there is nothing to be gained by organizing economic activity in large, durable and complex units . . . there is no economic justification for the existence of firms" (p. 28). We may mention that, indirectly, Scarf is interested in the question of what is a firm, like Alchian and Demetz, but from a quite different perspective.[6] Thirdly, Scarf provides a simple, but revealing example to show that in the presence of indivisibilities prices alone cannot identify the production plans that satisfy a given demand at minimum cost. Finally, Scarf sketches a "quantity test" to ascertain whether a production plan achieves cost minimisation.

The article by Telser rescues the theory of the core from the obscurity of general equilibrium theory and makes it both accessible and relevant. The central idea of the core is very simple: suppose there are n players each of whom can take some form of action with any number of players, ranging from 0 (meaning that the player acts on his/her own) to $n-1$ (where all players act together). Suppose also that individuals can compute (or more precisely, rank) the outcomes of their actions. Then we can ask the question: are there any outcomes that cannot be improved upon by individuals forming a different set of coalitions? The set of such unimprovable-upon outcomes is called *the core*. This set can contain no elements at all (empty core) or it may contain many (or indeed an infinitely large number of) elements or just a single outcome.

Telser provides some simple examples where the core is either non-empty (and so trade can take place) or does not exist (and thus a competitive market fails to produce a Pareto efficient outcome). He also tells a particularly revealing story that shows why in the textbook case of identical firms with U-shaped average cost curves a perfectly competitive market fails to achieve Pareto optimality and how the problem becomes more severe the greater the set-up costs are.

Having shown how easy it is for the core not to exist, especially when there are indivisibilities (examined in detail in the article by Scarf) Telser moves on to examine how this situation can be remedied. The "solution" typically involves forms of intervention that, *prima facie*, may appear counter-productive. In other words, as the core fails to exist when the constraints imposed by all the possible coalitions cannot all be satisfied simultaneously, the core can be "restored" by limiting the set of possible coalitions either directly (e.g., by vertical integration) or indirectly (by restricting output). Consider the following example. A technically complex good (e.g., personal computers, hi-fi equipment) is sold by two types of stores, assistance-and-sale shops that provide technical information to uninformed customers and sale-only shops that cater for the technically competent. Obviously the latter shops can sell at a lower price. This efficient equilibrium can be destroyed by opportunistic uninformed customers who could obtain the required technical information at low cost from the assistance-and-sale shops and then make a purchase at the (cheaper) sale-only stores. Even though such behaviour is obviously welfare-enhancing for the "opportunistic" customers, it typically ensures that the core is empty and thus imposing restrictions to prevent it can *increase* overall welfare.

PART II: GAME THEORY

The piece by Lyons and Varoufakis provides a bird's eye view of elementary game theory, with applications to oligopoly and bargaining. Its main virtue is that by using a discursive style and by emphasising the intuition more than the rigorous treatment of the various models analysed, it succeeds in drawing the student into game theory *as a way of thinking about microeconomics*. By its very nature, game theory is learnt (and more likely to be enjoyable[7]) by doing it, and this chapter entices the reader to pick up a pen and follow on paper the arguments sketched in the text. Given the fundamental role played by the notion of *Nash Equilibrium* in the whole of game theory, I should recommend that, as a supplement to this chapter, the reader consult the article by Johansen,[8] which explains in an elementary and yet rigorous way the status and analytical power of NE and, as a bonus, will allow the student to spot the many inaccuracies about this concept that still crop up in many micro textbooks.

The primer on auctions and bidding by one of the leading game theorists is undoubtedly more demanding, but will handsomely repay the reader willing to invest some time and attention in it. Paul Milgrom manages to explain in the simplest possible terms some of the intriguing and sometimes altogether surprising results that can be obtained by studying auctions rigorously. But why study auctions at all? If the economic theory of auctions were confined to analysing the esoteric topic of bidding for rare paintings, vintage ports, and pop memorabilia, it would amount to an amusing, but ultimately hardly relevant, field of investigation. Two main factors justify the sustained research interest in auction theory; first, a large and increasingly wide range of goods, services, and financial instruments are allocated by what are auction-type mechanisms. Just to mention a few examples: tracts for oil explorations, many types of government contracts (e.g., weapons, major infrastructural investment), social services,[9] government stocks, TV franchises, etc. Secondly, the feature of auctions that sets them apart from other methods of resource allocation—namely the fact that the return from participating in this form of activity does not depend on total, average, or marginal investment, but rather on the *relative* position (or *rank*) of a bid to others—is shared by the more general category of *contests*. These may range from the ephemeral (athletic races), to the catastrophic (wars), from the political arena (elections) to the technological (investment in research and development).

The article by Milgrom is an enticing introduction to this fascinating subject; the reader will learn about the "winner's curse", about the substantial equivalence of apparently different forms of auctions; about the circumstance under which by a suitable choice of auctions *both* the seller *and* the buyer can be made better off, etc.

PART III: UNCERTAINTY

The survey article by Hirshleifer and Riley (recently expanded to a book-length monograph[10]) provides a user-friendly introductory guide to the economics of uncertainty and information. The two authors undertake the welcome task of clearing some of the ambiguities surrounding the topic. For example, they unambiguously reject the crude Knightian distinction between "risk" (somehow objectively quantifiable) and "uncertainty" (incapable of being measured), by taking the sound viewpoint that probability is always subjective in so far as it is a degree of belief. Has a freshly minted £1 coin *really* a 50–50 chance of landing tails, if properly tossed? I may be willing to accept this probability as "objective" for some classes of problems (e.g., to decide whether to go to the cinema or to the races); but for others (e.g., if my life depended on the outcome), I may wish to acquire some additional information before acting on the basis of expected outcome of the coin toss.

Hirshleifer and Riley's attitude towards the expected-utility rule is also refreshingly straightforward. They start with the important distinction between the *utility* function $u(a)$ defined over *actions* and the *preference-scaling* function $v(c)$ defined over *consequences* and they frame the von Neumann–Morgenstern expected-utility rule as a procedure to move from preferences over outcomes (e.g., amounts of money) to preferences over actions (at what odds should I accept a given bet?). Instead of presenting the usual list of axioms on which expected-utility maximisation is based, Hirshleifer and Riley offer the student the opportunity to build his/her own preference-scaling function using the simple technique of the "reference lottery". Then the contingent-commodity approach is explained with the use of simple diagrams as is market equilibrium under uncertainty. The key concepts of *adverse selection* and *moral hazard* are examined briefly with a few examples from insurance. The second part of the article—The economics of information—introduces concepts (the value of information, complete and numeraire contingent markets) that probably are less familiar to students and perhaps more difficult to absorb at the first reading. The signalling/screening model sketches the standard treatment of the case of identical employers faced with employees of different ability (e.g., high- and low-productivity workers) who can either purchase a "signal" (e.g., educational credentials) or can be "screened" at a cost. Hirshleifer and Riley show how in this case there is no equilibrium, either of the "pooling" variety (when all workers are paid the same average wage), or of the "separating" variety when workers self-select into a low-education/low-wage group and a high-education/high-wage group. The non-existence of an equilibrium is proved by showing that when a pooling (separating) offer is made to workers, it will always pay a maverick firm to make a separating (pooling) offer. Unfortunately, Hirshleifer and Riley do not pursue this line of reasoning to its conclusion in so far as they do not hint that there may be cases in which competition amongst employers can produce a separating equilibrium *at zero cost*. I will sketch the logic of this result with reference to one of the seminal articles in the theory of screening.[11]

There are two types of workers, H and L, characterised by their marginal productivity, $v_H > v_L$. As employers are assumed to know the proportion of high-productivity workers in the population, λ, they can compute *average* productivity, $\bar{v} \equiv \lambda v_H + (1 - \lambda) v_L$. Moreover, although individual marginal productivity cannot be observed, the aggregate output produced by the assembly line to which workers are assigned is known to employers.[12] Let c be the cost of screening, whereby the screened worker's true productivity is revealed. Assuming that the following inequalities hold:

$$v_H - v_L > c > v_H - \bar{v} \tag{3}$$

consider the following screening/wage packages:

"*Pooling*" *package:* all workers are not screened and are paid their average productivity;

"*Separating*" *package:* high-productivity workers pay the screening cost c and receive a net wage of $v_H - c$: low-productivity workers are not screened and receive v_L.

Either package will yield zero-profits for employers and would be such that neither type of worker has the incentive to "lie" on its true productivity.

One common feature of the two employment packages is that neither makes use of the "aggregate" information on assembly line productivity.

Consider the following wage structure:

$$w_1 = \begin{cases} v_H & \text{if} & \sum_{i=1}^{N} v^i = N v_H \\[2ex] \underline{v} < v_L & \text{if} & \sum_{i=1}^{N} v^i < N v_H \end{cases} \tag{4}$$

$$w_2 = v_L$$

The idea behind the above wage structure is that workers are given the choice of joining either a high-productivity assembly line, where members are paid a wage equal to v_H, *provided all members are of the high-productivity type*; and a low-productivity line, where all members are paid v_L. Notice that under this scheme, workers will self-select *at zero cost* and firms earn zero profits.

The article by Mark Machina concentrates on the canonical model of choice under uncertainty, namely expected-utility theory, with special emphasis on its so-called "paradoxes" and the more recent work, both theoretical and empirical, on non-expected utility approaches. The standard model is presented in a fresh and accessible way: the key assumptions of expected-utility theory and their implications are spelt out in a way that makes clear the power and the limitations of the model, as well as the continuity between "old" and "newer" approaches. Supplying students with a menu of gambles and then pointing out the inconsistencies that inevitably result from their choice makes for lively tutorials, but whether it produces relevant evidence for "paradoxes" is less clear. The basic problem here is the "framing the question" syndrome. This is best seen with reference to one of the earliest and most influential of the "expected-utility paradoxes": the Allais paradox (see pp. 170–172 in Machina's article for details). A salutary experience for teachers and students alike is to ask students to select their preferred lottery in situations 1 and 2 as described in Table 1.

Table 1.

		Prize on ticket		
		1	2–11	12–100
Situation 1	a_1	£1m	£1m	£1m
	a_2	£0	£5m	£1m
Situation 2	a_4	£1m	£1m	£0
	a_3	£0	£5m	£0

The story behind Table 1 (adapted from Borch[13]) is this: under each of the four lotteries there are one hundred numbered tickets with a given prize on each ticket. So, for example, in the a_4 lottery, ticket no. 1 carries a £1m prize, tickets 2 to 11 a £5m prize and the remaining tickets no prize at all. Onc ticket only is drawn from the hat.

In my own, probably unrepresentative experience, I have never come across any inconsistent selections between situations 1 and 2, and yet, as the reader may easily verify, the menu of lotteries is *identical* to the one that, under a different framing, yields frequently the Allais paradox.[14]

PART IV: DEMAND THEORY

Robert Willig's unapologetic article on consumer's surplus is an indirect, but effective, way of introducing students to more advanced demand theory than the elementary indifference-curves-and-budget-constraint diagrams. The more technical aspects of this brief but "meaty" article and the actual calculations of the upper and lower bounds of the approximation involved in using consumer's surplus for welfare analysis can be skipped on a first reading without comprehension of the main points being adversely affected.

In my experience most students come to advanced micro classes with a strong antipathy for demand theory, due to the fact that protracted exposure to elementary micro textbooks typically insinuates the idea that, as consumer theory depends on unobtainable (if not meaningless) indifference curves, the whole edifice of demand theory is of no practical consequence. One of the pedagogical benefits of Willig's article is that it shifts emphasis on *observable* demand curves and on their use in welfare analysis. Suppose that government policy had increased the income of a group of consumers (e.g., old-age pensioners) while at the same time raising the price of a (non-inferior) good (e.g., by imposing VAT on fuel). Willig's work shows how, by relying on the observable changes in the demand curve for this good, one could obtain a fairly accurate measure of the resulting change in consumers' welfare.

The next piece, by Sah, shows the power of demand analysis to produce definite answers to complex policy issues. Suppose that if a given good or service were supplied at a marginal cost, this would create excess demand. This "deficit" good could be allocated to consumers either by a laissez-faire market mechanism (whereby supply and demand are brought in equilibrium by increasing the price) or by a "non-market" mechanism, e.g., queuing and rationing (with either convertible or non-convertible rations). Sah shows how these different systems of resources allocation can be ranked for two groups of individuals, the "poor" and the "rich".

PART V: PRICE DISCRIMINATION AND PRODUCT DIFFERENTIATION

The first three articles in this section, apart from their theoretical and practical interest, provide tangible evidence of the process of accretion and revision whereby economics as a discipline progresses. The reader will notice how the first article (by Varian), while building on august precursors, supplies a new insight into the widespread phenomenon of (third-degree) price discrimination. This, in turn, elicits a correction and further application by another economist (Layson). A third contribution (by Schwartz) extends the argument to cover the practically-relevant case of a price-discriminating monopolist operating under decreasing marginal cost. Demand theory and especially consumer's surplus appear again to provide the basis for determining under what conditions the ability to price-discriminate may *benefit* consumers.[15]

The article by Adams and Yellen on commodity bundling is an example of the increasingly rare case of an extremely simple analytical apparatus being used to deepen the understanding and policy implications of a widespread business practice. In my experience, students do enjoy working out the various pricing strategies open to a monopolist who can sell a number of good (and/or services) either individually or as a "bundle". Relying on a few diagrams and with no calculus at all, the teacher will be able to introduce a number of important notions, both theoretical and of policy significance, e.g., the effects of monopoly selling not only the wrong *level* of output (*allocative* inefficiency), but also to the wrong *people* (*distributive* inefficiency); the limitations of consumer's surplus analysis in the presence of bundling, the complexities of price regulation policies when monopolists apply sophisticated strategies, etc.

The article spawned a whole literature: an interesting extension is examined by Carbajo *et al.*[16] who consider the case of a two-product firm which monopolises the market for one product but competes with a second firm in the other. The authors show that the two-product firm has a *strategic* incentive to bundle, in the sense that bundling provides a form of *commitment* that can be used to elicit a favourable response by the competing firm. The welfare effects of strategic bundling depend on the nature of competition, i.e. whether firms choose output levels (Cournot duopoly) or prices (Bertrand duopoly).[17]

The theme of *product differentiation* is the topic of the final article in this section, the classic "circular market" model by Salop.

In one way or another any contribution on *horizontal*[18] product differentiation is a descendant of the seminal paper published in 1929 by Harold Hotelling.[19] Here Hotelling not only developed an analytical framework to analyse the choice of price and *location* by firms, but perhaps more importantly, drew the powerful analogy between physical space (location) and *quality* space (variety). Consider his famous "beach" model: on a beach of length l consumers are distributed uniformly and eager to purchase one (and only one) ice-cream. Two ice-cream vendors selling the same product appear. Where will they locate? Notice that now the good "ice-cream" not only has a price but also an "address" (a location): as customers have a positive (and constant) unit cost of transport t, they may be willing to trade a dearer ice-cream for a shorter journey to the vendor. Although Hotelling's own solution of this model, with the two vendors locating back-to-back at the socially inefficient location in the middle of the beach, is not correct,[20] the key idea that this location problem is formally identical to the case with consumers having different ideal varieties and firms choosing product quality[21] has proved correct and invaluable.

Salop extends Hotelling's insights in a number of directions: (i) by analysing a "circular market" (i.e., where firms locate on a circle[22]), Salop removes the artificial notion of market having "end-points" thus eliminating the artifice of a firm being able to supply all customers between its location and the end of the line (provided no other firm locates in between); (ii) by introducing an "outside option", Salop can distinguish betweeen inter-brand and inter-industry competition; (iii) using the notion of a symmetric zero-profit Nash equilibrium, the model provides substance to the often nebulous concept of "monopolistic competition".

PART VI: INFORMATION

In what was to turn out to be one of the most heavily cited papers in economics, George Akerlof provides an interest-grabbing account of the effects on introducing a specific form of uncertainty in economic transactions, namely when one of the two parties cannot identify some of the other party's relevant characteristics. As a result, the less informed party will face *adverse selection*. The example used in the article is the market for "lemons" (low-quality second-hand cars): the buyer is unable to distinguish whether the car offered for sale is a lemon or a "peach". The market may collapse altogether, in the sense that price changes may fail to equate supply and demand (if you are looking for a good-quality second-hand car, would you be *more* likely to buy my car if I *dropped* the price from £3000 to £500?) The reason for this market failure is that in a one-off transaction when product quality depends on price, the price mechanism alone is insufficient to determine both *quantity* and *quality*.

The short note by Heal suggests, by means of a somewhat contrived example, that the extension of the trading parties' horizon may assist the price system in achieving mutually satisfactory trades. The key idea is that if trade is modelled as an infinitely repeated game then, provided the relative incentive for a "quick buck" against the "returns from honesty" is not too large, the two trading partners may find it mutually beneficial to engage in a long-term arrangement whereby high-quality goods are exchanged.

The exchanges between Bond in the one corner and Pratt and Hoffer in the other are a vivid example of the perils encountered in trying to test empirically a theoretical model. Whereas most people have no difficulty in understanding the notion of a "lemon" (often drawing from bitter personal experience), how can you quantify the concept? As will become apparent reading the exchanges, Ackerlof's predictions on the market for lemons may be either confirmed or rejected depending on the definition of "lemon" (at least as far as the market for second-hand pick-up trucks is concerned).

The final article in this section is the excellent survey by Stiglitz of the wider problem of the dependence of quality on price. Here Stiglitz draws the more general and far-reaching consequences of prices carrying information on quality: traditional demand curves may have the "wrong" shape, may be difficult to disentangle from supply curves, and may give rise to "thin" markets. He also shows how pervasive the problem of asymmetric information is by examining models of the labour market (where employees may be of varying "quality"), of the capital market (where some borrowers may be more likely to default), of the product market. The prediction in the article's last section that the topic of the survey would provide scope for further research has been amply confirmed by the mushrooming of both theoretical and empirical work in the last ten years.

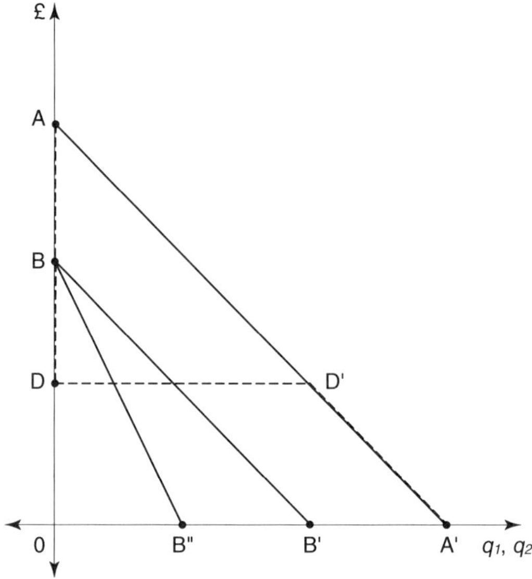

Figure 1. Bertrand versus Cournot.

PART VII: OLIGOPOLY: THEORY AND APPLICATION

With the irresistible rise of game theory the distinction between microeconomics and theoretical industrial organisation has become very blurred and nowhere so much as in the field of oligopoly theory. To mention but two, the concept of Cournot (quantity competition) and Bertrand (price competition) oligopoly and the notion of multi-stage game (with applications to *strategic* investment) are now part of every microeconomist's theoretical tool-kit.

Dixon provides a brief but lucid explanation of how the Cournot and Bertrand outcomes are just two different solutions of the same equilibrium concept (Nash equilibrium). Figure 1 (adapted from Shapiro[23]) may provide an intuitive explanation why it makes such a marked difference whether firms compete in quantities or prices.

Let demand be linear: $P = A - (q_1 + q_2)$ and marginal cost be constant (and normalised to zero). Under Cournot competition, each of the two identical firms produces $A/3$ units of output and the Cournot price, P^C, also equals $A/3$. Now perform the following experiment: suppose that firm 2 produces $A/3$ and thus firm 1 is faced by the *residual* demand curve BB′ in figure 1 (BB′ is obtained by subtracting $A/3$ from the market demand curve AA′). If, on the other hand, firm 2 were charging the Cournot price $A/3$ (= 0D in Figure 1), then firm 1 would be facing the *more elastic* demand curve ADD′A′ (see broken line in Figure 1). Whereas in the former case firm 1 cannot take the entire market by means of an output response, in the latter firm 1 can do so simply by charging a price a shade less than P^C.

These differences between quantity and price competition also apply to the case where firms produce differentiated products and become even more interesting in those circumstances in which firms can make strategic commitments. For example, whereas under Cournot competition it pays to be able to move first, under Bertrand competition there is a definite first-mover *dis*advantage.

The article by Fershtman and Judd, "Equilibrium Incentives in Oligopoly", is an "application" in two senses: (a) it is an illustration of the two-stage oligopoly model; and (b) it applies to oligopoly some of the basic concepts of principal-agent theory. In an earlier contribution[24] John Vickers had addressed the following problem: suppose that control of decisions either rests with me or can be delegated to an "agent". In the latter case, in order to maximise my own welfare, should I appoint someone whose preferences are as close as possible to mine or someone who will set out to maximise an objective function substantially different from mine? The somewhat surprising answer is that if I am engaged in some game with other players (i.e., if my payoff depends also on other people's actions), almost always I will want to appoint an agent whose objective is *different* from mine. Applying this principle to the case of the owner of a firm (principal) and a manager (agent), we obtain the result that in order to maximise profits the owner will delegate control to a *non*-profit-maximising manager.[25]

Fershtman and Judd consider the strategic possibilities offered by appointing a non-profit-maximising manager under both Cournot and Bertrand competition and examine the welfare effects of such choices.

PART VIII: SOCIAL CHOICE

"Social choice . . . is concerned with the relation between individuals and the society."[26] Slightly more specifically, most of social-choice theory deals with the attempt to aggregate some individual concept (e.g., welfare, judgement, interests) into its social counterpart. So typical applications of social-choice theory include: procedural rules for committees (who decides the agenda? how to choose between alternatives, should any country have a veto in an international deliberative body/ agency, etc.); choosing a "good" electoral scheme (e.g., proportional representation vs. first-past-the-post); formulating a constitution (see the experience of post-colonial and post-communist countries); designing ethically-meaningful indices of poverty/ inequality; etc.

Social-choice theory is also, and some would say mainly, a *method*: its axiomatic approach demands the explicit spelling out of assumptions and the logical derivation of their (often surprising) implications. As a result most of literature takes the peculiar form of *impossibility theorems*: a number of innocent-looking assumptions are shown to be mutually incompatible. This does not mean that social-choice theory is essentially destructive: a *significant* impossibility theorem forces the reader to take a deeper look at the issues involved. Two such theorems stand out for their far-reaching implications: Kenneth Arrow's *General (Im)Possibility Theorem* and Amartya Sen's *Impossibility of a Paretian Liberal*. Turning to the latter first, consider the following problem. Take the *least* demanding definition of individual liberty (e.g., individuals ought to be allowed to choose the colour of their shirts/blouses) and ask yourself whether it can be combined with the apparently innocuous stipulation that if every single individual in a society prefers a certain state of affairs *a* to a different state *b*, then society ought to reflect such unanimous preferences. A positive answer would not be an earth-shattering result: indeed, one would expect that any vaguely liberal (in a wide sense) constitution should be able to accommodate two such mild requirements. In the first article in this section Sen shows that a proper formulation of the question yields the inescapable and unpalatable conclusion that even the mildest concern for individual rights is incompatible with one of the pillars of welfare economics, namely the *Pareto Principle* (if everyone prefers *a* to *b*, so should society). The example chosen by Sen (who, if anyone, should read *Lady Chatterley's Lover*) may have little resonance with a contemporary audience, but the underlying dilemma of having to choose between the irresistible force of unanimity and the unmoveable requirement of (minimal) liberty has definitely stood the test of time, as witnessed by the almost continuous flow of contributions on this subject.[27]

The second article in the section, also by Sen, provides an assessment of the considerable achievements and still unresolved issues in social-choice theory and thus, inevitably, contains a statement and analysis of the other pillar of the theory I allude to above, namely Arrow's *General (Im)Possibility Theorem*. It is a non-technical and wide-ranging piece, which I have included with the hope that readers will be motivated to dwell further into a subject that many traditional textbooks tend to neglect.

The final piece by Levin and Nalebuff, "An Introduction to Vote-counting Schemes", looks in some detail (sixteen different ways of aggregating votes are examined) at a key problem of any democratic system, namely how to design a "good" electoral mechanism. We know from Arrow's impossibility theorem that there is no optimal voting scheme—the quest for the best must give way to the search for the not-too-flawed. The important lesson to be learnt from this survey is that choosing a voting scheme involves value judgements. Contrary to the belief that fired the founders of social-choice theory (Condorcet[28] and Borda) that in any election there is a "perfect" winner and the "proper" electoral system would identify him/her, if there is no consensus amongst voters, none can be created by means of any however sophisticated voting scheme.

NOTES

1. As Alchian and Demetz put it: the production function $Z = f(x_1, x_2)$ is separable into additive function if $\partial^2 Z / \partial x_1 \partial x_2 = 0$.
2. Interestingly, Alchian and Demetz do allude to non-verifiability, albeit not by name, in note 2.
3. B. Holmstrom. Moral Hazard in Teams. *Bell Journal of Economics*, 1982; **13**: 324–340.
4. The astute reader will notice that there are many such reward schemes that would achieve the first-best.
5. See for example the classic statement of take-over activity as a (typically under-supplied) public good in Grossman S.J. and Hart O.D. Takeover bids, the free rider problem, and the theory of the corporation. *Bell Journal of Economics*, 1980; **11**: 42–64.

6. An intriguing question is this: "if indivisibilities are a key explanation for the existence of firms, why are they not even mentioned in the Alchian and Demetz's article devoted at providing a rationale for firms?"

7. The reader wishing to examine game theory in more depth but without missing on the enjoyment should read the appropriately-titled *Fun and Games: a text on game theory*, by Ken Binmore, Lexington, Mass: D.C. Heath, 1992.

8. Lief Johansen. On the status of the Nash type of noncooperative equilibrium in economic theory. *Scandinavian Journal of Economics*, 1982; **84**(3): 421–441.

9. In the UK, for example, local authorities are compelled by law to "contract out" services like refuse collection, hospital and school cleaning, etc.

10. Hirshleifer J. and Riley J.G. *The analytics of uncertainty and information*, Cambridge: Cambridge University Press, 1992.

11. Stiglitz J. The theory of screening, education, and the distribution of income. *American Economic Review*, 1974; **64**: 283–300.

12. The astute reader will see a connection with Alchian and Demetz's notion of team production discussed above.

13. Borch K.H. *The economics of uncertainty*, Princeton, NJ: Princeton University Press, 1968.

14. For additional examples of differently framed Allais lotteries that typically produce no paradox at all, see Hirshleifer J. and Riley J.G. *The analytics of uncertainty and information*, Cambridge: Cambridge University Press, 1992, pp. 36–41.

15. The articles on demand theory and price discrimination refer to the standard duality approach to consumer theory that can be found in any micro textbook. The following reminders may be useful to follow the text:

When the consumer solves the problem of maximising $u(\boldsymbol{p},y)$ subject to the budget constraint $\boldsymbol{p}\cdot x = y$ where $\boldsymbol{p}$ and $\boldsymbol{x}$ are respectively a price and a commodity vector and y is income, we can express the maximum utility achieved as a function of prices and income, i.e. we can obtain the *indirect utility function* $v = v(\boldsymbol{p},y)$. As this relation holds for any $\boldsymbol{p}$ and u, we can write the minimum expenditure to achieve utility u at prices $\boldsymbol{p}$ as the *expenditure function* $e = e(\boldsymbol{p},u)$. This, in turn, can be seen as the product of prices times the *Hicksian* (or *utility-compensated*) *demand functions* $h(\boldsymbol{p},u)$, i.e., $e(\boldsymbol{p},u) = \boldsymbol{p}\cdot\mathbf{h}(\boldsymbol{p},u)$. Three properties of this function are used repeatedly in the text:

(i) $e(\boldsymbol{p},u)$ is *concave* in prices. Consider three vector prices: $\boldsymbol{p}^0$, $\boldsymbol{p}'$, and $\boldsymbol{p}'' \equiv a\boldsymbol{p}^0 + (1-a)\boldsymbol{p}''$ and suppose that at prices $\boldsymbol{p}''$ the cheapest way of attaining utility u is by buying the commodity vector $\boldsymbol{x}''$. This means that at prices $\boldsymbol{p}^0$ and $\boldsymbol{p}'$ buying $\boldsymbol{x}''$ would be at least as expensive, i.e.:

$$e(\boldsymbol{p}^{\,0}, u) \leq \boldsymbol{p}^{\,0} \cdot \boldsymbol{x}''; \tag{1}$$

$$e(\boldsymbol{p}', u) \leq \boldsymbol{p}' \cdot \boldsymbol{x}''. \tag{2}$$

Multiplying (1) by a and (2) by $(1-a)$ and adding up we obtain:

$$a\, e(\boldsymbol{p}^{\,0}, u) + (1-a)\, e(\boldsymbol{p}', u) \leq a\, \boldsymbol{p}^{\,0} \cdot \boldsymbol{x}'' + (1-a)\, \boldsymbol{p}' \cdot \boldsymbol{x}'' = e(a\, \boldsymbol{p}^{\,0} + (1-a)\, \boldsymbol{p}', u).$$

(ii) Suppose all prices but p_1 are kept constant: what is the cost to the consumer of maintaining her utility u if p_1 rises by a (small) unit? Intuitively, the answer is x_1, the amount of good 1 consumed before the change. Thus the *Hicksian* (compensated) *demand function* $h_1(\boldsymbol{p},u)$ equals $\partial e(\boldsymbol{p}, u)/\partial p_1$.

(iii) *Roy's identity.* This relationship enables us to retrieve the observable *Marshallian* demand function from the indirect utility function. Totally differentiate the indirect utility function $v(\boldsymbol{p},y)$ holding all prices by p_i constant and keeping utility also constant:

$$\frac{\partial v}{\partial p_i}\, dp_i + \frac{\partial v}{\partial y}\, dy = 0. \tag{3}$$

But as we have seen above, in order to keep utility constant, income must be increased by x_1 times the change in its price, i.e.,

$$dy = x_1 \, dp_1. \tag{4}$$

Combining (3) and (4), we obtain Roy's identity:

$$x_1(\boldsymbol{p}, y) = -\frac{\dfrac{\partial v}{\partial p_i}}{\dfrac{\partial v}{\partial y}}. \tag{5}$$

16. Carbajo J., De Meza D. and Seidmann D. A strategic motivation for commodity bundling. *Journal of Industrial Economics*, 1990; **38**(3): 283–298.
17. On the strategic value of commitments and the difference between Cournot and Bertrand oligopoly, see the contribution by Dixon in this volume (Chapter 19).
18. This type of product differentiation refers to the case where consumers differ as to their notion of "ideal" variety and thus two different varieties sold at the same price can achieve positive sales; *vertical* product differentiation, instead, covers the case where consumers agree on the ranking of varieties (but may differ on the quality premium they are willing to pay) and thus two different varieties cannot be supplied at the same price.
19. Hotelling H. Stability in competition. *Economic Journal*, 1929; **39**: 41–57.
20. See the corrected version of the model in d'Aspremont C., Gabszewicz J.J. and Thisse J.F. On Hotelling's stability in competition. *Econometrica*, 1979; **47**: 1145–1150.
21. Hotelling mentions the examples of political parties "locating" on a right-left spectrum, breweries selecting cider variety on a sweet-dry scale, Methodist and Presbyterian churches crowding each other on an imaginary "divine" line, etc.
22. A good example of how the physical space/product space analogy applies not only to a line, but also to a circle, is to imagine the circle as the face of a clock and the suppliers of transport services (i.e., airlines, railways, coach companies, etc.) choosing departure times.
23. Shapiro C. Theories of oligopoly behavior. In: Schmalensee R. and Willig R. (eds.) *Handbook of Industrial Organization*, 1989: Amsterdam and New York: North-Holland.
24. Vickers J. Delegation and theory of the firm. *Economic Journal*, 1985; **95** (Supplement): 138–147.
25. This result puts in an altogether different perspective the vast literature on "managerial theories of the firm", based on the assumption that the fact that managers typically may wish to pursue objectives other than profit-maximisation necessarily implies a conflict of interest with (profit-maximising) shareholders.
26. Sen A. Social choice. In: Eatwell J., Milgate M. and Newman P. (eds.) *The New Palgrave: A Dictionary of Economics*, 1987: vol. IV, pp. 382–393, p. 382.
27. The literature on the impossibility of a Paretian liberal runs into hundreds of contributions; two useful analytical surveys are: Sen A. Liberty, unanimity, and rights. *Economica*, 1976; **43**: 217–245; Sen A. Minimal liberty. *Economica*, 1992; **59**: 139–159.
28. The readers for whom the contemporary approach to election theory may appear slightly too detached and passionless will find in the writings of the enlightened forefathers of social-choice theory a powerful antidote; for an excellent collection of stirring contributions to the debate on voting raging at the time of the French Revolution, see *Condorcet: foundations of social choice and political theory*, translated and edited by Iain McLean and Fiona Hewitt, Aldershot: E. Elgar, 1994.

Part I

Resource Allocation

CONTENTS

1

Production, Information Costs, and Economic Organization

Armen A. Alchian and Harold Demsetz

The mark of a capitalistic society is that resources are owned and allocated by such nongovernmental organizations as firms, households, and markets. Resource owners increase productivity through cooperative specialization and this leads to the demand for economic organizations which facilitate cooperation. When a lumber mill employs a cabinetmaker, cooperation between specialists is achieved within a firm, and when a cabinetmaker purchases wood from a lumberman, the cooperation takes place across markets (or between firms). Two important problems face a theory of economic organization—to explain the conditions that determine whether the gains from specialization and cooperative production can better be obtained within an organization like the firm, or across markets, and to explain the structure of the organization.

It is common to see the firm characterized by the power to settle issues by fiat, by authority, or by disciplinary action superior to that available in the conventional market. This is delusion. The firm does not own all its inputs. It has no power of fiat, no authority, no disciplinary action any different in the slightest degree from ordinary market contracting between any two people. I can "punish" you only by withholding future business or by seeking redress in the courts for any failure to honor our exchange agreement. That is exactly all that any employer can do. He can fire or sue, just as I can fire my grocer by stopping purchases from him or sue him for delivering faulty products. What then is the content of the presumed power to manage and assign workers to various tasks? Exactly the same as one little consumer's power to manage and assign his grocer to various tasks. The single consumer can assign his grocer to the task of obtaining whatever the customer can induce the grocer to provide at a price acceptable to both parties. That is precisely all that an employer can do to an employee. To speak of managing, directing, or assigning workers to various tasks is a deceptive way of noting that the employer continually is involved in renegotiation of contracts on terms that must be acceptable to both parties. Telling an employee to type this letter rather than to file that document is like my telling a grocer to sell me

Reprinted with permission from *American Economic Review*, Vol. 62, No. 4, 1977, pp. 777–795

this brand of tuna rather than that brand of bread. I have no contract to continue to purchase from the grocer and neither the employer nor the employee is bound by any contractual obligations to continue their relationship. Long-term contracts between employer and employee are not the essence of the organization we call a firm. My grocer can count on my returning day after day and purchasing his services and goods even with the prices not always marked on the goods—because I know what they are— and he adapts his activity to conform to my directions to him as to what I want each day ... he is not my employee.

Wherein then is the relationship between a grocer and his employee different from that between a grocer and his customers? It is in a *team* use of inputs and a centralized position of some party in the contractual arrangements of *all* other inputs. It is the *centralized contractual agent in a team productive process*—not some superior authoritarian directive or disciplinary power. Exactly what is a team process and why does it induce the contractual form, called the firm? These problems motivate the inquiry of this paper.

THE METERING PROBLEM

The economic organization through which input owners cooperate will make better use of their comparative advantages to the extent that it facilitates the payment of rewards in accord with productivity. If rewards were random, and without regard to productive effort, no incentive to productive effort would be provided by the organization; and if rewards were negatively correlated with productivity the organization would be subject to sabotage. Two key demands are placed on an economic organization—metering input productivity and metering rewards.[1]

Metering problems sometimes can be resolved well through the exchange of products across competitive markets, because in many situations markets yield a high correlation between rewards and productivity. If a farmer increases his output of wheat by 10 percent at the prevailing market price, his receipts also increase by 10 percent. This method of organizing economic activity meters the *output directly*, reveals the marginal product and apportions the *rewards* to resource owners in accord with that direct measurement of their outputs. The success of this decentralized, market exchange in promoting productive specialization requires that changes in market rewards fall on those responsible for changes in *output*.[2]

The classic relationship in economics that runs from marginal productivity to the distribution of income implicitly *assumes* the existence of an organization, be it the market or the firm, that allocates rewards to resources in accord with their productivity. The problem of economic organization, the economical means of metering productivity and rewards, is not confronted directly in the classical analysis of production and distribution. Instead, that analysis tends to assume sufficiently economic—or zero cost—means, as if productivity automatically created its reward. We conjecture the direction of causation is the reverse—the specific system of rewarding which is relied upon stimulates a particular productivity response. If the economic organization meters poorly, with rewards and productivity only loosely correlated, then productivity will be smaller; but if the economic organization meters well productivity will be greater. What makes metering difficult and hence induces means of economizing on metering costs?

TEAM PRODUCTION

Two men jointly lift heavy cargo into trucks. Solely by observing the total weight loaded per day, it is impossible to determine each person's marginal productivity. With team production it is difficult, solely by observing total output, to either define or determine *each* individual's contribution to this output of the cooperating inputs. The output is yielded by a team, by definition, and it is not a *sum* of separable outputs of each of its members. Team production of Z involves at least two inputs, X_i and X_j, with $\partial^2 Z/\partial X_i \partial X_j \neq 0$.[3] The production function is *not* separable into two functions each involving only inputs X_i or only inputs X_j. Consequently there is no *sum* of Z of two separable functions to treat as the Z of the team production function. (An example of a *separable* case is $Z = aX_i^2 + bX_j^2$ which is separable into $Z_i = aX_i^2$ and $Z_j = bX_j^2$, and $Z = Z_i + Z_j$. This is not team production.) There exist production techniques in which the Z obtained is greater than if X_i and X_j had produced separable Z. Team production will be used if it yields an output enough larger than the sum of separable production of Z to cover the costs of organizing and disciplining team members—the topics of this paper.[4]

Usual explanations of the gains from cooperative behavior rely on exchange and production in accord with the comparative advantage specialization principle with separable additive production. However, as suggested above there is a source of gain from cooperative activity involving working as a *team*, wherein individual cooperating inputs do not yield identifiable, separate products which can be *summed* to measure the total output. For this cooperative productive activity, here called "team" production, measuring *marginal* productivity and making payments in accord therewith is more expensive by an order of magnitude than for separable production functions.

Team production, to repeat, is production in which (1) several types of resources are used and (2) the product is not a sum of separable outputs of each cooperating resource. An additional factor creates a team organization problem—(3) not all resources used in team production belong to one person.

We do not inquire into why all the jointly used resources are not owned by one person, but instead into the types of organization, contracts, and informational and payment procedures used among owners of teamed inputs. With respect to the one-owner case, perhaps it is sufficient merely to note that (a) slavery is prohibited; (b) one might assume risk aversion as a reason for one person's not borrowing enough to purchase all the assets of sources of services rather than renting them, and (c) the purchase-resale spread may be so large that costs of short-term ownership exceed rental costs. Our problem is viewed basically as one of organization among different people, not of the physical goods or services, however much there must be selection and choice of combination of the latter.

How can the members of a team be rewarded and induced to work efficiently? In team production, marginal products of cooperative team members are not so directly and separably (i.e., cheaply) observable. What a team offers to the market can be taken as the marginal product of the team but not of the team members. The costs of metering or ascertaining the marginal products of the team's members is what calls forth new organizations and procedures. Clues to each input's productivity can be secured by observing *behavior* of individual inputs. When lifting cargo into the truck, how rapidly does a man move to the next piece to be loaded, how many cigarette breaks does he take, does the item being lifted tilt downward toward his side?

If detecting such behavior were costless, neither party would have an incentive to shirk, because neither could impose the cost of his shirking on the other (if their cooperation was agreed to voluntarily). But since costs must be incurred to monitor each other, each input owner will have more incentive to shirk when he works as part of a team, than if his performance could be monitored easily or if he did not work as a team. If there is a net increase in productivity available by team production, net of the metering cost associated with disciplining the team, then team production will be relied upon rather than a multitude of bilateral exchange of separable individual outputs.

Both leisure and higher income enter a person's utility function.[5] Hence, each person should adjust his work and realized reward so as to equate the marginal rate of substitution between leisure and production of real output to his marginal rate of substitution in consumption. That is, he would adjust his rate of work to bring his demand prices of leisure and output to equality with their true costs. However, with detection, policing, monitoring, measuring or metering costs, each person will be induced to take more leisure, because the effect of relaxing on *his realized* (reward) rate of substitution between output and leisure will be less than the effect on the *true* rate of substitution. His realized cost of leisure will fall more than the true cost of leisure, so he "buys" more leisure (i.e., more nonpecuniary reward).

If his relaxation cannot be detected perfectly at zero cost, part of its effects will be borne by others in the team, thus making *his* realized cost of relaxation less than the true total cost to the team. The difficulty of detecting such actions permits the private costs of his actions to be less than their full costs. Since each person responds to his private realizable rate of substitution (in production) rather than the true total (i.e., social) rate, and so long as there are costs for other people to detect his shift toward relaxation, it will not pay (them) to force him to readjust completely by making him realize the true cost. Only enough efforts will be made to equate the marginal gains of detection activity with the marginal costs of detection; and that implies a lower rate of productive effort and more shirking than in a costless monitoring, or measuring world.

In a university, the faculty use office telephones, paper, and mail for personal uses beyond strict university productivity. The university administrators could stop such practices by identifying *the* responsible person in each case, but they can do so only at higher costs than administrators are willing to incur. The extra costs of identifying each party (rather than merely identifying the presence of such activity) would exceed the savings from diminished faculty "turpitudinal peccadilloes." So the faculty is allowed some degree of "privileges, perquisites, or fringe benefits". And the total of the pecuniary wages paid is lower because of this irreducible (at acceptable costs) degree of amenity-seizing activity. Pay is lower in pecuniary terms and higher in leisure, conveniences, and ease of work. But still every person would prefer to see detection made more effective (if it were somehow possible to monitor costlessly) so that he, as part of the now more effectively producing team, could thereby realize a higher pecuniary pay and less leisure. If everyone could, at zero cost, have his reward-realized rate brought to the true production possibility real rate, all could achieve a more preferred position. But detection of the responsible parties is costly; that costs acts like a tax on work rewards.[6] Viable shirking is the result.

What forms of organizing team production will lower the cost of detecting "performance" (i.e., marginal productivity) and bring personally realized rates of substitution closer to true rates of substitution? Market competition, in principle, could monitor some team production. (It already *organizes* teams.) Input owners who are not team members can offer, in return for a smaller share of the team's rewards, to replace excessively (i.e., overpaid) shirking members. Market competition among potential team members would determine team membership and individual rewards. There would be no team leader, manager, organizer, owner, or employer. For such decentralized organizational control to work, outsiders, possibly after observing each team's total output, can speculate about their capabilities as team members and, by a market competitive process, revised teams with greater productive ability will be formed and sustained. Incumbent members will be constrained by threats of replacement by outsiders offering services for lower reward shares or offering greater rewards to the other members of the team. Any team member who shirked in the expectation that the reduced output effect would not be attributed to him will be displaced if his activity is detected. Teams of productive inputs, like business units, would evolve in apparent spontaneity in the market—without any central organizing agent, team manager, or boss.

But completely effective control cannot be expected from individualized market competition for two reasons. First, for this competition to be completely effective, new challengers for team membership must know where, and to what extent, shirking is a serious problem, i.e., know they can increase net output as compared with the inputs they replace. To the extent that this is true it is probably possible for existing fellow team members to recognize the shirking. But, by definition, the detection of shirking by observing team output is costly for team production. Secondly, assume the presence of detection costs, and assume that in order to secure a place on the team a new input owner must accept a smaller share of rewards (or a promise to produce more). Then his incentive to shirk would still be at least as great as the incentives of the inputs replaced, because he still bears less than the entire reduction in team output for which he is responsible.

THE CLASSICAL FIRM

One method of reducing shirking is for someone to specialize as a monitor to check the input performance of team members.[7] But who will monitor the monitor? One constraint on the monitor is the aforesaid market competition offered by other monitors, but for reasons already given, that is not perfectly effective. Another constraint can be imposed on the monitor: give him title to the net earnings of the team, net of payments to other inputs. If owners of cooperating inputs agree with the monitor that he is to receive any residual product above prescribed amounts (hopefully, the marginal value products of the other inputs), the monitor will have an added incentive not to shirk as a monitor. Specialization in monitoring plus reliance on a residual claimant status will reduce shirking; but additional links are needed to forge the firm of classical economic theory. How will the residual claimant monitor the other inputs?

We use the term monitor to connote several activities in addition to its disciplinary connotation. It connotes measuring output performance, apportioning rewards, observing the input behavior of inputs as means of detecting or estimating their marginal productivity and giving assignments or instructions in what to do and how to do it. (It also includes, as we shall show later, authority to terminate or revise contracts.) Perhaps the contrast between a football coach and team captain is helpful. The coach selects strategies and tactics and sends in instructions about what plays to utilize. The captain is essentially an observer and reporter of the performance at close hand of the members. The latter is an inspector-steward and the former a supervisor manager. For the present all these activities are included in the rubric "monitoring." All these tasks are, in principle, negotiable across markets, but we are presuming that such market measurement of marginal productivities and job reassignments are not so cheaply performed for team production. And in particular our analysis suggests that it is not so much the costs of spontaneously negotiating contracts in the markets among groups for team production as it is the detection of the performance of individual members of the team that calls for the organization noted here.

The specialist *who receives the residual rewards* will be the monitor of the members of the team (i.e., will manage the use of cooperative inputs). The monitor earns his residual through the reduction in shirking that he brings about, not only by the prices that he agrees to pay the owners of the inputs, but also by observing and directing the actions or uses of these inputs. *Managing or examining the ways to which inputs are used in team production is a method of metering the marginal productivity of individual inputs to the team's output.*

To discipline team members and reduce shirking, the residual claimant must have power to revise the contract terms and incentives of *individual* members without having to terminate or alter every other input's contract. Hence, team members who seek to increase their productivity will assign to the monitor not only the residual claimant right but also the right to alter individual membership and performance on the team. Each team member, of course, can terminate his own membership (i.e., quit the team), but only the monitor may unilaterally terminate the membership of any of the other members without necessarily terminating the team itself or his association with the team; and he alone can expand or reduce membership, alter the mix of membership, or sell the right to be the residual claimant-monitor of the team. It is this entire bundle of rights: (1) to be a residual claimant; (2) to observe input behavior; (3) to be the central party common to all contracts with inputs; (4) to alter the membership of the team; and (5) to sell these rights, that defines the *ownership* (or the employer) of the *classical* (capitalist, free-enterprise) firm. The coalescing of these rights has arisen, our analysis asserts, because it resolves the shirking-information problem of team production better than does the noncentralized contractual arrangement.

The relationship of each team member to the *owner* of the firm (i.e., the party common to all input contracts *and* the residual claimant) is simply a "quid pro quo" contract. Each makes a purchase and sale. The employee "orders" the owner of the team to pay him money in the same sense that the employer directs the team member to perform certain acts. The employee can terminate the contract as readily as can the employer, and long-term contracts, therefore, are not an essential attribute of the firm. Nor are "authoritarian," "dictational," or "fiat" attributes, relevant to the conception of the firm or its efficiency.

In summary, two necessary conditions exist for the emergence of the firm on the prior assumption that more than pecuniary wealth enter utility functions: (1) It is possible to increase productivity through team-oriented production, a production technique for which it is costly to directly measure the marginal outputs of the cooperating inputs. This makes it more difficult to restrict shirking through simple market exchange between cooperating inputs. (2) It is economical to estimate marginal productivity by observing or specifying input behavior. The simultaneous occurrence of both these preconditions leads to the contractual organization of inputs, known as the *classical capitalist firms* with (a) joint input production; (b) several input owners; (c) one party who is common to all the contracts of the joint inputs; (d) who has rights to renegotiate any input's contract independently of contracts with other input owners; (e) who holds the residual claim, and (f) who has the right to sell his central contractual residual status.[8]

Other theories of the firm

At this juncture, as an aside, we briefly place this theory of the firm in the contexts of those offered by Ronald Coase and Frank Knight.[9] Our view of the firm is not necessarily inconsistent with Coase's; we attempt to go further and identify refutable implications. Coase's penetrating insight is to make more of the fact that markets do not operate costlessly, and he relies on the cost of using markets to *form* contracts as his basic explanation for the existence of firms. We do not disagree with the proposition that, *ceteris paribus*, the higher is the cost of transacting across markets the greater will be the comparative advantage of organizing resources within the firm; it is a difficult proposition to disagree with or to refute. We could with equal ease subscribe to a theory of the firm based on the cost of managing, for surely it is true that, *ceteris paribus*, the lower is the cost of managing the greater will be the comparative advantage of organizing resources within the firm. To move the theory forward, it is necessary to know what is meant by a firm and to explain the circumstances under which the cost of "managing" resources is low relative to the cost of allocating resources through market transaction. The conception of and rationale for the classical firm that we propose takes a step down the path pointed out by Coase toward that goal. Consideration of team production, team organization, difficulty in metering outputs, and the problem of shirking are important to our explanation but, so far as we can ascertain, not in Coase's. Coase's analysis insofar as it had heretofore been developed would suggest open-ended contracts but does not appear to imply anything more— neither the residual claimant status nor the distinction between employee and subcontractor status (nor any of the implications indicated below). And it is not true that employees are generally employed on the basis of long-term contractual arrangements any more than on a series of short-term or indefinite length contracts.

The importance of our proposed additional elements is revealed, for example, by the explanation of why the person to whom the control monitor is responsible receives the residual, and also by our later discussion of the implications about the corporation, partnerships, and profit sharing. These alternative forms for organization of the firm are difficult to resolve on the basis of market transaction costs only. Our exposition also suggests a definition of the classical firm—something crucial that was heretofore absent.

In addition, sometimes a technological development will lower the cost of market transactions while, at the same time, it expands the role of the firm. When the "putting out" system was used for weaving, inputs were organized largely through market negotiations. With the development of efficient central sources of power, it became economical to perform weaving in proximity to the power source and to engage in team production. The bringing in of weavers surely must have resulted in a reduction in the cost of negotiating (forming) contracts. Yet, what we observe is the beginning of the factory system in which inputs are organized within a firm. Why? The weavers did not simply move to a common source of power that they could tap like an electric line, purchasing power while they used their own equipment. Now team production in the joint use of equipment became more important. The measurement of marginal productivity, which now involved interactions between workers, especially through their joint use of machines, became more difficult though contract negotiating cost was reduced, while managing the *behavior* of inputs became easier because of the increased centralization of activity. The firm as an organization expanded even though the cost of transactions was reduced by the advent of centralized power. The same could be said for modern assembly lines. Hence the emergence of central power sources expanded the scope of productive activity in which the firm enjoyed a comparative advantage as an organizational form.

Some economists, following Knight, have identified the bearing of risks of wealth changes with the director or central employer without explaining why that is a viable arrangement. Presumably, the more risk-averse inputs become employees rather than owners of the classical firm. Risk averseness and uncertainty *with regard to the firm's fortunes* have little, if anything, to do with our explanation although it helps to explain why all resources in a team are not owned by one person. That is, the role of risk taken in the sense of absorbing the windfalls that buffet the firm because of unforeseen competition, technological change, or fluctuations in demand are not central to our theory, although it is true that imperfect knowledge and, therefore, risk, in *this* sense of risk, underlie the problem of monitoring team behavior. We deduce the system of paying the manager with a residual claim (the equity) from the desire to have efficient means to reduce shirking so as to make team production economical and not from the smaller aversion to the risks of enterprise in a dynamic economy. We conjecture that "distribution-of-risk" is not a valid rationale for the *existence* and organization of the *classical* firm.

Although we have emphasized team production as creating a costly metering task and have treated team production as an essential (necessary?) condition for the firm, would not other obstacles to cheap metering also call forth the same kind of contractual arrangement here denoted as a firm? For example, suppose a farmer produces wheat in an easily ascertained quantity but with subtle and difficult to detect quality variations determined by how the farmer grew the wheat. A vertical integration could allow a purchaser to control the farmer's behavior in order to more economically estimate productivity. But this is not a case of joint or team production, unless "information" can be considered part of the product. (While a good case could be made for that broader conception of production, we shall ignore it here.) Instead of forming a firm, a buyer can contract to have his inspector on the site of production, just as home builders contract with architects to supervise building contracts; that arrangement is not a firm. Still, a firm might be organized in the production of many products wherein no team production or jointness of use of separately owned resources is involved.

This possibility rather clearly indicates a broader, or complementary approach to that which we have chosen. (1) As we do in this paper, it can be argued that the firm is the particular policing device utilized when joint team production is present. If other sources of high policing costs arise, as in the wheat case just indicated, some other forms of contractual arrangement will be used. Thus to each source of informational cost there may be a different type of policing and contractual arrangement. (2) On the other hand, one can say that where policing is difficult across markets, various forms of contractual arrangements are devised, but there is no reason for that known as the firm to be uniquely related or even highly correlated with team production, as defined here. It might be used equally probably and viably for other sources of high policing cost. We have not intensively analyzed other sources, and we can only note that our current and readily revisable conjecture is that (1) is valid, and has motivated us in our current endeavor. In any event, the test of the theory advanced here is to see whether the conditions we have identified are necessary for firms to have long-run viability rather than merely births with high infant mortality. Conglomerate firms or collections of separate production agencies into one owning organization can be interpreted as an investment trust or investment diversification device—probably along the lines that motivated Knight's interpretation. A holding company can be called a firm, because of the common association of the word firm with any ownership unit that owns income sources. The term firm as commonly used is so turgid of meaning that we can not hope to explain every entity to which the name is attached in common or even technical literature. Instead, we seek to identify and explain a particular contractual arrangement induced by the cost of information factors analyzed in this paper.

TYPES OF FIRMS

Profit-sharing firms

Explicit in our explanation of the capitalist firm is the assumption that the cost of *managing* the team's inputs by a central monitor, who disciplines himself because he is a residual claimant, is low relative to the cost of metering the marginal outputs of team members.

If we look within a firm to see who monitors—hires, fires, changes, promotes, and renegotiates—we should find him being a residual claimant or, at least, one whose pay or reward is more than any others correlated with fluctuations in the residual value of the firm. They more likely will have options or rights or bonuses than will inputs with other tasks.

An implicit "auxiliary" assumption of our explanation of the firm is that the cost of team production is increased if the residual claim is not held entirely by the central monitor. That is, we assume that if profit sharing had to be relied upon for *all* team members, losses from the resulting increase in central monitor shirking would exceed the output gains from the increased incentives of other team members not to shirk. If the optimal team size is only two owners of inputs, then an equal division of profits and losses between them will leave each with stronger incentives to reduce shirking than if the optimal team size is large, for in the latter case only a smaller percentage of the losses occasioned by the shirker will be borne by him. Incentives to shirk are positively related to the optimal size of the team under an equal profit-sharing scheme.[10]

The preceding does not imply that profit sharing is never viable. Profit sharing to encourage self-policing is more appropriate for small teams. And, indeed, where input owners are free to make whatever contractual arrangements suit them, as generally is true in capitalist economies, profit sharing seems largely limited to partnerships with a relatively small number of *active*[11] partners. Another advantage of such arrangements for smaller teams is that it permits more effective reciprocal monitoring among inputs. Monitoring need not be entirely specialized.

Profit sharing is more viable if small team size is associated with situations where the cost of specialized management of inputs is large relative to the increased productivity potential in team effort. We conjecture that the cost of managing team inputs increases if the productivity of a team member is difficult to correlate with his behavior. In "artistic" or "professional" work, watching a man's activities is not a good clue to what he is actually thinking or doing with his mind. While it is relatively easy to manage or direct the loading of trucks by a team of dock workers where input activity is so highly related in an obvious way to output, it is more difficult to manage and direct a lawyer in the preparation and presentation of a case. Dock workers can be directed in detail without the monitor himself loading the truck, and assembly line workers can be monitored by varying the speed of the assembly line, but detailed direction in the preparation of a law case would require in much greater degree that the monitor prepare the case himself. As a result, artistic or professional inputs, such as lawyers, advertising specialists, and doctors, will be given relatively freer reign with regard to individual behavior. If the management of inputs is relatively costly, or ineffective, as it would seem to be in these cases, but, none the less if team effort is more productive than separable production with exchange across markets, then there will develop a tendency to use profit-sharing schemes to provide incentives to avoid shirking.[12]

Socialist firms

We have analyzed the classical proprietorship and the profit-sharing firms in the context of free association and choice of economic organization. Such organizations need not be the most viable when political constraints limit the forms of organization that can be chosen. It is one thing to have profit sharing when professional or artistic talents are used by small teams. But if political or tax or subsidy considerations induce profit-sharing techniques when these are not otherwise economically justified, then additional management techniques will be developed to help reduce the degree of shirking.

For example, most, if not all, firms in Jugoslavia are owned by the employees in the restricted sense that all share in the residual. This is true for large firms and for firms which employ nonartistic, or nonprofessional, workers as well. With a decay of political constraints, most of these firms could be expected to rely on paid wages rather than shares in the residual. This rests on our auxiliary assumption that general sharing in the residual results in losses from enhanced shirking by the monitor that exceed the gains from reduced shirking by residual-sharing employees. If this were not so, profit sharing with employees should have occurred more frequently in Western societies where such organizations are neither banned nor preferred politically. Where residual sharing by employees is politically imposed, as in Jugoslavia, we are led to expect that some management technique will arise to reduce the shirking by the central monitor, a technique that will not be found frequently in Western societies since the monitor retains all (or much) of the residual in the West and profit sharing is largely confined to small, professional-artistic team production situations. We do find in the larger scale residual-sharing firms in Jugoslavia that there are employee committees that can recommend (to the state) the termination of a manager's contract (veto his continuance) with the enterprise. We conjecture that the workers' committee is given the right to recommend the termination of the manager's contract precisely because the general sharing of the residual increases "excessively" the manager's incentive to shirk.[13]

The corporation

All firms must initially acquire command over some resources. The corporation does so primarily by selling promises of future returns to those who (as creditors or owners) provide financial capital. In some situations resources can be acquired in advance from consumers by promises of future delivery (for example, advance sale of a proposed book). Or where the firm is a few artistic or professional persons, each can "chip in" with time and talent until the sale of services brings in revenues. For the most part, capital can be acquired more cheaply if many (risk-averse) investors contribute small portions to a large investment. The economies of raising large sums of equity capital in this way suggest that modifications in the relationship among corporate inputs are required to cope with the shirking problem that arises with profit sharing among large numbers of corporate stockholders. One modification is limited liability, especially for firms that are large relative to a stockholder's wealth. It serves to protect stockholders from large losses no matter how they are caused.

If every stock owner participated in each decision in a corporation, not only would large bureaucratic costs be incurred, but many would shirk the task of becoming well informed on the issue to be decided, since the losses associated with unexpectedly bad decisions will be borne in large part by the many other corporate shareholders. More effective control of corporate activity is achieved for most purposes by transferring decision authority to a smaller group, whose main function is to negotiate with and manage (renegotiate with) the other inputs of the team. The corporate stockholders retain the authority to revise the membership of the management group and over major decisions that affect the structure of the corporation or its dissolution.

As a result a new modification of partnerships is induced—the right to sale of corporate shares without approval of any other stockholders. Any shareholder can remove his wealth from control by those with whom he has differences of opinion. Rather than try to control the decisions of the management, which is harder to do with many stockholders than with only a few, unrestricted salability provides a more acceptable escape to each stockholder from continued policies with which he disagrees.

Indeed, the policing of managerial shirking relies on across-market competition from new groups of would-be managers as well as competition from members within the firm who seek to displace existing management. In addition to competition from outside and inside managers, control is facilitated by the temporary congealing of share votes into voting blocs owned by one or a few contenders. Proxy battles or stock-purchases concentrate the votes required to displace the existing management or modify managerial policies. But is it more than a change in policy that is sought by the newly formed financial interests, whether of new stockholders or not. It is the capitalization of expected future benefits into stock prices that concentrates on the innovators the wealth gains of their actions if they own large numbers of shares. Without capitalization of future benefits, there would be less incentive to incur the costs required to exert informed decisive influence on the corporation's policies and managing personnel. Temporarily, the structure of ownership reformed, moving away from diffused ownership into decisive power blocs, and this is a transient resurgence of the classical firm with power again concentrated in those who have title to the residual.

In assessing the significance of stockholders' power it is not the usual diffusion of voting power that is significant but instead the frequency with which voting congeals into decisive changes. Even a one-man owned company may have a long term with just one manager—continuously being approved by the owner. Similarly a dispersed voting power corporation may be also characterized by a long-lived management. The question is the probability of replacement of the management if it behaves in ways not acceptable to a majority of the stockholders. The unrestricted salability of stock and the transfer of proxies enhances the probability of decisive action in the event current stockholders or any outsider believes that management is not doing a good job with the corporation. We are not comparing the corporate responsiveness to that of a single proprietorship; instead, we are indicating features of the corporate structure that are induced by the problem of delegated authority to manager-monitors.[14]

Mutual and nonprofit firms

The benefits obtained by the new management are greater if the stock can be purchased and sold, because this enables *capitalization* of anticipated future improvements into present *wealth* of new managers who bought stock and created a larger capital by their management changes. But in nonprofit corporations, colleges, churches, country clubs, mutual savings banks, mutual insurance companies, and "coops", the future consequences of improved management are not capitalized into present wealth of stockholders. (As if to make more difficult that competition by new would-be monitors, multiple shares of ownership in those enterprises cannot be bought by one person.) One should, therefore, find greater shirking in nonprofit, mutually owned enterprises. (This suggests that nonprofit enterprises are especially appropriate in realms of endeavor where more shirking is desired and where redirected uses of the enterprise in response to market-revealed values is less desired.)

Partnerships

Team production in artistic or professional intellectual skills will more likely be by partnerships than other types of team production. This amounts to market-organized team activity and to a nonemployer status. Self-monitoring partnerships, therefore, will be used rather than employer–employee contracts, and these organizations will be small to prevent an excessive dilution of efforts through shirking. Also, partnerships are more likely to occur among relatives or long-standing acquaintances, not necessarily because they share a common utility function, but also because each knows better the other's work characteristics and tendencies to shirk.

Employee unions

Employee unions, whatever else they do, perform as monitors for employees. Employers monitor employees and similarly employees monitor an employer's performance. Are correct wages paid on time and in good currency? Usually, this is extremely easy to check. But some forms of employer performance are less easy to meter and are more subject to employer shirking. Fringe benefits often are in nonpecuniary, contingent form; medical, hospital, and accident insurance, and retirement pensions are contingent payments or performances partly in *kind* by employers to employees. Each employee cannot judge the character of such payments as easily as money wages. Insurance is a contingent payment—what the employee will get upon the contingent event may come as a disappointment. If he could easily determine what other employees had gotten upon such contingent events he could judge more accurately the performance by the employer. He could "trust" the employer not to shirk in such fringe contingent payments, but he would prefer an effective and economic monitor of those payments. We see a specialist monitor—the union employees' agent—hired by them and monitoring those aspects of employer payment most difficult for the employees to monitor. Employees should be willing to employ a specialist monitor to administer such hard-to-detect employer performance, even though their monitor has incentives to use pension and retirement funds not entirely for the benefit of employees.

TEAM SPIRIT AND LOYALTY

Every team member would prefer a team in which no one, not even himself, shirked. Then the true marginal costs and values could be equated to achieve more preferred positions. If one could enhance a common interest in nonshirking in the guise of a team loyalty or team spirit, the team would be more efficient. In those sports where team activity is most clearly exemplified, the sense of loyalty and team spirit is most strongly urged. Obviously the team is better, with team spirit and loyalty, because of the reduced shirking—not because of some other feature inherent in loyalty or spirit as such.[15]

Corporations and business firms try to instill a spirit of loyalty. This should not be viewed simply as a device to increase profits by *over*-working or misleading the employees, nor as an adolescent urge for belonging. It promotes a closer approximation to the employees' potentially available true rates of substitution between production and leisure and enables each team member to achieve a more preferred situation. The difficulty, of course, is to create economically that team spirit and loyalty. It can be preached with an aura of moral code of conduct—a morality with literally the same basis as the ten commandments—to restrict our conduct toward what we would choose if we bore our full costs.

KINDS OF INPUTS OWNED BY THE FIRM

To this point the discussion has examined why firms, as we have defined them, exist? That is, why is there an owner-employer who is the common party to contracts with other owners of inputs in team activity? The answer to that question should also indicate the kind of the jointly used resources likely to be owned by the central-owner-monitor and the kind likely to be hired from people who are not team-owners. Can we identify characteristics or features of various inputs that lead to their being hired or to their being owned by the firm?

How can residual-claimant, central-employer-owner demonstrate ability to pay the other hired inputs the promised amount in the event of a loss? He can pay in advance or he can commit wealth sufficient to cover negative residuals. The latter will take the form of machines, land, buildings, or raw materials committed to the firm. Commitments of labor-wealth (i.e., human wealth) given the property rights in people, is less feasible. These considerations suggest that residual claimants—owners of the firm—will be investors of resalable capital equipment in the firm. The goods or inputs more likely to be invested, than rented, by the owners of the enterprise, will have higher resale values relative to the initial cost and will have longer expected use in a firm relative to the economic life of the good.

But beyond these factors are those developed above to explain the existence of the institution known as the firm—the costs of detecting output performance. When a durable resource is used it will have a marginal product and a depreciation. Its use requires payment to cover at least use-induced depreciation; unless that user cost is specifically detectable, payment for it will be demanded in accord with *expected* depreciation. And we can ascertain circumstances for each. An indestructible hammer with a readily detectable marginal product has zero user cost. But suppose the hammer were destructible and that careless (which is easier than careful) use is more abusive and causes greater depreciation of the hammer. Suppose in addition the abuse is easier to detect by observing the way it is used than by observing only the hammer after its use, or by measuring the output scored from a hammer by a laborer. If the hammer were rented and used in the absence of the owner, the depreciation would be greater than if the use were observed by the owner and the user charged in accord with the imposed depreciation. (Careless use is more likely than careful use—if one does not pay for the greater depreciation.) An absentee owner would therefore ask for a higher rental price because of the higher *expected* user cost than if the item were used by the owner. The expectation is higher because of the greater difficulty of observing specific user cost, by inspection of the hammer after use. Renting is therefore in this case more costly than owner use. This is the valid content of the misleading expressions about ownership being more economical than renting—ignoring all other factors that may work in the opposite direction, like tax provision, short-term occupancy and capital risk avoidance.

Better examples are tools of the trade. Watch repairers, engineers, and carpenters tend to own their own tools especially if they are portable. Trucks are more likely to be employee owned rather than other equally expensive team inputs because it is relatively cheap for the driver to police the care taken in using a truck. Policing the use of trucks by a nondriver owner is more likely to occur for trucks that are not specialized to one driver, like public transit buses.

The factor with which we are concerned here is one related to the costs of monitoring not only the gross product performance of an input but also the abuse or depreciation inflicted on the input in the course of its use. If depreciation or user cost is more cheaply detected when the owner can see its use than by only seeing the input before and after, there is a force toward owner use rather than renting. Resources whose user cost is harder to detect when used by someone else, tend on this count to be owner-used. Absentee ownership, in the lay language, will be less likely. Assume momentarily that labor service cannot be performed in the absence of its owner. The labor owner can more cheaply monitor any abuse of himself than if somehow labor-services could be provided without the labor owner observing its mode of use or knowing what was happening. Also his incentive to abuse himself is increased if he does not own himself.[16]

The similarity between the preceding analysis and the question of absentee landlordism and of sharecropping arrangements is no accident. The same factors which explain the contractual arrangements known as a firm help to explain the incidence of tenancy, labor hiring or sharecropping.[17]

FIRMS AS A SPECIALIZED MARKET INSTITUTION FOR COLLECTING, COLLATING, AND SELLING INPUT INFORMATION

The firm serves as a highly specialized surrogate market. Any person contemplating a joint-input activity must search and detect the qualities of available joint inputs. He could contact an employment agency, but that agency in a small town would have little advantage over a large firm with many inputs. The employer, by virtue of monitoring many inputs, acquires special superior information about their productive talents. This aids his *directive* (i.e., market hiring) efficiency. He "sells" his information to employee-inputs as he aids them in ascertaining good input combinations for team activity. Those who work as employees or who rent services to him are using him to discern superior combinations of inputs. Not only does the director-employer "decide" what each input will produce, he also estimates which heterogeneous inputs will work together jointly more efficiently, and he does this in the context of a privately owned market for forming teams. The department store is a firm and is a superior private market. People who shop and work in one town can as well shop and work in a privately owned firm.

This marketing function is obscured in the theoretical literature by the assumption of homogeneous factors. Or it is tacitly left for individuals to do themselves via personal market search, much as if a person had to search without benefit of specialist retailers. Whether or not the firm arose because of this efficient information service, it gives the director-employer more knowledge about the productive talents of the team's inputs, and a basis for superior decisions about efficient or profitable combinations of those heterogeneous resources.

In other words, opportunities for profitable team production by inputs already within the firm may be ascertained more economically and accurately than for resources outside the firm. Superior combinations of inputs can be more economically identified and formed from resources already used in the organization than by obtaining new resources (and knowledge of them) from the outside. Promotion and revision of employee assignments (contracts) will be preferred by a firm to the hiring of new inputs. To the extent that this occurs there is reason to expect the firm to be able to operate as a conglomerate rather than persist in producing a single product. Efficient production with heterogeneous resources is a result not of having *better* resources but in *knowing more accurately* the relative productive performances of those resources. Poorer resources can be paid less in accord with their inferiority; greater accuracy of knowledge of the potential and actual productive actions of inputs rather than having high productivity resources makes a firm (or an assignment of inputs) profitable.[18]

SUMMARY

While ordinary contracts facilitate efficient specialization according to comparative advantage, a special class of contracts among a group of joint inputs to a team production process is commonly used for team production. Instead of multilateral contracts among all the joint inputs' owners, a central common party to a set of bilateral contracts facilitates efficient organization of the joint inputs in team production. The terms of the contracts form the basis of entity called the firm— especially appropriate for organizing team production processes.

Team productive activity is that in which a union, or joint use, of inputs yields a larger output than the sum of the products of the separately used inputs. This team production requires—like all other production processes—an assessment of marginal productivities if efficient production is to be achieved. Nonseparability of the products of several differently owned joint inputs raises the cost of assessing the marginal productivities of those resources or services of each input owner. Monitoring or metering the productivities to match marginal productivities to costs of inputs and thereby to reduce shirking can be achieved more economically (than by across market bilateral negotiations among inputs) in a firm.

The essence of the classical firm is identified here as a contractual structure with: (1) joint input production; (2) several input owners; (3) one party who is common to all the contracts of the joint inputs; (4) who has rights to renegotiate any input's contract independently of contracts with other input owners; (5) who holds the residual claim; and (6) who has the right to sell his central contractual residual status. The central agent is called the firm's owner and the employer. No authoritarian control is involved; the arrangement is simply a contractual structure subject to continuous renegotiation with the central agent. The contractual structure arises as a means of enhancing efficient organization of team production. In particular, the ability to detect shirking among owners of jointly used inputs in team production is enhanced (detection costs are reduced) by this arrangement and the discipline (by revision of contracts) of input owners is made more economic.

Testable implications are suggested by the analysis of different types of organizations—nonprofit, proprietary for profit, unions, cooperatives, partnerships, and by the kinds of inputs that tend to be owned by the firm in contrast to those employed by the firm.

We conclude a highly conjectural but possibly significant interpretation. As a consequence of the flow of information to the central party (employer), the firm takes on the characteristic of an efficient market in that information about the productive characteristics of a large set of specific inputs is now more cheaply available. Better recombinations or new uses of resources can be more efficiently ascertained than by the conventional search through the general market. In this sense inputs compete with each other within and via a firm rather than solely across markets as conventionally conceived. Emphasis on interfirm competition obscures intrafirm competition among inputs. Conceiving competition as the *revelation and exchange* of knowledge or information about qualities, potential uses of different inputs in different potential applications indicates that the firm is a device for enhancing competition among sets of input resources as well as a device for more efficiently rewarding the inputs. In contrast to markets and cities which can be viewed as publicly or nonowned market places, the firm can be considered a privately owned market; if so, we could consider the firm and the ordinary market as competing types of markets, competition between private proprietary markets and public or communal markets. Could it be that the market suffers from the defects of communal property rights in organizing and influencing uses of valuable resources?

ACKNOWLEDGEMENTS

Acknowledgement is made for financial aid from the E. Lilly Endowment, Inc. grant to UCLA for research in the behavioral effects of property rights.

NOTES

1. Meter means to measure and also to apportion. One can meter (measure) output and one can also meter (control) the output. We use the word to denote both; the context should indicate which.

2. A producer's wealth would be reduced by the present capitalized value of the future income lost by loss of reputation. Reputation, i.e., credibility, is an asset, which is another way of saying that reliable information about expected performance is both a costly and a valuable good. For acts of God that interfere with contract performance, both parties have incentives to reach a settlement akin to that which would have been reached if such events had been covered by specific contingency clauses. The reason, again, is that a reputation for "honest" dealings—i.e., for actions similar to those that would probably have been reached had the contract provided this contingency—is wealth.

   Almost every contract is open-ended in that many contingencies are uncovered. For example, if a fire delays production of a promised product by A to B, and if B contends that A has not fulfilled the contract, how is the dispute settled and what recompense, if any, does A grant to B? A person uninitiated in such questions may be surprised by the extent to which contracts permit either party to escape performance or to nullify the contract. In fact, it is hard to imagine any contract, which when taken solely in terms of its stipulations, could not be evaded by one of the parties. Yet that is the ruling, viable type of contract. Why? Undoubtedly the best discussion that we have seen on this question is by Stewart Macaulay.

   There are means not only of detecting or preventing cheating, but also for deciding how to allocate the losses or gains of unpredictable events or quality of items exchanged. Sales contracts contain warranties, guarantees, collateral, return privileges and penalty clauses for specific nonperformance. These are means of assignment of *risks* of losses of cheating. A lower price without warranty—an "as is" purchase—places more of the risk on the buyer while the seller buys insurance against losses of his "cheating". On the other hand, a warranty or return privilege or service contract places more risk on the seller with insurance being bought by the buyer.

3. The function is separable into additive functions if the cross partial derivative is zero, i.e., if $\partial^2 Z/\partial X_i \partial X_j = 0$.

4. With sufficient generality of notation and conception this team production function could be formulated as a case of the generalized production function interpretation given by our colleague, E. A. Thompson.

5. More precisely: "if anything other than pecuniary income enters his utility function". Leisure stands for all nonpecuniary income for simplicity of exposition.

6. Do not assume that the sole result of the cost of detecting shirking is one form of payment (more leisure and less take home money). With several members of the team, each has an incentive to cheat against each other by engaging in more than the average amount of such leisure if the employer can not tell at zero cost which employee is taking more than average. As a result the total productivity of the team is lowered. Shirking detection costs thus change the form of payment and also result in lower total rewards. Because the cross partial derivatives are positive, shirking reduces other people's marginal products.

7. What is meant by performance? Input energy, initiative, work attitude, perspiration, rate of exhaustion? Or output? It is the latter that is sought—the *effect* or output. But performance is nicely ambiguous because it suggests both input and output. It is *nicely* ambiguous because as we shall see, sometimes by inspecting a team member's input activity we can better judge his output effect, perhaps not with complete accuracy but better than by watching the output of the *team*. It is not always the case that watching input activity is the only or best means of detecting, measuring or monitoring output effects of each team member, but in some cases it is a useful way. For the moment the word performance glosses over these aspects and facilitates concentration on other issues.

8. Removal of (b) converts a capitalist proprietary firm to a socialist firm.

9. Recognition must also be made to the seminal inquiries by Morris Silver and Richard Auster, and by H. B. Malmgren.

10. While the degree to which residual claims are centralized will affect the size of the team, this will be only one of many factors that determine team size, so as an approximation, we can treat team size as exogenously determined. Under certain assumptions about the shape of the "typical" utility function, the incentive to avoid shirking with unequal profit sharing can be measured by the Herfindahl index.

11. The use of the word active will be clarified in our discussion of the corporation, which follows below.

12. Some sharing contracts, like crop sharing, or rental payments based on gross sales in retail stores, come close to profit sharing. However, it is gross output sharing rather than profit sharing. We are unable to specify the implications of the difference. We refer the reader to S. N. Cheung.

13. Incidentally, investment activity will be changed. The inability to capitalize the investment value as "take-home" private property *wealth* of the members of the firm means that the benefits of the investment must be taken as annual income by those who are employed at the time of the income. Investment will be confined more to those with shorter life and with higher rates or pay-offs if the alternative of investing is paying out the firm's income to its employees to take home and use as private property. For a development of this proposition, see the papers by Eirik Furobotn and Svetozar Pejovich, and by Pejovich.

14. Instead of thinking of shareholders as joint *owners*, we can think of them as investors, like bondholders, except that the stockholders are more optimistic than bondholders about the enterprise prospects. Instead of buying bonds in the corporation, thus enjoying smaller risks, shareholders prefer to invest funds with a greater realizable return if the firm prospers as expected, but with smaller (possibly negative) returns if the firm performs in a manner closer to that expected by the more pessimistic investors. The pessimistic investors, in turn, regard only the bonds as likely to pay off.

If the entrepreneur-organizer is to raise capital on the best terms to him, it is to his advantage, as well as that of prospective investors, to recognize these differences in expectations. The residual claim on earnings enjoyed by shareholders does not serve the function of enhancing their efficiency as monitors in the general situation. The stockholders are "merely" the less risk-averse or the more optimistic member of the group that finances the firm. Being more optimistic than the average and seeing a higher mean value future return, they are willing to pay more for a certificate that allows them to realize gain on their expectations. One method of doing so is to buy claims to the distribution of returns that "they see" while bondholders, who are more pessimistic, purchase a claim to the distribution that they see as more likely to emerge. Stockholders are then comparable to warrant holders. They are not about the voting rights (usually not attached to warrants); they are in the same position in so far as voting rights are concerned as are bondholders. The only difference is in the probability distribution of rewards and the terms on which they can place their bets.

If we treat bondholders, preferred and convertible preferred stockholders, and common stockholders and warrant holders as simply different classes of investors—differing not only in their risk averseness but in their beliefs about the probability distribution of the firm's future earnings, why should stockholders be regarded as "owners" in any sense distinct from the other financial investors? The entrepreneur-organizer, who let us assume is the chief operating officer and sole repository of control of the corporation, does not find his authority residing in common stockholders (except in the case of a take over). Does this type of control make any difference in the way the firm is conducted? Would it make any difference in the kinds of behavior that would be tolerated by competing managers and investors (and we here deliberately refrain from thinking of them as owner-stockholders in the traditional sense)?

Investment old timers recall a significant incidence of nonvoting common stock, now prohibited in corporations whose stock is traded on listed exchanges. (Why prohibited?) The entrepreneur in those days could hold voting shares while investors held nonvoting shares, which in every other respect were identical. Nonvoting share holders were simply investors devoid of ownership connotations. The control and behavior of inside owners in such corporations has never, so far as we have ascertained, been carefully studied. For example, at the simplest level of interest, does the evidence indicate that nonvoting shareholders fared any worse because of not having voting rights? Did owners permit the nonvoting holders the normal return available to voting shareholders? Though evidence is prohibitively expensive to obtain, it is remarkable that voting and nonvoting shares sold for essentially identical prices, even during some proxy battles. However, our casual evidence deserves no more than interest-initiating weight.

One more point. The façade is deceptive. Instead of nonvoting shares, today we have warrants, convertible preferred stocks all of which are solely or partly "equity" claims without voting rights, though they could be converted into voting shares.

In sum, is it the case that the stockholder-investor relationship is one emanating from the *division* of *ownership* among several people, or is it that the collection of investment funds from people of varying anticipations is the underlying factor? If the latter, why should any of them be thought of as the owners in whom voting rights, whatever they may signify or however exercisable, should reside in order to enhance efficiency? Why voting rights in any of the outside, participating investors?

Our initial perception of this possibly significant difference in interpretation was precipitated by Henry Manne. A reading of his paper makes it clear that it is hard to understand why an investor who wishes to back and "share" in the consequences of some new business should necessarily have to acquire voting power (i.e., power to change the manager-operator) in order to invest in the venture. In fact, we invest in some ventures in the hope that no other stockholders will be so "foolish" as to try to toss out the incumbent management. We want him to have the power to stay in office, and for the prospect of sharing in his fortunes we buy nonvoting common stock. Our willingness to invest is enhanced by the knowledge that we can act legally via fraud, embezzlement and other laws to help assure that we outside investors will not be "milked" beyond our initial discounted anticipations.

15. *Sports Leagues:* Professional sports contests among teams is typically conducted by a *league* of teams. We assume that sports consumers are interested not only in absolute sporting skill but also in skills *relative* to other teams. Being slightly better than opposing teams enables one to claim a major portion of the receipts; the inferior team does not release resources and reduce costs, since they were expected in the play of contest. Hence, absolute skill is developed beyond the equality of marginal investment in sporting skill with its true social marginal value product. It follows there will be a tendency to overinvest in training athletes and developing teams. "'Reverse shirking'" arises, as budding players are induced to overpractice hyperactively relative to the social marginal value of their enhanced skills. To prevent overinvestment, the teams seek an agreement with each other to restrict practice, size of teams, and even pay of the team members (which reduces incentives of young people to overinvest in developing skills). Ideally, if all the contestant teams were owned by one owner, overinvestment in sports would be avoided, much as ownership of common fisheries or underground oil or water reserve would prevent overinvestment. This hyperactivity (to suggest the opposite of shirking) is controlled by the league of teams, wherein the league adopts a common set of constraints on each team's behavior. In effect, the teams are no longer really owned by the team owners but are supervised by them, much as the franchisers of some product. They are not full-fledged owners of their business, including the brand name, and can not "do what they wish" as franchises. Comparable to the franchiser, is the league commissioner or conference president, who seeks to restrain hyperactivity, as individual team supervisors compete with each other and cause external diseconomies. Such restraints are usually regarded as anticompetitive, antisocial, collusive-cartel devices to restrain free open competition, and reduce players' salaries. However, the interpretation presented here is premised on an attempt to avoid hyperinvestment in team sports production. Of course, the team operators have an incentive, once the league is formed and restraints are placed on hyper-investment activity, to go further and obtain the private benefits of monopoly restriction. To what extent over-investment is replaced by monopoly restriction is not yet determinable; nor have we seen an empirical test of these two competing, but mutually consistent interpretations. (This interpretation of league-sports activity was proposed by Earl Thompson and formulated by Michael Canes.) Again,

athletic teams clearly exemplify the specialization of monitoring with captains and coaches; a captain detects shirkers while the coach trains and selects strategies and tactics. Both functions may be centralized in one person.

16. Professional athletes in baseball, football, and basketball, where athletes having sold their source of service to the team owners upon entering into sports activity, are owned by team owners. Here the team owners must monitor the athletes' physical condition and behavior to protect the team owners' wealth. The athlete has *less* (not, *no*) incentive to protect or enhance his athletic prowess since capital value changes have less impact on his own wealth and more on the team owners. Thus, some athletes sign up for big initial bonuses (representing present capital value of future services). Future salaries are lower by the annuity value of the prepaid "bonus" and hence the athlete has *less* to lose by subsequent abuse of his athletic prowess. Any decline in his subsequent service value would in part be borne by the team owner who owns the players' future service. This does not say these losses of future salaries have no effect on preservation of athletic talent (we are not making a "sunk cost" error). Instead, we assert that the preservation is reduced, not eliminated, because the amount of loss of wealth suffered is smaller. The athlete will spend less to maintain or enhance his prowess thereafter. The effect of this revised incentive system is evidenced in comparisons of the kinds of attention and care imposed on the athletes at the "expense of the team owner" in the case where athletes' future services are owned by the team owner with that where future labor service values are owned by the athlete himself. Why athletes' future athletic services are owned by the team owners rather than being hired is a question we should be able to answer. One presumption is cartelization and monopsony gains to team owners. Another is exactly the theory being expounded in this paper—costs of monitoring production of athletes; we know not on which to rely.

17. The analysis used by Cheung in explaining the prevalence of sharecropping and land tenancy arrangements is built squarely on the same factors—the costs of detecting output performance of jointly used inputs in team production and the costs of detecting user costs imposed on the various inputs if owner used or if rented.

18. According to our interpretation, the firm is a specialized surrogate for a market for team use of inputs; it provides superior (i.e., cheaper) collection and collation of knowledge about heterogeneous resources. The greater the set of inputs about which knowledge of performance is being collated within a firm the greater are the present costs of the collation activity. Then, the larger the firm (market) the greater the attenuation of monitor control. To counter this force, the firm will be divisionalized in ways that economize on those costs—just as will the market be specialized. So far as we can ascertain, other theories of the reasons for firms have no such implications.

In Japan, employees by custom work nearly their entire lives with one firm, and the firm agrees to that expectation. Firms will tend to be large and conglomerate to enable a broader scope of input revision. Each firm is, in effect, a small economy engaging in "intranational and international" trade. Analogously, Americans expect to spend their whole lives in the United States, and the bigger the country, in terms of variety of resources, the easier it is to adjust to changing tastes and circumstances. Japan, with its lifetime employees, should be characterized more by large, conglomerate firms. Presumably, at some size of the firm, specialized knowledge about inputs becomes as expensive to transmit across divisions of the firms as it does across markets to other firms.

REFERENCES

Canes, M. A Model of a Sports League, unpublished doctoral dissertation, UCLA 1970.

Cheung, S. N. *The Theory of Share Tenancy*, Chicago 1969.

Coase, R. H. The Nature of the Firm, *Economica*, Nov. 1937, **4**: 386–405; reprinted in Stigler, G. J. and Boulding, K., eds., *Readings in Price Theory*, Homewood 1952, 331–351.

Furobotn, E. and Pejovich, S. Property Rights and the Behavior of the Firm in a Socialist State, *Zeitschrift für Nationalökonomie*, 1970, **30**: 431–454.

Knight, F. H. *Risk, Uncertainty and Profit,* New York 1965.

Macaulay, S. Non-Contractual Relations in Business: A Preliminary Study, *American Sociological Review,* 1968, **28**: 55–69.

Malmgren, H. B. Information, Expectations and the Theory of the Firm, *Quarterly Journal of Economics,* Aug. 1961, **75**: 399–421.

Manne, H. Our Two Corporation Systems: Law and Economics, *Virginia Law Review,* Mar. 1967, **53**: No. 2, 259–284.

Pejovich, S. The Firm, Monetary Policy and Property Rights in a Planned Economy, *Western Economic Journal,* Sept. 1969, **7**: 193–200.

Silver M. and Auster, R. Entrepreneurship, Profit, and the Limits on Firm Size, *Journal of Business,* July 1969, **42**: 277–281

Thompson, E. A. Nonpecuniary Rewards and the Aggregate Production Function, *Review of Economics and Statistics,* Nov. 1970, **52**: 395–404.

2

The Allocation of Resources in the Presence of Indivisibilities

Herbert E. Scarf

The major problem presented to economic theory by the presence of indivisibilities in production is the impossibility of detecting optimality at the level of the firm, or for the economy as a whole, using the criterion of profitability based on competitive prices. I will explore this issue in a rather leisurely way, beginning with a discussion of the role played by competitive prices in verifying optimality when production takes place under constant returns to scale; then illustrating the failure of prices to perform this task when indivisibilities are significant; and, finally, suggesting the replacement of the pricing test by a specific quantity test. It is my hope that continued study of these quantity tests will increase our understanding of the division of labor in a large firm.

USING PRICES TO DETECT OPTIMALITY UNDER CONSTANT RETURNS TO SCALE

One of the most important professional activities of economists is to carry out exercises in comparative statistics: to estimate the consequences and the merits of changes in economic policy or in our economic environment. We do comparative statics at the level of the firm when we calculate the effects of a change in factor endowments or in the price of a valuable input into production. We engage in comparative statics and dynamics for the economy as a whole when we examine the consequences of the dramatic increase in the price of imported oil in the latter part of 1973, or the second oil shock following the fall of the Shah, or the dismantling of AT&T, or a massive change in income taxation within the United States, or the NAFTA. If these consequences spread throughout the entire economy, we evaluate them by assessing their effects on the well-being of the members of the community.

We have a remarkable paradigm for assessing well-being that has been passed on to us by generations of economic theorists and utilitarian philosophers. The utilitarian

Reprinted with permission from *Journal of Economic Perspectives*, Vol. 8, No. 4, 1994, pp. 111–128

calculus, in its modern ordinal version, provides us with a simple test for evaluating the merits of a proposed change in economic activities: The change should be accepted if it has as an intermediate consequence—or one that can be brought about by a suitable redistribution of income—an increase in the well-being or utility of all of the members of society.

The utilitarian test requires the possibility of major income redistributions that may not be politically viable—the movement of a clothing manufacturer from a Northern mill town to a lower wage region of the South may result in a potential Pareto improvement, but I know of no instances of an appropriate compensation to those employees whose jobs have been lost. And there are serious problems about maintaining effective incentives if lump sum transfers of income are made independently of effort and the supply of productive factors.

In spite of these and other reservations, I personally consider the welfare test to be an extraordinary intellectual construction—one which permits us to focus our discussions about the potential merits of a novel economic proposal. Last summer, for example, I participated in an extended discussion with a distinguished high-energy physicist about the super-conducting super-collider. In that conversation, it became quite clear to me that the community of physicists in favor of the project had been unable to establish any ground rules about what constituted a compelling argument for the project. Of course, it wasn't the case that they had no arguments in favor of the collider; they had many of them. But most of these arguments could equally well have been presented for a project whose costs were orders of magnitude larger. There was no prior agreement or understanding between the proponents of the super-collider and their audiences about what constituted an acceptable argument for any particular level of expenditure.

Our profession does have such a line of discourse. It may, admittedly, be difficult to carry out the welfare test in an instance as complex as the super-collider; the collider is, after all, a public rather than a private good, and it is one whose potential benefits are extremely hard to predict. The utilitarian test is much easier to carry out when more conventional economic projects are proposed. The test actually leads to a simple exercise in the calculation of profitability, which, in my opinion, is one of the major theorems of microeconomic theory, a theorem which is not entirely obvious to the man on the street or even to professional economists.

Suppose that we are contemplating a hypothetical economic situation which is in equilibrium in the purest Walrasian sense. The production possibility set exhibits constant returns to scale so that there is a profit of zero at the equilibrium prices. Each consumer evaluates personal income (or wealth) at these prices and market demand functions are obtained by the aggregation of individual utility maximizing demands. The system is in equilibrium in the sense that demand equals supply for each of the goods and services in the economy.

Suppose that a technical advance is made resulting in the discovery of a new manufacturing activity subject to constant returns to scale—one which produces a good whose price is already known, at a new location, with different materials, with less expensive labor or with more sophisticated machinery. Shall the new activity be used at some positive level? The word "shall" in this question is the same word as in the question: "Shall the super-conducting super-collider be built?" The utilitarian test can be applied by inquiring whether the new activity can be combined with a plan of income redistributions in such a way as to make all consumers better off than they had previously been. On the face of it, this sounds as if we must solve a complex mathematical programming problem; but, in fact, the question has a remarkably simple answer: *If the activity if profitable at the old equilibrium prices, then there is a way to use the activity at a positive level so that with suitable income redistributions, the welfare of every member of society will increase.* There is no necessity to determine the new equilibrium prices arising after the activity is introduced; the current prices will do. And, conversely, *if the new activity makes a negative profit at the old equilibrium prices, then there is no way in which it can be used to improve the utility of all consumers, even allowing the most extraordinary schemes for income redistribution.* This is an astonishing mathematical theorem which I often ask about in graduate oral exams in microeconomics. The second assertation takes about two lines of proof; the first is more subtle; three lines of proof and a figure will do. I have never seen this theorem, which seems to me to be one of the important theoretical arguments in favor of private enterprise, in any textbook on economics.[1]

It may be worth remarking that if 17 new activities are presented simultaneously, the pricing test can be applied to the collection of activities in an arbitrary sequence, without regard to decisions made about the remaining activities. If none of the 17 activities makes a positive profit at the old equilibrium prices, then no subset of them can be used, along with income redistributions, so as to improve everyone's economic lot. If any one of the activities makes a positive profit, them some welfare improvement is surely possible. The activity can be introduced, a new equilibrium determined—with Pareto-improving income redistributions—and the pricing test can be applied to the remaining activities. This is an extraordinarily decentralized test; it presumably could be applied to every minor innovation on the shop floor of a large firm simply by evaluating its profitability in terms of prevailing market prices.

The market test sounds very much like a step in the simplex method for solving linear programs. An activity analysis model of the economy or a firm is given, along with a specified factor endowment and an objective function which is to be maximized subject to the constraint that the factor endowment is not exceeded. In a linear programming problem, a feasible solution to the constraints is proposed, and prices are found yielding a zero profit for the activities in use. The proposed solution is optimal if and only if the remaining activities make a profit less than or equal to zero.

The simplex method is an extremely efficient algorithm for solving linear programs: Programs involving thousands of variables can be solved routinely on a personal computer by high school students. But what is even more significant for economists is that this effective computational procedure is based on an evaluation of profitability identical to that performed by competitive markets. A visitor from another planet who was taught the simplex method for solving linear maximization problems would inevitably be led to the use of prices and profitability to detect optimality. An algorithm—a mathematical technique for solving maximization problems—suggests an institution—competitive markets—which is central to the way in which we organize our economic lives.

Is this suggestion of a major institutional structure an accident of the simplex method or can it be expected from other computational procedures as well? Is it a reasonable research strategy to address an area of economic theory which is not fully understood—at least by me—to cast it in the form of an optimization problem, and to hope that algorithms for its solution will produce a conceptual framework that is relevant to the original economic problem? I'm not sure, but it is a strategy that I have followed for a number of years in an attempt to increase my understanding of the problems posed for economic theory by indivisibilities and economies of scale.

THE FAILURE OF PRICES IN THE PRESENCE OF INDIVISIBILITIES

Both linear programming and the Walrasian model of equilibrium make the fundamental assumption that the production possibility set displays constant or decreasing returns to scale; that there are no economies associated with production at a high scale. I find this an absurd assumption, contradicted by the most casual of observations. Taken literally, the assumption of constant returns to scale in production implies that if technical knowledge were universally available we could all trade only in factors of production, and assemble in our own backyards all of the manufactured goods whose services we would like to consume. If I want an automobile at a specified future date, I would purchase steel, glass, rubber, electrical wiring and tools, hire labor of a variety of skills on a part-time basis, and simply make the automobile myself. I would grow my own food, cut and sew my own clothing, build my own computer chips and assemble and disassemble my own international communication system whenever I need to make a telephone call, without any loss of efficiency. Notwithstanding the analysis offered by Adam Smith more than two centuries ago, I would manufacture pins as I needed them.

If production really does obey constant returns to scale, there is nothing to be gained by organizing economic activity in large, durable and complex units; in short, there is no economic justification for the existence of firms. Competitive markets would set prices for manufactured goods at every stage of production and cash would be exchanged, or accounts would be reckoned, as goods moved from one task to another. Every step in a complex manufacturing process would be tested for profitability by itself, without regard to its relationship to other potential improvements.

I am, I believe, not alone in thinking that the essence of economies of scale in production is the presence of large and significant indivisibilities in production. What I have in mind are assembly lines, bridges, transportation and communication networks, giant presses and complex manufacturing plants, which are available in specific discrete sizes, and whose economic usefulness manifests itself only when the scale of operation is large. If the technology giving rise to a large firm is based on indivisibilities, then this technology can be described by, say, an activity analysis model in which the activity levels referring to indivisible goods are required to assume integral values, like $0, 1, 2 \ldots$, only. When factor levels are specified and a particular objective function is chosen, we are led directly to that class of difficult optimization problems known as integer programs.

For a theorist, the major problem presented by indivisibilities in production is the failure of the pricing test for optimality or for welfare improvements. Return to our previous discussion of the economy which is in full Walrasian equilibrium, and imagine, as before, that a new activity is discovered. But let us now assume, in contrast to our earlier example, that this new activity—perhaps a decision about the number of manufacturing plants of a particular type to be constructed—involves a discrete choice that can only be carried out at integral levels. One can argue easily that if the activity makes a negative profit at the old equilibrium prices, then there is no way to use it at a discrete or continuous level so as to improve the utility of every agent in the economy. The problem arises with the converse; it is perfectly possible that the activity make a positive profit at the old prices and still not be capable of being used at any discrete level to yield a Pareto improvement.

Even more problems arise if 17 activities are presented to us, all of which must be run at an integral level. A welfare improvement will typically require the selection of a subset of the activities, some of which are profitable at the old equilibrium prices, and some of which are not. There is no algorithm based on prices and profitability which permits us to make a sequence of welfare improvements by introducing one activity at a time, or even to detect which activities should ultimately be used. There is no pricing test in the presence of indivisibilities.

The absence of a pricing test is a truth that must be confronted. It certainly does imply that total decentralization by means of competitive prices is impossible if the technology involves serious indivisibilities. In my own view, this is a compelling reason for the existence of large firms, and it suggests that some serious insight about the large firm might be gained by considering such a firm to be essentially an algorithm for the solution of mathematical programming problems in which some of the variables are restricted to integer values. I hope that insights from this source would complement other insights about the functioning of large enterprises that are presented in a narrative rather than mathematical form, that are based on a careful analysis of particular historical cases, or that involve flows of information in hierarchical structures. The subject is sufficiently complex so that many voices should be heard.

AN EXAMPLE

An example may be useful. Consider a problem involving a single good that can be produced by a variety of technologies. Each technology is embodied in a particular type of manufacturing plant with a specific cost of construction, with a specific capacity, and with a specific unit cost of manufacturing. The level of demand for the product is given exogenously, and we are required to construct a series of plants and to manufacture sufficient product to satisfy this demand at minimum cost. We now have a mathematical programming problem in which some of the variables, the number of plants of each type to be constructed, are integral, and the remaining variables, the amounts manufactured at each plant, are continuous.

The example is artificial in many ways. Perhaps its most serious flaw is the obvious lack of any dynamic considerations. The construction cost is presumably paid at the time of construction, when a capacity for producing the maximum output per period is established. But demand for output manifests itself in a sequence of periods over time, possibly in a predictable though varying fashion, or possibly with a good deal of uncertainty. Moreover, it is plausible to assume that manufactured goods can be kept

Table 1. Production costs: Smokestack versus High Tech

	Smokestack	High Tech
Capacity	16	7
Construction cost	53	30
Marginal cost	3	2
Average cost	6.3125	6.2857

in inventory, at some cost, so as to satisfy future demand. These elements can certainly be introduced into our problem, but with a considerable increase in complexity. In order to make my points as simply as possible, I will assume that demand is constant over time and that no inventories are kept; the unit costs may then be thought of as the discounted sum of unit costs incurred over time as this constant demand is satisfied.

For fixed construction costs, capacities and unit costs, the optimal construction plan depends crucially on the level of demand. Some levels will call for considerable excess capacity in various plants, and other levels will not. How can we tell whether a proposed construction and manufacturing plan, which meets the demand requirement, does, in fact, minimize total cost? Competitive prices will not work for this class of problems. There is only one option: the price test must be supplemented, or replaced, by what can be called a "quantity test."

At this point, I have an expository difficulty about which I must be quite explicit. I would like to present an elementary example illustrating the particular quantity test required to demonstrate optimality without being cluttered by too much detail; this naturally leads to an example with a small number of plants, say, two. But programming problems with only two integer variables are easy to solve. In addition, when there are only two types of plants, the saving in cost achieved by a truly optimal solution is typically small compared to the cost of approximately optimal solutions, which are themselves quite easy to find. This is not true for larger problems, and I ask your indulgence on this issue.

With this caveat in mind, let us consider an example involving only two types of plants. The first type of plant—the Smokestack plant—is of ancient design, huge, made of red brick with steam pouring from its chimneys; it has a large capacity, is moderately inexpensive to construct per unit of capacity and has a fairly high marginal cost of production. The second plant—the High Tech plant—is a gleaming marvel of computerized technology; it has a capacity of medium size, is expensive to set up per unit of capacity, but has a lower marginal cost of production. Specific numerical values are provided in Table 1.

If capacity could be built continuously rather than in discrete units, the cost per unit of capacity in the Smokestack plant would be $53/16$ and the cost of supplying a unit of demand would be $53/16 + 3 = 6.3125$. The average construction and manufacturing cost from a High Tech plant is $30/7 + 2 = 6.2857$. What is, of course, uncomfortable about the example is the closeness of these two average costs.

If plants could be constructed at an arbitrary size, the market test—using either average or marginal cost as a criterion—would require that all demand be satisfied

Table 2. Cost minimizing choices of plants and output levels

Demand	# Smokestack	# High Tech	Output 1	Output 2	Total cost
55	3	1	48	7	347
56	0	8	0	56	352
57	1	6	15	42	362
58	1	6	16	42	365
59	2	4	31	28	375
60	2	4	32	28	378
61	3	2	47	14	388
62	3	2	48	14	391
63	0	9	0	63	396
64	4	0	64	0	404
65	1	7	16	49	409
66	2	5	31	35	419
67	2	5	32	35	422
68	3	3	47	21	432
69	3	3	48	21	435
70	0	10	0	70	440

from High Tech plants alone. But the optimal solution is considerably different if plants must be built in discrete sizes, and the pricing test for optimality fails dramatically. Table 2 illustrates the cost minimizing choices of plants and the aggregate output levels of each type of plant for an interval of demand values.

If the capacities at both plants were larger, the number of plants of each type would be considerably less sensitive to the level of demand; a given configuration of underutilized plants would be optimal for a large interval of demands. It can easily be shown that the number of Smokestack plants becomes a periodic function of demand after some point ($d = 91$ in this example). But it is clear from this table that the optimal integer solution cannot be obtained simply by rounding the fractional solution in which only High Tech plants are used.

QUANTITY TESTS FOR OPTIMALITY

Let us focus on a particular value of demand, say, 60, for which the optimal solution is to build two Smokestack plants, four High Tech plants, and manufacture 32 and 28 units respectively, for a cost of $378. Suppose that an alternative solution had been proposed: that we build three Smokestack plants (at a cost of $159 and providing a capacity of 48), two High Tech plants (at a cost of $60 and capacity of 14), and that we manufacture 46 units at the Smokestack plant and 14 units at the High Tech plant, for a total cost of $385. Is there a quantity test revealing that this proposal, which also satisfies the demand of 60, is not optimal?

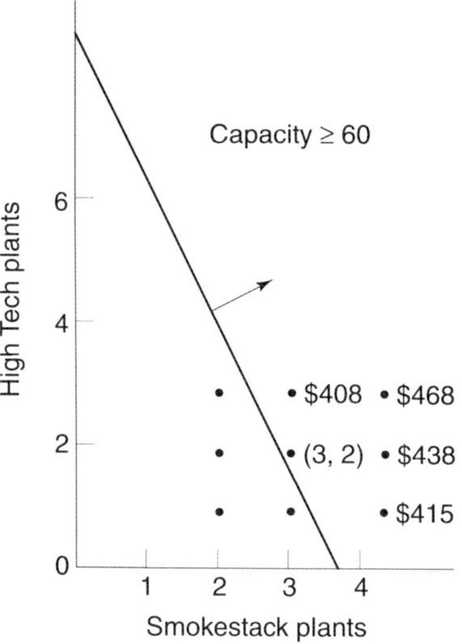

Figure 1. Looking in the immediate neighborhood.

The most elementary quantity test is to plot the point (3, 2) in the plane, and examine its 8 neighbors, which are obtained by increasing or decreasing the number of plants of each type of unity. In other words, for any particular feasible construction plan given by a pair (#Smokestack plants, #High Tech plants), we examine those alternative construction plans obtained by adding to this pair of integers each of the 8 vectors:

$$(1, 0), (1, 1), (0, 1), (-1, 1), (-1, 0), (-1, -1), (0, -1), (1, -1)$$

and testing each one of them to see whether it produces another feasible plan at lower cost.

In Figure 1, those combinations of Smokestack plants and High Tech plants which together provide a capacity of 60 units or more lie on or above the frontier—an unbounded region forming the constraint set for the two integer variables. (I have not drawn the iso-cost lines in this figure since cost depends not only on the number of plants of each type but also on the variables which do not appear in the figure: the levels of output from each type of plant.) The reader will notice that the four neighbors of (3, 2) given by (2, 2), (2, 1), (3, 1) and (2, 3) all lie below the frontier and therefore do not provide sufficient capacity to satisfy the demand of 60. The remaining four neighbors (4, 2), (4, 3), (3, 3) and (4, 1) do provide adequate capacity for the demand of 60, but their total costs—assuming that High Tech plants are used to full capacity—are each larger than the cost of $385 associated with (3, 2). The plan (3, 2) is therefore a *local minimum* for this very natural quantity test, but it is not the *global minimum* when the demand is 60. Some alternative to this particular quantity test is required, if we are looking for a test with the property that a local minimum is global for any demand specification.

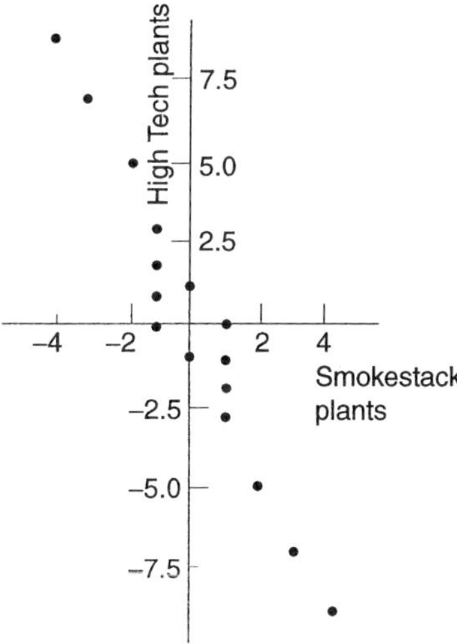

Figure 2. A global quantity test.

THE UNIQUE MINIMAL QUANTITY TEST

For a quantity test to detect optimality it must be based on an examination of a set of neighbors that are related in some intrinsic fashion to the underlying problem, rather than being merely adjacent in an elementary geometric sense. For our problem, there is a *unique, minimal* set of neighbors all of which must be examined to be certain about detecting optimality if we wish to use translates of the same set for all feasible points and all levels of demand. They are obtained by subtracting each of the following neighbors from the proposed plan:

$$(0, 1),$$
$$(1, 0), (1, -1), (1, -2),$$
$$(-1, 3), (-2, 5), (-3, 7),$$
$$(4, -9), (7, -16).$$

This set of neighbors, displayed along with its negatives in Figure 2, has the important property that if one of its translates is excluded from the test set, then there will be some level of demand and some feasible solution which is not optimal but which cannot be improved by moving to any neighbor in the smaller test set.[2] If all of them are examined, the local quantity test based on this set of neighbors will yield the global optimal solution for any level of demand.

To apply the neighborhood test of Figure 2, imagine that we lift up the set of those neighbors that decrease cost and translate them from the origin to the proposed solution (3, 2), as in Figure 3. The non-optimality of the plan (3, 2), for the demand of 60, is easily seen in the figure by noticing that if we subtract the neighbor $(1, -2)$

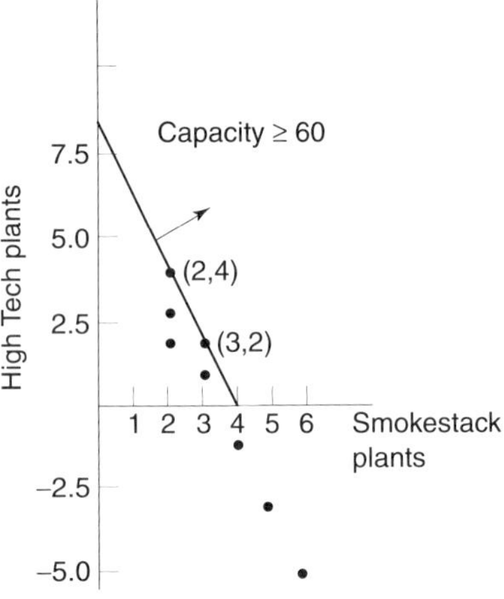

Figure 3. Applying the global quantity test.

from $(3, 2)$, we reach the new plan $(2, 4)$ which is feasible, lowers cost, and is, in this instance, optimal.

There is a clear algorithm suggested by these considerations: (1) Propose some construction plan which produces a capacity sufficient to meet demand; (2) if one of its neighbors in the unique minimal test set is also feasible and leads to a lower cost, move to that alternative plan; (3) if there are no such neighbors, the original proposal is optimal. This algorithm depends crucially on our requirement that the local test set be the same for every feasible point; the set of neighbors would otherwise have to be determined anew at each iteration.

It can be seen that these neighbors are closely related to the discrete analogue of marginal products. As the demand level increases, the optimal construction plan will either be unchanged or move to a new plan which is obtained from the previous plan by adding one of these neighbors.

The reader may feel, at this moment, that I've pulled this collection of neighbors out of a hat. I don't mean to be unduly mysterious, so let me be more specific about the role that neighbors play in detecting optimality. Consider the neighbor $(1, -2)$. If, as in our example, we *subtract* this neighbor from a proposed construction plan, we obtain a new plan with 1 less Smokestack plant and 2 more High Tech plants. There will be a net loss in capacity of two units and a net increase in construction costs of $7. But the 2 additional High Tech plants are capable of manufacturing 14 units at a cost of $28; these 14 units were previously manufactured at the Smokestack plant for an additional $1 per unit. It follows that there is a cost saving of $7 associated with this decrease in capacity of two units.

This "marginal" change would result in a decrease in cost if the original plan had at least 2 units of excess capacity and used at least one Smokestack plant; under these circumstances the change should certainly be adopted and we should move to a new solution with lower cost (as we did in our example in moving from the configuration $(3, 2)$ to $(2, 4)$). If the demand requirements had been 61 units rather than 60, the

Table 3. Decreases in capacity and cost for each
neighbor

Neighbor	Capacity	Cost
$(0, 1)$	7	23
$(1, 0)$	16	53
$(1, -1)$	9	30
$(1, -2)$	2	7
$(-1, 3)$	5	16
$(-2, 5)$	3	9
$(-3, 7)$	1	2
$(4, -9)$	1	5
$(7, -16)$	0	3

configuration (3, 2) would equally well have been feasible. But the excess capacity
would now be 1 unit rather than 2; we no longer can subtract the neighbor $(1, -2)$
and remain with sufficient capacity. On the other hand, it is easy to see that subtracting
the neighbor $(-3, 7)$ reduces capacity by only one unit, but we can only move to this
neighbor if we are currently contemplating a plan with seven or more High Tech
plants. Subtracting $(4, -9)$ also reduces capacity by a single unit, but for this change
to lead to a new feasible configuration, we must currently be constructing at least four
Smokestack plants. And, finally, if we build seven fewer Smokestack plants and 16 more
High Tech plants, there will be no change in capacity but a reduction in cost of \$3, an
option we should certainly take if the proposed plan involves building seven or more
Smokestack plants.

If we examine the members of the minimal test set, the decrease in capacity and cost
obtained by *subtracting* each of them from a proposed solution is given in Table 3,
assuming that all High Tech plants are used to full capacity. The set of neighbors
provides all of the discrete tradeoffs necessary to verify optimality. Of course, it is not
obvious—nor can I make it obvious without an argument that is quite straightforward,
but which I would rather not include in this chapter—precisely why no other discrete
tradeoffs are necessary.[3]

These observations are quite general. Subject to very mild conditions, an arbitrary
activity analysis model with integral activity levels has associated with it a unique,
minimal neighborhood system, which depends solely on the technology matrix and
not on the specific factor endowment, and such that a local maximum with respect to
this neighborhood system is a global maximum for any particular right-hand side
(Scarf, 1981a). The minimal neighborhood system is an intrinsic feature of the
discrete production possibility set and is fully independent of the particular factor
endowment. In suggesting a quantity test set which depends only on the specification
of technical possibilities, we are maintaining the distinction between the technical
knowledge and factor availability which has been so fruitful in economic analysis.

In our example, the technology is simply given by the cost structure, and aside from
non-negativity of the variables there is a single constraint requiring that output be

greater than or equal to demand. We would have more constraints if there were demands for output at several locations, or if we were explicit about a variety of factors of production. The neighborhood system would still be independent of the demand specification and factor endowments.

In the next section, I shall describe a few structural properties of neighborhood systems suggesting that they can be examined rapidly and systematically when there are only two integral variables. Other properties are known for higher dimensions, and many more remain to be discovered. To the extent that a firm can be viewed partially as an algorithm for the solution of discrete programming problems, the firm must either know this minimal test set explicitly—or in some implicit fashion—to test for optimality as the factor endowment varies. The optimal allocation of indivisible resources is essentially a combinatorial problem, addressed in this chapter by means of neighborhood systems. In a large firm, whose size arises from a technology involving indivisibilities, the resolution of these combinatorial problems must be reflected in the firm's organized decision-making procedures for selecting appropriate responses to changes in economic circumstances.

How, in general, are these neighbors to be determined for a given technology matrix? I find it astonishing that there is a canned computer program that can be found either in *Mathematica* or *Maple* which automatically calculates the set of neighbors if presented with the underlying activity and analysis matrix.[4] The program is not designed with this particular question in mind; its purpose is to compute a very sophisticated object in a field of mathematics known as algebraic geometry, a topic which is far removed from issues of economic theory. But here we see one of the remarkable, though rare, virtues of the translation into mathematical form of an everyday problem: words, phrases, and concepts which bear no apparent relationship to each other in ordinary discourse may become synonymous in the language of mathematics.

COMPARATIVE STATICS IN THE PRESENCE OF INDIVISIBILITIES

Can the minimal neighborhood system be used to analyze changes in optimal behavior resulting from a modification in our economic environment? One type of modification is an exogenous change in factor endowments or, in our example of plant selection, a change in demand for output. The minimal neighborhood system permits us to analyze this type of change quite readily in the sense that, for a general activity matrix, changes in the optimal solution associated with increases in the factor endowment or demand are given by precisely these neighbors.

A more complex change results from a modification in the technology rather than the factor endowment. In our earlier discussion in which production exhibited constant returns to scale, this feature was illustrated by the introduction of a new activity whose profitability could be tested at the old equilibrium prices. If indivisibilities are present, a new activity analysis matrix results in a new minimal neighborhood system.

Our numerical example is so elementary that the only changes in technology are modifications in the costs and capacities of the two competing types of plants. To see

Table 4. Changes which bring average costs closer

	Smokestack	High Tech
Capacity	1 609	700
Construction cost	5 300 000	3 000 000
Marginal cost	3 000	2 010
Average cost	6 293.97	6 295.71

the consequences for the minimal neighborhood system, let me first remark that the set of neighbors is unaltered if both capacities change by a common factor and if the average cost—the cost per unit of capacity plus marginal cost—are changed by a possibly different common factor for both types of plant.

Let us make such a rescaling, followed by slight increases in capacity at the Smokestack plant and marginal cost at the High Tech plant so that the parameters are now given by Table 4. At this point, the average cost at the Smokestack plant is slightly lower than that of the High Tech plant and the previous minimal test set is increased by four new neighbors; it is now given by:

$$(0, 1),$$
$$(1, 0), (1, -1), (1, -2),$$
$$(-1, 3), (-2, 5), (-3, 7),$$
$$(4, -9), (7, -16),$$
$$(-10, 23),$$
$$(17, -39), (27, -62), (37, -85).$$

The changes in capacities and costs obtained by subtracting each of these neighbors from a proposed feasible solution are given in Table 5. As we see, if the change in costs increases the competitiveness of the plants—causing their average costs to converge— the number of neighbors will expand. If the plants are closer in efficiency, a higher level of scrutiny is required to detect optimality.[5]

For integer programming problems with two variables, the set of neighbors can be linearly ordered, as in our examples. Small changes in the specification of the problem will always result in modifying our degree of resolution by adding or deleting an interval of neighbors at the end of the list. When the parameters change continuously, the unique procedure for detecting optimality changes in the most elementary fashion possible for a discrete, ordered set of points: the set grows or shrinks at one end. One of the major themes of my current research is to describe the ways in which the set of neighbors changes when the number of discrete choices is larger than two and the neighbors are no longer organized linearly. All of the present evidence suggests that, for the general integer programming problem, the minimal test set gains or loses members at a small number of locations on its boundary.

These examples also illustrate some unexpected structural elements of the set of neighbors: the set seems to be composed of a small number of linear segments. This is

Table 5. Decreases in capacity and cost for each neighbor

Neighbor	Capacity	Cost
$(0, 1)$	700	2 307 000
$(1, 0)$	1609	5 300 000
$(1, -1)$	909	2 993 000
$(1, -2)$	209	686 000
$(-1, 3)$	491	1 621 000
$(-2, 5)$	282	935 000
$(-3, 7)$	73	249 000
$(4, -9)$	136	437 000
$(7, -16)$	63	188 000
$(-10, 23)$	10	61 000
$(17, -39)$	53	127 000
$(27, -63)$	43	66 000
$(37, -85)$	33	5 000

a very desirable feature, since the question of whether a member of a linear set of neighbors can be added to a proposed feasible solution so as to retain feasibility and decrease cost is easy—rounding will do. It is not difficult to argue that this structure is valid for an arbitrary problem with two integer variables; the set of neighbors always consists of a small number of intervals (Scarf, 1981b). This observation permits us to construct what computer scientists call a "polynomial"—a really fast—algorithm for integer programs with two variables.

A remarkable accomplishment of mathematical programming is the generalization of this result to problems with an arbitrary number of integer variables. For any fixed number of integer variables, there is an integer programming algorithm which uses themes similar to, though not identical with minimal test sets, and which executes in "polynomial" time—very rapidly—as the other parameters of the problem vary. These algorithms have more than theoretical interest: they have been coded by experts, and seem to be among the best general purpose mixed integer programming algorithms currently available.[6]

FOR STUDYING LARGE FIRMS, PACK UP YOUR DERIVATIVES IN MOTHBALLS

But let us leave this example with only two discrete choices concerning types of plants, and remember that in a large manufacturing enterprise there will be many discrete choices involving a large menu of tasks and machinery, each of which has its own capacity, set-up cost and marginal cost. The equipment may be placed in a number of different locations on the shop floor; the work may be passed from one piece of machinery to another with complex requirements of scheduling and precedence, and the tasks may alter from one job lot to another as the product specification varies. Demands may be revised capriciously and unexpectedly over time; output may be shipped to many different regions. The enterprise may have a host of competitors or none at all. In the absence of internal market prices, combinatorial arguments and quantity tests are necessary to regulate the flow of activity inside the enterprise in an optimal fashion.

My message boils down to a simple straightforward piece of advice; if economists are to study economies of scale, and the division of labor in the large firm, the first step is to take our trusty derivatives, pack them up carefully in mothballs, and put them away respectfully; they have served us well for many a year. But derivatives are prices, and in the presence of indivisibilities in production, prices simply don't do the jobs that they were meant to do. They do not detect optimality; they aren't useful in comparative statics; and they tell us very little about the organized complexity of the large firm. Neighborhood systems are the discrete approximations to the marginal rates of substitution revealed by prices. They are relatively easy to compute, seem to behave pretty well under continuous changes in the technology, and will ultimately lead to even better algorithms than we have now.

We know much more about the structure of neighborhood systems than I have been able to describe here—not enough, perhaps, to derive a really satisfactory theory of the internal organization of the large firm at the present time. But my own intuition is that this is an important way to proceed. I am confident that serious, ultimately useful insights about the large firm will eventually be obtained by thinking very hard and long about indivisibilities in production.

ACKNOWLEDGEMENTS

I would like to thank my colleagues Truman Bewley, William Brainard, Alvin Klevorick, William Nordhaus, T.N. Srinivasan and James Tobin for their thoughtful comments.

NOTES

1. The second assertion: If the newly discovered activity is added to the old production possibility set, we obtain a new, and possibly larger, production possibility set. But the old equilibrium—which does not use the new activity—is still an equilibrium using the expanded production possibility set, because the new activity makes a non-positive profit at the old prices. By the first welfare theorem, the equilibrium must be Pareto optimal in the new setting with the larger set.

    The first assertion: Simply draw the old production possibility set, a cone which is separated by a plane—whose normal is the equilibrium price vector—from the convex set of net trades that can be allocated among the consumers so as to improve their utility levels. The new activity ray lies above this price plane and, subject to some mild assumptions, it can be connected to the old equilibrium production plan so as to yield a feasible production plan which intersects this set of net trades and increases all consumers' utilities.

2. Figure 2 displays eight of the nine neighbors listed above (I've left out $(7, -16)$ in order to keep the scale reasonable) and their negatives as well. These nine neighbors decrease cost when subtracted from a trial solution, and their negatives increase cost. The negatives are useful if an infeasible solution is given and we are searching for a feasible neighbor, or for a variant of the problem in which we are looking for a configuration of plants that maximizes output subject to a cost constraint.

3. A simple algorithm for constructing the set of neighbors when there are two integral variables is given in Scarf (1981b). There is sufficient regularity in Table 3 so that the reader might be able to guess what the algorithm is without looking at this paper.

4. The program finds a mathematical object known as a Groebner Basis for a polynomial ideal whose generators are defined by the columns of the activity analysis matrix.

5. Consider the new neighbor $(-10, 23)$ pointing in the direction of a cost reduction if excess capacity is 10 or more and if at least 23 High Tech plants are under consideration. Why is this not a neighbor under the previous cost structure? Under the cost structure of Table 1, if we had decided to build 10 more Smokestack plants and 23 fewer High Tech plants, there would have been a decrease in capacity of 1 unit. Construction costs would have decreased by \$160, but marginal costs would have increased by \$161, for a net increase in cost of \$1. This choice would not have lead to a decrease in cost even if there had been excess capacity in the original proposal.

   Of course, this argument might suggest that 10 fewer Smokestack and 23 more High Tech plants should have been built under the older cost regime, since this would result in a reduction in cost. But this would be feasible only if excess capacity was at least 1 unit and the number of contemplated Smokestack plants was 10 or more. If this had been so, the lack of optimality would already have been detected by the earlier neighbor leading to 7 fewer Smokestack and 16 more High Tech plants.

6. The seminal paper, exhibiting the first polynomial algorithm when the number of variables is fixed at an arbitrary level, is Lenstra (1983). Lenstra's argument requires the approximation by ellipsoids of many convex bodies in high dimensions. This approximation is avoided in Lovász and Scarf (August 1992). An elementary exposition of the Lovász and Scarf variant of Lenstra's algorithm may be found in Scarf (1990). Computational experience is discussed in Cook, Rutherford, Scarf, and Shallcross (1993).

REFERENCES

Cook, W., Rutherford, T., Scarf, H. E., Shallcross, D. An implementation of the generalized basis reduction algorithm for integer programming, *ORSA Journal on Computing*, Spring 1993, **5**: 206–212

Lenstra, H. W. Jr. Integer programming with a fixed number of variables, *Mathematics of Operations Research*, 1993, **8**: 538–548

Lovász, L. and Scarf, H. E. The generalized basis reduction algorithm, *Mathematics of Operations Research*, August 1992, **17**: 751–764

Scarf, H. E. Production sets with indivisibilities. Part I: Generalities, *Econometrica*, January 1981a, **49**: 1–32

Scarf, H. E. Production sets with indivisibilities. Part II: The case of two activities, *Econometrica*, March 1981b, **49**: 395–423

Scarf, H. E. Mathematical programming and economic theory, *Operations Research*, May–June 1990, **38**: 377–385

3

The Usefulness of Core Theory in Economics

Lester G. Telser

Core theory furnishes a useful framework for studying a wide variety of economic problems. It has an undeserved reputation of being too abstract, owing mainly to the manner in which it is employed in the theory of general equilibrium. In fact, core theory is a highly flexible way of looking at practical economic problems, especially problems in industrial organization. This paper seeks to show how simple numerical examples can illustrate the idea of the core, and, in turn, how the core can illustrate basic principles of economies.

PRINCIPLES OF THE CORE

The theory of the core begins with the assumption that there are n individuals who can do something either all together, individually or in small groups. For economic applications, a typical example is trade in a market, where all individuals may trade with each other in a single market, or in submarkets, or some may decide not to trade at all. The theory assumes that the individuals can measure the results of their actions. For the example of trade in a market, it is traditional to assume an individual measures the outcome by the utility from the bundle of commodities. Alternatively, an individual can measure the gains from trade in terms of money. For a buyer, this is the maximum amount the buyer would have been willing to pay for the quantities purchased minus the amount actually paid. For a seller, it is the actual receipts minus the amount the seller would have been willing to accept for what was sold. Thus the theory of the core has three elements; n individuals; the various groups they can form, called coalitions; and functions that measure the results of the actions taken by the individuals and coalitions.

There are some outcomes that the whole group of individuals cannot improve. These are the outcomes such that it is not possible to make one person better off without making at least one other person worse off. Such outcomes are called Pareto

Reprinted with permission from *Journal of Economic Perspectives*, Vol. 8, No. 2, 1994, pp. 151–164

optimal. They involve no deadweight loss. The originator of this theory, F. Y. Edgeworth (1881), went on to obtain remarkable results showing how competition among many traders and coalitions leads toward a Pareto efficient outcome. Edgeworth called the mechanism that produces this result "recontracting". The approach is to consider all possible coalitions of traders, recognizing that any coalition of traders will only participate in the markets as a whole if and only if they can do at least as well as they could be off by themselves in their own coalition. To put it another way, the best outcomes available to a coalition set lower bounds on what its members would be willing to accept as participants in the whole market. For example, the compete set of one-person coalitions implies the constraint that each individual will not trade in the market unless the trade makes that person better off. Next consider all two-person coalitions. In this case, any trades must make the individuals at least as well-off as they would be in choosing any possible two-person partnership. When this logic is extended from three-person on up to the n-person coalition, there is a total of $2^n - 1$ possible coalitions, with each coalition placing a constraint on the outcome of trade. The larger the number of traders, the smaller is the range of outcomes without deadweight losses. Under certain conditions, the terms of trade that can satisfy all these constraints constitute a competitive equilibrium.

Core theory examines this process systematically. Outcomes that are unacceptable to some coalition because it can do better for its members are said to be dominated. The set of undominated outcomes constitutes the core. Depending on the number of individuals and the process of recontracting, the core will sometimes consist of a range of outcomes, sometimes a single outcome and sometimes the core will not exist at all.

AN EXAMPLE OF PURE EXCHANGE WITH A NONEMPTY CORE

A simple example can illustrate these concepts. Say there are three individuals and the first two are potential buyers of a house from the third. The potential seller will not sell the house for less than \$100 000. Buyer 1 will not pay more than \$120 000 and buyer 2 not more than \$150 000. (From now on units are understood to be in \$1000.) Let x denote the return to the seller, y_1 the gain to buyer 1 and y_2 the gain to buyer 2. In case it turns out the owner of the house sells it, x is the price of the house. The owner can ensure $x \geq 100$ because retaining the house is an option worth at least 100. For the potential buyers, $y_1 \geq 0$ and $y_2 \geq 0$, because each buyer can refuse to make a purchase and thereby can ensure a net gain of zero, no matter what anyone else does. These three inequalities are the constraints for the three 1-person coalitions.

A coalition of both buyers can do the same as either one of them separately, and the coalition of this pair will have the same lower bound on the sum of their gains. As a result, the relevant constraint for the coalition of both buyers is that $y_1 + y_2 \geq 0$.

There are two more coalitions involving pairs of traders. Each is a coalition between the seller and either one of the buyers. A trade between the seller and buyer 1 must ensure them a return equal to the larger of the two values $\{100, 120\}$. The first value comes from the fact that the seller will only participate if the gain is at least 100; thus the gain to the coalition of the two must also be at least 100. But what determines the minimum gain is the willingness of buyer 1 to pay 120. Given the existence of an outside, higher offer for the house, with the possibility of reselling it to buyer 1 afterwards, the coalition between the seller and buyer 1 would reject any offer below the valuation either places on the house because each member of this coalition can bid for the house in competition with an outside offer. Similarly, the coalition between the seller and buyer 2 will demand a return of at least 150 because this is the larger of the two values $\{100, 150\}$ applicable to this coalition. These conditions set two additional constraints on the outcome: $x + y_1 \geq 120$ and $x + y_2 \geq 150$.

Lastly, the valuation for the coalition of all three traders equals the maximum of $\{100, 120, 150\}$. To put it another way, the cumulative return for the coalition of the whole must be at least as much as the most generous buyer is willing to pay. This condition puts an upper bound on the sum of the returns, given by $x + y_1 + y_2 \leq 150$.

Any triplet $\{x, y_1, y_2\}$ that can satisfy all these inequalities is undominated and said to be in the core of the market. As an example, consider the triplet $\{115, 0, 35\}$, where buyer 2 purchases the house at a price of 115. This triplet is not in the core; it does not satisfy the inequality that the gains to the coalition of the seller and buyer 1 must sum to at least 120. Thus, the seller and buyer 1 can form a coalition leading to the triplet $\{118, 2, 30\}$ in which buyer 1 buys the house from the seller for 118 and resells it to buyer 2 for 120 so that buyer 2 gains 30.

But this set of trades is not in the core either, because it does not fulfill the inequality that the gains to the coalition of the seller and buyer 2 must be at least 150. The imputation $\{120, 0, 30\}$, in which the seller deals directly with buyer 2, *is* in the core. It is undominated and satisfies all the constraints. More generally, all imputations in which $y_1 = 0$, $x + y_2 = 150$, $x \geq 120$ and $y_2 \geq 0$ are undominated and form the core of the market. Thus, any outcome where buyer 2 buys the house for at least 120, but no more than 150, is in the core and nothing else is in the core.

When a nonempty core exists, it means that any trader or group of traders prefers the outcome determined by the whole market to those they could get in any possible submarket involving a subset of traders. These submarkets present feasible alternatives that place limits on the prices that can emerge from the market as a whole. When the market has a nonempty core, it can survive all possible competing alternatives. In core theory, coalitions compete for members by making offers to individuals to induce them to join the coalition. The grand coalition, which includes all the members, can survive only by offering terms that are at least as good as any feasible offer coming from a subcoalition.

Although the example presented here illustrates only the simplest case of pure exchange, it can be extended into a comprehensive analysis of nearly everything there is to say on this topic. Because there is only one seller in the example, competition is present only between the two buyers. More complicated examples would have many sellers and buyers. The core is not empty for the more general case in which there are m sellers and n buyers who each seeks or offers at most one unit of the commodity. It can be shown that all those who sell the commodity must get the same price. This common price is determined by the constraints that emerge as a result of the terms that various coalitions could arrange by dealing among themselves. A still more general model allows the buyers and the sellers to seek or offer more than one unit of the commodity. If the demand schedules of the buyers are downward sloping and the supply schedules of the sellers are upward sloping then there is a nonempty core. Therefore, it remains true that each individual prefers the terms determined in the whole market to those that subsets of traders could agree upon by confining trade among themselves.

However, with multi-unit traders, a wider range of alternatives is consistent with the core constraints than if each trader were replaced by an equivalent set of single-unit traders. This is true because multi-unit traders do not make or tender offers for their commodities one unit at a time unless the forces of competition compel them to. In particular, it need no longer be true that a single price must prevail for the commodity throughout the market in this case. Different sellers could get different receipts per unit and different buyers could pay different prices per unit. In these cases core theory shows how the sizes of the traders could affect the outcome.

A still more general model allows the traders to deal in bundles of continuously divisible commodities. There is a nonempty core in this case if the valuation functions of the traders are continuously increasing concave functions of quantities. The most general analysis assumes a continuum of traders. Think of each trader as indexed by a real number and suppose there are as many traders as there are real numbers in the unit interval. An individual trader is infinitesimally small and has a correspondingly small effect on the outcome of trade. A nonempty core exists for this market under very general conditions on the preferences of the traders. Even with many "crazy" traders, who violate assumptions of rational choice such as transitivity or revealed preference, there is a nonempty core if the "sane" traders are sufficiently more numerous than the "crazy" ones.[1]

EXAMPLES OF AN EMPTY CORE

Sometimes it is not possible to satisfy the conditions for a nonempty core. This happens when the lower bounds on the terms that the coalitions would be willing to accept cannot all be met by the grand coalition. In this event, the core is empty. It means a fully competitive market fails to bring about a Pareto optimal result.

Consider an example which is easily visualized as applying to the cost conditions of the airline industry. Two sellers each operate an airline; they have one airplane apiece. The first airline, A_1, has a small airplane that can carry only two passengers at a total cost of 85. Or, to put it another way, not making the trip will save a cost of 85. (In the preceding example, this condition corresponds to the seller of the house retaining it, as if selling it to himself at the minimal price he would be willing to take for it, which is 100 in that example.) The second airline, A_2, has a bigger airplane that can carry up to three passengers at a total cost of 150. It can avoid this cost entirely by not making the trip. Note that the costs of the airlines are not dependent on whether they fly partly or entirely full, but only on whether they make the trip at all. In this example, let us agree to ignore both fixed and variable costs. This does not affect the validity of the results and it simplifies the arithmetic.

Let there be three potential travelers; B_1, who is willing to pay at most 55 for the trip; B_2, who is willing to pay at most 60 for the trip; and B_3, who is willing to pay up to 70.

The total number of coalitions in this example is $2^{2+3} - 1 = 31$. Let us again adopt the terminology that x represents the returns to the sellers while y represents the gains to the buyers. For starters, consider the 1-person coalitions; these have a buyer or a seller acting alone. To make a deal the sellers must receive enough to cover the costs of a trip: that is $x_1 \geq 85$ and $x_2 \geq 150$. The buyers must all perceive themselves as better off by making a purchase; therefore, y_1, y_2 and $y_3 \geq 0$.

Plainly, no coalition of a seller with only one buyer can cover the cost of a trip. Also, a coalition of either two or three buyers cannot gain more than zero. The remaining 2-person coalition, the two airlines without any passengers, cannot get more than the sum of what they could each get by themselves. Therefore, the interesting possibilities involve a seller with at least two buyers.

Consider the alternatives for the small airline A_1 with the three possible pairs of buyers. Again the return for each possible coalition is determined by the maximum of what the various purchasers might pay. For example, the potential gains for the coalition A_1, B_1, B_2 would be determined by the maximum of what the two buyers would pay and the seller would demand, that is the maximum of $\{55 + 60, 85\}$, which equals 115. Similarly, the gains for the coalition A_1, B_1, B_3 would be the maximum of $\{55 + 70, 85\}$ or 125 and the gains for the coalition A_1, B_2, B_3 would be the maximum of $\{60 + 70, 85\}$ or 130. These conditions lead to the following three constraints:

$$x_1 + y_1 + y_2 \geq 115,$$
$$x_1 + y_1 + y_3 \geq 125,$$
$$x_1 + y_2 + y_3 \geq 130.$$

Of course, seller 2 can also make a potential deal with all three buyers. Hence this coalition $\{A_1, B_1, B_2, B_3\}$ can guarantee itself a return of $185 = \max\{150, 55 + 60 + 70\}$. The constraint on the gains of this potential deal is $x_2 + y_1 + y_2 + y_3 \geq 185$.

Lastly, there is the maximum return available to the coalition of all five individuals, the three buyers and the two sellers. This coalition of everybody has two especially relevant alternatives: one where the first airplane flies full and the second does not fly at all; and the other where the second airplane flies full and the first does not fly at all. In the first, the two travelers who value the trip the most fly with the smaller airline; that is, B_2 and B_3 fly with A_1, B_1 does not make the trip and A_2 saves the avoidable cost of its service. For this alternative, the coalition of all five would get $60 + 70 + 150 = 280$. In the second alternative, A_1 does not fly thereby avoiding the cost of 85, and A_2 carries all three passengers generating a value of 185. For the second alternative, the return would be $185 + 85 = 270$. The value for the coalition of five is the larger of the returns under these two alternatives. This is given by $\max\{280, 270\}$. Therefore, the most efficient arrangement does not satisfy the demand of buyer 1; buyer 2 and buyer 3 make the trip on the airplane of seller 1; and seller 2 saves the cost of 150. Consequently, the upper bound on the x's and y's is given by

$$x_1 + x_2 + y_1 + y_2 + y_3 \leq 280.$$

There is no solution to this market; it is impossible to describe an outcome acceptable to every possible coalition. This is so because the set of inequalities given here has no solution. An outcome in the core must be Pareto optimal so that it gives the most efficient arrangement. Pareto optimality requires that

$$x_1 + y_2 + y_3 = 130, \quad x_2 = 150, \quad y_1 = 0 \quad \text{and} \quad x_1 + x_2 + y_1 + y_2 + y_3 = 280.$$

The first equation says that airline 1 carries passengers 2 and 3. The second says that airline 2 saves its avoidable cost, and the third says that buyer 1 gains zero either because of not making the trip or because of paying his maximal valuation of the trip, which is 55. The last equation makes the sum of everybody's gains as big as possible.

There are two constraints that set upper bounds on the gains of buyers 2 and 3 necessary to have a nonempty core. The coalition involving passengers 1 and 2 going on airplane 1 can ensure themselves a gain of 115. Since $y_1 = 0$ is necessary for a nonempty core, it follows that the sum of x_1 and y_2 is bounded below by 115. But $x_1 + y_2 + y_3 = 130$ is also necessary for a nonempty core so that the gain to passenger 3 cannot exceed 15 ($= 130 - 115$). Likewise, the coalition in which passengers 1 and 3 go on airplane 1 can guarantee themselves a return of 125. Again, for a nonempty core, $y_1 = 0$ and $x_1 + y_2 + y_3 = 130$. This puts an upper bound on the gain of passenger 2 given by 5 ($= 130 - 125$). Therefore, a nonempty core requires that the sum of the gains to passengers 2 and 3 does not exceed 20, or, in symbols, $y_2 + y_3 \leq 20$. However, the second airline can also offer a deal to the three buyers. The lower bound for this deal is 185, so the sum of the gains to the four participants in this coalition satisfies the inequality $x_2 + y_1 + y_2 + y_3 \geq 185$. A nonempty core requires that $y_1 = 0$ and $x_2 = 150$. Therefore, substituting in the preceding inequality, this competition from the second airline would set a lower bound on the gains to buyer 2 and buyer 3 which is

$$y_2 + y_3 \geq 35 = 185 - 150.$$

Consequently, the upper and lower bounds on the sum are contradictory, which proves the core is empty. Telser (1978, ch. 2) contains a detailed analysis of these airplane examples.

Admittedly, the cost conditions in this example are contrived in such a way as to make the core empty. It should be noted, for the record, that extending the model from pure exchange to production need not give an empty core. Also, in the example, the total capacity exceeds the total quantity demanded. Although capacity equal to demand is a sufficient condition for a nonempty core, it is not a necessary condition. The core can be empty for other reasons. The key lesson of this example is that introducing production into the model does add many complications to the theory, which in turn lead to important practical ramifications. To understand why this is so, let us look more closely at how the model treats coalitions.

The return to a coalition of n individuals stems from the activities of its members. The coalition can survive if and only if it can offer its members more than they could get by breaking away and forming their own subcoalition or joining another coalition. Each coalition must also ask whether it can make its present members better off by expanding its membership. There will be a gain if the incremental return from adding a member exceeds the current return per member. Or, to put it another way, at the optimal size of a coalition, the return per member is a maximum. When the coalition of everybody maximizes the return per member so that it is optimal for everybody to join the grand coalition, the core is not empty. Applied for markets, this means there is a core if the traders are better off with the terms they get in the whole market than they would be in any submarket. Therefore, a market with a nonempty core attracts all the trade.

Consider a coalition of individuals who constitute the demand for various commodities. The return to a member of such a coalition equals the valuation of the commodities minus the sum of the quantities bought at prices equal to the marginal cost of producing these commodities. An expansion of the size of the coalition corresponds to an increase in the demand for the commodities from the new members of the coalition. This does not harm the present members provided the marginal costs of the commodities they buy, which equals the prices they pay, do not increase when the demand expands. When adding more and more members to the coalition does not raise marginal costs, the optimal coalition is the coalition of everybody and the core exists. Therefore, a nonempty core requires constant or increasing returns to scale. Another way to see this is by starting with the coalition of everybody and asking whether it can survive. Survival means that it can offer its members a better deal than they could get in any subcoalition. However, with rising marginal cost, a subgroup of demanders has an incentive to break away from the grand coalition. By doing this, they can obtain their commodities at lower prices because marginal costs are lower.

A specific example of an empty core is an industry with identical firms having U-shaped average cost curves such that marginal cost rises with output and equals average cost at the positive output where average cost is a minimum. This case, presented in many textbooks on elementary economies, is familiar to readers of Jacob Viner's famous article (1931) on cost curves.[2] In an optimal coalition it must be true that firms are producing where their unit cost is at a minimum; otherwise, a coalition would form where the firm changes its output, produces at a lower unit cost, and sells to the demanders in this coalition at a lower price than they would have to pay in the grand coalition. But the efficient equilibrium for the market as a whole must be where the price at the quantity demanded equals the marginal cost of the total quantity produced by the firms. The problem arises because the efficient equilibrium for the industry also involves the optimal number of firms that must reckon with the fact that this number is an integer. Changing from n to $n + 1$ firms affects the total cost of production in two ways: it changes both the total variable cost and the total fixed cost of the industry. Optimality requires a comparison between the increase of the fixed cost from having one more firm and the reduction of the variable cost from having each of the firms producing a smaller output while the total output satisfies the total demand at a price equal to marginal cost. The efficient industry equilibrium will not in general be where the unit cost of the firm is at a minimum. The magnitude of the difficulty depends on size of the output per firm where unit cost is a minimum compared to the total equilibrium quantity. The gap between a nonempty and an empty core is smaller, the more numerous the firms in the optimal industry equilibrium. Therefore, there is a closer and closer approximation to the standard competitive equilibrium, the bigger the Pareto-optimal number of firms.

RESOLVING AN EMPTY CORE

What happens in a market when the core is empty? The answer to this question is referred to as "resolving" an empty core. For the type of cost conditions in the second example, a general method of resolving an empty core requires imposition of suitable upper bounds on the quantities that may be sold by certain sellers. Such bounds always exist.[3]

It may seem that a proposal for restricting output must be inefficient, since it has the character of a profit-maximizing cartel. However, in the situation where no core exists, such upper bounds can be efficient, if suitably chosen, in the sense that although removing the bounds can help some economic actors, it can do so only at the expense of creating a deadweight loss for the whole group. An example of this occurred in Hyde Park, which has a regular limo service to O'Hare Airport, 25 miles away. Going to O'Hare, this service makes scheduled stops at certain times and locations in the neighborhood where it picks up passengers. Demand is heavy at spring and Christmas breaks. Once, during spring break, we were waiting with several students for the 7 a.m. limo to O'Hare. Just before 7, a yellow taxi pulled up, flag down, meter off and offered to take up to five customers to O'Hare for $8 each, non-stop, which is below the limo price. The taxi got a full load and left for O'Hare. No one remained for the regular limo service. Although the taxi driver and those who accepted his offer were made better-off, the incentive for providing the regular limo service was impaired. The limo service would not continue, thereby harming the interest of any residents of Hyde Park desiring regular limo service to the airport, unless it could stop this skimming by taxis.

This example closely matches the situation facing shipping conferences. Here a group of shipping firms promises to furnish regular service and enough capacity to handle the cargo of the shippers at certain ports. The conference sets minimum rates. Cargoes accumulate at the port between arrivals of the regular freighters and are transported on the ships of the members of the conference. However, tramps may arrive at the port just before the scheduled stop and offer to take the freight at rates below the conference rates. The shippers who take advantage of these lower rates reduce the incentive for the conference to provide regular service. The lack of regular service would harm the shippers. Both the shippers and the carriers seek arrangement that can preserve regular service. One way that the conference deals with the problem of tramps is by offering shippers a deferred rebate for loyalty. Shippers who use members of the conference exclusively for a prescribed period, usually a year, get a rebate proportional to their total annual shipping costs at the end of the year. This helps ensure loyalty by the shippers to the conference members and thereby preserves regular service. Studies of shipping conferences by Sjostrom (1989) and Pirrong (1992) support the view that a cooperative arrangement among shipping firms is consistent with efficiency and a competitive return.

To demonstrate the flexibility of core theory as a tool of analysis, the airline example offered earlier can be adapted to illustrate how long-term (forward) contracts or vertical integration can sometimes resolve an empty core problem. Forward contracts work better when each party may have many interests other than the commodity involved in the particular exchange. Vertical integration entails closer relations between the two parties and usually needs agreement on many aspects of their operations so it works better when the two parties have a number of common interests.

Let B_1 own A_1, the smaller airline in the earlier example, and B_2 own A_2, the bigger airline. The third buyer, B_3, buys the service on the open or spot market. Neither B_1 nor B_2 has a big enough demand to cover the cost of using the airline for themselves exclusively. Hence each has an incentive to seek outside business. Notice that by this vertical integration, B_1 and B_2 become involved in the airline business. This would not happen if they made forward contracts for long-term service with the airlines as separate businesses. With three economic actors, there are three singleton coalitions; B_1 must receive the maximum of $\{85, 55\}$; the first for being willing to run its plane, the second for what it is willing to pay for a flight. Similarly, B_2 must receive the maximum of $\{150, 60\}$, and B_3 must not incur a loss by participating.

For the three groups, there are three coalitions of pairs. In a coalition between B_1 and B_2, there are two alternatives: either both fly in the smaller plane and save the cost of using the bigger one (which is 150) or neither flies so that they save $150 + 85$. The potential for gain will be the maximum of $\{55 + 60 + 150, 150 + 85\}$, which is 265. In a coalition between B_1 and B_3, both passengers must choose either to fly in the small plane owned by B_1, which has a value of $55 + 70$ or save the cost of the trip which has a value of 85. In this case, the maximum of $\{125, 85\}$ will be 125. Lastly, in a coalition between B_2 and B_3, the pair can either fly in the big plane, owned by B_2, where the trip has a value of $60 + 70$ or they can forego the trip and save 150. The potential for gain is the maximum of $\{130, 150\}$, or 150.

The remaining option is the grand coalition of all three. For this coalition, the best outcome will be a choice between flying in one plane or the other, or not flying at all, with the valuation as the maximum of $\{130 + 150, 185 + 85, 85 + 150\}$. The latter, $85 + 150$, is what would be gained by not flying at all. Notice that the maximum valuation of 280 is the same as in the case when the A's and B's were not vertically integrated.

Many solutions are possible that will satisfy all of these inequalities and so the core is nonempty in this case; one of them is the triplet $y_1 = 115$, $y_2 = 150$ and $y_3 = 15$.[4] This solution is based on a particular allocation of the property rights, but with three different buyers and the two airlines, there are actually five other allocations: B_1 owns A_2 and B_2 owns A_1; B_2 owns A_1 and B_3 owns A_2; B_2 owns A_2 and B_3 owns A_1; B_1 owns A_1 and B_3 owns A_2; B_1 owns A_2 and B_3 owns A_1. Allowing one buyer to own both airlines would provide three more allocations but with less competition than the six above. It is a general result that if any allocation of the property gives a nonempty core, then all will do so, although the imputation of the gains differs in each. Because the efficiency of the outcome does not depend on the allocation of the property, one may take this as an illustration of the Coase "theorem".[5]

Vertical integration gives a nonempty core in this example by eliminating certain potential contracts. These would confer gains on those who participate in them but such contracts would prevent the Pareto-optimal outcome. Ownership of an airline by a particular buyer means that the pair involved always operates together in a potential contract with other participants. Therefore, all the earlier constraints involving an x disappear, owing to the vertical integration. Only those constraints involving y's remain and there is a suitable adjustment of the lower bounds on the returns for the coalitions giving rise to these constraints.

The original situation in which the buyers and sellers are separate allows the most leeway for opportunistic behavior to the individuals. Vertical integration by joining certain pairs of buyers and sellers forces them to recognize their common interest and reduces their incentive to take temporary advantage of each other. Core theory shows this formally, when there is vertical integration, by removing some of the constraints from the original situation. However, this does not answer the question of how the members of a vertically integrated pair will divide their gain between them. Since divorce is possible because of disagreement, the situation can revert back to the empty core. Nor is this all. Even if the constituents in a vertical integration can reach amicable settlements, vertical integration cannot always resolve an empty core problem.

A change in the preceding example shows this. Say there is a third seller, A_3, with a capacity of 2 and an avoidable cost of 90. Also, let there be a fourth buyer, B_4, willing to pay at most 34. The core is empty with the addition of these two individuals. Vertical integration would not change the empty to a nonempty core, for instance, if B_4 integrates with A_3. The emptiness of the core in this new example is not affected by shuffling the property among the buyers (as the reader should be able to verify).

The original version of the airline coalition story can also illustrate how the gains to the participants change as the size of the coalition expands. To this end—and to show how the definition of the return to a coalition is malleable and therefore useful for many different purposes—now define the gain to a coalition as the total value of what they can produce, which is measured by what people are willing to pay for it, minus the cost of producing it. Assume vertical integration in the form that B_1 owns A_1 and B_2 owns A_2. Since no single passenger can cover the cost of a trip, no coalitions made up of a single member will form. Or to put it another way, the singleton coalitions can always decide to do nothing and each guarantees a gain of zero.

There are three possible pair coalitions. The coalition between B_1 and B_2 will either choose not to fly at all, for a gain of zero, or to pay $55 + 60$ to fly before subtracting 85 in costs for a gain of 30. Similarly, the coalition between B_1 and B_3 will either not fly at all for a gain of zero, or pay $55 + 70$ to fly, minus a cost of 85, for a gain of 40. Finally, the coalition between B_2 and B_3 will either not fly for a gain of zero or will fly the large plane, only two-thirds full, paying 130 with costs of 150. Notice that as this example moves from singleton to pair coalitions, the incremental gain is indeterminate because it depends on who joins whom.

The grand coalition of the three will choose the best of several possibilities. First, it may choose not to fly at all for a gain of zero. Second, it may choose to put the two highest-paying passengers in the small plane, for a gain of $130 - 85$. Or it may choose to put all three passengers in the largest plane, for a gain of $185 - 150$. The second alternative offers the biggest gain of 45, so that will be chosen.

Notice that adding B_1 to a coalition of B_2 and B_3 raises the gain from zero to 45, while adding B_2 to a coalition of B_1 and B_3 raises the gain only from 40 to 45 and adding B_3 to a coalition of B_1 and B_2 raises the gain from 30 to 45. It is a general proposition that when the core is empty, the return to each person cannot exceed that person's incremental contribution to the grand coalition. In this case, the return to B_1 cannot exceed 45, to B_2 the upper bound is 5 and to B_3 it is 15. These upper bounds are a good starting point to see whether there is an imputation of the gains in the core. Thus, try y_2 at its upper bound, which is 5, and y_3 at its upper bound, or 15. The sum of the gains must equal 45 because it is the maximum available to the grand coalition. Then for $y_2 = 5$ and $y_3 = 15$, y_1 must be $25(= 45 - 5 - 15)$. This gain for B_1 is admissible because it does not exceed the upper bound, which is 45. The triplet $\{25, 5, 15\}$ is in the core because it satisfies all the inequalities required by a nonempty core. It is an extreme imputation of the gains because it gives the largest possible amount consistent with the core to two of the three actors in this market. Another imputation in the core is at the other extreme where B_1 gets 45, the upper bound, and the other two get zero. Thus $\{45, 0, 0\}$ is also in the core and is the most favorable imputation for B_1. The theory does not determine which of these imputations or certain others in between will be chosen by the participants.

CONCLUSION

The existence of production introduces a number of complications into economic analysis. Set-up or avoidable costs are common, as illustrated in the airplane example, and coalitions will form to break down simple marginal cost in this case. There may be lower bounds on the scale of operation, as also illustrated in the airplane example. Continuous changes in output are often more expensive than discontinuous changes in discrete amounts, as in industries like auto assembly, electricity generation and railroad shipping. In addition, the least costly way to satisfy demand usually requires standby capacity available before the actual demand is known. This raises the problem of how to generate enough revenue to cover the cost of the stand-by capacity as well as the out-of-pocket costs of the demand that actually materializes. Both buyers and sellers have an interest in the resolution of these problems.

Core theory offers tools for confronting these challenges explicitly. It shows how opportunistic behavior by customers can destroy an efficient equilibrium and how suitable arrangements between customers and suppliers in the form of vertical integration can sometimes restore an efficient equilibrium.

Core theory has many other interesting uses in areas not discussed here (Telser, 1990). It gives new results that advance understanding of business organizations such as corporations. It explains why they have limited liability, fungible shares and how the nature of their investments relate to the preferences of their owners. Core theory also gives reasons other than the desire to pool risk for joint ventures such as mutual funds.

Rather than being treated as a somewhat arcane topic, suitable only for existence proofs in economic theory classes, the insights and examples of core theory should be brought into the undergraduate economics curriculum—and the tool-kit of every professional economist. Study and application of core theory will deepen understanding of how competition works in many situations ranging from organized markets to the matching of interns to hospitals (Roth and Sotomayor, 1990).

ACKNOWLEDGEMENTS

I am grateful to Alan Krueger, Carl Shapiro, Joseph Stiglitz and Timothy Taylor for their helpful comments and encouragement. I assume responsibility for all faults and errors that may still be present.

NOTES

1. Models of pure exchange using core theory are in Scarf and Debreu (1963). For a continuum of traders, see Aumann (1964, 1966) and Hildenbrand (1974). Simpler versions are in Telser (1972).
2. Such industries are called Viner industries and are studied in Telser (1978, ch. 3, sec. 4).
3. For a detailed analysis of suitable upper bounds on output that can give a nonempty core, see Telser (1987, ch. 5).
4. In particular, these are the relevant inequalities:

$$y_1 \geq 85; \quad y_2 \geq 150; \quad y_3 \geq 0; \quad y_1 + y_2 \geq 265; \quad y_1 + y_3 \geq 125;$$

$$y_2 + y_3 \geq 150 \quad \text{and} \quad y_1 + y_2 + y_3 \leq 280$$

5. The Coase "theorem" needs much repair when there is an empty core. Aivazian and Callen (1981) give an example with three firms: two factories that pollute the third, a laundry. They show there is an empty core because there is no undominated allocation of the gains among the three. Coase's elaborate analysis in his comment (1981) fails to come to grips with the issues raised by this example. Also, the allocation of the gains that Coase proposes is dominated by every 2-person coalition. Coase's most recent and authoritative exposition of his "theorem" (1988) is silent on the challenge posed by an empty core, although Chapter 6 discusses several criticisms of the theorem.

REFERENCES

Aivazian, V. A. and Callen, J. L. The Coase theorem and the empty core, *Journal of Law and Economics*, April 1981; **24**(1): 175–181

Aumann, R. Markets with a continuum of traders, *Econometrica*, January–April 1964; **32**: 39–50

Aumann, R. Existence of competitive equilibria in markets with a continuum of traders, *Econometrica*, January 1966; **34**: 1–17

Coase, R. H. The Coase theorem and the empty core: A comment, *Journal of Law and Economics*, April 1981; **24**(1): 183–187

Coase, R. H. *The Firm, the Market and the Law*, Chicago: University of Chicago Press, 1988.

Edgeworth, F. Y. *Mathematical Physics*, London: C. Kegan Paul, 1991.

Hildenbrand, W. *Core and Equilibria of a Large Economy*, Princeton: Princeton University Press, 1974.

Pirrong, S. C. An application of core theory to the analysis of ocean shipping markets, *Journal of Law and Economics*. April 1992; **35**: 89–131

Roth, A. E and Sotomayor, M. A. A. *Two-sided Matching: a Study in Game-theoretic Modeling and Analysis*, Cambridge: Cambridge University Press, 1990

Scarf, H. and Debreu, G. A limit theorem on the core of an economy, *International Economic Review*. September 1963; **4**: 235–246

Sjostrom, W. Collusion in ocean shipping: A test of monopoly and empty core models, *Journal of Political Economy*. October 1989; **97**(5): 1160–1179

Telser, L. G. *Competition, Collusion and Game Theory*, Chicago: Aldine-Atherton, 1972

Telser, L. G. *Economy Theory and the Core*, Chicago: University of Chicago Press, 1978

Telser, L. G. *A Theory of Efficient Cooperation and Competition*, Cambridge: Cambridge University Press, 1987

Telser, L. G. Theory of corporations: an application of the theory of the core, *Journal of Accounting, Auditing and Finance*. Spring 1990; **5**: 159–201

Viner, J. Cost curves and supply curves. *Zeitschrift für Nationalokonomie*, September 1931; **3**: 23–46. Reprinted in Stigler, G. J and Boulding, K., eds., *Readings in Price Theory*, American Economic Association Series of Reprinted Articles in Economics, vol. 6. Chicago: Irwin, 1952, 198–232.

Part II

Game Theory

CONTENTS

4

Game Theory, Oligopoly and Bargaining

Bruce Lyons and Yanis Varoufakis

INTRODUCTION

Game theory is currently having as much impact on certain topics in microeconomics as rational expectations has had on macroeconomics.[1] Yet whilst the modern undergraduate typically has a reasonable grasp of rational expectations macroeconomics, his or her understanding of game theory is likely to be both rudimentary and, even worse, faulty. Most microeconomic texts have a section on the "prisoners' dilemma" to highlight the problem of establishing cooperation; and somewhere else there will be an exposition of Cournot duopoly which suggests it could only apply to short-sighted firms which cannot predict a rival's reactions; and that is about it. It is one of the purposes of this chapter to point out the richness of the prisoners' dilemma game and another to correct the misperceptions surrounding Cournot. But our hope is that we can take the reader much further. Game theory provides a unifying framework with which to analyse properly any question involving the interation of rational agents. This includes topics as apparently diverse as oligopoly, externality, public goods, tariff-setting, bequests by parents to their children, wage-bargaining, Mrs Thatcher's macroeconomics, and much more besides. Clearly, there is insufficient space to treat each of these adequately here. Instead, we emphasise the underlying theory of games and give fairly detailed, but intuitive, expositions of just a few topics chosen from two of the best developed areas of research, those of oligopoly theory and wage-bargaining. The reader should then be adequately prepared to tackle other areas of particular interest.

The chapter is divided into three main parts. The first of these introduces the basic theory of non-cooperative games and includes a game theorist's view of the familiar prisoners' dilemma and Cournot models. This is followed by a section on various topics in noncooperative game theory. Oligopoly theory used to be a hotchpotch of

Reprinted with permission from *Current Issues in Microeconomics*, Hey J. D. (ed), pp. 79–126 unrelated models, but recent developments have begun to tie the various insights together within the unifying discipline of game theory. The next section introduces bargaining theory and emphasises the problem of understanding the emergence of conflict. This uses much the same game theoretic concepts as the two first parts, but a key difference is that individuals or groups are allowed to make binding agreements prior to taking any action. Interest surrounds the way such contracts come about and what division of the benefits is agreed. The final section offers some concluding comment.

THE THEORY OF NON-COOPERATIVE GAMES

Some basic definitions

A game is defined by a number of players each facing a set of possible actions and consequent pay-offs (or utilities). The structure of the game also specifies when each player may make a move. The pay-offs need not be precisely known and may depend on the state of nature. In that case, the players must place (possibly subjective) probability values on the various possible states of nature actually occurring. The motivating force behind game theory is that the pay-offs to one player depend on the actions of others.

Games are normally classified according to:

(1) the degree of inherent antagonism embodied in the pay-offs;
(2) whether or not binding agreements can be signed;
(3) the extent to which information is common to all players;
(4) the sequence in which players take decisions;
(5) the number of times a game is played.

Each of these can have an important influence on the analysis of the game.

(1) *Zero-sum games.* If the game essentially boils down to dividing a cake of pre-determined size then there is pure antagonism and we are in the realm of *zero-sum games*. These were the first games to be formally studied and the remarkable "minimax theorem" formulated by von Neumann (roughly speaking, that there is always a rational solution to zero-sum games) mesmerised a generation of game theorists. Most games of interest to economists, however, are not zero-sum but involve some mutuality of interests. For instance, oligopolists prefer a high price to a low price even though there remains a conflict of interests. It is the solution of *non-zero-sum games* that concerns us in this section and the next.

(2) *Cooperative and non-cooperative games.* In a cooperative game, players are free to communicate, before any actions are taken, and come to binding agreements on mutually beneficial courses of action, or strategies. The early effort of game theorists concerned economies with large numbers of players and resulted in the rigorous proof of Edgeworth's famous limit theorem: that as the number of players in an exchange

Prisoner 2

		"deny"	"confess"
		a_2	b_2
Prisoner 1	"deny" a_1	5, 5	0, 8
	"confess" b_1	8, 0	3, 3

Figure 1. Prisoners' dilemma.

economy becomes very large, then no coalition of players can guarantee themselves a better pay-off than arises from perfect competition. More recent work has concentrated on two-person cooperative games, which are known as bargaining games (discussed in the section "Bargaining and Conflict"). One characteristic that might reasonably be expected of the solution to a cooperative game is that it will be Pareto-optimal: if both players can be made better off by adopting a different strategy, then they should agree to do so.

In a *non-cooperative game*, in which binding agreements are not feasible, this is not always possible as will be seen in the examination of the prisoners' dilemma in Figure 1. The idea is that two criminals are caught and interrogated in separate rooms. If both confess (i.e. (b_1, b_2) is played) the police will be able to prosecute a major charge successfully, but will recommend lenient sentences. If neither confesses (a_1, a_2), it is likely that only a minor charge can be made to stick. If only one confesses and implicates the other who is denying involvement—i.e. (a_1, b_2) or (b_1, a_2)—the one who confesses gets an extremely light sentence, while the other gets "the book thrown at him". The set of actions implied by either denying or confessing is known as a *strategy*. Figure 1 gives the utility pay-offs to each choice with player 1's pay-off to his strategies a_1 and b_1 coming first in each pair. Notice that regardless of what player 2 does, player 1 does better by confessing than by denying the crime. In such cases, b_1 is called a *dominant strategy*. Similarly, confessing is also dominant for 2. Since b is dominant for each player, in the absence of binding contracts we must expect both to confess. Would it make any difference if the criminals could communicate prior to deciding whether to confess? Suppose they realise the police have found their hideout but they have a few moments for rational debate before being caught. 1 may begin by pointing out that although each has a dominant strategy, to confess would lead to a Pareto-inferior outcome, so why not agree to deny the crime? 2 likes the idea, agrees to it and they shake hands. Two hours later they are being interrogated. Despite their verbal agreement nothing in the pay-offs has changed, and to confess remains dominant. We must therefore expect rational players to confess. Pre-play communication without binding agreements cannot help to resolve the prisoners' dilemma.

(3) *Common knowledge.* If each player in the game has the same information—for instance, on the probability distributions assigned to various outcomes by each other—

and each knows that the others have this information, then the game is one of *common knowledge.* A critical piece of common knowledge is that all players are rational in the sense that when presented with the same information they will come to the same conclusion: in particular, they can duplicate each other's thought processes. As this will be seen later this idea that players can think through how others are working through the problem is the key to understanding equilibrium in game theory. A modification of this sort of reasoning can also be applied to games where either a rival's pay-offs, or his full rationality, is in doubt. If some players have private information, or even if they think that others might, then we have an *asymmetric information game.*[2] Such games are much more complex to analyse, but they have been the focus of considerable interest in the past few years, and they are introduced in the next section.

(4) *Simultaneous and sequential games.* In a *simultaneous game,* each player chooses his strategy before he knows the choice made by his rival. All decisions must be made on the basis of how one expects rivals to behave. In a *sequential game,* the initial actions of the first player are made known before the second player makes a move (the first player may then get a chance to move again and so on). This gives the first mover the opportunity to influence a rival's choice of strategy. Deliberate actions of this sort are known as *strategic behaviour* and this is discussed at the end of this section. Strategic behaviour can only be effective if the first mover's actions are irreversible. An action of this sort is known as a *commitment* (or credible threat), whereas an action which is reversible at a later stage in the game is known as an *empty threat.*

(5) *One-shot and super-games.* A *one-shot* game is played once only. If the game is played several times by different players then nothing material changes. However, if at least one of the players plays the same game repeatedly, and any new players can observe the results of previous plays, then history is introduced and the possibilities of implicit cooperation and learning arise. Such *repeated games* are sometimes known as *super-games,* though the latter term is more general and includes games which vary over time. The outcome of repeated games can depend crucially on whether the repetition is finite or infinite, and these cases are investigated below.

Equilibrium in non-cooperative games

Suppose we have defined an n-person, non-zero-sum, non-cooperative, common knowledge, one-shot game. Despite a long series of careful assumptions, we still need something else if we are to predict how rational players will play the game. What is needed is a solution concept that enables us to establish what assumptions one player will make about the behaviour of others so she can then act accordingly. It turns out that there is currently considerable, though not unanimous, agreement among economists about this. The *Nash equilibrium* (NE) concept is so widely accepted that it is often simply called the equilibrium point.

Let $U_i(s_1, s_2, \ldots, s_i, \ldots, s_n)$ be the pay-off to player i as a function of the strategies played by herself and all others. A Nash equilibrium is a vector of strategies $(s_1, \ldots, s_n)$

Player 2

	a_2	b_2	c_2
a_1	5, 5	3*, 6*	0, 4
b_1	4, 3*	2, 2	2, 0
c_1	7*, 0	1, 1*	4*, 0

(Player 1 labels the rows.)

Figure 2. Best replies and Nash equilibrium.

such that for each $i = 1, \ldots, n$, i selects the strategy s_i^* out of his set of feasible strategies such that

$$U_i(s_1^*, s_2^*, \ldots, s_i^*, \ldots, s_n^*) \geq U_i(s_1^*, s_2^*, \ldots, s_i, \ldots, s_n^*)$$

Thus, given the strategies played by rivals, s_i^* is i's *best reply*. At least one, and sometimes more than one, Nash equilibrium exists for all games in a very wide category. Sometimes, however, the NE may involve *mixed strategies* by which players do not definitely choose to play just one *pure strategy*, but a probability mix of various actions. In the prisoners' dilemma game, since b_1 and b_2 are both dominant, they are clearly best replies and so constitute the NE. In Figure 2: for player 1, c_1 is the best reply to a_2, a_1 is the best reply to b_2, and c_1 is the best reply to c_2; for player 2, b_2 is the best reply to a_1, a_2 is the best reply to b_1, and b_2 is the best reply to c_1. The pay-offs to these best replies are marked with a dot. To obtain the pure strategy NE, player 2 reasons as follows: I know my best replies and my rival's best replies. If these coincide then neither of us has any incentive to change what we are doing so (a_1, b_2) is the equilibrium. Any other strategy combination would leave one of us not optimising and so could not be expected to arise from play between rational players. Each of us is able to appreciate this so we will play our NE strategies.[3] Some game theorists claim that this is how rational players should behave; that is they argue that the equilibrium is *prescriptive*. Others go further to argue that this is how people actually do behave, that is to say, game theory is *descriptive*. The latter view can be justified either on the grounds that decision-makers are very clever or because there are evolutionary forces at work.

The oldest and most familiar example of a Nash equilibrium in microeconomics is the Cournot duopoly model. Two players each know both the demand curve for mineral water and each other's costs (common knowledge). Players must simultaneously choose quantities to supply to the market; so the set of feasible strategies is defined as rates of output between zero and some suitably high maximum (say, that which if supplied would reduce the demand price to zero). For any strategy chosen (output produced) by firm 2 it is straightforward to calculate firm 1's best reply from his costs and the residual demand curve (i.e. industry demand less 2's supply). For the

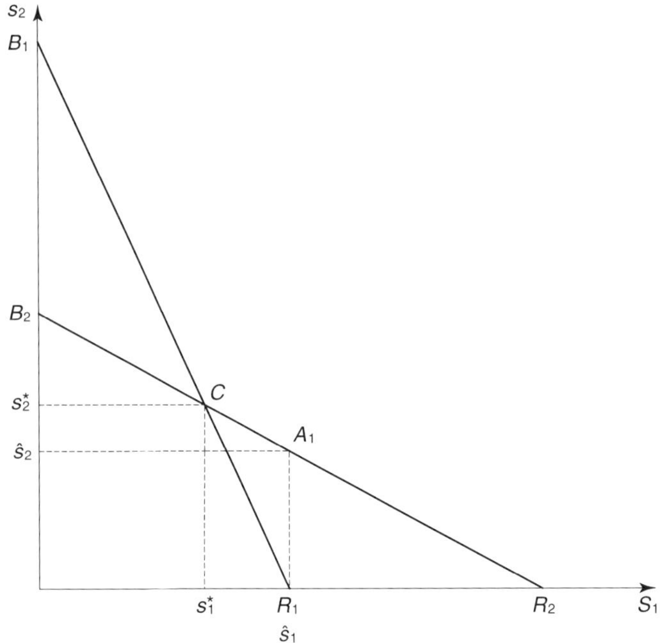

Figure 3. Cournot–Nash equilibrium.

linear-demand curve, $p = a - b[s_1 + s_2]$ where s_1 and s_2 are supplies by each firm, and constant costs, c, equal for both firms, 1's profits are $U_1 = [p - c]s_1 = [a - c - bs_1 - bs_2]s_1$. For any given s_2, profit-maximising firm 1's best reply is given by $\partial U_1/\partial s_1 = a - c - 2bs_1 - bs_2 = 0$, or $s_1^* = [a - c]/2b - [s_2/2]$. Now firm 2 faces a similar problem so her best reply is $s_2^* = [a - c]/2b - [s_1/2]$. Appreciating this, firm 1 can substitute $s_2 = s_2^*$ into his own best-reply function to get the NE which is $s_1^* = s_2^* = [a - c]/3b$. Note that in this linear example each firm supplies exactly one-third of the competitive output (found by setting $p = c = a - b[s_1 + s_2]$). Figure 3 plots firm 1's best-reply function as B_1R_1. B_2R_2 is firm 2's best reply to firm 1, and $C = (s_1^*, s_2^*)$ is the Cournot–Nash equilibrium. Had we defined price as the strategic variable, we would have arrived at the Bertrand–Nash equilibrium which is quite different. The fact that changing the set of feasible strategies changes the equilibrium outcome should be no surprise, but recent research discussed below has shown that under certain interesting circumstances the difference is less than is conventionally appreciated.

In deriving the Nash equilibrium, nothing has been said about how equilibrium is attained or how stable it is. Some otherwise very good undergraduate texts motivate the Cournot model by suggesting that firm 1 starts as a monopoly at R_1, whereupon firm 2 enters and produces vertically above R_1 on her best-reply curve, to which firm 1 responds until equilibrium is reached. The criticism that the duopolists are myopic and constantly being surprised by rivals' reactions inevitably follows. But this is the same as criticising standard supply and demand equilibrium on the grounds that you do not like the cobweb model! Yes, dynamics are important: but no, we need not rely on one particular version to motivate our equilibrium. It is far better to view the NE as the only logical result of careful analysis by the duopolists. Bearing in mind that they cannot come to a binding agreement, the attraction of the NE is that each is making the best reply to the other's strategy. With any other pair of strategies, at least one of them would have a unilateral incentive to change strategy.

Alternatives to the NE are not plausible for fully rational players. For instance, consider the case against the Stackelberg point for firm 1 as leader at A_1 in Figure 3. By choosing an output $\hat{s}_1 > s_1^*$, it might be argued that firm 1 could force firm 2 to a less advantageous position on her best reply curve at $\hat{s}_2$. Were this to be an equilibrium, firm 1 would be better off than at C. However, since each duopolist must choose output *before* the other's is known, this will never be tried by rational players because firm 1 must expect firm 2 to choose s_2^* (after all, firm 1's choice cannot influence firm 2) and the best reply to that is s_1^*.[4] It is the fact that rational players can duplicate each other's reasoning, and not some unspecified dynamics, that gives power to the NE concept. This is most definitely not to say that dynamics are unimportant, or that a satisfactory dynamic process is not desirable to give the NE credence when players are not trained game theorists, but it is to claim a special position for NE in our analysis of game situations. Binmore and Dasgupta (1986) go as far as to argue it is the *only* rational solution for a non-cooperative game, though Bernheim (1984) and Pearce (1984) suggest that some alternative strategies are "rationalisable" and so cannot be ignored.

What if firm 1 is able to announce his strategy before firm 2 decides what to do? Does this enable him to attain equilibrium at A_1? The answer depends, as with pre-play communication, on whether or not he can *commit* to $\hat{s}_1$ before 2 can make her decision. A simple announcement will be dismissed as a bluff by firm 2, and knowing this firm 1 will rationally react by reneging on his own announcement and going straight to the Cournot–Nash equilibrium. However, if firm 1 can somehow commit to $\hat{s}_1$, perhaps by signing contracts to supply $\hat{s}_1$ whatever the market price, then firm 2 is left with no option but to comply and produce her best reply of only $\hat{s}_2$. Note that we have not deviated from the Nash equilibrium concept. The rules of the game have changed so that we have sequential decision-making and credible commitment. The outcome in such circumstances is obviously different from the situation where the rules do not give one player an advantage, but the principle that each player adopts her best-reply strategy is maintained. Under the revised rules, A_1 is an NE; in fact, it is an example of a subgame perfect Nash equilibrium, a concept to which we now turn. But note well here that one of game theory's greatest virtues is that it imposes a considerable discipline on the economist to specify *exactly* the nature of the environment and other rules of the game before going on to say how individuals/firms/unions/governments/etc. should be expected to behave.

We earlier noted that there may exist multiple Nash equilibria. Some of these may be more "reasonable" than others, and recently there has been much intellectual effort in trying to define the term "reasonable" more explicitly. Consider Figure 4 which sets out a game in *normal* (or *strategic*) *form*. The normal form game often economises on the presentation of detailed strategies, and simply presents the ultimate pay-offs to all feasible strategy combinations without explicitly showing how actions lead to pay-offs. This particular game is called the entry game because it can be

Firm 2

	acquiesce	fight
enter	3, 3	−5, −5
stay out	0, 13	0, 13

Firm 1

Figure 4. Entry game in normal form.

interpreted as player 1 contemplating entry into a monopolist's (player 2's) market. 1's set of feasible strategies is simply either to enter or else stay out. The monopolist can either fight entry with an expensive price war, or else acquiesce to a passive duopoly. The pay-offs, or profits, are given in the boxes. Note that as long as 1 stays out, 2's pricing competitiveness remains hypothetical so the pay-offs are not affected. To search for Nash equilibria, consider each strategy pair in turn: (enter, acquiesce) is an NE because if 1 enters, 2's best reply is to acquiesce and if 2 acquiesces, 1's best reply is to enter; (enter, fight) is not an NE because fighting is not 2's best reply to entry, and a similar argument applies to (out, acquiesce); however, (out, fight) is another NE because staying out is the best reply to fighting and (threatened) fighting is a best reply to no entry.[5]

Closer examination of the entry game, however, suggests that the two Nash equilibria may not be equally plausible. This is brought out by studying a different presentation of the game, this time in *extensive form* such that the sequence of moves and the information available to each at the time of decision-making, are made explicit in the form of a *game tree*. Importantly, the extensive form explicitly introduces time into the model by specifying what information becomes available as the game progresses. *Decision nodes* are defined as points on the game tree at which one player or the other is able to make a move. Thus, in Figure 5 it is clear that 1 has the first move in deciding whether to enter or not (at node $1a$), and only with this information available to him does 2 have to respond (from node $2a$ or node $2b$). More formally, 2 is playing a proper *subgame* because he knows exactly where he is on the game tree (i.e. at $2a$ or $2b$), and there are no subsequent decision nodes that might be confused with some other subgame. He must therefore choose his strategy on this basis. This is often called a *two-stage game* because it can be divided into two separate parts.

A *subgame perfect Nash equilibrium* (SPNE) rules out all potential equilibria that are not Nash equilibria in each subgame (Selten, 1965). All SPNE are NE, but not necessarily vice versa. In the present case, once 1 has entered, 2's best reply is acquiescence so 1 can predict 2's rational response and (enter, acquiesce) is an SPNE. However (out, fight) is not an SPNE because player 1 would never choose to accept a pay-off of zero when she can earn three in the knowledge that it is not rational for the monopolist to fight once entry has actually occurred. Put another way, the threat to fight is not a *credible threat* in this game because it is never sensible to carry it out.

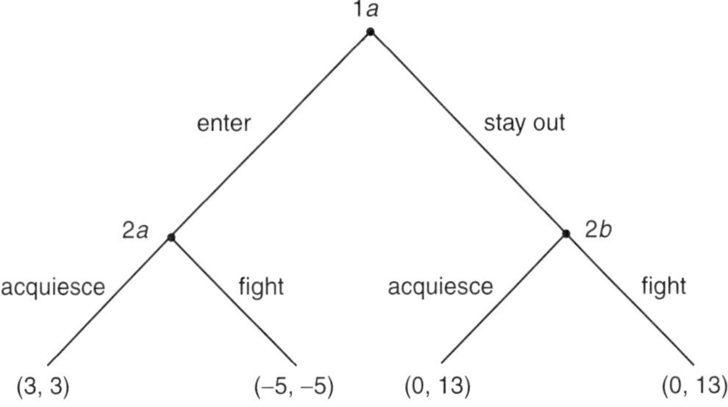

Figure 5. Entry game in extensive form.

The reader should be able to convince herself that reversing the order of moves, with 2 able to commit before 1, leads to (threatened) fighting and entry deterrence being the sole SPNE. However, although in the abstract this is a logical possibility, the economist is often able to impose a plausible structure on the sequence of moves such that one model is more appropriate than another. In the present case, for instance, it seems unlikely that incumbents are able to commit to fighting before entry takes place; while a commitment to entry prior to the choice of price seems quite plausible.

Sometimes, the economist may wish to add more features to the model to make it a little more realistic. For instance, even though the incumbent is unable credibly to threaten a fight on the basis of the game shown in Figure 5, he may have the opportunity to take some prior action (e.g. investing in excess capacity) that *would* make the threat credible. This is known as *strategic behaviour* which Schelling (1960) defines as an action "that influences the other person's choice [e.g. entry/stay out] in a manner favourable to one's self, by affecting the other person's expectations of how one's self will behave [e.g. acquiesce/fight]". As Dixit (1980) shows, this notion can be captured formally by introducing a third, prior stage to the entry game and looking for a new SPNE. For instance, suppose 2 can invest in excess capacity that would be needed in the event of a fight, but not otherwise. Figure 6 shows the game tree for the case where the extra investment costs nine. All 2's pay-offs, except that to actual fighting, are thus reduced by nine. At first sight this might seem a pretty stupid thing for the incumbent to do since most pay-offs fall and none rise. However, the cunning behind this strategic behaviour is that 2's pay-off to fighting in the event of entry is now greater than his pay-off to acquiescence ($-5 > -6$). 1 now faces a credible threat and must expect a fight if she enters. She will therefore stay out (since $0 > -5$). Finally, moving back to the first stage of the game, 1 prefers to commit the costly excess capacity because the pay-off to committed monopoly still exceeds that of duopoly which results from non-commitment ($4 > 3$). Thus (commit, stay out, threaten, fight) is an SPNE for the three-stage game. Note the welfare costs of strategic behaviour in this context: monopoly pricing remains but social welfare is worse than in the absence of the entry threat because of the unproductive investment. (A simple, but deeper, treatment of a strategic behaviour by firms is given in Lyons, 1987a, and the welfare

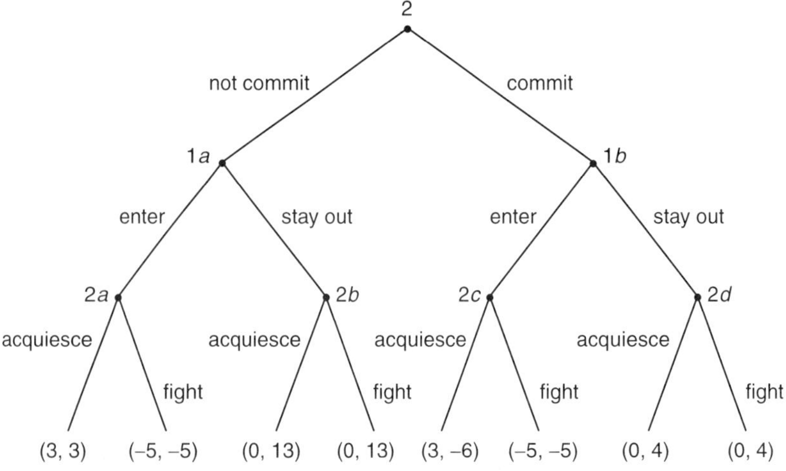

Figure 6. Pre-commitment in the entry game.

theme is picked up by Fudenberg and Tirole, 1987. An introduction to strategic behaviour by governments in the international arena of subsidies and tariff-setting can be found in Lyons, 1987b).

MICROECONOMIC APPLICATIONS OF NON-COOPERATIVE GAME THEORY

Simultaneous and sequential moves: the game theory of price competition

It is sometimes argued that in practice firms set prices not quantities as their strategic variables, and that this should be incorporated in oligopoly models. Although this presumption is far from empirically certain, we take it as true throughout this section.[6]

Suppose two duopolists can bottle any amount of homogeneous spring water at the same constant cost, c. Let the monopoly price be p_m. Suppose firm 2 charges a price $p_2 > p_m$, then firm 1's best reply is $p_1 = p_m$. Next suppose $c < p_2 \leq p_m$, then firm 1's best reply is to charge $p_1 = p_2 - e$ where e is very small but positive. In slightly undercutting firm 2, the entire market can be supplied whereas price-matching would necessitate less profitable market-sharing and any higher price would give zero market-share. If $p_2 \leq c$, then $p_1 = c$ is the best reply because any lower price would give negative returns. A similar analysis can be carried out for firm 2 and it is clear that $p_1 = p_2 = c$ is the unique (Bertrand−) Nash equilibrium. Notice that even with just two firms the market is fully competitive and no profits are earned. The best-reply curves are drawn in Figure 7, with the upward sloping parts being e away from the $p_1 = p_2$ line. Next suppose that costs differ such that $c_1 < c_2$. Similar reasoning gives the NE as $p_1 = c_2 - e$ and $p_2 = c_2$. Clearly firm 1 takes the whole market and makes positive profits. In terms of Figure 7, 2's best-reply curve becomes horizontal before 1's becomes vertical.

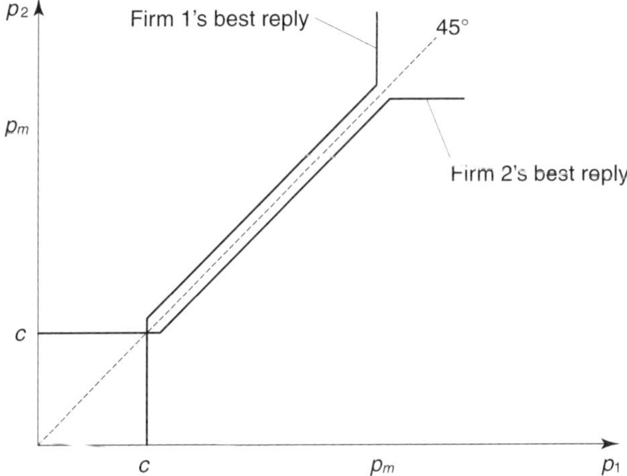

Figure 7. Bertrand–Nash duopoly with identical firms.

Now, return to the case of equal and constant marginal costs, but assume that there is some small cost of entry, f. The competitive process can be modelled as a three-stage game with first firm 1 deciding whether or not to enter, then firm 2, and finally the Bertrand–Nash pricing game is played. With extensive form, non-cooperative, full information games, we have already argued that a reasonable NE should also be an NE in all its subgames. The pricing decision constitutes a proper subgame, as does this plus firm 2's entry decision, so we look for an SPNE. The game is set out in Figure 8.

Working backwards, which is the appropriate way to solve all such games, we first calculate the pay-offs to the pricing game conditional on there being either one, two or no firms that choose to enter. Let V_m be the profit due to monopoly pricing, and for duopoly we have already shown that price equals marginal cost so net profits are $-f$ each. It should be straightforward to see that an SPNE involves firm 1 entering and firm 2 staying out.[7] In such potentially hyper-competitive markets the explicit modelling of entry plus the addition of even a tiny overhead cost completely changes the simple model of price competition to give monopoly profits instead of none at all! This is a clear example of what is known as a *first mover advantage* because firm 1 earns high profits simply because of the historical accident that he was given the first opportunity to enter the industry.

The public policy implications of this are discussed in Williamson (1987) and Dasgupta and Stiglitz (1988). Suppose the pricing game were changed such that the first firm to enter had by law to set a price that could not be altered, particularly *downwards*. If firm 2 decides to enter, then firm 1 would be forced to price competitively (at firm 2's potential average cost) in the first place. Failure to do so would induce entry at price $p_2 = p_1 - e$, so firm 1 would lose f. Paradoxically, then, a legal restraint on price cutting results in a more competitive market. This is an

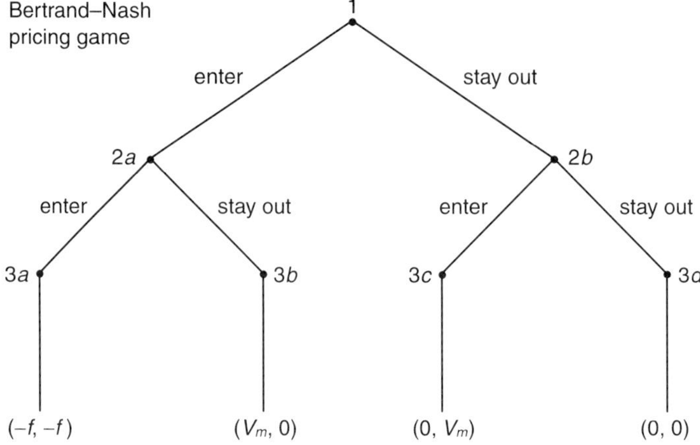

Figure 8. Bertrand competition with entry and fixed costs.

interesting and, on reflection, potentially important policy theme which also arises in a number of related game-theoretic models. For instance, an increasingly frequent strategy in retailing is to promise to match the price of any rival in the same town and this may discourage new entry.

Nevertheless, the hypersensitivity of the Bertrand model to the introduction of even a tiny fixed cost (the outcome switches from perfect competition to pure monopoly) contrasts with intuition and points to some fundamental misspecification of the pricing game. The implicit assumption so far has been that production follows the realisation of the pricing game. Once price has been determined, firms can produce however much they like. It turns out that if production takes place *before* the realisation of the pricing game, then the outcome is very different. Indeed, under certain quite strict but reasonable conditions, Cournot production levels will be chosen even when price competition is expected.

Before pursuing this line, however, it is necessary to investigate capacity-constrained Bertrand equilibria, a topic first tackled by Edgeworth, but which has only recently received rigorous treatment by game theorists. This example will also serve to introduce the idea of a *mixed strategy* equilibrium. For simplicity, assume a linear demand curve, DD' as in Figure 9. Furthermore, because a full analysis soon becomes very complex, we shall look only at symmetric situations with identical duopolists, each with capacity k. If $k \geq q_c$, where q_c is the competitive output, then there is no capacity constraint and the competitive Bertrand result goes through.

Next suppose $q_c > k > (1/3)q_c$. We assume throughout that if $p_1 = p_2$, then demand is shared equally between the two firms. If $p_1 > p_2$, then either firm 2 will be able to sell its entire capacity, leaving firm 1 with a residual demand, or if p_2 is too high firm 2 will be able to sell only part of her output and firm 1 will sell none. Assume the former case. It turns out to be very important exactly which units of demand firm 2 has satisfied. Two examples illustrate why. If 2 sells to the k units of demand that value the product most

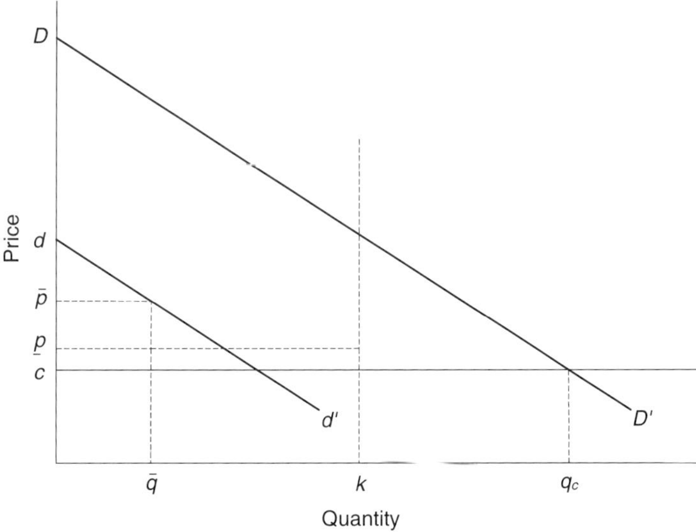

Figure 9. Capacity-constrained price competition with $q_c > k > \frac{1}{3} q_c$.

highly, then this leaves firm 1 with the residual demand curve dd' in Figure 9. In order to sell this entire capacity, it must be true that $p_2 \leq d$. Because the highest surplus units of demand have been satisfied, $p_1 > d$ would result in zero sales so for 1 to have positive sales we require $p_1 < d$. Alternatively, if firm 2 has sold its entire capacity to only the most marginal units of demand, this leaves firm 1 with the top of the DD' curve and some customers willing to pay as much as D. Thus the second allocation of customers, or rationing system, gives 2 higher expected sales at any chosen price. Having noted this range of possibilities, however, we proceed by analysing only the first rationing scheme (see Levitan and Shubik, 1971, for more detail on the alternatives).

Now consider 1's best reply to p_2 when $q_c > k > (1/3)q_c$. If $p_m \geq p_2 > d$ (i.e. 2 will not have sold her entire capacity), then for familiar Bertrand reasons undercutting is the profit-maximising response, so the best reply is $p_1 = p_2 - e$. If $p_2 \leq d$, then undercutting may still be appropriate, but there will come a point, when $p_2 \leq \underline{p}$, where firm 1 can do better by raising price to $\bar{p}$, which is the "monopoly" price for the residual demand curve. Although 1 will not then be producing to capacity, the profit earned from this strategy will be greater. $\bar{p}$ and the consequent demand $\bar{q}$ are given in the usual way by setting marginal residual revenue equal to marginal production cost, and $\underline{p}$ is defined by $(\underline{p} - c)k = (\bar{p} - c)\bar{q}$. Firm 1's best reply curve is drawn in Figure 10, as is that for firm 2 (drawn thinner) which is constructed in an identical manner.

A problem should be immediately apparent. Because of the discontinuities in the best-reply functions, they never actually cross. More formally, a Nash equilibrium in pure strategies does not exist because there is no pair of strategies (prices) for which

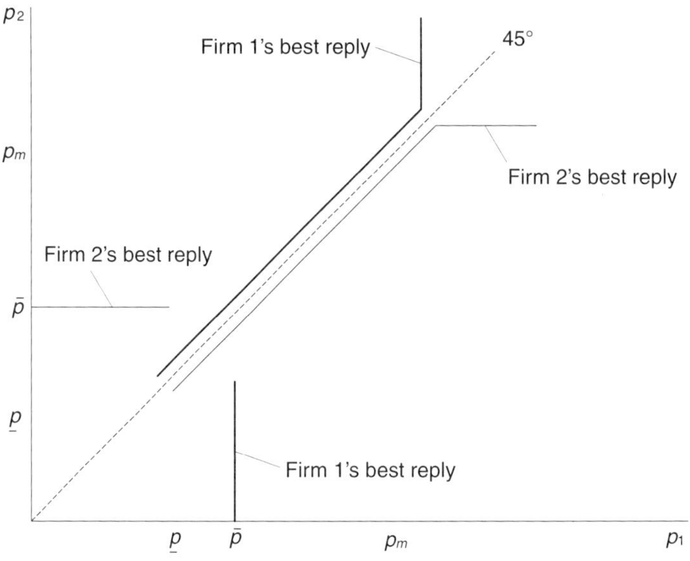

Figure 10. Discontinuous best-reply curves.

1's best reply to 2 is also 2's best reply to 1. For instance, suppose 2 chooses $\underline{p}$ and 1 chooses $\bar{p}$. 1 is making his best reply, but 2 could do better by choosing $\bar{p} - e$, in which case 1 should undercut, to which 2's best reply is to undercut and so on. No pure strategy equilibrium exists. The game theorist's answer to this problem of discontinuous games is to suggest a mixed strategy whereby each firm chooses prices according to a probabilistic formula; in this example it turns out that non-zero probabilities should be chosen to price over the range $[\underline{p}, \bar{p}]$. The essential idea is that if firm 2 is following the appropriate formula, it will leave firm 1 indifferent between choosing any price in the range. This constitutes an equilibrium from 1's point of view because it can do no better by taking unilateral action in choosing one particular price or mixture of prices. Note, however, that firm 1 must also adopt a mixed strategy so as to leave 2 indifferent, otherwise 2 could unilaterally improve her prospects by adjusting her probability formula. In terms of Figure 10, the effect of the mixed strategy is to bridge the discontinuity between the two parts of each firm's best-reply curve so that the two curves "intersect". Note that in a probabilistic sense, both firms will be operating with excess capacity because neither can expect to sell k *all* the time (even if the sum of capacities is less than q_c). Furthermore, even when the industry has capacity greater than the competitive level, price exceeds marginal cost (as long as $k < q_c$).

Mixed strategies can nearly always provide a Nash equilibrium in discontinuous games (see Dasgupta and Maskin, 1986, for a definitive treatment of the existence problem). Their use remains controversial to many economists, though others see mixed strategies as a natural extension of pure strategies and justify them in exactly the same ways as for any other NE.

If price competition is of the form just described, and if this constitutes the second stage of a game with a first stage in simultaneous output (or capacity) choice, then the outputs (or capacities) chosen will be exactly the same as in the simple case of Cournot quantity competition.

To see this, first suppose that all of marginal cost, c, is associated with capacity. In this case, although the *ex post* profits from the second stage will be different, the *ex ante* profits from the point of view of first stage decisions will be identical to those just described.[8] The first stage problem is to find the equilibrium in capacities in the light of the resulting price game. Again assume symmetric capacity choices. Suppose firm 2's capacity, $k_2 < (1/3)q_c$, then firm 1's best reply must be $k_1 > k_2$ because 1's residual demand curve leaves an expected marginal revenue greater than the marginal cost of capacity. Next suppose that $k_2 > (1/3)q_c$, then if $k_1 = k_2$ firm 1 will choose $p_1 > p$ with positive probability and would generally have preferred a smaller capacity. So $k_1 = k_2 > (1/3)q_c$ cannot be an SPNE. Only if firm 2 chooses $k_2 = (1/3)q_c$ is 1's best reply to choose the same capacity. This is, therefore, the only symmetric equilibrium. It is also true to say that a different rationing mechanism or modified cost assumptions can substantially alter the neatness of this result (see Dixon, 1988). Nevertheless, the careful specification of the sequence of output and price decisions does serve to capture the notion that although firms do, in practice, tend to set prices and not auction off predetermined quantities (as is suggested implicitly by the Cournot model) the Cournot model does give intuitively plausible results (e.g. duopoly generates a price somewhere between monopoly and competition).

The purpose of this extensive treatment of price competition in homogeneous goods markets has been more than simply to provide a thorough exposition of one area to which game theory has contributed. It has also been to illustrate the complications which the theorist must confront once real time is introduced into a model. The extensive form of a game forces the theorist to specify exactly what players know at which point in the decision-making process and how it is reasonable for them to anticipate the actions of rivals. Technological considerations must also enter the model explicitly, for instance through capacity constraints. In the remainder of this section, the importance of explicitly modelling demand is similarly brought out. It is *because* game-theoretic reasoning complicates the problem by forcing us to be so explicit that it contributes so much to our understanding of real-world phenomena. The simple textbook model of optimisation in a single-period world ignoring sequential decision-making hides a wealth of important detail, as the distance we have travelled from simple Bertrand duopoly shows. (For further thoughts along these lines, see Fudenberg and Tirole, 1987.)

So far we have considered only homogeneous products. What difference does product differentiation make? At a general level, a price cut by one firm is no longer able to entice all a rival's customers away so the firm's perceived demand curve is no longer perfectly elastic at equal prices. This blunts the edge of price competition and duopolists can expect to earn positive profits even in the simplest Bertrand model. However, the same effect also blunts the prospective competition faced by entrants, so a larger number of firms may enter the market even when there are economies of scale. Chamberlin (1933) christened this sort of market monopolistically competitive as long as it was large so that it could support numerous firms. Game theorists have recently challenged the basis for this conclusion, proving that not all "large" differentiated markets can support numerous firms even when scale economies are slight. One consequence is that it is dangerous to *assume* that zero profits will be earned in equilibrium (see for instance Shaked and Sutton 1982, 1983, 1984, 1987).

Infinitely repeated games: non-cooperative collusion

Consider again the prisoners' dilemma game. In Figure 1 substitute "collude" for "deny" and "cheat" for "confess". The only Nash equilibrium in this one-shot game (i.e. played only once) is if both play b. However, note that each could be better off if they could somehow agree to both play a. More formally, the strategy pair (a_1, a_2) Pareto-dominates the Nash equilibrium (b_1, b_2). One way to reach the Pareto-optimal solution would be if binding agreements could be signed. However, here we assume that this option is not possible, perhaps because it is illegal. Instead, we investigate simple intertemporal strategies that can sustain the cooperative outcome in infinitely repeated games without resort to binding agreements.

The essential idea is captured by a *trigger strategy* whereby player 1 chooses a_1 until player 2 chooses b_2, after which a_1 is played for ever (Friedman, 1977). If there is no discounting, this strategy clearly pays because the one-period gain to "cheating" on the a strategy is $8 - 5 = 3$, which must be compared with the loss thereafter of $5 - 3 = 2$ in each subsequent period when collusion has collapsed. That the trigger strategy is a subgame perfect Nash equilibrium is confirmed as usual by examining best replies. Consider player 1. If 2 chooses a_2 and this is expected to be part of her trigger strategy, then a_1 is the best reply because an infinite stream of pay-offs of 5 is better than a stream of pay-offs of 30. If 2 chooses b_2, then the best 1 can do from then on is to trigger the threat and play b_1. Identical arguments give player 2's best replies. The same proof can be applied at any point in time because infinitely repeated games always look the same, whatever the period. The threat implied by the trigger is credible (i.e. subgame perfect) because it is in each player's own best interests actually to trigger the "punishment" b; and each player can implicitly collude by always choosing a, because this pays more than triggering the punishment.[9] Note that although verbal pre-play communication to agree on the trigger strategy is not necessary in the strict theoretical sense for non-cooperative collusion to exist, such discussions make the result much more plausible.

Three strong assumptions have been made to get this result. First, the time horizon is infinite; second, players can observe each other's actions with certainty (possibly by their effect on own payoffs); and third, there is no discounting of future pay-offs. Let us consider these in reverse order.

Suppose future returns in period t are discounted by a factor $d^t < 1$. The conventional interpretation is $d = 1/(1 + r)$, where r is the interest rate. However, the effect is identical if there is no time discounting but it is expected that the infinitely repeated game will not, in fact, be definitely infinite and may end in any period with constant probability $(1 - d)$. Either way, with discounting the gains from "cheating" on implicit collusion now are weighted more highly than the gains from continued collusion in the future. Abiding by "collude" forever pays $5 + d5 + d^2 5 + \ldots = 5/(1 - d)$, while "cheating" pays at best

Player 2

	"carrot" a_2	b_2	"stick" c_2
"carrot" a_1	5, 5	0, 8	0, 0
b_1	8, 0	3, 3	2, 0
"stick" c_1	0, 0	0, 2	−1, −1

Figure 11. Stick and carrot.

$8 + d3 + d^2 3 + d^3 3 + \ldots = 8 - 3 + 3/(1 - d)$; so cheating will not pay as long as $5/(1 - d) > 5 + 3/(1 - d)$, which simplifies to $d > 0.6$.[10]

Recently, Abreu (1986) has argued that trigger strategies are unnecessarily restrictive in that they rely on perpetual reversion to the single-period NE. It will often be the case that a worse punishment can be invoked and this can be used to sustain a greater degree of cooperation. For instance, suppose an option c is introduced as in Figure 11. Abreu is able to prove the virtues of a "stick and carrot" strategy which, for player 1, is as follows: choose a_1 until 2 plays b_2, then play c_1 until 2 plays c_2, after which 2 is rewarded for cooperating in her punishment by playing a_1. We show that this can lead to the cooperative outcome for a wider range of discount factors than does simple trigger, and that it is an SPNE even though (c_1, c_2) is not an NE in the one-shot game. Indeed, c is a dominated strategy for both players. First, the threat of c_1 means that the cooperative pay-off exceeds the return to cheating and cooperating in one's own punishment as long as:

$$5 + d5 + d^2 5 + d^3 5 + \ldots > 8 - d1 + d^2 5 + d^3 5 \ldots$$

which implies the gain from cheating now is less than the discounted value of the punishment if, $d(5 + 1) > 8 - 5$ or $d > 0.5$. Second, it is worth cooperating in one's own punishment rather than cheating for two periods before cooperating as long as:

$$8 - d1 + d^2 5 + d^3 5 \ldots > 8 + d2 + d^2 1 + d^3 5 + \ldots$$

which implies that the gain from immediate remorse exceeds that of one-period recalcitrance if, $d(5 + 1) > 2 + 1$ or $d > 0.5$.[11] Thus, in the repeated game where the carrot can follow the stick, it is credible to threaten to wield the stick, and compliance is the best reply to the stick being used. It is straightforward to further compare the costs and benefits of postponing the end of the punishment period even longer and show that this does not alter the constraints on d. Thus, more sophisticated two-phase punishments which combine a harsher present with a rosier future, are more effective at sustaining non-cooperative collusion than is the single-phase trigger strategy. In a game which permits a wider choice of Pareto-superior strategies which are not single-period NE—for instance, output choice in Cournot duopoly—the "stick and carrot" permits a higher pay-off (i.e. combined output nearer the monopoly level) to be sustained for any given d. Furthermore, Abreu is able to demonstrate that in many cases not only is the "stick and carrot" very effective, it is also the best that can ever be done in a non-cooperative environment.[12]

Finitely repeated games: multiple equilibria, bounded rationality and reputation

It might be thought that games which are repeated a very large but finite number of times should exhibit equilibrium characteristics very similar to those just studied with infinite repetition. However, this turns out not to be true. We begin by introducing the "backward induction paradox" for finitely repeated games.

Suppose the prisoners' dilemma game in Figure 1 is to be played 100 times by the same two players. Could something like a trigger strategy sustain collusion? The answer is no. A finitely repeated game is a special type of extensive form, so as before we search for a subgame perfect Nash equilibrium by first considering the final play of the game. Clearly neither player has any incentive to play a because there is no future gain to inducing further collusion; so they will each play the one-shot Nash strategies (b_1, b_2). Next consider period 99. Each player knows that non-collusive choices will be made in period 100, so once more there is nothing to be gained from collusion in period 99. One-shot Nash actions in period 99 similarly mean that they will be optimal in period 98 and so in 97 and so on until period 1. Consequently, trigger strategies are not best replies to each other and they are not sub-game perfect in finitely repeated games. Notice that this backward induction argument is independent of the discount rate, and it can be applied to all conceivable punishment strategies (e.g. "stick and carrot", or "tit for tat" which is discussed below). It can also be applied whenever there is some finite date, however large, by which time the game will *certainly* have finished. For instance, if we and our descendants know for certain that the world will end in a trillion years, then unless we anticipate living on another planet, all games must be logically finite. However, if we believe that there is a small chance that the world will go on for ever, even though with probability $(1 - d)$ it will self-destruct in any one year, we can apply our earlier arguments for infinite supergames.[13] The critical point to grasp is that backward induction cannot be applied if the game always looks the same at each point in time, as it does with infinite repetition or a constant probability of ending; but it must take hold if an end-date is certain. This can be deemed a paradox for two main reasons. First, because the discontinuity in the logic behind very large numbers of repetitions and infinite repeats goes against intuition. Second, because experimental evidence suggests that collusion does emerge in the repeated prisoners' dilemma even when participants are sure that the experiment will not keep them playing for ever! We investigate three ways in which the *backward induction paradox* can be eliminated.

One way to break out of the paradox for finitely repeated games, and reinstate the possibility of non-cooperative collusion, is if there are multiple Nash equilibria in the one-shot game (Friedman, 1985). Consider the example in Figure 12 where both (b_1, b_2) and (d_1, d_2) are NE. Suppose the trigger strategy is to play a until the other

Player 2

	a_2	b_2	d_2
a_1	5, 5	0, 8	–2, –2
b_1	8, 0	3, 3	–2, –2
d_1	–2, –2	–2, –2	–1, –1

Figure 12. Multiple Nash equilibria in the one-shot (stage) game.

ceases to play a, whereafter play d. The threat to play d is credible because with multiple NE, there is no reason to expect one to transpire rather than another. Even if the game is repeated only twice (and bearing in mind that no one will collude in the last period), it is better for player 1 to play a_1 in the first period and b_1 in the second, rather than "cheat" straight away by playing b_1 then have to play d_1 in the last period as long as $5 + d_3 > 8 - d_1$ or $d > 0.75$. with more than one repetition, of course, collusion becomes even more sustainable. Benoit and Krishna (1987) extend this line of reasoning to the application of optimal "stick and carrot" disciplines to demonstrate that as long as there are multiple Nash equilibria, finitely repeated games generate results almost identical to the infinite supergame as long as the number of repetitions is large.

The second way around the backward induction paradox is to appeal to "bounded rationality". Radner (1986) defines an (epsilon) ε-best reply to be any strategy that pays within $\varepsilon \geq 0$ of the true best reply. An ε-equilibrium is then such that each player is making an ε-best reply. Suppose, for simplicity, that there is no discounting in the game in Figure 1 which is repeated T times. The pay-off to abiding by the trigger strategy when there are still t periods to go is $0 + 3(t - 1)$ if your rival cheats. The pay-off to cheating is at best $8 + 3(t - 1)$. Thus, cheating gains 8 or, in per period average terms, the gain is $8/t$. Now if players are interested in making ε-best replies of average pay-offs, collusion is sustainable as long as $\varepsilon > 8/t$. For instance, if $T = 100$ and $\varepsilon = 1$, collusion can be sustained for the first 92 periods but will collapse in the last eight. Although it is clearly very interesting to try to introduce bounded rationality into game theory, it is questionable that this is the best way to go about it. First, as Friedman (1986) points out, it might be just as reasonable to assume that players with bounded rationality can only calculate for a small number of periods ahead. In that case, games become even more finite and the backward induction becomes even more forceful. Second, we can question why players do not fully optimise. If this is because of calculation costs then these should be explicitly modelled. Although this might be rather complex, developments along such lines could lead to a better idea of whether ε-best replies or truncated time-horizons or some other approximation is the most appropriate stylisation of bounded rationality in any particular situation.

The third way of attacking the backward induction paradox is the one which has received most attention in recent years. It involves changing one of the most fundamental cornerstones of the game theory discussed so far (and arguably this makes it one of the most exciting developments in game theory since the war), namely the common knowledge assumption. Even a very small amount of *asymmetric information* can significantly alter the equilibrium in repeated games (and, more generally, in extensive form games).

Consider the repetition of the game in Figure 1 T times. Player 1 is perfectly rational, but suppose player 2 *might* be "irrational" in the sense that she fails to appreciate the backward induction argument and insists on playing trigger. Player 2 knows her own true character, but player 1 can only guess, at the beginning of the game, that 2 is rational with probability $(1 - p)$ and trigger with probability p. One might think that this asymmetric information game could be analysed fairly simply by calculating expected profits and proceeding as before. However, two interesting twists are immediately introduced. First, if player 1 is able to observe 2's play as the game unravels, he will pick up new information with which to revise his prior assessment of 2's true nature. Second, if player 2 is in fact rational, she will appreciate 1's ability to learn and may find it pays to bluff and act as if she were indeed a trigger strategist. Of course, 1 will appreciate 2's incentive to dissemble and build this into his expectations, etc. Straightforward application of NE or SPNE is unable to cope adequately with these possibilities, but a variant of subgame perfection known as *sequential equilibrium* (Kreps and Wilson, 1982b) has been developed as an appropriate and natural extension of games in which information is held asymmetrically. The essential insight gained from the formal game theory of asymmetric information games is that even a very small probability, p, is rapidly magnified by repeating the game, such that the incentives to cheat change and, at least for early plays of the game, the backward induction paradox disappears.

Unfortunately, asymmetric information models are very difficult to solve. One way to look at the asymmetric information model is to see it as a way in which reputation can be built. In the prisoners' dilemma game, the reputation is for irrational behaviour (or low pay-offs to cheating). The idea of reputation building can be seen even more clearly in a game known as the "chain-store paradox", which is a finite repetition of the extensive-form game illustrated in Figure 5. Recall that an entrant must decide whether to enter before the incumbent can commit to fighting. The only SPNE is for entry and no fighting because one entry has taken place the incumbent's best reply is to acquiesce. Fighting is an empty threat. Selten (1978) considers the finite repetition of this game and calls it the *chain-store paradox* because he uses the example of a chain-store which has a monopoly in N different towns and entry is threatened in each sequentially, one after the other. The threat to fight early entrants with a view to building a reputation for aggression cannot be part of an equilibrium strategy because of the familiar backward induction argument. In the last town to be threatened, the chain-store will always concede as in the one-off game. Thus, in the town before that it will have no reason to build a reputation and so must acquiesce, and so on. Once again, we encounter the paradox that no matter how many shops are owned by the chain-store, it cannot logically fight early entry in order to build a reputation for aggression and so deter later entrants. Milgrom and Roberts (1982) show that as long as there is a slight possibility that the incumbent is following a simple ("irrational") behavioural rule of "fight all entry", then entry can be dissuaded. Initially, there may be entry to test the incumbent's mentality. If he concedes, then entry will continue in all markets. But if there is a fight, further entry can be dissuaded at least until the number of towns into which there may be entry becomes small, when entrants may further test the resolve of the monopolist (who will eventually concede if rational).

BARGAINING AND CONFLICT

Introduction to bargaining theory

Two important questions in games where binding contracts are feasible are:

(1) Assuming we know the characteristics of each bargainer, is there a way of predicting the outcome?
(2) Moreover, have we anything to say about the occurrence of conflict?

At this point we must define our terms. Antagonism does not automatically lead to open conflict. From now on, the term conflict will be reserved for the "deadweight" loss, active-fight (e.g. wars, strikes, etc.) type of confrontation while conflict of interest will be referred to as antithesis.

Our two fundamental questions cannot be answered in isolation from each other. A complete theory of bargaining must predict both outcome *and* the peaceful or conflictual means by which it is achieved. A lot depends on the analyst's perception of what is rational.

Consider a simple game called the "race to twenty". A fair coin is tossed to decide who plays first. The first player says either "1" or "1, 2". The second responds with either one or two consecutive integers (e.g. "3" or "3, 4"); then the first player continues the same way. The player who says "20" first, wins £2. If you were invited to pay a fee in order to play "race to twenty" against an unknown opponent, how much should you be prepared to pay? The answer depends on your probability assessment of winning (p) as well as your risk-aversion. The expected pay-off from the game being $2p - x$ where x is the entry fee, it is not surprising that the more optimistic you are about your chances, the higher your valuation of the right to play. A game theorist would however quickly point out that $p = \frac{1}{2}$ and, therefore, the maximum fee consistent with non-negative returns—as well as risk-neutrality—is £1. The logic is straightforward: if you start first, there is no way you will lose. By saying "1, 2" you can get to 5, 8, 11, 14, 17 and 20 first whatever strategy your opponent chooses to follow. So provided that both players are aware of this strategy, the game is decided by the initial tossing of the coin: whoever starts will win. Game-theoretic analyses of human interaction begin by assuming that agents are capable of inferring from "perfect information" environments the dominant strategies for a win. In exactly the same way that "rational" players can in the "race to twenty" foresee the outcome and choose to end the game after the tossing of the coin, any two individuals with conflicting interests and perfect information can predict the future of any possible strategy. It would thus make very little sense for such well-informed and intelligent beings to allow confrontation to evolve into costly conflict since they can foresee the outcome of any "fight" and would prefer to reach it without having to suffer the costs associated with conflict. Models along these lines assuming peaceful resolutions, and thus strict Pareto-efficiency, have dominated early game theory. In this section we discuss these as well as sequential games with and without perfect information while retaining neoclassical rationality postulates. The built-in hyperrationality of such models inevitably leads to the conclusion that antithesis will invariably lead to a non-conflict outcome. The frequent emergence of conflict in the real world can then only be explained, within the game-theoretic paradigm, by unpredictable mistakes. But conflict often does seem to be predictable, for instance industrial disputes do not appear to be random, and this has led to discontent with the assumption of hyperrationality. We will also therefore illustrate two simple models of bargaining where disagreement leads to conflict as a result of bounded rationality, and outline an alternative approach suggesting that even with full rationality, costly confrontation can result if information is held asymmetrically and the game is finitely repeated. Finally we will discuss the normative implications of game theory and attempt to link it with a more general debate on the nature of human interaction.

The division game

Two relatives inherit a sum of money S although the Will does not specify how it should be divided. What it does specify is that, unless agreement on a division is reached, each gets nothing. Nash (1950) proposed a devastatingly simple distribution theory which predicts that the two sides will agree to the division which maximises the products of their utility gains. The solution follows from certain axioms that Nash regards as "fair" and "reasonable" conditions to be fulfilled when bargainers are rational. He first adopts von Neumann and Morgenstern's utility theory as an illustration of his conception of rationality. Briefly, this asserts that a person's preference between a certain pay-off and a given lottery is always consistent with the assumption of expected utility maximisation. In particular, a person has a neutral attitude towards risk if she is indifferent between a gift value g with probability p and a gift of value $p \cdot g$ with certainty. The second axiom on which the Nash solution depends is that of Pareto-efficiency. A distribution is said to be Pareto-optimal if it places the parties at some point on their utility frontier, which is defined as the locus where, for any given utility of one person, the other's utility is a maximum. In other words, Nash requires that the heirs avoid the "threat point" (i.e. zero pay-offs to both) by agreeing on a settlement consisting of two shares whose sum equals S. Having assumed that an optimal division will be reached, Nash proposes three critical axioms which uniquely lead to the Nash solution:

(a) *Symmetry axiom.* Utilities are set equal to zero at the threat point and are positive on the frontier (see Figure 13a). If the frontier is symmetric with respect to the line $u_1 = u_2$, the solution will lie on that line (i.e. it will be given by point N);

(b) *Transformation invariance.* Suppose that we decide to alter the dimensions of Figure 13a without changing the underlying pay-offs, e.g. by doubling the magnitude of u_2

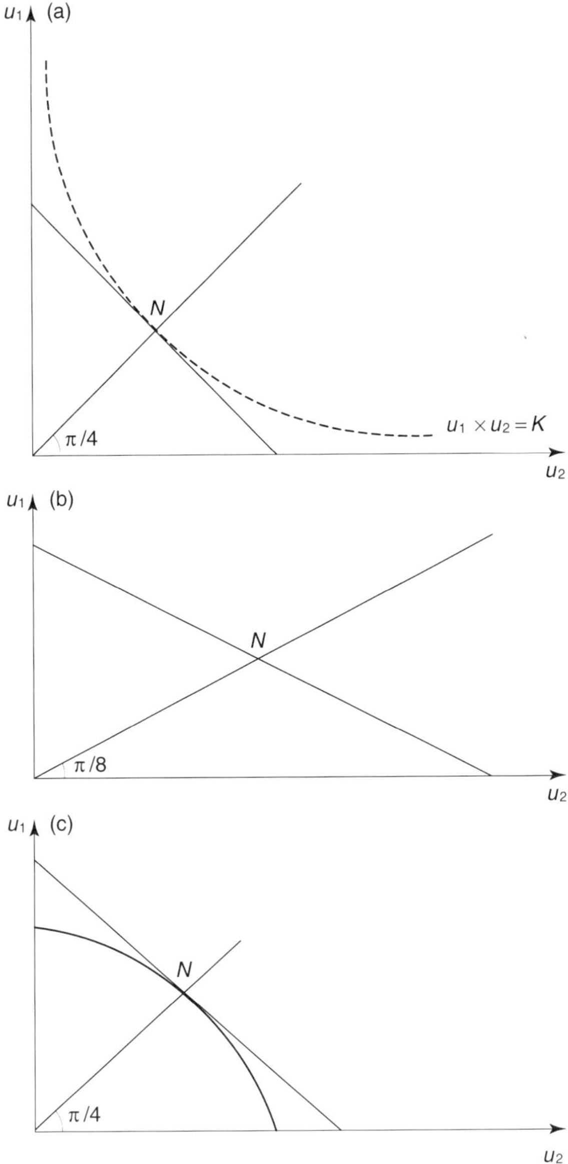

Figure 13. Nash equilibrium in the division game.

while we retain the same magnitude for u_1. Nash's second axiom is meant to preserve the original solution when transformations of this sort take place. It implies that if the midpoint of a linear utility frontier with slope -1 is the solution (Figure 13a) so is the midpoint of any other linear frontier (Figure 13b);

(c) *Independence of irrelevant alternatives.* While the previous axiom deals with linear transformations of the frontier, an additional axiom is needed to cover transitions from linear to non-linear frontiers. Consider the concave frontier in Figure 13c which is dominated by the original linear one everywhere except at the latter's solution point. The new frontier denies bargainers choices that they would not have made even if they were available. Nash suggests that their removal is not going to affect the outcome.

The appeal of Nash's solution stems from the incompatibility of any other solution with the above axioms/conditions. They are sufficient to establish that the Nash point N always occurs at a division maximising $u_1 \cdot u_2$.

Is the nature of Nash's solution descriptive, and thus positive, or prescriptive? Should we expect the inheritance to be split according to the utility–product maximisation rule, or should such a solution be forced upon the two relatives if they fail to agree? Luce and Raiffa (1957) argue that since any distribution theory depends on both sides behaving in accordance with it, and in view of possible rationality bounds, bargainers would seldom converge to the theoretical solution unaided; the theory should instead be utilised as a means of setting up guidelines for "fair" arbitration.[14] The debate on the normative implications of Nash's theory, and indeed of game theory as a whole, is interlinked with issues of rationality and its dependence on the social-physical environment in which "games" evolve. For the purposes of the present discussion it suffices to point out that whatever the normative implications of Nash's solution, it is only "fair" and "reasonable" in the context of relative advantage considerations, with no place for considerations of "right" or "wrong".

Returning to our two relatives, suppose that one of them is suffering from decreasing marginal utility—i.e. she is in such great need of money that failure to make a small gain is terribly painful as compared with a failure to make an even greater pain. If the second relative is reasonably affluent with constant marginal utility—or even a gambler with increasing marginal utility—the arbitrator who follows the Nash script will award most of the inheritance to the one who needs it less. Nash's theorem is essentially an intuitive result based on the idea that the more risk-loving a player, the higher the pay-off. As such, it is vulnerable to the criticism that imposing penalties on risk-aversion is not compatible with the assumption of perfect rationality since it would pay an intelligent player to pretend to be risk-loving. Nash's solution partially overcomes this criticism thanks to the assumption of perfect information about each other's utility functions. It does, however, point to possible benefits from self-persuasion: since the most desirable attribute seems to be a love for risk, it would be wise to take courses in throwing caution to the wind or, alternatively, to practice self-deception prior to the bargaining session. Objections to Nash's theory are not confined to the importance of exogenously given patterns of risk-taking. In particular there is widespread scepticism about the relevance of the proposed solution in view of the restrictiveness of axioms on which it relies.

Axiomatic approaches attempt to sidestep the issue of how bargains are actually reached by examining the properties of outcomes with only passing reference to the process which leads to them (see Nash, 1950; Luce and Raiffa, 1957; and Braithwaite, 1956). In doing so, they fail to describe the important process by which players move from disagreement to concession and, finally, agreement. Two decades before Nash,

Zeuthen (1930) had presented a solution to the division game which was geared towards explaining exactly this process. In an attempt to model convergence by considering the realistic uncertainties involved in bargaining, Zeuthen claimed that the one overriding characteristic of the final outcome is that, at the point of agreement, both sides are equally fearful of disagreement.[15] Having received an offer from player *B*, Zeuthen argues that *A* will deliberate between accepting it and holding out by making a counter-offer which may be accepted, or rejected, by *B*.[16] Zeuthen then asks "What is the maximum subjective probability of conflict that *A* will consider as reasonable and reject *B*'s offer?" The answer is "the level of probability that will make *A* indifferent between capitulating or persisting". The motivation that forces bargainers to concede is the fear that if they are too persistent the other side will choose the threat point—i.e. conflict in the form of a strike in the collective bargaining example or no agreement in the inheritance game. Zeuthen then postulates that the party whose "acceptable" subjective probability of conflict is lower will be forced to concede first that it will be just sufficient to motivate her opponent to concede. Hence, the process of convergence. An obvious disadvantage of Zeuthen's bargaining process is that in computing their subjective probabilities of conflict, bargainers irrationally assume that at every stage of the game they are faced with an all-or-nothing situation when clearly this is not the case. The implicit assumption here is that, during every stage, bargainers behave as if their opponents are either going to agree or head for the threat point. Bargainers are thus assumed to be myopic since their expectations are incompatible with the reality of disagreement often giving way, not to conflict, but to concessions. Despite this problem, however, it is interesting to compare the spirit of Zeuthen's solution with that of Nash. Intuitively they both seem to be telling the same story: the side which is more risk-averse will concede first (Zeuthen), or more (Nash), and there will be no actual conflict. Such coincidence of form and content is not accidental. In a notable proof, Harsanyi (1961) shows that, once von Neumann–Morgenstern utility functions are adopted, the two models generate the same solution: that which maximises the product of the parties' utility gains. The non-existence of conflict in the Nash–Zeuthen–Harsanyi (N–Z–H) solution is due to the ex-ante strict Pareto-optimality assumption rather than ex-post deduction. By defining rationality to be incompatible with conflict, cooperation emerges as the only optimal outcome of confrontation. If, however, one seeks a theory of conflict one should not attempt to read more into N–Z–H than it contains. Hicks (1932) had come to the same conclusion: if bargainers are well-informed about each other's preferences, then rationality is incompatible with conflict. The logic behind this argument is indestructible: perfect information coupled with hyperrationality should make agents capable of predicting the course of the dispute–strike–war. So when conflict does emerge it is "doubtless the result of faulty negotiation" (Hicks, 1932, p. 146). Hick's own theoretical contribution was the well-known "scissors diagram" depicting the two sides' concession schedules as a function of the duration of the dispute.

Sequential bargaining

Although Harsanyi's restatement of Zeuthen's sequential model confirms the Nash prediction about the final division, it is not clear whether agreement is going to be instantaneous or delayed. The reason behind this vagueness is that in the N–Z–H model there is only one type of waste: conflict. As long as conflict is averted, it does not matter whether convergence takes time. In an influential paper, Rubinstein (1982) explicitly introduced costs to the process of bargaining. The derivation of Rubinstein's SPNE requires a slight amendment of the Will. The heirs are told that a series of meetings has been arranged for them in which they are expected to reach a compromise if unable to agree a division immediately. However, the Will specifies that for every meeting that is broken off without a settlement a portion of the inheritance is donated to a charity—i.e. the final share of each is multiplied by a "discount rate" $\delta < 1$ and n indicates the number of meetings needed for an agreement. To enhance the generality of the analysis, it is useful to allow for different discount rates for the two parties (δ_1, δ_2) (by, for example, assuming that each heir's donation on the aftermath of an unsuccessful meeting should be proportional to her income). Rubinstein's SPNE requires that strategies within every bargaining round are also Nash equilibria (i.e. bargainers do not suffer from Zeuthenian myopia) and predicts immediate agreement with shares

$$\frac{1 - \delta_2}{1 - \delta_1 \delta_2}, \qquad \frac{\delta_2(1 - \delta_1)}{1 - \delta_1 \delta_2}$$

for A and B respectively (see Shaked and Sutton, 1984, for a proof).

The evolution of the game cannot be simpler: A demands an amount corresponding to the PE and B accepts any demand which does not exceed this amount. Predictably, the more impatient a player the smaller her share. Notice, however, that there is an unambiguous first-mover advantage (e.g. when $\delta_1 = \delta_2 = \delta$ A receives $(1 - \delta)^2 / 1 - \delta^2$ more than B). This imbalance disappears in the ex-ante sense if a coin is tossed to determine who starts first (see Binmore, 1987). The first-mover advantage also fades to zero, ex-post, as time delay between the two rounds vanishes. Letting the length of time between rounds tend to zero leads, in the limit, to equal shares for both sides (see Sutton, 1986, p. 710). The powerful implications of the SPNE can be illustrated by means of the so-called "outside option" (see Sutton, Shaked and Binmore, 1986).

Suppose that when B rejects A's offer, a random event may take place which would give B the option of receiving a fixed sum and leaving, thus ending A's hopes of a share of the inheritance. Nash's theory would predict that the effect of the availability of this option would be to shift the "threat point" in B's favour (i.e. the threat point would no longer mean a zero pay-off for B). An application of Rubinstein's SPNE, however, reveals that there are two possibilities: either B's outside option exceeds the expected pay-off from the original game or it does not. In the first case A's position is indeed worsened, whereas in the second, B's threat of taking the outside option is an empty one. It is thus clear that the "threat point" will not always shift.[17]

The sequential nature of Rubinstein's analysis is rather academic as far as a theory of conflict is concerned because his framework is incompatible with disagreement. Indeed, although an infinite number of potential stages is allowed, no dynamics ever develop as rational agreement is immediate and the potential costs of delay between stages only affect the size of the respective shares.

In spite of the analytical contribution of perfect equilibria, we are still left without a rationalisation of conflict. Could it be, however, that relaxing the assumption of common knowledge will generate "optimal" levels of conflict serving the purpose of information-gathering? Suppose, for example, that the size of the inheritance (S) to be divided is only known with certainty by A. B will then formulate a first-period offer that A should accept only if S is large. B's strategy is optimal since she would like as large a share as possible. A, however, can only credibly inform B of the real value of S by either accepting B's offer—in which case it is revealed that S is large—or rejecting it and thus persuading B that S is small by incurring the cost of disagreement (i.e. the price of conflict). Hence conflict may be optimal for at least some of the time.[18] The prospect of a rationalisation of conflict along these lines has naturally generated a lot of interest and the asymmetric information literature has recently proliferated.

The basic story is as follows. There are a buyer and a seller of a commodity whose value to the seller is known to be zero; the buyer's valuation is private information. In each period the seller announces a price and the buyer accepts or rejects it. Rejection leads to one period of costly conflict (such as a strike if the seller is the union and the buyer the firm) which may come to an end in the next bargaining round. The seller's assessment of the buyer's true valuation is updated every time an offer is rejected according to Bayes's rule. It is shown that if the seller's beliefs are consistent with Bayes's rule and the strategies of the two players at every stage of the game's history satisfy the condition of subgame perfection, the final solution will be a sequential equilibrium (see Kreps and Wilson, 1982b). Put simply, a sequential equilibrium can be described as follows: there is limited information on what your opponent's preferences are and therefore at every stage of the game you act fully rationally and you base your strategy on what information can be deduced from the opposition's actions. The only reason why the sequential equilibrium does not collapse to a perfect equilibrium without conflict is because there is imperfect information.

The restrictive requirement of asymmetry—where one side is well-informed while the other is in the dark—has recently been addressed by Crampton (1984), Gul, Sonnenschein and Wilson (1985) and Chatterjee and Samuelson (1987). Two-sided uncertainty is introduced by allowing each side to be one of two possible types (strong/weak or high/low valuation). However, the problem here is that equilibrium solutions are susceptible to variations in what is generally referred to as "out of equilibrium beliefs". The equilibrium price predicted by the analysis as the eventual point of agreement, will be dependent on how one bargainer interprets messages that might be received even if they are not the type of messages that would be in anybody's interest to send. Consequently, there is a plethora of equilibria—multiple equilibria—each one of them associated with how the analyst expects bargainers to respond to signals (offers) that will never be sent.[19]

Despite such problems, it does appear that the introduction of imperfect information has at long last produced a theory of conflict between rational agents. Unfortunately, such hopes are quickly dashed once we perform the following mental exercise: if, in any imperfect information model, we let the time-period between bargaining rounds go to zero then the duration of optimal conflict also goes to zero and our conflict theory disappears (see Gul and Sonnenschein, 1985). So, if bargaining is allowed to be continuous, then once more rationality is shown to be incompatible with conflict.[20]

An alternative possibility of salvaging a theory of impassive from imperfect information models is by adopting Crawford's (1982) adaptation of Schelling's

(1960) commitment theory. Suppose that there are two stages to every bargain: during the first, bargainers decide on whether they will attempt commitment, while in the second they find out the cost of backing down. Three possibilities exist: if both parties commit there is conflict; if only one side commits, it receives increased pay-offs; finally, if both choose not to commit there is immediate agreement with a solution resembling that of Nash. This type of imperfect information model preserves a positive probability of conflict by offering a rationale for the delay between periods. However, it does not explain what determines the duration of the commitment stage and therefore is again reduced to a non-theory of conflict once agents are allowed to make such decisions instantaneously (see Admarti and Perry, 1987).

In conclusion, it seems to be impossible to reconcile hyperrationality with wasteful conflict unless we are prepared to introduce exogenous restrictions to the process of bargaining. It would, however, be foolish to be surprised by this finding. Just as the "race to twenty" will not be played if there is full rationality, hyperrational agents will never "fight it out" provided that there are only two of them; they have nothing to learn about themselves from fighting and, there is no fixed time-horizon. Under such circumstances, it would be paradoxical if a fully rational theory of conflict were possible. If it were, rational agents would have had access to it and would be in a position to use it in order to predict the final outcome in which case there would be no need for conflict.

Bounded rationality models

The problem with these game-theoretic analyses of conflict then, is that they assume away the phenomenon they are supposed to be examining. One possible way out is to discard neoclassical hyperrationality, and recognise limitations on our own rationality. Even the smallest step away from hyperrationality, for instance some small uncertainty by rational agents concerning everyone else's rationality, can lead to major deviations from the equilibrium strategies of conventional game theory. Indeed, such uncertainty is synonymous with realistic interaction. Milgrom and Roberts (1982, 1987) argue that "since one doubts that everyone is always certain that everyone else is super-rational and, more generally, that the model of the world they are using is absolutely accurate . . . the study of how reasonable forms of bounded rationality affect the sensitivity of models assuming hyperrationality seems especially important" (Milgrom and Roberts, 1987, p. 190).

Ashenfelter and Johnson (1969) take a step along the path of bounded rationality in the context of a static marginalist model. They present a model of union–firm bargaining where a fully rational employer interacts with a myopic union. The firm maximises an intertemporal objective function and, in deciding to settle immediately or "take" a strike, balances the short-term costs of conflict against the long-term benefits of a reduced wage bill (reduced in comparison to what it would have been in the case of immediate settlement). Why is there conflict in this model? The reason is that there is nothing that can deflate labour's demand apart from a strike. Therefore, the decision by the employer to provoke conflict is no more than an investment decision. The model is of a one-sided bounded rationality nature. The union resists mechanically without even observing the firm's strategy while the hyperrational employer chooses the strike duration which maximises the firm's present value. Similar models have been presented by Johnston (1972) and Siebert, Bertrand and Addison (1985) (in which the union maximises an objective function while the firm resists mechanically) and some of them have been empirically tested (for a survey see Sapsford and Tzannatos, 1989). Because of their uncomplicated determinism, one-sided optimisation models of conflict have been received sceptically. A cynic would go as far as to argue that they purport to explain conflict by excluding actual bargaining from the analysis. Although it is true that bargaining does take a back seat, marginalist models can be shown to be more interesting than is generally recognised.

Consider, for example, the dynamic model of Cross (1969). A seller and a buyer bargain about the price of a commodity. Both incur bargaining costs proportional to the delay in reaching an agreement. Once an opening offer is reciprocated by an initial demand, each bargainer forms estimates of how long she will need to hold out for the other side to pay/accept the initial offer/demand. The formation of these estimates is equivalent to predicting each other's speed of concession. At the outset, each side's view of the rest of the game is identical to that of the employer in the Ashenfelter and Johnson game (i.e. they expect that the other side will be conceding at a given rate as the dispute progresses while *they* will remain unmoved). The significant difference is that in Cross' model *both* sides are capable of forming expectations about their opponent's future behaviour. Maximisation of each side's expected utility function subject to an expected concession pattern by the opposition yields the optimal offer and demand. Cross argues that at every point in time each side decides to prolong negotiations when their marginal return from an increase in their resistance to a lower pay-off is greater than their marginal cost of conflict. Once this kind of "optimal" disagreement is established, Cross addresses the process that leads to agreement. As the dispute goes on, at least one bargainer—possibly both—realise that their initial expectations concerning the opposition's readiness to concede were over-optimistic. The greater the discrepancy between the expected and the actual speed of concessions of the other side, the more extensively they update those inaccurate projections. These learning schemes—which are no more than adaptive expectations rules—when added to the first order conditions for the maximisation of the two sides' expected utility functions complete a system of four equations in four unknowns: the two predicted speeds of concession, the buyer's offer and the seller's demand. Potentially, this system can be solved for the time-paths of all four variables for every point in time. A plot of the time-paths of the offer and the demand provides a diagrammatic exposition of the solution which will be reached at the point of intersection of the two. Figure 14 depicts the history of the process and provides a possible rationalisation of Hick's concession curves.

There are two interesting observations to be made with regard to this solution. First, if the two bargainers are identical the Cross Solution coincides with the Nash distribution. Second, this model provides an intuitively appealing explanation of why bargainers do not attempt to settle immediately without delay or conflict: since offer adjustments do not depend on anything else but the discrepancy between expected and actual concessions, an attempt by one side to speed up the process by conceding more quickly will lead to a greater degree of intransigence by its opponent.

There are two fundamental problems with this type of model: first, it is not a genuine two-sided theory since the implicit assumption is that, when conceding,

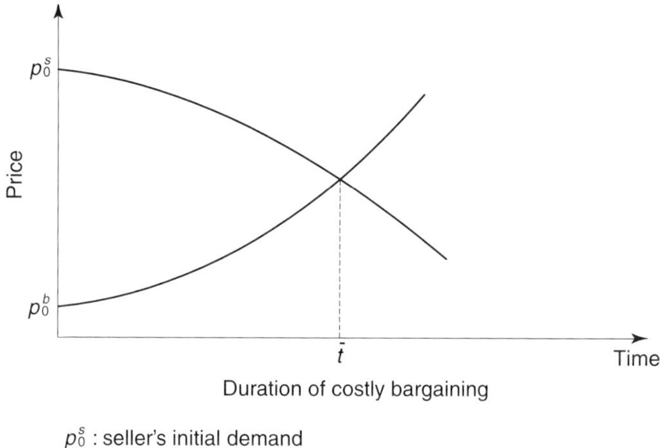

p_0^s : seller's initial demand

p_0^b : buyer's initial offer

$\bar{t}$: length of time before agreement is 'optimal'

Figure 14. Duration of costly bargaining.

bargainers are not aware of the fact that by doing so they are reshaping their opponents' behaviour—i.e. although the model allows for interdependence, bargainers behave as if it did not. In that respect, Cross's theory consists of two separate one-sided models stitched together by adaptive learning processes. The second problem is that of "eternal optimism". Bargainers never foresee forming erroneous expectations even if they have done so repeatedly in the past.[21] A dynamic rule-of-thumb model such as Cross's can potentially overcome the former problem by resorting to a synthesis of adaptive learning mechanisms and game-theoretic concepts although it is difficult to see how the inbuilt problem of ultra-optimism can be resolved.[22] The only available option is to wish it away by arguing that the best strategy for convincing one's opponent that no concessions should be expected, is first to convince oneself.

A reputation model of conflict

Clearly, if one is both to refrain from ruling out conflict by assumption and to ignore the entanglements of bargainers' webs of belief, then a tricky path between hyperrationality and crude bounded rationality must be trod. Kreps and Wilson (1982a) and Milgrom and Roberts (1982) have attempted just that.

Consider a union–firm bargaining relation where the existing *status quo* is characterised by consensus over a certain division of the producer surplus between capital and labour. The apparent tranquility is, however, thought to be in jeopardy in view of a recent development which imposes a finite—even if not fixed—horizon on the present circumstances. A recent example of such a development is the effect which

<table>
<tr><td></td><td></td><td colspan="2" align="center">Pay-offs to:</td></tr>
<tr><td></td><td></td><td align="center">Employer</td><td align="center">Union</td></tr>
<tr><td align="right">Union acquiesces</td><td></td><td align="center">$0 < h < 1$</td><td align="center">0</td></tr>
<tr><td align="right">Firm enforces plan</td><td></td><td></td><td></td></tr>
<tr><td align="right">Union goes on strike</td><td></td><td align="center">$h - 1$</td><td align="center">−1</td></tr>
<tr><td align="right">Firm continues to propose the plan but seeks
the Union's consent before implementing it.</td><td></td><td align="center">0</td><td align="center">$a > 1$</td></tr>
</table>

Figure 15. Pay-off matrix.

plans for a Channel Tunnel had on industrial relations in the British cross-Channel ferry labour market.[23]

Management proposes a "rationalisation" scheme which would involve employment and/or wage cuts. Figure 15 describes the pay-offs that will accrue to the two sides depending on the firm's decision to unilaterally enforce the scheme and also on whether the union chooses to acquiesce or to fight.

The above game, whether played only once or repeated a finite or an infinite number of times, can only have one outcome: the implementation of the plan followed by union acquiescence (a perfect equilibrium). Against the background of a finite horizon, would it be possible for the union to commit to strike and therefore prevent the firm from challenging? Consider the last time the game is to be played prior to the Chunnel's opening: as the firm is aware that there is no longer any scope for the union to attempt to preserve such commitment, it will choose to enforce the plan. By backward induction, it transpires that at no point in time will the union's threat be credible. That is, until a small amount of uncertainty is introduced concerning its actual pay-offs. When the firm chooses the aggressive strategy, union choice is limited between pay-offs 0 or -1, thus compelling its leaders to acquiesce. These values presumably reflect the fact that the net monetary returns from a strike for labour will be negative. What, however, if the union is known to value, in addition to income, the principle of consultation and thus derive utility from its reputation for being prepared to fight for its principles. In that case, the employer entertains the belief that the union's pay-offs from strike and acquiescence are 0 and -1 respectively with probability p. If $p = 1$, the firm will never challenge since it always expects an industrial dispute to ensue. The interesting twist here is that, not only will a union fight if it is "ideologically" committed, but it may also wish to do so when it is not, in order to build a belligerent reputation. The game starts at the moment the Channel Tunnel project is announced and is due to end after T periods (T being the length of time before the Tunnel's official opening to the public). Letting δt be the shortest period of time in which a challenge and a strike can materialise (say a day or a week), it will be assumed that when confronted by a massive picket line during period δt, the firm will back down. In the short interval $(t, t - \delta t)$—remember that time is moving backwards as the countdown to 1993 has commenced—the non-ideological union trying to build a reputation will strike with probability $1 - \Psi_t$ and, therefore, the firm will anticipate a strike with probability $1 - (1 - p_t)\Psi_t$.

In equilibrium, the firm is indifferent between challenging and staying put when the expected returns from the two are equal. So in the interval $(t, t - \delta t)$:

$$[h - 1] + [1 - (1 - p_t)\Psi_t] + (1 - p_t)\Psi] \times h = 0 \tag{1}$$

pay-off from strike in the interval $(t, t + \delta t)$	probability of a strike if the firm challenges	probability of union acquiescence	benefits to the firm in this case

is the condition for the firm to hesitate. The union must, therefore, strike with probability at least equal to

$$1 - \left(\frac{1 - h}{1 - p_t}\right) \tag{2}$$

if it is to prevent challenges.

Suppose that at time t the union has responded with a strike; how is this going to affect its reputation as measured by the firm's assessment p? Adopting Bayes's rule as a consistent means of updating beliefs we have that in every interval of δt length.[24]

$$p_t - \delta_t \equiv p_\delta(\text{Union is "ideological"})|\text{it fought at time } t) =$$

$$\frac{p_\delta(\text{fight}|\text{"ideological"}) \times p_\delta(\text{"ideological"})}{p_\delta(\text{fight})} = \frac{1 \times p_t}{1 - (1 - p_t)\Psi_t\delta_t} \tag{3}$$

Subtracting p_t from both sides, dividing by δt, and letting δt tend to zero, we derive the rate of increase in the union's reputation as challenges are met by strikes:

$$\dot{p}_t = p_t(1 - p_t)\Psi_t \tag{4}$$

Substitution of (2) in (4) leads to the time-path of the union's reputation ($p_t = \exp(h - 1)t$) as it responds to challenges aggressively. Figure 16 describes the game in its entirety.

At time $t = T$, the firm expects the union to prefer a strike if challenged with probability $[p_0]$ which can be thought of as the union's initial reputation for being ideological.[25] The union that is truly so will not hesitate to strike if its only alternative is to acquiesce. However, a union that would prefer to give in, on short-run considerations alone, will also strike if challenged as long as its initial reputation p_0 exceeds the level indicated by f (i.e. up to time-period $t = K$); this strategy is compatible with its goal of keeping managers at bay for as long as possible. The firm, knowing this, will never dare to challenge before $t = K$. At that point it will start thinking about challenging and will do so with a positive probability. When it does, (2) provides us with the probability that the "non-ideological" union will respond with a

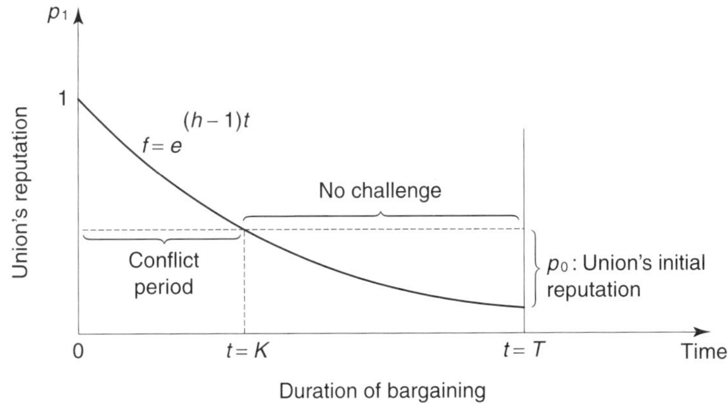

Figure 16. Duration of bargaining.

strike. As we approach the end, the union will eventually give in—unless of course it genuinely prefers a strike. It is interesting to note that the condition for conflict is not that combatants "prefer" fighting, but rather that given a small probability that they do, they choose to behave as if that were the case (see Kreps and Wilson, 1982a, for a full discussion). (The alert reader will notice that this rationale for conflict is exactly the same as that behind predatory pricing discussed in the previous section). An unfortunate disadvantage of this model is that, given the war-of-attrition nature of the game, there can be no room for compromise: concessions are ruled out by the requirement that a bargainer will be either a winner or a loser.

More recently there have been attempts to refine models similar to the above by allowing for a more realistic outflow of "signals" in place of the binary responses (e.g. strike or acquiescence) demonstrated here (see Crawford and Sobel, 1985, and Cho and Kreps, 1987) as well as the possibility that bargainers attempt to build multiple reputations (see Hargreaves–Heap and Varoufakis, 1987).

CONCLUDING COMMENTS

When a bargaining party consists of a group of heterogeneous individuals, uncertainty concerning their collective ability to combine in order to inflict costs on the other side will damage their bargaining strength. Furthermore, if there is a preconception that "fighting often means fighting well", conflict may emerge as a necessary condition for the creation of a future "threat point" (Hicks, 1932)—for example, acknowledged that "Weapons grow rusty if unused. . . . The most able union will embark on strikes occasionally" (Hicks, 1932, p. 146). The implication here is that if the ability to strike depends on striking experience, conflict has an investment role to play which is largely ignored. Collective participation in threatened conflict is undermined by the fact that the benefits are reaped by participants and non-participants alike. The common interest and the private interest pointing in different directions, free-riding will emerge with a detrimental effect on the group's bargaining power. The logic of collective action (see Olson (1965) for a definition) suggests that conflict may serve the purpose of freeing individuals from the prisoner dilemma preferences which prevent them from being collectively rational. If conflict encourages the adoption of common assurance preferences—i.e. individuals preferring to cooperate rather than defect (see Sen (1967))—then it may be the appropriate price for the formation of an effective coalition.

Akerlof (1980) offers a simple sociological model that relates the proportion of free-riders to the utility that agents derive from being "loyal" members of the community. If behaving according to a "social convention"—for example, not breaking a strike— affects one's preferences in proportion to the community's valuation of that convention, then it is shown that self interested individuals may be driven through the influences of society's values to prefer being selfless rather than egoistic. An alternative reason for not defecting (see Sugden (1987)) is that, if the coalition is fragile, agents choose to cooperate because they think that if they defect everyone will do likewise. However, refraining from being a "traitor" because you derive utility from being a "hero" is fundamentally different from doing so simply because you predict a collapse of a coalition whose success is only of pecuniary importance to you. In the former case, individuals are capable of a far-reaching transition from one set of preferences to another due to their experience of conflict, while in the latter, preferences remain unchanged.

The importance of such considerations transcends the study of organisations if it is recognised that, in making hard choices, the individual is presiding over an internal battle between conflicting tendencies. It is the suspicion that the outcome of this internal battle may be intrinsically linked with one's environment which raises doubts about the wisdom of exclusively construing conflict as the by-product of informational asymmetries.

Game theory's preference invariance to conflict is a strong assumption riddled with philosophical, as well as, ideological implications. Whereas it is consistent with— although not apologetic to—Hobbes's pessimistic perception of individuals being engaged in a perpetual war of all against all, it is incompatible with a wide class of alternative perceptions ranging from the Aristotle–Locke conservative consensus view of society which results from a benign view of human nature, to the radical conflict tradition of Plato, Rousseau and Marx who perceive conflict as an inescapable outcome of immature social organisation. The underlying Hobbesian–Humean leanings of game theory can thus be traced to the implicit assumption that individuals are unable to learn from social interaction anything more than the limitation of their bargaining power. This isolation of aspirations from experience is tantamount to a fundamental philosophical bias which prevents game theory from investigating the interdependence of personal development and social evolution.

In conclusion, game theory offers a fascinating insight into interdependent behaviour. However, if it is to constitute the bias for a comprehensive and relevant theory of conflict, it must mature and thus allow its subject matter to retain human nature's ability to undergo fundamental changes as a result of contact with the evolution in social relations.

NOTES

1. Rational expectations was introduced into macroeconomics in a blaze of controversy, largely because it was first applied to oversimplified, crude models of the labour market which inevitably threw up the implausible conclusion that involuntary unemployment could not exist. Had equally crude Keynesians been first to introduce rational expectations, then the force of fiscal policy would have been enhanced by rational expectations, and not neutered by it. For instance, in the simplest $YC = I + G$ model with exogenous investment and $C = a + by$, an increase in G would not need to await the laborious knock-on effects of the multiplier for consumption to increase and income with it: the rational expectation of income increases would entice consumers to raise demand immediately to its new equilibrium level. The reason for mentioning this is not to advance a particular macro model, but to divorce the analytical method from the policy stance.

2. Von Neumann and Morgenstern (1944) used the terms "complete information and incomplete information" games respectively. We follow modern terminology.

3. The NE is unique in this example. However, were 2's pay-off to (c_1, c_2) 5 instead of 0 then that would also be a pure strategy NE, as well as (a_1, b_2). In such cases of multiple equilibria, the game theorist is unable to say which is more likely to arise. Pre-play communication might help 1 and 2 to focus on one or the other, but unless one NE Pareto dominates the other (which it does not in this example) communication may be of little use.

4. Alternatively, if firm 1 thinks about playing $\hat{s}_1$ and duplicates 2's thought process expecting her to reason in the same way and set output B_2, then the conclusion would be that each would have higher than Cournot outputs and neither would be making best replies. This would also give worse profits than the NE. Interestingly, the Preto suboptimality of mutual Stackelberg leadership is not always the case. With upward-sloping best-reply curves, as typically arise from price competition, higher profits may obtain for both players as Stackelberg leadership involves higher prices. Nevertheless, this does not get round the essential point that best replies are not being played. These points relate to the simultaneous choice of strategies. See the text for the case where the "follower" is a genuine follower in that she chooses her strategy sequentially after the leader has declared his.

5. Incidentally, the pay-offs to entry and acquiescence in the example correspond to the linear Cournot game with parameter values $(a - c)^2/b = 72$ and fixed costs of 5. Actual fighting corresponds to setting price equal to marginal cost, c.

6. The recent game-theoretic literature on oligopoly has become known as the "New IO" (New Industrial Organisation). Both price and quantity have been utilised as strategic variables. For instance, much of the game-theoretic work on technological competition (see Dasgupta, 1987, for a good review) has firms choosing R&D expenditures to determine costs (i.e. process innovation) combined with Cournot quantity competition in the product market.

7. We have specified a three-stage game with sequential entry followed by pricing, because this yields a pure strategy equilibrium. If 1 and 2 must simultaneously decide on entry before they know what the other has done, we have a two-stage game but mixed strategies are required for equilibrium (see Fudenberg and Tirole, 1986). Mixed strategies are discussed in the pricing context later in this section.

8. If capacity costs are only a proportion of c and the remainder of costs can be postponed until a later date, this does not affect the problem from the point of view of the first stage.

9. This is an example of the so called 'folk theorem' which states that any individually rational outcome is sustainable in an infinitely repeated game without discounting (see Friedman, 1986, or Binmore and Dasgupta, 1986, for further references). Individual rationality eliminates only those strategies for which an alternative could guarantee the player a higher pay-off regardless of what rivals do. It is a very weak definition of rationality and generally permits multiple equilibria (e.g. both (a_1, a_2) and (b_1, b_2) in the one-shot prisoners' dilemma are individually rational equilibria). In the present, infinitely repeated example, trigger collusion, perpetual play of (b_1, b_2), and many other equilibria are

possible. Many game theorists are very wary of this Pandora's box of equilibria opened up by the folk theorem; though others are content that multiple equilibria are a more accurate reflection of real world situations.

10. It was earlier suggested that the practice of promising to match a rival's price could help deter entry. At the same time, in the present context, the same practice can help facilitate non-cooperative collusion between existing firms because it speeds up a price-cutting response by making it automatic. Thus, a superficially competitive strategy, in fact, reduces the incentive to cut price.

11. That we have $d > 0.5$ for both collusion and immediate remorse to be profitable is a contrivance of this particular example, but the general principle should be clear.

12. As such, it can claim to be the "best" equilibrium amongst the set given by the folk theorem (which can be modified to include discounting: see Fudenberg and Maskin, 1986).

13. Remember, d may be frighteningly low—it was only 0.5 in one of earlier examples!

14. See Farber and Bazerman (1987) for a recent survey of arbitration theories.

15. Aumann and Kurz (1977) present a similar interpretation of Nash's solution.

16. Here it is assumed that meetings are instantaneous consisting of one offer followed by either acceptance or rejection.

17. Consider a case of haggling between a buyer and a seller over the price of a commodity. The buyer is offer 200 while seller demands 250. if an outside option became available to the seller, it would, according to Nash, invariably shift the threat point in the seller's favour. In Rubinstein's analysis, however, it would only do so if its expected value exceeded 200.

18. One-sided asymmetric information bargaining models such as Fudenberg and Tirole (1986) have been modified to account for industrial disputes. For example, see Hayes (1984) and Tracy (1987).

19. The only way of deriving a single solution is by devising suitable restrictions on the players' beliefs. The model-builder has to find a fine balance between too strong and too weak restrictions or, otherwise, between non-existent and multiple equilibria. See Kreps (1986).

20. A parallel can be drawn here with the inheritance division game. Rubinstein shows that, in the presence of full information, the two relatives will come to an immediate agreement even if there is the possibility of many future, albeit instantaneous, negotiating stages separated by an exogenously fixed "delay". Uncertainty about each other—for example, concerning their discount rates—yields a positive probability of more than one stage before agreement. However, if we now allow them to enter the room and only come out when they have agreed, despite the presence of two-sided uncertainty, the probability of wasteful disagreement vanishes as there will be no need for a second meeting.

21. This type of myopia is not dissimilar to Zeuthen's implicit assumption that, at every round, bargainers fail to learn from past experience that since concessions have already been made by their opponents, further concessions may be forthcoming.

22. See Varoufakis (1987) where the Cross model is extended as a theory of strikes by incorporating two optimisation structures, one for each side. The crucial interdependence between bargainers—which is absent in models such as Ashenfelter and Johnson (1969)—is then restored as expectations on the opponent's concession rates, and therefore offers vary. Furthermore, strategic delay in conceding is explicitly modelled along the lines of models discussed in Part III Section 5 of Varoufakis (1987).

23. Finite horizons can be involved for a number of reasons. For example, it may be that a politician's term has an upper bound (R. Reagan?) or that it is common knowledge that, whatever protectionist measures from which a firm may be benefiting in an EEC country today, come 1992 it will be removed. Some oligopolistic games may thus be repeated over a finite period. In the analysis that follows T is assumed to be fixed. This need not be the case: Hargreaves-Heap and Varoufakis (1987) present a version of the models with stochastic horizons.

24. $0(\delta t)$ terms will be ignored throughout so as not to put off the non-technical student.

25. From equation (1) it can be shown that if the union's reputation (p_t) exceeds the value implicit in f, the firm will abstain from challenging.

REFERENCES

Abreu, D. Extremal equilibria of oligopolistic supergames, *Journal of Economic Theory*, 1986, **39**: 191–225.

Admab, A. R. and Perry, M. Strategic delay in bargaining, *Review of Economic Studies*, 1987, **54**(179): 315–364.

Akerlof, G. A. A theory of social custom of which unemployment may be one conscquence, *Quarterly Journal of Economics*, 1980, **94**: 749–775.

Ashenfelter, O. and Johnson, G. E. Bargaining theory, trade unions and industrial strike acitivty, *American Economic Review*, 1969, **59**, 35–49.

Aumann, R. J. and Kurz, H. Power and taxes, *Econometrica*, 1977, **45**: 1137–1161.

Benoit, J.-P. and Krishna, V. Dynamic du-poly: Prices and quantities, *Review of Economic Studies*, 1987, **54**: 23–35.

Binmore, K. G. and Dasgupta, P. (eds.) (1986) *Economic Organisations as Games*. Oxford: Basil Blackwell.

Braithwaite, R. B. (1956) *Theory of Games as a Tool for the Moral Philosopher*. Cambridge: Cambridge University Press.

Bernheim, B. D. Rationalizable strategic behaviour, *Econometrica*, 1984, **52**(4): 1007–1028.

Chamberlin, E. H. (1933) *The Theory of Monopolistic Competition*. Cambridge, Mass: Harvard University Press.

Chatterjee, K. and Samuelson, L. Bargaining with two-sided incomplete information: An infinite horizon model with alternating offers', *Review of Economic Studies*, 1987, **53**: 709–724

Cho, I. K. and Kreps, D. Signalling games and stable equilibria, *Quarterly Journal of Economics*, 1987, **CII**: 179–221.

Crampton, P. C. Bargaining with incomplete information: An infinite horizon model with continuous uncertainty, *Review of Economic Studies*, 1984, **51**: 579–594.

Crawford, V. P. A theory of disagreement in bargaining, *Econometrica*, 1982, **50**: 607–637.

Crawford, V. P. and Sobel, J. Strategic information transmission, *Econometrica*, 1982, **50**: 1431–1451.

Cross, J. *The Economics of Bargaining*, 1969. New York: Basic Books.

Dasgupta, P. The theory of technological competition. In: Stiglitz, J. and Mathewson, G. F., eds., *New Developments in the Analysis of Market Structure*, 1987. Basingstoke: Macmillan.

Dasgupta, P. and Maskin, E. Existence of equilibrium in discontinuous economic games: 1 and 2, *Review of Economic Studies*, 1986, **53**: 1–41.

Dasgupta, P. and Stiglitz, J. Learning by doing, *Oxford Economic Papers*, 1988, **40**: 246–268.

Dixit, A. Recent developments in oligopoly theory, *American Economic Review*, 1980, **72**: 12–17.

Dixon, H. Oligopoly Theory Made Simple. In: Davies, S. and Lyons, B. *et al., Economics of Industrial Organisation*, 1989. London: Longman.

Farber, H. S. and Bazerman, M. H. Why is there disagreement in bargaining?, *American Economic Review*, 1987, **77**: 347–352.

Friedman, J. W. *Oligopoly and the Theory of Games*, 1977. Amsterdam: North-Holland.

Friedman, J. W. *Game Theory with Applications to Economics*, 1986. Oxford: Oxford University Press.

Fudenberg, D. and Maskin, E. The Folk Theorem in Repeated Games with Discounting or with Incomplete Information, *Econometrica*, 1986, **54**: 533–54.

Fudenberg, D. and Tirole, J. A Theory of exit in duopoly, 1986, *Econometrica*, **54**: 943–960.

Fudenberg, D. and Tirole, J. Understanding rent dissipation: On the use of game theory in industrial organisation, *American Economic Association*, May 1987, **77**: 176–183.

Gul, F. and Sonnenschein, H. (1985) One-Sided Uncertainty Does Not Cause Delay, mimeo, Stanford University, Graduate Business School.

Gul, F. Sonnenschein, H and Wilson, R. (1985) Foundations of Dynamic Oligopoly and the Coase Conjecture, mimeo, Stanford University, Graduate Business School.

Hargreaves-Heap, S. and Varoufakis, Y. (1987) Multiple Reputations in Games with Uncertain Horizons, Discussion Paper No. 22, *Economics Research Centre*, University of East Anglia.

Harsanyi, J. On the rationality postulates underlying the theory of co-operative games, *Journal of Conflict Resolution*, 1961, **5**: 179–196.

Hayes, B. Unions and strikes and asymmetric information, *Journal of Labour Economics*, 1984, **2**: 57–83.

Hicks, J. R. (1932, reprinted in 1966) *The Theory of Wages*. London: Macmillan.

Johnston, J. A model of wage determination under bilateral monopoly, *Economic Journal*, 1972, **82**: 837–852

Kreps, D. (1986) Out of Equilibrium Beliefs and Out of Equilibrium Behaviour, mimeo, Stanford University, Graduate Business School.

Kreps, D. and Wilson, R. Reputation and imperfect information, *Journal of Economic Theory*, 1982a, **27**: 253–279.

Kreps D. and Wilson, R. Sequential equilibria, *Econometrica*, 1982b, **50**: 863–894.

Levitan, R. and Shubik, M. Price variation duopoly with differentiated products and random demand, *Journal of Economic Theory*, 1971, **3**(1): 23–39.

Luce, R. D. and Raiffa, H. *Games and Decisions*, 1957. New York: John Wiley.

Lyons, B. R. Strategic Behaviour, in R. Clarke and A. J. McGuinness (eds) *Economics of the Firm* 1987a. Oxford: Basil Blackwell.

Lyons, B. R. International Trade and Technology Policy. In *Economic Policy and Technological Performance*, 1987b. Cambridge: Cambridge University Press.

Milgrom, P. and Roberts, J. Predation, reputation and entry deterrence, *Journal of Economic Theory*, 1982, **27**: 280–312.

Milgrom, P. and Roberts, J. Informational asymmetries, strategic and industrial organisation, *American Economic Review*, 1987, **77**: 184–193.

Nash, J. F. The bargaining problem, *Econometrica*, 1950, **18**: 155–162.

Olson, M., Jr *The Logic of Collective Action*, 1965. Cambridge: Harvard University Press.

Pearce, D. G. Rationalizable strategic behavior and the problem of perfection, *Econometrica*, 1984, **52**(4): 1029–1050.

Radner, R. Repeated partnership games with imperfect monitoring and no discounting, *Review of Economic Studies*, 1986, **53**: 43–57.

Rubinstein, A. Perfect equilibrium in a bargaining model, *Econometrica*, 1982, **50**: 97–109.

Sapsford, D. and Tzannatos, Z. *Current Issues in Labour Economics*, 1989. London: Macmillan.

Schelling, T. C. *The Strategy of Conflict*, 1960. Cambridge, Mass: Harvard University Press.

Selten, R. The chain store paradox, *Theory and Decision*, 1978, **9**: 129–159.

Sen, A. K. Isolation, assurance and the social rate of discount, *Quarterly Journal of Economics*, 1967, **80**: 112–124.

Shaked, A. and Sutton, J. Relaxing price competition through product differentiation, *Review of Economic Studies*, 1982, **459**: 3–14.

Shaked, A. and Sutton, J. Natural oligopolies, *Econometrica*, 1983, **51**: 1469–1484.

Shaked, A. and Sutton, J. Natural oligopolies and international trade. In: H. Kierzkowski (ed.) *Monopolistic Competition and Internal Trade*, 1984. Oxford: Oxford University Press.

Shaked, A. and Sutton, J. Involuntary unemployment as a perfect equilibrium in a bargaining model, *Econometrica*, 1984, **52**: 1351–1364.

Shaked, A. and Sutton, J. Product differentiation and industrial structure, *Journal of Industrial Economics*, 1987, **36**: 131–146.

Siebert, W. S. Bertrand, P. V. and Addison, J. T. The political model of strikes: A new twist, *Southern Journal of Economics*, July 1985, **52**(1): 23–33.

Sugden, R. *The Economics of Rights, Co-operation and Welfare*, 1987. Oxford: Blackwell.

Sutton, J. Shaked, A. and Binmore, K. An outside option experiment, *American Economic Review*, 1986, **76**: 57–63.

Sutton, J. Non-cooperative bargaining theory: An introduction, *Review of Economic Studies*, 1986, **53**: 709–724.

Tracy, J. S. An empirical test of an asymmetric information model of strikes, *Journal of Labour Economics*, 1987, **5**: 149–173.

Varoufakis, Y. Optimisation and Strikes, Ph.D thesis, 1987, University of Essex.

von Newmann, John and Morgenstern, Oskar, *Theory of Games and Economic Behavior*, 1947. Princeton: Princeton University Press, 1944; 2nd edn., 1947; 3rd edn., 1953.

Williamson, O. E., *Antitrust Economics: Mergers, Contracting, and Strategic Behaviour*, 1987. Oxford: Basil Blackwell.

Zeuthen, F. *Problems of Monopoly and Economic Warfare*, 1. New York: Augustus M. Kelley reprint 1968.

5

Auctions and Bidding: A Primer

Paul Milgrom

A painting contractor once complained to me that the jobs put up for competitive bids are unlike other painting jobs.

> I do most of my work for a few builders that I've known for years. My estimates of what it will cost to do a job for one of them come out about right. Sometimes a little high, sometimes low, but about right overall. Occasionally, when business is slow, I bid on a big job for another builder, but those jobs are different: They always run more than I expect.

Maybe the contractor was right to think bid jobs are different, but it is more likely that he suffered from too simple a view of what is involved in preparing a competitive bid. Our analysis will show that even an experienced estimator working in familiar terrain can lose money if he doesn't understand the subtleties of competitive bidding.

The phenomenon experienced by the painting contractor, known as the "Winner's Curse", is just one of the surprising and puzzling conclusions that have been turned up by modern research into auctions. Another is the theoretical proposition (supported also by some experimental evidence) that, for example, a sealed-bid Treasury bill auction in which each buyer pays a price equal to the highest rejected bid would yield more revenue to the Treasury than the current procedure in which the winning bidder pays the seemingly higher amount equal to his own bid. There are also subtle results that demonstrate the equivalence of such apparently different institutions as the standard sealed-bid auction, in which the auctioneer/seller sells the goods to the highest bidder for a price equal to his bid, and the Dutch auction, in which the auctioneer/seller begins by asking a high price and gradually lowers the price until some bidder shouts "Mine" to claim the item. Other results explain the use of standard auctions as the selling schemes that maximize the welfare of the bid-taker, or as schemes that lead to efficient allocations, minimize transaction costs, guard against corruption by the bid-taker's agents or mitigate the effects of collusion among the bidders. Finally, for some environments, the theory makes sharp, testable predictions about the bids and profits of various classes of bidders. This paper relies

Reprinted with permission from *Journal of Economic Perspectives*, Vol. 3, No. 3, 1989, pp. 3–22

mainly on theory to study these issues, but it will also review some experimental evidence and recent empirical studies testing the predictions of the theory.

PITFALLS FOR BIDDERS

One of the earliest operations research studies of competitive bidding was made by Lawrence Friedman (1956). He argued that a bidder should study the past behavior of its competitors to discover the patterns that governed their bidding. This information could be used, in any particular competition, to estimate the probability distribution of any particular competitor i's bid b_i, as represented by the function describing how likely the bid b_i is to be less than any particular amount b. This is the cumulative distribution function: $F_i(b) = \text{Prob}(b_i \leq b)$.

Suppose that the bidders are vying for a road construction contract and that the usual rules of sealed bid auctions apply, so that it is the lowest bid that wins. Examine the problem of just one of the contractors. If it bids b and wins and if its cost of completing the contract is c, then its profits will be $b - c$; if it loses the auction, its profits will be zero. The contractor's bid of b will win precisely when *all* the other contractors make higher bids. The probability that the ith competing contractor makes a higher bid is $1 - F_i(b)$. Thus, if there are N other bidders, the probability that a bid of b beats them all is $P(b) = (1 - F_i(b)) \dots (1 - F_N(b))$ and the contractor's expected profit is equal to that probability times the profit margin in the bid: $P(b)(b - c)$. Friedman recommends that the bid b be chosen to maximize that expression.

This expression for expected profits depends on two important assumptions. One is that the bids made by competitors are statistically independent (the *independence assumption*) and that their distributions can be somehow estimated from history. The other is that the bidder actually knows the amount c that it will cost him to complete the contract (the *private values assumption*). The independence assumption means that there is no unobserved common factor affecting all of the competitor's bids while the private values assumption allows the contractor to ignore the competitors' information in forming its cost estimate. These assumptions make collecting data, constructing the model, and solving the optimization problem easy, but they may often fail to portray the auction environment accurately.

An alternative model that violates both of these assumptions was used by ARCO in preparing bids for offshore oil tracts sold by the US government. The detailed logic of their model has been described by Capen, Clapp, and Campbell (1971). As applied to the problem of bidding for construction contracts, ARCO's model would say that a contractor doesn't really know what the job will cost, and regards the actual cost C of the job as a random variable. Uncertainties about cost arise from uncertainties about factors that will affect all bidders like the number of tons of concrete that will be required, blasting difficulties, cold weather construction delays, changing factor prices, and so on in addition to factors that are idiosyncratic and vary from bidder to bidder. Each contractor's cost estimate is just an estimate, subject to error. No contractor knows what its cost will be and each realizes that the other bidders may possess information or analyses that the contractor would find useful for its own cost estimation, so the private values assumption fails.

The simplest way to illustrate the consequence of this sort of estimation error is to replace the private values assumption by the *common values assumption* that the contractors are all equally capable and that each could, if called upon, do the job at the same cost *C*. Although this assumption is special, it makes it possible to illustrate some general phenomena rather simply. For additional simplicity, suppose that the bidders make unbiased estimates $X_i = C + \tilde{\varepsilon}_i$, where the estimation errors are independent.

Despite the independence of the estimation *errors*, the bidders' *estimates* are not independent, because the estimates in this Bayesian model are the sums of the common random term *C* and the independent errors.[1] As we shall later argue, this failure of the independence assumption has important consequences for the comparative performance of alternative auctioning rules.

Now comes a crucial observation. Even though each contractor's individual estimate is unbiased (that is, equal on average to the expected cost), the *lowest* estimate is biased downward. Indeed, because the expected value of the individual estimation errors is zero, the expected value of the minimum estimation error must be less than zero, and that implies the claimed estimation bias.

Now suppose all bidders determine their bids by adding the same fixed and/or percentage markup to their estimated costs, or using any other markup rule for which higher costs lead to higher bids. Then the winning bidder will be the one with the lowest estimate of project completion costs, and the winner's cost estimate will be too low on average.

The phenomenon just described is known as the winner's curse. It forms the basis of the explanation and advice that I might have offered to the painting contractor quoted in the introduction: "There may be nothing unusual about the painting jobs on which you have bid and nothing terribly wrong with your cost estimates. The problem is that in competitive bidding, your bid usually loses when you overestimate your actual costs. Often, when you win a job, it will be because your cost estimates were too low. To make money in competitive bidding, you will need to mark up your bids twice: once to correct for the underestimation of costs on the projects you win and a second time to include a margin for profit. Don't let the presence of several competing bidders push you into making too aggressive a bid. The markup to adjust for underestimation will have to be larger the larger is the number of your competitors and the more you respect the accuracy of their cost estimation; you may, however, want to make the profit markup smaller when there are more competitors. Also, the payoff to careful cost estimation in competitive bidding is great, because it allows you to bid aggressively without great risk. If you can also develop a reputation among your competitors for being an unusually savvy estimator, that's even better for you, because it will compel sensible competitors to bid more cautiously against you and allow you either to increase your profit markup or to win more bids."[2]

Since the contractor (who was my father) was retired by the time I understood these lessons, I have not tried my explanation on him.

Students are quite rightly reluctant to accept these results as proof that it is always best to bid cautiously. "You can't make any money if you never win a bid, and you can't win if you are too catious" is a common response. The most important lessons to be learned from both the theory and the experiments are that the returns in bidding come from cost and information advantages, that naive bidding strategies can squander these advantages, and that bidders without some advantage have little hope of earning much profit, but could with a little bit of carelessness suffer large losses.

EQUIVALENCES AMONG AUCTION INSTITUTIONS

To fix the terminology for this section, let us assume that the auctioneer is selling some goods and the bidders are the potential buyers. The first general question to ask about auction markets is to what extent the details of the institution matter. Should sealed bids be used, with the contract being awarded to the highest bidder for a price equal to its bid? Would the price be higher or the outcome more efficient if an open outcry auction of the kind used by the English auction houses were adopted, where bidders call out increasing bids until only the highest bidder remains? How do these alternatives compare with the Dutch auction, in which the auctioneer initially calls a high price and then lowers it continuously until some bidder claims the goods?

In one of the earliest and most remarkable economic analyses of auctions, William Vickrey (1961) studied those questions (and others). Let us review first Vickrey's analysis of the Dutch and sealed bid auctions.

In a sealed bid auction, each bidder independently and privately picks a price and offers to buy the goods at that price. The one who bids the highest price wins. The Dutch auction is seemingly quite different. The auctioneer calls the prices, beginning with a high price and proceeding to successively lower ones. The bidder listens to the prices called, notices whether any other bidder has accepted a price, and finally accepts some price if no other bidder has done so first.

Despite the seeming complexity of the Dutch auction bidder's task, a bidder who plans his actions in advance will find that his problem is identical to that facing a bidder in a sealed bid auction. For regardless of how the bidder approaches the calculations, the only genuine choice open to him is to select the highest price at which he will be willing to claim the goods. An example will help to illustrate this point. Suppose the bidder decides to proceed as follows. First, he will wait until the price has fallen to some level p_0 and then infer what he can from the failure of the others to bid at that point. Then, depending on the outcome of some calculation, he may choose to claim the item or he may choose to wait. In the latter case, he will perform some other calculation given the then available information to select another (lower) price p_1 at which to reevaluate, and the process then repeats itself. The outcome of this algorithm is entirely predictable. The upshot is that there is a single number p that represents the first price at which the bidder will claim the item. Let us call p the "bid". Using this language, we find that under the rules of the Dutch auction, the goods will be awarded to the "highest bidder" at a price equal to his bid. But those are precisely the rules of the standard sealed bid auction! The apparent complexity of the possible bidding strategies in the Dutch auction is a chimera; the only real choice a bidder has is to select his "bid" p.

Putting this conclusion somewhat differently, what this argument shows is that when the Dutch and sealed bid auctions are each modeled as "strategic form games," the games are identical.[3] That is, the sets of strategies are identical and the outcome rules that transform strategies into allocations are identical. Since solution concepts like the

Nash equilibrium work on strategic forms, these concepts predict powerfully that the identity of the winner and the price the winner pays will always be the same for these two kinds of auctions.

In small stakes laboratory experiments, however, this prediction appears not to hold: winning bidders in these experiments tend to pay a lower price in the Dutch auction than in the sealed bid auction. Why might this happen? One hypothesis, which I favor, is that the Dutch auction format discourages planning by the subjects: Dutch auctions are not "played" in the normal form. This hypothesis could be tested by manipulating the experimental conditions to encourage articulation of a plan before bidding in the Dutch auction to see if that reduces or eliminates the price disparity. For example, the experiment could have pairs of subjects who must place a joint bid; this is likely to encourage discussion of how to bid and may provide direct evidence on whether the subjects express their strategies as single numbers. An alternative hypothesis is that the subjects do not maximize expected utility, but instead use some other decision criterion. Finally, given the small stakes in most experimental conditions, the excitement of playing the game may lead the subjects in the Dutch auction game to prolong the game by holding out longer, which would account for the lower price. In this case, raising the stakes would tend to diminish the differences in the outcomes between the two alternative auction forms.[4]

Next, consider the common form of auction used by English auction houses, often called the English open outcry auction. Here, the auctioneer begins with the lowest acceptable price—the *reserve price*—and proceeds to solicit successively higher bids from the customers until no one will increase the bid. Then the item is "knocked down" (sold) to the highest bidder. Suppose that the bidders know the value to themselves of the item being auctioned. This is the private values assumption: it rules out the possibilities that the value of the goods to one bidder depends on its resale value to other bidders, or on the availability of substitutes regarding which the other bidders may have private information, or on how much others may admire the item, and so on. With the private value assumption, the bidder's dominant strategy in an English auction is to bid until the price exceeds his willingness to pay. Evidently, at equilibrium, the item will be awarded to the bidder who values it most highly for a price equal to the second highest valuation. This outcome is efficient.

Vickrey observed that the outcome of the English auction could also be achieved by means of a sealed-bid auction with the following rules: Each bidder submits a bid. The item is awarded to the highest bidder at a price equal to the second highest bid, or to the reserve price if that is higher. The bidders in this Vickrey *second-bid* auction are price takers—the price that the winning bidder pays is determined by the competitors' bids alone and does not depend on any action the bidder undertakes. From a single bidder's point of view, a bid in the Vickrey auction determines which "price offers" the bidder would be willing to accept; he will accept any "offers" up to the price he has bid. It is thus a dominant strategy for a bidder in this auction to submit a bid equal to his true reservation price, for he then accepts all offers which are below his reservation price and none that are above. When each bidder adopts his dominant strategy, the outcome will be that the item is awarded to the bidder with the highest valuation for price equal to the second highest valuation. The existence of a *dominant strategy* in this auction means that the bidder can choose his sealed bid without regard for how others bid. Thus, the second-bid auction duplicates the principal characteristics of the English open outcry auction. For that reason, it is customary to model the English auction as a second-bid auction, a custom we shall respect in this essay.

We cannot specify "optimal" bidding strategies for the Dutch auction and the standard sealed-bid ("first-bid") auction in the same way that we did for the English and second-bid auctions, because the profit-maximizing bid in these auctions depends on what bids the competitors make. To analyze this problem, let us shift attention from "bids" to "bidding strategies." A (pure) *strategy* for a bidder specifies what bid to make as a function of the information the bidder has. As illustrations, the construction contractor in our earlier example makes its bid as a function of its estimate of the cost of performing the contract and of any information it has about its competitors, and the oil company makes its bid for drilling rights as a function of its geologists' estimates of hydrocarbon potential. If each bidder correctly anticipates the bidding strategies his competitors will use and selects his own optimal strategy accordingly, then the collection of strategies form a *Nash equilibrium* of the bidding game. To say that a bidder correctly anticipates his competitors' *strategies* is not to say that he correctly anticipates their *bids*, but only how they would bid if they had some particular information. We will use the Nash equilibrium solution concept to analyze the auction games here.

The first thing to note about the first-bid auction, whether run using sealed bids or using a Dutch descending auction, is that there is no assurance that the equilibrium outcome will be efficient. In fact, in any environment where the bidders have observably different characteristics, the equilibrium outcome of sealed bidding is inefficient with some positive probability. To illustrate, suppose there are two bidders, one who is known to have a personal reservation price, or *valuation*, of $101 and a second whose valuation is either $50 with probability 4/5 or $75 with probability of 1/5. The first bidder is assumed not to know the valuation of the second, but he knows its distribution. If the first bidder bids $51, he will win $50 (his valuation minus his bid) at least 4/5 of the time, yielding an expected profit of at least $40. If he bids $62 or more, he can win no more than $39 (= $101 − $62), so he will never make that choice. Since the first bidder never bids as much as $62, an optimizing second bidder must win sometimes when his valuation is $75, and the allocation then is inefficient. This stands in contrast to the English auction, which would always lead to an efficient allocation in this environment.

Much of auction theory has analyzed "symmetric" environments where the bidders cannot discern differences among their competitors. For example, one popular formulation assumes that the bidders' private valuations are independent and indentically distributed random variables. In this case, as Vickrey first showed, there is an equilibrium in which each bidder adopts the same *strategy*; that is, each bids the same increasing function of his personal valuation. As a consequence, the bidder with the highest personal valuation will make the highest actual bid and the equilibrium allocation will be efficient.

Given that the English and second-price auctions and the Dutch and sealed bid (first-bid) auctions are both efficient in this environment, what can be said about how the total surplus will be divided between profits for the bidders and revenue for the seller? If the auctioneer/seller has the power to set the rule, the answer to this distribution question will predict which type of auction will be seen in practice. Will the first-bid auction, in which a winning bidder pays the amount of his own bid, lead to higher payments on average than the second-bid auction, in which the price is set equal to the second highest bid? The matter is not an obvious one, because the bidder in the first-bid auction will optimally shade his bid down to allow a margin for profit, while (as argued earlier) the bidder in a second-bid auction will find it optimal to bid the full amount of his valuations. Is the profit margin deducted by the bidder in the first-bid auction greater or less than his expected profit when he wins in the second-bid auction?

To illustrate the surprising answer, let us adopt an indirect approach. In any auction, the bids made by the bidders can be viewed as labels that are processed through the rules of the auction to determine the outcome. The actual items of interest to a bidder here are the probability P that his bid will win and the expected payments that he will be required to make if he wins or loses. Let us assume for simplicity that only winners pay, and denote the winning bidder's expected payment, given his bid, by E. Then, a bid is really just an indirect way to choose among the real items of interest—the pairs (P, E) where the set of possible pairs is determined jointly by the rules of the auction and the strategies adopted by one's competitors. At an equilibrium of the bidding game, the bidder correctly perceives how his bids map into (P, E) pairs.

Suppose a bidder's valuation (reservation price) for the goods being offered is X. If he wins the auction, his expected profits are just the difference between this valuation and his expected payment: $X - E$. So if he selects the point (P, E), his expected profits corresponding will be:

$$U[P, E; X] = P \cdot (X - E) \tag{1}$$

The bidder's optimal choice of (P, E) will clearly depend on his reservation level X. Let $(P^*(X), E^*(X))$ denote the optimal choice for the bidder and let the corresponding maximal expected profits be $U^*(X) = U[P^*(X), E^*(X); X]$. By studying the function U^*, we learn how the expected gains from trade are divided among the seller and the various possible types of bidders in each auction format. The main conclusion is this:

Revenue Equivalence Theorem: The English and sealed bid auctions yield exactly the same expected profit for every bidder valuation and the same expected revenue for the seller. Indeed, every auction that allocates the goods efficiently and offers no profit to a zero valuation bidder has the same expected profits for every bidder valuation and the same expected revenue for the seller.

Proof is given below. The proofs in this paper highlights the general techniques which are used repeatedly in auction theory. The proofs may be omitted by readers without any loss of continuity in the development.

Proof. Applying the Envelope Theorem to (1), we have:

$$U^{*\prime}(X) = U_X[P^*(X), E^*(X); X] = P^*(X) \tag{2}$$

Given the hypothesis of the Theorem that $U^*(0) = 0$, we may integrate (2) to obtain:

$$U^*(X) = \int_0^X P^*(s)\,ds. \tag{3}$$

For any auction where the allocation is always efficient, $P^*(X)$ is just the probability that the other bidders' valuations are less than X. Thus, by (3), all such auctions yield identical expected profits for the bidders. Since the total surplus generated by trade is the same in all such auctions and the bidders' profits are the same, the seller's expected revenues must be the same, too. QED.

The conclusion in the foregoing model that standard auctions like the first-bid auction, the Dutch auction, and the English auction all lead to the same expected revenues for the seller and expected profits for the bidders has spawned a number of analyses that tweak the model in some way to explain why one auction rule or another might be expected to perform better in practice. Two variations are reviewed in the next sections which seem especially interesting because they help to explain in plausible ways why open outcry auctions like the English auction are by far the most prevalent auctions in the world, yet industrial procurement auctions are almost always first-bid auctions.

AUCTIONS WITH ENDOGENOUS QUANTITIES

This section presents and analyzes the auction model introduced by Hansen (1988) to explain the use of first-bid auctions for industrial procurement. For this application, we flip back to the contracting perspective: The bidders are again sellers, the bid-taker is a buyer, and the lowest bidder will be declared the winner.

The model retains all of the assumptions of the preceding model but one: rather than purchasing a single unit, the buyer who solicits bids can purchase as many units as he wishes at the price fixed by the auction. The buyer's quantity decision is modelled by a demand function $q(p)$; if the price determined by the auction is p then the bidder will actually purchase $q(p)$ units. Each bidder's private valuation in this model is its unit cost parameter c; it is assumed that the bidder can produce as many units as are demanded at cost c per unit.

The rules of the variable-quantity first-bid auction are as follows. Privately and simultaneously, each bidder submits a price bid; the lowest bidder is declared the winner; the price p is set equal to the lowest bid; and the buyer purchases the quantity $q(p)$. The rules of the second-bid auction are the same, except that the price p is set equal to the second lowest bid. One could recover the model analyzed in the preceding section as a special case of this model by setting $q(p) = 1$. However, the objective here will be to analyze the extra effects caused by elastic demand, so we shall assume that the demand curve slopes downward: $q' < 0$ and that there is a "choke price" $\bar{p}$ such that $q(\bar{p}) = 0$. As in the simpler model, there again exists an equilibrium for each auction game in which all the bidders adopt the same strategy and the bids are an increasing function of the production cost parameter. So, parallel to our earlier finding that the goods are sold to the highest evaluator, we find in this model that the contract is awarded to the low cost producer. However, because the equilibrium price will generally exceed marginal cost, the final allocation will *not* be efficient. Our first task is therefore to analyze and compare the expected prices, quantities, and surplus in the two auction formats. Then, we will look at how the gains to the more efficient format are distributed between the bidders and the bid-taker.

In the second-bid auction, even with variable quantities, bidders are price takers; the price a winning bidder will receive depends not on his own bid but on the bid of his nearest competitor. From the perspective of an individual bidder, the price he names merely specifies the lowest price at which he will be willing to undertake production. So it is a dominant strategy for each bidder to name a price equal to his marginal cost c; that way he accepts all offers to produce output at a price exceeding his cost per unit, and no other offers. Thus far, the analysis is unchanged from the case in which the quantity demanded is always one unit.

What is new is that, in the first-bid auction, the winner will have an additional incentive to shade his bid. For consider the problem facing an individual bidder. Suppose that $P(p)$ is the probability that a price bid of p will be lowest and suppose that the bidder's production cost per unit is c. Then he will choose his bid p to maximize expected profits, calculated as the probability the bid will win times the quantity sold in that case times the profit per unit sold. Compared with the case where $q' = 0$, the bidder in a first-bid auction with $q' < 0$ finds it more profitable to reduce his bid price p, because there is the additional effect that reducing the bid causes the quantity sold to rise when he wins.[5] The upshot is that the equilibrium bids in the first-bid auction are reduced by the introduction of elastic demand. When demand is inelastic, we already know that the first-bid and second-bid auctions leads to the same average price. *In this model, for every level of cost of the winning bidder, the first-bid auction leads to a lower average price than the second-bid auction.*[6]

Recalling that bids are really just ways of parameterizing the choice among the objects of real interest, we can perform the same analysis on the bidder's choice of expected quantities sold. The upshot is that *for every level of cost of the winning bidder, the quantity $q_F(c)$ sold in the first-bid auction is greater than the expected quantity $q_S(c)$ sold in the second-bid auction.*

Finally, to compare the efficiency of the two auction formats, observe that whenever demand is downward sloping, society is risk averse about the quantity to be produced; total surplus is higher when a fixed quantity q is produced than when a random quantity with mean q is produced. We have already argued that, for every level of c, the expected quantity is higher in the first-bid auction and, unlike the second-bid auction, the quantity given c in the first-bid auction is not random. So, *for every level c of the cost of the winning bidder, the expected total surplus is greater in the first-bid auction than in the second-bid auction.*

Who captures the gains generated by switching to a first-bid auction? One might guess that since the first-bid auction generates lower average prices, the bidders are made worse off. In fact, the reverse is true.

Proposition. Although the average price is lower and the expected quantity is greater in the first-bid auction than in the second-bid auction, the bidder/sellers' expected profit is greater as well.

Proof. The proof is quite similar to that of the Revenue Equivalence Theorem. Let Q denote the expected quantity sold by a bidder who makes any particular bid, defined as the probability of making sale times the expected quantity given that a sale is made, and let E be the expected price per unit. Then if a bidder with marginal production cost c selects a bid corresponding to (Q, E), his expected profits are:

$$U[Q, E; c] = Q(E - c) \tag{4}$$

This expression is analogous to the one given earlier (in (1)) for the case where quantity was fixed at a single unit. Let $U^*(c) = U[Q^*(c), E^*(c); c]$.

Applying the Envelope Theorem to (4), we have:

$$U^{*\prime}(c) = U_c[Q^*(c), E^*(c); c] = Q^*(c) \tag{5}$$

Observing that $U^*(\bar{p}) = 0$, we may integrate (5) to obtain:

$$U^*(c) = \int_c^{\bar{p}} Q\ ^*(s)\,ds. \tag{6}$$

For the first-bid auction, $Q^*(s) = q_F(s)$; for the second-bid auction, $Q^*(s) = q_s(s)$. Since we have argued above that $q_F(s) > q_s(s)$, it is evident from (6) that $U_F^*(c) > U_S^*(c)$, and the Proposition is proved. QED.

One can show, as well, that under any of a variety of mild restrictions on the demand function, the buyer enjoys greater expected consumer surplus with the first-bid auction. When these conditions hold, both sides of the market prefer this auction mechanism. This relatively simple model therefore provides a straightforward explanation of why first-bid auctions are so widely used in procurement.

CORRELATED BIDDER INFORMATION

In many auction settings, the quantity to be supplied is specified in advance, so that the effects explained in the last section are absent. In these settings, the English (open, ascending) auctions are much more common than any other form. Here we relax the independence assumption of the standard model in order to explain the prevalence of English auctions and of certain other auction practices.

What are we to use in place of the independence assumption? When the bidders' costs or valuations depend on some common random factors, so that all the bidders are estimating the same variables, their estimates will be positively correlated even if their estimation *errors* are independent. Positive correlation has been especially prominent in models of auctions for oil and gas drilling rights, where the rights being acquired are, to a first approximation, of equal value to each of the bidders, and the main uncertainties concern such common factors as the quantities of recoverable hydrocarbons, the costs of recovery, the costs of transporting the product to market (perhaps through as yet undeveloped pipelines over the Arctic Slope), future world energy prices, and so on. The common uncertainties found in these auctions also play a large role in the sale of items like wine or art which are purchased at least partly for their savings or investment value, as the parties estimate what it would cost to purchase the same vintage in the future or what the eventual resale price for the painting will be. So there is good reason to believe that positive correlations among value estimates will often be present.

The actual equilibrium analysis relies on a stronger notion than positive correlation. The appropriate concept, known as *affiliation,* was introduced by Milgrom and Weber (1982). Affiliation of the bidders' value estimates in the auction model captures the idea that as a bidder's value estimate rises, he expects others' estimates to rise as well, in the sense that higher values for other bidders' estimates become relatively more likely.[7]

Turning now to the model formulation, since English auctions are mostly used by sellers of goods, it is most natural to switch back to the model formulation where there is a single item or bundle of goods being offered for sale. Thus, bidders are once again buyers, and the auctioneer is the seller or his representative. The bidders each have an estimate of the value of the goods to themselves; these estimates are assumed to be symmetrically distributed and affiliated. The value of the goods may be a common value, identical to all the bidders, or it may be a private value, or some mixture of these. Each bidder chooses his bid as a function of his value estimate to maximize the expected excess of value received minus payments made.

Parts of the analysis are unchanged by the new assumption of affiliation. First, the equilibrium bids are still increasing functions of the bidders' valuations, so the winner is the bidder with the highest valuation in both auction formats. Consequently, the total surplus does not differ between the two auction forms. Second, the profits of a marginal bidder who is just willing to participate in the auction is zero in both formats. Let $U^*(X)$ be the expected profits of a bidder with valuation X in the auction. Then if the valuation of a marginal bidder is X, the second conclusion can be stated as $U_F^*(\underline{X}) = U_S^*(\underline{X}) = 0$. The point of the present analysis is to compare how affiliation affects the auctioneer's ability to extract the incremental profits associated with larger value estimates, that is, how it affects the slopes $U_F^{*\prime}$ and $U_S^{*\prime}$ of the profit functions.

Heuristically, the comparison is easy. In a first-bid auction, when a bidder with valuation X submits a bid of b and wins, the price he pays is b; it does not depend on X. In an English or second-bid auction, the expected payment by a winning bidder whose private valuation of the good is X depends on his bid b, *but it also depends on his private valuation X to the extent that the distribution of the remaining bids depends on X.* This extra effect raises the slope $U_S^{*\prime}$ but not $U_F^{*\prime}$, tending to result in higher average prices in the English auction. One still needs to verify, though, that these effects are not eliminated by equilibrium adjustments.

Proposition. The expected total surplus is the same in the English and sealed-bid auctions in the model, but for every value of X the bidder's expected profit $U^*(X)$ is smaller in the English auction and the seller's expected revenue is correspondingly higher.

Proof. To emphasize the parallel with the preceding proofs, we add the private values assumption to the list of hypotheses. We continue, however, to assume that the bidders' estimates are affiliated. Then for a bidder whose value estimate is X and who bids just enough to win when the highest estimate of an opposing bidder is Z, the expected payoff is:

$$U[Z, E; X] = P(Z|X)(X - E) \tag{7}$$

where E is the bidder's expected payment when he wins and $P(Z|X)$ is the probability that all the other bidders have value estimates less than Z, given that the present bidder has value estimate X. Given the strategies of the other bidders, the expected payment E is some function $E(Z, X)$ of the bid (parameterized by Z) and the information X of the bidder. So,

$$U[Z, E(Z, X); X] = P(Z|X)(X - E(Z, X)) \tag{8}$$

Let $U^*(X)$ be the maximized value of (8). At equilibrium, we know that $Z^* = X$ is the optimal choice of Z. So, the Envelope Theorem implies that:

$$\begin{aligned}
U^{*\prime}(X) = U_X &= P(Z^*|X)(1 - E_X(Z^*,X)) + P_X(Z^*|X)(X - E(Z^*,X)) \\
&= P(X|X)(1 - E_X(X, X)) + P_X(X|X)(X - E(X, X)) \\
&= P \cdot (1 - E_X) + (P_X/P)U^* \tag{9}
\end{aligned}$$

where the arguments X are suppressed in the last line to improve readability. Affiliation implies that P_X is negative. It is then a standard exercise in differential equations to show that, given the fixed boundary condition $U^*(\underline{X}) = 0$, all the values of $U^*(X)$ fall if the coefficient function E_X is increased.

Notice, however, that for the first-bid auction $E_X = 0$, that is, the bidder's expected payment depends only on his bid and not on his value estimate. For the second-bid auction, $E_X \geq 0$, because (holding the bid fixed) a higher value estimate makes higher bids by the other bidders relatively more likely. Hence, raising E_X by switching to the second- bid (English) auction causes $U^*(X)$ to fall for all X, and the Proposition is proved. QED.

Our formal proof directly mirrors the intuitive argument given earlier. The difference between the expected payoffs in the two kinds of auctions is directly traceable to the fact that the bidder's expected payment in the second-bid auction rises with his value estimate, because the payment depends on the value estimate of a competitor which is affiliated with his own estimate. No such effect is present in the first-bid auction, which is therefore less effective in extracting surplus from the bidders. If one supposes that the auctioneer (representing the seller) sets the rules, then the Proposition provides a possible explanation of why English auctions are so much more prevalent than sealed-bid auctions.

The sort of analysis we have just employed can be applied in a variety of ways. The main general insight of the analysis is the *Linkage Principle.* According to this informal principle, the bidders are made worse off and the seller better off if the price paid by the buyer can be more effectively linked to exogenous variables that are affiliated with the bidder's private information. For example, the Principle implies that the use of royalties in the selling of mineral rights or publication rights—a practice that links the price paid to the actual value—will increase the seller's average receipts. It also implies that if the auctioneer/seller has private information about the item being sold that is affiliated with the bidders' estimates of value, then a policy of always revealing that information increases average receipts compared to a policy of never revealing that information. For if a policy of revealing information is adopted, the price becomes linked to the seller's information, which extracts more of the winning bidder's surplus.[8]

Another application of the Linkage Principle arises in a simple model of the weekly Treasury bill auction. In the model, there are N bidders and $M < N$ items for sale, and each buyer wants to buy only one unit. The brokers who bid in the T-bill auction all estimate the future market price at which they will be able to resell the bills to their customers. So, it may be sensible to assume that their estimates are affiliated. That suggests that, in place of the present "discriminatory" auction rule where each bidder pays the amount of his own bid, the Treasury might do better to adopt an auction in which the price paid by each bidder is linked to the bids made by others. Among the possibilities are the uniform price auctions in which the price charged to all bidders is, for example, the lowest accepted bid, or the highest rejected bid, or the average accepted bid. Each is in fact predicted by the theory to generate a higher average price than the auction at which each bidder pays the amount of his own bid.

The analysis in this section is subject to a number of important qualifications. First, we have developed the arguments only for symmetric bidding models. There was a good reason for that: the theory makes no sharp predictions about the outcome in asymmetric environments. Second, we assumed that the bidders were risk neutral. In "private values" models, risk aversion raises receipts in the first-bid auction but not in the second-bid auction; that could reverse some of the auction rankings. However, in general value environments, the effects of risk aversion are ambiguous. Although most auctions do not require the bidder to commit a significant fraction of his wealth, some (like construction bids) do often carry the risk of insolvency, and risk aversion may be important in these cases. Third, we assumed that equilibrium strategies would be adopted by the bidders. The computation of equilibrium strategies for first-bid auctions in the environments we have studied is not a simple matter, and there is no assurance that these bidding strategies would, in fact, be used.

COMPARISONS AMONG AUCTIONS

The emphasis of much of recent bidding theory has been on ranking auctions on the basis of the expected receipts they generate. Sometimes this approach is taken to the extreme of determining the institutions that maximize expected receipts, on the grounds that such institutions will be the ones chosen by the auctioneer/seller. The results of these maximization problems are, for all but the simplest environments, auctions of outlandishly complicated forms involving payments by the seller to losers, required side bets among the bidders, and so on. That such forms are not observed in practice indicates that the "optimal auctions" theory in which the auctioneers can tailor a specific institution to each environment may be a poor way to explain actual institutions. The common auction institutions are all simple and robust, working well in a variety of environments, used by desperate sellers as well as by those with market power bordering on a monopoly, and usually leading to a tolerably efficient allocation of the items being sold. Comparisons of robustness, efficiency, transaction costs, and immunity to cheating offer an important alternative to the revenue-based approaches for explaining the popularity of specific auction institutions.

We have already seen that the various models differ in their conclusions about the efficiency of the allocations resulting from various kinds of auctions. The Hansen endogenous quantities model assumes symmetry among the bidders before the auction and predicts that the outcome of the first-bid auction is more efficient. When the quantity traded is fixed and the bidders are not symmetrical, the second-bid auction always assigns the goods to the proper bidder, but the first-bid auction may fail to do so.

Of course, the final allocation itself is only one aspect of the efficiency of auctions. Another important aspect is the cost of preparing a bid. Complicated auctions and those that provide large returns to information gathering are likely to increase bid preparation costs. The English auction system, in which a bidder's optimal bidding strategy does not depend on how his competitors bid, economizes on information gathering and bid preparation costs.

In summary, at least for fixed quantity environments, the English auction possesses a variety of characteristics that help to explain its popularity. It generates more receipts on average than the Dutch/sealed-bid auction. It leads to efficient outcomes in a wider range of environments. And, it economizes on information gathering and bid preparation costs.

English auctions also have some characteristic disadvantages, however. First, being open outcry auctions, they require the actual presence of the bidders, which may be expensive. One might think that this disadvantage could be overcome by substituting the equivalent second-bid auction, which is a sealed-bid auction and so does not require the presence of the bidders. However, when the auctioneer opens the bids in a second-bid auction and learns what the bidders are willing to pay, what is to prevent him from inserting a false bid to drive up the price? This susceptibility to manipulation may account for the unpopularity of second-bid auctions. (Interestingly, a second-bid auction in which the auctioneer is free to insert extra bids after opening the sealed bids is virtually identical to a first-bid auction, because the highest bidder wins and winds up paying a price approximately equal to his bid.)

A second disadvantage of English auctions is their easy susceptibility to *rings* of bidders.[9] A ring is a group of bidders who agree to re-auction the items they purchase among themselves, dividing the proceeds among the bidders. One member, representing the ring, bids up to the ring's reservation price (the highest of the members' reservation prices) in competition with other bidders, while the ring members refrain from bidding. In an English auction, no member of a ring can successfully exploit the ring agreement to gain a bargain for himself. For if a ring member were to have an anonymous associate bid aggressively on his behalf, the ring representative would continue to bid up to the ring's reservation price, and the selling price would be just as high as if no ring had been formed.[10] Rings of bidders are comparatively much less effective in the first-bid auction, in which a single defector from a ring agreement could reap a substantial gain by bidding slightly more than the agreed price. This observation favors the selection by auctioneers of the sealed-bid auction when the threat of rings is great, as when the bidders are well known to each other. It supplements Hansen's argument, that first-bid auctions lead to more efficient allocations when purchase quantities are endogenous, to explain the use of first-bid auctions for industrial procurement.

COMPARISONS WITH NON-AUCTION AND HYBRID INSTITUTIONS

So far, we have compared only alternative auction institutions for selling a single item. However, most trades are not made using auctions. There are goods for which stores post prices and others over which people haggle. High volume securities trading is conducted on organized exchanges using a complicated set of auction-like rules. These alternatives only scratch the surface in describing the huge variety of terms and institutions that govern trade in the modern world. What is it about the circumstances in each case that make one or another trading institution most appropriate? Unfortunately, that question has received less attention from researchers than the others we have asked. Nevertheless, some informed guesses are possible.

Posted prices are commonly used for standardized, inexpensive items sold in stores. Often, these are manufactured items for which there is no need to compare competing bids: all comers can be served. Even when the suppliers are limited, unlike organized auctions, the competing buyers are not all present at the store at any given time. If it is too expensive to gather the competing buyers together or if the item is storable and the timing of buyer demands varies, auctions are not a practicable selling institution. The alternative to posted prices, then, is individual bargaining. Bargaining, however, is a costly way to determine prices in societies where time is especially valuable. Also, when the salesman is not an owner, the lack of a fixed price makes it easy for the salesman to steal or take kickbacks from the buyer. These defects of bargaining are especially great when the opportunity to gain from price discrimination in individual sales is low. These observations explain why sales of consumer goods in developed economies so often utilize the posted price institution.

When goods are not standardized or when the market clearing prices are highly unstable, posted prices work poorly, and auctions are usually preferred. Thus, livestock are sold at auction because the value of individual animals varies, and needs to be determined separately. Similarly, the assets of bankrupt firms are valued depending on their age, condition, location, and so on. Fresh fish, being perishable, is sold at auction so that prices can be responsive to daily variations in the catch and demand.

Bargaining is a trading institution that is best avoided when there is enough competition for auctions to be used, Coase's theorem notwithstanding. It is well-known, for example, that in bargaining to divide a fixed surplus with some or all of the surplus being lost if agreement is delayed, there can be a problem of indeterminacy, with the outcome of bargaining depending on the bargainers' expectations (Roth and Schoumaker, 1983). If one bargainer demands 75 percent of the surplus, the other can do no better than to settle for 25 percent. Each, knowing this, may be tempted to play a game of brinkmanship, demanding the lion's share in the hope that the other party will back down. Disagreement and inefficiency can, and sometimes does, result. In contrast, when a seller employs an English auction to sell an item worth $100 to himself to one of a pair of potential buyers with reservation values of $170 and $200, the equilibrium theory predicts the sale will occur at a price of $170.[11] Not only is the result efficient, but the seller gets a good price: By bargaining singly with the $200 evaluator, the seller can at best hope to split the gains, getting a price of $150, and he may lose some of those gains if the parties fail to reach agreement.

As compared to bargaining, auctions have the additional advantage of being institutions whose conduct can be delegated to an unsupervised agent. Public auctions offer fewer opportunities for kickbacks and behind-the-scenes agreements between the seller's agent and a single buyer than do negotiated agreements. In the early New England textile trade, established merchants sponsored laws against auction sales, thus indicating their awareness of how effectively auctions narrow their margins and prevent them from extracting better terms from the cotton farmers.

These simple comparisons of the pure forms of auctions and bargaining tell only part of the story. Often, is it necessary to combine bargaining and bidding to support efficient trade. For example, in the problem of soliciting bids for a contract to build a bridge, to install a cable television service, or to perform R&D on a new weapons system, it would be foolish to invite bids from all comers and just take the lowest bid. Before the final bid can be made, there may be a round of negotiations over the specifications and then another round to determine which of the potential bidders are qualified to produce a product meeting the specifications. Then, the evaluation of the bid may take into account design or quality differences, service capabilities, the ability to deliver on time, and perhaps the need to maintain multiple sources of supply, as well as price. These appendages to the basic auction institution require a substantial element of managerial judgement and open again the possibilities for influence, favoritism, and bribes.

RECENT EMPIRICAL STUDIES OF THE WINNER'S CURSE

In a pair of recent papers, Hendricks, Porter and Boudreau (1987) and Hendricks and Porter (1987) have studied empirically the prediction of auction theory concerning price and profit for federal sale of leases of the Outer Continental Shelf. In lease sales, the government divides a map of an area with hydrocarbon potential into square areas called *tracts*. Periodically, the government conducts an auction sale of a group of tracts. Rights to the individual tracts are sold separately, by first-bid auction.

Both empirical studies focus on the bidding for *drainage tracts*, which are tracts adjacent to one on which deposits of oil and gas have already been found. A characteristic feature of these tracts is that the owner of the adjacent tract has better information about the underlying geologic structure than do any of the competitors. The theoretical analysis of competitive bidding under such conditions was initiated by Wilson (1967) and developed further by Weverburgh (1979), Engelbrecht-Wiggans, Milgrom, and Weber (1983), and Milgrom and Weber (1982a). The distinguishing assumption of drainage tract models is that all the bidders but one have access only to public records. A number of testable predictions are derived, including these: (1) The best informed firm wins at least half the auctions (exactly half if there are no economies of scope in developing adjacent tracts); (2) given the informed bid, the uninformed bids are uncorrelated with the actual value of the tract; and (3) the average profits of uninformed bidders are zero, being negative on the tracts where the informed bidders fail to bid (that is, where the reserve price exceeds the informed's value estimate) and positive on the tracts where the informed do bid.

The empirical investigations of these hypotheses involves the study of 11 drainage tracts adjacent to a single producing tract auctioned in the period 1954–69. There are various empirical and theoretical issues to be faced in attributing profit levels to firms over the producing period of the wells, during which world oil prices jumped sharply. Still, the results are encouraging, leading Hendricks and Porter to conclude that their analysis "has provided strong, but not necessarily definitive, support" for the model.

FURTHER READING

The interested reader can turn to several recent survey papers covering auction theory for additional details. McAfee and McMillan (1987) thoroughly survey both the theoretical and empirical literatures on auctions. Milgrom (1987) explores the connections between auctions and bargaining and gives a precise mathematical account of the Linkage Principle. Wilson's (1987) survey pursues the links between auction research and research into market mechanisms when there are many buyers and sellers of a homogeneous good. Much of the work in experimental economies has been focused on tests of auction theory. Useful surveys of that field can be found in Plott (1982) and Smith (1982). The influential "optimal auctions" theory is not fully developed in any of the surveys cited above. A highly readable introductory account of it has been given by Riley and Samuelson (1981), and a new account that analyzes the problem using familiar economic tools is given by Bulow and Roberts (1988). Finally, any serious student of auction theory must read the paper by Vickrey (1961). His analysis, which compared auctions on the basis of expected receipts, allocational efficiency, bid preparation costs, and vulnerability to cheating by the auctioneer and others, and which extended the analysis to procurement problems where the government needs to use multiple suppliers, provided the outline for much of what has been reported in this paper.

NOTES

1. Indeed, the covariance of any two different estimates X_i and X_j is equal to the variance of C.
2. Formal propositions to this effect are provided by Milgrom and Weber (1982a).
3. In the language of game theory, the Dutch and sealed-bid auctions have the same "reduced normal form".
4. See Cox, Smith, and Walker (1983) for a report of an experiment along these lines.
5. The constrained optimization problem looks this way:

$$\max_{p} P(p)q(p)(p - c)$$

The derivative of this objective function consists of two terms that do not depend on $q'(p)$ and one term that does:

$$P'(p)q(p)(p - c) + P(p)q(p) + q'(p)P(p)(p - c)$$

Moving from the case $q'(p) = 0$ to $q'(p) < 0$ reduces the slope of the objective everywhere and therefore reduces the maximizing bid p.
6. There are more steps to the formal analysis than indicated here. If other competitors lower their bid prices, then one must account for the change in the first bidder's choice problem. With price competition, one might expect that more aggressive bidding by competitors

    reinforces the incentive to cut one's own bid price, and the full equilibrium analysis given by Hansen confirms that intuition.

7.   A collection of random variables $(X_1, \ldots, X_N)$ with symmetric joint density f is affiliated if for any $y \geq y'$ in $\mathcal{R}^{n-1}$, the ratio of densities $f(y|x)/f(y'|x)$ rises in x; this is the basis of the statement in the text that higher values y become relatively more likely at x increases.

8.   For experimental evidence that tends to confirm this prediction, see Kagel and Levin (1986).

9.   This discussion of the problem of rings is based largely on Graham and Marshall (1987).

10.   This is not to say that an auctioneer is helpless when faced by a ring. He can set high reserve prices and take bids from the chandelier to force some competition when he suspects that a ring is at work. Still, these devices are not complete remedies, so auctions that make secret and profitable violations of ring agreements possible have obvious advantages in cases where rings are a real problem.

11.   Indeed, he may get more if the $170 evaluator considers that he may be able to resell the item to the $200 party, dividing the $30 surplus equally. When resale is possible, the item is worth about $185 to this party, and the initial auction may lead to a price of $185. See Milgrom (1987) for more on auctions with resale.

REFERENCES

Bulow, Jeremy and Roberts, John. The simple economics of optimal auctions. *Journal of Political Economy*, October 1989; **97**: 1060–1090.

Capen, E. C., Clapp, R. B. and Campbell, W. M. Competitive bidding in high risk situations. *Journal of Petroleum Technology*, June 1971; **23**: 641–653.

Cox, James, Smith, Vernon and Walker, James. A test that discriminates between two models of the Dutch-First auction non-isomorphism. *Journal of Economic Behavior and Organization*, 1983; **4**: 205–219.

Engelbrecht-Wiggans, Richard, Milgrom, Paul and Weber, Robert. Competitive bidding and proprietary information. *Journal of Mathematical Economics*, June 1983; **11**: 161–169.

Friedman, Lawrence. A competitive bidding strategy. *Operations Research*, 1956; **4**: 104–112.

Graham, Daniel and Marshall, Robert. Collusive bidder behavior at single-object second-price and English auctions. *Journal of Political Economy*, 1987; **95**: 1217–1239.

Hansen, Robert. Auctions with endogenous quantity, *Rand Journal of Economics*, Spring 1988, **19**(4) 516–537.

Hendricks, Kenneth and Porter, Robert. An empirical study of an auction with asymmetric information. *American Economic Review*, December 1988; **78**: 865–883.

Hendricks, Kenneth, Porter, Robert and Boudreau, Bryan. Information, returns and bidding behavior in OCS auctions: 1954–1969. *Journal of Industrial Economics*, June 1987; **35**: 517–542.

Kagel, John and Levin, Dan. The winner's curse and public information in common value auctions. *American Economic Review*, December 1986; **76**: 894–920.

McAfee, Preston, R. and McMillan, John. Auctions and bidding. *Journal of Economic Literature*. June 1987; **25**: 699–738.

Milgrom, Paul and Weber, Robert. A theory of auctions and competitive bidding. *Econometrica*, November 1982; **50**: 1089–1122.

Milgrom, Paul and Weber, Robert. The value of information in a sealed-bid auction. *Journal of Mathematical Economics*, June 1982a; **10**: 105–114.

Milgrom, Paul. Auction theory. In Bewley, Truman, ed., *Advances in Economic Theory, 1985: Fifth World Congress*. London: Cambridge University Press, 1987, pp. 1–32.

Plott, Charles. Industrial organization theory and experimental economics. *Journal of Economic Literature*, December 1982; **20**: 1485–1527.

Riley, John and Samuelson, William. Optimal auctions. *American Economic Review*, June 1981; **71**: 381–392

Roth, Alvin and Schoumaker, Francoise. Expectations and reputations in bargaining: an experimental study. *American Economic Review*, June 1983; **73**: 362–372.

Smith, Vernon. Microeconomic systems as experimental science. *American Economic Review*, December 1982; **72**: 923–955.

Vickery, William. Counterspeculation, auctions, and competitive sealed tenders. *Journal of Finance*, March 1961; **16**: 8–37.

Weverburgh, M. Competitive bidding with asymmetric information reanalyzed. *Management Science*, March 1979; **25**: 291–294.

Wilson, Robert. Competitive bidding with asymmetric information. *Management Science*, July 1967; **13**: 816–820.

Wilson, Robert. Auction theory. In Eatwell, J., Milgate, M. and Newman, P. eds., *The New Palgrave: A Dictionary of Economic Theory and Doctrine*. London: Mcmillan, 1987.

Part III

Uncertainty

CONTENTS

6

The Analytics of Uncertainty and Information— An Expository Survey

Jack Hirshleifer and John G. Riley

That human endeavors are constrained by our limited and uncertain knowledge of the world has always been recognized by leading economic thinkers, far too numerous to be cited here. (An extended historical bibliography is contained in Fritz Machlup [81, 1980]. But despite this longstanding *recognition*, until relatively recently there was no rigorous foundation for the *analysis* of individual decision-making and market equilibrium under uncertainty. This foundation lacking, the standard analytical models of our textbooks (typified by the familiar apparatus of supply and demand) made no explicit provision for uncertainty. It is not surprising, therefore, that the world of affairs often found academic economics to be of little operational value.

Recent explosive progress in the economics of uncertainty has changed this picture. The subject now flourishes not only in economics departments, but in professional schools and programs oriented toward business, government and administration, and public policy. In the world of commerce, stockmarket analysts now regularly report measures of share-price uncertainty devised by economic theorists. Even in government and the law, formal analysis of uncertainty is beginning to appear in dealing with such problems as safety and health, allowable return on investment, and income distribution. And academic economists, armed with the new developments in the economics of uncertainty, are much more successfully analyzing previously intractable phenomena such as insurance, research and invention, advertising, speculation, and the functioning of financial markets.

It will be impossible to provide any adequate review here of all the important developments under the headings of uncertainty and information. What we hope to do is to expound the central underlying ideas in nontechnical fashion; to introduce the novel tools of analysis that have proved fruitful in this area; and to go somewhat more deeply into selected applications in order to convey some impression of the potential richness and power of the theory. Wherever possible, we will provide citations to major branches of the literature that we have been unable to survey here.

Reprinted with permission from *Journal of Economic Literature*, Vol. 17, December 1979, pp. 1375–1421

The theoretical developments that have brought about this intellectual revolution have two main foundation stones: (1) the theory of preference for uncertain contingencies and in particular the "expected-utility theorem" of John von Neumann and Oskar Morgenstern [103, 1944], and (2) the formulation of the ultimate goods or objects of choice in an uncertain universe as *contingent* consumption claims: entitlements to particular commodities or commodity baskets valid only under specified "states of the world" (more briefly, "states") [4, Kenneth J. Arrow, 1953; 7, 1964; 29, Gerard Debreu, 1959]. Just as intertemporal analysis requires subscripting commodity claims *by date*, uncertainty analysis requires subscripting commodity claims *by state*. Among objects of choice so defined, as we shall see, production and exchange and consumption all take on recognizable forms as generalizations of the corresponding processes in the familiar world of certainty.

An alternative conceptualization of the objects of choice under uncertainty runs in terms of the *statistical parameters* of the probability distributions of commodity or income claims. In that formulation it is assumed that individuals prefer greater *mean* income but smaller *variance* of income; attention may or may not be paid to higher moments of the distribution [83, Harry M. Markowitz, 1959]. It has been shown that the more general "state-preference" representation of the objects of choice under uncertainty can be reduced to such a "parameter-preference" representation by making a number of specializing assumptions [141, James Tobin, 1958; 17, Karl Borch, 1968; 39, Martin S. Feldstein, 1969]. In the particularly simple form of choice between mean return and variance of return on investment, the parameter-preference model has provided the basis for important modern developments in the theory of finance [83, Markowitz, 1959; 130, William F. Sharpe, 1964; 75, John Lintner, 1965; 99, Jan Mossin, 1966]. We will not be able to pursue the parameter-preference approach here; for recent surveys see Michael C. Jensen [65, 1972] and Robert C. Merton [96, 1980].

The modern analytical literature on uncertainty and information divides into two rather distinct branches. The first branch deals with *market uncertainty*. Each individual is supposed to be fully certain about his own endowment and productive opportunities; what he is unsure about are the supply–demand offers of other economic agents. In consequence, on the individual level the search for trading partners and at the market level disequilibrium and price dynamics take the center stage—replacing the traditional assumption of costless exchange at market-clearing prices [136, George J. Stigler, 1961; 137, 1962; 94, John J. McCall, 1965]. Explicit analysis of market uncertainty is leading toward a more realistic treatment of market "imperfections," with implications not only for microeconomics but for macro-economics as well [106, Edmund S. Phelps, 1970]. The second branch of literature deals with *technological uncertainty* or (a preferable designation) *event uncertainty*. Here individuals are uncertain not about the terms on which they might make market exchanges but rather about exogenous events—such as resource endowments (will the wheat crop be large or small?) or productive opportunities (will fusion power be available?) or public policy (will taxes be cut?). Put another way, market uncertainty concerns the *endogenous* variables of the economic system, event uncertainty the *exogenous* data.

The present survey is limited to the relatively more tractable topic of *event uncertainty*. This limitation permits us to employ the simpler traditional model of perfect markets in which all dealings take place costlessly at equilibrium prices. Recent studies of the complex search and disequilibrium phenomena that emerge under market uncertainty are reviewed in Michael Rothschild [117, 1973] and Steven A. Lippman and McCall [76, 1976].

The chapter is divided into two main parts, the first covering the economics of *uncertainty* and the second the economies of *information*. The two categories correspond to what might be called passive versus active responses to our limitations of knowledge. In the first part individuals may be said to *adapt* to the fact of uncertainty; in the second part they are allowed also to *overcome* uncertainty by engaging in informational activities.

THE ECONOMICS OF UNCERTAINTY

Decision under uncertainty

In decision-making under uncertainty the individual chooses among acts, while Nature may metaphorically be said to "choose" among *states*. In principle both acts and states may be defined over a continuum, but for simplicity here a discrete representation will ordinarily be employed. Table 1 pictures an especially simple 2×2 situation. The individual's alternative acts $a = (1, 2)$ are shown along the left margin, and Nature's alternative states $s = (1, 2)$ across the top. The body of the table shows the *consequences* c resulting from the interaction of each possible act and state.

Table 1. Consequences of alternative acts and states

	States		
	$s=1$	$s=2$	Utility of acts
Acts			
$a=1$	c_{11}	c_{12}	u_1
$a=2$	c_{21}	c_{22}	u_2
Beliefs as to states	π_1	π_2	

More generally, the individual's decision problem requires him to specify: (1) *a set of acts* $a = (1,\ldots,A)$; (2) *a probability function* expressing his beliefs $\pi(s)$ as to Nature's choice of state $s = (1,\ldots,S)$; (3) *a consequence function* $c(a, s)$ showing outcomes under all combinations of acts and states; and, finally (4) a preference-scaling or *utility function* $v(c)$ defined over consequences. Using these as elements, the "expected-utility rule" enables him to order the available acts in terms of preferences, i.e., to assign a utility function over *acts* $u(a)$ so as to determine the one most highly preferred.

The menu of acts

We shall consider here two main classes of acts: *terminal,* and non-terminal or *informational.*

Terminal actions represent making the best of one's existing combination of information and ignorance. For example, you might decide whether or not to take an umbrella on the basis of your past history of having been caught in the rain. In statistical theory, terminal action is exemplified by the balancing of Type I and Type II errors in coming to a decision (whether to accept or reject the null hypothesis) on the basis of the evidence or data now in hand. In contrast with the classical statistical problem, which may be likened to the decision situation of an isolated Robinson Crusoe, in the world of affairs studied by economists there are interpersonal arrangements—insurance contracts, futures markets, guarantees and collateral, the corporation and other forms of combined enterprise—which serve to widen the terminal-act options available to individuals. These market processes provide a variety of ways for *sharing* risks and returns among the decision-making agents in the economy.

Informational actions are non-terminal in that a final decision is deferred while awaiting or actively seeking new evidence which will, it is anticipated, reduce uncertainty. In statistics, informational actions involve decisions as to new data to be collected: choice of sampling technique, sample size, etc. Again, in the world of affairs, interpersonal transactions open up ways of acquiring information apart from the sampling techniques studied in statistics: information may be purchased, or inferred by monitoring the behavior of others, or even stolen. To a degree, information acquisition and dissemination have become specialized functions (the "knowledge industry" [79, Machlup, 1962]) whose practitioners are rewarded by exchanges with other economic agents in the economy.

The first part of this chapter will, apart from introductory discussions, cover only *terminal actions*—decisions made under fixed probability beliefs ("the economics of uncertainty"). The enlarged range of issues generated by admitting also non-terminal actions will be examined in the second part ("the economics of information").

The probability function

We will assume that each individual is able to represent his *beliefs* as to the likelihood of the different states of the world (e.g., as to whether Nature will choose Rain or Shine) by a "subjective" probability distribution [40, Irving Fisher, 1912, ch. 16; 126, Leonard J. Savage, 1954]. That is, an assignment to each state of a number between zero and one (end-points not excluded) whose sum equals unity. Subjective *certainty* would be represented by attaching the full probabilistic weight of unity to only one of the outcomes. The degree of subjective *uncertainty* is reflected in the dispersion of probability weights over the possible states.

Frank Knight [72, 1921] attempted to distinguish between "risk" and "uncertainty," depending upon whether probability estimates are or are not calculable on the basis of an objective classification of instances. At times he suggested [72, 1921, 20, 226] that the probability concept is inapplicable under true uncertainty, for example, to such questions as whether or not a cure for cancer will be discovered in the next decade. It will not be possible to review here the philosophical and operational underpinnings of the probability concept; for our purposes, it is sufficient that the "subjective" or "degree of belief" interpretation has proved fruitful even for Knightian uncertainty situations. But elsewhere Knight's discussion is much more in line with modern developments, as when he suggests [72, 1921, p. 227] that a man's actions may depend upon his estimate of the chance that his beliefs are correct—or, we shall say, upon his *confidence* in his beliefs. We will show explicitly in the second part of this chapter that degree of confidence is an essential element in *non-terminal* (information) actions; the estimated value of acquiring information varies inversely with prior confidence.

The consequence function

By *consequence* is meant a full definition of all relevant characteristics of the individual's environment resulting from the interaction of the specified act and state. A consequence can be regarded as a multicommodity multi-date consumption basket. However, we will sometimes assume that it corresponds simply to the amount of a single summary variable like income.

In the case of a *terminal* action, the consequences contingent upon each state might either be certain or probabilistic—depending upon the definition of "states of the world" for the problem at hand. If the states are defined deterministically, as in "Coin shows Heads" versus "Coin shows Tails," and supposing the act is "Bet on Heads," the contingent consequences are the simple certainties "Win" in the one state and "Lose" in the other. But states of the world might sometimes represent alternative probabilistic processes. For example, the two alternative states might be "Coin is fair (has 50 percent chance of coming up Heads)" versus "Coin is biased to come up Heads with 75 percent chance." In this situation the act "Bet on Heads" will have probabilistic consequences: "50 percent chance of winning" in one state of the world, "75 percent chance" in the other.

For an *informational* action, on the other hand, the consequences will in general be probabilistic even if the states of the world are defined deterministically, since acquisition of information does not ordinarily eliminate all uncertainty. If the states are "Rain" versus "Shine," and the informational action is "Look at barometer," the consequences will only be improved likelihoods of behaving appropriately—since the barometer reading is not a perfect predictor of Rain or Shine.

The utility function and the expected utility rule

In the theory of decision under uncertainty, utility as an index of preference attaches both to consequences c and to acts a. We distinguish the two by the notations $v(c)$ and $u(a)$, the problem being to derive the $u(a)$ for evaluating actions from the primitive preference scaling $v(c)$ for consequences.

To choose an act is to choose a row of the consequence matrix, as in Table 1. Given the assignment of probabilities to states, this is also choice of a probability distribution or "prospect." A convenient notation for the "prospect" associated with an act a, whose consequences $c_a = (c_{a1}, \ldots, c_{aS})$ are to be received with respective probabilities $\pi = (\pi_1, \ldots, \pi_S)$, is:

$$a \equiv (c_{a1}, \ldots, c_{aS}; \pi_1, \ldots, \pi_S)$$

The connection between the utility ordering of acts and the preference scaling of consequences is provided by the Neumann–Morgenstern "expected-utility rule":

$$\begin{aligned} u(a) &\equiv \pi_1 v(c_{a1}) + \ldots + \pi_S v(c_{aS}) \\ &\equiv \sum_{s=1}^{S} \pi_s v(c_{as}) \end{aligned} \tag{1}$$

That is, the utility of each act $u(a)$ is the mathematical expectation or probability-weighted average of the utilities of the associated consequences $v(c_{as})$.

The expected-utility rule is of course a very specific and special procedure for inferring preferences $u(a)$ over acts from the primitive preference scaling of consequences $v(c)$. What is its justification? It turns out that the expected-utility rule is usable *if and only if the $v(c)$ function is determined in a particular way that has been termed the assignment of "cardinal" utilities to consequences.* More specifically, the underlying theorem can be stated as follows:

> Given certain "postulates of rational choice", there is a way of assigning a cardinal preference-scaling function $v(c)$ over consequences such that the preference ranking of any pair of prospects a', a'' coincides with the ranking under the expected-utility rule.

The "postulates of rational choice" therefore justify the *joint* use of cardinal utilities and the expected-utility rule in dealing with choices among risky prospects—a point worth emphasizing, since it would be quite invalid to infer that the theorem warrants or provides a cardinal utility measure for choices *not* involving risk (see the discussions in William Baumol [14, 1951]; Armen A. Alchian [2, 1953]; Robert H. Strotz [139, 1953]).

The "postulates of rational choice" serving as basis for the theorem have been set forth in a number of different ways in the literature [42, Milton Friedman and Savage, 1948; 78, R. Duncan Luce and Howard Raiffa, 1957; 83, Markowitz, 1959; 85, Jacob Marschak, 1968] and involve technicalities that cannot be pursued here. Instead, what follows is an informal presentation (based mainly on Robert Schaifer [128, 1959]) illustrating, by direct construction, the development of personal cardinal preference-scaling function for use with the expected-utility rule (equation 1).

For the purposes of this discussion, we will assume that the contingent consequences c are certainties and also that c represents simply the quantity of generalized income. Let $\hat{c}$ represent the worst consequence (lowest level of income) contemplated by the individual, and $\hat{\hat{c}}$ the best consequence (highest level of income). As "cardinal" preference scales allow free choice of zero and unit interval, we can let $v(\hat{c}) = 0$ and $v(\hat{\hat{c}}) = 1$. Now consider some intermediate level of income c^*. We can suppose that the individual is indifferent between (assigns equal utility to) having c^* for certain versus having some particular chance of success π^* in a "reference lottery" involving $\hat{c}$ and $\hat{\hat{c}}$. What numerical value can we attach to this common level of utility to allow use of the

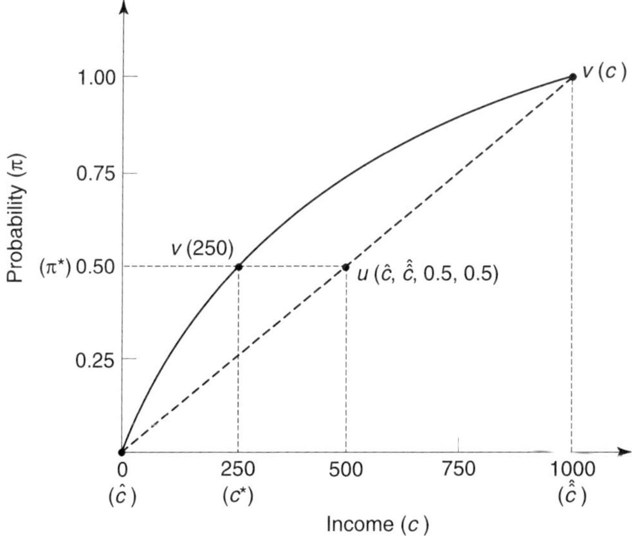

Figure 1. The preference-scaling function $v(c)$ derived by the "reference lottery technique".

expected-utility rule? The answer is, simply, the probability $\pi*$ of success in the reference lottery. Making use of "prospect" notation:

$$u(c)* \equiv u(\hat{\hat{c}}, \hat{c}; \pi*, 1 - \pi*) \equiv \pi* \tag{2}$$

Figure 1 illustrates a situation in which $\hat{c} = 0$, $\hat{\hat{c}} = 1000$, $c* = 250$, and $\pi* = \frac{1}{2}$. That is, this individual is indifferent between a sure income of \$250 and a 50 percent chance of winning in a lottery whose alternative outcomes are \$1000 or nothing. Then the utility assigned to the sure consequence \$250 is just $\frac{1}{2}$, so $v(250) = 0.5$. Repeating this process, the reference-lottery technique generates the individual's entire $v(c)$ curve of Figure 1, which is his preference-scaling function for consequences.

The expected-utility rule, combined with the constructed $v(c)$ function, works because the latter is *scaled as a probability*. The formula (1) for finding an overall $u(a)$ by weighting the utilities of contingent consequences $v(c)$ is exactly the formula for finding the overall probability associated with a set of contingent probabilities.

We have forgone presenting a formal statement of the "postulates of rational choice" that underly the expected-utility rule. But a few comments are in order here:

(1) We have assumed that the $v(c)$ scale is unique, applicable to every state of the world. This will be reconsidered below under the heading of "state-dependent utility."

(2) We have implicitly ruled out complementarities in utility, whereby a higher income c_s in a state s might affect the v score attached to income c_t in another state t. The justification is that c_s and c_t are not to be received in *combination* but

only *as alternatives*; no complementarity can exist because c_s and c_t can never be enjoyed simultaneously.

(3) While we have emphasized that $v(c)$ should be intuitively thought of as scaled in terms of probability, any fixed positive linear transformation of the $v(c)$ scale would be equally satisfactory—because cardinality permits free choice of zero and unit interval.

Risk-aversion and the risk-bearing optimum of the individual

The "concave" form of the cardinal preference-scaling $v(c)$ function in Figure 1 shows diminishing marginal utility of income—$v''(c) < 0$—for this individual. Such a person is said to be *risk-averse*: he would always prefer a sure consequence (level of certain income) to any probabilistic mixture of consequences (lottery or prospect) having the same mathematical expectation. Figure 1 illustrated a situation where the reference lottery with equal chances of $1000 or zero (and thus with a mathematical expectation of $500) is the utility equivalent of a sure income of only $250. Such a person must then prefer a sure income of $500 to this risky lottery whose mathematical expectation is $500. It is intuitively evident that this generalizes: any point P on a concave $v(c)$ curve will lie *above* the corresponding (vertically aligned) point along the straight line connecting any pair of positions on $v(c)$ that bracket P. The point *on the curve* represents the utility of a given sure income; the vertically aligned point *on the straight line* represents the utility of a lottery with a mathematical expectation equal to that given amount.

It follows immediately that a risk-averse individual endowed with a given sure income would never accept a *fair gamble*, a lottery whose mathematical expectation of net return equals zero (since it would shift him from a position *on* the $v(c)$ curve to a vertically aligned point on a straight line below it). A gamble would have to be somewhat better than fair, i.e., offer some positive mean return (just how much depends upon his degree of risk-aversion) to be acceptable. On the other hand an individual whose $v(c)$ function had the opposite "convex" curvature, representing *increasing* marginal utility of income—$v''(c) > 0$—would be happy to accept any fair gamble and even, up to a point, gambles worse than fair (offering a negative mean return). Such an individual is said to display *risk-preference*. An individual on the borderline, with a $v(c)$ function that is linear (constant marginal utility of income or $v''(c) = 0$) is said to be *risk-neutral*. A risk-neutral individual would accept, reject, or be indifferent to gambles that are respectively better than fair, worse than fair, or just fair.

It might be thought that the "concave" $v(c)$ function of Figure 1 applies only to one psychological type of person, or perhaps only to people at particular times or stages in the life cycle, so that the world would consist of a mixture of risk-averse, risk-neutral, and risk-preferring types. But the observed fact of *diversification of assets* suggests that risk-aversion is normal. An individual who is risk-neutral, for example, would plunge all of his wealth in that single asset which—regardless of its riskiness—offered the highest mathematical expectation of return. But we scarcely ever see this behavior pattern, and do observe more typically that individuals hold a variety of assets, thereby reducing their risk of ending up with an extremely low level of income.

What of the seemingly opposed evidence that fair gambles (and, indeed, gambles generally worse than fair) are accepted by bettors at Las Vegas and elsewhere? There have been some attempts to construct preference-scaling functions $v(c)$ that would be consistent with gambling over certain ranges of income *and* with avoiding gambles over other ranges [42, Friedman and Savage, 1948; 82, Markowitz, 1952]. These constructs run against the difficulty that if gambles are available on a fair or nearly-fair basis, no one could ever be at an optimum in any risk-preferring range of his $v(c)$ curve. To leave such a range, individuals would accept even enormous riches-or-ruin gambles. Such behavior is surely rare, and there is no indication of ranges of income that are thus depopulated. Except in more or less pathological cases, therefore, gambling at fair or adverse odds appears to be a recreational rather than income-status-determining activity for individuals. As evidence, we observe that actual gambling as in Las Vegas is mostly of a repetitive small-stakes nature, more or less guaranteed *not* to change income status in the long run.

That risk-aversion is the normal situation is indicated in a different way by Figure 2. Here the familiar-looking indifference curves u^0, u', u, ... show the expected utilities of gambles, for the individual characterized by the preference-scaling function $v(c)$ in Figure 1, in *state-claim* space. Following Arrow's formulation [4, 1953; 7, 1964], the commodities c_1 and c_2 on the two axes represent claims to income (claims to the unique consumption good) *contingent* upon the occurrence of the subscripted state of the world. (For simplicity here, we assume only two states, s_1 and s_2, with

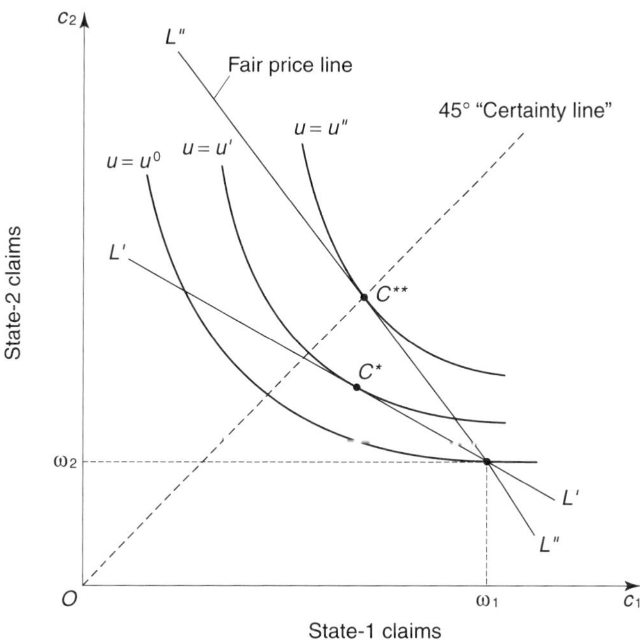

Figure 2. The preference map in contingent consumption or state-claim space (probability fixed)

corresponding fixed probabilities π_1 and $\pi_2 \equiv 1 - \pi_1$.) Then the expected-utility equation (1) takes the special form (1'):

$$u \equiv \pi_1 v(c_1) + \pi_2 v(c_2) \tag{1'}$$

This family of equations corresponds to the indifference curves of the diagram. The indifference-curve slopes in Figure 2 are related to the marginal utilities $v'(c)$ via:

$$\left. \frac{dc_2}{dc_1} \right|_{du\,=\,0} \equiv -\frac{\pi_1 v'(c_1)}{\pi_2 v'(c_2)} \tag{3}$$

It is elementary though tedious to show that the indifference curves have the normal "convex to the origin" curvature if and only if $v''(c) < 0$—i.e., only if the preference-scaling function $v(c)$ is "concave."

Now let us suppose that the individual is a price-taker in a market where contingent claims c_1 and c_2 can be exchanged in the ratio P_1/P_2. He has an initial endowment position (ω_1, ω_2) in state-claim space, his starting portfolio of contingent income claims—a risky position in the diagram, since $\omega_1 \neq \omega_2$. The price ratio, together with the endowment position, determined his budget line $L'L'$ in Figure 2. It is then geometrically evident that, given the standard indifference-curve curvature that stems from risk aversion, the risk-bearing optimum position C^* will normally be in the interior—i.e., the individual will want to "diversify" his holdings of state-claims. Following standard techniques, C^* along the budget line is the tangency determined by the condition:

$$-\left. \frac{dc_2}{dc_1} \right|_{du\,=\,0} \equiv \frac{\pi_1 v'(c_1)}{\pi_2 v'(c_2)} = \frac{P_1}{P_2} \tag{4}$$

We can arrive at a much stronger result for the special case where the price ratio P_1/P_2 equals the probability ratio π_1/π_2. Since the condition for "fair" gambles can be expressed as $\pi_1 \Delta c_1 + \pi_2 \Delta c_2 = 0$—the mathematical expectation of gain is zero—and since in market exchange $\Delta c_2/\Delta c_1 \equiv -P_1/P_2$, this equality of the price ratio and the probability ratio corresponds to the market offering fair gambles. Then the condition (4) simplifies to:

$$\frac{v'(c_1)}{v'(c_2)} = 1 \tag{4'}$$

Given the state-independent form of the $v(c)$ curve as in Figure 1, equation (4') corresponds to a solution where $c_1 = c_2$—i.e., to a tangency optimum like C^{**} at the intersection of the budget line $L''L''$ with the 45° "certainty line" in Figure 2.

Thus, confirming our earlier result, starting from a certainty position the individual would never accept any gamble at fair odds. And, if endowed with a risky situation he would use the fair-odds condition to "insure" by moving to a certainty position. That is, he would accept just that risk contract, offering income in one state in exchange for income in another, which exactly offsets his endowed gamble. (Correspondingly, if the market odds are not fair, the individual *would* accept some risk so that C^* would lie off the 45° line.) Note that mere acceptance of a risky contract does not tell us whether the individual is moving away or toward a certainty position (enlarging or reducing his risk exposure)—the riskiness of his *endowment* position must also be taken into account.

A natural next step would be to explore the responses of the individual's risk-bearing optimum C^* (and thus of his implied state-claim transactions) to a variety of parametric shifts: to changes in prices, in probability beliefs, in the size of endowed income and its state-distribution, and in the riskiness of the prospects available to him. It has proved useful to define measures of *relative* and *absolute risk-aversion* [107, John W. Pratt, 1964; 8, Arrow, 1965] that help characterize the individual's response to such parametric shifts. Limited space unfortunately precludes coverage of this large topic.

Market equilibrium under uncertainty

We now shift the level of analysis, from the decisions of the individual to market interactions and the conditions of equilibrium. Recall however that we are not dealing with what is called *market uncertainty* (with its characteristic phenomena of search and of trading at non-clearing prices). Rather, we are dealing with *event uncertainty*. And we shall generally be assuming perfect but not necessarily complete markets: trading in consumption claims contingent upon alternative states of the world takes place at market-clearing prices, but not all definable claims may be separately tradable.

Risk sharing

If both parties in some transaction are risk-averse, they will generally contract to share the total risks and returns. This can be illustrated by the Edgeworth box in Figure 3 [18, William C. Brainard and F. Trenery Dolbear, Jr., 1971; 92, John M. Marshall, 1976], which for concreteness may be thought of as illustrating a "share cropping" problem [20, Steven N. S. Cheung, 1969; 112, Joseph D. Reid, Jr., 1976]. The alternative states of the world are "good crop" or non-loss state N and "bad crop" or loss state L, with associated contingent claims c_N and c_L. Because of the difference in social totals of income in the two states, the box is vertically elongated.

Given agreed-upon probabilities π_L, π_N ($\pi_N = 1 - \pi_L$), the indifference curves for each agent have the same absolute slope π_L/π_N along their respective 45° certainty lines. It is obvious that the two traders (Landlord I and Worker II) cannot both attain certainty positions. At a position like E the Landlord is bearing all the risk (the Worker is receiving a fixed wage independent of which state obtains). At a position like V the opposite holds; the Landlord is receiving a fixed rent regardless of state, while the Worker bears the risk. Starting from a position like E, state-claim trading will lead to an equilibrium at a point like C on the contract curve TT within the region of mutual advantage. It is geometrically evident that the contract curve necessarily lies between the two 45° certainty lines, so some of the risk will be borne by each party.

If the individuals were constrained to strict *proportionate* crop-sharing, the equilibrium would have to lie along the main diagonal of the Edgeworth box. (This would represent a kind of "incomplete market" for the trading of contingent claims.)

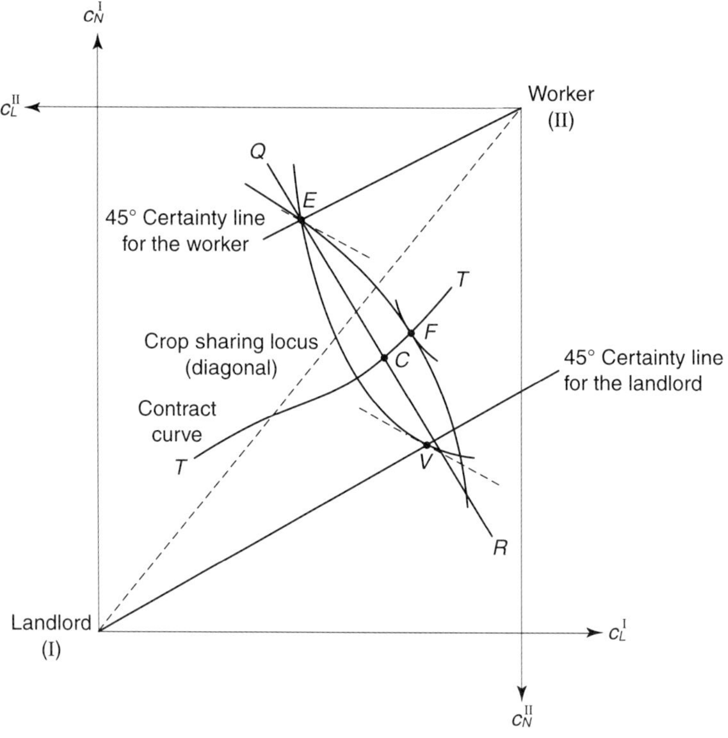

Figure 3. Risk sharing.

Such a solution would not in general be Pareto-optimal, but it might be a rather close approximation of a point on the contract curve. Proportionate sharing in a world of unequal social totals of income would be strictly consistent with a Pareto-optimal solution only if conjoined with side payments from one party to another.

Insurance

The Edgeworth box interaction in Figure 3 can be given another interpretation: the risk-sharing that takes place there can be regarded as "mutual insurance." Indeed, all insurance is best thought of as mutual [91, Marshall, 1974]; insurance companies are only intermediaries in the risk-sharing process. We will be providing here a relatively extended discussion of insurance markets in order to illustrate in somewhat greater depth a number of the salient issues of uncertainty theory.

In the insurance context, once again the Edgeworth box will in general be elongated; we can imagine a social "loss" state of the world L (e.g., an earthquake occurs) versus a "non-loss" state N. From any given endowment point like E, price-taking traders arrive at a risk-sharing equilibrium like C on the contract curve. The absolute slope $(= P_L/P_N)$ of the equilibrium market line (OR) exceeds the absolute slope of the dashed lines representing the fair prices or probability ratio $(= \pi_L/\pi_N)$. That is, claims to income in the less affluent state L command a relatively high price, the marginal utility of income in that state being higher in equation (4) for the representative individual.

In economic analyses of insurance there has been a tendency to assume that fair or "actuarial" insurance terms would be normal were it not for the transaction costs ("loading") [33, Isaac Ehrlich and Gary S. Becker, 1972]. In what follows we shall survey some of the major elements, transaction costs aside, that generally lead to *nonfair* equilibrium prices.

Social risk. Suppose two individuals I and II have equal initial incomes, but there is a hazard that will surely impose a fixed loss ξ on exactly one of them (with fixed, but not necessarily equal probabilities for each). The Edgeworth box would be square. Then the two 45° lines collapse into the single main 45° diagonal, which also becomes the contract curve. Here there is private risk without social risk. The two states of the world are "loss strikes I" versus "loss strikes II." Each party will want to exchange income in *his* non-loss state (the "premium") for compensation to be received in his loss state (the "indemnity"). The equilibrium price ratio (premium/indemnity ratio) corresponds to the respective probabilities; at these fair prices, all private risk is eliminated by mutual insurance.

Apart from this extreme special case of perfect negative correlation of risks, *four* distinct states of the world can be defined in a two-party situation—the loss may be suffered by neither person, by I alone, by II alone, or by both. And the social total of losses can be 0, 1, or 2. Evidently, there is no way of arranging affairs so that everyone can have the same income regardless of state; universal *full insurance* (whereby everyone attains his "certainty line") is generally impossible. It follows that equilibrium prices cannot be "fair"; each person's premium/indemnity ratio must exceed the odds that he will suffer a loss.

For larger insurance pools with M members, the Law of Large Numbers is sometimes thought to justify treating the per-capita loss $\gamma = 1/M \sum_{i=1}^{M} \xi i$ as approximately constant over states. As M increases, the variance of γ declines and thus the error committed by assuming away social risk diminishes. Nevertheless this error does *not* tend toward zero unless the separate risks are on average uncorrelated [83, Markowitz, 1959, p. 111]. If the variance of loss has the same value σ^2 for each individual, and if the correlations between all pairs of risks equal some common r (which can only hold if $r \geq 0$), the variance of the per-capita loss γ equals:

$$\sigma_\gamma^2 = \frac{1}{M^2}(M\sigma^2 + M(M-1)r\sigma^2) \tag{5}$$

In the limit as M increases, the variance of per capita loss approaches the value $r\sigma^2$, which remains positive unless $r = 0$.

We see, therefore, that "social risk" is not exclusively due to small numbers; it persists even with large numbers if risks are on average correlated. In the language of portfolio theory, risks have a "diversifiable" element, which can be eliminated by purchasing shares in many separate securities (equivalent to mutual insurance among a large number of individuals) and an "undiversifiable" element due to the average correlation between risks. It follows then that a particular asset will be more valuable the less is the correlation of *its* returns over states with the aggregate returns of all assets together—the variability of which is the source of undiversifiable risk. As this concept is applied in modern investment theory, the correlation of returns from the "market portfolio" consisting of all securities together is indicated by that security's "beta" parameter [131, Sharpe, 1978, chap. 6]. Securities with low or, even better, negative betas trade at relatively high prices (i.e., investors are satisfied with low expected rates of return on these assets) because they provide their holders with relatively large returns in just those states of the world where aggregate incomes are low (where marginal utilities are high).

The "social risk" phenomenon therefore provides two reasons why insurance prices may not be fair or actuarial, so that purchase of coverage is ordinarily less than complete: (1) if the number of risks in the insurance pool is small, so that the Law of Large Numbers cannot fully work, or (2) even with large numbers, if risks are on average correlated.

State-dependent utilities. Our discussion to this point has been based upon the unique state-independent preference-scaling function of Figure 1. More generally, however, the utility we attach to income c may vary with the state of the world. In the insurance context, we may have a $v_N(c)$ curve for the non-loss state N and a separate (lower) $v_L(c)$ curve for the loss state L (Figure 4a). This will be appropriate wherever the object insured cannot be regarded simply as an income-equivalent—for example if it is an irreplaceable heirloom, or your own life, or your child's. There is no contradiction with the development above that led to the picture in Figure 1, for there it was assumed (merely as a simplification) that utility was a function of a single generalized

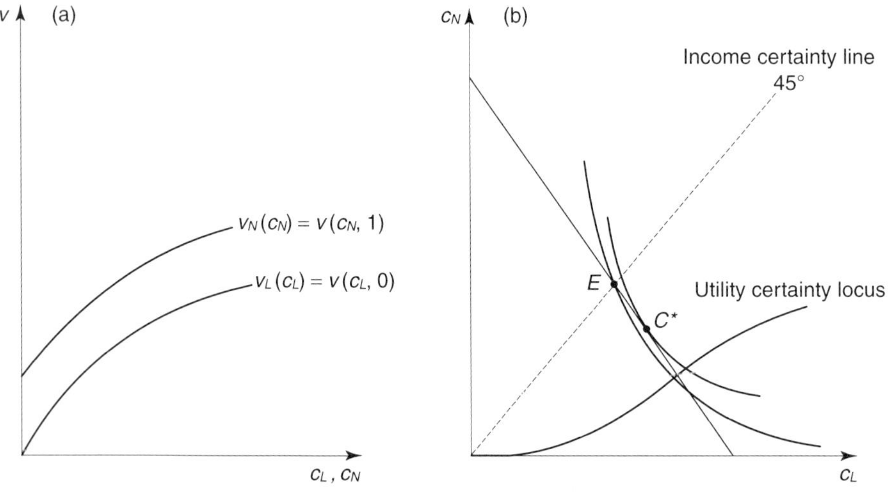

Figure 4. (a) State-dependent utility. (b) "Heirloom" insurance.

"income" commodity c. Here utility is a function of both c and an "heirloom" variable h, where $h=0$ defines the loss state L and $h=1$ the non-loss state N. Hence the two curves $v_N(c)$ and $v_L(c)$ do not represent distinct utility functions, but different sections through a single $v(c, h)$ function.

With state-dependent utility, the 45° *income* certainty line (ICL) is no longer the individual's utility certainty locus (UCL). Someone on the 45° line would not be indifferent as to whether state N or L occurs. In Figure 4b, the UCL lies toward the c_L axis, since the individual requires more income in state L than in state N if he is to "fully insure utility" [25, Philip J. Cook and Daniel A. Graham, 1977].

The individual optimization condition will, apart from the N or L subscripts attaching to the marginal utilities v', have the same form as equation (4):

$$\frac{\pi_L v'_L(c_L)}{\pi_N v'_N(c_N)} = \frac{P_L}{P_N} \tag{6}$$

Assuming, as a benchmark, that prices are fair, (6) reduces to:

$$v'_L(c_L) = v'_N(c_N) \tag{6'}$$

With actuarial insurance available, the individual thus equates his marginal utilities in the two states as before, but these marginal utilities are now slopes along different $v(c)$ curves.

With uncertainty only over the possible loss of the "heirloom," the individual has an initial endowment point E on the 45° income certainty line. Therefore insurance against the loss state is optimal, at actuarial prices, if and only if the indifference curve through E is steeper at this point than the budget line, that is if:

$$v'_L(c_E) = \frac{\partial v}{\partial c}(c_E, 0) > v'_N(c_E) = \frac{\partial v}{\partial c}(c_E, 1)$$

The desirability of insuring against the loss state thus depends upon whether or not income c and the "heirloom" variable h are Edgeworth substitutes—i.e., whether the cross-derivative of the two-dimensional cardinal preference-scaling function $v(c, h)$ is negative. For an heirloom such as an ancestral painting with negligible cash value it is hard to establish an *a priori* case either way. We can thus expect to find that some people insure such objects while others, similarly situated, do not.

But suppose $h=0$ represents a major injury. Then the marginal utility of income will probably be higher in the loss state (one "needs" income c more than before). In such cases the optimum $C*$ lies to the southeast of the income certainty line, though not necessarily southeast of the utility certainty locus. The individual will buy insurance against injury, but not necessarily so much as to be "fully insured" in the sense of not caring whether or not the injury occurs.

The situation is very different if the variable h represents the life of one's child. It then seems plausible that h and c are complements; if your child dies ($h=0$) you have *less* need for income, since you planned to spend it largely on him. In such a case it is optimal to transfer income from the loss state to the non-loss state. That is, to "reverse insure"—to bet that the loss would not occur. (Contractually, instead of insuring your child's life you might buy a life annuity for him.)

We see that once allowance is made for state-dependent utility, it can no longer be presumed that individuals offered actuarial insurance terms will move to certainty positions—either certainty with respect to income, or with respect to utility.

Adverse selection and moral hazard. We now turn back to the simple assumption of state-independent utility, and also assume away "social risk," in order to isolate another force operating upon individual decisions and market equilibrium: the inability of insurers to perfectly monitor the behavior or identify the risk-status of insureds. (Since this is a kind of *informational* problem, our analysis here has close ties with topics to be taken up below.)

To stick to essentials, we need only consider two risk classes with the same initial wealth ω and facing the same potential loss ξ. In the absence of insurance the high-risk class, with loss probability π', has an expected utility of $\pi' v(\omega - \xi) + (1 - \pi') v(\omega)$. This is represented by the distance $A'B'$ in Figure 5. If members of this risk class are identifiable by the insurers (by the other members of the mutual insurance pool), fair insurance will result in their being offered full coverage for a premium of $\pi'\xi$—equal to the mathematical expectation of loss. These individuals then choose certainty position C' in Figure 5 (equivalent to being on the 45° line in Figure 2). Expected utility is $v(\omega - \pi'\xi)$, equal to the distance $A'C'$ in the diagram.

Similarly, if members of a low-risk class with loss probability π'' can be identified, insurance at actuarial terms will raise their expected utility from $A''B''$ to $A''C''$.

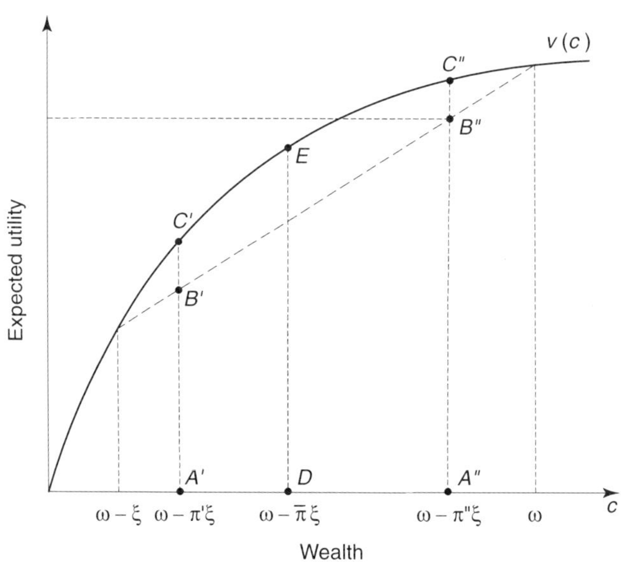

Figure 5. Adverse selection.

But what if the insurers have no way of distinguishing individuals belonging to different risk classes? Suppose they offer insurance on a full-coverage-or-none basis, initially using the average probability of loss $\bar{\pi}$. The resulting expected utility of those purchasing the insurance, $v(\omega - \bar{\pi}\xi)$, is given by the distance DE in Figure 5. The high-risk class would be getting a bargain, but the low-risk class *may* (as shown here) be better off without any coverage ($A''B'' > DE$). If so, the latter drop out of the insurance pool; only the high risks insure. The premium in equilibrium would of course be $\pi'\xi$, reflecting the loss probability of the high-risk class.

This is the problem of *adverse selection*. While we have described it in the insurance context, it is a much more general phenomenon. Whenever buyers can only observe average quality, there is a tendency for sellers not fully rewarded for high quality to withdraw from the market. In one extreme model George A. Akerlof [1, 1970] showed that even if the used cars in existence represent a merit continuum, only the lowest-quality "lemons" would actually be traded.

More generally, however, the equilibrium may not be quite so extreme. With somewhat greater risk-aversion, in Figure 5 the $v(c)$ curve might have warranted participation even of the low-risk class in the insurance pool, at prices based on the average odds $\bar{\pi}$. With a risk continuum also, the pool of participants may include everyone from the lowest quality up to some cutoff point [149, Richard Zeckhauser, 1974]. Returning to Figure 5, suppose now that the risks are distributed over a range of loss probabilities, the interval $[\pi'', \pi']$. Since insurance yields an expected-utility gain of $B'C'$ to the highest risk class, those with not too dissimilar loss probabilities are also better off purchasing the same type of policy. Such participation lowers the average probability of loss and improves the actuarial premium, thereby drawing still better risks into the insurance pool. The process continues until the marginal risk class is just indifferent between no coverage and full coverage at a premium reflecting the average probability of loss for all those in the pool.

So far we have been assuming, in effect, a world of pure exchange: we have allowed people to *trade* risks (to engage in mutual insurance) but not to *modify* risks by productive activities. Such modifications might take the form of committing resources to *loss reduction* (reducing the gap between c_N and c_L) or to *loss prevention* (reducing the loss-probability π_L) [33, Ehrlich and Becker, 1972; 92, Marshall, 1976]—apart from or in addition to purchase of market insurance. More commonly the problem is viewed the other way. Might individuals who purchase insurance be inclined not to undertake protective measures that would reduce the scale or chance of loss? This is what is called *moral hazard*.

Since efficient prices are proportioned only to the *probability* of loss, if π_L is known and fixed there is no need for insurers to guard against inadequate loss-reduction activity by price-taking risk-owners; the decisions of the insureds lead automatically to a Pareto-efficient *production and distribution* of risks [92, Marshall, 1976]. And if π_L is variable but subject to costless monitoring by insurers, prices would respond appropriately and thus would continue to induce efficient loss-prevention activity as well as market risk-sharing transactions [135, Michael Spence and Zeckhauser, 1971]. Another way of looking at this is to note that, in principle, variation of *probability* of loss is equivalent to variations in the *amounts* of loss under a suitably extensive specification of states of the world [57, Hirshleifer, 1970, p. 217]. Thus, with perfect monitoring, insurance terms can always be based upon the fixed probabilities of the true underlying states. If insurers could offer suitably different premium/indemnity ratios for losses under perfectly observable contingencies like a 10-foot flood, a 20-foot flood, etc., they need not be concerned with how high a dike the insured chooses to build.

Realistically speaking, however, monitoring of states will be imperfect. Insurers cannot be certain about the true flood hazards, fire hazards, or medical hazards experienced by insureds. Consequently, very often contracts have to be written in terms of "result-states" [92, Marshall, 1976]—actual observed losses—rather than the true underlying states. Then, if in the extreme case price did not respond at all to loss-prevention activity, no such activity would be undertaken.

Insurers have two main ways of coping with the problem [6, Arrow, 1963; 104, Mark Pauly, 1968; 148, Zeckhauser, 1970]. The first is to require the insured party to bear some portion of the risk, for example, by a "deductible" provision (indemnity will be less than the loss by a fixed amount) or by "coinsurance" (indemnity will be a proper fraction of the loss). Then insurance will be provided, but moral hazard persists in that insureds will engage in less preventive activity than would be efficient with costless monitoring. In addition, risk-spreading through insurance is less than ideal. The second way of coping is to price insurance in accordance with the *actual loss-prevention behavior* of insureds (the height of the dike built), the idea being that to monitor behavior may be easier than monitoring the underlying states. Again, as this process is subject to slippage and uncertainty, there is less preventive activity and less risk-spreading through insurance than would be optimal.

Complete and incomplete market regimes, the stockmarket economy, and optimal production decisions

We have briefly alluded above to the possibility that, under uncertainty, a complete set of markets may not be available to economic agents. More formally, a regime of Complete Contingent Markets (CCM) will exist if, with S distinct states of the world, the S elementary state-claims c_s ($s = 1, \ldots, S$) are all separately tradable. In such a regime each individual i with endowment $\omega^i \equiv (\omega^i_p, \ldots, \omega^i_s)$ and facing prices $P \equiv (P_1, \ldots, P_S)$ chooses some vector of trades t^i satisfying $P \cdot t^i = 0$. Equating marginal rates of substitution with the corresponding price ratios, the necessary condition for a utility-maximizing consumption choice of $c^i \equiv \omega^i + t^i$ is then:

$$\frac{\pi_s v'(c^i_s)}{\pi_1 v'(c^i_1)} = \frac{P_s}{P_1} \quad \text{for all } s. \tag{7}$$

This is of course a generalization of equation (4) above. More generally, trading in any S distinct *assets* representing combinations or packages of the c_s-claims will also constitute a CCM regime provided the assets are linearly independent (i.e., that none of them can be expressed as a linear combination of the others). For, any desired vector c^i can then be attained by holding an appropriate combination of the S assets.

There is however a rather large gap between the CCM model and reality. Given the infinite variety of conceivable contingencies of economic interest (possible inventions, disasters, political developments, taste changes, etc.), in practice market regimes will necessarily be severely incomplete. Economic agents cannot in fact trade, directly or indirectly, in every distinct contingent claim. There are a number of different incomplete market regimes, some of which will be studied in more detail in the second part of this chapter. For example, it might be the case that for some or all commodities only *certainty* claims rather than *contingent* claims are tradable; one might be able to contract to deliver wheat, but there might be no effective market in wheat contingent upon the Republicans winning the next election.

We will consider here one interesting regime of incomplete markets: a "stockmarket economy." Here each individual i has an untradable endowment $\omega^i = (\omega^i_P, \ldots, \omega^i_S)$ plus endowed amount of tradable *shares* $(\bar{\alpha}^i_l, \ldots, \bar{\alpha}^i_F)$ of the F "firms" in the economy. Each firm corresponds to a state-claim vector $\omega^f = (\omega^f_1, \ldots, \omega^f_S)$.

If each firm's holding has market value V_f, the individual's decision problem is to choose a portfolio $(\alpha^i_l, \ldots, \alpha^i_F)$ subject to his marketable wealth constraint:

$$\Sigma_f \alpha^i_f V_f = \Sigma_f \bar{\alpha}^i_f V_f \tag{8}$$

His final consumption is $c^i \equiv \omega^i + t^i$ where:

$$t^i = \Sigma_f (\alpha^i_f - \bar{\alpha}^i_f)\omega^t \tag{9}$$

The individual then chooses a portfolio to maximize:

$$u(\alpha^i_l, \ldots, \alpha^i_F) = \Sigma_s \pi_s v(c^i_s) \tag{10}$$

subject to (8) and (9). To achieve this he expands or contracts his holdings in the different firms until the expected marginal utility of a dollar invested in each asset is equated to his expected marginal utility of wealth, λ^i, that is:

$$\frac{\Sigma_s \pi_s v'(c^i_s)\omega^f_s}{V_f} = \lambda^i \quad \text{for all } f \text{ and all } i. \tag{11}$$

This directly implies:

$$\frac{\Sigma_s \pi_s v'(c^i_s)\omega^f_s}{\Sigma_s \pi_s v'(c^i_s)\omega^1_s} = \frac{V_f}{V_1} \quad \text{for all } f \text{ and } i. \tag{12}$$

This relation, in comparison with (7), indicates an optimization constrained by the set of assets or claims packages (firms $f = 1, \ldots, F$) through which trading may take place. Unless the set of tradable assets constitutes a Complete Contingent Market (which cannot be the case if $F < S$, or more generally if the F asset vectors fail to span the full S-dimensional space), it will not in general be possible for individuals to achieve the Pareto-efficient vector of net trades by purchase and sale of shares. However, it can be shown that the stockmarket economy is efficient in the restricted sense of achieving Pareto-preferred allocations of the tradable shares of different firms [30, Peter A. Diamond, 1967].

Two related questions have received considerable attention: (1) Will shareholders in general be *unanimous* in support of the firm's production decision, and (2) if so, will the optimal decision be such as to maximize the firm's *market value* V_f? In the simpler model of certainty choices, it is well known that unanimous support for maximization of market value follows when a "separation theorem" holds. If there are perfect competitive markets and no technological externalities among firms, maximization of firm value implies that every shareowner's wealth and thus his consumption opportunities will be maximized. In the absence of the stated conditions, the separation theorem does not in general hold. For example, if the firm has significant monopoly power, the shareowner must balance increases in wealth against the loss he suffers as a consumer having to pay higher prices. And if differing shareowners have different tastes or endowments, the failure of separation will imply non-unanimity as well.

Very much the same holds for the firm's decisions in a world of uncertainty. In a stockmarket economy, in particular, shareowners will unanimously support value maximization if the firm's decision can have only a negligible perceived effect upon their marginal utilities in the different states. This condition will be violated if the firm can have a significant effect upon the aggregate supply of claims to any particular state s, akin to its having a degree of monopoly over c_s-claims. As an important special case, the condition will fail if the productive options before the firm enable it to create otherwise unavailable patterns (ratios) of state-claims. And again, unanimity fails if there is technological interdependence between this firm and any other firm, since there generally will be overlapping ownership between the two [30, Diamond, 1967; 34, Steinar Ekern and Robert Wilson, 1974; 28, Harry DeAngelo, 1979].

Other applications

In this part I we have provided a relatively extensive treatment of insurance; under that heading we have been able to expound and illustrate, in rather simple format, most of the basic ideas of modern uncertainty theory. (Of course, we have scarcely been able to hint at the many exciting developments of a more advanced nature.) We have also referred briefly to other applications of uncertainty theory such as sharecropping and portfolio selection. A number of other significant applications can only be mentioned here: (1) optimal contracts between agent and principal, for example, to elicit ideal performance on the part of corporate managers [88, Jacob Marschak and Roy Radner, 1972; 51, Milton Harris and Artur Raviv, 1978; 133, Steven Shavell, 1978; 21, Steven N. S. Cheung, 1969; 49, Theodore Groves, 1973; 3, Armen A. Alchain and Harold Demsetz, 1972; 66, Michael C. Jensen and William A. Meckling, 1976; 150, Thomas S. Zorn, 1978]; (2) corporate finance and, in particular, the balance between debt and equity funding [98, Franco Modigliani and Merton H. Miller, 1958; 74, John Lintner, 1962; 56, Jack Hirshleifer, 1966; 37, Eugene F. Fama and Merton H. Miller, 1972, chap. 4]; (3) optimal behavior and equilibrium with respect to accidents [143, William Vickrey, 1968; 19, Guido Calabresi, 1970; 15, William Baumol, 1972; 31, Peter A. Diamond, 1974]; (4) the "value of life" appropriate for risk-taking decisions [97, Ezra J. Mishan, 1971; 140, Richard H. Thaler and Sherwin Rosen, 1976; 24, Bryan C. Conley, 1976; 127, Thomas C. Schelling, 1968; 68, Michael Jones-Lee, 1976; 73, Joanne

Linnerooth, 1979; 16, Theodore Bergstrom, 1974]; and (5) choice of discount rate for public investment [56, J. Hirshleifer, 1966; 11, Kenneth J. Arrow and Robert C. Lind, 1970; 124, Agnar Sandmo, 1972; 12, Martin J. Bailey and Michael C. Jensen, 1972; 93, Joram Mayshar, 1977].

THE ECONOMICS OF INFORMATION

In the first part individuals were limited to terminal actions, permitting them only to *adapt* to uncertainty. In this part we examine the consequences of informational actions, which allow them to *overcome* uncertainty. Paralleling the sequence of topics in the first part, we first analyze the optimizing choices of the decision-making unit. We then cover market equilibrium and, in particular, the interrelated prior and posterior equilibria associated with the receipt of *public* information. This is followed by a discussion of the incentives to seek out *private* information, as in inventive effort. We then examine processes by which information is revealed in market prices. Finally, there is a brief discussion of rational expectations and informational efficiency.

Informational decision-making

Acquisition of information

We continue to assume that the set of acts $a = (1, \ldots, A)$, the set of states of the world $s = (1, \ldots, S)$, and the associated consequences $c(a,s)$ are all known to the individual. He has, as before, a prior probability distribution of initial beliefs π_s as to the states of the world. The new element is that he can acquire information, receiving one of a known set of possible *messages* $m = (1, \ldots, M)$ that in general will lead to a revision of probability beliefs. And thus in turn, to a possible revised choice of action.

In the extreme case, a message m might be *conclusive* to the occurrence of some particular state s^*—in which case the revised or posterior belief distribution will attach probability of unity to state s^* and zero to all other states. More generally, the warranted revised probability belief $\pi_{s,m}$ attaching to state s after receiving message m is determined by Bayes' Theorem:

$$\pi_{s,m} = \Pr\{s|m\} = \frac{\Pr\{m|s\}\Pr\{s\}}{\Pr\{m\}} \\ = \frac{q_{m,s}\pi_s}{q_m} \tag{13}$$

The probability q_m of receiving message m is related to the conditional probabilities or "likelihoods" $q_{m,s}$ (of receiving message m in each state s) by:

$$q_m = \sum_{s=1}^{S} q_{m,s}\pi_s \tag{14}$$

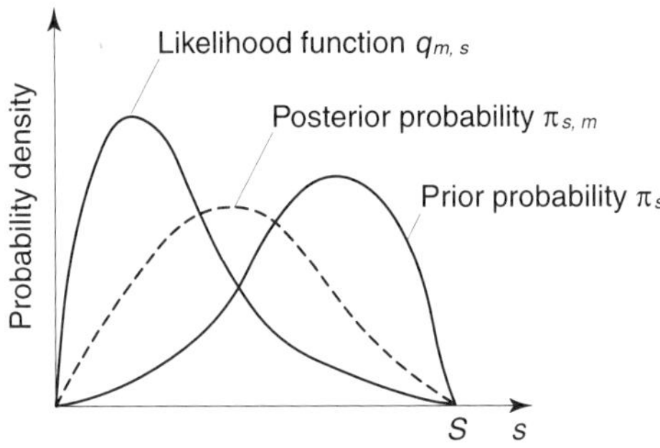

Figure 6. Bayesian probability recalculation.

Figure 6 is a suggestive illustration of Bayesian recalculation of probabilities on the basis of a given message m, where the possible states of the world are a continuum of values of s from zero to some upper limit S. In the prior distribution pictured, the bulk of the initial probability weight is assumed to lie toward the high end. But, as the likelihood function indicates, a message (evidence) has been received that is much more likely if s has a small rather than a large value. The posterior probability distribution is a compromise or average of the other two curves, derived by multiplying (for each s) the prior probability π_s and the likelihood $q_{m,s}$—as indicated in the numerator of equation (13)—and then rescaling by the denominator factor so that the probability integral comes to unity.

The individual's *confidence* in his initial beliefs is indicated by the "tightness" of his prior probability distribution—the degree to which he approaches assigning 100 percent prior probability to some single possible value for s. Evidently, the higher the prior confidence the more the posterior probability distribution will resemble the prior for any given weight of evidence. As we shall see in detail below, *greater confidence implies attaching lesser value to acquiring evidence.*

We now turn to the revision of optimal terminal actions consequent upon acquisition of information. The terminal-action decision problem discussed above, for any given set of probability beliefs π, can be written:

$$\max_{(a)} u(a, \pi) = \sum_{s=1}^{S} \pi_s v(c_{as}) \tag{15}$$

The values of *informational* actions are essentially based upon the expected utility gains from shifting to better choices among the set of *terminal* actions. In particular, denote as a_0 the optimal terminal action that would be chosen before receiving any message—i.e., using the prior probabilities π_s in equation (15). If now a particular message m is received, the decision-maker would use (15) again, but with revised probabilities $\pi_{s,m}$ possibly leading to a new choice of terminal action a_m. Then Δ_m, the "value of the message m" can be written:

$$\Delta_m = u(a_m, \pi_{s,m}) - u(a_0, \pi_{s,m}) \tag{16}$$

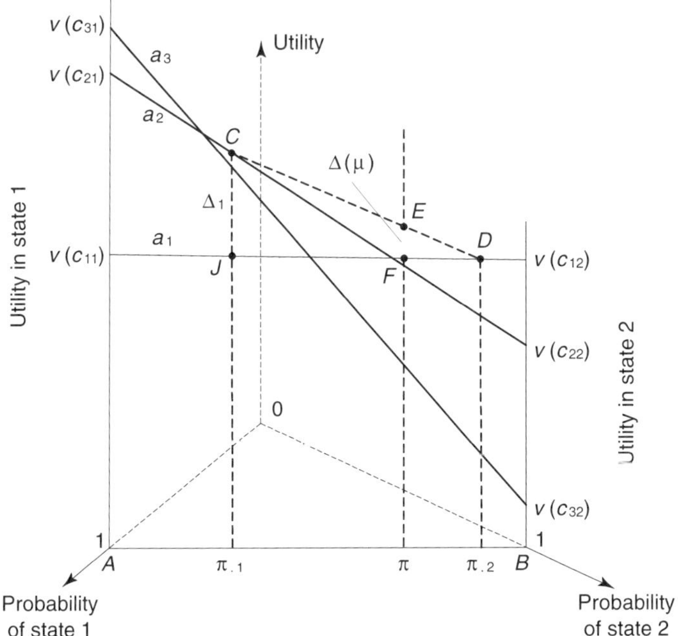

Figure 7. The value of information.

Note that Δ_m, which is necessarily non-negative, is an *ex post* valuation. It represents the expected gain from revision of best action, estimated in terms of the revised probabilities.

However, the decision to seek information must necessarily be made *ex ante*. One is never in the position of choosing whether or not to receive the particular message m; the essence of the problem is that the information-seeker does not know in advance which of the set of possible messages $m = (1, \ldots, M)$ he will obtain. What the agent can actually purchase is not a particular message but an *information service* μ— generating a probability distribution of messages m [87, Jacob Marschak and Koichi Miyasawa, 1968].

An information service μ is "objectively" characterized by its matrix of likelihoods $Q = [q_{m,s}]$. As we have seen, matrix Q together with the individual's subjective prior probability vector $\pi = [\pi_s]$ imply a posterior probability matrix $\Pi = [\pi_{s,m}]$ and message probability vector $q = [q_m]$. Then (Π, q) represents a *personal* characterization of μ. Utilizing the message probabilities, the individual can calculate the *value* $\Delta(\mu)$ *of the information service* to him as the expectation of its associated message values Δ_m:

$$\Delta(\mu) = E(\Delta_m)$$
$$= \Sigma_m q_m [u(a_m, \pi_{s,m}) - u(a_0, \pi_{s,m})] \tag{17}$$

Since, as already indicated, each Δ_m represented by the bracket in (17) is non-negative, an information service can never lower the agent's expected utility (before allowing for the cost of acquiring that service).

In Figure 7 the determination of $\Delta(\mu)$ is illustrated for a special case in which there are two states of the world ($s = 1, 2$), three available terminal actions ($a = 1, 2, 3$), and an information service μ with two possible messages ($m = 1, 2$). In the diagram utility is measured vertically, while the probabilities of the two states are scaled along the horizontal axes. Each possible assignment of probabilities to states is represented by a point along AB, a 135° line in the base plane whose equation is simply $\pi_1 + \pi_2 = 1$.

The utilities of consequences $v(c_{a1})$ attaching to the different actions if state 1 occurs are indicated by the points labelled $v(c_{11})$, $v(c_{21})$, and $v(c_{31})$ lying vertically above A in the diagram. Similarly, the utilities of outcomes in state 2—$v(c_{a2})$ for $a = 1, 2, 3$—lie above point B. The expected utility $u(a; \pi)$ of any action a given any probability vector π is indicated by the vertical distance from the point $\pi = (\pi_1, \pi_2)$ along AB to the line joining $v(c_{a1})$ and $v(c_{a2})$ for that action. In the diagram, if π is the *prior* probability vector, then the best terminal action is $a = 1$ and the associated utility is indicated by the height of point F above the base plane.

Suppose for simplicity that the information service μ is costlessly acquired. Each of the possible messages $m = 1, 2$ will lead to a revised probability vector $\pi_{.m} = (\pi_{1.m}, \pi_{2.m})$. If $m = 1$, the revised optimal action in Figure 7 is $a = 2$ (point C) with Δ_1 (*ex post* utility gain over $a = 1$) equal to the vertical distance CJ. If $m = 2$, the best action in the diagram remains $a = 1$ (point D), so $\Delta_2 = 0$. Weighting Δ_1 and Δ_2 by the message probabilities q_1 and q_2, the value $\Delta(\mu)$ of the information service is represented by the vertical distance EF above the point π along the line AB.

Figure 7 also helps us see why higher prior confidence implies lower value of information. Higher confidence—a tighter prior probability distribution in Figure 6— means that any given message or evidence will have a smaller impact upon the posterior probabilities. Then, in Figure 7, the posterior probability vectors $\pi_{.1}$ and $\pi_{.2}$ would both lie closer to the original π. It is evident that the effect (if any) can only be to shrink the distance EF that represents the expected value of acquiring evidence.

One information service $(\hat{\Pi}, \hat{q})$ is said to be "more informative" than another (Π, q), from the point of view of an economic agent, if it yields sometimes higher and never lower expected utility regardless of the menu of actions [86, Jacob Marschak, 1971]. Between some information services an informativeness ordering is clearly possible: a random sample of 2, we know, must be more informative than a sample of 1. But, in general, informativeness can only be partially ordered. The condition for $(\hat{\Pi}, \hat{q})$ to be more informative than (Π, q) is that the posterior probability vector associated with each message under the latter must be a convex combination of the posterior probabilities under the more informative service. For example, with two messages in each case, $(\hat{\Pi}, \hat{q})$ is more informative than (Π, q) if for some α, β between zero and unity:

$$\pi_{.1} = \alpha\hat{\pi}_{.1} + (1 - \alpha)\hat{\pi}_{.2}$$

and

$$\pi_{.2} = \beta\hat{\pi}_{.1} + (1 - \beta)\hat{\pi}_{.2} \tag{18}$$

One interpretation of these conditions is that the recipient of the information service (Π, q) knows that the true messages 1 and 2 would imply revised probabilities $\hat{\pi}_{.1}$ and $\hat{\pi}_{.2}$. However the messages have become garbled in transmission, so that he is not sure which message he has actually received. For example, his received message 1 has chance $(1 - \alpha)$ or really being the true message 2.

These conditions are easily visualized in terms of Figure 7, which pictures a particular information service (Π, q) leading to posterior probability vectors $\pi_{.1}$ and $\pi_{.2}$. Suppose an alternative information service $(\hat{\Pi}, \hat{q})$ also had two possible messages 1 and 2, but $\hat{\pi}_{.1}$ were to lie to the left of $\pi_{.1}$ and $\hat{\pi}_{.2}$ to the right of $\pi_{.2}$. The alternative service must lead to higher utility so long as there is any change in best conditional action under either message. If on the other hand the two posterior probability vectors of one service do not bracket the two posterior vectors of another which one will be found "more informative" by an individual will depend upon the specifics of his personal situation.

Figure 7 also illustrates a general "non-concavity" (condition of *increasing* marginal returns) in the valuation of information services [110, Radner and Joseph E. Stiglitz, 1976]. Starting with the null information service with posterior probabilities equal to the prior π, suppose a slightly informative μ comes along with posterior probabilities $\hat{\pi}_{.1}$ just barely to the left of π and $\hat{\pi}_{.2}$ barely to the right. If the probability revisions are small, neither message changes the associated best action and there can be no utility gain. So the *marginal* return of improved information may be zero over a certain range, before becoming positive at the point where the improvement begins to affect action.

A number of interesting complications, which unfortunately cannot be pursued here, arise when the informational decision process has multipersonal aspects. One important example is the use of "expert opinion"—the problems being to disentangle what is genuinely new in the information provided, and also to allow for possible conflict of interest between expert and client [132, Shavell, 1976; 105, Judea Pearl, 1978; 46, Jerry Green, forth.]. Other issues arise when a *group* of people must jointly make an information decision [111, Raiffa, 1968, chap. 8]. The problems here stem once again from possible conflicts of interest (differences in utilities attached to consequences), but also from conflicts of opinion (differences in probability beliefs). Depending upon the circumstances, these factors may lead either to overinvestment or underinvestment in information.

Other informational activities

So far, under the heading of informational action we have only considered the *acquisition* of evidence—as by generation of sample data (the production of socially "new" information) or the receipt of expert advice (the interpersonal transfer of "old" information). But other types of informational activities can also be very important. The possibility of acquiring information from others, as discussed in connection with expert opinion above, immediately suggests the reverse activity—the *dissemination* of information to other economic agents. This might be done for a price, as when one is hired as an expert, but (as we shall see below) sometimes it may pay to disseminate gratuitously, or even to incur cost to "push" information to others [60, Hirshleifer, 1973]. Advertising is an obvious example. There is also a choice between disseminating publicly ("publishing"), or else privately to a select audience. As a question of authenticity might arise in all such cases, the receiver of information may devote effort to the process of *evaluation*, possibly assisted by *authentication* activities (or hampered by *deception* activities) on the part of the disseminator. There is also the possibility of unintended dissemination, achieved by *espionage* or *monitoring* on the part of information-seekers—possibly leading to countermeasures in the form of *security* (secrecy-maintaining) activities by the possessors of information.

Finally, there are classes of activities, apart from those involved with acquisition or dissemination of information, that are indirect consequences of informational patterns. Wagering, for example, typically follows from differences of opinion in a situation where conclusive information is anticipated (so as to determine who wins and who loses). *Speculation* is a somewhat analogous activity, which turns on a prospective revision of prices in consequence of the arrival of information. Another form of activity, which will be considered in the next section below, involves the adoption of more or less "flexible" positions in anticipation of ability to make use of future information when it arrives.

Emergent information and the value of flexibility

In the sections preceding we thought of information as being newly generated by an informational action like a sampling experiment or, alternatively, as acquired from others via a transaction like the purchase of expert opinion. But in some cases information may autonomously *emerge* simply with the passage of time, without requiring any direct action by recipients. Tomorrow's weather is uncertain today, but the uncertainty will be reduced as more meteorological data flow in and will in due course be conclusively resolved when tomorrow arrives. Direct informational actions might still be useful, by providing knowledge *earlier* than it would autonomously arrive. But under conditions of emergent information, one might choose a kind of indirect informational action—adopting a flexible position and *waiting* before taking terminal action.

Suppose a choice must be made now between immediate terminal action and awaiting emergent information. This choice can only be interesting where there is a trade-off between two costs: (1) a cost of waiting, versus (2) an "irreversible" element in the possible loss suffered from mistaken early commitment. Exactly these elements have been involved in analyzing the benefit of actions that irreversibly transform the environment [10, Arrow and Anthony C. Fisher, 1974; 54, Claude Henry, 1974] and in discussions of the value of "liquidity" [84, Jacob Marschak, 1949; 59, Hirshleifer, 1972] or of "flexibility" [89, Thomas Marschak and Richard Nelson, 1962; 67, Robert A. Jones and Joseph Ostroy, 1976].

To illustrate these ideas, consider again Figure 7. Suppose an action is to be chosen in each of two time periods ($t = 0$, 1), but information is to emerge that might improve the decision at $t = 1$. Let the payoff to the different actions be the same in each period. With no cost of switching, the diagram shows that the best action at $t = 0$ is a_1. At $t = 1$ this action will again be optimal unless message 1 is received, in which case a_2 becomes superior.

However, suppose that the cost of switching from action a_1 to a_2 exceeds the cost of switching from a_2 to a_1. So a_2 is the more "flexible" choice. If a_2 is chosen at $t=0$ there would be an initial-period loss in expected utility. But if this cost is sufficiently small relative to the differential in switching cost and the expected value of the emerging information, a_2 may become the preferred initial-period action. Here the initial-period loss (reduction in payoff due to choice of a_2) is the cost of waiting (or of maintaining flexibility); the counterbalancing "irreversible" loss, due to early commitment to a_1, is the extra cost of switching should that be required.

Public information and market equilibrium

Emergence of new public information will affect prices. In particular, relative market values will rise for those assets paying off more handsomely in states of the world now regarded as more likely. The anticipated arrival of public information requires economic agents to contemplate market exchanges in two distinct rounds—*trading prior to and posterior to receipt of the message.* The equilibria of the two trading rounds will generally be interrelated, but the form of the relationship depends upon the completeness of markets (see 134–136) in each round.

Equilibrium in complete versus incomplete market regimes

In the first part of the paper we mainly considered models with S states of the world and a single consumption good c. In the realm of the *economics of uncertainty,* where arrival of public information is not anticipated, a regime of Complete Contingent Markets (CCM) was said to exist if all the distinct c_s claims (S in number) are separately tradable at prices P_s. (Trading in any set of S linearly independent asset combinations of the underlying c_s-claims would also constitute a CCM regime, but we will generally ignore this complication). In equilibrium, the optimality condition (7) holding for each individual can conveniently be repeated here:

$$\frac{\pi_2 v'(c_s)}{\pi_1 v'(c_1)} = \frac{P_s}{P_1} \qquad (s = 2, \ldots, S) \tag{19}$$

To achieve this condition, individuals will generally undertake *productive transformations* (e.g., loss-reduction and loss-prevention activities) as well as *market exchanges* (e.g., purchase of insurance).

Now consider that public information is expected to arrive before the close of trading. We will generally be assuming, however, that the message is not timely enough to permit *productive* adaptations to the changed probabilities. For example, a message as to increased flood danger comes in time to affect the market terms of flood-insurance transactions, but not in time to permit construction of dikes.

As an initial special case, assume it is known that the message will be *conclusive* as to which state of the world will obtain. Then to each and every state s corresponds exactly and one message m. In these circumstances Complete Contingent Markets (CCM) in the *prior round* will, just as before, provide for separate trading in the S distinct c_s-claims at prices P_s. Under the timing assumption of the previous paragraph, posterior trading is in general possible. But such trading would be meaningless in this special case; once it becomes known that some single state s^* is the true one, c_s^* is the only state-claim retaining any market value, and there is nothing available for exchanging against it. So equation (19) in the prior round are the *only* relevant conditions of equilibrium.

A more interesting model, continuing to assume that traders anticipate *conclusive* information, allows for multiple consumptive goods $g = 1, \ldots, G$. Here a regime of Complete Contingent Markets (CCM) in the prior round would allow trading in the $G \cdot S$ different claims c_{gs}—claims to any good g under any state s—at prices P_{gs}. After the conclusive message arrives that some state s^* will obtain, complete *posterior* markets would permit exchanges among the G commodity claims $c_{gs}*$. But suppose for the moment that individuals were not aware, in their prior-round dealings, of this possibility of posterior trading. Then the prior-round optimality conditions would have included ratios of the following form, where g' and g are any two goods:

$$\frac{\dfrac{\partial v}{\partial c_{g's}}}{\dfrac{\partial v}{\partial c_{g''s}}} = \frac{P_{g's}}{P_{g''s}} \tag{20}$$

Note that π_s, whatever its value may be, is not involved in the optimality condition between different goods *contingent upon state s*. It follows that receipt of the incoming message, revising the probabilities π_s (in this particular case, making $\pi_{s^*} = 1$) does not affect this condition. Therefore the price ratio on the right-hand side of (20) continues to sustain the solution arrived at in the prior round.

Thus we see that even though posterior exchanges are *possible* among the G remaining tradable claims c_{gs^*}, with CCM in the prior round no one will find such exchanges *advantageous*. Trading in the G posterior claims is "not needed" if there have been markets for $G \cdot S$ prior claims. We must however emphasize a very important qualification to this result: prior-round traders must *correctly forecast* that the price ratio on the right-hand side of (20) will remain unchanged in the posterior-round. If they mistakenly thought that it would change, they would be led to make "erroneous" prior-round transactions, affecting the market equilibrium and thus requiring corrective posterior-round transactions. The result would be a loss of efficiency. So CCM in the prior round (without posterior trading) suffices for Pareto-optimality, but subject to a proviso of "correct conditional price forecasting" [62, Hirshleifer, 1977]. (This proviso corresponds to one of the meanings of that Delphic phrase, "rational expectations," to be discussed below.)

We can now generalize still further to the case where messages are *not conclusive* as to the advent of any particular state. With Complete Contingent Markets in the prior round, there would be $G \cdot S \cdot M$ distinct tradable claims g_{gsm}. And there remain $G \cdot S$ valid claims c_{gsm^*} in the posterior-round after receipt of message m^*. But here also it is not difficult to verify that CCM in the prior round permits every agent to attain his optimum at one fell swoop—provided once again that everyone correctly predicts that the relevant posterior-round price ratios are unchanged [38, George Feiger, 1976]. So quite generally, given "correct conditional price forecasting" and a CCM regime for prior-round trading, posterior-round markets are available but not necessary for Pareto efficiency.

Very interesting and important issues arise, however, when we analyze prior-round market regimes that are *incomplete* (as of course they actually must be in the world). To maintain simplicity, we will however return to the particular case of *conclusive* information. Then the set of M messages collapses into the set of S states so that individuals are concerned only with c_{gs} claims, $G \cdot S$ in the number.

Among the many possible patterns of market incompleteness, three will be briefly discussed here.

Absence of prior-round markets. Total absence of prior-round markets is of course the most extreme form of incompleteness. In effect, what has happened is that the information arrives before *any* exchanges have taken place, while individuals are still at their endowment positions.

This situation has aroused considerable interest, as it implies, the surprising result that incoming public information may be socially disadvantageous in the sense that everyone in the economy might be willing to pay *not* to have it! [58, Hirshleifer, 1971; 90, Marshall, 1974; 149, Zeckhauser, 1974; 50, Nils H. Hakansson, J. Gregory Kunkel, and James A. Ohlson, 1979.] As among a group of traders who would otherwise have mutually insured against fire, a conclusive message (as to whose houses would actually burn down) would negate the possibility of mutually advantageous risk-sharing through insurance. The prospective arrival of such information prior to the opening of markets imposes an undiversifiable wealth-redistribution risk on the economy; no one can hedge against the price impact of the message to be received. (On the other hand, if earlier arrival of information permits more effective *productive* adaptations, as in loss-reduction measures against fire, this socially valuable feature must be weighed against elimination of the ability to spread risks.)

Numeraire contingent markets (NCM). Suppose instead that there is prior-round trading, but only in contingent claims to a *single* commodity–which might as well be taken as the numeraire good $g = 1$. In the prior market, individuals cannot purchase claims to *any* good contingent upon state s, but can purchase claims to (say) *corn* contingent upon state s. Under this Numeraire Contingent Markets (NCM) regime, these purchases are in effect side-bets as to which state of the world is going to obtain, whose outcome will determine the individual's posterior wealth. After receipt of the message, of course, the individual will use his enhanced or reduced wealth to purchase a preferred consumption basket in the *posterior* round of trading.

Arrow [7, 1964] has shown that the same equilibrium allocation as indicated by conditions (2.8) under CCM (with prior trading in $G \cdot S$ claims) is achievable under NCM with prior contingent trading only in the S claims to a single commodity. But given the prior-round incompleteness of this NCM regime, the availability of G markets in the posterior round becomes now quite essential. And once again, we must also specify the important proviso of "correct conditional price forecasting." Furthermore, this proviso here becomes more stringent than under CCM, where the correct forecast was simply "no change" from the prior price ratio P_{gs^*}/P_{1s^*} to the posterior ratio $P_{g \cdot s^*}/P_{1 \cdot s^*}$ (for the particular state s^* pointed to by the incoming message). Here, under NCM, the correct price forecast *is not in general computable from data available to* *traders in the prior round* [108, Radner, 1968; 32, Jacques H. Drèze, 1970–71]. The conditional relative supplies and demands determining the posterior ratios $P_{g \cdot s^*}/P_{1 \cdot s^*}$ are not publicly "visible" in the prior round, where only claims to $g = 1$ are being traded. (Only the absence of utility complementarities between the numeraire and other goods could make the noncomputability of posterior prices irrelevant for prior decisions.)

Futures markets (FM). The CCM and NCM regimes both allow trading in state-contingent claims. Such trading does take place to some extent in the actual world, directly as in some insurance transactions or indirectly via trading in assets like corporate shares that can be regarded as packages of state-claims. But most of the trading observed in the world represents exchange of *unconditional* claims to goods. In a market regime allowing only the exchange of unconditional claims to G consumptive goods, under conclusive emergent information the prior and posterior rounds can be respectively identified with current "futures" markets versus later "spot" markets.

Under such a regime of unconditional or, as we shall say, Futures Markets (FM) there will be just G tradable claims in the prior round followed by possible re-trading in the same claims in the posterior round. Since it is reasonable to assume that $G < S$ (there are many more conceivable contingencies than goods), it is evident that the $G + G$ markets in two rounds under FM cannot in general achieve the same efficiency as the $S + G$ markets under NCM (or, *a fortiori*, as the $G \cdot S$ markets under CCM) [142, Robert M. Townsend, 1978].

This negative conclusion is somewhat mitigated, however, once we allow for the fact that emergent information in the world is only rarely *conclusive*. If improved though not yet conclusive public information emerges repeatedly, the multiplication of rounds of trading recreated after each informational input increases the effectiveness of FM relative to NCM and CCM. (Once again, the proviso as to correct conditional price forecasting retains its relevance and is indeed increasingly difficult of achievement.) Also, in general, multiple rounds can only partially offset market incompleteness, so that full Pareto efficiency is not achieved. More troubling, there may be different *self-fulfilling predictions* about prices in future trading rounds, leading to different equilibrium allocations—and these allocations may be Pareto-rankable [52, Oliver D. Hart, 1975].

Speculation

The term "speculation" has caused a good deal of confusion. Some authors loosely apply the word to arbitrage between markets, or to storage of goods over time or carriage over space—activities that do not involve uncertainty in any essential way. For our purposes, speculation is purchase with the intention of re-sale, or sale with the intent of re-purchase, where the *uncertainty of the future spot price* is a source of both risk and gain. The probabilistic variability of price is in turn *due to anticipated emergence of information.* Each possible message (in the conclusive information case that we shall be assuming here, this is equivalent to the advent of a single possible state) leads to an associated equilibrium posterior price vector, benefiting agents who adopted trading positions generating relatively high conditional wealths for that state.

Among the possible determinants of speculative activity, John Maynard Keynes [70, 1930] and John Hicks [55, 1946] followed by many others have emphasized differential *risk-aversion*. In their view, in the prior round of a Futures Markets (FM) regime the relatively risk-tolerant speculators accept risks of price variability from relatively risk-intolerant "hedgers." In the prior trading round, speculators buy commodity futures, achieving on average a small gain (excess of later mean spot price over futures price), which represents the return they receive from suppliers unwilling to bear the price risk. For example, a wheat-grower hedges by accepting a firm price now from a speculator, both of them anticipating that the unknown spot price will on average be a little higher. Later developments along this line [63, Hendrik S. Houthakker, 1957; 64, 1968; 26, Paul H. Cootner, 1968] have brought out that hedgers can be on either side of the futures market; speculators need bear only the imbalance between "long" and "short" hedgers' commitments, so that the risk-compensating average price movement could go either way. In contrast with these views, Holbrook Working [146, 1953; 147, 1962] has denied that there is any systematic difference as to risk-tolerance between those conventionally called speculators and hedgers. Working emphasizes, instead, differences of *belief* (optimism or pessimism) as motivating futures trading.

The Keynes–Hicks concentration upon *aversion to "price risk"* is seriously misleading. Individuals' prior-round trading decisions are affected by "quantity risk" (variability of endowments over states), as well as by price risk [95, Ronald I. McKinnon, 1967]. Indeed, from the social point of view, price uncertainty is the (inverse) reflection of an underlying uncertainty as to the future aggregate commodity totals. And these risks tend to be offsetting, reducing the need to engage in prior-round hedging activity. For example, when the crop of a representative wheat-grower is big (good news) he will find that the wheat price tends to be low (bad news) and vice versa. In a Futures Markets (FM) regime it is in general not possible to divest oneself of *quantity risk* (since only certainty claims can be traded); consequently, traders might well find it preferable *not* to hedge against the offsetting *price risk*.

In a world where people have a spectrum of beliefs as to probabilities of future states, an individual's speculative activity proper (his adoption of a trading position in anticipation of arriving public information that will change market prices) depends in a rather complex way upon the degree of deviation of his beliefs from average opinion, upon his willingness to tolerate risks, and upon his endowment position cojoined with the trading limitations imposed by a regime of incomplete markets [61, Hirshleifer, 1975; 62, 1977]. With regard to the first of these determinants, a speculator with strongly deviant beliefs thinks that *others* will be surprised by the incoming message (and thus will be forced to make unanticipated posterior transactions). He will in consequence have adopted a trading position enabling him to benefit from these transactions. With regard to the second determinant, degree of risk-aversion affects the *scale* of preferred speculative exposure. As to the regime of markets, we saw in the preceding section that (assuming "correct conditional price forecasting") re-trading possibilities are not needed under Complete Conditional Markets (CCM). Thus, incompleteness of prior-round markets is also a necessary condition for speculation [122, Stephen W. Salant, 1976; 38, George Feiger, 1976].

The economics of research and invention

Research and invention activities are prime instances of the *informational* actions studied, on the level of the individual economic agent, above. We are not dealing here with situations like those examined earlier, where public information simply emerges with the passage of time. Since Nature will not autonomously reveal her secret, it must be sought out by costly (generally "private) search for the still-unknown "message." The topic of concern here however is not the informational decisions of an isolated Robinson Crusoe, but rather of individuals in a market environment facing rivalrous competition from some agents, but also having opportunities for mutually advantageous exchanges with others. In particular, as we shall see, successful private search generally leads to more or less universal dissemination of the discovery, with price impacts akin to that of the public information studied earlier.

The central problem considered by modern analysts [80, Fritz Machlup, 1968; 5, Arrow, 1962] has been the conflict between the social goals of *achieving efficient use of information once produced* versus *providing ideal motivation for production of information.* With regard to optimal use, already-produced information is a "public good" in the sense that its availability to any member of society does not reduce the amount that could be made available to others. Then any barrier to use, as may stem from legal enforcement of patents or copyrights or property in trade secrets, is inefficient. On the other hand, as in the standard public-good situation, there will be inadequate motivation to invest in production of information if the product cannot be reduced to legally protected property.

Under ideal conditions the efficient-use problem could be solved by charging perfectly-discriminating fees to license (non-exclusively) all uses of a given idea. If the discoverer were granted full property rights in the idea, as by a perpetual copyright or patent, he in turn would have the optimal incentive to produce (search for) ideas. But in practice owners of copyrights or patents cannot impose perfectly-discriminating royalty fee structures on licensees. A patentee might instead maximize returns by granting *exclusive* licenses (in which case the social value of the excluded uses is of course lost) or by imposing fee structures that distort the marginal production decisions of licensees. On the other side of the picture, because of the elusiveness of property in ideas, there is uncertainty and unreliability in the legal protection of patents and copyrights, and even less protection for trade secrets not covered by patent or copyright. The result is that unlicensed uses often escape control. Short of ideal conditions there will be losses from *both* underproduction and underutilization, and in practice something of a trade-off: provision of greater legal protection to inventors tends to ameliorate the underproduction problem, but to worsen the underutilization problem.

More recent investigations have indicated, however, that not all the important elements of the picture have been captured by this analysis. These newer results turn upon the possibility of *over*investment in the production of ideas ("a rush to invent").

The first such factor is the *fugitive resource* (or *common-property resource*) nature of undiscovered ideas [13, Yoram Barzel, 1968]. For concreteness, we can use a metaphor the "over-fishing" model of H. Scott Gordon [43, 1954]. Suppose there are perfect property rights in fish caught, but complete free entry into fishing (i.e., there are no property rights that exclude others from engaging in fishing as an activity). Then in competitive equilibrium there will be over-fishing; private marginal cost will equal price, but the true social marginal cost in fishing exceeds the private marginal cost. The reason is that a certain fraction of each fisherman's catch consists of fish that would have been caught anyway, by other fishermen—so the true social product of fishing effort is less than appears in private calculations. The upshot is that too many fish are caught, too soon. Among the remedies discussed in the fugitive-resource literature are the imposition of taxes or production quotas to reduce the amount of fishing activity, or alternatively the assignment of exclusive property rights to engage in such activity.

This last point may be clarified by explicitly distinguishing rights *in* fish (the right to exclude others from a fish you have caught) from rights *of* fishing (the right to exclude others from competing with you in fishing activity). Assuming fully protected rights *in* fish, the fugitive-resource problem can be solved by also vesting rights *of* fishing—for example, by auctioning the right to exclusively exploit a fishery. Indeed, once rights *of* fishing are defined such an auction would tend to occur of its own, via Coase's theorem negotiations. In the context of research, the equivalent distinction is between a right *in* an idea and a right *of* engaging in search for an idea. Again, one might imaging auctioning off the right *of* searching for an idea—for example, the right of inventing an alloy with specified properties. As the lowest-cost inventor would bid highest for this right, the "rush to invent" problem would be solved [22, Cheung, 1979; 23, 1979].

In research, the difficulty of defining the nature of an "uncaught" idea seems to make the assignment of rights *of* searching for them unfeasible. (Even in fishing, it is often impractical to define exclusive rights *of* hunting for such a wandering resource.) In contrast with fishing, however, property rights *in* ideas when caught are also very far from perfect. But, in the circumstances, this is not necessarily bad; being somewhat like a tax on inventive activity, defective rights *in* ideas reduce what otherwise might be an excessive "rush to invent".

Recapitulating at this point, we have seen two distinct possible justifications for limiting property rights in ideas—for example, by granting patents only for a term of years. The first is that some protection to inventors is traded off against protection to users of invention. The second is that the "rush to invent" tendency is moderated by reducing the capturable value of the invention itself.

There is still another motivation that may lead to excessive devotion of resources to invention. Ideas of course vary enormously in their significance, and some among them will have far-reaching consequences. This opens up a new channel of reward for inventors. Instead of, or possibly in addition to, selling the information via patent license or otherwise, an inventor might be able to *speculate* by taking long or short positions in assets whose values will be affected by the invention [58, Hirshleifer, 1971]. An oil firm that has developed a new method of deep recovery might, for example, reap a speculative payoff by buying up options on tracts whose petroleum now lies too deep to be recovered. One important implication of the speculative reward of invention is that it motivates the possessor of information to disseminate it widely and even gratuitously—after having made his speculative commitment.

Looking at this more generally, individual ideas will—unlike individual fish, or whole boatloads of fish—often have important *pecuniary* externalities. The "ideal conditions" referred to above, which would have reserved for the inventor the entirety of the technological benefit flowing from his idea, would then generally lead to *overcompensation* if the inventor could also capture some fraction of the pecuniary externalities as well.

There are classes of research activity for which the reward element stemming from the technological benefit is negligible, where the potential pecuniary return is almost the whole picture. Stockmarket research ("security analysis"), whether engaged in by full-time professionals or by ordinary investors, is essentially of this nature [36, Fama and Laffer, 1971]. While there may be a technological benefit (improvement in society's productive opportunities) due to accurate security *analysts* stems almost entirely from the pecuniary revaluations—the correctly interpreted rises or falls in the stock prices themselves.

Recognition of the "rush to invent" problem, while undermining the traditional argument for patents (or other forms of protection for discoverers of ideas) that was based upon a presumption of *underinvestment* in research, does not warrant going to the other extreme. It would not be in order to conclude that patent protection is *not* justified, but only that the arguments pro and con are more complex than had previously been realized.

Informational advantage and market revelation of information

In the preceding sections we have considered situations in which an individual could profit by timely publication of knowledge in his private possession. For example, an agent obtaining new information might transact at existing prices (take a speculative position), planning to sell out at the revised prices that ensue once he publicly discloses his knowledge. But there are two problems here. First, the agent must be able to move to a trading position (make a speculative commitment) without thereby revealing his secret—this is the problem of *information leakage.* Second, at the disclosure stage he must be able to authenticate the information he is trying to publicize—that is the problem of *signalling.* We shall consider these two problems, in reverse order, in the sections following.

Signalling

The particular signalling problem that has aroused greatest interest arises when sellers of a higher-quality product or service are attempting to convey that message (that their product *is* high-quality) to buyers. Of course, any seller is motivated to *claim* that his is a high-quality product. Signalling as a solution to this difficulty takes place when sellers of truly higher-quality products engage in some activity *that would not be rational for those selling lower-quality products.* Any activity is a potential signal if sellers of higher-quality products can engage in it at lower marginal cost (or higher marginal return) than producers of lower-quality products. For example, it has been argued [101, Phillip Nelson, 1974; 102, 1975] that advertising tends to be especially advantageous for producers of higher-quality goods, in contexts where *repeat purchases* are a significant consideration. Since the high-quality firm will be acquiring a pool of satisfied customers, its marginal advertising cost per unit of sales will be lower. Even if there is zero information content in the advertising itself, a message is thus being conveyed: *that the product is worth promoting.*

For the labor market, Spence [134, 1974], Stiglitz [138, 1975], and John G. Riley [114, 1976; 116, 1979] have argued that educational credentials constitute signals with regard to jobs in which productivity is difficult to determine. As long as there is a negative correlation between productivity and the (money and time) costs involved in achieving any education level, *the marginal cost of education is lower for the higher-quality workers.* The latter are then able to signal by attaining higher educational credentials. On the other side of the market, the process complementary to signalling is called *screening*; employers are able to use education signals to *screen* for quality differentials.

Rothschild and Stiglitz [120, 1976] and Charles A. Wilson [144, 1977] make parallel arguments for the insurance market. 'Adverse selection and moral hazard' (132–134) illustrated how, in the absence of ability to distinguish between better and poorer risks, insurance premiums reflect the average risk quality. Hence *adverse selection* occurs, with lower-quality risk classes tending to insure more than others. However, the higher the probability of loss, the higher is the marginal loss in utility associated with accepting less than full coverage. Thus, the marginal cost of accepting a large "deductible" is greater for low-quality risks (those with high loss probabilities). In effect, then, high-quality risks can signal by willingness to accept a big deductible. Insurance companies can thus screen for differences in risk: policies with large deductibles can be offered at the low premiums appropriate for high-quality risks, while others with smaller deductibles but steeper premiums will be appropriate for and purchases by low- quality risks.

In contrast to the autonomously emergent information situations examined earlier, in signalling models the flow of information from seller to buyer is generated endogenously. This has important consequences for the stability of informational equilibria. It has been established that unless the gap between the quality of different products is sufficiently large, there is no Cournot–Nash equilibrium [120, Rothschild and Stiglitz, 1976; 113, Riley, 1975; 115, 1979]. That is, starting from a situation in which all traders adopt some complementary signalling/screening pattern, there is always an alternative that yields someone greater profit.

Figure 8 illustrates this for the simple case in which there are only two quality levels of the item for sale (insurance risk, consumer good, labor service, etc.) For concreteness we shall use the labor market interpretation. The dashed indifference curves $u_1(e, w)$ represent, for a low-quality (low marginal productivity) worker, equivalent combinations of the price of his labor services (lifetime earnings) w and the level e of signalling activity (education). For a high-quality worker the solid indifference curves $u_2(e, w)$ will be applicable. The lesser slope of the latter indicates the condition for signalling to come about: that a more qualified worker can more easily or cheaply acquire the educational attainment that serves as signal. Put the other way, for any offer profile of lifetime earnings as related to educational credentials e, the higher- quality worker would be willing to acquire more e.

It is supposed here that, with full information, buyers (employers) would be willing to pay the marginal products θ_1 for the low-quality worker and θ_2 for the high-quality worker. If only average quality were known, however, their maximum offer is $\bar{\theta}$. Suppose that initially all workers are offered the same signal-wage pair $Z^* = \langle e^*, w^* \rangle$ as depicted in Figure 8, where w^* is no greater than $\bar{\theta}$.

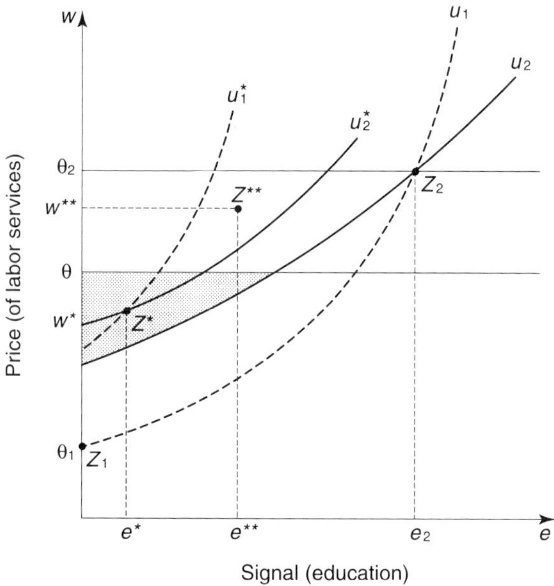

Figure 8. Reactive signalling equilibrium.

The low-quality workers would then be on their indifference curve u_1^*, and the high-quality workers on u_2^*. Some firm would then be motivated to make the new offer Z^{**}. For, this would attract only the high-quality workers and, since $w^{**} < \theta_2$, such an offer would generate a positive profit. This proves that the position Z^*, pooling the different quality levels, is not a Cournot–Nash equilibrium.

Alternatively, suppose the two classes of workers are successfully separated with the pair of offers $Z_1 = \langle 0, \theta_1 \rangle$ and $Z_2 = \langle e^{**}, \theta_2 \rangle$ depicted in Figure 8. Acting as price-takers, the lower-quality workers will accept the offer Z_1 and the higher-quality workers the offer Z_2. On the other side of the market the buyers, also acting as price-takers, find that the products purchased have the anticipated characteristics. The pair of offers $\{Z_1, Z_2\}$ is thus an equilibrium in the Walrasian sense (and in the sense of Spence [134, 1974]). It is also efficient in the sense that all other pairs of offers (more generally all other wage schedules) that yield zero profit and that separate workers provide lower utility to the high-quality workers.

However, this equilibrium does not have the Cournot–Nash stability property either. A firm can now enter offering the signal-wage pair Z^*, which is strictly preferred by both classes of workers and yields an expected profit to the entering firm. As we have already seen that an offer like Z^* is not itself an equilibrium, there is no Cournot–Nash equilibrium.

How then would such a market behave? Plausibly, in the absence of collusion, each buyer would eventually expect some *reaction* by other agents to changes in his own list of offers. Suppose that a new offer would be profitable in the absence of any reaction, but leads to loss once another buyer reacts with a strictly profitable counteroffer.

Suppose furthermore that the latter's response is riskless, in the sense that *further* response by any other buyers would not impose losses on the first reactor. Then it seems reasonable that the potential initial "defector" would eventually recognize that his new offer would bring on such a reaction, and hence would be deterred from making it. This suggests the following strategic equilibrium concept [115, Riley, 1979], which builds on the development by Charles A. Wilson [144, 1977].

Reactive equilibrium. A set of offers is a reactive equilibrium if, for any additional offer that yields an expected gain to the agent making the offer, there is another that yields a gain to a second agent and losses to the first. Moreover, no further addition to or withdrawal from the set of offers generate losses to the second agent.

The general derivation of the existence and uniqueness of the reactive equilibrium is somewhat delicate. However, it is relatively easy to check that, in Figure 8, $\{Z_1, Z_2\}$ is a reactive equilibrium. The initial "defector" must make an offer like Z^* to generate an expected profit. But then another buyer can counter with Z^{**}, thereby attracting away some high-quality workers. As this process continues, $\bar{\theta}$ will fall until Z^* generates losses, while Z^{**} remains strictly profitable, since $w^{**} < \theta_2$.

To conclude, the endogenous revelation of information via markets is, after all, explainable as a noncooperative equilibrium phenomenon. While in general there is no Cournot–Nash equilibrium, recognition of reasonable reactions by other agents always results in a stable equilibrium.

Informational inferences from market prices

We now consider the problem of *information leakage.* The process of speculation was interpreted above as largely due to differences of information and belief. Nevertheless, the problem of *leakage* did not arise there because no trader regarded any other individual's knowledge or beliefs as intrinsically superior to his own. Here, we will suppose instead, everyone recognizes that some traders do and others do not possess an *informational advantage.* (Though traders with an informational advantage may not be publicly identified as such.) In the section above, better-informed individuals were seeking to *overcome* the informational disparity by signalling to potential trading partners. In this section, in contrast, the better-informed individuals are trying to *capitalize* on the disparity, by adopting a speculative position before their informational advantage disappears.

For concreteness, we can imagine that an information service μ is available which, at a certain price k, will (non-exclusively) provide any purchaser with conclusive information as to which state of the world will obtain. Initially, all the potential traders (speculators) may be assumed to have the same beliefs. But *anyone* can become better informed, and *everyone* knows that this is the case. The first, rather obvious point is that the speculative profit to those who become better informed will decrease the larger the number purchasing the information. Figure 9 illustrates a 2-state situation. An individual has an endowment $E = (\omega_1, \omega_2)$ and beliefs (π_1, π_2). With initial state-claim prices (P_1, P_2), his optimal consumption point is C_0. If he purchases information at a price k (to be paid regardless of state), his endowment shifts to $E' = (\omega_1 - k, \omega_2 - k)$. He then anticipates that with probability π_1 he will learn that the true state is $s = 1$. In

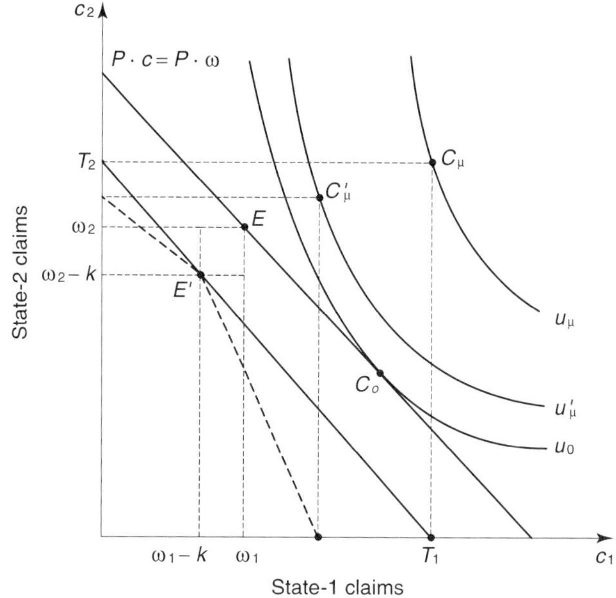

Figure 9. Trading by informed agents.

this case he will exchange all his state-2 claims for additional consumption in state 1 (point T_1). Similarly, with probability π_2 he anticipates learning that the true state is $s = 2$, in which case he sells all his state-1 claims (point T_2). The final consumption vector C_μ yields him an expected utility gain of $u_\mu - u_0$.

But, of course, the higher expected utility associated with the information service μ attracts other individuals. If the message is that the true state is $s = 1$, *all* the informed individuals will be in the market purchasing state-1 claims. This pushes up the relative price of these claims (steeper dashed budget line through E'). Similarly if the true state is $s = 2$ the price of state-2 claims is bid up (flatter dashed budget line). Final consumption is thus lower in each state, reducing the expected utility of informed agents from u_μ to u'_μ. As there is still a gain over u_0, purchase of information continues—until the utility gain due to informed trading is exactly offset by the cost k of obtaining and processing the information.

So far, it looks as if there may be an equilibrium in terms of a fraction of traders that choose to become informed. But there is a further complication. Should the true state be $s = 1$, as long as any traders at all are buying the information, the price of state-1 claims will tend to rise in comparison with the initial uninformed situation—and, of course, the reverse if $s = 2$ is going to obtain. So individuals not purchasing the information can *infer* it, simply by observing the movement of market prices! [44, Green, 1973; 45, 1977; 48, Sanford J. Grossman and Stiglitz, 1976]. They will therefore speculate in the same direction as those who have paid to become informed. With sufficiently hair-trigger reaction functions on the part of the uninformed, there will not even be a gross profit to those choosing to buy the information—so that, on net, these latter must lose.

In general, of course, prices may depend upon a great number of unknown or partially known determinants or parameters, apart from the uncertain element here that defines the state (e.g., the weather). But the same general result will continue to hold, so long as the price vector $p(I)$, which would prevail if *all* agents had all the available information I, differs for each different I. Then the function $p(I)$ is invertible, and $I = f^{-1}(p)$. That is, the information can be computed from the prices; or, the price vector p is a sufficient statistic for I [71, Richard E. Kihlstrom and Leonard J. Mirman, 1975; 47, Grossman, 1977]. With a finite number of states, it is almost certainly the case that even in very incomplete markets the function $p(I)$ is invertible [109, Radner, 1979]. Thus there is almost certainly a "fulfilled-expectations" equilibrium in which each agent correctly infers aggregate information from the price vector p. However, this conclusion relies on a rather extreme "correct conditional price forecasting" assumption, in which each trader is able to *compute* the equilibrium price vector associated with each state of the world.

As in the case of the signalling models considered above, there is a market externality here that tends to break down any equilibrium in which information is obtained only at a cost. If none are informed, there is potential profit in becoming informed; yet if anyone invests in information and trades accordingly, he loses relative to those who have invested. The analog of the "reactive equilibrium" concept here would evidently be the corner solution with no informational investments. However, in contrast with the signalling case, an interior solution can be obtained by introducing noise or lags. If only imperfect information about the state of nature can be inferred by observing prices (as will generally be the case with a continuum of states [47, Grossman, 1977; 69, James S. Jordan, 1976]), or if the informed individual can make his commitments before the uninformed can fully react, there will tend to be an equilibrium *fraction* of traders who choose to become informed.

Rational expectations and informational efficiency

There is much confusion about both the logical meaning and the descriptive realism of the interrelated concepts of "rational expectations" and "informational efficiency."

The original idea of rational expectations is that anticipations "are essentially the same as the predictions of the relevant economic theory" [100, John F. Muth, 1961, p. 316]. This can be visualized in a very simple temporal model without *exogenous* uncertainty—that is, a world where present and future endowed supplies, productive opportunities, utility functions, etc., are all perfectly known and determinate. In such a world there would, in general, be trading at different dates. And since the relative supply-demand situations for the various goods may change as the economy moves on its world-line, there is no reason to expect the *spot* price ratios to remain constant over time.

Suppose that, despite universal knowledge of the exogenous data, traders have divergent beliefs about the implied solution values for *endogenous* variables—in particular, about future spot prices. This possibility is of interest in connection with the problem of incompleteness of market regimes discussed above. For concreteness, think of a two-period world. *Complete* markets at the current date (the analog of *Complete Conditional* Markets as discussed earlier, but in the absence of exogenous uncertainty there is only one state) would provide for trading in the $2G$ claims c_{tg} at prices P_{tg}^0—where the first subscript represents the effective date of the claim ($t = 0$, 1) and the second designates the good ($g = 1, \ldots, G$), while the superscript indicates the *trading date*. In an *incomplete* market regime with *no* futures markets, the future-dated claims c_{1g} would not be tradable at $t = 0$, so that the prices P_{1g}^0 would not exist. (In either case, however, there could be later spot trading at $t = 1$, at prices P_{1g}^1).

In either market regime, individuals' trading decisions today will depend upon their anticipations as to the later spot prices P_{1g}^1, since there will in general be both productive interdependencies (e.g., storage possibilities) and utility complementarities between the two dates. And, in consequence, the equilibrium prices in today's and tomorrow's markets will generally both depend upon the anticipations that the individuals hold today. But, following a familiar theme of the previous discussion, a *complete* regime at $t = 0$ makes "correct price forecasting" at $t = 1$ easy: "no change" will be the correct prediction. That is, if all traders forecast that the *later spot* price ratios will equal the *current futures* price ratios—$P_{1g'}^0 / P_{1g''}^0 = P_{1g'}^1 / P_{1g''}^1$—and make their current trading decisions accordingly, their anticipations will be borne out.

It is thus the absence of futures markets that creates the forecasting problem envisaged by the rational expectations literature [9, Arrow, 1978]. We have seen that, strictly speaking, with incomplete markets today individuals cannot compute (from information privately available to them) tomorrow's spot prices necessary to guide today's productive and consumptive decisions. The model of rational expectations nevertheless assumes that, at least on average, they *can* do so. Each person in effect makes a guess on the basis of his private bit of information (as well as his general knowledge of relationships such as the law of supply and demand), and the errors of the various independent guesses balance out in the aggregate:

> ... allowing for cross-sectional differences in expectations is a simple matter, because their aggregate effect is negligible as long as the deviation from the rational forecast ... is not strongly correlated with those of the others. [Muth, 1961, p. 321.]

The central idea of rational expectations can of course be applied more generally than in our bare-bones illustrative example: there can be more than two dates, not *all* futures markets need be lacking, individuals can have subjective probability distributions rather than simple point estimates for the unknown future spot prices, and finally some agreed patterns of exogenous uncertainty might be introduced—as in a random shift factor for future supply and/or demand. These generalizations lead to complications that cannot be pursued here. But even in the simplest version the assumption remains a strong one, whose virtue is in enabling us to close our intertemporal models and force out solutions. We shall not attempt to comment here on the descriptive validity of these models; just how validity might be tested is not at all evident and has been the subject of controversy. One interesting point brought out by Arrow [9, 1978] is that the rational-expectations assumption in effect stands on its head the famous argument by Friedrich A. Hayek [53, 1945] about the informational function of the market system. Hayek's view was that market prices convey to traders all they need to know about the vastly detailed particular circumstances of other economic agents. Without a price system, a central planner would require an impossibly elaborate data-gathering and data-analyzing scheme to reproduce its results. But rational expectations implies that the price signals from the missing markets are not needed after all; traders can, at least on average, reproduce the missing signals on their own!

In these microeconomic applications, rational expectations essentially means correct prediction of the prices that will reign given different objective exogenous contingencies—what we have called "correct conditional price forecasting". No restrictions are placed upon subjective beliefs as to the probabilities of the different states. In contrast, a central feature of *macro*economic applications [77, Robert E. Lucas, Jr., 1972; 125, Thomas J. Sargent and Neil Wallace, 1975] has been that individuals are not only superior econometricians but clairvoyant about events as well. Frank H. Knight seems to have anticipated this view: "We are so built that what seems to us reasonable is likely to be confirmed by experience, or we could not live in the world at all" [72, 1921, p. 227]. In the present context, it is supposed that in addition to being able to analyze the macroeconomic effects of any given monetary policy, individuals can also decipher the actual monetary rule being followed.

This Lincolnesque idea that "the people can't be fooled" may be based upon viewing the underlying world process as stochastically stationary, so that individuals can gradually learn both about the effects of events upon prices and about the probability distribution of events. However, this learning evolution does not imply that beliefs would be on average correct except in the limit.

Prices in an economy will be related to the knowledge and beliefs of all participating traders—possibly weighted by endowed wealths, degree of risk-aversion, etc. Under the heading of *informational efficiency*, the issue has been raised as to whether prices "fully reflect" people's current information [35, Fama, 1970].

Unfortunately, the meaning of the term "fully reflect" has proved elusive. Mark E. Rubinstein has proposed that information be said to be already reflected in prices if, upon arrival of the message, traders have no incentive to revise portfolios [121, 1975]. On this definition, he shows that prices can almost never "fully reflect information". There are two main reasons: (1) even with agreed beliefs, incomplete regimes of *prior* markets generally make posterior trading (portfolio revision) unavoidable, and (2) with diverging beliefs and consequent speculative prior trading, it will be necessary to close out speculative positions in the posterior round.

The most widely held interpretation—what has been called the "weak form" of the proposition—is that markets are "informationally efficient" if, as a pragmatic matter, there is no way to make a profit (more precisely, to achieve an expected utility gain) from information already in the public domain. In particular, there is no way to outsmart the stockmarket by detecting patterns of price movement in the historic record.

This interpretation in effect asserts that, at least on average, individuals can *process* available information correctly. (While costs of processing may prevent perfect adjustment, errors tend to cancel out.) More specifically, this has been taken to imply that prices should follow a *martingale* process. That is, except perhaps for time and risk adjustment factors, the price today should be the mathematical expectation of the price tomorrow [123, Paul A. Samuelson, 1965]. However, it has been shown that even supposing known or agreed probabilities (without which it would be impossible to calculate mathematical expectations), only under very special conditions does a martingale in prices result [145, Susan E. Woodward, 1979]. First of all, prices are *ratios*; if a given ratio followed the martingale property, in general its reciprocal (the ratio taken the other way) would not. And even if expressed in terms of some standard numeraire commodity, prices would not follow a martingale unless there were no utility complementarities between the numeraire and other goods [122, Salant, 1976]. It has also sometimes been argued that failure of prices to follow a martingale would by definition create an arbitrage-like profit opportunity in the sense of a positive expectation of gain from holding an asset, over and above the normal interest yield. But, as we have seen from our early discussion of "private and social risk", a higher *mathematical expectation* of income does not in general represent higher *expected utility*, so this argument is erroneous.

The "strong form" of the efficient market hypothesis has been taken to mean that even *private* information cannot be profitably used (compare our discussion of "information leakage" above). This form of the hypothesis does not seem consistent with the evidence—for example, of gains from insider trading (surveyed in Thomas E. Copeland and J. Fred Weston [27, 1979, chap. 9]). As for the "weak form," numerous econometric studies have concluded that it is not possible to reject the hypothesis that price changes are independent of past prices. However, there does not yet seem to be a sufficiently well-specified model to allow testing the hypothesis that price changes are independent of *all* public information (but see Stephen Figlewski [39a, 1979]).

Informational activities, finally, have an unusual relation to economic equilibrium. Information generation is in large part a disequilibrium-creating process [129, Joseph A. Schumpeter (1911) 1936], and information dissemination a disequilibrium-repairing process. The two are intertwined, as we have seen, in very complex ways. It does not yet seem that we are very close to having an efficiency concept that can usefully be employed to measure the dynamically optimal level of such activities.

ACKNOWLEDGEMENTS

Among the very large number of people who provided comments and suggestions, we would like to thank most especially Fritz Machlup, Robert A. Jones, Mark Perlman, and Richard J. Zeckhauser. Hirshleifer's work on this paper was supported in part by National Science Foundation grant No. SOC75-15697 and by a grant from the Foundation for Research in Economics and Education. Riley's work was supported in part by National Science Foundation grant No. SOC79-07573.

REFERENCES

1. Akerlof, George A. The market for lemons: Qualitative uncertainty and the market mechanism, *Quarterly Journal of Economics*, August 1970; **84**(3): 488–500.

2. Alchian, Armen A. The meaning of utility measurements, *American Economic Review*, March 1953, **43**: 26–50.

3. Alchian, Armen A. and Demesetz, Harold. Production information costs, and economic organization, *American Economic Review*, Dec. 1972, **62**(5), 777–795.

4. Arrow, Kenneth J. Le rôle des valeurs boursières pour la répartition la meilleure des Risques. In *International Colloquium on Econometrics*, 1952. Paris: Centre National de la Recherche Scientifique, 1953. (For the English translation, see 6.)

5. Arrow, Kenneth J. Economic welfare and the allocation of resources for invention. In *The Rate and Direction of Inventive Activity: Economic and Social Factors*. Universities-NBER Conference Series. Princeton, NJ: Princeton University Press, 1962, pp. 609–625.

6. Arrow, Kenneth J. Uncertainty and the welfare economics of medical care, *American Economic Review*, Dec. 1963, **53**: 941–973.

7. Arrow, Kenneth J. The role of securities in the optimal allocation of risk-bearing, *Review of Economic Studies*, April 1964, **31**: 91–96.

8. Arrow, Kenneth J. Aspects of the theory of risk-bearing. Helsinki: Yrjö Jahnssonin Säätio, 1965.

9. Arrow Kenneth J. The future and the present in economic life, *Economic Enquiry*, April 1978, **16**(2): 157–169.

10. Arrow, Kenneth J and Fisher, Anthony C. Environmental preservation, uncertainty and irreversibility, *Quarterly Journal of Economics*, May 1974, **88**(2): 312–319.

11. Arrow, Kenneth J. and Lind, Robert C. Uncertainty and the evaluation of public investment, *American Economic Review*, June 1970, **60**(3): 364–378.

12. Bailey, Martin J. and Jensen, Michael C. Risk and the discount rate for public investment. In Michael C. Jensen ed., *Studies in the Theory of Capital Markets*. New York: Praeger, 1972, pp. 269–293.

13. Barzel, Yoram. Optimal timing of innovations, *Review of Economic Statistics*, August 1968, **50**: 348–355.

14. Baumol, William. The Neumann-Morgenstern Utility Index: An ordinalist view, *Journal of Political Economy*, Feb. 1951, **59**: 61–66.

15. Baumol, William. On taxation and the control of externalities, *American Economic Review*, June 1972, **62**(3): 307–322.

16. Bergstrom, Theodore. Preference and choice in matters of life and death, Appendix 1 of *Applying cost-benefit concepts to projects which affect human mortality*. By Jack Hirshleifer, Theodore Bergstrom, and Edward Rappaport. UCLA School of Engineering and Applied Science, ENG-7478, Nov. 1974.

17. Borch Karl. Indifference curves and uncertainty, *Swedish Journal of Economics*, March 1968, **70**: 19–24.

18   Brainard, William C. and Dolbear, F. Trenery Jr. Social risk and financial markets, *American Economic Review*, May 1971, **61**(2): 360–370.

19. Calabresi, Guido. *The Costs of Accidents: A Legal and Economic Analysis*. New Haven: Yale University Press, 1970.

20. Cheung, Steven N. S. *The Theory of Share Tenancy: With Special Application to Asian Agriculture and the First Phase of Taiwan Land Reform*. Chicago: University of Chicago Press, 1969.

21. Cheung Steven N. S. Transaction costs, risk aversion, and the choice of contractual arrangements, *Journal of Law and Economics*, April 1969, **12**(1): 23–42.

22. Cheung, Steven N. S. *Property Rights and Inventions*, University of Washington Institute of Economic Research, Report No. 79–11, 1979.

23. Cheung, Steven N. S. *The Right To Invent and the Right To an Invention*, University of Washington Institute of Economic Research, Report No. 79–13, 1979.

24. Conley, Bryan C. The value of human life in the demand for safety, *American Economic Review*, March 1976, **66**(1): 45–55.

25. Cook, Philip J. and Graham, Daniel A. The demand for insurance and protection: The case of irreplaceable commodities, *Quarterly Journal of Economics*, Feb. 1977, **91**(1): 143–156.

26. Cootner, Paul H. Speculation, Hedging and Arbitrage. In *International Encyclopaedia of the Social Sciences*. Vol. 15. New York: Macmillan, Free Press, 1968, 117–121.

27. Copeland, Thomas E. and Weston, J. Fred. *Financial Theory and Corporate Policy*. Reading, MA: Addison-Wesley, 1979.

28. DeAngelo, Harry. *Three Essays in Financial Economics*. UCLA Ph.D. dissertation, 1979.

29. Debreu, Gerard. *Theory of Value: An Axiomatic Analysis of Economic Equilibrium*. New York. Wiley, 1959.

30. Diamond, Peter A. The role of a stock market in a general equilibrium model with technological uncertainty, *American Economic Review*, Sept. 1967, **57**: 759–776.

31. Diamond, Peter A. Accident law and resource allocation, *Bell Journal of Economics*, Autumn 1974, **5**(12): 366–405.

32. Drèze, Jacques H. Market allocation under uncertainty, *European Economic Review*, Winter 1970–71, **2**(2): 133–165.

33. Ehrlich, Isaac and Becker, Gary S. Market insurance, self-insurance, and self-protection, *Journal of Political Economy*, July-August 1972, **80**(4): 623–648.

34. Ekern, Steinar and Wilson, Robert. On the Theory of the firm in an economy with incomplete markets, *Bell J. Econ*, Spring 1974, **5**(1): 171–180.

35. Fama, Eugene F. Efficient capital markets: A review of theory and empirical work, *Journal of Finance*, May 1970, **25**(2): 383-417.

36. Fama, Eugene F. and Laffer, Arthur B. Information and capital markets, *Journal of Business*, July 1971, **44**(3): 289–298.

37. Fama, Eugene F. and Miller, Merton H. *The theory of finance*. New York: Holt, Rinehart Winston, 1972.

38. Feiger, George. What Is speculation? *Quarterly Journal of Economics*, Nov. 1976, **90**(4): 677–688.

39. Feldstein, Martin S. Mean-variance analysis in the theory of liquidity preference and portfolio selection, *Review of Economic Studies*, Jan. 1969, **36**(105): 5–12.

39a. Figlewski, Stephen. Subjective information and market efficiency in a betting market, *Journal of Political Economy*, Feb. 1979, **87**(1): 75–88.

40. Fisher Irving. *The Nature of Capital and Income*. New York: Macmillan, 1912.

41. Fisher, Irving *The Theory of Interest*. New York: Macmillan, 1930.

42. Friedman Milton and Savage, Leonard J. The utility analysis of choices involving risks, *Journal of Political Economy*, August 1948, **56**: 279–304.

43. Gordon H. Scott. The economic theory of a common property resource: The fishery, *Journal of Political Economy*, April 1954, **62**: 124–142.

44. Green, Jerry. Information, Efficiency and Equilibrium. Harvard Institute of Economic Research, Discussion Paper no. 284, March 1973.

45. Green, Jerry. The non-existence of informational equilibria, *Review of Economic Studies*, Oct. 1977, **44**(3), 451–463.

46. Green, Jerry. Statistical decision theory requiring incentives for information transfer. In John J. McCall, ed. *The Economics of Information and Uncertainty*. Universities-NBER Conference Series. Chicago, University of Chicago Press, 1982.

47. Grossman, Sanford J. The existence of futures markets, noisy rational expectations and informational externalities, *Review of Economic Studies*, Oct. 1977, **44**(3): 431–449.

48. Grossman, Sanford J. and Stiglitz, Joseph E. Information and competitive price systems, *American Economic Review*, May 1976, **66**(2): 246–253.

49. Groves, Theodore. Incentives in teams, *Econometrica*, July 1973, **41**(4): 617–631.

50. Hakansson, Nils H., Kunkel, J. Gregory and Ohlson, James A. Sufficient and Necessary Conditions for Information to Have Social Value in Pure Exchange, School of Business Administration, University of California, Berkeley, June 1979.

51. Harris, Milton and Raviv, Arthur. Some results on incentive contracts with applications to education and employment, health insurance, and law enforcement, *American Economic Review*, March 1978, **68**(1): 20–30.

52. Hart Oliver D. On the optimality of equilibrium when the market structure is incomplete, *Journal of Economic Theory*, Dec. 1975, **11**(3): 418–443.

53. Hayek Friedrich A. The use of knowledge in society, *American Economic Review*, Sept. 1945, **35**: 519–530.

54. Henry, Claude. Investment decisions under uncertainty: The irreversibility effect, *American Economic Review*, Dec. 1974, **64**(6): 1006–1012.

55. Hicks, John. *Value and Capital.* Second edition. Oxford: Oxford University Press, Clarendon Press, 1946.

56. Hirshleifer, Jack. Investment decision under uncertainty: Applications of the state-preference approach, *Quarterly Journal of Economics*, May 1966, **80**: 252–277.

57. Hirshleifer, Jack. *Investment, Interest, and Capital*, Englewood Cliffs, NJ: Prentice-Hall, 1970.

58. Hirshleifer, Jack. The private and social value of information and the reward to inventive activity, *American Economic Review*, Sept. 1971, **61**(4): 561–574.

59. Hirshleifer Jack. Liquidity, uncertainty, and the accumulation of information. In C. F. Carter and J. L. Ford, (eds), *Uncertainty and expectations in economics: Essays in honour of G. L. S. Shackle.* Oxford: Blackwell, 1972, pp. 136–147.

60. Hirshleifer, Jack. Where are we in the theory of information? *American Economic Review*, May 1973, **63**(2), 31–39.

61. Hirshleifer, Jack. Speculation and equilibrium: Information, risk, and markets, *Quarterly Journal of Economics*, Nov. 1975, **89**(4): 519–542.

62. Hirshleifer, Jack. The theory of speculation under alternative regimes of markets, *Journal of Finance*, Sept. 1977, **32**(4), 975–999.

63. Houthakker, Hendrik S. Can speculators forecast prices? *Review of Economic Statistics*, May 1957, **39**: 143–151.

64. Houthakker, Hendrik S. Normal Backwardation, in *Value, Capital, and Growth: Papers in Honour of Sir John Hicks.* Edited by James N. Wolfe. Edinburgh: Edinburgh University Press, 1968, pp. 193–214.

65. Jensen, Michael C. Capital Markets: Theory and Evidence, *Bell Journal of Economics*, Autumn 1972, **3**(2), 357–398.

66. Jensen, Michael C. and Meckling, William H. Theory of the firm: managerial behavior, agency costs and ownership structure, *Journal Financial Economics*, Oct. 1976, **3**(4): pp. 305–360.

67. Jones Robert A. and Ostroy, Joseph. Uncertainty and Flexibility, UCLA Discussion Paper no. 73, July, 1976.

68. Jones-Lee, Michael W. *The Value of Life: An Economic Analysis.* Chicago: University of Chicago Press, 1976.

69. Jordan, James S. *Expectations Equilibrium and Informational Efficiency for Stochastic Environments.* University of Minnesota, Centre for Economic Research, Discussion Paper no. 71, August 1976.

70. Keynes, John Maynard. *A Treatise on Money.* New York: Harcourt Brace, 1930.

71. Kihlstrom, Richard E. and Mirman, Leonard J. Information and market equilibrium, *Bell Journal of Economics*, Spring 1975, **6**(1): 357–376.

72. Knight, Frank H. *Risk, Uncertainty and Profit.* New York: Houghton Mifflin, 1921.

73. Linnerooth, Joanne, The value of human life: A review of the models, *Economic Inquiry*, Jan. 1979, **17**(1): 52–74.

74. Lintner, John. Dividends, Earnings, leverage, stock prices and the supply of capital to corporations, *Review of Economic Statistics*, August 1962, **44**: 243–269.

75. Lintner, John. The valuation of risk assets and the selection of risky investments in stock portfolios and capital budgets, *Review of Economic Statistics*, Feb. 1965, **47**: 13–37.

76. Lippman, Steven A. and McCall, John J. The economics of job search: A survey, *Economic Inquiry*, June 1976, **14**(2): 155–189.

77. Lucas, Robert E., Jr. Expectations and the neutrality of money, *Journal of Economic Theory*, April 1972, **4**(2): 103–124.

78. Luce, R. Duncan and Raiffa, Howard. *Games and Decisions: Introduction and Critical Survey.* New York: Wiley, 1957.

79. Machlup, Fritz. *The Production and Distribution of Knowledge in the United States.* Princeton, NJ: Princeton University Press, 1962.

80. Machlup, Fritz. *Patents, International Encyclopaedia of the Social Sciences. Vol. 11.* New York: Macmillan, Free Press, 1968, pp. 461–72.

81. Machlup, Fritz. Knowledge: Its creation, distribution, and economic significance. 2 vols, Princeton, NJ: Princeton University Press, 1980 and 1982, part seven: The Economics of Knowledge and Information.

82. Markowitz, Harry M. The utility of wealth, *Journal of Political Economics*, April 1952, **60**: 151–158.

83. Markowitz, Harry M. *Portfolio selection: Efficient diversification of investments.* Cowles Foundation for Research in Economics, Yale University, Monograph 16. New York: Wiley, 1959.

84. Marschak, Jacob. Role of liquidity under complete and incomplete information, *American Economic Review*, May 1949, **39**: 182–195.

85. Marschak, Jacob. Decision-making: Economic Aspects, *International Encyclopedia of the Social Sciences. Vol. 4.* New York: Macmillan, Free Press, 1968, 42–55.

86. Marschak, Jacob. Economics of information systems. In: Intriligator, M. D., ed. *Frontiers of Quantitative Economics.* Amsterdam: North-Holland, 1971, pp. 32–107.

87. Marschak, Jacob and Miyasawa, Koichi. Economic comparability of information systems, *International Economic Review*, June 1968, **9**, 137–174.

88. Marschak, Jack and Radner, Roy. *The economic theory of teams.* Cowles Foundation for Research in Economics, monograph no. 22. New Haven: Yale University Press, 1972.

89. Marschak, Thomas and Nelson, Richard. Flexibility, uncertainty, and economic theory, *Metroeconomica*, April–Dec. 1962, **14:** 42–58.

90. Marshall, John M. Private incentives and public information, *American Economic Review*, June 1974, **64**(3): 373–390.

91. Marshall, John M. Insurance theory: reserves versus mutuality, *Econ. Inquiry*, Dec. 1974, **12**(4): 476–492.

92. Marshall, John M. Moral hazard, *American Economic Review*, Dec. 1976, **66**(5): 880–890.

93. Mayshar, Joram. Should government subsidize risky private projects? *American Economic Review*, March 1977, **67**(2): 20–28.

94. McCall, John J. The economics of information and optimal stopping rules, *J. Bus.*, July 1965, **38**, 300–317.

95. McKinnon, Ronald I. Futures markets, buffer stocks, and income stability for primary producers, *Journal of Political Economy*, Dec. 1967, **75**: 844–861.

96. Merton, Robert C. Investment theory. In Arrow, K. J. and Intriligator, M. D., eds. *Handbook of Mathematical Economics.* Amsterdam: North-Holland, 1980.

97. Mishan, Ezra J. Evaluation of life and limb, *Journal of Political Economy*, July/August 1971, 79(4): 687–705.

98. Modigliani, Franco and Miller, Merton H. The cost of capital, corporation finance and the theory of investment, *American Economic Review*, June 1958, **48**, 261–297.

99. Mossin, Jan. Equilibrium in a capital asset market, *Econometrica*, Oct. 1966, **34**: 768–783.

100. Muth, John F. Rational expectations and the theory of price movements, *Econometrica*, July 1961, **29**: 315–335.

101. Nelson, Phillip. Advertising as information, *Journal of Political Economy*, July/August 1974, **82**(4): 729–754.

102. Nelson, Phillips. The economic consequences of advertising, *Journal of Business*, April 1975, **48**(2): 213–241.

103. von Neumann, John and Morgenstern, Oskar. *Theory of Games and Economic Behavior.* Princeton, NJ: Princeton University Press, 1944.

104. Pauly, Mark V. The economics of moral hazard: Comment, *American Economic Review*, June 1968, **58**: 531–536.

105. Pearl, Judea. An economic basis for certain methods of evaluating probabilistic forecasts, *International Journal Man-Machine Studies*, 1978, **10**, 175–183.

106. Phelps, Edmund S., *et al. Microeconomics Foundations of Employment and Inflation Theory.* New York: Norton, 1970.

107. Pratt, John W. Risk aversion in the small and in the large, *Econometrica*, Jan–April 1964, **32**: 122–136.

108. Radner, Roy. Competitive equilibrium under uncertainty, *Econometrica*, Jan. 1968, **36**: 31–58.

109. Radner, Roy. Rational expectations equilibrium: Generic existence and the information revealed by prices, *Econometrica*, May 1979, **47**(3): 655–678.
110. Radner, Roy and Stiglitz, Joseph E. A Nonconcavity in the Value of Information, unpublished manuscript, July 1976.
111. Raiffa, Howard. *Decision Analysis: Introductory Lectures on Choices Under Uncertainty*. Reading, Mass.: Addison-Wesley, 1968.
112. Reid, Joseph D., Jr. Sharecropping and agricultural uncertainty, *Economic Development and Cultural Change*, April 1976, **24**(3): 549–576.
113. Riley, John G. Competitive signalling, *Journal of Economic Theory*, April 1975, **10**(2): 174–186.
114. Riley, John G. Information, screening and human capital, *American Economic Review*, May 1976, **66**(2): 254–260.
115. Riley, John G. Informational equilibrium, *Econometrica*, March 1979, **47**(2): 331–359.
116. Riley, John G. Testing the educational screening hypothesis, *Journal of Political Economy*, Oct. 1979, **87**(5): Part 2, 227–244.
117. Rothschild, Michael. Models of market organization with imperfect information: A survey, *Journal of Political Economy*, Nov./Dec. 1973, **81**(6): 1283–1308.
118. Rothschild, Michael and Stiglitz, Joseph E. Increasing risk: I. A definition, *Journal of Economic Theory*, Sept. 1970, **2**(3): 225–243.
119. Rothschild, Michael and Stiglitz, Joseph E. Increasing risk: II. Economic consequences, *Journal of Economic Theory*, March 1971, **3**(1): 66–84.
120. Rothschild, Michael and Stiglitz, Joseph E. Equilibrium in competitive insurance markets: An essay on the economics of imperfect information, *Quarterly Journal of Economics*, Nov. 1976, **90**(4): 629–649.
121. Rubinstein, Mark E. Securities market efficiency in an Arrow–Debreu economy, *American Economic Review*, Dec. 1975, **65**(5): 812–824.
122. Salant, Stephen W. Hirshleifer on speculation, *Quarterly Journal of Economics*, Nov. 1976, **90**(4): 667–676.
123. Samuelson, Paul A. Proof that properly anticipated prices fluctuate randomly, *Industrial Management Review*, Spring 1965, **6**(2): 41–49.
124. Sandmo, Agnar. Discount rates for public investment under uncertainty, *International Economic Review*, June 1972, **13**(2): 287–302.
125. Sargent, Thomas J. and Wallace, Neil. Rational expectations, the optimal monetary instrument, and the optimal money supply rule, *Journal of Political Economy*, April 1975, **83**(2): 241–254
126. Savage, Leonard J. *The Foundations of Statistics*. New York: Wiley, 1954.
127. Schelling, Thomas C. The life you save may be your own. In: Chase, Samuel B., Jr. ed. *Problems in Public Expenditures Analysis*. Washington, D.C.: Brookings Institution, 1968, pp. 127–162.
128. Schlaifer, Robert. *Probability and Statistics for Business Decisions*. New York: McGraw-Hill, 1959.
129. Schumpeter, Joseph A. *The Theory of Economic Development*. Translated from the German by Redvers Opie. Cambridge, MA: Harvard University Press, [1911] 1936.
130. Sharpe, William F. Capital asset prices: A theory of market equilibrium under conditions of risk, *Journal of Finance*, Sept. 1964, **19**: 425–442.
131. Sharpe, William F. *Investments*, Englewood Cliffs, NJ: Prentice-Hall, 1978.
132. Shavell, Steven. On valuable opinion and the efficiency of the price system under uncertainty, Harvard Institute of Economic Research, Discussion Paper #458, March 1976.
133. Shavell, Steven. Do managers use their information efficiently? *American Economic Review*, Dec. 1978, **68**(5): 935–937.
134. Spence, A. Michael. *Market Signaling: Informational Transfer in Hiring and Related Processes*. Cambridge, MA: Harvard University Press, 1974.
135. Spence, A. Michael and Zeckhauser, Richard. Insurance, information, and individual action, *American Economic Review*, May 1971, **61**(2): 380–387.
136. Stigler, George J. The economics of information, *J. Polit. Econ.*, June 1961, **69**: 213–225.
137. Stigler, George J. Information in the labor market, *J. Polit. Econ.*, Oct. 1962, **70**(5): 94–105.

138. Stiglitz, Joseph E. The theory of screening, education, and the distribution of income, *American Economic Review*, June 1975, **65**(3): 283–300.
139. Strotz, Robert H. Cardinal utility, *American Economic Review*, May 1953, **43**, 384–397.
140. Thaler, Richard H. and Rosen, Sherwin. The value of saving a life: Evidence from the labor market, in household production and consumption: Papers. Edited by Nestor E. Terleckyj. National Bureau of Economic Research, Studies in Income and Wealth, Vol. 40. New York: NBER, 1976, pp. 265–98.
141. Tobin, James. Liquidity preference as behavior towards risk, *Review of Economic Study*, Feb. 1958, **25**: 65–86.
142. Townsend, Robert M. On the optimality of forward markets, *American Economic Review*, March, 1978, **68**(1): 54–66.
143. Vickrey, William. Automobile accidents, tort law, externalities, and insurance: An economist's critique, *Law and Contemporary Problems*, summer 1968, **33**(3): 464–487.
144. Wilson, Charles A. A model of insurance markets with incomplete information, *Journal of Economic Theory*, Dec. 1977, **16**(2): 167–207.
145. Woodward, Susan E. *Two Essays in the Theory of Competitive Markets for Contingent Claims.* UCLA Ph.D. dissertation, 1979.
146. Working Holbrook. Futures trading and hedging, *American Economic Review*, June 1953, **43**: 314–343.
147. Working, Holbrook. New concepts concerning futures markets and prices, *American Economic Review*, June 1962, **52**: 431–59.
148. Zeckhauser, Richard. Medical insurance: A case study of the trade-off between risk spreading and appropriate incentives, *Journal of Economic Theory*, March 1970, **2**(1): 10–26.
149. Zeckhauser, Richard. Risk spreading and distribution. In: Hochman, Harold M. and Peterson, George E., eds. *Redistribution Through Public Choice*. New York: Columbia University Press, 1974, 206–228.
150. Zorn, Thomas S. *Information differences, the stockmarket, and management incentives.* UCLA Ph.D. dissertation, 1978.

7

Choice Under Uncertainty: Problems Solved and Unsolved

Mark J. Machina

Fifteen years ago, the theory of choice under uncertainty could be considered one of the "success stories" of economic analysis: it rested on solid axiomatic foundations, it had seen important breakthroughs in the analytics of risk, risk aversion and their applications to economic issues, and it stood ready to provide the theoretical underpinnings for the newly emerging "information revolution" in economics.[1] Today choice under uncertainty is a field in flux: the standard theory is being challenged on several grounds from both within and outside economics. The nature of these challenges, and of our profession's responses to them, is the topic of this chapter.

The following section provides a brief description of the economist's canonical model of choice under uncertainty, the expected utility model of preferences over random prospects. I shall present this model from two different perspectives. The first perspective is the most familiar, and has traditionally been the most useful for addressing standard economic questions. However the second, more modern perspective will be the most useful for illustrating some of the problems which have beset the model, as well as some of the proposed responses.

Each of the subsequent sections is devoted to one of these problems. All are important, some are more completely "solved" than others. In each case I shall begin with an example or description of the phenomenon in question. I shall then review the empirical evidence regarding the uniformity and extent of the phenomenon. Finally, I shall report on how these findings have changed, or are likely to change, or ought to change, the way we view and model economic behavior under uncertainty. On this last topic, the disclaimer that "my opinions are my own" has more than the usual significance.[2]

Reprinted with permission from *Journal of Economic Perspectives*, Vol. 1, No. 1, 1987, pp. 121–154

THE EXPECTED UTILITY MODEL

The classical perspective: cardinal utility and attitudes toward risk

In light of current trends toward generalizing this model, it is useful to note that the expected utility hypothesis was itself first proposed as an alternative to an earlier, more restrictive theory of risk-bearing. During the development of modern probability theory in the 17th century, mathematicians such as Blaise Pascal and Pierre de Fermat assumed that the attractiveness of a gamble offering the payoffs $(x_1, \ldots, x_n)$ with probabilities $(p_1, \ldots, p_n)$ was given by its expected value $\bar{x} = \sum x_i p_i$. The fact that individuals consider more than just expected value, however, was dramatically illustrated by an example posed by Nicholas Bernoulli in 1728 and now known as the *St Petersburg Paradox*:

> Suppose someone offers to toss a fair coin repeatedly until it comes up heads, and to pay you $1 if this happens on the first toss, $2 if it takes two tosses to land a head, $4 if it takes three tosses, $8 if it takes four tosses, etc. What is the largest sure gain you would be willing to forgo in order to undertake a single play of this game?

Since this gamble offers a $1/2$ chance of winning $1, a $1/4$ chance of winning $2, etc., its expected value is $(1/2) \cdot \$1 + (1/4) \cdot \$2 + (1/8) \cdot \$4 + \cdots = \$1/2 + \$1/2 + \$1/2 + \cdots = \$\infty$, so it should be preferred to any finite sure gain. However, it is clear that few inividuals would forgo more than a moderate amount for a one-shot play. Although the unlimited financial backing needed to actually make this offer is somewhat unrealistic, it is not essential for making the point: agreeing to limit the game to at most one million tosses will still lead to a striking discrepancy between most individuals' valuations of the modified gamble and its expected value of $500 000.

The resolution of this paradox was proposed independently by Gabriel Cramer and Nicholas's cousin Daniel Bernoulli (Bernoulli, 1738/1954). Arguing that a gain of $200 was not necessarily "worth" twice as much as a gain of $100, they hypothesized that the individual possesses what is now termed a *von Neumann–Morgenstern utility function* $U(\cdot)$, and rather than using expected value $\bar{x} = \sum x_i p_i$, will evaluate gambles on the basis of expected utility $\bar{u} = \sum U(x_i) p_i$. Thus the sure gain ξ which would yield the same utility as the Petersburg gamble, i.e. the certainty equivalent of this gamble, is determined by the equation

$$U(W + \xi) = (1/2) \cdot U(W + 1) + (1/4) \cdot U(W + 2) + (1/8) \cdot U(W + 4) + \cdots \quad (1)$$

where W is the individual's current wealth. If utility took the logarithmic form $U(x) \equiv \ln(x)$ and $W = \$50\,000$, for example, the individual's certainty equivalent ξ would only be about $9, even though the gamble has an infinite expected value.

Although it shares the name "utility," $U(\cdot)$ is quite distinct from the ordinal utility function of standard consumer theory. While the latter can be subjected to any monotonic transformation, a von Neumann–Morgenstern utility function is cardinal in that it can only be subjected to transformations of the form $a \cdot U(x) + b \; (a > 0)$, i.e. transformations which change the origin and/or scale of the vertical axis, but do not affect the "shape" of the function.[3]

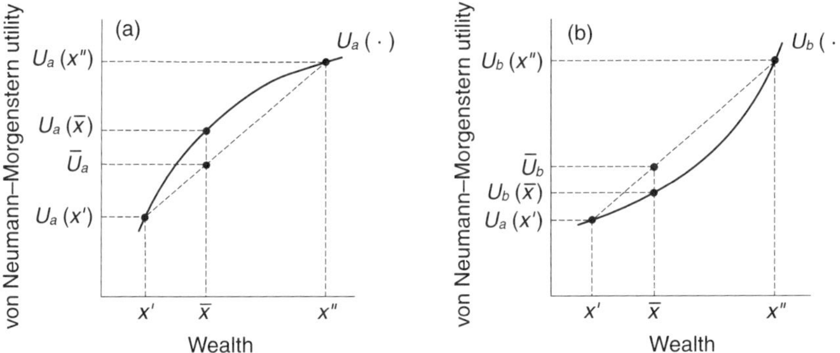

Figure 1. (a) Concave utility function of a risk averter. (b) Convex utility function of a risk lover.

To see how this shape determines risk attitudes, consider Figures 1a and 1b. The monotonicity of $U_a(\cdot)$ and $U_b(\cdot)$ in the figures reflects the property of stochastic dominance preference, where one lottery is said to stochastically dominate another one if it can be obtained from it by shifting probability from lower to higher outcome levels.[4] Stochastic dominance preference is thus the probabilistic analogue of the attitude that "more is better."

Consider a gamble offering a $2/3:1/3$ chance of the outcomes x' or x''. The points $\bar{x} = (2/3) \cdot x' + (1/3) \cdot x''$ in the figures give the expected value of this gamble, and $\bar{u}_a = (2/3) \cdot U_a(x') + (1/3) \cdot U_a(x'')$ and $\bar{u}_b = (2/3) \cdot U_b(x') + (1/3) \cdot U_b(x'')$ give its expected utilities for $U_a(\cdot)$ and $U_b(\cdot)$. For the concave utility function $U_a(\cdot)$ we have $U_a(\bar{x}) > \bar{u}_a$, which implies that this individual would prefer a sure gain of x (which would yield utility $U_a(\bar{x})$) to the gamble. Since someone with a concave utility function will in fact always prefer receiving the expected value of a gamble to the gamble itself, concave utility functions are termed risk averse. For the convex utility function $U_b(\cdot)$ we have $\bar{u}_b > U_b(\bar{x})$, and since this preference for bearing the risk rather than receiving the expected value will also extend to all gambles, $U_b(\cdot)$ is termed risk loving. In their famous article, Friedman and Savage (1948) showed how a utility function which was concave at low wealth levels and convex at high wealth levels could explain the behavior of individuals who both incur risk by purchasing lottery tickets as well as avoid risk by purchasing insurance. Algebraically, Arrow (1965) and Pratt (1964) have shown how the degree of concavity of a utility function, as measured by the curvature index $-U''(x)/U'(x)$, determines how risk attitudes, and hence behavior, will vary with wealth or across individuals in a variety of situations. If $U_c(\cdot)$ is at least as risk averse as $U_d(\cdot)$ in the sense that $-U_c''(x)/U_c'(x) \geq -U_d''(x)/U_d'(x)$ for all x, then an individual with utility function $U_c(\cdot)$ would be willing to pay at least as much for insurance against any risk as would someone with utility function $U_d(\cdot)$.

Since a knowledge of $U(\cdot)$ would allow us to predict preferences (and hence behavior) in any risky situation, experimenters and applied decision analysts are frequently interested in eliciting or recovering their subjects' (or clients') von Neumann–Morgenstern utility functions. One method of doing so is termed the fractile method. This approach begins by adopting the normalization $U(0) = 0$ and $U(M) = 1$ (see Note 3) and fixing a "mixture probability" $\bar{p}$, say $\bar{p} = 1/2$. The next step involves finding the individual's certainty equivalent ξ_1 of a $1/2 : 1/2$ chance of M or 0, which implies that $U(\xi_1) = (1/2) \cdot U(M) + (1/2) \cdot U(0) = 1/2$. Finding the certainty equivalents of the $1/2 : 1/2$ chances of ξ_1 or 0 and of M or ξ_1 yields the values ξ_2 and ξ_3 which solve $U(\xi_2) = 1/4$ and $U(\xi_3) = 3/4$. By repeating this procedure (i.e. $1/8$, $3/8$, $5/8$, $7/8$, $1/16$, $3/16$, etc.), the utility function can (in the limit) be completely assessed.

Our discussion so far has paralleled the economic literature of the 1960s and 1970s by emphasizing the flexibility of the expected utility model compared to the Pascal–Fermat expected value approach. However, the need to analyze and respond to growing empirical challenges has led economists in the 1980s to concentrate on the behavioral restrictions implied by the expected utility hypothesis. It is to these restrictions that we now turn.

A modern perspective: linearity in the probabilities as a testable hypothesis

As a theory of individual behavior, the expected utility model shares many of the underlying assumptions of standard consumer theory. In each case we assume that the objects of choice, either commodity bundles or lotteries, can be unambiguously and objectively described, and that situations which ultimately imply the same set of availabilities (e.g. the same budget set) will lead to the same choice. In each case we also assume that the individual is able to perform the mathematical operations necessary to actually determine the set of availabilities, e.g. to add up the quantities in different sized containers or calculate the probabilities of compound or conditional events. Finally, in each case we assume that preferences are transitive, so that if an individual prefers one object (either a commodity bundle or a risky prospect) to a second, and prefers this second object to a third, he or she will prefer the first object to the third. We shall examine the validity of these assumptions for choice under uncertainty in some of the following sections.

However, the strongest implication of the expected utility hypothesis stems from the form of the expected utility maximand or preference function $\sum U(x_i)p_i$. Although this preference function generalizes the expected value form $\sum x_i p_i$ by dropping the property of linearity in the payoffs (the x_i's), it retains the other key property of this form, namely linearity in the probabilities.

Graphically, we may illustrate the property of linearity in the probabilities by considering the set of all lotteries or prospects over the fixed outcome levels $x_1 < x_2 < x_3$, which can be represented by the set of all probability triples of the form $P = (p_1, p_2, p_3)$ where $p_i = \text{prob}(x_i)$ and $\sum p_i = 1$. Since $p_2 = 1 - p_1 - p_3$, we can represent these lotteries by the points in the unit triangle in the (p_1, p_3) plane, as in Figure 2.[5] Since upward movements in the triangle increase p_3 at the expense of p_2 (i.e. shift probability from the outcome x_2 up to x_3) and leftward movements reduce p_1 to the benefit of p_2 (shift probability from x_1 up to x_2), these movements (and more generally, all northwest movements) lead to stochastically dominating lotteries and would accordingly be preferred. Finally, since the individual's indifference curves in the (p_1, p_3) diagram are given by the solutions to the linear equation

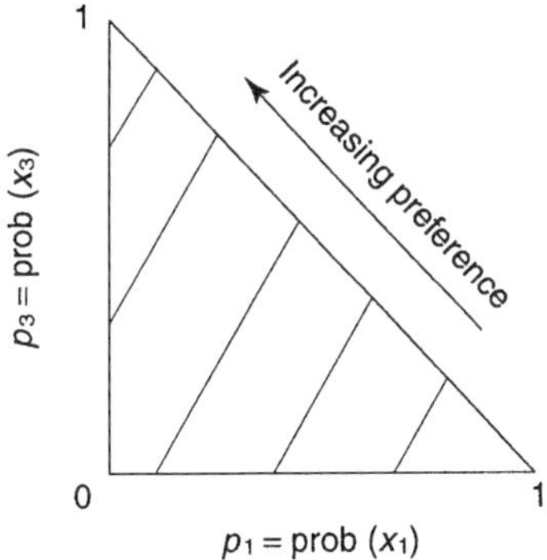

Figure 2. Expected utility indifference curves in the triangle diagram.

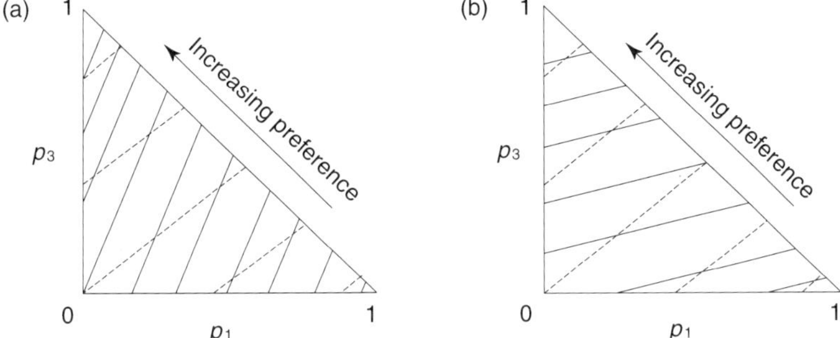

Figure 3. (a) Relatively steep indifference curves of a risk averter. (b) Relatively flat indifference curves of a risk lover. (Solid lines are expected utility indifference curves; dashed lines are iso-expected value lines.)

$$\bar{u} = \sum_{i=1}^{3} U(x_i)p_i = U(x_1)p_1 + U(x_2)(1 - p_1 - p_3) + U(x_3)p_3 = \text{constant} \qquad (2)$$

they will consist of parallel straight lines of slope $[U(x_2) - U(x_1)]/[U(x_3) - U(x_2)]$, with more preferred indifference curves lying to the northwest. This implies that in order to know an expected utility maximizer's preferences over the entire triangle, it suffices to know the slope of a single indifference curve.

To see how this diagram can be used to illustrate attitudes toward risk, consider Figures 3a and 3b. The dashed lines in the figures are not indifference curves but rather *iso-expected value lines*, i.e. solutions to

$$\bar{x} = \sum_{i=1}^{3} x_i p_i = x_1 p_1 + x_2(1 - p_1 - p_3) + x_3 p_3 = \text{constant} \qquad (3)$$

Since northeast movements along these lines do not change the expected value of the prospect, but do increase the probabilities of the tail outcomes x_1 and x_3 at the expense of the middle outcome x_2, they are examples of *mean preserving spreads* or "pure" increases in risk (Rothschild and Stiglitz, 1970). When the utility function $U(\cdot)$ is concave (i.e. risk averse), its indifference curves can be shown to be steeper than the iso-expected value lines as in Figure 3a,[6] and such increases in risk will lead to lower indifference curves. When $U(\cdot)$ is convex (risk loving), its indifference curves will be flatter than the iso-expected value lines (as in Figure 3b) and increases in risk will lead to higher indifference curves. If we compare two different utility functions, the one which is more risk averse (in the above Arrow-Pratt sense) will possess the steeper indifference curves.

Behaviorally, we can view the property of linearity in the probabilities as a restriction on the individual's preferences over probability mixtures of lotteries. If $P^*=(p_1^*,\ldots,p_n^*)$ and $P=(p_1,\ldots,p_n)$ are two lotteries over a common outcome set $\{x_1,\ldots,x_n\}$, the $\alpha:(1-\alpha)$ probability mixture of P^* and P is the lottery $\alpha P^*+(1-\alpha)P=(\alpha p_1^*+(1-\alpha)p_1,\ldots,\alpha p_n^*+(1-\alpha)p_n)$. This may be thought of as that prospect which yields the same ultimate probabilities over $\{x_1,\ldots,x_n\}$ as the two-stage lottery which offers an $\alpha:(1-\alpha)$ chance of winning either P^* or P. Since linearity in the probabilities implies that $\sum U(x_i)(\alpha p_i^*+(1-\alpha)p_i)=\alpha\cdot\sum U(x_i)p_i^*+(1-\alpha)\cdot\sum U(x_i)p_i$, expected utility maximizers will exhibit the following property, known as the *Independence Axiom* (Samuelson, 1952):

> If the lottery P^* is preferred (resp. indifferent) to the lottery P, then the mixture $\alpha P^*+(1-\alpha)P^{**}$ will be preferred (resp. indifferent) to the mixture $\alpha P+(1-\alpha)P^{**}$ for all $\alpha>0$ and P^{**}.

This property, which is in fact equivalent to linearity in the probabilities, can be interpreted as follows:

> In terms of the ultimate probabilities over the outcomes $\{x_1,\ldots,x_n\}$ choosing between the mixtures $\alpha P^*+(1-\alpha)P^{**}$ and $\alpha P+(1-\alpha)P^{**}$ is the same as being offered a coin with a probability of $1-\alpha$ of landing tails, in which case you will obtain the lottery P^{**}, and being asked before the flip whether you would rather have P^* or P in the event of a head. Now either the coin will land tails, in which case your choice won't have mattered, or else it will land heads, in which case you are "in effect" back to a choice between P^* or P, and it is only "rational" to make the same choice as you would before.

Although this is a prescriptive argument, it has played a key role in economists' adoption of expected utility as a descriptive theory of choice under uncertainty. As the evidence against the model mounts, this has lead to a growing tension between those who view economic analysis as the description and prediction of what they consider to be rational behavior and those who view it as the description and prediction of observed behavior. We turn now to this evidence.

VIOLATIONS OF LINEARITY IN THE PROBABILITIES

The Allais paradox and "fanning out"

One of the earliest and best known examples of systematic violation of linearity in the probabilities (or equivalently, of the independence axiom) is the well-known *Allais*

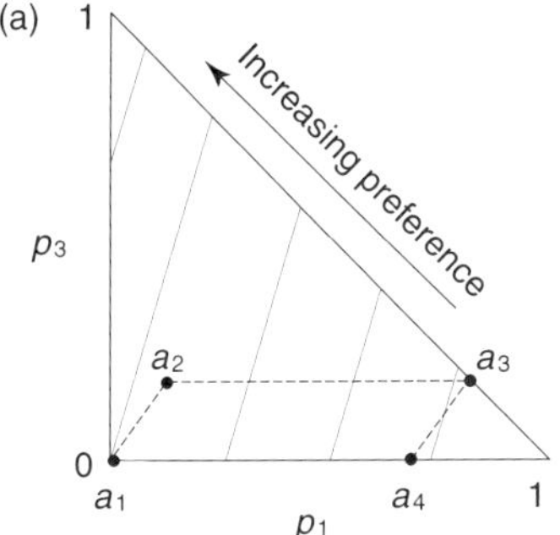

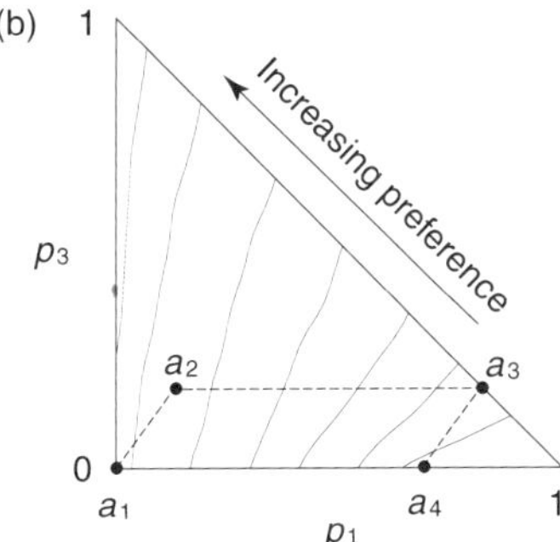

Figure 4. (a) Expected utility indifference curves and the Allais Paradox. (b) Indifference curves which "fan out" and the Allais Paradox.

Paradox (Allais, 1953, 1979). This problem involves obtaining the individual's preferred option from each of the following two pairs of gambles (readers who have never seen this problem may want to circle their own choice from each pair before proceeding):

$$a_1: \left\{ 1.00 \text{ chance of } \$1\,000\,000 \right. \quad \text{versus} \quad a_2: \left\{ \begin{array}{l} .10 \text{ chance of } \$5\,000\,000 \\ .89 \text{ chance of } \$1\,000\,000 \\ .01 \text{ chance of } \$0 \end{array} \right.$$

and

$$a_3: \left\{ \begin{array}{l} .10 \text{ chance of } \$5\,000\,000 \\ .90 \text{ chance of } \$0 \end{array} \right. \quad \text{versus} \quad a_4: \left\{ \begin{array}{l} .11 \text{ chance of } \$1\,000\,000 \\ .89 \text{ chance of } \$0 \end{array} \right.$$

Defining $\{x_1, x_2, x_3\} = \{\$0; \$1\,000\,000; \$5\,000\,000\}$, these four gambles are seen from a parallelogram in the (p_1, p_3) triangle, as in Figures 4a and 4b. Under the expected utility hypothesis, therefore, a preference for a_1 in the first pair would indicate that the individual's indifference curves were relatively steep (as in Figure 4a), and hence a preference for a_4 in the second pair. In the alternative case of relatively flat indifference curves, the gambles a_2 and a_3 would be preferred.[7] However, researchers such as Allais (1953), Morrison (1967), Raiffa (1968) and Slovic and Tversky (1974) have found that the modal if not majority preferences of subjects has been for a_1 in the first pair and a_3 in the second, which implies that indifference curves are not parallel but rather fan out, as in Figure 4b.

One of the criticisms of this evidence has been that individuals whose choices violated the independence axiom would "correct" themselves once the nature of their violation was revealed by an application of the above coin-flip argument. Thus, while even Savage chose a_1 and a_3 when first presented with this example, he concluded upon reflection that these preferences were in error (Savage, 1954, pp. 101–103).

Although his own reaction was undoubtedly sincere, the hypothesis that individuals would invariably react in such a manner has not been sustained in direct empirical testing. In experiments where subjects were asked to respond to Allais-type problems and then presented with arguments both for and against the expected utility position, neither MacCrimmon (1968), Moskowitz (1974) nor Slovic and Tversky (1974) found predominant net swings toward the expected utility choices.

Additional evidence of fanning out

Although the Allais Paradox was originally dismissed as an isolated example, it is now known to be a special case of a general empirical pattern termed the *common consequence effect*. This effect involves pairs of probability mixtures of the form:

$$b_1: \alpha\delta_x + (1-\alpha)P^{**} \quad \text{versus} \quad b_2: \alpha P + (1-\alpha)P^{**}$$

and

$$b_3: \alpha\delta_x + (1-\alpha)P^* \quad \text{versus} \quad b_4: \alpha P + 1(1-\alpha)P^*$$

where δ_x denotes the prospects which yields x with certainty, P involves outcomes both greater and less than x, and P^{**} stochastically dominates P^*.[8] Although the independence axiom clearly implies choices of either b_1 and b_3 (if δ_x is preferred to P) or else b_2 and b_4 (if P is preferred to δ_x), researchers have found a tendency for subjects to choose b_1 in the first pair and b_4 in the second (MacCrimmon, 1968; MacCrimmon and Larsson, 1979; Kahneman and Tversky, 1979; Chew and Waller, 1986). When the distributions δ_x, P, P^* and P^{**} are each over a common outcome set $\{x_1, x_2, x_3\}$, the prospects b_1, b_2, b_3 and b_4 will again form a parallelogram in the (p_1, p_3) triangle, and a choice of b_1 and b_4 again implies indifference curves which fan out, as in Figure 4b.

The intuition behind this phenomenon can be described in terms of the above "coin-flip" scenario. According to the independence axiom, preferences over what would occur in event of a head should not depend upon what would occur in the event of a tail. In fact, however, they may well depend upon what would otherwise happen.[9] The common consequence effect states that the better off individuals would be in the event of a tail (in the sense of stochastic dominance), the more risk averse they become over what they would receive in the event of a head. Intuitively, if the distribution P^{**} in the pair $\{b_1, b_2\}$ involves very high outcomes, I may prefer not to bear further risk in the unlucky event that I don't receive it, and prefer the sure outcome x over the distribution P in this event (i.e. choose b_1 over b_2). But if P^* in $\{b_3, b_4\}$ involves very low outcomes, I may be more willing to bear risk in the (lucky) event that I don't receive it, and prefer the lottery P to the outcome x in this case (i.e. choose b_4 over b_3). Note that it is not my beliefs regarding the probabilities in P which are affected here, merely my willingness to bear them.[10]

A second class of systematic violations, stemming from another early example of Allais (1953), is known as the *common ratio effect*. This phenomenon involves pairs of

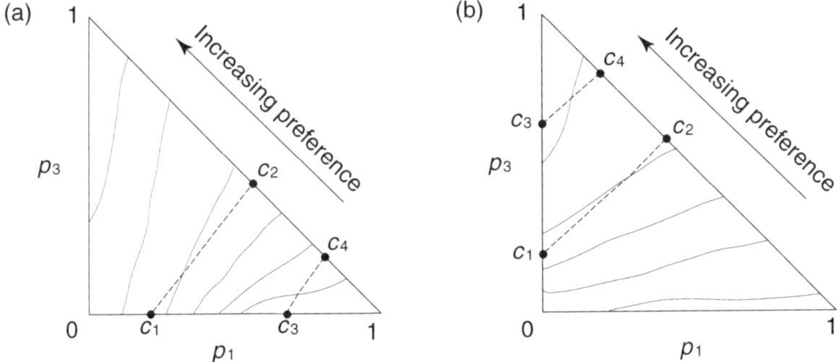

Figure 5. (a) Indifference curves which fan out and the common ratio effect. (b) Indifference curves which fan out and the common ratio effect with negative payoffs.

prospects of the form:

$$c_1: \begin{cases} p \text{ chance of } \$X \\ 1 - p \text{ chance of } \$0 \end{cases} \quad \text{versus} \quad c_2: \begin{cases} q \text{ chance of } \$Y \\ 1 - q \text{ chance of } \$0, \end{cases}$$

and

$$c_3: \begin{cases} rp \text{ chance of } \$X \\ 1 - rp \text{ chance of } \$0 \end{cases} \quad \text{versus} \quad c_4: \begin{cases} rq \text{ chance of } \$Y \\ 1 - rq \text{ chance of } \$0, \end{cases}$$

where $p > q$, $0 < X < Y$ and $r \in (0, 1)$, and includes the "certainty effect" of Kahneman and Tversky (1979) and the ingenious "Bergen Paradox" of Hagen (1979) as special cases.[11] Setting $\{x_1, x_2, x_3\} = \{0, X, Y\}$ and plotting these prospects in the (p_1, p_3) triangle, the segments $\overline{c_1 c_2}$ and $\overline{c_3 c_4}$ are seen to be parallel (as in Figure 5a), so that the expected utility model again predicts choices of c_1 and c_3 (if the individual's indifference curves are steep) or else c_2 and c_4 (if they are flat). However, experimental studies have found a systematic tendency for choices to depart from these predictions in the direction of preferring c_1 and c_4,[12] which again suggests that indifference curves fan out, as in the figure (Tversky, 1975; MacCrimmon and Larsson, 1979; Chew and Waller, 1986). In a variation on this approach, Kahneman and Tversky (1979) replaced the gains of $\$X$ and $\$Y$ in the above gambles with losses of these magnitudes, and found a tendency to depart from expected utility in the direction of c_2 and c_3. Defining $\{x_1, x_2, x_3\}$ as $\{-Y, -X, 0\}$ (to maintain the condition $x_1 < x_2 < x_3$) and plotting these gambles in Figure 5b, a choice of c_2 and c_3 is again seen to imply that indifference curves fan out. Finally, Battalio, Kagel and MacDonald (1985) found that laboratory rats choosing among gambles which involved substantial variations in their actual daily food intake also exhibited this pattern of choices.

A third class of evidence stems from the elicitation method described in the previous section. In particular, note that there is no reason why the mixture probability $\bar{p}$ must

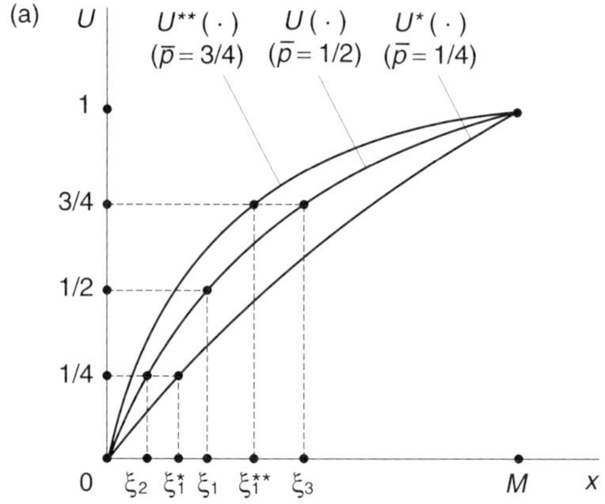

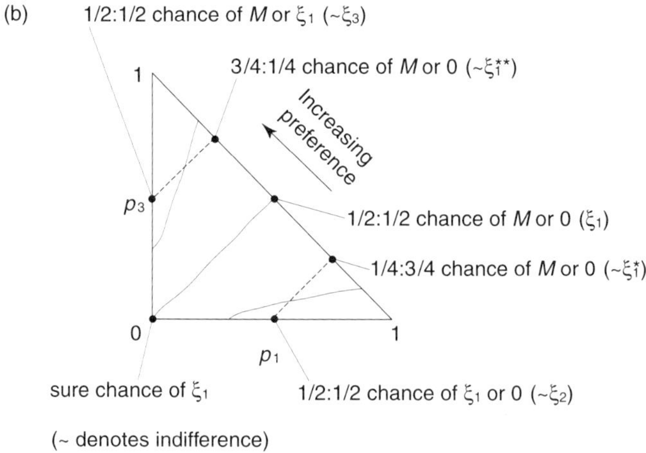

Figure 6. (a) 'Recovered' utility functions for mixture probabilities 1/4, 1/2 and 3/4. (b) Fanning out indifference curves which generate the responses of Figure 6(a).

be $1/2$ in this procedure. Picking any other $\bar{p}$ and defining ξ_1^*, ξ_2^* and ξ_3^* as the certainty equivalents of the $\bar{p}:(1 - \bar{p})$ chances of M or 0, ξ_1^* or 0, and M or ξ_1^* yields the equations $U(\xi_1^*) = \bar{p}$, $U(\xi_2^*) = \bar{p}^2$, $U(\xi_3^*) = \bar{p} + (1 - \bar{p})\bar{p}$, etc., and such a procedure can also be used to recover $U(\cdot)$.

Although this procedure should recover the same (normalized) utility function for any mixture probability $\bar{p}$, researchers such as Karmarkar (1974, 1978) and McCord and de Neufville (1983, 1984) have found a tendency for higher values of $\bar{p}$ to lead the "recovery" of higher valued utility functions, as in Figure 6a. By illustrating the gambles used to obtain the values ξ_1, ξ_2 and ξ_3 for $\bar{p}=1/2$, ξ_1^* for $\bar{p}=1/4$ and ξ_1^{**} for

$\bar{p}=3/4$, Figure 6b shows that, as with the common consequence and common ratio effects, this *utility evaluation effect* is precisely what would be expected from an individual whose indifference curves departed from expected utility by fanning out.[13]

Non-expected utility models of preferences

The systematic nature of these departures from linearity in the probabilities have led several researchers to generalize the expected utility model by positing nonlinear functional forms for the individual preference function. Examples of such forms and researchers who have studied them include:

$$\sum v(x_i)\pi(p_i) \qquad \text{Edwards (1955); Kahneman and Tversky (1979)} \qquad (4)$$

$$\frac{\sum v(x_i)\pi(p_i)}{\sum \pi(p_i)} \qquad \text{Karmarkar (1978)} \qquad (5)$$

$$\frac{\sum v(x_i)p_i}{\sum \tau(x_i)p_i} \qquad \text{Chew (1983); Fishburn (1983)} \qquad (6)$$

$$\sum v(x_i)[g(p_1 + \cdots + p_i) - g(p_1 + \cdots + p_{i-1})] \qquad \text{Quiggin (1982)} \qquad (7)$$

$$\sum v(x_i)p_i + \left[\sum \tau(x_i)p_i\right]^2 \qquad \text{Machina (1982)} \qquad (8)$$

Many (though not all) of these forms are flexible enough to exhibit the properties of stochastic dominance preferences, risk aversion/risk preference and fanning out, and (6) and (7) have proven to be particularly useful both theoretically and empirically. Additional analyses of these forms can be found in Chew, Karni and Safra (1987), Fishburn (1964), Segal (1984) and Yaari (1987).

Although such forms allow for the modelling of preferences which are more general than those allowed by the expected utility hypothesis, each requires a different set of conditions on its component functions $v(\cdot)$, $\pi(\cdot)$, $\tau(\cdot)$ or $g(\cdot)$ for the properties of stochastic dominance preference, risk aversion/risk preference, comparative risk aversion, etc. In particular, the standard expected utility results linking properties of the function $U(\cdot)$ to such aspects of behavior will generally not extend to the corresponding properties of the function $v(\cdot)$ in the above forms. Does this mean that the study of non-expected utility preferences requires us to abandon the vast body of theoretical results and intuition we have developed within the expected utility framework?

Fortunately, the answer is no. An alternative approach to the analysis of non-expected utility preferences proceeds not by adopting a specific nonlinear function, but rather by considering nonlinear functions in general, and using calculus to extend

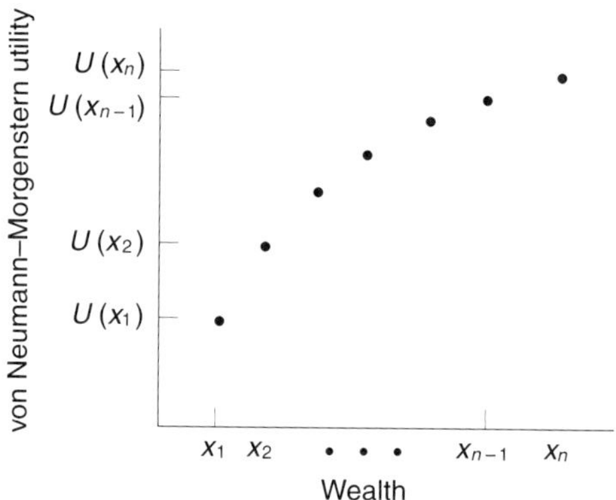

Figure 7. von Neumann–Morgenstern utilities as coefficients of the expected utility preference function $V(p_1, \ldots, p_n) \equiv \Sigma U(x_i)p_i$.

the results from expected utility theory in the same manner in which it is typically used to extend results involving linear functions.[14]

Specifically, consider the set of all probabililty distributions $P = (p_1, \ldots, p_n)$ over a fixed outcome set $\{x_1, \ldots, x_n\}$, so that the expected utility preference functions can be written as $V(P) = V(p_1, \ldots, p_n) \equiv \sum U(x_i)p_i$, and think of $U(x_i)$ not as a "utility level" but rather as the coefficient of $p_i = \text{prob}(x_i)$ in this linear function. If we plot these coefficients against x_i as in Figure 7, the expected utility results of the previous section can be stated as:

Stochastic dominance preference: $V(\cdot)$ will exhibit global stochastic dominance preference if and only if the coefficients $\{U(x_i)\}$ are increasing in x_i, as in the figure.

Risk aversion: $V(\cdot)$ will exhibit global risk aversion if and only if the coefficients $\{U(x_i)\}$ are concave in x_i,[15] as in the figure.

Comparative risk aversion: The expected utility preference function $V^*(P) \equiv \sum U^*(x_i)p_i$ will be at least as risk averse as $V(\cdot)$ if and only if the coefficients $\{U^*(x_i)\}$ are at least as concave in x_i as $\{U(x_i)\}$.[16]

Now take the case where the individual's preference function $\mathscr{V}(P) = \mathscr{V}(p_1, \ldots, p_n)$ is not linear (i.e. not expected utility) but at least differentiable, and consider its partial derivatives $\mathscr{U}(x_i; P) \equiv \partial\mathscr{V}(P)/\partial p_i = \partial\mathscr{V}(P)/\partial \text{ prob}(x_i)$. Pick some probability distribution P_0 and plot these $\mathscr{U}(x_i; P_0)$ values against x_i. If they are again increasing in x_i, it is clear that any infinitesimal stochastically dominating shift from P_0, such as a decrease in some p_i and matching increase in p_{i+1}, will be preferred. If they are again concave in x_i, any infinitesimal mean preserving spread, such as a drop in p_i and (mean preserving) rise in p_{i-1} and p_{i+1}, will make the individual worse off. In light of this correspondence between the coefficients $\{U(x_i)\}$ of an expected utility preference function $V(\cdot)$ and the partial derivatives $\{\mathscr{U}(x_i; P_0)\}$ of the non-expected utility preference function $\mathscr{V}(\cdot)$ we refer to $\{\mathscr{U}(x_i; P_0)\}$ as the individual's local utility indices at P_0.

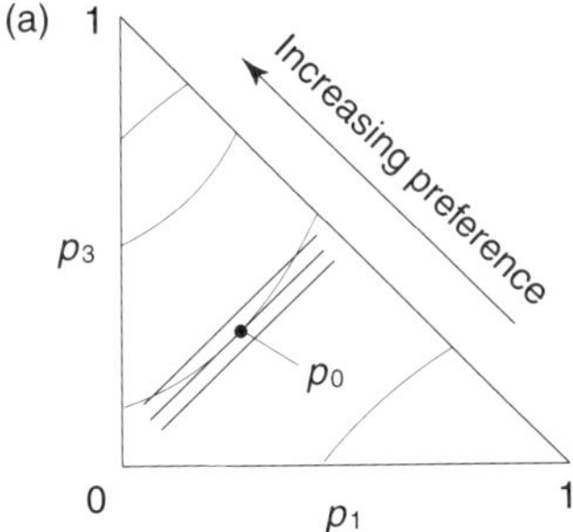

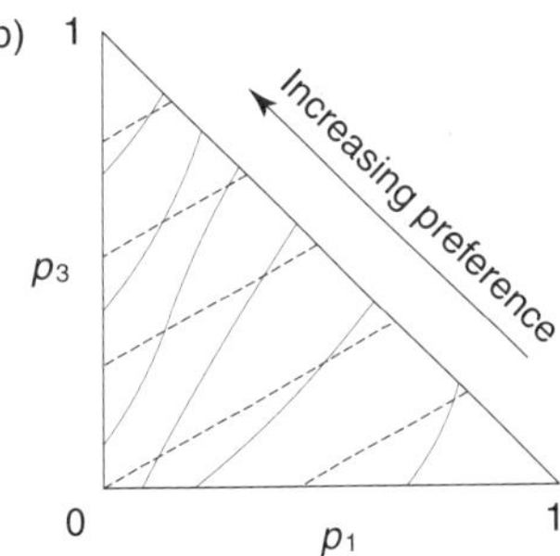

Figure 8. (a) Tangent "expected utility" approximation to non-expected utility indifference curves. (Solid lines are local expected utility approximation to non-expected utility indifference curves at P_0.) (b) Risk aversion of every local expected utility approximation is equivalent to global risk aversion. (Dashed lines are iso-expected value lines.)

Of course, the above results will only hold precisely for infinitesimal shifts from the distribution P_0. However, we can exploit another result from standard calculus to show how "expected utility" results may be applied to the exact global analysis of non-expected utility preference. Recall that in many cases, a differentiable function will exhibit a specific global property if and only if that property is exhibited by its linear approximations at each point. For example, a differentiable function will be globally nondecreasing if and only if its linear approximations are non-decreasing at each point. In fact, most of the fundamental properties of risk attitudes and their expected utility characterizations are precisely of this type. In particular, it can be shown that:

Stochastic dominance preference: A non-expected utility preference function $\mathscr{V}(\cdot)$ will exhibit global stochastic dominance preference if and only if its local utility indices $\{\mathscr{U}(x_i; P)\}$ are increasing in x_i at each distribution P.

Risk aversion: $\mathscr{V}(\cdot)$ will exhibit global risk aversion if and only if its local utility indices $\{\mathscr{U}(x_i; P)\}$ are concave in x_i at each distribution P.

Comparative risk aversion: The preference function $\mathscr{V}^*(\cdot)$ will be globally at least as risk averse as $\mathscr{V}(\cdot)$[17] if and only if its local utility indices $\{\mathscr{U}^*(x_i; P)\}$ are at least as concave in x_i as $\{\mathscr{U}(x_i; P)\}$ at each P.

Figures 8a and 8b give a graphical illustration of this approach for the outcome set $\{x_1, x_2, x_3\}$. Here the solid curves denote the indifference curves of the non-expected utility preference function $\mathscr{V}(P)$. The parallel lines near the lottery P_0 denote the tangent "expected utility" indifference curves that correspond to the local utility indices $\{\mathscr{U}(x_i; P_0)\}$ at P_0. As always with differentiable functions, an infinitesimal change in the probabilities at P_0 will be preferred if and only if they would be preferred by this tangent linear (i.e. expected utility) approximation. Figure 8b illustrates the above "risk aversion" result: It is clear that these indifference curves will be globally risk averse (averse to mean preserving spreads) if and only if they are everywhere steeper than the dashed iso-expected values lines. However, this is equivalent to all their *tangents* being steeper than these lines, which is in turn equivalent to all of their local expected utility approximations being risk averse, or in other words, to the local utility indices $\{\mathcal{U}(x_i; P)\}$ being concave in x_i at each distribution P.

My fellow researchers and I have shown how this and similar techniques can be applied to extend further the results of expected utility theory to the case of non-expected utility preferences, to characterize and explore the implications of preferences which "fan out" and to conduct new and more general analyses of economic behavior under uncertainty (Machina, 1982; Chew, 1983; Fishburn, 1984; Epstein, 1985; Allen, 1987; Chew, Karni and Safra, 1987). However, while I feel that they constitute a useful and promising response to the phenomenon of non-linearities in the probabilities, these models do not provide solutions to the more problematic empirical phenomena of the following sections.

THE PREFERENCE REVERSAL PHENOMENON

The evidence

The finding now known as the preference reversal phenomenon was first reported by psychologists Lichtenstein and Slovic (1971). In this study, subjects were first presented with a number of pairs of bets and asked to choose one bet out of each pair. Each of these pairs took the following form:

$$\text{P-bet:} \begin{cases} p \text{ chance of } \$X \\ 1 - p \text{ chance of } \$x \end{cases} \quad \text{versus} \quad \text{\$-bet:} \begin{cases} q \text{ chance of } \$Y \\ 1 - q \text{ chance of } \$y, \end{cases}$$

where X and Y are respectively greater than x and y, p is greater than q, and Y is greater than X (the names "P-bet" and "\$-bet" come from the greater probability of winning in the first bet and greater possible gain in the second). In some cases, x and y took on small negative values. The subjects were next asked to "value" (state certainty equivalents for) each of these bets. The different valuation methods used consisted of (1) asking subjects to state their minimum selling price for each bet if they were to own it; (2) asking them to state their maximum bid price for each bet if they were to buy it, and (3) the elicitation procedure of Becker, DeGroot and Marschak (1964), in which it is in a subject's best interest to reveal his or her true certainty equivalents.[18] In the latter case, real money was used.

The expected utility model, as well as each of the non-expected utility models of the previous section, clearly implies that the bet which is actually chosen out of each pair will also be the one which is assigned the higher certainty equivalent.[19] However, Lichtenstein and Slovic found a systematic tendency for subjects to violate this prediction by choosing the P-bet in a direct choice but assigning a higher value to the \$-bet. In one experiment, for example, 127 out of 173 subjects assigned a higher sell price to the \$-bet in every pair in which the P-bet was chosen. Similar findings were obtained by Lindman (1971), and in an interesting variation on the usual experimental setting, by Lichtenstein and Slovic (1973) in a Las Vegas casino where customers actually staked (and hence sometimes lost) their own money. In another real-money experiment, Mowen and Gentry (1980) found that groups who could discuss their (joint) decisions were, if anything, more likely than individuals to exhibit the phenomenon.

Although the above studies involved deliberate variations in design in order to check for the robustness of this phenomenon, they were nevertheless received skeptically by economists, who perhaps not unnaturally felt they had more at stake than psychologists in this type of finding. In an admitted attempt to "discredit" this work, economists Grether and Plott (1979) designed a pair of experiments which, by correcting for issues of incentives, income effects, strategic considerations, ability to indicate indifference and other items, would presumably not generate this phenomenon. They none the less found it in both experiments. Further design modifications by Pommerehne, Schneider and Zweifel (1982) and Reilly (1982) yielded the same results. Finally, the phenomenon has been found to persist (although in mitigated form) even when subjects are allowed to engage in experimental market transactions involving the gambles (Knez and Smith, 1986), or when the experimenter is able to act as an arbitrageur and make money off of such reversals (Berg, Dickhaut and O'Brien, 1983).

Two interpretations of this phenomenon

How you interpret these findings depends on whether you adopt the worldview of an economist or a psychologist. An economist would reason as follows: Each individual possesses a well-defined preference relation over objects (in this case lotteries), and information about this relation can be gleaned from either direct choice questions or (properly designed) valuation questions. Someone exhibiting the preference reversal phenomenon is therefore telling us that he or she (1) is indifferent between the P-bet and some sure amount ξ_P; (2) strictly prefers the P-bet to the \$-bet, and (3) is indifferent between the \$-bet and an amount $\xi_\$$ greater than ξ_P. Assuming they prefer $\xi_\$$ to the lesser amount ξ_P, this implies that their preferences over these four objects are cyclic or intransitive.

Psychologists on the other hand would deny the premise of a common underlying mechanism generating both choice and valuation behavior. Rather, they view choice and valuation (even different forms of valuation) as distinct processes, subject to possibly different influences. In other words, individuals exhibit what are termed *response mode effects*. Excellent discussions and empirical examinations of this phenomenon and its implications for the elicitation of probabilistic beliefs and utility functions can be found in Hogarth (1975); Slovic, and Lichtenstein (1983); Hershey and Schoemaker (1985) and MacCrimmon and Wehrung (1986). In reporting how the response mode study of Slovic and Lichtenstein (1968) led them actually to predict the preference reversal phenomenon, I can do no better than quote the authors themselves:

> The impetus for this study [Lichtenstein and Slovic (1971)] was our observation in our earlier 1968 article that choices among pairs of gambles appeared to be influenced primarily by

probabilities of winning and losing, whereas buying and selling prices were primarily determined by the dollar amounts that could be won or lost. ... In our 1971 article, we argued that, if the information in a gamble is processed differently when making choices and setting prices, it should be possible to construct pairs of gambles such that people would choose one member of the pair but set a higher price on the other. (Slovic and Lichtenstein, 1983)

Implications of the economic worldview

The issue of intransitivity is new neither to economics nor to choice under uncertainty. May (1954), for example, observed intransitivities in pairwise rankings of three alternative marriage partners, where each candidate was rated highly in two of three attributes (intelligence, looks, wealth) and low in the third. In an uncertain context, Blyth (1972) has adapted this approach to construct a set of random variables $(\tilde{x}, \tilde{y}, \tilde{z})$ such that $\mathrm{prob}(\tilde{x} > \tilde{y}) = \mathrm{prob}(\tilde{y} > \tilde{z}) = \mathrm{prob}(\tilde{z} > \tilde{x}) = 2/3$, so that individuals making pairwise choices on the basis of these probabilities would also be intransitive. In addition to the preference reversal phenomenon, Edwards (1954, pp. 404–405) and Tversky (1969) have also observed intransitivities in preferences over risky prospects. On the other hand, researchers have shown that many aspects of economic theory, in particular the existence of demand functions and of general equilibrium, are surprisingly robust to dropping the assumption of transitivity (Sonnenschein, 1971; Mas-Colell, 1974; Shafer, 1974).

In any event, economists have begun to develop and analyze models of nontransitive preferences over lotteries. The leading example of this is the "expected regret" model developed independently by Bell (1982), Fishburn (1982) and Loomes and Sugden (1982). In this model of pairwise choice, the von Neumann–Morgenstern utility function $U(x)$ is replaced by a *regret/rejoice function* $r(x, y)$ which represents the level of satisfaction (or if negative, dissatisfaction) the individual would experience if he or she were to receive the outcome x when the alternative choice would have yielded the outcome y (this function is assumed to satisfy $r(x, y) \equiv - r(y, x)$). In choosing between statistically independent gambles $P^* = (p_1^*, \ldots, p_n^*)$ and $P = (p_1, \ldots, p_n)$ over a common outcome set $\{x_1, \ldots, x_n\}$, the individual will choose P^* if the expectation $\sum_i \sum_j r(x_i, x_j) p_i^* p_j$ is positive, and P if it is negative.

Note that when the regret/rejoice function takes the special form $r(x, y) \equiv U(x) - U(y)$ this model reduces to the expected utility model, since we have

$$\sum_i \sum_j r(x_i, x_j) p_i^* p_j \equiv \sum_i \sum_j [U(x_i) - U(x_j)] p_i^* p_j \equiv \sum_i U(x_i) p_i^* - \sum_j U(x_j) p_j \qquad (9)$$

so that the individual will prefer P^* to P if and only if $\sum_i U(x_i) p_i^* > \sum_j U(x_j) p_j$.[20] However, in general such an individual will neither be an expected utility maximizer nor have transitive preferences.

However, this intransitivity does not prevent us from graphing such preferences, or even applying "expected utility" analysis to them. To see the former, consider the case when the individual is facing alternative independent lotteries over a common outcome set $\{x_1, x_2, x_3\}$, so that we may again use the triangle diagram to illustrate

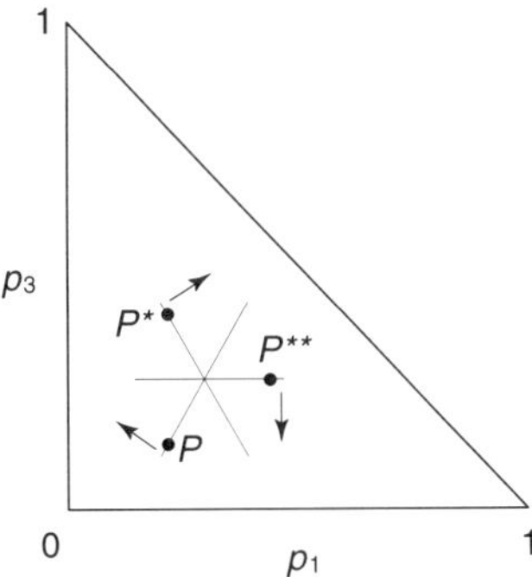

Figure 9. "Indifference curves" for the expected regret model.

their "indifference curves," which will appear as in Figure 9. In such a case it is important to understand what is and is not still true of these indifference curves. The curve through P will still correspond to the set of lotteries that are indifferent to P, and it will still divide the set of lotteries that are strictly preferred to P (the points in the direction of the arrow) from the ones to which P is strictly preferred. Furthermore, if (as in the figure) $P*$ lies above the indifference curve through P, then P will lie below the indifference curve through $P*$ (i.e. the individual's ranking of P and $P*$ will be unambiguous). However, unlike indifference curves for transitive preferences, these curves will cross,[21] and preferences over the lotteries P, $P*$ and $P**$ are seen to form an intransitive cycle. But in regions where the indifference curves do not cross (such as near the origin) the individual will be indistinguishable from someone with transitive (albeit non-expected utility) preferences.

To see how expected utility results can be extended to this nontransitive framework, fix a lottery $P = (p_1, \ldots, p_n)$ and consider the question of when an (independent) lottery $P*=(p_1^*, \ldots, p_n^*)$ will be preferred or not preferred to P. Since $r(x, y) \equiv - r(y, x)$ implies $\sum_i \sum_j r(x_i, x_j)p_j \equiv 0$, we have that $P*$ will be preferred to P if and only if

$$0 < \sum_i \sum_j r(x_i, x_j)p_i^*p_i = \sum_i \sum_j r(x_i, x_j)p_i^*p_j = \sum_i \sum_j r(x_i, x_j)p_ip_j$$

$$= \sum_i \left[\sum_j r(x_i, x_j)p_j\right]p_i^* - \sum_i \left[\sum_j r(x_i, x_j)p_j\right]p_i \qquad (10)$$

$$= \sum_i \phi(x_i; P)p_i^* - \sum_i \phi(x_i; P)p_i$$

In other words, $P*$ will be preferred to P if and only if it implies a higher expectation of the "utility function" $\phi(x_i; P) \equiv \sum_j r(x_i, x_j)p_j$ than P. Thus if $\phi(x_i; P)$ is increasing in x_i for all lotteries P the individual will exhibit global stochastic dominance preference, and if $\phi(x_i; P)$ is concave in x_i for all P the individual will exhibit global risk aversion, even though he or she is not necessarily transitive (these conditions will clearly be satisfied if $r(x, y)$ is increasing and concave in x). The analytics of expected utility theory are robust indeed.

The developers of this model have shown how specific assumptions on the form of the regret/rejoice function will generate the common consequence effect, the common ratio effect, the preference reversal phenomenon, and other observed properties of choice over lotteries. The theoretical and empirical prospects for this approach accordingly seem quite impressive.

Implications of the psychological worldview

On the other hand, how should economists respond if it turns out that the psychologists are right, and the preference reversal phenomenon really is generated by some form of response mode effect (or effects)? In that case, the first thing to do would be to try to determine if there were analogues of such effects in real-world economic situations.[22] Will individuals behave differently when determining their valuation of an object (e.g. reservation bid on a used car) than when reacting to a fixed and non-negotiable price for the same object? Since a proper test of this would require correcting for any possible strategic and/or information-theoretic (e.g. signalling) issues, it would not be a simple undertaking. However, in light of the experimental evidence, I feel it is crucial that we attempt it.

Say we found that response mode effects did not occur outside of the laboratory. In that case we could rest more easily, although we could not forget about such issues completely: experimenters testing other economic theories and models (e.g. auctions) would have to be forever mindful of the possible influence of the particular response mode used in their experimental design.

On the other hand, what if we did find response mode effects out in the field? In that case we would want to determine, perhaps by going back to the laboratory, whether the rest of economic theory remained valid provided the response mode is held constant. If this were true, then with further evidence on exactly how the response mode mattered, we could presumably incorporate it as a new independent variable into existing theories. Since response modes tend to be constant within a given economic model, e.g. quantity responses to fixed prices in competitive markets, valuation announcements (truthful or otherwise) in auctions, etc., we should expect most of the testable implications of this approach to appear as cross-institutional predictions, such as systematic violations of the various equivalency results involving prices versus quantities or second price-sealed bid versus oral English auctions. In such a case, the new results and insights regarding our theories of institutions and mechanisms could be exciting indeed.[23]

FRAMING EFFECTS

Evidence

In addition to response mode effects, psychologists have uncovered an even more disturbing phenomenon, namely that alternative means of representing or "framing" probabilistically equivalent choice problems will lead to systematic differences in

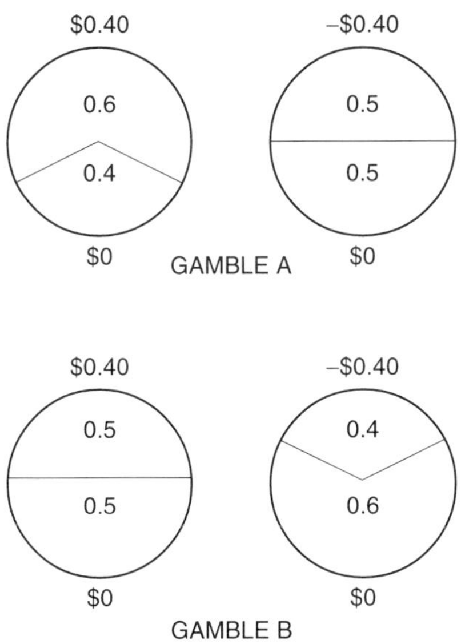

Figure 10. Duplex gambles with identical underlying distributions.

choice. An early example of this phenomenon was reported by Slovic (1969), who found that offering a gain or loss contingent on the joint occurrence of four independent events with probability p elicited different responses than offering it on the occurrence of a single event with probability p^4 (all probabilities were stated explicitly). In comparison with the single-event case, making a gain contingent on the joint occurrence of events was found to make it more attractive, and making a loss contingent on the joint occurrence of events made it more unattractive.

In another study, Payne and Braunstein (1971) used pairs of gambles of the type illustrated in Figure 10. Each of the gambles in the figure, known as a *duplex gamble*, involves spinning the pointers on both its "gain wheel" (on the left) and its "loss wheel" (on the right), with the individual receiving the sum of the resulting amounts. Thus an individual choosing Gamble A would win $0.40 with probability 0.3 (i.e. if the pointer in the gain wheel landed up and the pointer in the loss wheel landed down), would lose $0.40 with probability 0.2 (if the pointers landed in the opposite positions), and would break even with probability 0.5 (if the pointers landed either both up or both down). An examination of Gamble B reveals that it has an identical underlying distribution, so that subjects should be indifferent between the two gambles regardless of their risk preferences. However, Payne and Braunstein found that individuals in fact chose between such gambles (and indicated nontrivial strengths of preference) in manners which were systematically affected by the attributes of the component wheels. When the probability of winning in the gain wheel was greater than the probability of losing in the loss wheel for each gamble (as in the figure), subjects tended to choose the gamble whose gain wheel yielded the greater probability of a gain (Gamble A). In cases where the probabilities of losing in the loss wheels were respectively greater than the probabilities of winning in the gain wheels, subjects tended toward the gamble with the lower probability of losing in the loss wheel.

Finally, although the gambles in Figure 10 possess identical underlying distributions, continuity suggests that a slight worsening of the terms of the preferred gamble could result in a pair of non-equivalent duplex gambles in which the individual will actually choose the one with the stochastically dominated underlying distribution. In an experiment where the subjects were allowed to construct their own duplex gambles by choosing one from a pair of prospects involving gains and one from a pair of prospects involving losses, stochastically dominated prospects were indeed chosen (Tversky and Kahneman, 1981).[24]

A second class of framing effects involves the phenomenon of a *reference point*. Theoretically, the variable which enters an individual's von Neumann–Morgenstern utility function should be total (i.e. final) wealth, and gambles phrased in terms of gains and losses should be combined with current wealth and re-expressed as distributions over final wealth levels before being evaluated. However, economists since Markowitz (1952) have observed that risk attitudes over gains and losses are more stable than can be explained by a fixed utility function over final wealth, and have suggested that the utility function might be best defined in terms of changes from the "reference point" of current wealth. This stability of risk attitudes in the face of wealth variations has also been observed in several experimental studies.[25]

Markowitz (p. 155) also suggested that certain circumstances may cause the individual's reference point to temporarily deviate from current wealth. If these circumstances include the manner in which a given problem is verbally described, then differing risk attitudes over gains and losses can lead to different choices depending upon the exact description. A simple example of this, from Kahneman and Tversky (1979), involves the following two questions:

> In addition to whatever you own, you have been given 1000 (Israeli pounds). You are now asked to choose between a $1/2 : 1/2$ chance of a gain of 1000 or 0 or a sure gain of 500.

and

> In addition to whatever you own, you have been given 2000. You are now asked to choose between a $1/2 : 1/2$ chance of loss of 1000 or 0 or a sure loss of 500.

These two problems involve identical distributions over final wealth. However, when put to two different groups of subjects, 84 percent chose the sure gain in the first problem but 69 percent chose the $1/2 : 1/2$ gamble in the second. A nonmonetary version of this type of example, from Tversky and Kahneman (1981, 1986), posits the following scenario:

> Imagine that the U.S. is preparing for the outbreak of an unusual Asian disease, which is expected to kill 600 people. Two alternative programs to combat the disease have been proposed. Assume that the exact scientific estimate of the consequences of the programs are as follows:
>
> If program A is adopted, 200 people will be saved.
> If Program B is adopted, there is 1/3 probability that 600 people will be saved, and 2/3 probability that no people will be saved.

Seventy-two percent of the subjects who were presented with this form of the question chose Program A. A second group was given the same initial information, but the descriptions of the programs were changed to read:

> If Program C is adopted 400 people will die.
> If Program D is adopted there is 1/3 probability that nobody will die, and 2/3 probability that 600 people will die.

Although this statement of the problem is once again identical to the former one, 78 percent of the respondents chose Program D.

In other studies, Schoemaker and Kunreuther (1979), Hershey and Schoemaker (1980), McNeil, Pauker, Sox and Tversky (1982) and Slovic, Fischhoff and Lichtenstein (1982) have found that subjects' choices in otherwise identical problems will depend upon whether they are phrased as decisions whether or not to gamble or whether or not to insure, whether the statistical information for different therapies is presented in terms of cumulative survival probabilities or cumulative mortality probabilities, etc. For similar examples of this phenomenon in non-stochastic, situations, see Thaler (1980).

In a final class of examples, not based on reference point effects, Moskowitz (1974) and Keller (1982) found that the proportion of subjects choosing in conformance with or in violation of the independence axiom in examples like the Allais Paradox was significantly affected by whether the problems were described in the standard matrix form (e.g. Raiffa, 1968, p. 7), decision tree form, or as minimally structured written statements. Interestingly enough, the form which was judged the "clearest representation" by the majority of Moskowitz's subjects (the tree form) led to the lowest degree of consistency with the independence axiom, the highest proportion of fanning out choices, and the highest persistency rate of these choices (pp. 234, 237–38).

Two issues regarding framing

The replicability and pervasiveness of the above types of examples is indisputable. However, before being able to assess their implications for economic modelling we need to resolve two issues.

The first issue is whether these experimental observations possess any analogue outside of the laboratory. Since real-world decision problems do not present themselves as neatly packaged as the ones on experimental questionnaires, monitoring such effects would not be as straightforward. However, this does not mean that they do not exist, or that they cannot be objectively observed or quantitatively measured. The real-world example which comes most quickly to mind, and is presumably of no small importance to the involved parties, is whether gasoline price differentials should be represented as "cash discounts" or "credit surcharges." Similarly, Russo, Krieser and Miyashita (1975) and Russo (1977) found that the practice, and even method, of displaying unit price information in supermarkets (information which consumers could calculate for themselves) affected both the level and distribution of consumer expenditures. The empirical marketing literature is no doubt replete with findings that we could legitimately interpret as real-world framing effects.

The second, more difficult issue is that of the independent observability of the particular frame that an individual will adopt in a given problem. In the duplex gamble and matrix/decision tree/written statement examples of the previous section, the different frames seen unambiguously determined by the form of presentation. However, in instances where framing involves the choice of a reference point, which presumably include the majority of real-world cases, this point might not be objectively determined by the form of presentation, and might be chosen differently, and what is worse, unobservably, by each individual.[26] In a particularly thorough and insightful study, Fischhoff (1983) presented subjects with a written decision problem which allowed for different choices of a reference point, and explored different ways of predicting which frame individuals would adopt, in order to be able to predict their actual choices. While the majority choice of subjects was consistent with what would appear to be the most appropriate frame, Fischhoff noted "the absence of any relation within those studies between [separately elicited] frame preference and option preference". Indeed to the extent that frame preferences varied across his experiments, they did so inversely to the incidence of the predicted choice.[27] If such problems can occur in predicting responses to specific written questions in the laboratory, imagine how they could plague the modelling of real-world choice behavior.

Framing effects and economic analysis: have we already solved this problem?

How should we respond if it turns out that framing actually is a real-world phenomenon of economic relevance, and in particular, if individual's frames cannot always be observed? I would argue that the means of responding to this issue can already be found in the "tool box" of existing economic analysis.

Consider first the case where the frame of a given economic decision problem, even though it should not matter from the point of view of standard theory, can at least be independently and objectively observed. I believe that economists have in fact already solved such a problem in their treatment of the phenomenon of "uninformative advertising". Although it is hard to give a formal definition of this term, it is widely felt that economic theory is hard put to explain a large proportion of current advertising in terms of traditional informational considerations.[28] However, this has hardly led economists to abandon classical consumer theory. Rather, models of uninformative advertising proceed by quantifying this variable (e.g. air time) and treating it as an additional independent variable in the utility and/or demand function. Standard results like the Slutsky equation need not be abandoned, but rather simply reinterpreted as properties of demand functions holding this new variable constant. The amount of advertising itself is determined as a maximizing variable on the part of the firm (given some cost curve), and can be subjected to standard comparative static analysis.

In the case when decision frames can be observed, framing effects can presumably be modelled in an analogous manner. To do so, we would begin by adopting a method of quantifying, or at least categorizing, frames. The second step, some of which has of course already been done, is to study both the effect of this new independent variable holding the standard economic variables constant, and conversely, to retest our standard economic theories in conditions where we carefully held the frame fixed.

With any luck we would find that, holding the frame constant, the Slutsky equation still held.

The next step in any given modelling situation would be to ask "who determines the frame?" If (as with advertising) it is the firm, then the effect of the frame upon consumer demand, and hence upon firm profits, can be incorporated into the firm's maximization problem, and the choice of the frame as well as the other relevant variables (e.g. prices and quantities) can be simultaneously determined and subjected to comparative static analysis, just as in the case of uninformative advertising.

A seemingly more difficult case is when the individual chooses the frame (for example, a reference point) and this choice cannot be observed. Although we should not forget the findings of Fischhoff (1983), assume that this choice is at least systematic in the sense that the consumer will jointly choose the frame and make the subsequent decision in a manner which maximizes a "utility function" which depends both on the decision and the choice of frame. In other words, individuals make their choices as part of a joint maximization problem, the other component of which (the choice of frame or reference point) cannot be observed.

Such models are hardly new to economic analysis. Indeed, most economic models presume that the agent is simultaneously maximizing with respect to variables other than the ones being studied. When assumptions are made on the individual's joint preferences over the observed and unobserved variables, the well-developed *theory of induced preferences*[29] can be used to derive testable implications on choice behavior over the observables. With a little more knowledge on exactly how frames are chosen, such an approach could presumably be applied here as well.

The above remarks should not be taken as implying that we have already solved the problem of framing in economic analysis or that there is no need to adapt, and if necessary abandon, our standard models in light of this phenomenon. Rather, they reflect the view that when psychologists are able to hand us enough systematic evidence on how these effects operate, economists will be able to respond accordingly.

OTHER ISSUES: IS PROBABILITY THEORY RELEVANT?

The manipulation of subjective probabilities

The evidence discussed so far has primarily consisted of cases where subjects have been presented with explicit (i.e. "objective") probabilities as part of their decision problems, and the models which have addressed these phenomena possess the corresponding property of being defined over objective probability distributions. However, there is extensive evidence that when individuals have to estimate or revise probabilities for themselves they will make systematic mistakes in doing so.

The psychological literature on the processing of probabilistic information is much too large even to summarize here. However, it is worth noting that experimenters have uncovered several "heuristics" used by subjects which can lead to predictable errors in the formation and manipulation of subjective probabilities. Kahneman and Tversky (1973), Bar-Hillel (1974) and Grether (1980), for example, have found that probability updating systematically departs from Bayes Law in the direction of underweighting prior information and overweighting the "representativeness" of the current sample. In a related phenomenon termed the "law of small numbers," Tversky and Kahneman (1971), found that individuals overestimated the probability of drawing a perfectly representative sample out of a heterogeneous population. Finally, Bar-Hillel (1973), Tversky and Kahneman (1983) and others have found systematic biases in the formation of the probabilities of conjunctions of both independent and non-independent events. For surveys, discussions and examples of the psychological literature on the formation and handling of probabilities see Edwards, Lindman and Savage (1963), Slovic and Lichtenstein (1971), Tversky and Kahneman (1974) and the collections in *Acta Psychologica* (December 1970), Kahneman, Slovic and Tversky (1982) and Arkes and Hammond (1986). For examples of how economists have responded to some of these issues see Arrow (1982), Viscusi (1985) and the references cited there.

The existence of subjective probabilities

The evidence referred to above indicates that when individuals are asked to formulate probabilities they do not do it correctly. However, these findings may be rendered moot by evidence which suggests that when individuals making decisions under uncertainty are not explicitly asked to form subjective probabilities, they might not do it (or even act as if doing it) at all.

In one of a class of examples due to Ellsberg (1961), subjects were presented with a pair of urns, the first containing 50 red balls and 50 black balls and the second also containing 100 red and black balls but in an unknown proportion. When faced with the choice of staking a prize on: (R_1) drawing a red ball from the first urn; (R_2) drawing a red ball from the second urn; (B_1) drawing a black ball from the first urn; or (B_2) drawing a black ball from the second urn; a majority of subjects strictly preferred (R_1) over (R_2) and strictly preferred (B_1) over (B_2). It is clear that there can exist no subjectively assigned probabilities $p: (1 - p)$ of drawing a red vs. black ball from the second urn, even $1/2:1/2$, which can simultaneously generate both of these strict preferences. Similar behavior in this and related problems has been observed by Raiffa (1961), Becker and Brownson (1964), Slovic and Tversky (1974) and MacCrimmon and Larsson (1979).

Life (and economic analysis) without probabilities

One response to this type of phenomenon has been to suppose that individuals "slant" whatever subjective probabilities they might otherwise form in a manner which reflects the amount of confidence/ambiguity associated with them (Fellner, 1961; Becker and Brownson, 1964; Fishburn, 1986; Hogarth and Kunreuther, 1986). In the case of the complete ignorance regarding probabilities, Arrow and Hurwicz (1972), Maskin (1979) and other have presented axioms which imply principles such as ranking options solely on the basis of their worst and/or best outcomes (e.g. maximin, maximax), the unweighted average of their outcomes ("principle of insufficient reason"), or similar criteria.[30] Finally, generalizations of expected utility theory which drop the standard additivity and/or compounding laws of probability theory have been developed by Schmeidler (1986) and Segal (1987).

Although the above models may well capture aspects of actual decision processes, the analytically most useful approach to choice in the presence of uncertainty but the absence of probabilities is the so-called *state-preference* model of Arrow (1953/1964), Debreu (1959) and Hirshleifer (1966). In this model uncertainty is represented by a set of mutually exclusive and exhaustive *states of nature* $S = \{s_i\}$. This partition of all possible unfoldings of the future could be either very coarse, such as the pair of states {it rains here tomorrow, it doesn't rain here tomorrow} or else very fine, so that the definition of a state might read "it rains here tomorrow and the temperature at Gibraltar is 75° at noon and the price of gold in New York is below \$700.00/ounce". Note that it is neither feasible nor desirable to capture all conceivable sources of uncertainty when specifying the set of states for a given problem: it is not feasible since no matter how finely the states are defined there will always be some other random criterion on which to further divide them, and not desirable since such criteria may affect neither individuals' preferences nor their opportunities. Rather, the key requirements are that the states be mutually exclusive and exhaustive so that exactly one will be realized, and (for purposes of the present discussion) that the individual cannot influence which state will actually occur.

Given a fixed (and say finite) set of states, the objects of choice in this framework consist of alternative *state-payoff bundles*, each of which specifies the outcome the individual will receive in every possible state. When the outcomes are monetary payoffs, for example, state-payoff bundles take the form $(c_1, \ldots, c_n)$, where c_i denotes the payoff the individual would receive should state s_i occur. In the case of exactly two states of nature we could represent this set by the points in the (c_1, c_2) plane. Since bundles of form (c, c) represent prospects which yield the same payoff in each state of nature, the 45° line in this plane is known as the *certainty line*.

Now if the individual did happen to assign probabilities $\{p_i\}$ to the states $\{s_i\}$, each bundle $(c_1, \ldots, c_n)$ would imply a specific probability distribution over wealth, and we could infer his or her preferences (i.e. indifference curves) over state-payoff bundles. However, since these bundles are defined directly over the respective states and without reference to any probabilities, it is also possible to speak of preferences over these bundles without making any assumptions regarding the coherency, or even existence, of such probabilistic beliefs. Researchers such as the ones cited above as well as Yaari (1969), Diamond and Yaari (1972) and Mishan (1976) have shown how this indifference curve-based approach can be used to derive results from individual demand behavior through general equilibrium in a context which requires neither the expected utility hypothesis nor the existence or commonality of subjective probabilities. In other words, life without probabilities does not imply life without economic analysis.

Final thoughts

Welfare implications

Although the theme of this chapter has been the descriptive theory of choice under uncertainty, another important issue is the implications of these developments for normative economics. Can welfare analysis be conducted in the type of world implied by the above models?

The answer to this question depends upon the model. Fanning-out behavior and the non-expected utility models used to characterize it, as well as the state-payoff approach of the previous section, are completely consistent with the assumption of well-defined, transitive individual preference orderings, and hence with traditional welfare analysis along the lines of Pareto, Bergson and Samuelson (e.g. Samuelson, 1947/1983, Ch. VIII). For example, the proof of Pareto-efficiency of a system of complete contingent-commodity markets (Arrow, 1953/1964; Debreu, 1969, Ch. 7) requires neither the expected utility hypothesis nor the assumption of well-defined probabilistic beliefs. On the other hand, it is clear that the preference reversal phenomenon and framing effects, and at least some of the non-transitive and/or non-economic models used to address them, will prove much more difficult to reconcile with welfare analysis, at least as currently practised.

A unified model?

Another issue is the lack of a unified model capable of simultaneously handling all of the phenomena described in this paper: fanning-out, the preference reversal phenomenon, framing effects, probability biases and the Ellsberg paradox. After all, it is presumably the same ("typical") individuals who are exhibiting each of these phenomena—shouldn't there be a single model out there capable of generating them all?

Although I am doubtful of our present ability to do this, I am also doubtful about the need to establish a unified model as a prerequisite for continued progress. The aspects of behavior considered in this paper are very diverse, and if (like the wave versus particle properties of light) they cannot be currently unified, this does not mean that we cannot continue to learn by studying and modelling them separately.

An essential criterion

The evidence and theories reported in this chapter have taken us a long way from the classical expected utility approach presented at the outset. To what extent will these new models be incorporated into mainstream economic thought and practice? I believe the answer will depend upon a single factor: the extent to which they can address the important issues in the economics of uncertainty, such as search, investment, bargaining or auctions, to which the expected utility model has been so usefully applied.

ACKNOWLEDGEMENTS

I am grateful to Brian Binger, John Conlisk, Jim Cox, Vincent Crawford, Gong Jin Dong, Elizabeth Hoffman, Michael Rothschild, Carl Shapiro, Vernon Smith, Joseph

Stiglitz, Timothy Taylor and especially Joel Sobel for helpful discussions on this material, and the Alfred P. Sloan Foundation for financial support.

NOTES

1. E.g. von Neumann and Morgenstern (1947) and Savage (1954) (axiomatics); Arrow (1965), Pratt (1964) and Rothschild and Stiglitz (1970) (analytics); Akerlof (1970) and Spence and Zeckhauser (1971) (information).

2. In keeping with the spirit of this journal, references have been limited to the most significant examples of and/or most useful introductions to the literature in each area. For further discussions of these issues see Arrow (1982), Machina (1983a, 1983b), Sugden (1986) and Tversky and Kahneman (1986).

3. Such transformations are often used to normalize the utility function, for example to set $U(0) = 0$ and $U(M) = 1$ for some large value M.

4. Thus, for example, a $2/3:1/3$ chance of \$100 or \$20 and a $1/2:1/2$ chance of \$100 or \$30 both stochastically dominate a $1/2:1/2$ chance of \$100 or \$20.

5. Thus if $x_1 = \$20$, $x_2 = \$30$ and $x_3 = \$100$, the prospects in Note 4 would be represented by the points $(p_1, p_3) = (1/3, 2/3)$, $(p_1, p_3) = (0, 1/2)$ and $(p_1, p_3) = (1/2, 1/2)$ respectively. Although it is fair to describe the renewal of interest in this approach as "modern," versions of this diagram go back at least to Marschak (1950)

6. This follows since the slope of the indifference curves is $[U(x_2) - U(x_1)]/[U(x_3) - U(x_2)]$, the slope of the iso-expected value lines is $[x_2 - x_1]/[x_3 - x_2]$, and concavity of $U(\cdot)$ implies $[U(x_2) - U(x_1)]/[x_2 - x_1] > [U(x_3) - U(x_2)]/[x_3 - x_2]$ whenever $x_1 < x_2 < x_3$.

7. Algebraically, these cases are equivalent to the expression $[.10 \cdot U(5\,000\,000) - .11 \cdot (1\,000\,000) + .01 \cdot U(0)]$ being negative or positive, respectively.

8. The Allais Paradox choices a_1, a_2, a_3, and a_4 correspond to b_1, b_2, b_4 and b_3, where $\alpha = .11$, $x = \$1\,000\,000$, P is a $10/11:1/11$ chance of \$5\,000\,000 or \$0, P^* is a sure chance of \$0, and P^{**} is a sure chance of \$1\,000\,000. The name of this phenomenon comes from the "common consequence" P^{**} in $\{b_1, b_2\}$ and P^* in $\{b_3, b_4\}$.

9. As Bell (1985) notes, in "winning the top prize of \$10\,000 in a lottery may leave one much happier than receiving \$10\,000 as the lowest prize in a lottery".

10. In a conversation with the author, Kenneth Arrow has offered an alternative phrasing of this argument: The widely maintained hypothesis of decreasing absolute risk aversion asserts that individuals will display more risk aversion in the event of a loss, and less risk aversion in the event of a gain. In the common consequence effect, individuals display more risk aversion in the event of an opportunity loss, and less risk aversion in the event of an opportunity gain.

11. The former involves setting $p = 1$, and the latter consists of a two-step choice problem where individuals exhibit the effect with $Y = 2X$ and $p = 2q$. The name "common ratio effect" comes from the common value of $\text{prob}(X)/\text{prob}(Y)$ in the pairs $\{c_1, c_2\}$ and (c_3, c_4).

12. Kahneman and Tversky (1979), for example, found that 80 percent of their subjects preferred a sure gain of 3000 Israeli pounds to a .80 chance of winning 4000, but 65 percent preferred a .20 chance of winning 4000 to a .25 chance of winning 3000.

13. Having found that ξ_1 which solves $U(\xi_1) = (1/2) \cdot U(M) + (1/2) \cdot U(0)$, choose $\{x_1, x_2, x_3\} = \{0, \xi_1, M\}$ so that the indifference curve through $(0,0)$ (i.e. a sure gain of ξ_1) also passes through $(1/2, 1/2)$ (a $1/2:1/2$ chance of M or 0). The order of $\xi_1, \xi_2, \xi_3, \xi^*, \xi^{**}$ in Figure 6a is derived from the individual's preference ordering over the five distributions in Figure 6b for which they are the respective certainty equivalents.

14. Readers who wish to skip the details of this approach may proceed to the next section.

15. As in Note 6, this is equivalent to the condition that $[U(x_{i+1}) - U(x_i)]/[x_{i+1} - x_i] < [U(x_i) - U(x_{i-1})]/[x_i - x_{i-1}]$ for all i.

16. This is equivalent to the condition that $U^*(x_i) \equiv \rho(U(x_i))$ for some increasing concave function $\rho(\cdot)$.

17. For the appropriate generalizations of the expected utility concepts of "at least as risk averse" in this context, see Machina (1982, 1984).

18. Roughly speaking, the subject states a value for the item, and then the experimenter draws a random price. If the price is above the stated value, the subject forgoes the item and receives the price. If the drawn price is below the stated value, the subject keeps the item. The reader can verify that under such a scheme it can never be in a subject's best interest to report anything other than his or her true value.

19. Economic theory tells us that income effects could cause an individual to assign a lower bid price to the object which, if both were free, would actually be preferred. However, this reversal should not occur for either selling prices or the Becker, DeGroot and Marschak elicitations. For evidence on sell price/bid price disparities, see Knetsch and Sinden (1984) and the references cited there.

20. When $r(x, y)$ takes the form $r(x, y) \equiv v(x)\tau(y) - v(y)\tau(x)$, this model will reduce to the (transitive) model of equation (6). This is the most general form of the model which is compatible with transitivity.

21. In this model the indifference curves will all cross at the same point. This point will thus be indifferent to all lotteries in the triangle.

22. It is important to note that neither the evidence of response mode effects (e.g. Slovic, 1975) nor their implications for economic analysis are confined to the case of choice under uncertainty.

23. A final "twist" on the preference reversal phenomenon: Holt (1986) and Karni and Safra (1987) have shown how the procedures used in most of these studies will only lead to truthful revelation of preferences under the added assumption that the individual satisfies the independence axiom, and has given examples of transitive non-expected utility preference rankings which lead to the typical "preference reversal" choices. How (and whether) experimenters will be able to address this issue remains to be seen.

24. Subjects were asked to choose either (A) a sure gain of $240 or (B) a 1/4:3/4 chance of $1000 or $0, and to choose either (C) a sure loss of $750 or (D) a 3/4:1/4 chance of −$1000 or 0. 84 percent chose A over B and 87 percent chose D over C, even though B + C dominates A + D, and choices over the combined distributions were unanimous when they were presented explicitly.

25. See the discussion and references in Machina (1982, pp. 285–286).

26. This is not to say that well-defined reference points never exist. The reference points involved in credit surcharges vs. cash discounts, for example, seem unambiguous.

27. Fischhoff (1983, pp. 115–116). Fischhoff notes that "If one can only infer frames from preferences after assuming the truth of the theory, one runs the risk of making the theory itself untestable."

28. A wonderful example, offered by my colleague Joel Sobel, are milk ads which make no reference to either price or a specific dairy. What could be a more well-known commodity than milk?

29. E.g. Milne (1981). For an application of the theory of induced preferences to choice under uncertainty, see Machina (1984).

30. For an excellent discussion of the history, nature and limitations of such approaches, see Arrow (1951).

REFERENCES

Akerlof, George A. The market for lemons: Quality, uncertainty and the market mechanism, *Quarterly Journal of Economics*, August 1970, **84**: 488–500.

Allais, Maurice, Le comportement de l'homme rationel devant le risque, critique des postulates et axiomes de l'École Americaine, *Econometrica*, October 1953, **21**: 503–546.

Allais, Maurice. The Foundations of a Positive Theory of Choice Involving Risk and a Criticism of the Postulates and Axioms of the American School, in Allais and Hagen (1979).

Allais, Maurice and Ole Hagen, eds. *Expected Utility hypotheses and the Allais Paradox.* Dordrecht, Holland: D. Reidel, 1979.

Allen, Beth. Smooth preferences and the expected utility hypothesis, *Journal of Economic Theory,* 1987, **41**: 340–355.

Arkes, Hal R. and Hammond, Kenneth R. eds. *Judgement and Decision Making: An Interdisciplinary Reader.* Cambridge: Cambridge University Press, 1986.

Arrow, Kenneth J. Alternative approaches to the theory of choice in risk-taking situations, *Econometrica,* October, 1951, **19**: 404–437. Reprinted in Arrow (1965).

Arrow, Kenneth J. Le rôle des valeurs boursières pour la répartition le meilleure des risques, *Économetrie,* Colloques Internationaux du Centre National de la Recherche Scientifique, Paris, 1953, **40**: 41–47. English translation: *Review of Economic Studies,* April 1964, **31**: 91–96.

Arrow, Kenneth J. *Aspects of the Theory of Risk-bearing,* Helsinki: Yrjo Jahnsson Saatio, 1965.

Arrow, Kenneth J. Risk Perception in Psychology and Economics, *Economic Inquiry,* January 1982, 20, 1–9.

Arrow, Kenneth J and Hurwicz, Leonid. An optimality criterion for decision-making under ignorance. In: Carter, C. F. and J. L. Ford, eds. *Uncertainty and Expectations in Economics.* Oxford: Basil Blackwell, 1972.

Bar-Hillel, Maya, On the subjective probability of compound events, *Organizational Behavior and Human Performance,* June 1973, **9**: 396–406.

Bar-Hillel, Maya. Similarity and probability, *Organizational Behavior and Human Performance,* April 1974, **11**: 277–282.

Battalio, Raymond C., Kagel, John H. and MacDonald, Don N. Animals' choices over uncertain outcomes, *American Economic Review,* September 1985, **75**: 597–613.

Becker, Gordon M. and Brownson, Fred O. What price ambiguity? Or the role of ambiguity in decision-making, *Journal of Political Economy,* February 1964, **72**: 62–73.

Becker, Selwyn W., DeGroot, Morris H. and Marschak, Jacob. Measuring utility by a single-response sequential method, *Behavioural Science,* July 1964, **9**: 226–232.

Bell, David E. Regret in decision making under uncertainty, *Operations Research,* September–October 1982, **30**: 961–981.

Bell, David E. Disappointment in decision making under uncertainty, *Operations Research,* January–February 1985, **33**: 1–27.

Berg, Joyce E., Dickhaut, John W. and O'Brien, John R. Preference Reversal and Arbitrage, manuscript, University of Minnesota, September 1983.

Bernoulli, Daniel. Specimen Theoriae novae de mensura sortis, *Commentarii Academiae Scientiarum Imperialis Petropolitanae,* 1738, **5**: 175–192. English translation: *Econometrica,* January 1954, **22**: 23–36.

Blyth, Colin R. Some probability paradoxes in choice from among random alternatives, *Journal of the American Statistical Association,* June 1972, **67**: 366–373.

Chew Soo Hong. A generalization of the quasilinear mean with applications to the measurement of income inequality and decision theory resolving the Allais Paradox, *Econometrica,* July 1983, **51**: 1065–1092.

Chew Soo Hong, Karni Edi and Safra Zvi. Risk aversion in the theory of expected utility with rank dependent probabilities, *Journal of Economic Theory,* 1987, **42**: 370–381.

Chew Soo Hong and Waller, William. Empirical tests of weighted utility theory, *Journal of Mathematical Psychology,* March 1986, **30**: 55–72.

Debreu, Gerard. *Theory of Value: An Axiomatic Analysis of General Equilibrium.* New Haven: Yale University Press, 1959.

Diamond, Peter A. and Yaari, Menahem. Implications of the theory of rationing for consumer choice under uncertainty, *American Economic Review,* June 1972, **62**: 333–343.

Edwards, Ward. The theory of decision making, *Psychological Bulletin,* July 1954, **51**: 380–417.

Edwards, Ward, The prediction of decisions among bets, *Journal of Experimental Psychology,* September 1955, **50**: 201–214.

Edwards, Ward, Lindman, Harold and Savage, Leonard J. Bayesian statistical inference for psychological research, *Psychological Review,* May 1963, **70**:, 193–242.

Ellsberg, Daniel. Risk, ambiguity and the savage axioms, *Quarterly Journal of Economics*, November 1961, **75**: 643–669.

Epstein, Larry. Decreasing risk Aversion and mean-variance analysis, *Econometrica*, 1985, **53**: 945–961.

Fellner William. Distortion of subjective probabilities as a reaction to uncertainty, *Quarterly Journal of Economics*, November 1961, **75**: 670–689.

Fischhoff, Baruch. Predicting frames, *Journal of Experimental Psychology: Learning, Memory and Cognition*, January 1983, **9**: 103–116.

Fishburn Peter C. Nontransitive measurable utility, *Journal of Mathematical Psychology*, August 1982, **26**: 31–67.

Fishburn, Peter C. Transitive measurable utility, *Journal of Economic Theory*, December 1983, **31**: 293–317.

Fishburn, Peter C. SSB utility theory: An economic perspective, *Mathematical Social Sciences*, 1984, **8**: 63–94.

Fishburn, Peter C. A new model for decisions under uncertainty, *Economics Letters*, 1986, **21**: 127–130.

Friedman, Milton and Savage, Leonard J. The utility analysis of choices involving risk, *Journal of Political Economy*, August 1948, **56**: 279–304.

Grether, David M. Bayes Rule as a descriptive model: The representatives heuristic, *Quarterly Journal of Economics*, November 1980, **95**: 537–557.

Grether, David M. and Plott, Charles R. Economic theory of choice and the preference reversal phenomenon, *American Economic Review*, September 1979, **69**: 623–638.

Hagen, Ole. Towards a positive theory of preferences under risk. In: Allais and Hagen (1979).

Hershey, John C. and Schoemaker, Paul J. H. Risk-taking and problem context in the domain of losses—An expected utility analysis, *Journal of Risk and Insurance*, March 1980, **47**: 111–132.

Hershey, John C. and Schoemaker, Paul J. H. Probability versus certainty equivalence methods in utility measurement: Are they equivalent?, *Management Science*, October 1985, **31**: 1213–1231.

Hirshleifer, Jack. Investment decision under uncertainty: Applications of the state-preference approach, *Quarterly Journal of Economics*, May 1966, **80**: 252–277.

Hogarth, Robin. Cognitive processes and the assessment of subjective probability distributions, *Journal of the American Statistical Association*, June 1975, **70**: 271–289.

Hogarth, Robin and Kunreuther, Howard. Decison making under ambiguity, *Journal of Business*, October 1986, Prt. 2, **4**: 225–250.

Holt, Charles A. Preference reversals and the independence axiom, *American Economic Review*, June 1986, **76**: 508–515.

Kahneman, Daniel, Slovic, Paul and Tversky, Amos, eds. *Judgement Under Uncertainty: Heuristics and Biases*, Cambridge: Cambridge University Press, 1982.

Kahneman, Daniel and Tversky, Amos, On the psychology of prediction, *Psychological Review*, July 1973, **80**: 237–251.

Kahneman, Daniel and Tversky, Amos, Prospect theory: An analysis of decision under risk, *Econometrica*, March 1979, **47**: 263–91.

Karmarkar, Uday S. *The Effect of Probabilities on the Subjective Evaluation of Lotteries*, Massachusetts Institute of Technology Sloan School of Business Working Paper, 1974.

Karmarkar, Uday S. Subjectively weighted utility: A descriptive extension of the expected utility model, *Organizational Behavior and Human Performance*, February 1978, **21**: 61–72.

Karni, Edi and Safra, Zvi. Preference reversal and the observability of preferences by experimental methods, *Econometrica*, 1987, **55**: 675–685.

Keller, Robin L. *The Effects of Decision Problem Representation on Utility Conformance*, manuscript, University of California, Irvine, 1982.

Knetsch, Jack L. and Sinden, J. A. Willingness to pay and compensation demanded: Experimental evidence of an unexpected disparity in measures of value, *Quarterly Journal of Economics*, August 1984, **99**: 507–521.

Knez, Marc and Smith, Vernon L. *Hypothetical Valuations and Preference Reversals in the Context of Asset Trading*, manuscript, University of Arizona, 1986.

Lichtenstein, Sarah and Slovic, Paul. Reversals of preferences between bids and choices in gambling decisions, *Journal of Experimental Psychology*, July 1971, **89**: 46–55.

Lichtenstein, Sarah and Slovic, Paul. Response-induced reversals of preference in gambling: An extended replication in Las Vegas, *Journal of Experimental Psychology*, November 1973, **101**: 16–20.

Lindman, Harold. Inconsistent preferences among gambles, *Journal of Experimental Psychology*, May 1971, **89**: 390–397.

Loomes, Graham and Sugden, Robert. Regret theory: An alternative theory of rational choice under uncertainty, *Economic Journal*, December 1982, **92**: 805–824.

MacCrimmon, Kenneth R. Descriptive and normative implications of the decision-theory postulates. In: Borch, Karl H. and Jan Mossin, eds., *Risk and Uncertainty:* Proceedings of a Conference Held by the International Economic Association. London: Macmillan, 1968.

MacCrimmon, Kenneth R and Larsson, Stig. Utility theory: Axioms versus paradoxes. In: Allais and Hagen (1979).

MacCrimmon, Kenneth R. and Wehrung, Donald A. *Taking Risks: The Management of Uncertainty.* New York: The Free Press, 1986.

Machina, Mark J. Expected utility analysis without the independence axiom, *Econometrica*, March 1982, **50**: 277–323.

Machina, Mark J. *The Economic Theory of Individual Behavior Toward Risk: Theory, Evidence and New Directions*, Stanford University Institute for Mathematical Studies in the Social Sciences Technical Report, 1983a.

Machina, Mark J. Generalized expected utility analysis and the nature of observed violations of the independence axiom, 1983b. In: Stigum and Wenstøp, 1983.

Machina, Mark J. Temporal risk and the nature of induced preferences, *Journal of Economic Theory*, August 1984, **33**: 199–231.

Markowitz, Harry. The utility of wealth, *Journal of Political Economy*, April 1952, **60**: 151–158.

Marschak, Jacob. Rational behaviour, uncertain prospects, and measurable utility, *Econometrica*, April 1950, **19**: 111–41. Errata, *Econometrica*, July 1950, **18**: 312.

Mas-Colell, Andreu. An equilibrium existence theorem without complete or transitive preferences, *Journal of Mathematical Economics*, December 1974, **3**: 237–246.

Maskin, Eric. Decision making under ignorance with implications for social choice, *Theory and Decision*, September 1979, **11**: 319–337.

May, Kenneth O. Intransitivity, utility, and the aggregation of preference patterns, *Econometrica*, January 1954, **22**: 1–13.

McCord, Marc and de Neufville, Richard. Empirical demonstration that expected utility analysis is not operational. In: Stigum and Wenstøp (1983).

McCord, Marc and de Neufville, Richard. Utility dependence on probability: An empirical demonstration, *Large Scale Systems*, February 1984, **6**: 91–103.

McNeil, Barbara J., Pauker, Stephen G., Sox, Harold C. and Tversky, Amos. On the elicitation of preferences for alternative therapies, *New England Journal Medicine*, May 1982, **306**: 1259–1262.

Milne, Frank. Induced preferences and the theory of the consumer, *Journal of Economic Theory*, April 1981, **24**: 205–217.

Mishan, E. J. Choices involving risk: Simple steps toward an ordinalist analysis, *Economic Journal*, December 1976, **86**: 759–777.

Morrison, Donal G. On the consistency of preferences in Allais' Paradox, *Behavioural Science*, September 1967, **12**: 373–83.

Moskowitz, Herbert. Effects of problem representation and feedback on rational behavior in Allais and Morlat-type problems, *Decision Sciences*, 1974, **5**: 225–242.

Mowem, John C. and Gentry, James W. Investigation of the preference-reversal phenomenon in a new product introduction task, *Journal of Applied Psychology*, December 1980, **65**: 715–722.

Payne, John W. and Braunstein, Myron L. Preferences among gambles with equal underlying distributions, *Journal of Experimental Psychology*, January 1971, **87**: 13–18.

Pommerehne, Werner W., Schneider, Friedrich and Zweifel, Peter. Economic theory of choice and the preference reversal phenomenon: A reexamination, *American Economic Review*, June 1982, **72**: 569–574.

Pratt, John W. Risk aversion in the small and in the large, *Econometrica*, January/April 1964, **32**: 122–136.

Quiggin, John. A theory of anticipated utility, *Journal of Economic Behavior and Organization*, December 1982, **3**: 323–343.

Raiffa, Howard. Risk, ambiguity, and the Savage axioms, *Quarterly Journal of Economics*, November 1961, **75**: 690–694.

Raiffa, Howard. *Decision Analysis: Introductory Lectures on Choice Under Uncertainty*. Reading, MA.: Addison-Wesley, 1968.

Reilly, Robert J. Preference reversal: Further evidence and some suggested modifications of experimental design, *American Economic Review*, June 1982, **72**: 576–584.

Rothschild, Michael and Stiglitz, Joseph E. Increasing risk: I. A definition, *Journal of Economic Theory*, September 1970, **2**: 225–243.

Russo, J. Edward. The value of unit price information, *Journal of Marketing Research*, May 1977, **14**: 193–201.

Russo, J. Edward, Krieser, Gene and Miyashita, Sally. An effective display of unit price information, *Journal of Marketing*, April 1975, **39**: 11–19.

Sanuelson, Paul A. *Foundations of Economic Analysis*. Cambridge MA: Harvard University Press, 1947. Enlarged Edition, 1983.

Savage, Leonard J. *The Foundations of Statistics*, New York: Wiley, 1954. Revised and Enlarged Edition, New York: Dover, 1972.

Schmeidler, David. *Subjective Probability and Expected Utility Without Additivity*, manuscript, Tel-Aviv University, 1986.

Schoemaker, Paul J. H. and Kunreuther, Howard. An experimental study of insurance decision, *Journal of Risk and Insurance*, December 1979, **46**: 603–618.

Segal, Uzi. *Nonlinear Decision Weights with the Independence Axiom*, manuscript, University of California, Los Angeles, November 1984.

Segal, Uzi. The Ellsberg paradox and risk aversion: An anticipated utility approach, *International Economic Review*, 1987, **28**: 175–202.

Shafer, Wayne J. The nontransitive consumer, *Econometrica*, September 1974, **42**: 913–919.

Slovic, Paul. Manipulating the attractiveness of a gamble without changing its expected value, *Journal of Experimental Psychology*, January 1969, **79**: 139–145.

Slovic, Paul. Choice between equally valued alternatives, *Journal of Experimental Psychology: Human Perception and Performance*, August 1975, **1**: 280–287.

Slovic, Paul, Fischhoff, Baruch and Lichtenstein, Sarah. Reponse mode, framing, and information processing effects in risk assessment. In: Hogarth, Robin ed., *New Directions for Methodology of Social and Behavioral Science: Question Framing and Response Consistency*. San Francisco: Jossey-Bass, 1982.

Slovic, Paul, Fischhoff, Baruch and Lichtenstein, Sarah. Relative importance of probabilities and payoffs in risk taking, *Journal of Experimental Psychology*, November 1968, Prt 2, **78**: 1–18.

Slovic, Paul, Fischhoff, Baruch and Lichtenstein, Sarah. Comparison of Bayesian and regression approaches to the study of information processing in judgement, *Organizational Behavior and Human Performance*, November 1971, **6**: 649–744.

Slovic, Paul, and Lichtenstein, Sarah. Preference reversals: A broader perspective, *American Economic Review*, September 1983, **73**: 596–605.

Slovic, Paul and Tversky, Amos. Who accepts Savage's axiom?, *Behavioural Science*, November 1974, **19**: 368–373.

Sonnenschein, Jugo F. *Demand Theory Without Transitive Preferences, With Applications to the Theory of Competitive Equilibrium*. In: Chipman, John S., Hurwicza, Leonid, Richter, Marcel K. and Sonnenschein, Hugo F., eds. *Preferences, Utility and Demand*. New York: Harcourt Brace Jovanovich, 1971.

Spence, A. Michael and Zeckhauser, Richard J. Insurance, information and individual action, *American Economic Review (Papers and Proceedings)*, May 1971, **61**: 380–387.

Stigum, Bernt and Wenstøp, Fred. *Foundations of Utility and Risk Theory with Applications*, Dordrecht, Holland: D. Reidel, 1983.

Sugden, Robert. New developments in the theory of choice under uncertainty, *Bulletin of Economic Research*, January 1986, **38**: 1–24

Thaler, Richard. Toward a positive theory of consumer choice, *Journal of Economic Behavior and Organization*, March 1980, **1**: 39–60.

Tversky, Amos. Intransitivity of preferences, *Psychological Review*, January 1969, **76**: 31–48.

Tversky, Amos. A critique of expected utility theory: Descriptive and normative considerations, *Erkenntnis*, 1975, **9**: 163–173.

Tversky, Amos and Kahneman, Daniel. Belief in the Law of Small Numbers, *Psychological Bulletin*, July 1971, **2**: 105–110.

Tversky, Amos and Kahneman, Daniel. Judgement under uncertainty: Heuristics and biases, *Science*, September 1974, **185**: 1124–1131.

Tversky, Amos and Kahneman, Daniel. The framing of decisions and the psychology of choice, *Science*, January 1981, **211**: 453–458.

Tversky, Amos and Kahneman, Daniel. Extensional vs. intuitive reasoning: The conjunction fallacy in probability judgement, *Psychological Review*, October 1983, **90**: 293–315.

Tversky, Amos and Kahneman, Daniel. Rational choice and the framing of decisions, *Journal of Business*, October 198, Prt. 2, **4**: 251–278.

Viscusi, W. Kip. Are individuals Bayesian decision makers? *American Economic Review (Papers and Proceedings)*, May 1985, **75**: 381–385.

von Neumann, John and Morgenstern, Oskar. *Theory of Games and Economic Behavior*. Princeton: Princeton University Press, 1944, 2nd Ed., 1947. 3rd Ed., 1953.

Yaari, Menahem. Some remarks on measures of risk aversion and on their uses, *Journal of Economic Theory*, October 1969, **1**: 315–329.

Yaari, Menahem. The Dual theory of choice under risk, *Econometrica*, January 1987, **55**: 95–115.

Part IV

Demand Theory

CONTENTS

8

Consumer's Surplus Without Apology

Robert D. Willig

The purpose of this paper is to settle the controversy surrounding consumer's surplus[1] and, by so doing, to validate its use as a tool of welfare economics. I will show that observed consumer's surplus can be rigorously utilized to estimate the unobservable compensating and equivalent variations—the correct theoretical measures of the welfare impact of changes in prices and income on an individual.

I derive precise upper and lower bounds on the percentage errors of approximating the compensating and equivalent variations with consumer's surplus. These bounds can be explicitly calculated from observable demand data, and it is clear that in most applications the error of approximation will be very small. In fact, the error will often be overshadowed by the errors involved in estimating the demand curve. The results in no way depend upon arguments about the constancy of the marginal utility of income.

Consequently, this chapter supplies specific empirical criteria which can replace the apologetic caveats frequently employed by those who presently apply consumer's surplus. Moreover, the results imply that consumer's surplus is usually a very good approximation to the appropriate welfare measures.

To preview, below I establish the validity of these rules of thumb: For a single[2] price change, if $|\bar{\eta}A/2m^0| \leq 0.05$, $|\underline{\eta}A/2m^0| \leq 0.05$, and if $|A/m^0| \leq 0.9$, then

$$\frac{\underline{\eta}|A|}{2m^0} \leq \frac{C - A}{|A|} \leq \frac{\bar{\eta}|A|}{2m^0} \tag{1}$$

and

$$\frac{\underline{\eta}|A|}{2m^0} \leq \frac{A - E}{|A|} \leq \frac{\bar{\eta}|A|}{2m^0} \tag{2}$$

Here,

$A =$ consumer's surplus area under the demand curve and between the two prices (positive for a price increase and negative for a price decrease);

$C=$ compensating variation corresponding to the price change;
$E=$ equivalent variation corresponding to the price change;
$m^0=$ consumer's base income;
$\bar{\eta}$ and $\underline{\eta}=$ respectively the largest and smallest values of the income elasticity of demand in the region under consideration.

The formulae place observable bounds on the percentage errors of approximating the C or E conceptual measures with observable A. For example, if the consumer's measured income elasticity of demand is 0.8 and if the surplus area under the demand curve between the old and new prices is 5 percent of income, then the compensating variation is within 2 percent of the measured consumer's surplus.

The ratio $|A|/m^0$ can be interpreted as a measure of the proportional change in real income due to the price change.[3] In most applications, the ratio will be very small. Measured income elasticities of demand tend to cluster closely about 1.0, with only rare outliers. Thus it can be expected that $\bar{\eta}|A|/2m^0$, the most important of the terms in (1) and (2), will usually be small enough to permit conscious and unapologetic substitution of A for C or E in studies of individual welfare.[4]

Should $\underline{\eta}|A|/2m^0$ be large, A would not be close to C and E. For such rare cases, formulae are provided below in Section IV which enable the estimation of C and E from the observable $\bar{\eta}$, $\underline{\eta}$, m^0 and A.

THE COMPENSATING AND EQUIVALENT VARIATIONS

In this section, I present definitions of conceptual tools to measure the costs or benefits of price changes to an individual consumer. While these theoretical measures are not directly observable, the analysis that follows in succeeding sections will show that they can be empirically estimated with consumer's surplus.

Throughout I will be assuming that the consumer behaves as though he were choosing his consumption bundle $X = X^1, X^2, \ldots, X^n$ to maximize an increasing strictly quasi-concave ordinal utility function $U(X)$ subject to the budget constraint $\sum p_i X^i = m$. The resulting demand function, denoted $X^i(p, m)$, are assumed to be differentiable. The indirect utility function, defined by

$$l(p, m) \equiv U[X^1(p, m), X^2(p, m), \ldots, X^n(p, m)]$$

relates the price and income parameters to the maximum level of utility the consumer can achieve under the resulting budget constraint. Clearly, by nonsatiation, $l(p, m)$ is monotone increasing in income m, and decreasing in prices p.

The indirect utility function can be used to make statements above individual welfare. Let the base, initial situation be characterized by prices p^0 and income m^0 while an alternative situation can be summarized by p', m'. The economic well-being of the consumer in the different situations can be compared by means of the ordinal ranking of the numbers $l(p^0, m^0)$ and $l(p', m')$.

Another way to effect this welfare test is to compare the income change $m' - m^0$ to the smallest income adjustment needed to make the consumer indifferent to the change in prices from p^0 to p'. If $m' - m^0$ is larger, then welfare is greater in the new situation, and inversely.

This test level of income adjustment is called the compensating income variation, denoted by C below. Symbolically,

$$l(p^0, m^0) = l(p', m^0 + C) \tag{3}$$

The welfare test above

$$l(p', m') \gtreqless l(p^0, m^0) \quad \text{as} \quad m' - m^0 \gtreqless C \tag{4}$$

follows immediately from (3) by nonsatiation. Thus the compensating variation is an individual's cost-benefit concept which makes price changes perfectly commensurable with changes in income.

Similarly, the equivalent variation in income (E) can be defined[5] by

$$l(p^0, m^0 - E) = l(p', m^0) \tag{5}$$

In words, $-E$ is the income change which has the same welfare impact on the consumer in the base situation as have the changes in prices from p^0 to p'. It reduces the impacts of different price changes down to the single dimension of income. As such, the equivalent variation concept can be used to rank the consumer's levels of well-being under various sets of prices. With the definitions $l(p^0, m^0 - E') = l(p', m^0)$ and $l(p^0, m^0 - E'') = l(p'', m^0)$, these welfare tests, too follow from nonsatiation:

$$l(p', m^0) \gtreqless l(p'', m^0) \quad \text{as} \quad E'' \gtreqless E' \tag{6}$$

$$l(p', m^0) \gtreqless l(p^0, m') \quad \text{as} \quad m^0 - E \gtreqless m'$$

The welfare tests (4) and (6) show that the compensating and equivalent variations are cost-benefit concepts which can be used to evaluate the impact of microeconomic policy on an individual.[6] These concepts derive practical importance from the fact that they can be estimated from observable consumer's surplus.

CONSUMER'S SURPLUS

The compensating and equivalent variations can be most incisively studied and related to consumer's surplus by means of the income compensation function.[7] This is denoted by $\mu(p|p^0, m^0)$ and is defined to be the least income required by the consumer when he faces prices p to achieve the same utility level he could enjoy (by maximizing behavior) under the parameters p^0, m^0. Thus, by definition,

$$l[p, \mu(p|p^0, m^0)] = l(p^0, m^0) \tag{7}$$

Trivially, we have

$$\mu(p^0|p^0, m^0) = m^0 \tag{8}$$

Now, we can see that the compensating and equivalent variations can be expressed or redefined in terms of the income compensation function. From (3), $m^0 + C = \mu(p'|p^0, m^0)$, or combining with (8),

$$C = \mu(p'|p^0, m^0) - \mu(p^0|p^0, m^0) \tag{9}$$

Similarly, from (5), $m^0 - E = \mu(p^0|p', m^0)$, or

$$E = \mu(p'|p', m^0) - \mu(p^0|p', m^0) \tag{10}$$

These relationships serve as the bridge to consumer's surplus.

It is well known[8] that

$$\frac{\partial\mu(p|p^0, m^0)}{\partial p_i} = X^i(p, \mu(p|p^0, m^0)) \tag{11}$$

This system of partial differential equations, together with the boundary condition (8), is the heart of analytical welfare economics.[9] The compensating and equivalent variations, or any measure of individual welfare that accepts the individual's own consumption preferences, can be calculated from the complete demand functions via (11) and (8).

Restricting attention to changes in a single price, p_1, let $p^0 = (p_1^0, p_2^0, \ldots, p_n^0)$ and $p' = (p_1', p_2^0, \ldots, p_n^0)$. Use the Fundamental Theorem of Calculus and (11) to rewrite (9) and (10) as

$$C = \int_{p_1^0}^{p_1'} X^1(p_1, p_2^0, \ldots, p_n^0, \mu(p_1, p_2^0, \ldots, p_n^0|p_1^0, p_2^0, \ldots, p_n^0, m^0))\,dp_1 \tag{12}$$

$$E = \int_{p_1^0}^{p_1'} X^1(p_1, p_2^0, \ldots, p_n^0, \mu(p_1, p_2^0, \ldots, p_n^0|p_1', p_2^0, \ldots, p_n^0, m^0))\,dp_1 \tag{13}$$

These formulae express the compensating and equivalent variations as areas under demand curves, between the old and new price horizontals. The demand curves are not Marshallian in that the income parameters are not constant. Instead, they are Hicksian compensated demand curves, because the income parameters include compensation which varies with the price to keep the consumer at a constant level of utility. The only distinction between C and E in (12) and (13) is the level of utility the compensation is designed to reach.

Referring to Figure 1, C is the area $p_1^0 p_1'$ be under the demand curve compensated to $l(p^0, m^0)$. This curve crosses the Marshallian curve $X^1(p, m^0)$ at p_1^0, since $\mu(p^0|p^0, m^0) = m^0$. With $p_1' > p_1^0$, if X^1 is noninferior $(\partial X^1/\partial m \geq 0)$ this compensated curve lies above the Marshallian one for $p_1 > p_1^0$, since $\mu(p_1, p_2^0, \ldots, p_n^2|p^0, m^0) \geq m^0$ whenever $p_1 > p_1^0$. Similarly, E is the area $p_1^0 p_1'$ af under the demand curve

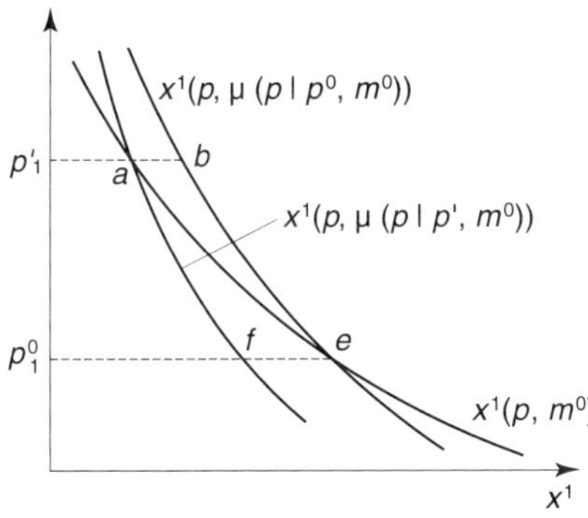

Figure 1.

compensated to $l(p', m^0)$. This Hicksian curve crosses the Marshallian one at p_1', and lies below it for $p_1 < p_1'$. The area usually called consumer's surplus is $p_1^0 p_1' ae$, defined by the observable Marshallian demand curve. Denoting this area by A, we have, then, $C \geq A \geq E$, for noninferior X^1 (the inequalities reverse for X^1 inferior). Of course, it also follows immediately that if there is no income effect ($\partial X^1 / \partial m \equiv 0$), $C = A = E$.

These qualitative results may be useful for some cost-benefit analyses. For example, suppose a policy would raise both an individual's income and the price of non-inferior good. If the observable consumer's surplus area A were greater than the income boost, it could be inferred from the inequality that C also would be greater. Then, from the welfare test (4), an analyst could conclude that the policy would be injurious to the consumer.

However, usually more information than this is needed about C and E. What is required is a methodology to estimate the welfare measures from observable data. In the next section I show how C and E can be explicitly calculated from observables when the income elasticity of demand is constant.

CONSTANT INCOME ELASTICITY

Constant income elasticity of demand for X^1 means that

$$\frac{\partial X^1(p, m)}{\partial m} \frac{m}{X^1(p, m)} \equiv \eta$$

Then, we have the simple differential equation $dX^1/X^1 = \eta(dm/m)$ which can be integrated from $X^1(p, m^0)$ to yield

$$X^1(p, m) = X^1(p, m^0) \left[\frac{m}{m^0}\right]^\eta$$

The entire income compensation function can be derived by substituting this expression into (11) and solving the resulting differential equation with boundary condition (8). We have, suppressing unchanging arguments,

$$\frac{d\mu}{dp_1} = X^1(p_1, \mu) = X^1(p_1, m^0)\left[\frac{\mu}{m^0}\right]^{\eta}$$

or

$$\mu^{-\eta}\,d\mu = (m^0)^{-\eta}X^1(p_1, m^0)\,dp_1$$

Then, integration between p_1^0 and p_1', remembering that $\mu(p_1^0) = m^0$, yields

$$\frac{[\mu(p_1')]^{1-\eta} - [m^0]^{1-\eta}}{1-\eta} = (m^0)^{-\eta}\int_{p_1^0}^{p_1'} X^1(p_1, m^0)\,dp_1 \tag{14}$$

for $\eta \neq 1$, and for $\eta = 1$,

$$\ln \mu(p_1') - \ln m^0 = \frac{1}{m^0}\int_{p_1^0}^{p_1'} X^1(p_1, m^0)\,dp_1$$

Hence, after rearranging we have these explicit expressions for the income compensation function:

$$\mu(p_1'|p_1^0, m^0) = m^0\left[1 + \left(\frac{1-\eta}{m^0}\right)\int_{p_1^0}^{p_1'} X^1(p_1, m^0)\,dp_1\right]^{1/1-\eta} \qquad \eta \neq 1 \tag{15}$$

$$\mu(p_1'|p_1^0, m^0) = (m^0)\exp\left[\frac{1}{m^0}\int_{p_1^0}^{p_1'} X^1(p_1, m^0)\,dp_1\right] \qquad \eta = 1 \tag{16}$$

These give the welfare measure μ in terms of the potentially observable constant income elasticity of demand and the consumer's surplus area under the Marshallian demand curve. Let us denote this area by

$$A \equiv \int_{p_1^0}^{p_1'} X^1(p_1, m^0)\,dp_1 \tag{17}$$

From (15), we see that if $\eta = 0$, $\mu(p_1'|p_1^0, m^0) = m^0 + A$. However, from (16) we see that if preferences are homothetic, the consequent unitary η does not imply any equalities among C, E, and A. Below, for expositional convenience, I ignore the case $\eta = 1$.

Recalling the definitions of C and E, (9) and (10), and loosely applying to (15) this Taylor approximation,

$$(1+t)^{1/1-\eta} \approx 1 + \frac{t}{1-\eta} + \frac{\eta t^2}{2(1-\eta)^2}$$

(where $\approx$ means "approximately equal to"), we get:

$$C \approx A + \frac{\eta A^2}{2m^0}, \qquad E \approx A - \frac{\eta A^2}{2m^0}, \qquad \frac{C-A}{A} \approx \frac{\eta A}{2m^0} \qquad \text{and} \qquad \frac{A-E}{A} \approx \frac{\eta A}{2m^0}$$

This was the striking result on the percentage error of approximating C with A which was previewed in the introduction. The next section will establish this formula rigorously for nonconstant income elasticity of demand.

ESTIMATION RESULTS

Assume that in the region of price-income space under consideration,[10] $\bar{\eta}$ and $\underline{\eta}$ are upper and lower bounds, respectively, on $(\partial X^1(p, m)/\partial m)(mX^1(p, m))$, with neither equal to 1.[11] It follows from the Mean Value Theorem that

$$\left(\frac{m_2}{m_1}\right)^{\underline{\eta}} \leq \frac{X^1(p, m_2)}{X^1(p, m_1)} \leq \left(\frac{m_2}{m_1}\right)^{\bar{\eta}} \qquad \text{for } m_2 \geq m_1 \tag{18}$$

Let us consider the welfare impact of a price increase from p_1^0 to p_1'. Since $\mu(p_1|p^0, m^0) \geq \mu(p_1^0|p^0, m^0)$ for $p_1 \geq p_1^0$, we can set $m_2 = \mu(p_1)$ and $m_1 = \mu(p_1^0) = m^0$ in (18):

$$\left[\frac{\mu(p_1)}{m^0}\right]^{\underline{\eta}} \leq \frac{X^1(p_1, \mu(p_1))}{X^1(p_1, m^0)} \leq \left[\frac{\mu(p_1)}{m^0}\right]^{\bar{\eta}}$$

Rearranging, and substituting from (11) yields

$$0 \leq X^1(p, m^0)^{-\underline{\eta}} \leq \frac{\partial \mu(p)}{\partial p_1}[\mu(p)]^{-\underline{\eta}} = \partial\left[\frac{\mu(p)^{1-\underline{\eta}}}{1-\underline{\eta}}\right]/\partial p_1$$

and

$$0 \leq \partial\left[\frac{\mu(p)^{1-\bar{\eta}}}{1-\bar{\eta}}\right]/\partial p_1 = \frac{\partial \mu(p)}{\partial p_1}\mu(p)^{-\bar{\eta}} \leq X^1(p, m^0)(m^0)^{-\bar{\eta}}$$

Integrating these relationships with respect to p_1 between p_1^0 and p_1' (as in (14)) preserves the inequalities. Rearrangement of the resulting relationships yields these bounds:

$$m^0\left[1 + (1-\underline{\eta})\frac{A}{m^0}\right]^{1/1-\underline{\eta}} \leq \mu(p'|p^0, m^0) \leq m^0\left[1 + (1-\bar{\eta})\frac{A}{m^0}\right]^{1/1-\bar{\eta}} \tag{19}$$

provided

$$\underline{\eta}, \bar{\eta} \neq 1, 1 + (1-\underline{\eta})\frac{A}{m^0} > 0$$

and

$$1 + (1-\bar{\eta})\frac{A}{m^0} > 0$$

For the case of a price decrease from p_1^0 to p_1', since $\mu(p_1|p_1^0, m^0) \leq m^0$ for $p_1 \leq p_1^0$, we can set $m_2 = m^0$ and $m_1 = \mu(p_1)$ in (18), and then follow the same sequence of steps. Once again, (19) emerges, but reference to (17) shows that here A is negative.

Invoking the definition (9), (19) can be rewritten as

$$\frac{\left[1 + (1 - \underline{\eta})\frac{A}{m^0}\right]^{1/1-\underline{\eta}} - 1 - \frac{A}{m^0}}{|A|/m^0} \leq \frac{C - A}{|A|} \leq \frac{\left[1 + (1 - \bar{\eta})\frac{A}{m^0}\right]^{1/1-\bar{\eta}} - 1 - \frac{A}{m^0}}{|A|/m^0} \tag{20}$$

Also, using (10) and reversing the roles of p' and p^0 in (19) (but not in the definition of A) gives

$$\frac{\left[1 - (1 - \underline{\eta})\frac{A}{m^0}\right]^{1/1-\underline{\eta}} - 1 + \frac{A}{m^0}}{|A|/m^0} \leq \frac{A - E}{|A|} \leq \frac{\left[1 - (1 - \bar{\eta})\frac{A}{m^0}\right]^{1/1-\bar{\eta}} - 1 + \frac{A}{m^0}}{|A|/m^0} \tag{21}$$

The measures of a consumer's welfare can be tightly estimated from observables via (19)–(21), regardless of the size of A/m^0, if $1 \pm (1 - \underline{\eta})A/m^0 > 0$, $1 \pm (1 - \bar{\eta})A/m^0 > 0$, and if $\underline{\eta}$, and $\bar{\eta}$ are sufficiently close in value.[12] Of course, in the limit, as $\underline{\eta}$ approaches $\bar{\eta}$, (19) reduces to the constant elasticity formula (15). Moreover, we shall see that if the absolute values of $\underline{\eta}A/2m^0$ and $\bar{\eta}A/2m^0$ are small, then (20) and (21) reduce to elegant rules of thumb.

Table 1 displays the numerical values of the following coefficients for selected choices of η and a:

$$\frac{\eta a}{2}, \quad \frac{[1 + (1 - \eta)a]^{1/1-\eta} - 1 - a}{a}$$

and

$$\frac{[1 - (1 - \eta)a]^{1/1-\eta} - 1 + a}{a}$$

The latter two expressions encompass the forms of the bounds in (20) and (21), when a is interpreted as $|A|/m^0$.[13] It can be readily seen from the table that for the ranges of parameter values studied,[14] when $|\eta a/2|$ is small (say less than 0.05), $\eta a/2$ is close enough (within 0.005) to the actual bounds for most practical purposes. This numerical observation corroborates the loose application to (15) of the Taylor Series expansion in the previous section. More importantly, it establishes the rules of thumb previewed in (1) and (2).[15]

Addition of (1) and (2) yields a check on the numerical proximity of C and E: when $|\underline{\eta}A/2m^0| \leq 0.05$, $|\bar{\eta}A/2m^0| \leq 0.05$, and $|A/m^0| \leq 0.9$,

$$\frac{\underline{\eta}|A|}{m^0} \leq \frac{C - E}{|A|} \leq \frac{\bar{\eta}|A|}{m^0} \tag{23}$$

So, the analysis hinges on the magnitudes of η and A/m^0. As discussed in the introduction, in most practical applications $|\eta A/2m^0|$ and $|A/m^0|$ are likely to be small

Table 1[a]

η \ a	.001	.005	.010	.020	.030	.040	.050	.075	.100	.150	.200	.250
	$-.001$	$-.005$	$-.010$	$-.020$	$-.030$	$-.040$	$-.050$	$-.075$	$-.100$	$-.150$	$-.200$	$-.250$
$-.200$	$-.001$	$-.005$	$-.010$	$-.019$	$-.029$	$-.038$	$-.046$	$-.067$	$-.086$	$-.121$	$-.152$	$-.180$
	$-.001$	$-.005$	$-.010$	$-.021$	$-.032$	$-.043$	$-.054$	$-.086$	$-.121$	$-.205$	$-.316$	$-.480$
	$-.001$	$-.003$	$-.005$	$-.010$	$-.015$	$-.020$	$-.025$	$-.038$	$-.051$	$-.076$	$-.101$	$-.126$
-1.01	$-.001$	$-.003$	$-.005$	$-.010$	$-.015$	$-.019$	$-.024$	$-.035$	$-.046$	$-.066$	$-.085$	$-.102$
	$-.001$	$-.003$	$-.005$	$-.010$	$-.016$	$-.021$	$-.027$	$-.041$	$-.056$	$-.090$	$-.129$	$-.174$
	.000	.001	.002	.003	.005	.006	.008	.011	.015	.023	.030	.038
.30	.000	.001	.002	.003	.005	.006	.008	.011	.015	.023	.029	.036
	.000	.001	.002	.003	.005	.006	.008	.011	.015	.023	.031	.039
	.000	.001	.003	.005	.008	.010	.013	.019	.025	.038	.050	.063
.50	.000	.001	.003	.005	.008	.010	.013	.019	.025	.038	.050	.063
	.000	.001	.003	.005	.008	.010	.013	.019	.025	.038	.050	.063
	.000	.002	.004	.007	.011	.014	.018	.026	.035	.053	.070	.088
.70	.000	.002	.004	.007	.011	.014	.018	.027	.035	.054	.072	.090
	.000	.002	.004	.007	.010	.014	.017	.026	.035	.051	.068	.085
	.000	.002	.005	.009	.014	.018	.023	.034	.045	.068	.090	.113
.90	.000	.002	.005	.009	.014	.018	.023	.034	.046	.070	.095	.120
	.000	.002	.004	.009	.013	.018	.022	.033	.044	.065	.085	.105
	.001	.003	.005	.010	.015	.020	.025	.038	.051	.076	.101	.126
1.01	.001	.003	.005	.010	.015	.020	.026	.039	.052	.080	.108	.138
	.001	.003	.005	.010	.015	.020	.025	.037	.049	.072	.094	.116
	.001	.003	.006	.011	.017	.022	.028	.041	.055	.083	.110	.138
1.10	.001	.003	.006	.011	.017	.022	.028	.043	.057	.088	.119	.152
	.001	.003	.006	.011	.016	.022	.027	.040	.053	.078	.102	.125
	.001	.003	.006	.012	.018	.024	.030	.045	.060	.090	.120	.150
1.20	.001	.003	.006	.012	.018	.024	.031	.047	.063	.097	.132	.169
	.001	.003	.006	.012	.018	.024	.029	.043	.057	.084	.110	.134
	.001	.004	.008	.015	.023	.030	.038	.056	.075	.113	.150	.188
1.50	.001	.004	.008	.015	.023	.031	.039	.059	.080	.125	.173	.224
	.001	.004	.007	.015	.022	.029	.036	.054	.070	.102	.132	.160
	.001	.005	.010	.020	.030	.040	.050	.075	.100	.150	.200	.250
2.00	.001	.005	.010	.020	.031	.042	.053	.081	.111	.176	.250	.333
	.001	.005	.010	.020	.029	.038	.048	.070	.091	.130	.167	.200
	.002	.008	.015	.030	.045	.060	.075	.113	.150	.225	.300	.375
3.00	.002	.008	.015	.031	.047	.064	.082	.129	.180	.302	.455	.657
	.002	.008	.015	.029	.043	.056	.069	.100	.129	.180	.226	.266
	.003	.013	.025	.050	.075	.100	.125	.188	.250	.375	.500	.625
5.00	.003	.013	.026	.053	.082	.114	.147	.244	.362	.716	1.477	**
	.002	.012	.024	.047	.069	.089	.109	.154	.193	.261	.317	.364
	.005	.025	.050	.100	.150	.200	.250	.375	.500	.750	1.000	1.250
10.00	.005	.026	.053	.115	.186	.271	.374	.774	1.916	**	**	**
	.005	.024	.047	.089	.126	.160	.191	.257	.312	.396	.460	.509

[a] Each group of three numbers includes, from the top, $\eta a/2$, $[(1+(1-\eta)a)^{1/1-\eta}-1-a]/a$, and $[(1-(1-\eta)a)^{1/1-\eta}-1+a]/a$. The entry ** indicates that $(1+(1-\eta)a) < 0$.

enough for the rules of thumb to apply. If not, equations (19)–(21) and Table 1 will be useful. Even if the calculated error bounds are too large to be ignored, the compensating and equivalent variations may still be usefully estimated from the data via the formulae.

INDIVIDUAL WELFARE AND CONSUMER'S SURPLUS

With the approximation results in hand, let us return to the question of how to make statements about individual welfare, based on observable data. Remember from (4) that $l(p', m') \geq / \leq l(p^0, m^0)$ as $m' - m^0 \geq / \leq C$. With the empirical information that $\underline{C} \leq C \leq \bar{C}$, where $\underline{C}$ and $\bar{C}$ can be calculated from (20) or (22), it can be concluded that

$$
\begin{aligned}
l(p', m') &> l(p^0, m^0), &\quad \text{if} \quad & m' - m^0 > \bar{C} \\
l(p', m') &< l(p^0, m^0), &\quad \text{if} \quad & m' - m^0 < \underline{C}
\end{aligned}
\tag{24}
$$

If $\underline{C}$ and $\bar{C}$ are close in value, (24) provides a welfare test of considerable power.[16] If $|\bar{\eta}A/2m^0|$ and $|\underline{\eta}A/2m^0|$ are small enough, both $\underline{C}$ and $\bar{C}$ can be safely replaced in (24) by A. Otherwise, they can be calculated from $\bar{\eta}$, $\underline{\eta}$, A, and m^0.

To conclude, at the level of the individual consumer, cost-benefit welfare analysis can be performed rigorously and unapologetically by means of consumer surplus.

ACKNOWLEDGEMENTS

This chapter is drawn from doctoral research done at Stanford University under the guidance of Jim Rosse. I am grateful for his support and for the standards of professional excellence he tried to teach me. I would also like to thank Megina Jack for considerable editorial assistance.

NOTES

1. Throughout, the term consumer's surplus is used to refer to the area to the left of an individual's fixed-income (Marshallian) demand curve and between the relevant price horizontals. The concept of consumer's surplus originated in 1844 (see Jules Dupuit) and has been controversial ever since. Alfred Marshall, who popularized the tool, stipulated that for it to be validly used the marginal utility of money must be constant (Marshall, p. 842 or David Katzner, p. 152). However, Harold Hotelling wrote that consumer's surpluses "give a meaningful measure of social value. This breaks down if the variations under consideration are too large a part of the total economy of the person . . ." (p. 289). John Hicks too, stated only a gentle caution: "In order that the Marshallian measure of consumer's surplus should be a good measure, one thing alone is needful—that the income effect should be small" (p. 177). More recently, though, Paul Samuelson (pp. 194–95) concluded that consumer's surplus is a worse than useless concept (because it confuses), and I. M. D. Little

(p. 180) agreed, calling it no more than a "theoretical toy." None the less, theorists and cost-benefit analysts have persisted in their use of the tool. For justification they resort (see E. J. Mishan, pp. 337–38, for example), with no formal theoretical support, to statements similar to those quoted above from Hotelling and Hicks.

2. While I restrict attention to single price changes here, analogous, but more complex formulae are derived for multiple price changes in my papers (1973a,b).

3. Or the ratio can be interpreted using the words of Hotelling quoted in Note 1 as the relative size of the variation.

4. Formulae (1) and (2) reflect the cautions (see Note 1) of both Hotelling and Hicks.

5. The definitions (3) and (5) correspond to those of Hicks, p. 177, and Samuelson, p. 199.

6. They also can serve as building blocks for methodologies to make social welfare judgements. The Compensation Principle is a well-known example (see Tibor Scitovsky).

7. This theoretical tool was introduced by Lionel McKenzie, and definitively studied by Leonid Hurwicz and Hirofumi Uzawa.

8. See Hurwicz and Uzawa for a state-of-the-art derivation. Heuristically, (11) says that the first-order income change, $d\mu$, required to compensate for the price increase, dp_1, is just the augmentation needed to buy the old consumption bundle, $X(p, \mu, (p|p^0, m^0))$, at the new prices $p_1 + dp_1, p_2, \ldots, p_n$, rather than at the old prices p. The irrelevance to this calculation of the concomitant substitution effects is the result of the envelope theorem.

9. This point of view was taken by Herbert Mohring.

10. This region is $\{(p, m) : p_1 = \alpha p_1^0 + (1 - \alpha)p_1', 0 \leq \alpha \leq 1; \quad p_i = p_i^0, i \neq 1; \quad m = \gamma m^0 + (1-\gamma)\mu(p|p^0, m^0), 0 \leq \gamma \leq 1 \quad \text{and} \quad X_1(p, m) > 0\}$.

11. Either $\bar{\eta}$ or $\underline{\eta}$ can be arbitrarily close to 1.

12. The most plausible cause of the negation of these conditions is $(\partial X^1/\partial m)(m/X^1) \to \infty$. However, regions in which X^1 is identically zero can be ignored, since there both μ and A are unchanging. To handle the case in which $X^1 = 0$ and $\partial X^1/\partial m \neq 0$ near the boundary of the relevant region, bounds on μ can be derived from bounds on $\partial X^1/\partial m$. Because these are generally more gross than (19), the best approach is to take this tack only in the vicinity of the singularity, use (19) on the rest of the path of integration, and splice the sets of inequalities together. The formulae for such procedures can be found in my 1973a,b papers. An explicit solution for μ when $\partial X^1/\partial m$ is independent of m is also reported there.

13. For example, the value of the lower bound in (20) when $\eta = 2$ and $A/m^0 = -0.05$ is 0.048. This can be found in Table 1 as the value of $[(1 - (1 - \bar{\eta})a)^{1/1-\eta} - 1 + a]/|a|$ when $\eta = 2$ and $a = 0.05$.

14. These seem to include most values that would be found for these parameters in actual applications.

15. When $|\eta A/2m^0| \leq 0.05$ and $|\bar{\eta}A/2m^0| \leq 0.05$, it suffices for $1 \pm (1 - \underline{\eta})A/m^0 > 0$ and $1 \pm (1 - \bar{\eta})A/m^0 > 0$ that $|A/m^0| < 0.9$.

16. Another welfare comparison (which may be useful for an analysis of social welfare with a Bergsonian social welfare function) is made possible by the fact (see Hurwicz and Uzawa) that $\mu(p^0|p, m)$, viewed as a function of p and m, is a proper indirect utility function.

$$\mu(p^0|p, m) = E + m$$

where E is the equivalent variation associated with a change from p^0 to p. Hence this particular ordinal indirect utility function can be exactly expressed by areas under compensated demand curves, as in (13), or it can be estimated from consumer's surplus via (19), (21), or (2).

REFERENCES

Arrow, K. J. and Scitovsky, T. *Readings in Welfare Economics*, vol. 12, Homewood 1969.

Dupuit, J. On the measurement of the utility of public works, (1844), translated and reprinted in Arrow, K. J. and Scitovsky, T. eds., *Readings in Welfare Economics*, vol. 12, Homewood 1969, 255–283.

Hicks, J. R. *A Revision of Demand Theory*, London 1956.

Hotelling, H. The general welfare in relation to problems of taxation and of railway and utility rates, reprinted in Arrow, K. J. and Scitovsky, T. eds., *Readings in Welfare Economics*, vol. 12, Homewood 1969.

Hurwicz, L. and Uzawa, H. On the integrability of demand functions. In: Chipman, J. S. et al., eds., *Preferences, Utility, and Demand*, New York 1971, 114–148.

Katzner, D. *Static Demand Theory*, New York 1970

Little, I. M. D., *A Critique of Welfare Economics*, London 1957.

Marshall, A., *Principles of Economics*, 9th ed., New York 1961.

McKenzie, L. W. Demand theory without a utility index, *Review of Economic Studies*, June 1957, **24**: 185–89.

Mishan, E. J., *Cost-Benefit Analysis: An Introduction*, New York 1971.

Mohring, H. Alternative welfare gain and loss measures, *Western Economic Journal*, Dec. 1971, **9**: 349–368.

Samuelson, P. A., *Foundations of Economic Analysis*, Cambridge 1947.

Scitovsky, T., A note on welfare propositions in economics, reprinted in Arrow, K. J. and Scitovsky, T., eds., *Readings in Welfare Economics*, vol. 12, Homewood 1969.

Willig, R. (1973a) Consumer's Surplus: A Rigorous Cookbook, tech. rep. no. 98, Economics Series, Inst. for Mathemat. Stud. in the Soc. Sci., Stanford Univ. 1973.

Willig, R. Welfare Analysis of Policies Affecting Prices and Products, memo. no. 153, Center for Research in Econ. Growth, Stanford Univ. 1973.

9

Queues, Rations, and Market: Comparisons of Outcomes for the Poor and the Rich

Raaj Kumar Sah

This chapter compares outcomes of alternative allocation systems (queues, convertible and nonconvertible rations, and unhindered market) to distribute limited quantity of a deficit good among heterogeneous individuals. It is shown that, for the poor, the ranking of systems (from better to worse) is convertible rations, nonconvertible rations, queues, and nonintervention. The rich are better off under nonintervention than under other systems. These and other positive results are robust to certain types of commodity taxes and administrative costs.

"Nonmarket" allocation systems such as rationing and queues are not only extensively employed in many less developed countries and centrally planned economies, but also their consequences are issues of important controversies. There is a wide range of features that such allocation systems exhibit; for instance, the rationed good is not convertible (i.e., individuals cannot exchange this good in secondary markets) in some rationing and queue systems, whereas it is partly or fully convertible in others.[1]

Each of the above allocation systems leads to a markedly different distribution of welfare among various individuals in the economy, and these welfare distributions are quite different, in turn, from the one that would emerge if the government were not intervening. The primary objective of this paper is to compare the welfare of specific groups of individuals (particularly the poor and the rich) when the limited supply of a good (the deficit good) is allocated though alternative allocation systems, including non-intervention. I do this in two steps: (i) I ascertain the utilities of various groups of individuals under each allocation system, and then (ii) I take each pair of allocation systems and attempt to determine whether a specific group of individuals is better off under one allocation system or another.

My analysis is *positive*, and it is not my objective here to determine the societal desirability of alternative allocation systems. I believe, however, that analyses of the kind developed in the present paper can contribute significantly to typical political or normative debates about whether, when, and how governments ought to intervene in

Reprinted with permission from *American Economic Review*, Vol. 77, No. 1, 1987, pp. 69–77

markets. For instance, a main argument often given in favor of the queue or the ration system is that (since direct income subsidies to the poor are not feasible) these allocation systems might be effective ways of helping the poor. My comparisons of the welfare of the poor under alternative allocation systems can help to recognize some of the circumstances when such arguments are useful and when they are not.

The specific allocation systems which I compare here are: nonintervention, convertible and nonconvertible rations, and the queue system (without secondary trade).[2] I show that

(1) *For the poor, the ranking of allocation systems (from better to worse) is convertible rations, nonconvertible rations, the queue system, and nonintervention.* The queue system, thus, does not turn out to be relatively as beneficial to the poor as it is often thought to be. Also, governments frequently attempt to enforce nonconvertibility of rations. Such an emphasis is potentially harmful to the poor.

(2) *The rich are better off under nonintervention than they are under other allocation systems. Also, the rich are better off under convertible rations than they are under the queue system.* These results as we shall see, are understandable consequences of the high wages and large endowments that the rich typically have.

It is often believed that no one can be worse off, and some individuals must be better off, under convertible rations than nonconvertible rations, because there are gains to trade in the former system. But this view is incorrect because, as James Tobin (1952) had rightly argued, the convertibility of rations may alter individuals' incentives to buy the rationed good. Consequently, convertible rations are not always weakly Pareto superior to nonconvertible rations. I demonstrate this important aspect of rationing.

A methodological aspect of this chapter is that the standard tools of marginal analysis are not usable here because alternative allocation systems result in equilibria which cannot be assumed to be in the neighborhood of one another. Yet, as we shall see, my results are robust not only to many parameters of the economy but also to certain types of commodity taxes and administrative costs. An additional strength of my pairwise comparisons among alternative systems is that the comparison between any two systems does not depend on whether a third system is considered feasible or not. For instance, nonintervention may not be a realistic alternative in centrally planned economies. In these contexts, the relevant comparisons are those among alternative government managed systems (i.e., among the rationing system and the queue system).

A central contribution to the comparison of allocation systems is by Martin Weitzman (1977, pp. 517–19) in which he compared, based on a normative criterion of "satisfying the needs of the population", the allocation of a fixed quantity of the deficit good through nonconvertible rations versus a "price system". My analysis is different in not only the scope (I compare several important allocation systems in addition to the two that he does) and the emphasis (mine is on obtaining positive results, whereas his is on normative analysis based on a specific social criterion), but also in a critical aspect of the model of the price system (discussed later).

This chapter is not related to the important literature which has extended the theory of second-best to instruments such as rations and queues. For instance, Roger

Guesnerie and Kevin Roberts (1984) show that, starting from a second-best situation, a government can do better under certain circumstances if nonconvertible rations are partly introduced into an economy. Sam Bucovetsky (1984) shows that the same is possible if a queue system is partly introduced into an economy. The underlying economic reason is simple: the government cannot do worse by having additional policy instruments (whatever the instruments might be, provided it is assumed that there are no administrative costs) and it may do strictly better under some circumstances, regardless of what the social criterion might be.

The present paper has a different aim. My motivation here is not to study rations or queue as *additional* (and costless) policy instruments through which the government can do better, based on some criterion. Instead, my motivation is to examine and compare rations, queues, and market as *alternative* allocation systems.[3] In the following section, I derive the expressions for individuals' utilities under alternative systems. Then the method for comparing an individual's utility is summarized. Finally, alternative systems are then compared to one another.

INDIVIDUALS' UTILITIES UNDER ALTERNATIVE ALLOCATION SYSTEMS

First, I determine the utility levels of different individuals under four allocation systems: nonintervention (market), nonconvertible rations, convertible rations, and the queue system. These system are respectively denoted by superscripts $I = M, R, C,$ and Q. Individuals are denoted by the superscript h. The variable n^h is the proportion of individuals of type h in the economy, $n^h > 0$, and $\sum_h n^h = 1$.

Denote the available supply (per capita) of the deficit good by X, and its unit cost by p. For individual h, x^h, and V^h, respectively, denote the demand function for the deficit good, and the indirect utility function. I assume that the market demand for the deficit good would exceed the available quantity (i.e., there would be a "shortage") if its market price were to be set equal to its unit cost.[4] That is,

$$\sum_h n^h x^h(p, m^h) > X, \tag{1}$$

where m^h is the (full) income of individual h if the market price of the deficit good is p.[5]

Under nonintervention, therefore, private firms (owners of the deficit good) adjust the consumer price of the deficit good to equate its demand and supply. Under a government-managed system, the government procures the available quantity of the deficit good at its unit cost p, and distributes it through one or another allocation system.[6] I assume at present that the price of the deficit good that the government charges at its shops is also p; issues concerning administrative costs and commodity taxes are discussed later.

For individual h, let x^{hI} and V^{hI} denote the quantity of the deficit good consumed, and the utility obtained, under the allocation system I. The economywide consumption of the deficit good equals its available quantity under each system;

that is,

$$\sum_h n^h x^{hI} = X, \qquad \text{for} \qquad I = M, R, C, Q. \tag{2}$$

I now obtain the expressions for V^{hI} for various systems, which are needed for later comparisons.

Nonintervention

The individual h owns (through partial ownership of firms) $\alpha^h X$ units of the deficit good. Naturally, $\alpha^h \geq 0$, and $\sum_h n^h \alpha^h = 1$. If the market-clearing price is p^M, then the full income of individual h is $m + \alpha^h(p^M - p)X$.[7] Thus

$$V^{hM} = V^h(p^M, m^h + \alpha^h(p^M - p)X) \tag{3}$$

and

$$x^{hM} = x^h(p^M, m^h + \alpha^h(p^M - p)X).$$

The market price p^M is obtained by substituting the expression for x^{hM} into (2). We restrict our analysis to those situations where the aggregate market demand curve for the deficit good is downward sloping in its price. The relevant implication of this restriction, from (1) and (2), is that the market price p^M is higher than p. This implication is consistent with the intuition that systems such as rationing are typically employed in those situations where the market allocation would entail a significant rise in the price of the deficit good.

Nonconvertible rations

Under this system, individuals can buy (at government shops) up to a fixed quantity, X^R, of the deficit good, but no more, and resale is not permitted. Naturally, the population self-selects itself into two groups. The first group consists of those who wish to buy the deficit good in quantities smaller than or equal to X^R. These individuals are not constrained by rationing. For them,

$$V^{hR} = V^h(p, m^h). \tag{4}$$

The second group consists of those who want to consume more deficit good than X^R, but are constrained to consume only X^R. A convenient representation of an individual's utility under a rationing constraint is to define the virtual price of the deficit good for person h to be p^{hR}, which is obtained from $x^h(p^{hR}, m^h + (p^{hR} - p)X^R) = X^R$. Then, this person's consumption behavior under rationing is the same as that in the hypothetical case when he faces price p^{hR}, receives an income transfer $(p^{hR} - p)X^R$, and faces no rationing. Therefore, the utility level of person h can be expressed as

$$V^{hR} = V^h(p^{hR}, m^h + (p^{hR} - p)X^R),\tag{5}$$

where $p^{hR} > p$.[8]

I assume that there are at least some individuals in the economy (the poorest persons are among them) who do not (or cannot) buy the maximum ration quantity X^R. This I believe, is a more accurate representation in most situations (particularly in *LDCs*) than to assume that everyone buys the maximum ration quantity. It follows then that

$$X^R > X.\tag{6}$$

Convertible rations

If rations purchased from the government shops can be subsequently traded, and if the resulting equilibrium price of the deficit good is higher than p, then everyone would buy the full quantity of available ration. The ration per person is thus X. If p^C denotes the equilibrium price, then

$$V^{hC} = V^h(p^C, m^h + (p^C - p)X).\tag{7}$$

The price p^C is obtained by substituting $x^{hC} = x^h(p^C, m^h + (p^C - p)X)$ into (2). Comparison of (7) with (3) shows, as one might expect, that the key difference between nonintervention and convertible rations is that, in the latter system, the government intervention has effectively equalized the ownership of the deficit good. Since the income distribution in these two cases is different, p^C and p^M are not the same, in general. But $p^C > p$, given my earlier restriction that the aggregate demand curve for the deficit good is downward sloping in price.

Queues

The wage rate for individual h is denoted by w^h. I assume for brevity that the waiting time per unit purchase, t, is not significantly affected by the quantity purchased. This representation approximates those cases where individuals make several purchases within a single decision period; for instance, because the deficit good is dispensed in small lots, or because private storage of the good is expensive.[9] The opportunity price of the deficit good to individual h is $p + tw^h$, and his utility level is

$$V^{hQ} = V^h(p + tw^h, m^h),\tag{8}$$

where t is determined from $x^{hQ} = x^h(p + tw^h, m^h)$ and (2).

I assume that the prices of the nondeficit goods (i.e., of goods other than the deficit good) and the wage rate of any given individual are not significantly different under the four allocation systems described above. This would be the case if, for example, the supply elasticities of the nondeficit goods and the demand elasticities for different types of labor are large.

METHOD FOR COMPARING AN INDIVIDUAL'S UTILITY

If I and J represent two different allocation systems, then I want to ascertain whether the individual h is better off or worse off under I; that is, whether V^{hI} is larger or smaller than V^{hJ}. For notational brevity, let p^{hI} and m^{hI} denote the price of the deficit good and income, corresponding to individual h, under the system I. Let p^{hJ} and m^{hJ} denote the respective variables under the system J. Then the individual is obviously better off under the system J if $m^{hI} \geq m^{hJ}$ and $p^{hI} \leq p^{hJ}$, with at least one strict inequality. This is because a higher income or a lower price (or both) yield a higher utility.

To deal with the remaining cases, in which one of the two allocation systems entails a higher price but also higher income for an individual, define the metric

$$\Delta^h(I,J) = (m^{hI} - m^{hJ}) + (p^{hJ} - p^{hI})x^{hJ} \tag{9}$$

Then it can be shown that

$$V^{hI} > V^{hJ}, \quad \text{if} \quad \Delta^h(I,J) \geq 0. \tag{10}$$

A revealed preference argument underlying (10) is as follows. If $\Delta^h \geq 0$, then (9) implies that this individual could have purchased, in allocation system I, the same bundle of goods as he did in the allocation system J. The individual's actual purchase under the allocation system I, however, was different. Therefore, the individual h must be better off under I.[10]

Note that this method does not yield a verdict when the metric (9) is negative or when its sign cannot be ascertained based on the available information, but it is the best available method for comparing an individual's utility under two different situations, without restricting his preferences. In the analysis below, therefore, I compare as many pairs of allocation systems as are possible based on the above method.

COMPARISONS AMONG ALTERNATIVE ALLOCATION SYSTEMS

In this section, I compare the outcomes of the allocation systems described earlier. I do this first for the poor, then for the rich. I then compare certain aspects of convertible vs. nonconvertible rations. Issues concerning commodity taxation and administrative costs are examined at the end.

Comparisons for the poor

The poor are denoted by $h = 1$. Since the poor belong to the lower tail of the distribution of incomes and wages, their demand for the deficit good under nonconvertible rations is smaller than the per capita available quantity. That is,

$$x^{1R} < X. \tag{11}$$

No special assumption is needed for the poor to behave this way; the budget constraint itself will generate such a demand behavior at sufficiently low incomes. Also the poor do not get any part of the profit under nonintervention; this is a reasonable assumption because the poor do not typically possess ownership of firms. That is $\alpha^1 = 0$, and from (3): $V^{1M} = V^1(p^M, m^1)$. I now derive the following result: The ranking of allocation systems for the poor (from better to worse) is convertible rations, nonconvertible rations, the queue system, and nonintervention.

Begin by comparing convertible rations to nonconvertible rations. Expressions (4), (7) and (9) yield

$$\Delta^1(C, R) = (p^C - p)(X - x^{1R}). \tag{12}$$

Using (11) and recalling that $p^C > p$, it follows that (12) is positive. Therefore, the poor are better off under the ration system with convertibility than they are if rations are nonconvertible. The reason for this is as follows. Convertibility of rations brings an income gain to the poor, but it also entails a higher price for the deficit good. On the whole, the poor are better off with convertibility because the (income-producing) ration quantity they can get under this system exceeds the quantity of the deficit good they consume under nonconvertible rations.

The comparison between nonconvertible rations and the queue system is straightforward since, from (4) and (8), the poor have the same income under these two systems, but they face a higher price of the deficit good under the latter. This is because the queue system entails an *extra* cost of waiting, small though this extra cost may be for the poor. Thus, $V^{1R} > V^{1Q}$. Finally, compare $V^{1M} = V^1(p^M, m^1)$ to (8). The poor have the same income under the queue system and nonintervention, but the respective prices for the deficit good are $p + tw^1$ and p^M. Now recall that $p^M > p$. It follows then that a person with sufficiently low wage is better off under the queue system than under nonintervention.

Comparisons for the rich

The rich are denoted by $h = r$, and they belong to the upper tail of the distribution of incomes and wages. As one would expect, the comparisons between nonintervention and other systems depend, in part, on the ownership of the deficit good that the rich have under nonintervention. I show here that: the rich are better off under nonintervention than under other allocation systems, if their ownership of the deficit good under nonintervention is large; specifically if

$$\alpha^r X \geq x^{rI}, \quad \text{for} \quad I = R, C, Q. \tag{13}$$

That is, if the rich own more deficit good under nonintervention than what they consume under other systems.

The condition (13) is automatically satisfied in a two-class economy because, in this case, the rich own all of the deficit good under nonintervention, but (regardless of the allocation system) the poor consume at least some of the deficit good. In fact, we expect the condition (13) to be satisfied in a multiclass economy as well, because the rich typically own proportions of firms' shares which are far in excess of the proportions of the outputs of firms that they consume.

To establish the above results, I obtain the following from (3), (5), (7), (8), and (9)

$$\Delta^r(M, R) = (p^M - p)(\alpha^r X - X^R) \tag{14}$$

$$\Delta^r(M, C) = (p^C - p)(x^{rC} - X) + (p^M - p)(\alpha^r X - x^{rC}) \tag{15}$$

$$\Delta^r(M, Q) = (p^M - p)(\alpha^r X - x^{rQ}) + tw^r x^{rQ}. \tag{16}$$

Recall that $p^M > p$, and $p^C > p$. Using (13), thus, (14) and (16) are nonnegative. Further, under convertible rations, the consumption of the deficit good by the rich would typically not be less than the economywide average consumption; that is $x^{rC} \geq X$.[11] Hence, (15) is also nonnegative.

We can also show that those with very high wages (which includes the rich) are better off under convertible rations than under the queue system. Specifically, expressions (7), (8) and (9) yield:

$$\Delta^h(C, Q) = (p^C - p)X + [tw^h - (p^C - p)]x^{hQ}.$$

Since $p^C > p$, the preceding expression is positive if $w^h \geq (p^C - p)/t$.

Convertible vs. nonconvertible rations

To show that certain individuals are better off under nonconvertible rations than under convertible rations, I consider those whose consumption of the deficit good under convertible rations is between X and X^R; that is, $X^R \geq x^{hC} \geq X$. Among these individuals, there could be two types: those whose consumption is not constrained under nonconvertible rations, and those whose consumption is constrained. For the former type, expressions (4), (7) and (9) yield

$$\Delta^h(R, C) = (p^C - p)(X^{hC} - X). \tag{17}$$

For the latter type, expressions (5), (7), and (9) yield

$$\Delta^h(R, C) = (p^{hR} - p)(X^R - x^{hC}) \\ + (p^C - p)(x^{hC} - X). \tag{18}$$

Both (17) and (18) are nonnegative because $p^C > p$, and $p^{hR} > p$. Thus, this entire group of individuals is better off under nonconvertible rations than under convertible rations.

The intuition behind this result can be seen in two steps. First, under convertible rations, everyone has an incentive to buy the maximum quantity of rations available; consequently, this quantity equals X. There is no corresponding incentive under nonconvertible rations. Therefore, the maximum ration quantity, X^R, is larger than X, because there are individuals who do not buy the maximum ration quantity. Second, recall that the convertibility of rations implies a higher price of the deficit good, but also an income gain $(p^C - p) X$. Thus, for those individuals whose consumption under convertible rations is larger than X but smaller than X^R, the loss due to higher price exceeds the income gain from convertibility.

Note that the above result is based on my assumption that some individuals in the economy do not (or cannot) buy the maximum ration quantity under the nonconvertible ration system. Under the less realistic assumption that everybody buys the maximum quantity under the nonconvertible ration system, on the other hand, it is easily verified that convertible rations are weakly Pareto superior to nonconvertible rations.

Commodity taxes and administrative costs

An important generalization of the results presented earlier is that they remain unchanged if there is a tax (or subsidy) on the deficit good, provided the same tax applies under all allocation systems. To see this, let s denote the tax per unit of the deficit good. That is: (i) under a government-managed system, the price of the deficit good at government shops is $p + s$; (ii) under nonintervention, s is the difference between the market price of the deficit good and the price which firms owning this good receive; and (iii) the resulting budget surplus (or deficit) to the government, in each case, is sX per capita. Then, it can be verified that my comparisons among alternative systems are unaffected, regardless of what s is. This is because s cancels out when an individual's utility under alternative systems is compared.

My results are also unaffected by administrative costs, if these costs are not significantly different under alternative systems (i.e., the sum of storage, personnel, and other transaction costs accruing to the government as well as private intermediaries depends primarily on the total quantity of the deficit good), and if these costs are passed on to consumers through the price of the deficit good. This is simply because the effect of administrative cost, in this case, is analogous to that of a commodity tax.

Additional generalizations of the following kind are, therefore, straightforward. Suppose we find that $V^{hI} > V^{hJ}$ when systems I and J are hypothetically assumed to have the same administrative cost, then the same conclusion holds if in fact the system J has a higher administrative cost than that of I. As a specific example, my result that convertible rations are better for the poor than nonconvertible rations holds not only when these two systems entail the same administrative cost, but also when the latter system entails a larger administrative cost (for instance, if the cost of enforcing nonconvertibility exceeds the cost of transacting secondary trades).[12]

CONCLUDING REMARKS

Allocation systems such as rationing and queues are extensively employed in many *LDCs* and centrally planned economies. In this paper, I have compared the outcomes of such systems with one another, and with that of unhindered market. My analysis has concentrated on *positive* comparisons: I have attempted to ascertain, for each pair of allocation systems, whether a specific group of individuals (particularly the poor and the rich) is better off under one system or another. The results and insights obtained from these comparisons are valid, as well as informative for policy debates on these issues, regardless of the social criterion or political pressures (resulting, for instance, in an unwillingness to allow the market price to increase) based on which a government might want to choose an allocation system.

I recognize that there is a great diversity in the structures and the economic outcomes of the allocation systems that are employed in different contexts.[13] In this paper, I have used relatively simple models to depict alternative allocation systems and have focused on the comparisons of their outcomes within a narrow but important class of circumstances when the supply of a good is limited.[14] Within this class, however, most of my results are robust not only to parameters such as the cost and the quantity of the deficit good available in the economy, and the nature of heterogeneity in individuals' tastes, but also to certain types of commodity taxes and administrative costs. Moreover, my comparisons among alternative government- managed systems are relevant even when the quantity of the deficit good to be distributed among individuals is a policy choice, rather than a datum for the economy.

ACKNOWLEDGEMENTS

I thank Martin Weitzman and three anonymous referees for comments on an earlier version of this chapter.

NOTES

1. These systems have been employed and debated in developed countries as well, particularly in the context of external hostilities.
2. See a more detailed version of the present chapter (1986) for positive comparisons of some other systems such as the queue system with secondary trade, and the bundling system (where the deficit good is bundled with some other good).
3. I do not consider mechanisms such as nonlinear pricing schemes (with arbitrary nonlinearities) because such schemes are not feasible for consumption goods. In fact, only simple allocation systems, such as those considered in this paper, are typically feasible because of reasons such as the unavailability of information, and the limitations on third-party enforceability. My forthcoming paper with Joseph Stiglitz discusses some of the sources and the consequences of the restrictions on policy instruments available in *LCDs*.
4. In fact, it is under these conditions that governments typically intervene by employing allocation systems such as rations or queues.

5. For notational convenience, an individual's wage rate and the prices of nondeficit goods are suppressed in the arguments of his demand function and his indirect (individualistic) utility function.

6. In those contexts where nonintervention is not a feasible alternative (for instance, when the deficit good is produced in the public sector), p is the unit cost to the government.

7. Where $\alpha^h(p^M - p)X$ is the profit from ownership which nonintervention brings to individual h. Weitzman's model of a price system assumes for simplicity that these profits disappear altogether. But as we shall see, these profits (no matter how they are distributed among individuals) play a critical role in determining not only the welfare and the consumption of individuals but also the market-clearing price.

8. To see that $p^{hR} > p$, note from (5) that $\partial V^{hR}/\partial X^R = \mu^h(p^{hR} - p)$, where μ^h is the positive marginal utility of income for this person. Also, $\partial V^{hR}/\partial X^R$ is positive because this person wants to consume more of the deficit good. Hence, $p^{hR} > p$. See J. Peter Neary and Roberts (1980) for additional details of this representation.

9. My analysis is readily extended, however, to a more general specification in which t differs across individuals and it is determined in part by individual's decisions concerning the quantity and the frequency of their purchases. In fact, it can be easily verified that if t^h donates the waiting time per unit purchase, then a sufficient condition under which the results I derive later remain unaffected is that the waiting cost per unit purchase, $t^h w^h$, is very small (but positive) at the lower end of the wage distribution, and that this cost is relatively large at the upper end of the wage distribution.

10. Expression (10) can also be established by using the standard concavity properties of expenditure functions. See my 1986 paper.

11. Sufficient conditions for this to be the case are that the deficit good is normal, and that the individuals' tastes are similar.

12. Note that this chapter does not take a position on whether the total administrative cost under a particular system is larger or smaller than that in another system. This is because the empirical or conceptual basis for such a generalized assertion appears to be inadequate at present. Attention to administrative costs is nevertheless a step in the right direction because these costs are important in practice but, as I indicated earlier, they have been ignored in much of the literature.

13. See Janos Kornai (1980) for a description of some of the effects of nonprice controls in centrally planned economies; this work, however, does not emphasize a comparison of the outcomes of alternative controls.

14. Supply responses, on the other hand, have critical implications (for prices as well as individuals' earnings) in many situations. See, for instance, my article with T. N. Srinivasan (1986) for an analysis of the role of supply responses in determining the distributional consequences of partial food rationing in *LDC* cities.

REFERENCES

Bucovetsky, Sam. On the use of distributional waits, *Canadian Journal of Economics*, November 1984, **17**: 699–717.

Guesnerie, Roger and Roberts, Kevin. Effective policy tools and quantity controls, *Econometrica*, January 1984, **52**: 59–86.

Kornai, J. *Economics of Shortage*, Amsterdam: North-Holland, 1980.

Neary, J. Peter and Roberts, Kevin. The theory of household behaviour under rationing, *European Economic Review*, March 1980, **13**: 25–42.

Sah, Raaj Kumar. *Queues, Rations, and Market: Comparisons of Outcomes for the Poor and the Rich*, Economic Growth Center Discussion Paper 504, Yale University, 1986.

Sah, Raaj Kumar and Srinivasan, T. N. *Distributional Consequences of Rural Food Levy and Subsidized Urban Rations*, Economic Growth Center Discussion Paper 505, Yale University, 1986.

Sah, Raaj Kumar and Stiglitz, Joseph E. The taxation and pricing of agricultural and industrial goods in developing economies. In: Newbery D. O. G. and Stern, Nicholas H., eds. *Modern Tax Theory for Developing Countries*, Oxford: Oxford University Press, 1987.
Tobin, James. A survey of the theory of rationing, *Econometrica*, October 1952, **20**: 521–553.
Weitzman, Martin L. Is the price system or rationing more effective in getting a commodity to those who need it most, *Bell Journal of Economics*, Autumn 1977, **8**: 517–24.

Part V

Price Discrimination and Product Differentiation

CONTENTS

10

Price Discrimination and Social Welfare

Hal R. Varian

The effect on social welfare of third-degree price discrimination was first investigated by Joan Robinson (1933). Richard Schmalensee (1981) has recently reexamined this question and presented several new results. In particular, he noted that a *necessary* condition for price discrimination to increase social welfare—defined as consumers' plus producers' surplus—is that output increase.

Schmalensee established this result only in the case of independent demands and constant marginal costs. However, it turns out to be true in much more general circumstances. In this chapter I show how simple methods from duality theory can be used to establish this result and several other new results on the welfare effect of price discrimination.

A RESERVATION PRICE MODEL

Before proceeding to an examination of price discrimination in a general context, it is worth pausing to consider the special case of a reservation price model. I will describe the model in the context of discrimination by age—as in senior citizen discounts or youth discounts— but several other interpretations are possible. Assume that we have a set of consumers of different ages, and that one unit will be demanded by the consumers of age a if the price facing these consumers $p(a)$, is less than or equal to $r(a)$, the reservation price of these consumers. Suppose that the slope of $r(a)$ is of one sign, which without loss of generality we take to be negative. For simplicity, it is assumed that costs are zero, or equivalently, that constant marginal costs are incorporated into the definition of $r(a)$.

Suppose first that the monopolist must choose one price p_0 that will apply to all consumers. Then the maximization problem facing the monopolist is to choose a_0 to

Reprinted with permission from *American Economic Review*, Vol. 75, No. 4, 1985, pp. 870–875

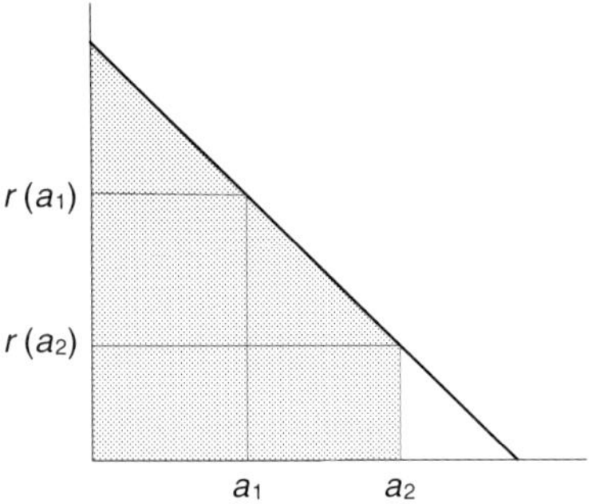

Figure 1. Surplus in reservation price model.

solve:

$$\max r(a_0)a_0.$$

Now suppose that the monopolist is allowed to price discriminate; that is, he can choose critical ages a_1, a_2 and prices p_1, p_2 such that the consumers younger than a_1 face price p_1 and consumers between a_1 and a_2 face price p_2. The problem facing the monopolist now is to solve:

$$\max r(a_1)a_1 + r(a_2)(a_2 - a_1).$$

In this model it is easy to see that consumers' plus producers' surplus is given by the area below the reservation price function, as depicted in Figure 1. Thus the total welfare rises when price discrimination is allowed if and only if total output goes up. And, as shown below, output must always rise in this sort of model.

Fact 1. If $r(a)$ is a decreasing function, then output and thus welfare must increase when price discrimination is allowed.

Proof. Assume not so that $a_0 > a_2$ and thus: $-r(a_0)a_1 > -r(a_2)a_1$. By profit maximization: $r(a_0)a_0 \geq r(a_2)a_2$. Adding these two inequalities together, and adding $r(a_1)a_1$ to each side of the resulting inequality gives

$$r(a_1)a_1 + r(a_0)(a_0 - a_1) > r(a_1)a_1 + r(a_2)(a_2 - a_1).$$

which contradicts profit maximization.

This result easily generalizes to the choice of many regimes of price discrimination as well: allowing more price discrimination always increases output and welfare. As the number of prices increases to infinity, we converge to perfect price discrimination and thus maximal social welfare.

In this model we have a very simple story about price discrimination: price discrimination always increases output and an increase in output is always associated with an increase in welfare. But the reservation price model is a very special sort of demand structure and it is worth investigating whether these results carry over to more general demand specifications. As Schmalensee shows, in general, output and welfare may increase or decrease when price discrimination is allowed, although an increase in output remains a necessary condition for welfare increase. This result provides an observable criterion for when welfare has gone down under price discrimination, but how can we recognize those circumstances in which welfare has increased? I provide some answers to this question and related questions below.

QUASI-LINEAR UTILITY AND CONSUMERS' SURPLUS

I want to continue to use the classical measure of consumers' plus producers' surplus, and the most general preference structure for which that is possible is that of quasi-linear utility, which is also known as the case of "constant marginal utility of income". For this class of preferences it is well known that not only does consumers' surplus serve as a legitimate measure of individual welfare, but also that the individual consumers' utility functions can be added up to form a social utility function, so that aggregate *consumers'* surplus is also meaningful. For a discussion of consumers' surplus and indirect utility, see my 1984 book (ch. 7). These observations imply that we can treat the aggregate demand function as though it were generated by a representative consumer with an indirect utility function of the form:

$$V(\mathbf{p}, y) = v(\mathbf{p} + y.$$

The aggregate consumer's income, y, is composed of some exogenous income which we take to be zero and the profits of the firm. Thus the appropriate form of the social objective function becomes:

$$V(\mathbf{p}, y) = v(\mathbf{p}) + \pi(\mathbf{p}).$$

By Roy's law the demand for good i is given by the negative of the derivative of $v(\mathbf{p})$ with respect to p_i—since the marginal utility of income is one. Thus the integral of demand is just $v(\mathbf{p})$. It follows that the above expression is nothing but the classical welfare measure of consumers' plus producers' surplus.

As a general principle, it is easier to differentiate to find demands than to integrate to find surplus; thus starting with the properties of the indirect utility function rather than the demand functions tends to simplify most problems in applied welfare economics. The most important property for our purposes concerns the curvature of the indirect utility function. The indirect utility function is always a quasiconvex function of prices, but in the case of quasi-linear utility, it is not hard to show that it is in fact a *convex* function of prices. (Proof: the expenditure function is $e(\mathbf{p}, u) = u - v(\mathbf{p})$ and it is necessarily a concave function of prices.)

UPPER AND LOWER BOUNDS ON WELFARE CHANGE

I turn now to the welfare effects of price discrimination for demand structures generated by quasi-linear utility. I start by describing a general result about such demands which can then be specialized in a number of ways. Consider an initial set of prices $\mathbf{p}^0$ and a final set of prices $\mathbf{p}^1$, and let $c(\mathbf{x}(\mathbf{p}^0))$ and $c(\mathbf{x}(\mathbf{p}^1))$ denote the total costs of production at the two different output levels associated with the price vectors $\mathbf{p}^0$ and $\mathbf{p}^1$. Let $\Delta\mathbf{x}$ denote the vector of changes in demand (i.e., $\Delta\mathbf{x} = \mathbf{x}(\mathbf{p}^1) - \mathbf{x}(\mathbf{p}^0)$, and let Δc denote the change in the total costs of production.

Fact 2. The change in welfare, ΔW, satisfies the following bounds:

$$\mathbf{p}^0\Delta\mathbf{x} - \Delta c \geq \Delta W \geq \mathbf{p}^1\Delta\mathbf{x} - \Delta c.$$

Proof. Since the indirect utility function is a convex function of prices, we have:

$$v(\mathbf{p}^0) \geq v(\mathbf{p}^1) + \mathbf{D}v(\mathbf{p}^1)(\mathbf{p}^0 - \mathbf{p}^1)$$

where $\mathbf{D}v(\mathbf{p})$ stands for the gradient of $v(\mathbf{p})$. Using Roy's law, and rearranging:

$$\mathbf{x}(\mathbf{p}^1)(\mathbf{p}^0 - \mathbf{p}^1) \geq v(\mathbf{p}^1) - v(\mathbf{p}^0) = \Delta v.$$

The change in profits is given by

$$\mathbf{x}(\mathbf{p}^1)\mathbf{p}^1 - \mathbf{x}(\mathbf{p}^0)\mathbf{p}^0 - \Delta c = \Delta\pi.$$

Adding these expressions together we have

$$[\mathbf{x}(\mathbf{p}^1) - \mathbf{x}(\mathbf{p}^0)]\mathbf{p}^0 - \Delta c = \mathbf{p}^0\Delta\mathbf{x} - \Delta c \geq \Delta v + \Delta\pi = \Delta W.$$

The other bound can be derived in a similar manner.

Now think of the n goods as being one good sold in n different markets and produced at constant marginal cost. I want to compare a uniform pricing policy to a policy of price discrimination. Making the necessary substitutions in the bounds given in Fact 2, we have the following:

Fact 3. Let $\mathbf{p}^0 = (p_0, \ldots, p_0)$, $\mathbf{p}^1 = (p_1, \ldots, p_n)$, and let c be the constant level of marginal costs. Then the bounds on welfare change become:

$$(p_0 - c) \sum_{i=1}^{n} \Delta x_i \geq \Delta W \geq \sum_{i=1}^{n} (p_i - c)\Delta x_i.$$

Note that the upper bound in Fact 3 immediately gives Schmalensee's result that an increase in output is a necessary condition for welfare to increase. The lower bound in Fact 3 was not discussed by Schmalensee. It implies that if the profitability of the new

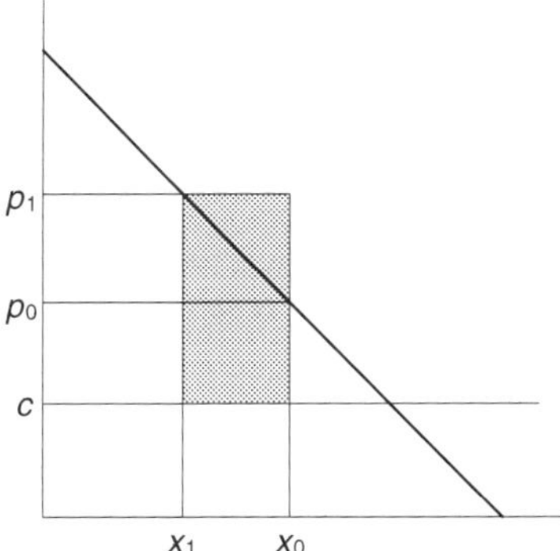

Figure 2. Bounds on welfare change in single market.

output exceeds the profitability of the old output, *valued at the new prices*, then welfare must have risen at the discriminatory equilibrium. This is basically a revealed preference relationship.

Both of these facts hold in complete generality, for independent and dependent demands, as long as one is willing to assume quasilinear utility; that is, that aggregate consumers' surplus serves as an acceptable welfare measure. The bounds have a simple geometric interpretation in the case of a single demand curve which is given in Figure 2. However, it is worth emphasizing that these results are purely statements about demand and utility functions and hold for arbitrary configurations of prices. The fact that the prices are chosen by a profit-maximizing monopolist has not been used in their derivation.

BOUNDS ON WELFARE CHANGE WITH OPTIMAL PRICE DISCRIMINATION

I now ask what results can be derived that *use* the conditions implied by *profit-maximizing* price discrimination. Let us specialize the notation above to consider only three prices, the initial price p_0 that is charged in both markets, and the final prices p_1 and p_2 that are profit-maximizing prices in their respective markets. We also continue to suppose that the good is produced at constant marginal cost c.

Fact 3 holds for all prices and all demand structures. If we consider only profit-maximizing prices and restrict ourselves to the textbook case of independent demands, we can apply the standard marginal revenue equals marginal cost formulae to find:

Fact 4. If demand functions are independent, welfare is bounded by

$$\frac{c[\Delta x_1 + \Delta x_2]}{\epsilon_0 - 1} \geq \Delta W \geq \frac{c\Delta x_1}{\epsilon_1 - 1} + \frac{c\Delta x_2}{\epsilon_2 - 1},$$

where ε_0, ε_1, ε_2 are the (absolute values of the) respective elasticities of demand, evaluated at p_0, p_1, and p_2.

This result may be of use if one has estimates of the elasticities of demand in the various submarkets. However the independent demand case is rather restrictive. Profit maximization *alone* yields the following sufficient condition for a welfare increase.

Fact 5. A sufficient condition for welfare to increase under profit-maximizing price discrimination is that

$$(p_0 - c)[x_1(p_0, p_0) + x_2(p_0, p_0)] > (p_1 - c)x_1(p_0, p_0) + (p_2 - c)x_2(p_0, p_0).$$

Proof. By profit maximization at (p_1, p_2) we have

$$(p_1 - c)x_1(p_1, P_2) + (p_2 - c)x_2(p_1, p_2) \geq (p_0 - c)x_1(p_0, p_0) + (p_0 - c)x_2(p_0, p_0).$$

Combining this with the hypothesis and rearranging, we have $(p_1 - c)\Delta x_1 + (p_2 - c)\Delta x_2 > 0$. By Fact 3 this yields a welfare increase.

The interesting thing about Fact 5 is that it only involves a condition on the nondiscriminatory levels of output. If you can forecast the prices that would be charged under discrimination and those prices satisfy the condition given in Fact 5, you can be assured that welfare will rise when discrimination is allowed.

It might be worthwhile to give an example of how these bounds can be used to verify that a welfare increase or decrease has occurred. The simplest example is the case of linear demands described by Schmalensee. If both markets are served in the single price regime, then it is easy to show by direct calculation that total output with discrimination is the same as in the single price regime. Hence, as noted by Schmalensee, welfare must decline when discrimination is allowed.

However, suppose we are in a situation where market 2 is not served in the single price regime. Then when discrimination is allowed, $p_1 = p_0$, $\Delta x_1 = 0$, and $\Delta x_2 > 0$. By Fact 3 welfare must increase. Note also that in this situation the sufficient condition given in Fact 5 is satisfied as an equality.[1]

Thus Fact 3 verifies that welfare will increase when price discrimination is allowed in the linear demand case if a new market is served. However, Fact 3 also shows that for *arbitrary* independent demands, welfare goes up if a new market is served when price discrimination is allowed. The argument is simply that of the above paragraph: $\Delta x_1 = 0$ and $\Delta x_2 > 0$, so welfare must increase.

These examples give some intuition for the case where both markets are served in both the discriminatory and nondiscriminatory regimes as in Figure 4. What is needed for welfare to increase when price discrimination is allowed is that one of the markets has small demand over the price range where the other market has large demand.

Another test case for the bounds is the reservation price model described earlier. Here we should think of each consumer as being a different market with demand function $x_a(p)$. If there are a_0 consumers purchasing the good in the single-price regime and $a_2 > a_0$ under price discrimination, then we know that $\Delta x_a = 0$ for $a \leq a_0$ and $\Delta x_a = 1$ for $a_2 > a > a_0$, which by Fact 3 implies welfare must increase when discrimination is allowed.

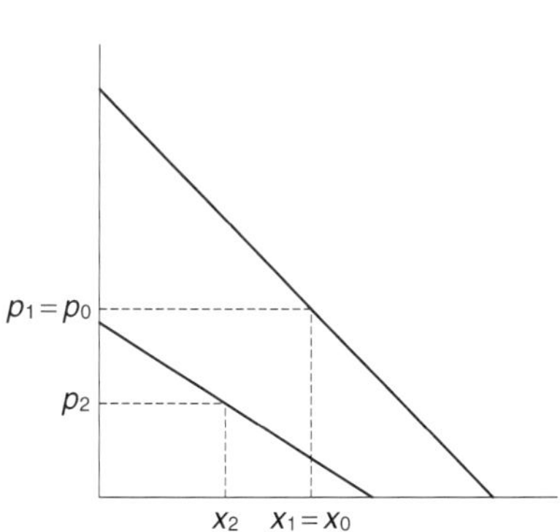

Figure 3. Increase in welfare (Boundary Case).

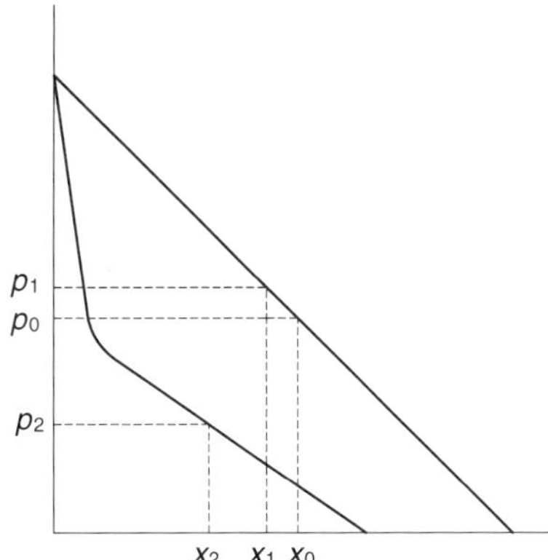

Figure 4. Increase in welfare (Interior Case).

The bounds can also be used to show that marginal cost pricing and perfect price discrimination are welfare optima in the reservation price model. For if price equals marginal cost, the upper bound on welfare change is zero. And if each consumer is being charged his reservation price, then Δx_a is either 0 or -1 which implies the upper bound nonpositive.

The welfare bounds given above take a nice form if we are willing to make curvature assumptions on the demand functions. Let us restrict ourselves to the case of independent demands and focus on the market for good 1. Then the argument of Fact 2 implies that the welfare effect of a price change of good 1 is bounded by $(p_0 - c)\Delta x_1 \geq \Delta W_1 \geq (p_1 - c)\Delta x_1$. Suppose that the demand for good 1 is a concave function of its own price. Then we have $\Delta x_1 \geq x_1'(p_1)(p_1 - p_0)$. Combining these two inequalities we have $\Delta W_1 \geq (p_1 - c)x_1'(p_1)[p_1 - p_0]$. The first-order conditions for profit maximization imply that $(p_1 - c)x_1'(p_1) + x_1(p_1) = 0$. Substituting we have $\Delta W_1 \geq x_1(p_1)(p_0 - p_1)$. If both markets have concave demand curves we can write:

$$\Delta W \geq x_1(p_1)(p_0 - p_1) + x_2(p_2)(p_0 - p_2) = p_0[x_1(p_1) + x_2(p_2)] - [p_1 x_1(p_1) + p_2 x_2(p_2)].$$

Add and subtract $(p_0 - c)[x_1(p_0) + x_2(p_0)] - c[x_1(p_1) + x_2(p_2)]$ to get $\Delta W \geq (p_0 - c)\Delta x - \Delta\pi$, where Δx is the total change in output and $\Delta\pi$ is the total change in profits. Thus the change in welfare is at least as large as the change in profit valued at the old prices minus the change in actual profit. Or, to put it another way, $\Delta x > \Delta\pi/(p_0 - c)$ is a sufficient condition for welfare to increase when price discrimination is allowed if all demand curves are independent and concave. Combining this with Fact 3 we can conclude:

Fact 6. If all demand curves are independent and concave the welfare bounds can be written as

$$(p_0 - c)\Delta x \geq \Delta W \geq (p_0 - c)\Delta x - \Delta\pi.$$

Note that Facts 5 and 6 use profit maximization at p_1 and p_2, but do *not* use profit maximization at p_0. Thus these results are independent of firm behavior at the nondiscriminatory equilibrium.

If the demand curves are concave and convex (i.e., linear), then the inequality in Fact 6 becomes an equality so that $\Delta W = -\Delta \pi$. Thus in the case of linear demands, the change in welfare is exactly the negative of the change in profits. Of course this can also be verified by direct calculation.

MORE GENERAL COST STRUCTURES

The above results were all derived in the case of constant marginal cost but they can be partially extended to the case of increasing marginal costs; that is, the case of a *convex* cost function. By the standard convexity inequality:

$$\mathbf{Dc}(\mathbf{x}(\mathbf{p}^1))\Delta\mathbf{x} \geq \Delta c \geq \mathbf{Dc}(\mathbf{x}(\mathbf{p}^0))\Delta\mathbf{x}.$$

Combining this with the inequality given in Fact 2 we have

$$[\mathbf{p}^0 - \mathbf{Dc}(\mathbf{x}(\mathbf{p}^0))]\Delta\mathbf{x} \geq [\mathbf{p}^1 - \mathbf{Dc}(\mathbf{x}(\mathbf{p}^1))]\Delta\mathbf{x}.$$

Again, these are general bounds which hold for all pairs of price vectors $\mathbf{p}^0$ and $\mathbf{p}^1$ as well as for arbitrary convex cost functions; in particular the cost function can be a function of the vector of outputs rather than just the total output. Thus the bounds can be useful in more general contexts. For example, they give a simple proof of the optimality of marginal cost pricing in the presence of convex costs: if $\mathbf{p}^0 = \mathbf{Dc}(\mathbf{x}(\mathbf{p}^0))$ then any movement from $\mathbf{p}^0$ must decrease social welfare.

If costs depend only on total output, denoted by x_0 and x_1, and $\mathbf{p}^0$ is a vector of constant prices p_0 as above, we can write these bounds as

$$[p_0 - c'(x_0)] \sum_{i=1}^{n} \Delta x_i \geq \Delta W \geq \sum_{i=1}^{n} [p_i - c'(x_1)]\Delta x_i.$$

Thus in the case of increasing marginal costs, Schmalensee's proposition still holds: price must be greater than marginal cost at the nondiscriminatory price, so an increase in output is still a necessary condition for welfare to increase.

ACKNOWLEDGEMENTS

This research was supported in part by the National Science Foundation. I thank Richard Schmalensee, Louis Philips, Andreu Mas-Collel, and an anonymous referee for helpful comments on an earlier draft.

NOTES

1. Of course, total output rises as well. The reader might wonder what is wrong with the "direct calculation" mentioned above. The problem is that what economists call "linear" demand curves are not really linear functions; instead they have the form: $Q = \max\{A - BP, 0\}$.

REFERENCES

Robinson, Joan. *Economics of Imperfect Competition*, London: Macmillan, 1933.
Schmalensee, Richard. Output and welfare implications of Monopolistic third-degree price discrimination, *American Economic Review*, March 1981, **71**: 242–247.
Varian, Hal R. *Microeconomic Analysis*, 2nd ed., New York: W. W. Norton, 1984.

11

Third-Degree Price Discrimination, Welfare and Profits: A Geometrical Analysis

Stephen Layson

This note introduces a new geometrical method of measuring the welfare effects of third-degree price discrimination that builds on earlier work by Richard Schmalensee (1981). The geometrical technique presented here suggests a simple empirically useful formula for the calculation of the welfare effects of third-degree price discrimination under linear demand. This geometrical technique also demonstrates the special relationship between the welfare and profit effects of price discrimination under linear demand and in this regard corrects an error in Hal Varian (1985).

Figure 1 illustrates the profit-maximizing solution for a monopolist that faces two independent linear demands. In Figure 1 the demand and marginal revenue curves for group 1 are drawn with respect to the left-hand side origin, O_1, while the demand and marginal revenue curves for group 2 are drawn with respect to the right-hand side origin, O_2. The width of Figure 1 represents the total profit-maximizing output under both price discrimination and simple monopoly.[1] At this output level marginal cost is MC_0.

Under simple monopoly each group is charged a price per unit of P^s. At this price group 1 purchases Q_1^s and group 2 purchases Q_2^s. In general the marginal revenues of selling to the two groups will not be the same at the simple monopoly allocation. For example, in Figure 1, $MR_2 > MR_1$ at the simple monopoly allocation. Starting from this situation the price-discriminating monopolist will increase sales to group 2 to Q_2^d and decrease sales to group 1 to Q_1^d. At this allocation $MR_1 = MR_2 = MC_0$ and profits are maximized under price discrimination. The prices charged to groups 1 and 2 under price discrimination, are, respectively, P_1^d and P_2^d.

Because total output is the same under price discrimination and simple monopoly, the profit gain from price discrimination is the additional revenue from increased sales to group 2 minus the revenue forgone from reduced sales to group 1. In Figure 1 the shaded triangular area ABC represents the profit gain from price discrimination. The welfare loss from price discrimination in Figure 1 is represented by the shaded triangular area between the two demand curves labeled DEF. This welfare loss stems

Reprinted with permission from *American Economic Review*, Vol. 78, No. 5, 1988, pp. 1131–1132

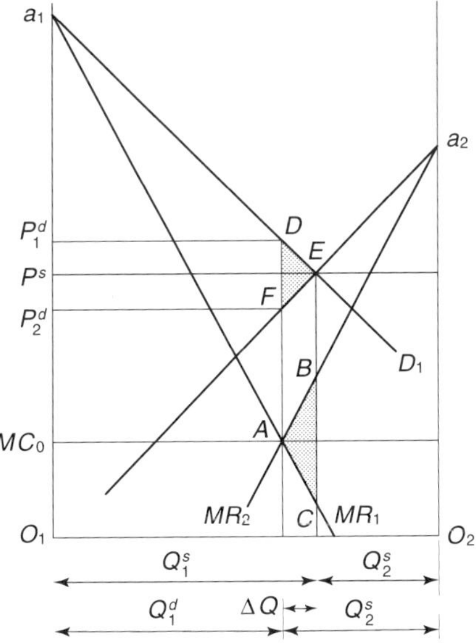

Figure 1.

from the transfer of ΔQ units from group 1, who values the good more highly, to group 2 who values the good less highly.[2]

Referring to Figure 1, the welfare loss triangle and the profit triangle have heights of equal length, ΔQ. The base of the profit triangle, however, is twice the base of the welfare loss triangle. The reason for this is that the slopes of the marginal revenue curves are twice the slopes of their respective demand curves. It follows that the area of the profit triangle is exactly twice the area of the welfare loss triangle. Varian's (1985, p. 875) result that the welfare loss is equal to the profit gain in the linear demand case is incorrect.[3]

The mathematical derivations of the profit gain and welfare loss from price discrimination in the linear demand case are straightforward and revealing. Let the demand curves be given by

$$P_i = a_i - b_i Q_i; \quad a_i, b_i > 0 \quad i = 1, 2. \tag{1}$$

Assuming profit maximization and linear demands, it can be shown that the relationship between the profit change, $\Delta\pi$, and the welfare change, ΔW, from price discrimination is given by[4]

$$\Delta W = -1/2\Delta\pi = -(a_1 - a_2)^2/[(8(b_1 + b_2)]. \tag{2}$$

The profit gain and the welfare loss are directly proportional to the squared difference in the price intercepts of the demand curves and inversely proportional to the sum of the demand slopes. For the linear demand case we see from equation (2) that price discrimination is most harmful when it is most profitable, and hence most likely to be undertaken. An alternative empirically useful formula for the welfare change suggested by the triangular measure in Figure 1 is $-1/2(P_1^d - P_2^d)\Delta Q$. Solving for ΔQ in terms of observable variables under price discrimination yields equation (3):

$$\Delta W = -\tfrac{1}{2} Q_1^d Q_2^d (P_1^d - P_2^d)^2 / [Q_1^d (P_2^d - MC_0) + Q_2^d (P_1^d - MC_0)]. \tag{3}$$

Note that calculation of the expression for the welfare change in equation (3) does not require that one observe the transition from simple monopoly to price discrimination. Data are required only on variables observed under price discrimination. Furthermore, equation (3) does not require that the demand curves be globally linear; it requires linearity only in the output range between simple monopoly and price discrimination. The validity of equation (3) like equation (2) discussed previously assumes profit maximization, however.

The geometrical technique presented in this note may also be used to measure the welfare effects of price discrimination when demands are nonlinear. When demands are nonlinear there are two welfare effects: (1) a welfare effect due to the transfer of sales from one group to the other, and (2) a welfare effect due to the net change in total output. For a discussion of the nonlinear case and other extensions, see my paper (1987).

ACKNOWLEDGEMENTS

I wish to thank John P. Formby for stimulating my interest in this subject and for helpful comments.

NOTES

1. See Joan Robinson (1933, p. 192) for a proof of this proposition. It is assumed in this note that both markets are served under simple monopoly.
2. The interested reader may wish to compare Figure 1 in this note to the geometric treatment in Schmalensee (1981, p. 246).
3. His mathematical demonstration shows only that $\Delta W \geq \Delta \pi$ for the linear demand case.
4. Derivations of equations (2) and (3) are available from the author on request: Department of Economics, University of North Carolina at Greensboro, Greensboro, NC 27412.

REFERENCES

Layson, Stephen, Third Degree Price Discrimination Welfare and Profits: A Geometrical Analysis, Working Paper Series No. ECO870402, Center for Applied Research, University of North Carolina, Greensboro, April 1987.

Robinson, Joan. *The Economics of Imperfect Competition*, London: Macmillan, 1933.

Schmalensee, Richard. Output and welfare implications of monopolistic third-degree price discrimination, *American Economic Review*, March 1981, **71**: 242–247.

Varian, Hal. Price discrimination and social welfare, *American Economic Review*, September 1985, **75**: 870–875.

12

Third-Degree Price Discrimination and Output: Generalizing a Welfare Result

Marius Schwartz

One of the best-known conjectures in the economics of price discrimination is that a move by a monopolist from uniform pricing to third-degree price discrimination—charging different prices in different exogenously identifiable markets—reduces the sum of consumer surplus and profit (hereafter "welfare") if total output decreases. This conjecture can be found, at least implicitly, as far back as A. C. Pigou (1920). It is of some interest, since it suggests a welfare test that only requires knowledge of observable magnitudes. Richard Schmalensee (1981) proves the conjecture assuming that the monopolist can perfectly separate markets and that marginal cost is constant. Hal Varian (1985) extends the result by allowing imperfect arbitrage, so that demand in any market can depend on prices in other markets, and by allowing marginal cost to be constant or increasing. (Schmalensee and Varian establish additional useful results on the welfare effects of third-degree price discrimination.) Using a revealed-preference argument, this note generalizes the result to the case in which marginal cost is decreasing, a serious possibility in the context of monopoly.

In order to motivate the revealed-preference approach, it is helpful to review the intuition for the result when marginal cost is constant or increasing and show why that intuition can break down when marginal cost is decreasing. Suppose that the monopoly output under uniform pricing is q^u and that moving to discrimination yields a total output q^d below q^u. Welfare under discrimination will be no higher than if the same output q^d is allocated through uniform pricing: uniform pricing allocates a given total output optimally (it leaves no unexploited gains from reshuffling output between markets), while discriminatory pricing in general will induce misallocations by distorting consumers' choices. Also, welfare achieved if q^d is allocated through uniform pricing will be lower than if the higher output q^d is allocated through uniform pricing. This follows because q^u is the monopolist's choice under uniform pricing, so the demand curve lies above the marginal cost curve at q^u. If marginal cost is nondecreasing, demand will lie above marginal cost also at lower outputs; hence, reducing output below q^u will reduce welfare.

Reprinted with permission from *American Economic Review*, Vol. 80, No. 5, 1990, pp. 1259–1262

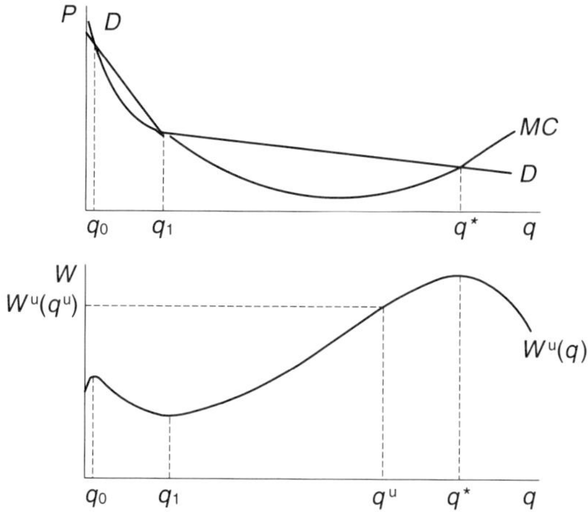

Figure 1. Welfare and output under uniform pricing: Example in which welfare function is not single-peaked.

If marginal cost is decreasing, this type of argument is inconclusive. At some outputs below q^u the demand curve might now lie below the marginal cost curve, as illustrated in Figure 1. Thus, welfare under uniform pricing, $W^u(q)$, can increase over some range as output falls below q^u. I therefore proceed along a different tack, using a revealed-preference argument that relies on q^u being a profit-maximizing output under uniform pricing.

Consider a monopolist selling to n exogenously identifiable markets. Let p_i and q_i respectively denote the price and output sold in market i, $i = 1, \ldots, n$. The monopolist's total cost function is $C(\Sigma q_i)$; that is, total cost depends only on total output and not on its distribution among markets. The markets can be viewed, for example, as different types of customers (e.g., students, senior citizens), different times of purchase (e.g., lunch vs. dinner), or different locations to which the monopolist ships its output. (In the last case, cost can be independent of the output's distribution among markets if, for example, markets are equidistant to the monopolist's plant and transport cost is constant.) Following Varian (1985), I allow imperfect arbitrage among markets (with perfect arbitrage, of course, price discrimination would be impossible). That is, if price differentials are sufficiently high, then goods or customers might move between locations, nonstudents might obtain fake student IDs, and dinner patrons might switch to lunch.

It is not necessary to get into details of the arbitrage technology. One simply thinks of the n markets as representing different goods to consumers and allows each individual's indirect utility function to depend on the prices of all n goods. In order to use the classical welfare measure of total consumer surplus plus profit, each individual's indirect utility function is assumed to be quasi-linear in the vector of n prices and in all other goods, which are treated as a composite commodity y and used as the numeraire. Under the quasi-linear preferences, one can also aggregate across consumers and think of the indirect utility function of a representative individual whose endowment in the numeraire is y_0: $f(p_1, \ldots, p_n, y_0) = v(p_1, \ldots, p_n) + y_0$. The function v embodies whatever substitutability exists among the n goods or, equivalently, whatever arbitrage is possible among the n markets. (For discussions of consumer surplus, aggregation, quasi-linear utility, and the composite commodity theorem see Angus Deaton and John Muellbauer (1980) or Varian (1984).)

If the monopolist's n goods are sold under uniform pricing ($p_i = p$ for all i), then one can simplify further and think also of these n goods as a composite commodity whose price is p, and write the indirect utility function as

$$F(p, y_0) = V(p) + y_0.$$

Note that $V(p)$ gives consumer surplus from purchasing the monopolist's composite good at price p (if one normalizes V) by setting $V(p \to 0$ as $p \to \infty$). $V(p)$ is always strictly decreasing and weakly convex. Since F is linear in y_0, the negative of the derivative of V, where it exists, gives the demand function for the composite good: $q = D(p) = -V'(p)$. The only substantive assumption is that $V(p)$ is strictly convex, that is, that the demand for the monopolist's composite good is a strictly decreasing function of price.

Let $W^u(q)$ denote welfare when the monopolist maximizes profit subject to being constrained to charge uniform prices and to sell a given total quantity q:

$$W^u(q) = V(h(q)) + \Pi(q) \tag{1}$$

where $h(q)$ is the inverse demand function and $\Pi(q) = h(q)q - C(q)$ is profit and where, for simplicity, we omit from welfare the endowment term y_0, which is constant. Observe that V is strictly increasing in q, since it is strictly decreasing in p and since the inverse demand function is strictly decreasing. That is, given a downward-sloping demand curve, consumer surplus is higher if a higher output is sold. Whether pricing is uniform or not, welfare (again ignoring y_0) can also be expressed as utility minus cost:

$$W(q_1, \ldots, q_n) = U(q_1, \ldots, q_n) - C(\Sigma q_i). \tag{2}$$

It is now possible to establish the welfare result.

Proposition 1. Suppose that p^u $q^u = D(p^u)$ are a profit-maximizing price and output pair when the monopolist is constrained to charge uniform prices. Consider any discriminatory price vector $\mathbf{p}^d = (p_1, \ldots, p_n)$, $p_i \neq p_j$ for at least some $i \neq j$, which yields an associated output vector $\mathbf{q}^d = (q_1, \ldots, q_n)$, and denote the total output by $q^d = \Sigma q_i$. If total output is lower under discrimination, then welfare also is lower. That is, if $q^d < q^u$, then $W(\mathbf{q}^d) < W^u(q^u)$.

Proof. I show that $W(\mathbf{q}^d) \leq W^u(q^d) < W^u(q^u)$. Consider the first inequality. For any total output q, let $W^*(q)$ denote the solution to the planner's problem: $\max U(q_1, \ldots, q_n) - C(\Sigma q_i)$ subject to $\Sigma q_i = q$. Since cost is fixed, the planner's problem is equivalent to $\max U(q_1, \ldots, q_n)$ subject to $\Sigma q_i = q$. Now consider $W^u(q)$. Since q is the quantity of the monopolist's composite good, $q = D(p) = \Sigma q_i(p)$, where the outputs $[q_1(p), \ldots, q_n(p)]$ maximize utility given $p_i = p$. This means that $D(p)$ solves max $U(q_1, \ldots, q_n)$ subject to $p\Sigma q_i = pq$, which coincides with the planner's problem. Thus, $W^u(q) = W^*(q)$. Since $W^*(q)$ is the maximum feasible welfare given the constraint $\Sigma q_i = q$, the first inequality is established.

Consider the second, more novel inequality. Given $q^d < q^u$, it is known that $V(h(q^d)) < V(h(q^u))$. Since q^u is a profit-maximizing output (not necessarily unique) under uniform pricing, $\Pi(q^d) \leq \Pi(q^u)$. Thus, by expression (1), $q^d < q^u$ implies $W^u(q^d) < W^u(q^u)$.

Intuitively, the first inequality reflects the fact that, if the cost function depends only on total output and not on its distribution among goods or markets, then the constraint $\Sigma q_i = q$ can be interpreted as a particular transformation function, one with marginal transformation rates of unity. Uniform pricing reflects these marginal rates of transformation. Thus, a uniform-price equilibrium will maximize welfare for the given level of total output, while discriminatory prices generally will not. This is just the same logic that underlies the first welfare theorem.

The second inequality is where the revealed preference argument comes in. It shows that—regardless of the shape of the cost function—welfare under uniform pricing is higher at a profit-maximizing output q^u than at any lower output q^d. For more intuition, express welfare under uniform pricing as total valuation minus total cost: $W^u(q) = B(q) - C(q)$, where B is the integral under the demand curve from 0 to q. Since q^u maximizes profit, moving from a lower output q^d to q^u must increase revenue by at least as much as cost: $\Delta R \geq \Delta C$. Since increasing quantity demanded from q^d to q^u would require lowering price, total valuation would increase by more than revenue: $\Delta B > p^u(q^u - q^d) > \Delta R$. Therefore, $\Delta W = \Delta B - \Delta C > \Delta R - \Delta C \geq 0$, so welfare must increase if, under uniform pricing, output is raised to a profit-maximizing level. Correspondingly, Figure 1 shows welfare at q^u to be higher than at any lower output.

Note that if marginal cost is decreasing and the comparison is of two *arbitrary* outputs, both below the efficient level, then one cannot be sure that welfare will be higher at the higher output. When the cost function is concave, welfare—value minus cost—need not be concave everywhere (even though value is concave) and therefore need not be single-peaked. It is because the higher output represents a profit maximum that one can be sure that welfare there is higher.

I conclude with two remarks about the policy relevance of the analysis. First, the welfare result rests on the assumption that demand curves faced by the monopolist generate adequate measures of welfare. This condition can fail, for example, when the monopolist is selling to distorted intermediate-good markets rather than to final consumers. Consider an input monopolist selling at a uniform price to several unrelated intermediate-good industries. Suppose that in equilibrium the proportional price-cost markups are different in the various industries due to different degrees of competition (rather than different demand elasticities). Then, allocating a given quantity of the input through uniform pricing does not maximize welfare for that input quantity; lower input prices should be charged to the industries with the higher markups. If price discrimination by the input monopolist results in such a pattern, then welfare can be higher under discrimination even if the total quantity of the input is lower. (Such desirable discrimination might be profit-maximizing for the monopolist if, for instance, those industries with the higher markups also have greater ability to substitute in production away from the monopolist's input.) That is, price discrimination by the input monopolist could help counteract the downstream distortions. This is a standard second-best ambiguity.

The second remark concerns the information needed for my result and for those of Schmalensee (1981) and Varian (1985) to provide useful welfare tests in practice (assuming that areas under demand curves do accurately reflect welfare). What must the policymaker know in order to infer that welfare is lower under discrimination if output is observed to be lower? My proposition requires the policymaker to be confident that the monopolist knows demand and cost and that the output observed under uniform pricing, q^u, is profit-maximizing. Schmalensee (1981) and Varian (1985) require only that marginal cost at q^u be less than price (q^u need not be profit-maximizing, because of the monopolist's imperfect knowledge about cost and demand), provided the policymaker knows also that marginal cost is nondecreasing at lower outputs. Thus, more information is required for the monopolist but less for the policymaker: the policymaker must know only that the monopolist possesses the requisite information needed to maximize profit under uniform pricing.

ACKNOWLEDGEMENTS

For helpful discussions and comments, I thank Tim Brennan, Maxim Engers, Martin Richardson, Marilyn Simon, Bert Smiley, and Jean Tirole.

REFERENCES

Deaton, Angus and Muellbauer, John. *Economics and Consumer Behaviour*, Cambridge: Cambridge University Press, 1980.
Pigou, A. C. *The Economics of Welfare*, 1st ed., London: Macmillan.
Schmalensee, Richard. Output and welfare implications of monopolistic third-degree price discrimination, *American Economic Review*, March 1981, **71**: 242–247.
Varian, Hal R. *Microeconomic Analysis*, 2nd ed., New York: Norton, 1984.
Varian, Hal R. Price discrimination and social welfare, *American Economic Review*, September 1985, **75**: 870–875.

13

Commodity Bundling and the Burden of Monopoly

William James Adams and Janet L. Yellen

INTRODUCTION

Firms often sell their goods in packages: sporting and cultural organizations offer season tickets, restaurants provide complete dinners, banks offer checking, safe deposit, and travelers' check services for a single fee, and garment manufacturers sell their retailers clothing grab bags comprised of assorted styles, sizes, and colors. We shall refer to the practice of package selling as commodity bundling. A firm that sells goods only in package form has adopted a *pure* bundling strategy. A firm that sells the same goods separately as well as in packages has adopted a *mixed* bundling strategy.

Commodity bundles sometimes include goods that cannot be sold separately in the market place. For example, an automobile can be interpreted as a package of luxury and transport services. The transport services could be offered without luxury (in the form of a stripped down car), but luxury must be sold in conjunction with motive power. Similarly, aspirin can be sold with or without a well-known brand name, but the brand name cannot be sold alone. In general, firms offering several incarnations of the same product, differing in either real or perceived quality, practice mixed bundling.

Commodity bundling also occurs when firms sell the same physical commodity in different container sizes. For example, toothpaste, detergent, and cereal are sold in small and large packages. In such cases, a bundle consists of multiple units[1] of the same commodity. Offering both sizes constitutes mixed bundling, while offering just the large size constitutes pure bundling.[2]

Why is commodity bundling such a prevalent marketing strategy? Some observers focus on the cost savings in production, transactions, and information associated with package selling.[3] Others dwell on the complementarity in consumption of bundle components. We shall demonstrate that commodity bundling can be profitable even

Reprinted with permission from *Quarterly Journal of Economics*, Vol. 90, No. 3, 1976, pp. 475–498

when these motivations are absent. In particular, we show that the profitability of commodity bundling can stem from its ability to sort customers into groups with different reservation price characteristics, and hence to extract consumer surplus.[4] We choose to emphasize this rationale for commodity bundling for several reasons.

First, in the real world firms cannot always resort to conventional forms of price discrimination in order to extract consumer surplus: reservation prices of specific customers are typically unknown; even if they were known, laws like the Robinson-Patman Act might prevent a seller from using them in an overtly discriminatory scheme. Commodity bundling can overcome these two practical problems associated with conventional price discrimination. We demonstrate this in the following section. In some circumstances, bundling is just as profitable as Pigouvian price discrimination of the first degree. In most circumstances, it is more profitable than simple monopoly pricing.[5]

Second, bundling motivated by price discrimination has distinctive normative consequences. On the one hand, bundling could lead monopolists to oversupply as well as undersupply specific commodities: equilibrium output could fall on *either* side of ideal output. On the other hand, bundling could lead monopolists to sell whatever output is produced to the wrong people, in the sence that potential gains from trade among consumers would exist in equilibrium. Hence the conditions for distributive efficiency as well as those for allocative efficiency might be violated. Neither Pigouvian first-degree price discrimination nor simple monopoly pricing results in either of these problems. These findings are discussed in the section "The model: normative properties".

Third, the existence of commodity bundling seriously complicates public appraisal of monopoly, for it impairs the validity of major tools of applied welfare economics, such as consumer-producer surplus analysis and hedonic price indices. Finally, prohibition of bundling in monopolistic markets, without elimination of monopoly, can either increase or decrease the deadweight loss arising in the relevant markets. This reinforces the desirability of structural, as opposed to conduct, attack on market power. We discuss these implications of commodiity bundling in the concluding section.

THE MODEL: POSITIVE PROPERTIES

Consider a model with the following characteristics. Technology is such that A1 holds.

A1 (Technology). The marginal cost of supplying each good separately (c_1, c_2) is invariant with respect to output, and the marginal cost of supplying the two goods in a bundle is the sum of the component costs ($c_B = c_1 + c_2$). There are no fixed costs.

Tastes are such that for all individuals A2 and A3 hold.

A2 (Indivisibility). The marginal utility of a second unit of either commodity is zero.

A3 (Independence). The reservation price for a package comprised of one unit of each commodity (r_B) is equal to the sum of their separate reservation prices (r_1, r_2).[6]

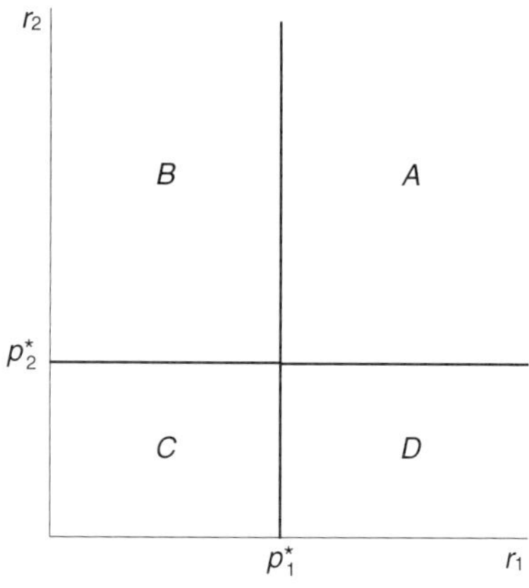

Figure 1.

By assumption, therefore, this model excludes both economies in the bundling process and complementarity in consumption. If bundling is found to be profitable, it cannot be explained by these phenomena.

If the monopolist knows the reservation price of each consumer for each commodity, his profit-maximizing strategy is simply Pigouvian first-degree price discrimination with respect to each commodity separately. If the monopolist knows only the distribution of reservation prices in the population, however, or if he is legally prevented from engaging in pure price discrimination, then his ideal pricing strategy is more difficult to establish. Three options open to him are as follows.

(1) Set the single price on each commodity separately (p_1^*, p_2^*), which yields the greatest profits. We call this a pure components strategy, or simple monopoly pricing.

(2) Offer the two commodities for sale only in a package comprised of one unit of each at the price p_B^* chosen so as to maximize profits. This is the pure bundling strategy.

(3) Combine strategies one and two by offering each commodity separately and a package of both, at a set of prices (p_1^*, p_2^*, p_B^*), which maximizes overall profits. This is the mixed bundling strategy. Since the value of a bundle to consumers is no greater than the value of its components, mixed bundling is a distinct strategy only if the package is sold at a discount relative to its components.

Each of these strategies is easily represented in diagrammatic form.

The reservation price of each consumer for each commodity can be represented as a point in Figure 1. If the monopolist adopts the pure components strategy, and sets component prices p_1^* and p_2^* (Figure 1), the population is sorted into four groups: individuals with reservation prices at least equal to market prices for both commodities (area A in Figure 1), individuals with reservation prices less than market prices for

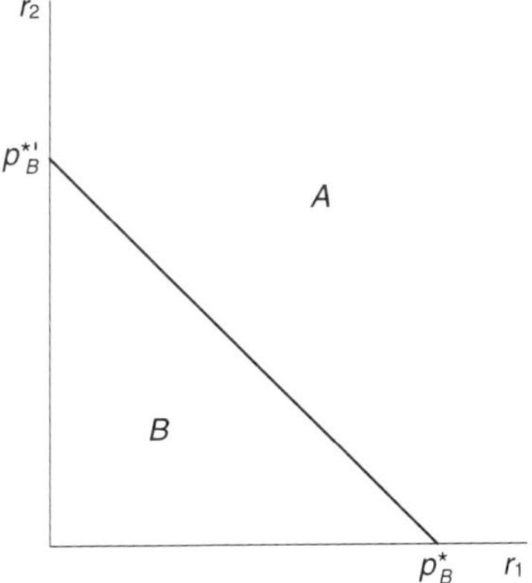

Figure 2.

both commodities (area C), and individuals with reservation price at least equal to market price for one but not the other commodity (areas B and D). Those in area A purchase both goods, those in areas B and D purchase goods 2 and 1, respectively, and individuals in area C purchase neither good.

If instead the monopolist adopts the pure bundling strategy, the population is sorted into only two groups: those whose reservation price for the bundle ($r_B = r_1 + r_2$) is at least equal to the bundle's market price, and those for whom the opposite is true. In Figure 2 the bundle price appears in reservation price space as a straight line with both intercepts equal to the bundle price p_B^* and hence with slope of minus one. Those in area A buy the bundle and hence consume both goods. Those in area B do not buy the bundle and hence consume neither good.[7]

Finally, if the monopolist adopts the mixed bundling strategy, customers are again sorted into four groups. These appear in Figure 3. Individuals in area $Op_2^*XYp_1^*$ consume nothing. They are characterized by $r_1 \leq p_1^*$, $r_2 \leq p_2^*$, and $r_B \leq p_B^*$. Individuals southeast of p_1^*YZ consume only good 1. They are characterized by $r_1 \geq p_1^*$ and $r_2 \leq p_B^* - p_1^*$. The reason is that $(p_B^* - p_1^*)$ represents the implicit price of good 2 to an individual already prepared to buy good 1.[8] For similar reasons those northwest of p_2^*XW consume only good 2. They are characterized by $r_2 \geq p_2^*$ and $r_1 \leq (p_B^* - p_1^*)$. The last group comprises those northwest of $WXYZ$, who consume the bundle. They are characterized by $r_1 + r_2 > p_B^*$, $r_1 \geq (p_B^* - p_2^*)$, and $r_2 \geq (p_B^* - p_1^*)$. In words, the bundle is consumed by those who not only derive positive consumer surplus from purchase of the bundle but also derive more surplus from the bundle ($r_B - p_B^*$) than they would from purchase of either component separately ($r_i - p_i^*$, $i = 1, 2$).

The profit-maximizing monopolist chooses among these sorting mechanisms by calculating the most remunerative configuration of prices under each strategy and then by comparing the resulting profits. The relative profitability of the three strategies depends on the distribution of consumers in reservation price space and the structure of costs. Each conceivable ranking of the three is in fact possible.[9] The reason is that each strategy has both strengths and weaknesses *vis à vis* its rivals.

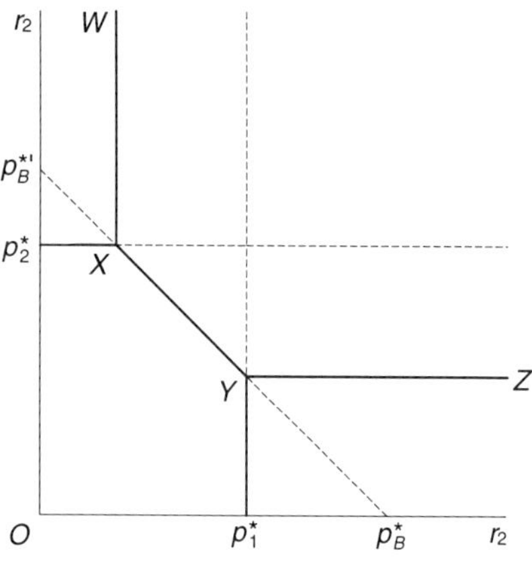

Figure 3.

In order to assess the virtues and defects of each strategy, a benchmark is required. Since pure price discrimination is known to be the most remunerative pricing strategy available to a firm, it provides a benchmark for appraising the profitability of other pricing schemes. In the context of our model pure price discrimination satisfies three conditions:

C1 (Complete Extraction). No individual realizes any consumer surplus on his purchases.

C2 (Exclusion). No individual consumes a good if the cost of that good exceeds his reservation price for it.

C3 (Inclusion). Any individual whose reservation prices for a good exceeds its cost in fact consumes that good.

To what extent does simple monopoly pricing, or bundling in some form, also satisfy these conditions?

The pure components strategy never violates Exclusion because within the framework of our model prices in component markets are never set below cost.[10] As we show below, this virtue of simple monopoly pricing is not shared by its bundling rivals. On the other hand, the pure components strategy violates Extraction or Inclusion as long as customers are distributed in reservation price space such that the monopolist faces downward-sloping demand curves in both component markets: the finite elasticity of demand curves implies that monopolists cannot extract all consumer surplus on a particular good without preventing some individuals with valuation in excess of cost from consuming it. This violates Inclusion.

If the bundle demand curve is extremely elastic while the component demand curves are not, pure bundling avoids excessive violation of Inclusion and Extraction. This proposition is illustrated in Figure 4. The four consumers—*A, B, C,* and *D*—are distributed in reservation price space along a straight line with slope minus one. The value of the bundle is the same to all customers so that the bundle demand curve is

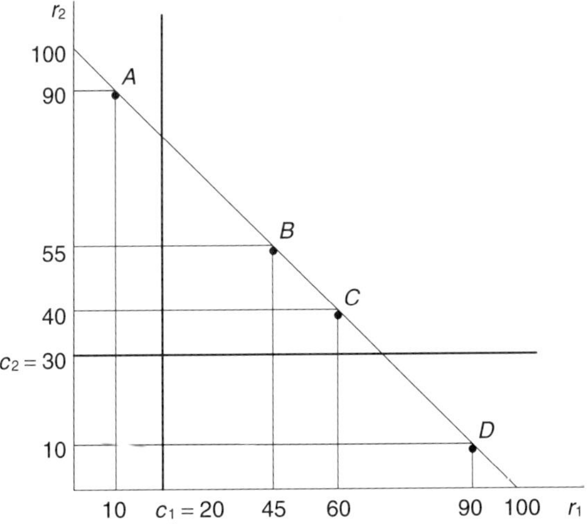

	$p_1^\star$	$p_2^\star$	$p_B^\star$	Profits
Pure components strategy	60	90	–	140
Pure bundling strategy	–	–	100	200
Mixed bundling strategy	90	90	100	230

Figure 4.

perfectly elastic. The relative value of the components differs among customers, however, so that each component demand curve is downward-sloping. If the monoplist knows the common valuation of the bundle by his customers, he can satisfy the extraction and inclusion requirements simultaneously by charging each customer a price equal to that amount for the bundle.[11]

The chief defect of pure bundling is its difficulty in complying with Exclusion. The greater the cost of supplying either good, the greater the possibility of supplying some individuals with commodities for which reservation price falls short of cost. In Figure 4, A and D are individuals with $r < c_i$ for some commodity. Thus, pure bundling is perferred to simple monopoly pricing only if the greater profits accruing from more complete extraction or inclusion are not outweighcd by the lower profits due to less complete exclusion. The more negligible are costs relative to reservation prices, the less of a problem this poses for pure bundling.

The mixed bundling strategy is more profitable than its pure counterpart whenever Exclusion is violated in the pure bundling equilibrium. The reason is that creation of separate component markets adds two categories into which the monopolist can sort his customers. In Figure 4, for example, he can charge prices $p_1^\star=90$ and $p_2^\star=90$ in the component markets, thereby inducing individuals A and D to cease consuming the good they value above cost. In general, *whenever the exclusion requirement is violated in a*

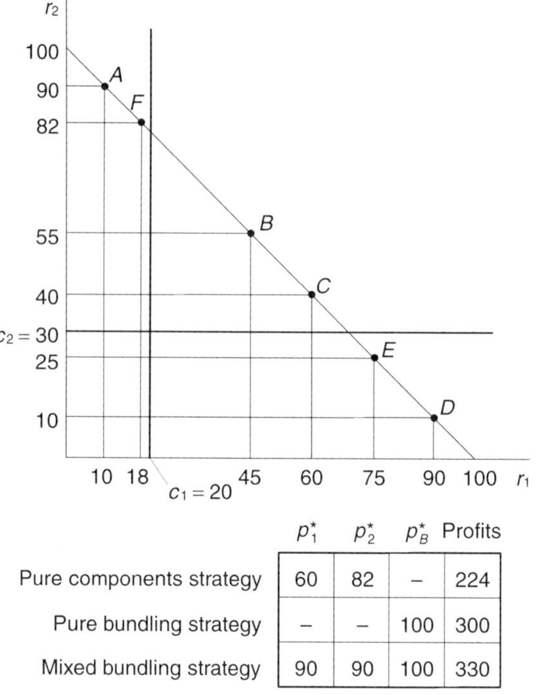

	p_1^*	p_2^*	p_B^*	Profits
Pure components strategy	60	82	–	224
Pure bundling strategy	–	–	100	300
Mixed bundling strategy	90	90	100	330

Figure 5.

pure bundling equilibrium, mixed bundling is necessarily preferred to pure bundling.[12] That mixed bundling satisfies Exclusion more completely than does pure bundling, however, does not mean that mixed bundling avoids the problem altogether. Rarely does a monopolist find it profitable to exclude every individual whose reservation price for a good falls short of its cost. The reason is apparent in Figure 5, which is identical to Figure 4 except for the presence of consumers E and F. Mixed bundling is still the most profitable strategy, but Exclusion is unfulfilled in the cases of E and F. To exclude them from the bundle market proves too costly in terms of consumer surplus foregone on A and D. Another way of putting this is that the component demand curves are downward-sloping and hence successive price reductions on a given component usually reduce total revenue in that component market. Like pure bundlers, therefore, mixed bundlers face a trade-off between more complete extraction and complete exclusion. The dilemma is simply less pronounced in the case of mixed bundling.

If customers are distributed in reservation price space such that people with high reservation prices for the package exhibit small variance in their valuations of the components, and vice versa, then mixed bundling has another virtue relative to pure bundling: it facilitates the monopolist's attempts to extract the consumer surplus of individuals with high reservation prices for both goods. The reason is that a mixed bundler can charge a high bundle price and yet extract via separate markets the consumer surplus associated with customers valuing one but not both goods highly.

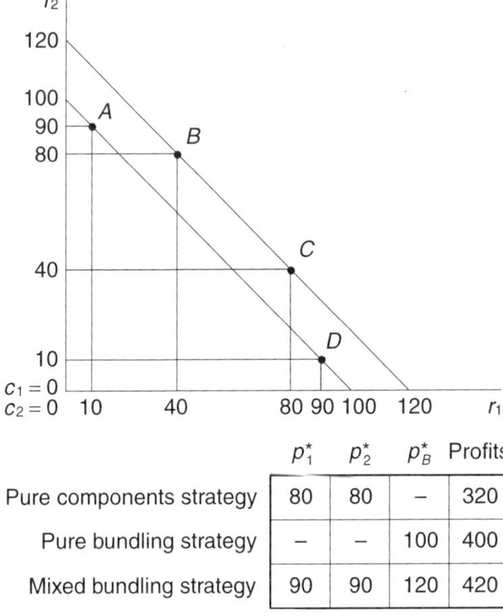

	p_1^*	p_2^*	p_B^*	Profits
Pure components strategy	80	80	–	320
Pure bundling strategy	–	–	100	400
Mixed bundling strategy	90	90	120	420

Figure 6.

This is illustrated in Figure 6. The bundle is priced to extract all the surplus of B and C, while the separates markets are used to extract the surplus of A and D. If the distribution of consumers in reservation price space is the opposite of that assumed here, however, pure bundling could be preferred to its mixed counterpart.[13]

Turning to comparison of mixed bundling with simple monopoly pricing, if the correlation coefficient linking an individual's valuation of one good to his valuation of the other good is not strongly positive, we can see that the mixed bundling strategy is better able to satisfy Extraction and Inclusion simultaneously. This is possible in Figure 7. The monopolist adopting a pure components strategy sets $p_1^*=p_2^*=10$ in this situation, earning 40 in profits. If he then offers a bundle at $p_B = 16$, without changing the component prices, he entices people currently consuming nothing (i.e., E), as well as people currently consuming just one good (i.e., D, F), to purchase the bundle, while retaining other customers (i.e., A, B, C, G, H, I) in the separates markets. More generally, strong negative correlation helps the monopolist to achieve greater Inclusion by insuring that numerous individuals like F, E and D exist. In the case at hand, simply adding the bundle at a price of 16 generates profits of 48 rather than 40. Profits are not maximized, however, by leaving component prices at their pre-bundle level. The bundle option permits the monopolist to raise prices in component markets, in pursuit of more complete extraction, without driving as many customers entirely out of the market. In Figure 7, for example, introduction of a bundle at a price of 16 makes it profitable to raise each component price from 10 to 14. This involves sacrifice of customers at A and I. Without the bundle, however, D and F would also exit from the market. On balance, introduction of a bundle, when coupled with elevation

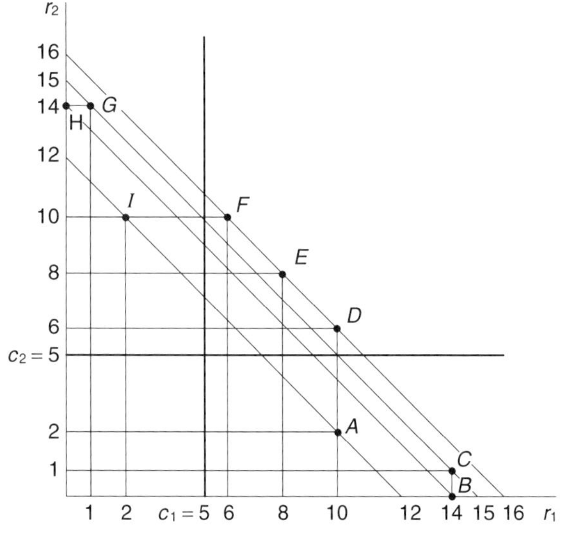

	$p_1^\star$	$p_2^\star$	$p_B^\star$	Profits
Pure components strategy	10	10	–	40
Pure bundling strategy	–	–	14	28
Mixed bundling strategy	14	14	16	54

Figure 7.

of component market prices, permits achievement of 54 in profits. These are the highest attainable under any of the three strategies. In effect, negative correlation guarantees the existence of individuals with extreme tastes (e.g., *B, C, G, H*) who realize substantial consumer surplus in pure components equilibrium.

A major defect of mixed bundling *vis à vis* simple monopoly pricing is its difficulty in accomplishing Exclusion and Complete Extraction simultaneously. In Figure 8, for example, if costs are $c_1 = c_2 = 45$, exclusion is such an important desideratum that pure components pricing is more profitable than mixed bundling. If $c_1 = c_2 = 30$, by contrast, so that exclusion is no longer a serious problem, simple monopoly pricing is less profitable than mixed bundling. This illustrates the general proposition that pure components pricing is a more desirable strategy the greater the cost of violating Exclusion.[14]

In sum, each of the three pricing strategies has both advantages and disadvantages in relation to the other two. Whether one generates more profits than another depends on the prevailing level of costs and on the distribution of customers in reservation price space. In numerous experiments with plausible cost structures and continuous distributions of reservation prices, we found some form of bundling to be more profitable than simple monopoly pricing.[15] Thus, commodity bundling can be

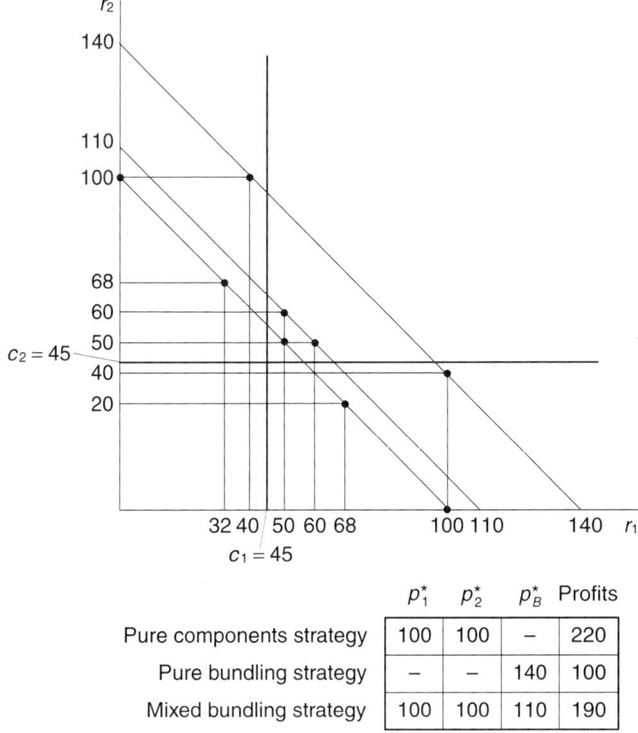

	p_1^*	p_2^*	p_B^*	Profits
Pure components strategy	100	100	–	220
Pure bundling strategy	–	–	140	100
Mixed bundling strategy	100	100	110	190

Figure 8.

expected to occur in the real world under more than the highly particular circumstances discussed here.[16]

We are now in a position to understand why a restaurant might offer complete dinners as well as an *à la carte* menu. Some people value an appetizer relatively highly (soup on a cold day), others may value dessert relatively highly (Baked Alaska, unavailable at home), but all might wish to pay roughly the same amount for a complete dinner. The *à la carte* menu is designed to capture consumer surplus from those gastronomes with extremely high valuations of particular dishes, while the complete dinner is designed to retain those with lower variance in their reservation prices.

With slight changes in interpretation, our model can be used to explain why products like toothpaste are sold in multiple container sizes. The horizontal axis in such cases measures an individual's reservation price for a first unit of the good, while the vertical axis measures his reservation price for an additional unit of the same good, given that he consumes a first unit. These definitions guarantee that assumptions A1–A3 can be satisfied.[17] Note, however, that what comprises "one unit" of a good is inherently arbitrary. Moreover, customers must lie below the 45-degree line in reservation price space so as to comply with the law of diminishing marginal rates of substitution. Finally, the monopolist must charge the same price in both separates markets. Whenever mixed bundling occurs in toothpaste-type situations, the monopolist is engaging in price discrimination by offering quantity discounts. Individuals with high reservation prices for the first ounce and low reservation prices for the second ounce have lower price elasticities of demand than do those with more equal valuations of successive units. Offering both one- and two-ounce containers thus induces individuals with inelastic demand to pay a high unit price in the component market, while individuals with elastic demand pay a low unit price in the bundle market.[18]

Our model also provides a plausible explanation of why automobile manufacturers add luxury to at least some of their vehicles. If the horizontal axis of reservation price space is defined as valuation of transport services, while the vertical axis is defined as the valuation of added luxury, assumptions A1–A3 can be satisfied.[19] In such situations the monopolist could offer just a basic car, just a luxury car, or both. Since the last strategy is equivalent to mixed bundling, it is usually the most profitable of the three.[20] That explains why consumer goods' manufacturers typically sell their product in both differentiated and undifferentiated form.[21]

In conclusion, we have shown that commodity bundling is more profitable than simple monopoly pricing in a wide variety of circumstances. The reason is that if often permits more complete extraction of consumer surplus than is possible under a pure components strategy. Price discrimination is another technique designed to achieve that result. What are the relative merits of these two schemes? Package selling has two virtues when compared with price discrimination. First, it requires far less information to implement. For example, Pigouvian first-degree price discrimination could be practised only if the monopolist knows the reservation prices of each individual for each commodity. Needless to say, individuals have a strong incentive to conceal such information whenever possible. Commodity bundling, on the other hand, can be practised even if the monopolist knows only the joint distribution of reservation prices in the population. Such information is sufficient to calculate the most profitable bundle and component prices. In a bundling context the price structure is such that individuals automatically sort themselves into distinct reservation price groups and thereby reveal truthful information concerning their tastes. In this sense commodity bundling serves as a self-selection device.[22]

Second, since each person pays the same price for what he consumes as do all others purchasing the same market basket, price discrimination laws based on price differentials alone are not violated. Unlike pure price discrimination, therefore, commodity bundling leaves its practitioner immune from prosecution.

THE MODEL: NORMATIVE PROPERTIES

Two requirements of Pareto optimality in the model in the preceding section are that commodities be distributed among consumers in such a way that no mutual gains from trade are possible, and that output of each commodity be just sufficient to supply all consumers with reservation prices at least equal to the marginal cost of that commodity. It is well known that simple monopoly pricing violates the second but not

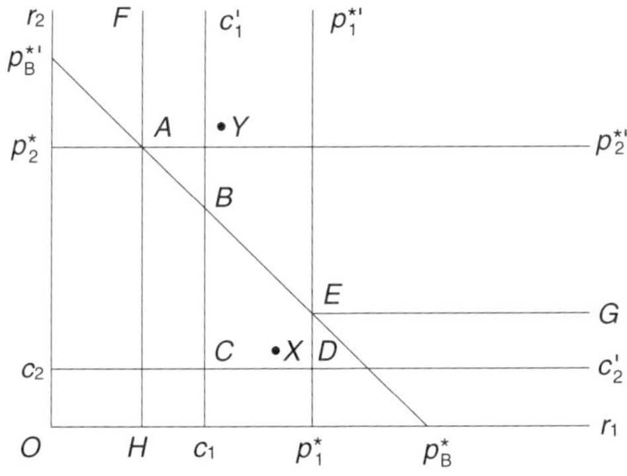

Group	Actually consumes good 1	Should consume good 1	Actually consumes good 2	Should consume good 2
Oc_2Cc_1	no	no	no	no
Southeast of $c_2'Dp_1^*$	yes	yes	no	no
Northwest of p_2^*AF	no	no	yes	yes
$c_1'BEG$	yes	yes	yes	yes
$c_2\,p_2^*ABC$	no	no	no	yes
$c_1GDp_1^*$	no	yes	no	no
$GEDc_2'$	yes	yes	no	yes
$FAB\,c_1'$	yes	no	yes	yes
$GBED$	no	yes	no	yes

Figure 9.

the first of these requirements. Commodity bundling can violate either or both. Since the precise defects of bundling depend on which case—restaurant, toothpaste, or car—is under consideration, we shall discuss the normative consequences of each case separately.

In cases of the restaurant type, where each component can in principle be disembodied from the bundle, package selling typically results in distributive inefficiency. This is illustrated in Figure 9.[23] Consumers located in the area AHp_1^*E, for example, do not consume good 1, while individuals northeast of $FAEp_1^{*\prime}$ do. And yet, some individuals in the former area (e.g., X) value good 1 more highly than do some individuals in the latter area (e.g., Y). Thus, mutual gains from trade of good 1 for money between X and Y are possible, violating the distributive efficiency criterion. The same reasoning applies to distribution of good 2. Insofar as it leads to distributive inefficiency, commodity bundling shares certain normative properties with (imperfect) price discrimination.[24]

In cases of the restaurant type commodity bundling also results in allocative inefficiency. Unlike simple monopoly pricing, however, bundling can lead to

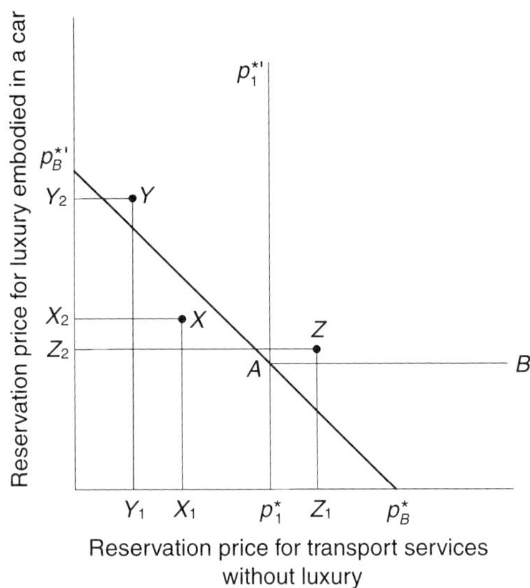

Figure 10.

oversupply as well as undersupply of either or both commodities. This, too, is illustrated in Figure 9. All consumers located east of $c_1 c_1'$ should consume good 1. In mixed bundling equilibrium, though, it is individuals northeast of $FAEp_1^*$ who in fact consume good 1. If $FABc_1'$ contains more customers than does $c_1 BEp_1^*$, then good 1 is oversupplied. If not, the reverse is true. Economically, a necessary if insufficient condition for oversupply of good 1 is that equilibrium prices bear the relationship $p_B^* - p_2^* < c_1$ so that the shadow price of good 1 when consumed in bundles is less than its opportunity cost. By similar reasoning the necessary and sufficient[25] conditions for undersupply of good 1 are $p_1^* > c_1$ and $p_B^* - p_2^* > c_1$. Since the same logic prevails in analyzing good 2, commodity bundling can lead to oversupply of both commodities, undersupply of both commodities, or oversupply of one and undersupply of the other. Figure 5 illustrates the first possibility, Figures 6 and 7 illustrate the second, while Figure 9 could be used to illustrate the last.[26] That monopolists can produce too much as well as too little output implies that the conventional view of monopoly output lacks general validity.

The welfare implications of bundling of the toothpaste variety are identical to those of the restaurant variety: both distributive inefficiency and allocative inefficiency typically occur, and equilibrium output might exceed optimal output. Therefore, no separate treatment of this case if required.

Bundling of the automobile variety, however, does possess distinctive normative characteristics. These can be illustrated in Figure 10. If both the basic car and the luxury car are offered at prices p_1^* and p_B^*, respectively, individuals in the area southeast of $p_1^* AB$ consume the basic car, and individuals northeast of $p_B^{*\prime} AB$ consume the luxury car. Because luxury is valued only by those who also consume transport services, no mutually beneficial trades among potential customers are possible, even

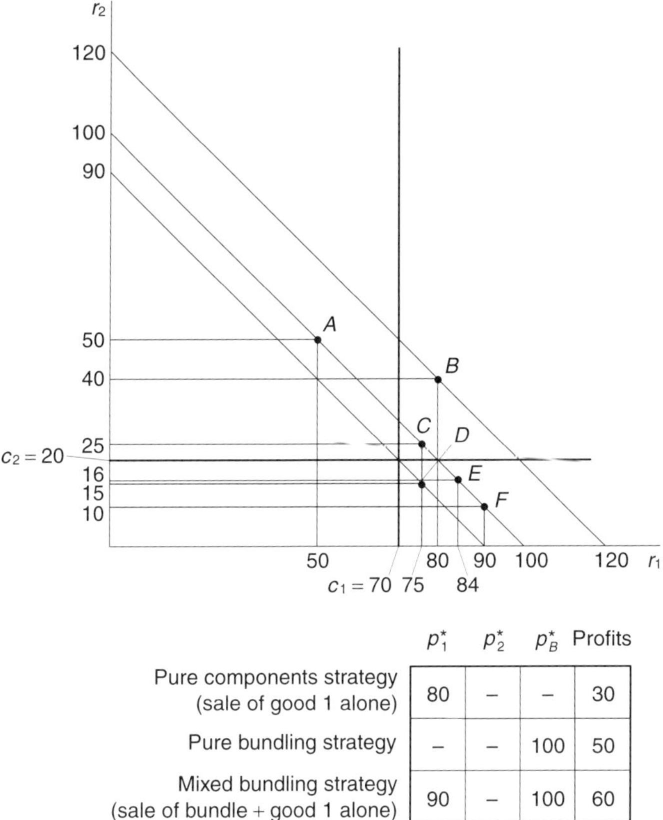

	p_1^*	p_2^*	p_B^*	Profits
Pure components strategy (sale of good 1 alone)	80	–	–	30
Pure bundling strategy	–	–	100	50
Mixed bundling strategy (sale of bundle + good 1 alone)	90	–	100	60

Figure 11.

though some who do not consume a commodity value it more highly than others who do. For example, X values transport more highly than does Y, and luxury more highly than does Z. Nevertheless, Y would not sell the transport services of his car to X at a price of Y_1, even if he could retain the luxury (e.g., in the form of chrome).[27] For the same reason, X would be unwilling to pay X_2 for the chrome of Z's car if that chrome were disembodied from the vehicle. Thus, no distributive inefficiency results from bundling in the car-type situation.

Allocative inefficiency is possible, however, even if some components cannot be disembodied from the bundle. This can be illustrated in Figure 11. In this situation A, B, and C should consume a luxury car, while D, E, and F should consume a basic car. The monopolist's profit-maximizing strategy, however, results in A, B, C, and E consuming the luxury car, F consuming the basic car, and D consuming nothing. Hence luxury is oversupplied, while transport services are undersupplied by the firm. More generally, in cases of the automobile type basic transport is never oversupplied, although the production of luxury can either exceed or fall short of ideal output.

In sum, commodity bundling generally leads to welfare losses when compared with perfect competition. But this does not imply that banning package selling *per se* decreases the burden of monopoly. In Figure 5, for example, mixed bundling is the most profitable strategy. The associated deadweight welfare loss is 7.[28] If bundling were prohibited and the monopolist forced to adopt a pure components strategy, the associated welfare loss would be 60 instead. Thus, prohibition of bundling without more might make society worse off. In fact, within the framework of our model, whenever mixed bundling is equivalent to pure price discrimination, it is Pareto optimal. Simple monopoly pricing never is. The possibility that mixed bundling is Pareto optimal is illustrated in Figure 4.

The deadweight loss associated with bundling might also exceed the corresponding loss associated with simple monopoly pricing. This possibility is illustrated in Figure 7. The profit-maximizing strategy for a monopolist is mixed bundling. And yet, the deadweight loss associated with that strategy (i.e., 10) exceeds that associated with the most profitable pure components strategy (i.e., 8). In this case, therefore, inability to bundle on the part of the monopolist would decrease the burden of monopoly.

IMPLICATIONS AND CONCLUSION

In the movie *Five Easy Pieces*, Jack Nicholson enters a diner to purchase some toast and coffee. The waitress informs him that toast alone is not available, even though both bread and toaster are on the premises. Nicholson is forced to order a chicken salad sandwich without chicken, lettuce, or mayonnaise.

Our purpose here has been to explain this and other forms of commodity bundling, such as vacation packages, chrome on cars, and quantity discounts. We have demonstrated that a monopolist's urge to charge customers their reservation prices for each of his products could lead to package selling. We have also demonstrated that bundling is inefficient by Pareto standards: it can lead to oversupply or undersupply of particular goods, and it can lead to the wrong people consuming each good. In this section we present some implications of commodity bundling for public policy analysis.

The first step in social appraisal of monopoly is to ascertain the sources and magnitude of the welfare loss it generates. That is the function of certain tools of applied welfare economics, such as consumer–producer surplus analysis and hedonic price indices. Unfortunately, the reliability of both such tools is seriously jeopardized when monopolists practice commodity bundling.

Looking first at consumer–producer surplus analysis, we estimate the burden of monopoly as

$$\Delta W = \int_0^{z^*} \sum_i D_i(z) \frac{\partial x_i}{\partial z} \, dz, \tag{1}$$

where D_i represents the excess of marginal social benefit over marginal social cost per unit level of activity i, x_i represents the number of units of activity i, and z denotes the extent of monopoly power. In effect, this formula measures the excess of consumer surplus lost over producer surplus gained from simple monopoly, as compared with competitive, pricing.

Where monopolists practice commodity bundling, equation (1) has two defects. First, it focuses exclusively on allocative inefficiency, ignoring the distributive inefficiency characteristic of the situation. Second, the formula is inaccurate even in its estimation of allocative inefficiency. To take the simplest and most dramatic example, assume that individuals are uniformly distributed in reservation price space along the line $r_1 + r_2 = 1$, and that both component costs are positive. Suppose also that the monopolist adopts a pure bundling strategy.[29] The profit-maximizing price is $P_B^* = 1$, and all individuals consume the package. Resource misallocation exists, since some consumers have reservation prices below cost for one component, while other consumers have reservation prices below cost for the other component. No distributive inefficiency exists. Yet as long as equation (1) is applied at the bundle level, $\partial x_i / \partial z = 0$, so that estimated welfare loss is zcro. This follows from the fact that the bundle demand curve is completely inelastic at prices below unity; hence the usual "triangle" measuring the deadweight loss vanishes entirely. In this example the formula not only underestimates welfare loss but fails even to detect its presence.

These defects of the consumer–producer surplus approach have two implications for public policy analysis. First, society may be unaware of the true extent of the burden of monopoly.[30] Second, even if society knows the extent of welfare loss, it may fail to pinpoint its source.[31] This could set governments on the wrong policy track, since distributive inefficiency requires social intervention of a sort different from that designed to eliminate resource misallocation.

Commodity bundling also affects certain conclusions that may be drawn from hedonic price indices. The reason is that practitioners of that art often discuss whether consumers are willing to pay for the quality change they consume. The standard treatment is to suggest that consumers either are willing to pay for improvements they consume, or else are not fully understanding of the cost they bear.[32] Bundling analysis suggests a third explanation of why quality might be consumed. Some people value it highly; others do not. The seller finds it profitable to offer quality in a bundle with characteristics consumers uninterested in quality wish to have. As a result, not everyone who buys quality is willing to pay for it. The normative interpretation of quality indices would accordingly seem ambiguous.

Once the sources and extent of welfare loss have been ascertained, the second step in policy analysis is to determine whether public intervention can reduce the loss. If the goods sold in the market place cannot be decomposed for separate purchase, for example, government is powerless to stop the evils of bundling.[33] To the extent that package goods can be decomposed, however, it becomes possible to guarantee that shadow prices on all components are the same for all customers. Hence the distributive inefficiency of bundling could be prevented. Moreover, pure components selling could reduce the waste associated with individuals consuming commodities for which they are unwilling to pay cost. Hence at least some of the allocative inefficiency of bundling could also be prevented.

What specifically, then, should governments do? Clearly they must embark on policies that achieve competitive supply of each decomposable good separately. As some have long, if unpopularly, argued, this might reduce rather than increase the output of firms with market power. The argument that modern industrial societies produce too much product differentiation need not rest on the hypothesis that advertising changes consumer tastes.

In any event public policy must take account of the fact that prohibition of commodity bundling without more may increase the burden of monopoly. This is consistent with the general theorem of second best: when one distortion exists (e.g., monopoly), elimination of other distortions (e.g., bundling) may either enhance or diminish social welfare. The implication is that monopoly itself must be eliminated to achieve high levels of social welfare.

ACKNOWLEDGEMENTS

We are indebted to Richard Caves, Jerry Green, Zvi Griliches, Rachel McCulloch, and Steven Shavell for their comments. Yellen's research was financed by the National Science Foundation via Grant SOC74-19459.

NOTES

1. Whenever a commodity is infinitely divisible, the choice of a "standard unit" is essentially arbitrary.
2. Thus, a telephone company that offers local calling only for a fixed monthly fee is engaged in pure bundling. A telephone company that offers local calling on both a fee for service and a monthly basis is engaged in mixed bundling.
3. This is one implication of the transaction cost literature. See, for example, R. Coase. The Problem of Social Cost, *Journal of Law and Economics*, III (Oct. 1960), 1–44; and H. Demsetz, The Cost of Transacting, *Quarterly Journal of Economics*, LXXXII (Feb. 1968), 33–53.
4. This view was first articulated in G. Stigler. United States v. Loew's Inc.: A Note on Block Booking, in P. Kurland, *The Supreme Court Review: 1963* (Chicago: University of Chicago Press, 1963), 152–57, See Also R. Markovits. Tie-Ins, Reciprocity and Leverage Theory, *Yale Law Journal*, LXXVI (June 1967), 1397–1472. Several recent papers illustrate the relevance of this phenomenon in a variety of institutional and market settings: R. Parks. The Demand and Supply of Durable Goods and Durability, *American Economic Review*, LXIV (March 1974), 37–55; S. C. Salop. The Noisy Monopolist: Imperfect Information, Price Dispersion and Price Discrimination, unpublished manuscript, 1973; J. K. Salop and S. C. Salop. Self-Selection and Turnover in the Labour Market, paper presented to the Econometric Society Meetings, Toronto, 1972; A. M. Spence. *Market Signaling* (Cambridge, MA: Harvard University Press, 1974); A. M. Spence. Time and Communication in Economic and Social Interaction, *Quarterly Journal of Economics*, LXXXVII (Nov. 1973), 651–60; and J. Stiglitz, Monopoly and Imperfect Information: the Insurance Market, unpublished manuscript, 1973. Commodity bundling is not the only sophisticated strategy a monopolist can use to enhance profit and complicate welfare judgements. The most similar practices are full-line forcing and all-or-non offers, although conventional price discrimination, the multipart tariff, and product differentiation are all related. See, respectively, M. Burstein. The Economics of Tie-In Sales, *Review of Economics and Statistics*, XLII (Feb., 1960), 68–73; and R. Markovits. *op. cit.*; R. Baldwin. Equilibrium in International Trade, *Quarterly Journal of Economics*, LXII (Nov. 1948), 748–62; E. Clemens. Price Discrimination and the Multiple Product Firm, *Review of Economic Studies*, XIX (Jan. 1951), 1–11; W. Oi. A Disneyland Dilemma: Two-Part Tariffs for a Mickey Mouse Monopoly, *Quarterly Journal of Economics*, LXXXV (Feb. 1971), 77–96; and E. Chamberlin. *The Theory of Monopolistic Competition* (Cambridge, MA: Harvard University Press, 1933).

5. Simple monopoly pricing involves setting those prices for each component that maximize profit. In general, the monopolist must take account of any interdependencies among product demand curves in his computation of these prices. This point is developed in M. Bailey, Price and Output Determination by a Firm Selling Related Products, *American Economic Review*, XLIV (March 1954), 82–93.

6. We assume here that any individual would be indifferent between consuming both goods 1 and 2 and a package consisting of these two goods. In other words, a package is identical to the sum of its component parts from the consumer's point of view.

7. The sorting of consumers depicted in Figure 2 assumes that resale of components is impossible.

8. Note that $p_1^* p_B^*$ must equal $p_1^* Y$, since the slope of $p_B^* p_B^*$ is -1.

9. An appendix to this effect is available upon request from the authors.

10. This follows from assumption A3. If an individual's reservation price for one good depends on the amount of the other he consumes, the profit-maximizing pure components strategy might involve violation of Exclusion. The loss leader is a classic case of this proposition.

11. The pure bundling strategy is analytically equivalent to an all-or-none offer. In both cases a package of commodities if offered to the consumer on a take it or leave it basis.

12. The proof of this assertion proceeds as follows. Assume that the monopolist adopts a pure bundling strategy and sets a price of p_B^*. Assume further that there exists some consumer i for whom $r_1 = r_2 \geq p_B^*$ and $r_2 < c_2 - \epsilon$, where $\epsilon > 0$. If the monopolist now adopts a mixed bundling strategy, with prices p_B^* and $p_1 = p_B^* - c_2 + \epsilon$, he necessarily earns more profits than under pure bundling: profits are unchanged on individuals for whom $r_1 + r_2 \geq p_B^*$ and $r_2 > p_B^* - p_1$, since they consume the bundle in both cases. Profits are increased, however, on individuals for whom $r_1 + r_2 > p_B^*$ and $r_2 < p_B^* - p_1$, since they bring in $p_1 - c_1 = p_B^* - c_B + \epsilon$ apiece instead of just $p_B^* - c_B$. Profits are also increased on individuals for whom $r_1 + r_2 < p_B^*$ and $r_1 \geq p_1$, since they previously consumed nothing but now generate $p_1 - c_1$ in profits apiece. All other individuals consume nothing in both cases.

13. For example, if $c_1 = c_2 = 0$ and consumers A, B, C, and D have reservation prices equal to $(30, 90)$, $(40, 60)$, $(60, 40)$, and $(90, 30)$, respectively, the pure bundling strategy generates profits of 400, while the mixed bundling strategy yields profits of 340. Hence pure bundling could be preferred to mixed bundling.

14. It is also possible, although less probable, that taste considerations alone render pure components pricing more profitable than mixed bundling. This is illustrated by the following example. Assume that five consumers—A, B, C, D, and E—have reservation prices of $(80, 80)$, $(75, 75)$, $(45, 45)$, $(75, 5)$, and $(5, 75)$. Assume that $c_1 = c_2 = 0$. The pure components strategy with $p_1^* = p_2^* = 75$ generates profits of 450. Although a bundle could be offered at a price of 90 in order to induce C to enter the market, gains from the inclusion of C would be outweighed by the loss of revenue on sales to A and B. Furthermore, increasing prices in components markets in conjunction with introduction of a bundle would not increase profits either. The point of this example is to suggest that there exist some distributions of tastes consistent with any strategy ranking as long as Exclusion is violated by none of the options.

15. To demonstrate this, we explored the profitability of bundling when individual reservation prices for the two components follow the joint normal distribution. Our experiments covered a wide range of parameters of the taste distribution and a wide range of cost structures. Suffice it to say that, for every characterization of tastes we studied, bundling in some form was preferred to pure components pricing for some cost conditions. Less complete explorations of tastes following the uniform and chi-square distributions were consistent with this result.

16. Using attendance data on first-run movies for various cities, Stigler attempted to show that real world tastes are such that the block booking practice of movie distributors can be explained by a model of this type. See Stigler, *op. cit.*

17. Note how this incarnation of the model can be used to treat divisible goods, even though they appear to be excluded by assumption A2. In the limiting case of perfect divisibility, bundling is equivalent to imposing non-linear budget constraints on consumers. The nonlinearity stems from the fact that the average unit price of toothpaste depends on the

    quantity of toothpaste consumed. The important point here is that bundling can be profitable in a world of divisible commodities for exactly the reasons set forth here.

18. This point is made in Salop, *op. cit.*

19. Note how this incarnation of the model can be used to treat complementarity even though it appears to be excluded by Assumption A3. Two goods are complements in consumption if an individual's reservation price for a unit of one depends on the quantity consumed of the other. By this definition luxury and transport services are complements in our model, since we assume that no individual would pay anything for luxury if he does not consume transport. Hence, by defining the vertical axis as we have, it is possible to analyze complementary goods.

20. In this situation it is rarely in the monopolist's interest to offer only a basic car. The reason is that as long as some consumer values luxury in excess of cost, profits can be increased by offering a luxury, as well as a basic, car. The proof is as follows. Assume that the monopolist offers a basic car at price p_1^*. Assume further that there exists an individual with $r_1 \geq p_1^*$ and $r_2 > c_2 + \epsilon, \epsilon > 0$. If the monopolist introduces a luxury car with price $p_B = p_1^* + c_2 + \epsilon$, all consumers with $r_1 \geq p_1^*$ and $r_2 \leq p_B - p_1^*$ continue to purchase only good 1. Profits on these sales are unchanged. All consumers with $r_1 \geq p_1^*$ and $r_2 > p_B - p_1^*$ now purchase the bundle instead of the basic car. Profits on these sales rise from $(p_1^* - c_1)$ to $(p_B - c_1 - c_2 = p_1^* - c_1 + \epsilon)$. In addition, individuals with $r_1 < p_1^*$ and $r_1 + r_2 > p_B$ now consume the bundle instead of nothing. Since $p_B > c_B$, greater profits are earned on these individuals. In situations of the car variety pure bundling is likely to be more profitable relative to mixed bundling than in cases of the restaurant type. However, the existence of any consumer in pure bundling equilibrium with $r_2 < c_2$ still suffices to guarantee the superiority of mixed bundling.

21. In the industrial organization literature it is usually argued that product differentiation is profitable because it raises barriers to new competition. Our results suggest that product differentiation might be profitable even if entry barriers are unaffected. On the market structure explanation see W. Comanor and T. A. Wilson, Advertising, Market Structure and Performance, *Review of Economics and Statistics*, XLIV (Nov. 1967), 423–40.

    One major class of automobile-type situations, sometimes discussed in other contexts, involves bundling of a good and a bad. Two bad cannot be disembodied from the package. The bad could be the search costs or waiting time required to purchase a commodity. See, respectively, Salop, *op. cit.*; and Spence, Time and Communication in Economic and Social Interaction.

22. See Spence, Time and Communication in Economic and Social Interaction, and Salop and Salop, *op. cit.*

23. The prices and costs depicted in Figure 9 were selected to permit simultaneous illustration of all potential sources of welfare loss under commodity bundling.

24. Whenever bundling occurs, the shadow price an individual faces for one commodity depends on his reservation price for the other commodity. Hence shadow prices on particular goods typically differ among consumers. This is what can lead to distributive inefficiency.

25. Sufficient as long as the mixed bundling equilibrium violates Inclusion in any way.

26. In Figure 9 good 1 can be either oversupplied or undersupplied, but good 2 must, by construction, be undersupplied.

27. This follows from our assumption that no individual has a positive reservation price for chrome when disembodied from transport services.

28. We calculated welfare loss as follows: the total loss is equal to the difference between consumer surplus in pure competition and the sum of consumer surplus and profits in the monopoly equilibrium.

29. Mixed bundling generates more profits in this situation, but its appraisal via equation (1) is more complicated.

30. The Harberger formula provides neither a floor not a ceiling to the true burden of monopoly; it can be shown that in situations where bundling is profitable, dead-weight loss can be overestimated or underestimated by equation (1).

31. Conceptually, the loss associated with allocative inefficiency should be measured as the net gain in producer and consumer surplus that results from increasing (decreasing) component outputs to their optimal levels, given the correct distribution of output among individuals. The loss associated with distributive inefficiency should be measured as the net gain in consumer surplus that results from redistribution of existing output.

32. Consider, for example, the stance adopted in F. Fisher, Z. Griliches, and C. Kaysen, The Costs of Automobile Model Changes Since 1949, *Journal of Political Economy*, LXX (Oct. 1952), 433–51. In discussing consumer expenditures on automobile model changes, they assert that "the model changes of the last decade seem to have been largely those desired by the consuming public, at least until the last years of the horsepower race. There are thus grounds for believing that car owners (at the time of purchase) thought model changes worth most of the cost. The general presumption of consumer sovereignty thus implies that these model changes *were* worth their cost" (p. 450). But they also aver that "the fact that model change costs for the late 1950s (about $700 in the purchase price per car, or more than 25 percent, and $40 per year in gasoline expenses) will probably seem surprisingly high to consumers is an indication that the costs in question were not fully understood by the consuming public" (p.450).

33. Where no component can be sold separately, bundling is equivalent to the Lancaster formulation of consumer theory. See K. Lancaster. A New Approach to Consumer Theory, *Journal of Political Economy*, LXXIV (April 1966) 132–57. Apart from the differences in normative interpretation, our model can be distinguished from Lancaster's in the sense that we provide some explanation for the range of products firms choose to offer in the market place. Our model integrates consumer and producer behavior.

14

Monopolistic Competition with Outside Goods

Steven C. Salop

The Chamberlinian monopolistically competitive equilibrium has been explored and extended in a number of recent papers. These analyses have paid only cursory attention to the existence of an industry outside the Chamberlinian group. In this chapter I analyze a model of spatial competition in which a second commodity is explicitly treated. In this two-industry economy, a zero-profit equilibrium with symmetrically located firms may exhibit rather strange properties. First, demand curves are kinked, although firms make "Nash" conjectures. If equilibrium lies at the kink, the effects of parameter changes are perverse. In the short run, prices are rigid in the face of small cost changes. In the long run, increases in costs lower equilibrium prices. Increases in market size raise prices. The welfare properties are also perverse at a kinked equilibrium.

INTRODUCTION

The Chamberlinian (1931) zero-profit monopolistically competitive equilibrium has been explored and extended in a number of recent papers. These analyses have focused on the monopolistically competitive industry and have paid only cursory attention to the existence of an industry outside the Chamberlinian group. In this chapter, a model of spatial competition is analyzed in which a second commodity is explicitly treated.

In this two-industry economy, a zero-profit equilibrium with symmetrically located firms may exhibit rather strange properties. First, demand curves are kinked, even though firms make "Nash" conjectures. If equilibrium is a tangency solution away from the kink, the short- and long-run responses to parameter changes are conventional. However, if equilibrium lies at the kink, the effects of parameter changes are perverse. In the short run, prices are rigid in the face of small cost changes. In the long run, increases in costs lower equilibrium prices. Interpreting the cost increase as an excise tax, this result states that the incidence of the tax is negative. Increases in market size raise prices. The welfare properties are also perverse at a kinked equilibrium. Decreases in cost and increases in market size lower both consumer and aggregate welfare.

In the next section the formal model is presented and the symmetric zero-profit Nash equilibrium (SZPE) is defined. Conditions for existence of the SZPE are then derived and comparative statics and welfare properties are explored. The chapter concludes with a short discussion of the deterrence equilibrium concept.

THE BASIC MODEL

In this section we analyze a variant of the traditional Hotelling (1929) model of spatial competition which is derived from Lerner and Singer (1937). In this variant the economy that is envisioned consists of two industries. The one upon which we focus is monopolistically competitive with differentiated brands and decreasing average costs; the other is a competitive industry producing a homogeneous commodity. Each of L consumers purchases either one unit or none[1] of the differentiated commodity according to preference, prices, and the distribution of brands in product space. Remaining income is spent on the homogeneous commodity.

Each consumer has a most-preferred brand specification l^*. A brand l different from the most preferred specification is valued lower according to preferences in product space $U(l, l^*)$. The product space of the industry is taken to be an infinite line or the unit-circumference of a circle. While neither assumption is realistic, both allow the "corner" difficulties of the original Hotelling model to be ignored and an industry equilibrium with identical prices by equally-spaced firms to obtain. Eliminating the technical difficulties makes it simpler to analyze the qualitative equilibrium properties of the model. Thus, the model is a benchmark for subsequent analyses with nonuniform preferences across empirically validated product spaces. By eliminating technical problems, this model allows a focus on the essential interactions of firms in an industry.

If there are n brands of the differentiated commodity available at prices p_i and locations l_i, a consumer whose most preferred specification is l^* will purchase one unit from some brand if the maximum surplus of utility less price across brands outweighs the surplus from the homogeneous other good. Denoting that surplus by $\bar{s}$, we have the decision rule: Purchase one unit of the brand satisfying

$$\max_i \left[U(l_i, l^*) - p_i \right] \geq \bar{s}. \tag{1}$$

The traditional model of constant transport costs is captured with preferences given by

$$U(l_i, l^*) = u - c|l_i - l^*|, \tag{2}$$

where the "distance" $|l_i - l^*|$ refers to the shortest arc length between l_i and l^*. In

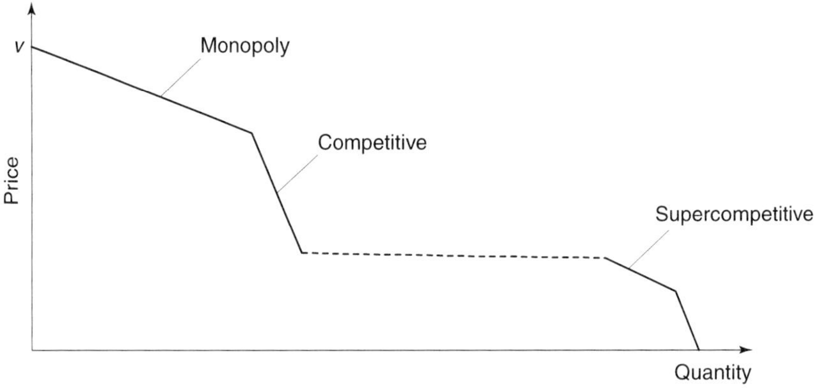

Figure 1. Typical demand curve.

this case, equation (1) may be rewritten as follows:

$$\max_i \left[v - c|l_i - l^*| - p_i \right] \geq 0, \tag{3}$$

where the effective reservation price is given by

$$v = u - \bar{s} > 0. \tag{4}$$

We now explore the existence and properties of a symmetric zero-profit Nash equilibrium (SZPE). By symmetric we mean an equilibrium in which the brands are equally spaced around the circular product space and charge identical prices. By zero profits, we mean an equilibrium in which free entry leads to a situation of each brand earning zero profits. The equilibrium is Nash in that each brand chooses a best price, given a perception that all other brands hold their prices constant. The conclusion discusses the requirement that the number of brands be integer-valued.

The methodology here consists of deriving the perceived demand curve for a single representative brand as a function of other brands' prices and locations and then finding a tangency between that demand curve and the average cost curve. Three regions of the representative brand's demand curve may be distinguished: the "monopoly," "competitive," and "supercompetitive" regions. The "monopoly" region consists of those prices in which the brand's entire market consists of consumers for whom the surplus of no other brand exceeds the surplus of the homogeneous outside good. The "competitive" region is composed of those prices in which customers are attracted who would otherwise purchase some other differentiated brand. The "supercompetitive" region consists of those prices in which all the customers of the closest neighboring brand are captured. These three regions of a typical demand curve are illustrated in Figure 1.

Suppose the representative brand charges price p and its nearest competitors located at distance $1/n$ charge $\bar{p}$, as shown in Figure 2. We derive the regions of the demand curve as follows. In the absence of competition from other differentiated

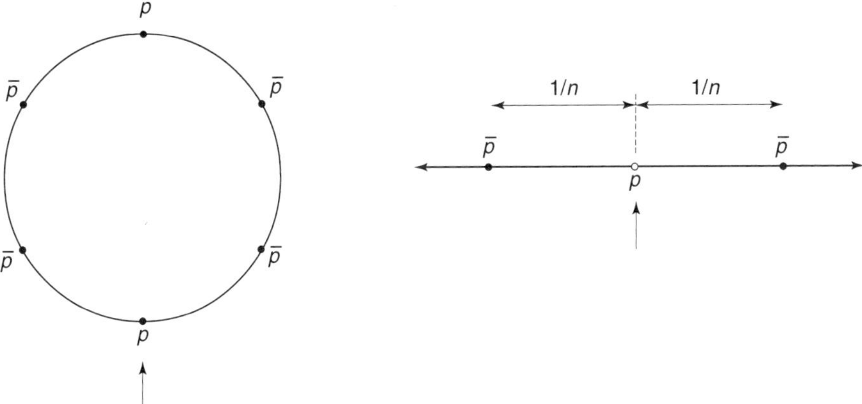

Figure 2. The circular market.

brands, the representative brand captures all consumers living within a distance where the net surplus given in (3) is nonnegative. Denoting the maximum distance by $\hat{x}$ and substituting into (3) we have,

$$\hat{x} = \frac{v - p}{c}. \tag{5}$$

If there are L consumers around the circle, since the brand captures customers within a distance $\hat{x}$ on each side, its monopoly demand q^m is given by

$$q^m = \frac{2L}{c}(v - p). \tag{6}$$

This defines the potential monopoly market of the representative brand. Those consumers residing in the potential monopoly market of two brands purchase from the one offering higher net surplus. If the brands are located a distance apart of $1/n$ and the neighboring brand on one side charges a price $\bar{p}$, then from (3) the representative brand captures all those consumers within a distance x given by

$$v - cx - p \le v - c\left(\frac{1}{n} - x\right) - \bar{p}. \tag{7}$$

Denoting by $\bar{x}$, the value for which (7) holds with equality, we have

$$\bar{x} = \frac{1}{2c}(\bar{p} + c/n - p) \tag{8}$$

and hence a firm's competitive demand $q^c = 2L\bar{x}$ is given by

$$q^c = \frac{L}{c}(\bar{p} + c/n - p). \tag{9}$$

Figure 3. Market segments.

Figure 4. Market overlap.

Differentiating (6) and (9), the slopes $sl(D)$ of the demand curve in these two regions are given by

$$sl(D^m) = -c/2L \tag{10}$$

$$sl(D^c) = -c/L. \tag{11}$$

Thus, we have the unusual result that demand is more elastic in the monopoly region than in the competitive region. Moreover, as illustrated in Figure 1, the monopoly region comes at higher prices.

The two regions fit together as follows. Suppose the right-side neighbor has a potential monopoly market illustrated in Figure 3. At prices above v, the representative brand obtains no customers. As it begins lowering prices below v, it captures demand from the homogeneous good according to the monopoly slope $c/2L$. Eventually its price becomes low enough that its monopoly market overlaps the monopoly market of its neighbor as illustrated in Figure 4. Now as it lowers price further, it begins to capture customers from its neighbor according to the steeper competitive slope c/L. At the kink in Figure 2, the monopoly regions just touch. Note that the kink arises here from the existence of the other industry, not from the non-Nash perceptions discussed by Sweezy (1939). It generalizes to higher dimensional spaces.[2]

At some lower price, even those customers residing at the neighbor are indifferent between the representative firm at p and the neighbor at $\bar{p}$ (and additional surplus $c(1/n)$). This price p_z is given by

$$p_z = \bar{p} - c/n. \tag{12}$$

At prices below p_z, the representative firm captures the entire market of its neighbor, for not only are those consumers residing at the neighbor willing to incur the surplus loss c/n for the price differential $\bar{p} - p$, but so are all the customers of the neighbor. Thus the representative brand's demand has a discontinuity at p_z from this "predatory" pricing.

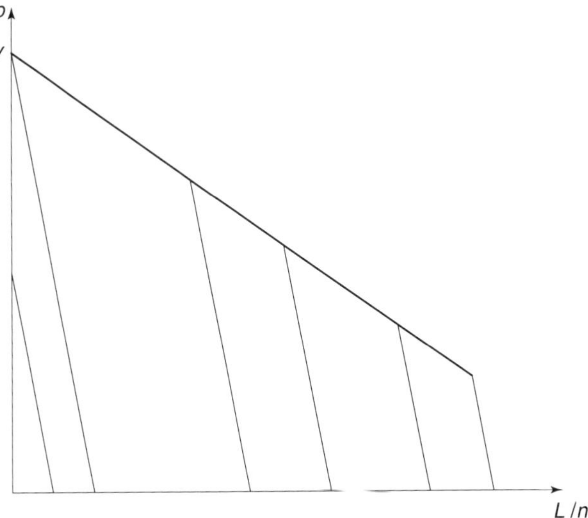

Figure 5. Family of demand curves.

The demand curve in Figure 2 displays the typical shape of these three regions. It shifts according to the prices and locations of the neighboring brands. Since demand can never exceed the monopoly demand, the kink always lies on that monopoly curve, as illustrated in Figure 5 (with supercompetitive regions deleted). Note that the market may be so competitive as to make the kink nonexistent. This occurs when the neighbors' potential monopoly market includes the location of the representative brand.

EXISTENCE OF A SYMMETRIC ZERO-PROFIT EQUILIBRIUM (SZPE)

An SZPE is defined as a price p and a number of brands n such that every equally spaced[3] Nash price setter's maximum profit price choice earns zero profits. We ignore the additional requirement that the number of brands must be an integer and discuss it later. In addition, the potential nonexistence of equilibrium arising from the discontinuity in demand is also postponed. If an equilibrium exists, the representative brand's demand curve and average cost curve will be tangent, for then the zero-profit point is surely also one of maximum profits. Three equilibrium configurations are possible, as illustrated in Figure 6, where the monopoly, kinked, and competitive equilibrium prices are denoted by subscripts (m, k, c), respectively.

At the monopoly equilibrium, some consumers lying between two neighboring brands may not purchase the differentiated commodity. Thus, the markets of neighbors may not overlap and each can act as a monpolist, constrained only by the outside commodity. Monopoly equilibria with and without overlap are pictured in

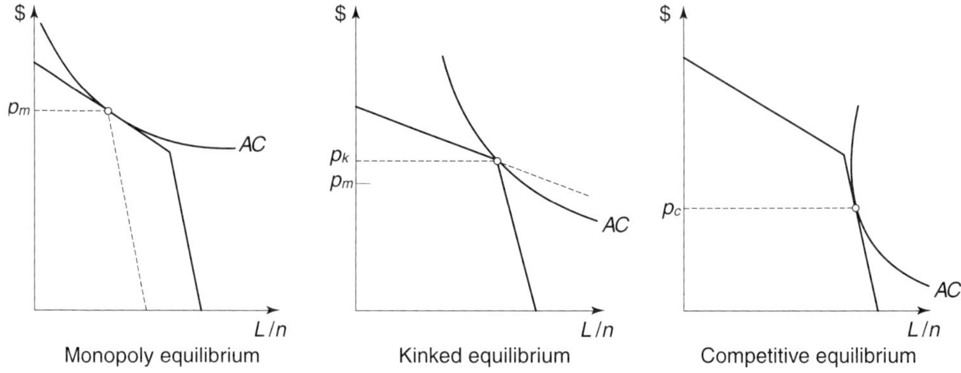

Figure 6. Equilibrium configurations.

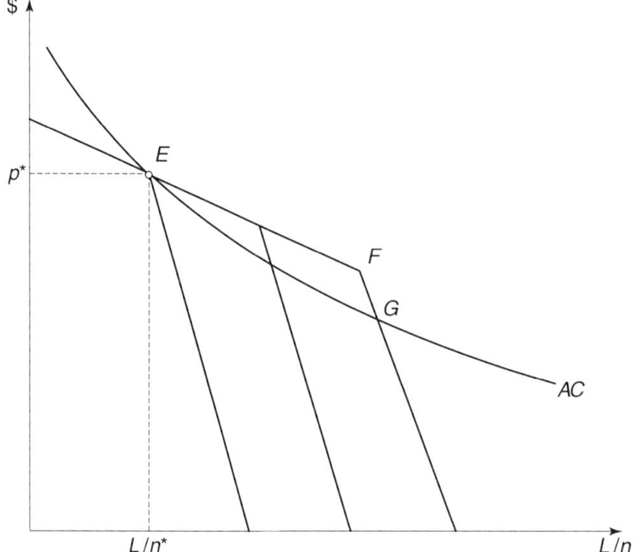

Figure 7. Existence of equilibrium.

Figure 6. At a kinked equilibrium, markets just touch. As illustrated in Figure 6, since the extension of the monopoly demand curve lies above the average cost curve, the monopoly price p_m lies below the kinked equilibrium price p_k. At the competitive equilibrium configuration, monopoly markets completely overlap. However, p_c may be above or below p_m, depending on demand and technologies.

It is easy to show graphically which equilibrium configuration obtains for any set of technology and demand parameters f, m, v, c, L. Simply drawing the average cost curve and the entire family of demand curves, existence of an equilibrium configuration requires maximum profits equal to zero-point E in Figure 7. A zero-profit point like G does not satisfy maximum profits because it is dominated by a point like F.

The SZPE satisfies two conditions: marginal revenue (less than or) equal to marginal cost and price equal to average cost. For constant marginal cost m and fixed cost F, the SZPE is given by

$$p + q\frac{dp}{dq} \leq m \tag{13}$$

$$p = m + F/q, \tag{14}$$

and from symmetry, if the equilibrium has no gaps,

$$q = L/n. \tag{15}$$

At the monopoly equilibrium dp/dq is given by $sl(D^m)$ in (10); at the competitive equilibrium by $sl(D^c)$ in (11); and at the kinked equilibrium by a slope between $sl(D^m)$ and $sl(D^c)$. Substituting (15) and (10) into (13) and (14), the monopoly price and number of brands[4] are given by

$$p_m = m + c/2n_m \tag{16}$$

$$n_m = \frac{1}{\sqrt{2}}\sqrt{cL/F}. \tag{17}$$

Using (11) instead of (10), the competitive equilibrium is given by[5]

$$p_c = m + c/n_c \tag{18}$$

$$n_c = \sqrt{cL/F}. \tag{19}$$

The values (p_k, n_k) for a kinked equilibrium lie between the values given in (16)–(19). Since there is no tangency at a kinked equilibrium, (13) holds as an inequality. Instead of being given by the equality in (13), price is given by the monopolistic demand function, or

$$p_k = v - (c/L)q = v - c/n. \tag{20}$$

Solving (20) and the price equal to average cost condition given by equation (14) for equilibrium variety n_k, we have

$$\frac{F}{L}n_k + c/n_k = v - m. \tag{21}$$

The monopoly equilibrium configuration requires the very restrictive condition that the exogenously given average cost curve be tangent to the exogenously given demand curve or $v - m = \sqrt{2cF/L}$.[6] We ignore this limiting case for the remainder of the analysis. The competitive equilibrium configuration occurs for all parameter values such that $v - m \geq \frac{3}{2}\sqrt{cF/L}$.[7] The kinked equilibrium configuration occurs for values of $v - m$ in the interval $\left[\sqrt{2cF/L}, \frac{3}{2}\sqrt{cF/L}\right]$, which is small relative to the range of values $v - m$ can assume.[8]

The demand discontinuity can imply the nonexistence of any SZPE.[9] Recalling from (12) that the representative firm can capture its neighbor's entire market at prices below $\bar{p} - c/n$, an additional condition for existence of an SZPE is that such pricing behavior is unprofitable. A sufficient condition for this is that the predatory price $\bar{p} - c/n$ does not exceed marginal cost m, for price equal to or below marginal cost necessarily is a losing strategy in the presence of fixed costs. Referring to (16) and (18), supercompetitive behavior is not profitable, since the equilibrium price is no greater than $m + c/n$. Similarly, if marginal costs are increasing, as with U-shaped AC curves, then the market-capturing price lies below the minimum AC price. However, if marginal costs are decreasing, then such price cuts may be profitable and cause nonexistence of an SZPE.

COMPARATIVE STATICS

As the exogenous technological or demand parameters $\{F, m, v, c, L\}$ vary, the equilibrium price-variety pair also changes. These changes may be calculated from the equilibrium values in equations (16)–(19).

Competitive equilibria

The comparative statics at competitive equilibria are straightforward and traditional. Substituting (19) into (18) we have

$$p_c = m + \sqrt{\frac{cF}{L}} \tag{22}$$

$$n_c = \sqrt{\frac{cL}{F}}. \tag{23}$$

As fixed costs (F) rise, price rises and equilibrium variety falls. Changes in marginal costs (m) are fully shifted onto consumers; equilibrium variety remains the same. Surprisingly perhaps, changes in the net valuation v have no effect on the equilibrium. The market is competitive enough that aggregate demand is unaffected by changes in this demand price.

As the value of product differentiation (c) falls, prices fall and variety falls. As market size (L) rises, prices fall and variety rises. As c/L decreases, demand becomes more elastic and price moves toward marginal cost. Thus, the ratio c/L is the relevant measure of monopolistic product differentiation in the model. For U-shaped average

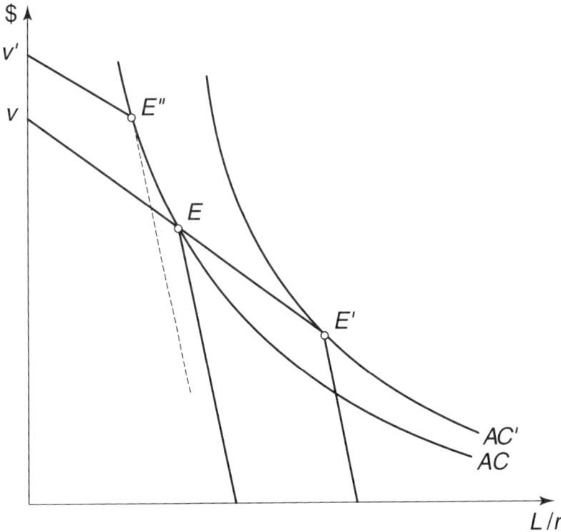

Figure 8. Comparative statics of (v, m, F): kinked equilibrium.

costs, perfect competition obtains when $c/L = 0$, for then every brand faces a perfectly elastic demand function.

Kinked equilibria

The comparative statics at kinked equilibria are all perverse. An increase in either fixed or marginal costs lowers prices. This is illustrated diagrammatically, in Figure 8, as a movement from E to E'. Intuitively, cost increases reduce the equilibrium number of brands, allowing the remaining brands to further exploit scale economies. This is a very striking result. If the increase in costs is interpreted as an excise tax levied on the industry, then the incidence of that excise tax is negative at the kinked equilibrium. In terms of consumer welfare, the lower price is offset by the decline in variety, of course. However, it is shown in the next section that consumer welfare does rise from the tax, even if the proceeds of the tax are ignored.

It should be emphasized that this perverse reaction to a cost increase is a long-run response that results from the exit of marginal firms. In the short run, there is no reaction at all. Since the marginal revenue curve is discontinuous at the kinked equilibrium, a small change in marginal costs induces no price response. Thus, the industry responds to a small marginal cost increase as follows. In the short run, prices and quantities do not change, though profits fall below normal (zero). These losses induce some firms to exit, resulting in higher demand for those that remain. This increased demand allows the remaining firms to better exploit scale economies, resulting in decreased long-run prices.

An increase in the valuation (v) raises price and variety, as illustrated by the movement from E to E''. As may be seen from Figure 8, price rises by more than the increase in valuation, as scale economies are lost. As with cost increases, the welfare

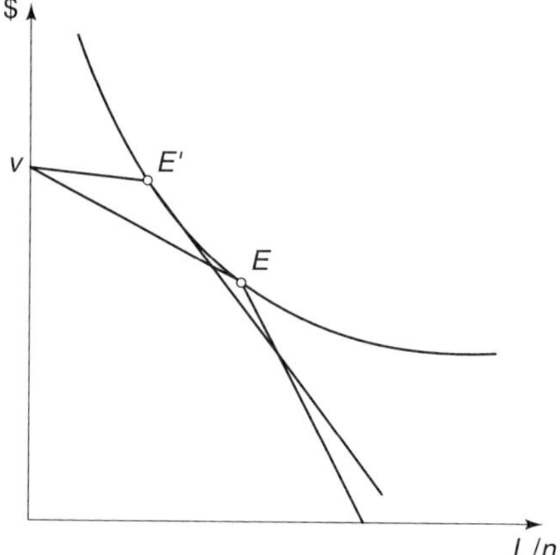

Figure 9. Comparative statics of c/L: kinked equilibrium.

effect of this increase in valuation is also perverse; it may be shown that consumer welfare falls. Interpreting the increase in valuation as arising from informative advertising and the cost increase as the cost of that informative advertising, the valuation effect lowers welfare, while the cost effect raises welfare.

Decreases in c/L, arising from either an increase in market size (L) or a decrease in the value of product differentiation (c), raise prices in equilibrium, as illustrated in Figure 9 as a movement from E to E'. As with the other comparative statics discussed, this result is the reverse of what occurs in the competitive equilibrium configuration.

WELFARE ANALYSIS

Product selection

It has been pointed out by Spence (1976) and others that the production of some unprofitable commodities may be optimal and the production of some profitable commodities may be nonoptimal. For the circular market, this may be tested by comparing the condition under which a segment of the market will be served by a monopolist (the profitability condition) with the condition under which service yields positive net surplus (the optimality condition).

Suppose each brand produces up to the point where the net benefit to the marginal consumer, who is at a distance x^* from the brand serving him, is zero. Then, the net social benefit per brand of serving the entire circular market is:

$$B = 2L \int_0^{x^*} (v - cx - m)dx - F, \tag{24}$$

where the marginal consumer's benefit is given by

$$v - cx^* - m = 0. \tag{25}$$

Substituting (25) into (24) and integrating, we have

$$B = \frac{L}{c}(v - m)^2 - F, \tag{26}$$

and this surplus is nonnegative ($B \geq 0$) if and only if the following optimality condition is satisfied:

$$v - m \geq \sqrt{\frac{cF}{L}}. \tag{27}$$

On the other hand, a monopolistic firm will choose to serve any segment of the market only if its profits are nonnegative,[10] where profits for the monopoly portion of the demand function are given by

$$\Pi_m = \left(v - \frac{c}{2L}q - m\right)q - F. \tag{28}$$

Maximizing (28) with respect to q, we have

$$q_m = \frac{L}{c}(v - m). \tag{29}$$

Substituting (29) into (28), profits are given by

$$\Pi_m = \frac{L}{2c}(v - m)^2 - F. \tag{30}$$

Profits are nonnegative ($\Pi_m \geq 0$) if and only if the following profitability condition is satisfied:

$$v - m \geq \sqrt{\frac{2cF}{L}}. \tag{31}$$

Comparing the optimality and profitability conditions, we see that profitability is sufficient but not necessary for optimality. All markets served should be served, but not vice versa.

Optimal vs. equilibrium variety

Given that the entire circular market should be served, the optimal price-variety pair may be compared with the equilibrium price-variety pair. A tradeoff between price and variety exists because of the scale economies present in production.

If n firms operate and serve the entire unit-circumference market, then the marginal consumer travels a distance $\frac{1}{2n}$ and a consumer located at $x \leq \frac{1}{2n}$ obtains a surplus in excess of marginal cost of $v - m - cx$. Since there are L consumers per unit distance and $2n$ intervals of length $\frac{1}{2n}$, total surplus is given by

$$W = 2n \int_0^{1/2n} (v - m - cx)L dx - nF. \tag{32}$$

Integrating, we have:

$$W = \left(v - m - \frac{1}{4}\frac{c}{n}\right)L - nF. \tag{33}$$

The interpretation of (33) is the following. Since (i) the marginal consumer travels a distance of $\frac{1}{2}n$ in product space; (ii) the consumer who travels the shortest distance (zero) obtains his most preferred brand, and (iii) L consumers are distributed uniformly in product space, the average distance travelled is $\frac{1}{4}n$ at an imputed cost of c per unit. Then the average net surplus per consumer is $v - m - c/4n$. Total fixed costs are nF. Maximizing (33) with respect to the number of brands n to find the optimal price-variety mix, we have

$$n^* = \frac{1}{2}\sqrt{\frac{cL}{F}}. \tag{34}$$

Comparing this optimum to the possible equilibria given by (17), (19), and (21) we have

$$n^* < n_m < n_k < n_c. \tag{35}$$

That is, optimal variety is less than equilibrium variety for this circular market, if the market should be served.

This result of too many brands is not robust, but rather depends crucially on the distribution of consumers and preferences. As Spence (1976) and others[11] have pointed out, the optimum depends on the difference between the average surplus and the surplus of the marginal consumer relative to fixed costs; the value of adding an extra brand (and respacing the others) effectively converts marginal consumers to average ones, at fixed cost F.[12]

Graphically, the comparison of the equilibrium with the optimum may be made as follows. The planning problem in (33) is equivalent to maximizing average consumer welfare minus price $W(n,p)$ subject to the price equal to average cost breakeven constraint.[13] Since the average consumer travels a distance $\frac{1}{4n}$ in product space, we have

$$\max W(n,p) = v - p - \frac{1}{4}\frac{c}{n} \tag{36}$$

$$\text{subject to} \quad p = m + \frac{F}{L}n. \tag{37}$$

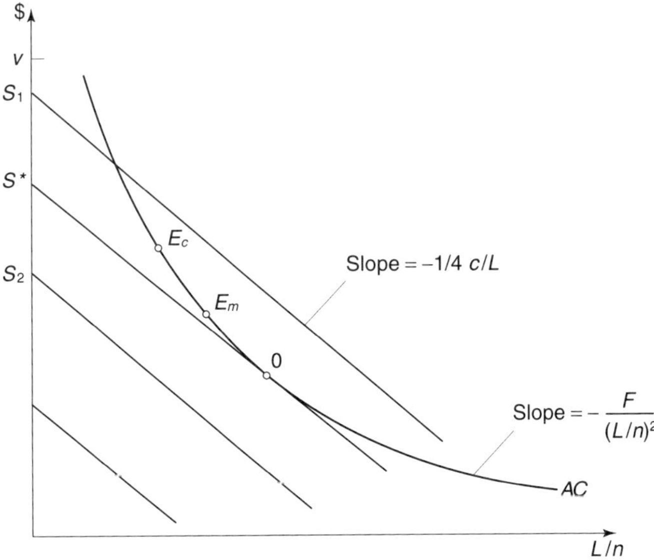

Figure 10. Equilibrium vs. optimal variety.

Equation (36) defines linear indifference curves in $(p, L/n)$ space with slope of $-\frac{1}{4}(c/L)$ while (37) expresses the constraint. As illustrated in Figure 10, a smaller value of S expresses a higher surplus $v - S$. Then, the optimum lies at the point where the average cost has slope equal to $-\frac{1}{4}(c/L)$, whereas equilibrium lies at the point where the average cost curve has slope between $-\frac{1}{2}(c/L)$ (for monopoly equilibrium) and $-c/L$ (for competitive equilibrium).

A graphical representation of the optimum vs. equilibrium price-variety pair may be used to show the welfare effects of the comparative statics at the kinked equilibrium (See Figure 11.) For example, an increase in costs from AC to AC' that lowers prices will improve welfare, since the slope of the indifference curve $(-\frac{1}{4}c/L)$ is flatter than the slope of the monopoly demand curve $(-\frac{1}{2}c/L)$. Thus, movements down the demand curve represent higher welfare as illustrated below by comparing S to S'. Similar analysis will show that an increase in valuation (v) and an increase in market size (L) lowers consumer welfare.

Finally, we can determine the optimal number of brands given monopolistically competitive pricing. Spence (1976) shows that for his partial equilibrium model, the market solution is optimal. For the circular model studied here, the optimum is either the market equilibrium or complete monopoly. We may prove this as follows. First we derive the Nash equilibrium price for different (exogenously given) numbers of symmetrically spaced brands. We denote this relationship by $p(L/n)$.[14] The $p(L/n)$ function is illustrated in Figure 12 as $EE'M$, where we assume the SZPE (point E) is competitive. The complete monopoly equilibrium is labeled M, and $E'M$ is a portion of the monopoly demand curve.

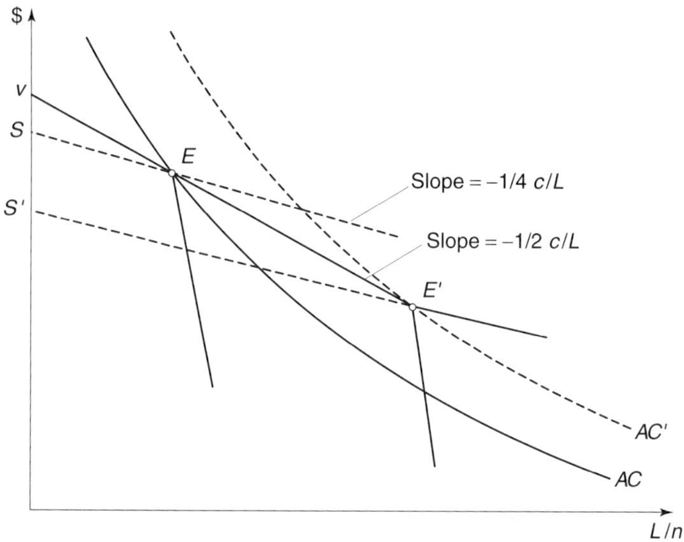

Figure 11. Derivation of optimal variety.

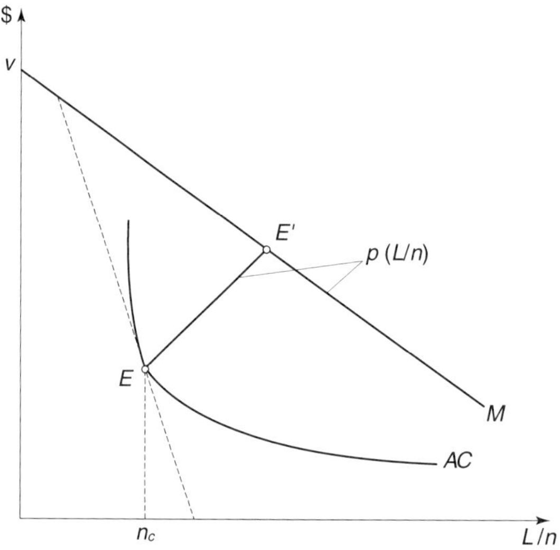

Figure 12. Derivation of the $p(L/n)$ function.

The consumer welfare maximum could then be found by placing indifference curves, which have slope $-\frac{1}{4}(c/L)$, in Figure 12. It is clear that the optimum must lie at E or M. If the SZPE were kinked, say at E', the $p(L/n)$ would be the portion $E'M$, and the optimum would lie at the complete monopoly point. Thus, for the circular industry, optimal entry policy is either free entry or entry restricted to the point of each brand having a complete monopoly market.

CONCLUSIONS

In the example studied here, explicit attention has been paid to the role a second industry (outside goods) plays in determining the properties of monopolistically competitive equilibrium. This focus required us to ignore the possibility of non-uniform preferences across more complicated and realistic product spaces or different technologies across brands.

The major contribution of the approach taken here, which was first noted by Lerner and Singer (1937), is to provide a rationalization of the kinked demand curve in terms of symmetric "Nash" conjectural variations. Previous rationalizations by Sweezy (1939) and others were based upon asymmetric competitive responses to price increases and decreases. This paper goes beyond Lerner and Singer by deriving the industry equilibrium and analyzing its properties.

The industry equilibrium model displays conventional properties when equilibrium occurs at a Chamberlinian tangency away from the kink. On the other hand, the properties of equilibria occurring at the kink are perverse. In the short run, industry prices do not adjust to small cost changes, as noted by Sweezy in his model. It is only through the process of entry and exit that the industry adjusts to cost changes. Moreover, at the kinked equilibrium, the long-run response to a cost increase is exit by some brands followed by a decrease in industry prices, as remaining brands better exploit scale economies.

The short-run price rigidity of the kinked equilibrium accords with casual empiricism. However, the long-run properties are more difficult to confirm or reject, since they depend on longer run entry adjustments. Moreover, the actual symmetric example analyzed entails the abstract and unrealistic assumptions of uniform preferences around a circular product space and identical cost functions and valuations among competing brands. While these assumptions considerably simplify the theoretical analysis, they make empirical confirmation more difficult.

Other shortcomings of the approach taken here are the zero-profit and costless relocation assumptions we have made. Because the technology is characterized by an indivisible fixed cost, the number of brands must be integer-valued. Therefore, free entry need not lead to a zero-profit equilibrium, as originally pointed out by Kaldor (1935) and analyzed by Eaton (1976). An interesting "deterrence" equilibrium concept built on these foundations has been explored for a circular market by Hay (1976) and Schmalensee (1977) and for other spatial markets by Prescott and Visscher (1977). In a deterrence equilibrium sequential entrants locate in such a way that no new entrant wishes to locate in the interval between two firms. As a result, the deterrence equilibrium has half the number of brands as the SZPE.

In the model analyzed here, the deterrence equilibrium configuration is generally that point in the $p(L/n)$ curve with the number of brands n equal to $\frac{1}{2}$ the number at the SZPE.[15] If the SZPE is competitive, the deterrence equilibrium may be competitive, kinked, or at the monopoly point; which equilibrium occurs depends on the particular parameter values. Hay showed that if the deterrence equilibrium is competitive, prices are higher than at the SZPE. However, kinked or monopoly deterrence equilibria may result in lower prices than the competitive SZPE. Finally, if the SZPE is kinked, the deterrence equilibrium lies at the monopoly point and entails lower prices and unserved segments of the circular market.

In closing, it should be reemphasized that the exact results derived here merely reflect the example used. That there is excess variety at equilibrium is not robust. The kink appears robust as the number of dimensions of product space increases. However, as Archibald–Rosenbluth (1975) and Weiss (1977) point out, equilibrium may not exist with higher dimensional product spaces.

ACKNOWLEDGEMENTS

I am indebted to Don Hester, Lew Johnson, Bob Mackay, Perry Quick, Steve Salant, Joe Stiglitz, Andy Weiss, the referee and editor, for helpful comments and to Mary Ann Henry for editing and typing.

NOTES

1. The model easily generalizes to elastic demands.
2. This may be confirmed in a two-dimensional product space. The monopoly market is circular, while competitive markets are polygonal.
3. This equilibrium concept is static. In a dynamic context, it assumes that firms may costlessly relocate in response to entry and, in fact, do relocate. Thus, equal spacing is maintained. For a discussion of an alternative equilibrium concept, see the conclusions.
4. There may be gaps at a monopoly equilibrium. This calculation yields the maximum number of brands at a monopoly equilibrium.
5. See Grubel (1963) for a short derivation of the competitive equilibrium.
6. For the derivation, see the derivation of equation (31) below when profits are zero.
7. The derivation is as follows. Referring to Figure 6, the equilibrium p_c derived in (18) and (19) must lie below the monopoly portion of the demand curve, or $v - \frac{1}{2}(c/L)(L/n_c) \geq p_c$. Substituting for p_c and n_c, the stated condition obtains.
8. This interval may be larger for alternative technological and demand specifications.
9. See Roberts-Sonnenschein (1977) for examples of discontinuous reaction functions leading to nonexistence of equilibrium.
10. It should be noted that if one monopolist does not wish to serve one segment, no monopolist will serve any segment since the circular market is symmetric.
11. For example, Dixit and Stiglitz (1977) and Lancaster (1975).
12. It can be shown that any utility function that is concave in distance will yield excess variety, for a uniform consumer distribution. Convex functions are necessary for deficient variety.
13. Since consumers have inelastic demands in this example, that price does not equal marginal cost introduces no distortion.
14. The derivation of $p(L/n)$ relies on the following observation. For any number of brands n, there exists a level of fixed costs F' such that an n-brand SZPE obtains (or the market is not served). Thus, an n-brand Nash equilibrium, when fixed costs are F, yields equilibrium price $p(L/n)$ and excess profits per brand of $\Pi = F' - F$.
15. The exception arises when this point on $p(L/n)$ lies below the monopoly point on the monopoly portion of the demand curve. In this case, while the number of brands is still

halved, the remaining brands raise price and lower output to the monopoly point. Hence, the deterrence equilibrium entails unserved segments of the circular market.

REFERENCES

Archibald, G.C. and Rosenbluth, G. The 'new' theory of consumer demand and monopolistic competition, *Quarterly Journal of Economics*, 1975, **89**.
Chamberlin, E. H. *The Theory of Monopolistic Competition*. Cambridge, MA: Harvard University Press, 1931.
Dixit, A. K. and Stiglitz, J. E. Monopolistic competition and optimum product diversity, *American Economic Review*, 1977, **67**.
Eaton, B. C. Free entry in one-dimensional models: Pure profits and multiple equilibria, *Journal of Regional Science*, 1976.
Grubel, H. G. *Wastes of Monopolistic Competition*. (Based on a lecture by J. Tobin.) Yale University, 1963.
Hotelling, H. Stability in competition, *Economic Journal*, 1929, **39**.
Kaldor, N. Market imperfection and excess capacity. *Economica*, 1935, **2**.
Lancaster, K. Socially optimal product differentiation, *American Economic Review*, 1975, **65**.
Lerner, A. P. and Singer, H. W. Some notes on duopoly and spatial competition, *Journal of Political Economy*, 1937, **45**.
Prescott, E. and Visscher, M. Sequential location decisions among firms with foresight, *Bell Journal of Economics*, 1977, **8**.
Roberts, J. and Sonnenschein, H. On the foundations of the theory of monopolistic competition, *Econometrica*, 1977, **75**.
Schmalensee, R. Entry deterrence in the ready-to-eat breakfast cereal industry, *Bell Journal of Economics*, 1978, **9**.
Spence, A. M. Product selection. Fixed costs and monopolistic competition, *Review of Economic Studies*, 1976, **43**.
Sweezy, P. M. Demand under Conditions of Oligopoly, *Journal of Political Economy*, 1939, **47**.
Weiss, A. Spatial competition with two dimensions. Unpublished manuscript, Bell Laboratories, 1977.

Part VI

Information

CONTENTS

15

The Market for "Lemons": Quality Uncertainty and the Market Mechanism

George A. Akerlof

INTRODUCTION

This chapter relates quality and uncertainty. The existence of goods of many grades poses interesting and important problems for the theory of markets. On the one hand, the interaction of quality differences and uncertainty may explain important institutions of the labor market. On the other hand, this chapter presents a struggling attempt to give structure to the statement: "Business in underdeveloped countries is difficult"; in particular, a structure is given for determining the economic costs of dishonesty. Additional applications of the theory include comments on the structure of money markets, on the notion of "insurability," on the liquidity of durables, and on brand-name goods.

There are many markets in which buyers use some market statistic to judge the quality of prospective purchases. In this case there is incentive for sellers to market poor quality merchandise, since the returns for good quality accrue mainly to the entire group whose statistic is affected rather than to the individual seller. As a result there tends to be a reduction in the average quality of goods and also in the size of the market. It should also be perceived that in these markets social and private returns differ, and therefore, in some cases, governmental intervention may increase the welfare of all parties. Or private institutions may arise to take advantage of the potential increases in welfare which can accrue to all parties. By nature, however, these institutions are nonatomistic, and therefore concentrations of power—with ill consequences of their own—can develop.

The automobile market is used as finger exercise to illustrate and develop these thoughts. It should be emphasized that this market is chosen for its concreteness and ease in understanding rather than for its importance or realism.

Reprinted with permission from *Quarterly Journal of Economics*, Vol. 84, No. 3, 1970, pp. 488–500

THE MODEL WITH AUTOMOBILES AS AN EXAMPLE

The automobiles market

The example of used cars captures the essence of the problem. From time to time one hears either mention of or surprise at the large price difference between new cars and those which have just left the showroom. The usual lunch table justification for this phenomenon is the pure joy of owning a "new" car. We offer a different explanation. Suppose (for the sake of clarity rather than reality) that there are just four kinds of cars. There are new cars and used cars. There are good cars and bad cars (which in America are known as "lemons"). A new car may be a good car or a lemon, and of course the same is true of used cars.

The individuals in this market buy a new automobile without knowing whether the car they buy will be good or a lemon. But they do know that with probability q it is a good car and with probability $(1 - q)$ it is a lemon; by assumption, q is the proportion of good cars produced and $(1 - q)$ is the proportion of lemons.

After owning a specific car, however, for a length of time, the car owner can form a good idea of the quality of this machine; i.e., the owner assigns a new probability to the event that his car is a lemon. This estimate is more accurate than the original estimate. An asymmetry in available information has developed: for the sellers now have more knowledge about the quality of a car than the buyers. But good cars and bad cars must still sell at the same price—since it is impossible for a buyer to tell the difference between a good car and a bad car. It is apparent that a used car cannot have the same valuation as a new car—if it did have the same valuation, it would clearly be advantageous to trade a lemon at the price of new car, and buy another new car, at a higher probability q of being good and a lower probability of being bad. Thus the owner of a good machine must be locked in. Not only is it true that he cannot receive the true value of his car, but he cannot even obtain the expected value of a new car.

Gresham's law has made a modified reappearance. For most cars traded will be the "lemons," and good cars may not be traded at all. The "bad" cars tend to drive out the good (in much the same way that bad money drives out the good). But the analogy with Gresham's law is not quite complete: bad cars drive out the good because they sell at the same price as good cars; similarly, bad money drives out good because the exchange rate is even. But the bad cars sell at the same price as good cars since it is impossible for a buyer to tell the difference between a good and a bad car; only the seller knows. In Gresham's law, however, presumably both buyer and seller can tell the difference between good and bad money. So the analogy is instructive, but not complete.

Asymmetrical information

It has been seen that the good cars may be driven out of the market by the lemons. But in a more continuous case with different grades of goods, even worse pathologies can exist. For it is quite possible to have the bad driving out the not-so-bad driving out the medium driving out the not-so-good driving out the good in such a sequence of events that no market exists at all.

One can assume that the demand for used automobiles depends most strongly upon two variables—the price of the automobile p and the average quality of used cars traded, μ, or $Q^d = D(p, \mu)$. Both the supply of used cars and also the average quality μ will depend upon the price, or $\mu = \mu(p)$ and $S = S(p)$. And in equilibrium the supply must equal the demand for the given average quality, or $S(p) = D(p, \mu(p))$. As the price falls, normally the quality will also fall. And it is quite possible that no goods will be traded at any price level.

Such an example can be derived from utility theory. Assume that there are just two groups of traders: groups one and two. Give group one a utility function

$$U_1 = M + \sum_{i=1}^{n} x_i$$

where M is the consumption of goods other than automobiles, x_i is the quality of the ith automobile, and n is the number of automobiles.

Similarly, let

$$U_2 = M + \sum_{i=1}^{n} \frac{3}{2} x_i$$

where M, x_i and n are defined as before.

Three comments should be made about these utility functions: (1) without linear utility (say with logarithmic utility) one gets needlessly mired in algebraic complications. (2) The use of linear utility allows a focus on the effects of asymmetry of information; with a concave utility function we would have to deal jointly with the usual risk-variance effects of uncertainty and the special effects we wish to discuss here. (3) U_1 and U_2 have the odd characteristic that the addition of a second car, or indeed a kth car, adds the same amount of utility as the first. Again realism is sacrificed to avoid a diversion from the proper focus.

To continue, it is assumed (1) that both type one traders and type-two traders are von Neumann–Morgenstern maximizers of expected utility; (2) that group one has N cars with uniformly distributed quality x, $0 \leq x \leq 2$, and group two has no cars; (3) that the price of "other goods" M is unity.

Denote the income (including that derived from the sale of automobiles) of all type one traders as Y_1 and the income of all type-two traders as Y_2. The demand for used cars will be the sum of the demands by both groups. When one ignores indivisibilities, the demand for automobiles by type-one traders will be

$$
\begin{aligned}
D_1 &= Y_1/p && \mu/p > 1 \\
D_1 &= 0 && \mu/p < 1.
\end{aligned}
$$

And the supply of cars offered by type one traders is

$$S_2 = pN/2 \qquad\qquad p \leq 2 \tag{1}$$

with average quality

$$\mu = p/2. \tag{2}$$

(To derive (1) and (2), the uniform distribution of automobile quality is used.)
Similarly the demand of type two traders is

$$
\begin{aligned}
D_1 &= Y_2/p && 3\mu/2 > p \\
D_2 &= 0 && 3\mu/2 < p
\end{aligned}
$$

and

$$S_2 = 0.$$

Thus total demand $D(p,\mu)$ is

$$
\begin{aligned}
D(p,\mu) &= (Y_2 + Y_1)/p && \text{if } p < \mu \\
D(p,\mu) &= Y_2/p && \text{if } \mu < p < 3\mu/2 \\
D(p,\mu) &= 0 && \text{if } p > 3\mu/2.
\end{aligned}
$$

However, with price p, average quality is $p/2$ and therefore at no price will any trade take place at all: in spite of the fact that *at any given price* between 0 and 3 there are traders of type one who are willing to sell their automobiles at a price which traders of type two are willing to pay.

Symmetric information

The foregoing is contrasted with the case of symmetric information. Suppose that the quality of all cars is uniformly distributed, $0 \le x \le 2$. Then the demand curves and supply curves can be written as follows:
Supply

$$
\begin{aligned}
S(p) &= N && p > 1 \\
S(p) &= 0 && p < 1.
\end{aligned}
$$

And the demand curves are

$$
\begin{aligned}
D(p) &= (Y_2 + Y_1)/p && p < 1 \\
D(p) &= (Y_2/p) && 1 < p < 3/2 \\
D(p) &= 0 && p > 3/2.
\end{aligned}
$$

In equilibrium

$$p = 1 \quad \text{if } Y_2 < N \tag{3}$$

$$p = Y_2/N \qquad \text{if } 2Y_2/3 < N < Y_2 \tag{4}$$

$$p = 3/2 \qquad \text{if } n < 2Y_2/3. \tag{5}$$

If $N < Y_2$ there is a gain in utility over the case of asymmetrical information of $N/2$. (If $N > Y_2$, in which case the income of type two traders is insufficient to buy all N automobiles, there is a gain in utility of $Y_2/2$ units.)

Finally, it should be mentioned that in this example, if traders of groups one and two have the same probabilistic estimates about the quality of individual automobiles—though these estimates may vary from automobile to automobile—(3), (4), and (5) will still describe equilibrium with one slight change: p will then represent the expected price of one quality unit.

EXAMPLES AND APPLICATIONS

Insurance

It is a well-known fact that people over 65 have great difficulty in buying medical insurance. The natural question arises: why doesn't the price rise to match the risk?

Our answer is that as the price level rises the people who insure themselves will be those who are increasingly certain that they will need the insurance; for error in medical check-ups, doctors' sympathy with older patients, and so on make it much easier for the applicant to assess the risks involved than the insurance company. The result is that the average medical condition of insurance applicants deteriorates as the price level rises—with the result that no insurance sales may take place at any price.[1] This is strictly analogous to our automobiles case, where the average quality of used cars supplied fell with a corresponding fall in the price level. This agrees with the explanation in insurance textbooks:

> Generally speaking policies are not available at ages (materially) greater than sixty-five. ... The term premiums are too high for any but the most pessimistic (which is to say the least healthy) insureds to find attractive. Thus there is a severe problem of adverse selection at these ages.[2]

The statistics do not contradict this conclusion. While demands for health insurance rise with age, a 1956 national sample survey of 2809 families with 8898 persons shows that hospital insurance coverage drops from 63 per cent of those aged 45 to 54, to 31 per cent for those over 65. And surprisingly, this survey also finds average medical expenses for males aged 55 to 64 of $88, while males over 65 pay an average of $77.[3] While noninsured expenditure rises from $66 to $80 in these age groups, insured expenditure declines from $105 to $70. The conclusion is tempting that insurance companies are particularly wary of giving medical insurance to older people.

The principle of "adverse selection" is potentially present in all lines of insurance. The following statement appears in an insurance textbook written at the Wharton

School:

> There is potential adverse selection in the fact that healthy term insurance policy holders may decide to terminate their coverage when they become older and premiums mount. This action could leave an insurer with an undue proportion of below average risks and claims might be higher than anticipated. Adverse selection "appears (or at least is possible) whenever the individual or group insured has freedom to buy or not to buy, to choose the amount or plan of insurance, and to persist or to discontinue as a policy holder".[4]

Group insurance, which is the most common form of medical insurance in the United States, picks out the healthy, for generally adequate health is a precondition for employment. At the same time this means that medical insurance is least available to those who need it most, for the insurance companies do their own "adverse selection".

This adds one major argument in favor of medicare.[5] On a cost-benefit basis medicare may pay off: for it is quite possible that every individual in the market would be willing to pay the expected cost of his medicare and buy insurance, yet no insurance company can afford to sell him a policy—for at any price it will attract too many "lemons". The welfare economics of medicare, in this view, is *exactly* analogous to the usual classroom argument for public expenditure on roads.

The employment of minorities

The Lemons Principle also casts light on the employment of minorities. Employers may refuse to hire members of minority groups for certain types of jobs. This decision may not reflect irrationality or prejudice—but profit maximization. For race may serve as a good *statistic* for the applicant's social background, quality of schooling, and general job capabilities.

Good quality schooling could serve as a substitute for this statistic; by grading students the schooling system can give a better indicator of quality than other more superficial characteristics. As T. W. Schultz writes, "The educational establishment *discovers* and cultivates potential talent. The capabilities of children and mature students can never be known until *found* and cultivated."[6] (Italics added.) An untrained worker may have valuable natural talents, but these talents must be certified by "the educational establishment" before a company can afford to use them. The certifying establishment, however, must be credible; the unreliability of slum schools decreases the economic possibilities of their students.

This lack may be particularly disadvantageous to members of already disadvantaged minority groups. For an employer may make a rational decision not to hire any members of these groups in responsible positions—because it is difficult to distinguish those with good job qualifications from those with bad qualifications. This type of decision is clearly what George Stigler had in mind when he wrote, "in a regime of ignorance Enrico Fermi would have been a gardener, Von Neumann a checkout clerk at a drugstore".[7]

As a result, however, the rewards for work in slum schools tend to accrue to the group as a whole—in raising its average quality—rather than to the individual. Only insofar as information in addition to race is used is there any incentive for training.

An additional worry is that the Office of Economic Opportunity is going to use cost-benefit analysis to evaluate its programs. For many benefits may be external. The benefit from training minority groups may arise as much from raising the average quality of the group as from raising the quality of the individual trainee; and, likewise, the returns may be distributed over the whole group rather than to the individual.

The costs of dishonesty

The Lemons model can be used to make some comments on the costs of dishonesty. Consider a market in which goods are sold honestly or dishonestly; quality may be represented, or it may be misrepresented. The purchaser's problem, of course, is to identify quality. The presence of people in the market who are willing to offer inferior goods tends to drive the market out of existence—as in the case of our automobile "lemons". It is this possibility that represents the major costs of dishonesty—for dishonest dealings tend to drive honest dealings out of the market. There may be potential buyers of good quality products and there may be potential sellers of such products in the appropriate price range; however, the presence of people who wish to pawn bad wares as good wares tends to drive out the legitimate business. The cost of dishonesty, therefore, lies not only in the amount by which the purchaser is cheated; the cost also must include the loss incurred from driving legitimate business out of existence.

Dishonesty in business is a serious problem in underdeveloped countries. Our model gives a possible structure to this statement and delineates the nature of the "external" economies involved. In particular, in the model economy described, dishonesty, or the misrepresentation of the quality of automobiles, costs 1/2 unit of utility per automobile; furthermore, it reduces the size of the used car market from N to 0. We can, consequently, directly evaluate the costs of dishonesty—at least in theory.

There is considerable evidence that quality variation is greater in underdeveloped than in developed areas. For instance, the need for quality control of exports and State Trading Corporations can be taken as one indicator. In India, for example under the Export Quality Control and Inspection Act of 1963, "about 85 per cent of Indian exports are covered under one or the other type of quality control".[8] Indian housewives must carefully glean the rice of the local bazaar to sort out stones of the same color and shape which have been intentionally added to the rice. Any comparison of the heterogeneity of quality in the street market and the canned qualities of the American supermarket suggests that quality variation is a greater problem in the East than in the West.

In one traditional pattern of development the merchants of the pre-industrial generation turn into the first entrepreneurs of the next. The best-documented case is Japan,[9] but this also may have been the pattern for Britain and America.[10] In *our* picture the important skill of the merchant is identifying the quality of merchandise; those who can identify used cars in our example and can guarantee the quality may profit by as much as the difference between type two traders' buying price and type one traders' selling price. These people are the merchants. In production these skills are equally necessary—both to be able to identify the quality of inputs and to certify the quality of outputs. And this is one (added) reason why the merchants may logically become the first entrepreneurs.

The problem, of course, is that entrepreneurship may be a scarce resource; no development text leaves entrepreneurship unemphasized. Some treat it as central.[11] Given, then, that entrepreneurship is scarce, there are two ways in which product variations impede development. First, the pay-off to trade is great for would-be entrepreneurs, and hence they are diverted from production; second, the amount of entrepreneurial time per unit output is greater, the greater are the quality variations.

Credit markets in underdeveloped countries

Credit markets in underdeveloped countries often strongly reflect the operation of the Lemons Principle. In India a major fraction of industrial enterprise is controlled by managing agencies (according to a recent survey, these "managing agencies" controlled 65.7 per cent of the net worth of public limited companies and 66 per cent of total assets).[12] Here is a historian's account of the function and genesis of the "managing agency system":

> The management of the South Asian commercial scene remained the function of merchant houses, and a type of organization peculiar to South Asia known as the Managing Agency. When a new venture was promoted (such as a manufacturing plant, a plantation, or a trading venture), the promoters would approach an established managing agency. The promoters might be Indian or British, and they might have technical or financial resources or merely a concession. In any case they would turn to the agency because of its reputation, which would encourage confidence in the venture and stimulate investment.[13]

In turn, a second major feature of the Indian industrial scene has been the dominance of these managing agencies by caste (or, more accurately, communal) groups. Thus firms can usually be classified according to communal origin.[14] In this environment, in which outside investors are likely to be bilked of their holdings, either (1) firms establish a reputation for "honest" dealing, which confers upon them a monopoly rent insofar as their services are limited in supply, or (2) the sources of finance are limited to local communal groups which can use communal—and possibly familial—ties to encourage honest dealing *within* the community. It is, in Indian economic history, extraordinarily difficult to discern whether the savings of rich landlords failed to be invested in the industrial sector (1) because of a fear to invest in ventures controlled by other communities; (2) because of inflated propensities to consume; or (3) because of low rates of return.[15] At the very least, however, it is clear that the British-owned managing agencies tended to have an equity holding whose communal origin was more heterogeneous than the Indian-controlled agency houses, and would usually include both Indian and British investors.

A second example of the workings of the Lemons Principle concerns the extortionate rates which the local moneylender charges his clients. In India these high rates of interest have been the leading factor in landlessness; the so-called "Cooperative Movement" was meant to counteract this growing landlessness by setting up banks to compete with the local moneylenders.[16] While the large banks in the central cities have prime interest rates of 6, 8, and 10 per cent, the local moneylender charges 15, 25, and even 50 per cent. The answer to this seeming paradox is that credit is granted only where the granter has (1) easy means of enforcing his contract or (2) personal knowledge of the character of the borrower. The middleman who tries to arbitrage between the rates of the moneylender and the central bank is apt to attract all the "lemons" and thereby make a loss.

This interpretation can be seen in Sir Malcolm Darling's interpretation of the village moneylender's power:

> It is only fair to remember that in the Indian village the money-lender is often the one thrifty person amongst a generally thriftless people; and that his methods of business, though demoralizing under modern conditions, suit the happy-go-lucky ways of the peasant. He is always accessible, even at night; dispenses with troublesome formalities, asks no inconvenient questions, advances promptly, and if interest is paid, does not press for repayment of principal. He keeps in close personal touch with his clients, and in many villages shares their occasions of weal or woe. *With his intimate knowledge of those around him he is able, without serious risk, to finance those who would otherwise get no loan at all.* [Italics added.][17]

Or look at Barbara Ward's account:

> A small shopkeeper in a Hong Kong fishing village told me: "I give credit to anyone who anchors regularly in our bay; but if it is someone I don't know well, then I think twice about it unless I can find out all about him."[18]

Or, a profitable sideline of cotton ginning in Iran is the loaning of money for the next season, since the ginning companies often have a line of credit from Teheran banks at the market rate of interest. But in the first years of operation large losses are expected from unpaid debts—due to poor knowledge of the local scene.[19]

COUNTERACTING INSTITUTIONS

Numerous institutions arise to counteract the effects of quality uncertainty. One obvious institution is guarantees. Most consumer durables carry guarantees to ensure the buyer of some normal expected quality. One natural result of our model is that the risk is borne by the seller rather than by the buyer.

A second example of an institution which counteracts the effects of quality uncertainty is the brand-name good. Brand names not only indicate quality but also give the consumer a means of retaliation if the quality does not meet expectations. For the consumer will then curtail future purchases. Often too, new products are associated with old brand names. This ensures the prospective consumer of the quality of the product.

Chains—such as hotel chains or restaurant chains—are similar to brand names. One observation consistent with our approach is the chain restaurant. These restaurants, at least in the United States, most often appear on interurban highways. The customers are seldom local. The reason is that these well-known chains offer a better hamburger than the *average* local restaurant; at the same time, the local customer, who knows his area, can usually choose a place he prefers.

Licensing practices also reduce quality uncertainty. For instance, there is the licensing of doctors, lawyers, and barbers. Most skilled labor carries some certification indicating the attainment of certain levels of proficiency. The high school diploma, the baccalaureate degree, the Ph.D, even the Nobel Prize, to some degree, serve this function of certification. And education and labor markets themselves have their own "brand names".

CONCLUSION

We have been discussing economic models in which "trust" is important. Informal unwritten guarantees are preconditions for trade and production. Where these guarantees are indefinite, business will suffer—as indicated by our generalized Gresham's law. This aspect of uncertainty has been explored by game theorists, as in the Prisoner's Dilemma, but usually it has not been incorporated in the more traditional Arrow-Debreu approach to uncertainty.[20] But the difficulty of distinguishing good quality from bad is inherent in the business world; this may indeed explain many economic institutions and may in fact be one of the more important aspects of uncertainty.

ACKNOWLEDGEMENTS

The author would especially like to thank Thomas Rothenberg for invaluable comments and inspiration. In addition he is indebted to Roy Radner, Albert Fishlow, Bernard Saffran, William D. Nordhaus, Giorgio La Malfa, Charles C. Holt, John Letiche, and the referee for help and suggestions. He would also like to thank the Indian Statistical Institute and the Ford Foundation for financial support.

NOTES

1. Arrow's fine article, "Uncertainty and Medical Care" (*American Economic Review*, 53, 1963), does not make this point explicitly. He emphasizes "moral hazard" rather than "adverse selection". In its strict sense, the presence of "moral hazard" is equally disadvantageous for both governmental and private programs; in its broader sense, which includes "adverse selection," "moral hazard" gives a decided advantage to government insurance programs.
2. O. D. Dickerson. *Health Insurance* (Homewood, IL: Irwin, 1959), p. 333.
3. O. W. Anderson (with J. J. Feldman). *Family Medical Costs and Insurance* (New York: McGraw-Hill, 1956).
4. H. S. Denenberg, R. D. Eilers, G. W. Hoffman, C. A. Kline, J. J. Melone, and H. W. Snider. *Risk and Insurance* (Englewood Cliffs, NJ: Prentice Hall, 1964), p. 446.

5. The following quote, again taken from an insurance textbook, shows how far the medical insurance market is from perfect competition:

   ... insurance companies must screen their applicants. Naturally it is true that many people will voluntarily seek adequate insurance on their own initiative. But in such lines as accident and health insurance, companies are likely to give a second look to persons who voluntarily seek insurance without being approached by an agent (F. J. Angell. *Insurance, Principles and Practices*, New York: The Ronald Press, 1957, pp. 8–9).

   This shows that insurance is not a commodity for sale on the open market.

6. T. W. Schultz. *The Economic Value of Education* (New York: Columbia University Press, 1964), p. 42.

7. G. J. Stigler. Information and the Labor Market, *Journal of Political Economy*, 70 (Oct. 1962), Supplement, p. 104.

8. *The Times of India*, Nov. 10, 1967, p. 1.

9. See M. J. Levy, Jr. "Contrasting Factors in the Modernization of China and Japan," in *Economic Growth: Brazil, India, Japan*, ed. S. Kuznets, *et al.* (Durham, NC: Duke University Press, 1955).

10. C. P. Kindleberger, *Economic Development* (New York: McGraw-Hill, 1958), p. 86.

11. For example, see W. Arthur Lewis. *The Theory of Economic Growth* (Homewood, IL: Irwin, 1955), p. 196.

12. *Report of the Committee on the Distribution of Income and Levels of Living*, Part I, Government of India, Planning Commission, Feb. 1964, p. 44.

13. H. Tinker. *South Asia: A Short History* (New York: Praeger, 1966), p. 134.

14. The existence of the following table (and also the small per cent of firms under mixed control) indicates the communalization of the control of firms. *Source*: M.M. Mehta. *Structure of Indian Industries* (Bombay: Popular Book Depot, 1955), p. 314.

Distribution of industrial control by community (number of firms)

	1911	1931	1951
British	281	416	382
Parsis	15	25	19
Gujratis	3	11	17
Jews	5	9	3
Muslims	–	10	3
Bengalis	8	5	20
Marwaris	–	6	96
Mixed control	28	28	79
Total	341	510	619

Also, for the cotton industry see H. Fukuzawa, "Cotton Mill Industry," in V.B. Singh (ed). *Economic History of India, 1857–1956* (Bombay: Allied Publishers, 1965).

15. For the mixed record of industrial profits, see D. H. Buchanan, *The Development of Capitalist Enterprise in India* (New York: Kelley, 1966, reprinted).

16. The leading authority on this is Sir Malcolm Darling. See his *Punjabi Peasant in Prosperity and Debt*. The following table may also prove instructive:

	Commonest rates for		
	Secured loans (per cent)	Unsecured loans (per cent)	Grain loans (per cent)
Punjab	6 to 12	12 to 24 ($18\frac{3}{4}$ commonest)	25
United Provinces	9 to 12	24 to $37\frac{1}{2}$	25 (50 in Oudh)
Bihar		$18\frac{3}{4}$	50
Orissa	12 to $18\frac{3}{4}$	25	25
Bengal	8 to 12	9 to 18 for "respectable clients" $18\frac{3}{4}$ to $37\frac{1}{2}$ (the latter common to agriculturists)	
Central provinces	6 to 12	15 for proprietors 24 for occupancy tenants $37\frac{1}{2}$ for ryots with no right of transfer	25
Bombay	9 to 12	12 to 25 (18 commonest)	
Sind		36	
Madras	12	15 to 18 (in insecure tracts 24 not uncommon)	20 to 50

Source: Punjabi Peasant in Prosperity and Debt, 3rd ed. (Oxford University Press, 1932), p. 190.

17. Darling, *op. cit.*, p. 204.
18. B. Ward. "Cash or Credit Crops," *Economic Development and Cultural Change*, 8 (Jan. 1960), reprinted in *Peasant Society: A Reader*, ed. G. Foster, *et al.* (Boston: Little Brown and Company, 1967). Quote on p. 142. In the same volume, see also G. W. Skinner, "Marketing and Social Structure in Rural China," and S. W. Mintz, "Pratik: Haitian Personal Economic Relations".
19. Personal conversation with mill manager, April 1968.
20. R. Radner. "Équilibre de Marchés à Terme et au Comptant en Cas d'Incertitude," in *Cahiers d'Econometrie*, Vol. 12 (Nov. 1967), Centre National de la Recherche Scientifique, Paris.

16

Do Bad Products Drive Out Good?

Geoffrey Heal

INTRODUCTION

In a thought-provoking article[1] Akerlof argued that in a situation where samples of a product might vary in quality and where the consumer at the time of purchase was unable to tell the quality of the particular sample he was buying, there might be a tendency for bad products to drive out good, possibly even to the point where there was no market at all in the good. The phenomena involved in such a process are clearly of intellectual interest and practical importance, and my aim in this paper is to examine certain of their aspects in more detail than has been done hitherto.

One can show that Gresham's law—that bad products drive out good—may not always be valid: to be precise, in a dynamic context it is valid only if traders are sufficiently shortsighted, in the sense of discounting future benefits at a sufficiently high rate.

AKERLOF'S PROBLEM AND THE PRISONER'S DILEMMA

As Akerlof suggested,[2] some aspects of the problem can be captured by the conventional prisoner's dilemma model. Consider two traders A and B, each endowed with the entire stock of commodity a or b, respectively. These stocks are not homogeneous, but may be divided into high-quality a (respectively b) and low-quality a (respectively b): only the owner of a stock can tell which elements of the stock are of

Reprinted with permission from *Quarterly Journal of Economics*, Vol. 90, No. 3, 1976, pp. 498–503

high or low quality. *A* and *B* meet and agree to exchange one *a* for one *b*. Suppose that *A* values the various possible trades as follows:

Gaining a high-quality *b* is worth α
Gaining a low-quality *b* is worth β
Losing a high-quality *a* is worth γ
Losing a low-quality *a* is worth δ,

and let *B*'s valuations be the same with *a* and *b* interchanged. Each trader has two strategies—to trade a high- or low-quality item—and the payoff matrix is

| | | *B*'s strategy | |
		High *b*	Low *b*
A's strategy	(High *a*	$\gamma+\alpha$, $\gamma+\alpha$	$\beta+\gamma$, $\alpha+\delta$
	(Low *a*	$\alpha+\delta$, $\beta+\gamma$	$\beta+\delta$, $\beta+\delta$

A will supply a low-quality *a* if $\alpha+\delta>\alpha+\gamma$ and $\beta+\delta>\beta+\gamma$: this reduces to $\delta>\gamma$, and this condition also ensures that *B* supplies a low-quality *b*. Of course, δ and γ are both negative: hence bad products drive out good whenever parting with a bad product causes the trader a smaller utility loss than parting with a good product. It is difficult to conceive of a situation where this condition is *not* satisfied. Note that, if we complicate the exercise by having separate valuations $\alpha(A)$, $\alpha(B)$, etc. for the two traders, the condition just takes the equivalent form $\delta(A)>\gamma(A)$ and $\delta(B)>\gamma(B)$.

If the exchange of products is treated as noncooperative game, then the strategy pair (low quality, low quality) is a Nash equilibrium, whereas of course the pair (high quality, high quality) is not. But now let us suppose that the traders do not expect to trade just once, but to continue trading with each other once each period for all subsequent time periods: in this case we are dealing with a supergame—that is, a game that is repeated infinitely many times. As an example of such a situation, one might consider two neighboring peasant farms, one specializing in crop *A* and one in crop *B*. At the end of each harvest they meet to exchange some fraction of their crops so that each family will have a mixed diet throughout the winter, and they expect to continue this custom indefinitely. Following a fairly standard argument,[3] we can show that although (low quality, low quality) is the only noncooperative equilibrium for the once-off game, and is still one of the noncooperative equilibria for the supergame, there exist noncooperative equilibrium strategies for the supergame that will result in the outcome (high quality, high quality). Consider the following strategy pair:

For *A*, trade a high-quality product in the first period. In the *t*-th period ($t>1$), trade a bad product if and only if in some previous period *B* traded a low-quality product. (Call this strategy S_A.)

For *B*, as above with *B* replaced by *A*. (Strategy S_B.)

Let both traders discount future payoffs at a rate $\Delta, 0 < \Delta < 1$, and return to the original example. The payoff to A from strategy S_A, if B plays strategy S_B, is simply

$$(\gamma + \alpha) \sum_{t=1}^{\infty} \Delta^t. \tag{1}$$

If B plays S_B, could A ever gain by departing from S_A? Suppose that from $t = 1$ to $t = T$, A played "good," but at $t = T + 1$ played "bad". As B is following S_B, he will play "bad" from $t = T + 2$ onward, and of course when B plays "bad", the best A can possibly do is to play "bad" also. So the highest payoff A could gain by departing from S_A at time $T + 1$ is

$$(\gamma + \alpha) \sum_{t=1}^{T} \Delta^t + (\alpha + \delta) \Delta^{T+1} + (\beta + \delta) \sum_{t=T+2}^{\infty} \Delta^t \tag{2}$$

We wish to know whether it is better for A to follow S_A or to depart, i.e., we wish to know whether $(1) - (2)$ is positive or negative. It is easily seen to be positive if and only if

$$\Delta > \frac{\delta - \gamma}{\alpha - \beta}.$$

Thus, if this condition holds, the strategy pair (S_A, S_B) forms a Nash equilibrium, and one might expect that only high-quality products would be traded. The weight given to future gains increases as Δ increases, so that the chances of bad products driving out good fall as the weight that traders give to future benefits rises: in other words, we can only be sure that bad products will drive out good if traders are sufficiently shortsighted.

What constitutes sufficient shortsightedness depends on the ratio of the difference between parting with a bad product and parting with a good one, to the difference between gaining a good product and gaining a bad one. It should be clear that it is sufficient to have just one shortsighted trader in a market for the inefficient outcome to result. It should also be evident that the argument is sufficiently robust to withstand some slackening of the assumptions. For example, it was implicit above that each agent could trade only with the other: in practice of course the response when a trading partner supplies inferior products may be to take one's business elsewhere rather than to try retaliating. This extension could easily be accommodated by introducing as a third strategy "trade elsewhere."

This relationship between the stability of trade in high-quality products and the shortsightedness or otherwise of traders is of course in keeping with what one might call "business mythology" on this subject: in this it is customarily argued that the danger to quality comes from "upstarts" and "fly-by-nights" who are in the market only for a quick gain. In contrast, established businesses with a reputation to protect (and by implication a long time horizon) are supposed to realize that their long-term interests lie in maintaining standards. This raises another important point: in a market with many sellers with varying discount rates, and thus varying propensities to sell reliable products, the consumer has an incentive to classify traders by discount rate-and traders with low discount rates have an incentive to reveal themselves as such, for example, by emphasizing the established nature of their business. Of course, if these identifications are carried out successfully, the problems discussed in this paper may not be serious in practical terms and indeed one of the premises of the Akerlof model (the nonidentifiability of sellers) will be violated.

NOTES

1. G. Akerlof, "The Market for Lemons," *Quarterly Journal of Economics*, LXXXIX (Aug. 1970), 488–500.
2. *Ibid.*, p. 500, last paragraph.
3. See, for example, R. D. Luce and H. Raiffa. *Games and Decisions* (New York: John Wiley and Sons, Inc., 1957), esp. p. 102.

17a

A direct Test of the "Lemons" Model: the market for Used Pickup Trucks

Eric W. Bond

This chapter provides an empirical test of one of the implications of models of markets with asymmetric information. In the seminal paper on markets with asymmetric information, George Akerlof (1970) pointed out two possible outcomes that may occur where sellers have better information about the quality of products than do buyers. One possibility is that bad products will drive out good products. If buyers cannot distinguish quality until after the purchase has been made, there will be no incentive for sellers to provide good quality products, and the average quality in the market will decline. In the case of cars, an often-cited example of this phenomenon, owners who discover that they have a "lemon" will attempt to sell it in the used car market to an unsuspecting buyer. The owner of a "creampuff" will not sell his car, since it is indistinguishable from a lemon to buyers and must therefore sell for the price of a car of average quality. The effect of quality uncertainty is to reduce the volume of transactions in the used car market below the socially optimal level.

A second possibility suggested by Akerlof is that institutions may develop to counteract the effects of quality uncertainty. Warranties and brand names can be used to give the buyer some assurance of quality. These institutions may prevent good products from being driven from the market, but they will not necessarily eliminate the inefficiency. These institutions may be costly, and sellers may overinvest in signalling the quality of their product to buyers (for example, see Akerlof, 1976).

The purpose of this chapter is to test whether bad products drive out good products in the market for used pickup trucks, a market similar to the used car market. The measure of quality chosen here is the amount of maintenance required on a truck, with a lemon being a truck that requires significantly more maintenance than average. Owners will have an idea of the truck's quality from past maintenance experience, but it may be difficult for a potential buyer to predict future maintenance from inspecting the truck. If this informational asymmetry is significant and counteracting institutions do not develop, the lemons model would predict that owners of high maintenance trucks would sell them in the used market. The used truck market would then become

Reprinted with permission from *American Economic Review*, Vol. 72, No. 4, 1982, pp. 836–840.

a market for lemons, with the abundance of high maintenance trucks driving out sellers of low maintenance trucks as described above. The empirical implication of this model is that a sample of trucks that has been purchased used should have required more maintenance (since it should contain more lemons) than a sample of trucks with similar characteristics that have not been traded. The following section reports the results of such a test using data from the *1977 Truck Inventory and Use (TIU Survey)*.

The results indicate that if the effects of age and lifetime mileage on maintenance are controlled for, there is no difference in maintenance between trucks acquired new and trucks acquired used. This leads to a rejection of the hypothesis that bad products have driven out good, since there is no evidence of an overabundance of lemons among used trucks. One explanation for this finding is that the counteracting institutions of the type discussed by Akerlof may have developed. The provision of warranties on used trucks and the seller's concern about his reputation may prevent sellers from supplying low quality products. A second possible explanation is that buyers are able to obtain enough information from search to eliminate the asymmetry. While the finding that the average quality of original owner and used trucks is the same is consistent with the operation of an efficient market for used trucks, the market could still be inefficient if the informational asymmetry is eliminated through costly counteracting institutions or costly search by buyers.

TESTING THE LEMONS MODEL

As discussed above, the hypothesis that the used truck market contains an overabundance of lemons was tested by comparing the frequency of maintenance between trucks that were acquired used and those that were acquired new in the *TIU Survey*. This section describes the data obtained from the *TIU Survey* and reports the results of the test.

The *TIU Survey* is part of the Census of Transportation. It is based on a stratified probability sample of all trucks registered at motor vehicle departments in the fifty states, and requests information about the characteristics and usage of the trucks. With regard to maintenance, respondents were asked whether their truck had required major maintenance in any of five categories (engine, transmission, brakes, rear axle, and other) in the preceding twelve months.[1] Since the maintenance variable is a dichotomous variable, the frequency of maintenance of a given type in a sample of trucks can be modeled with a binomial distribution if the trucks in the sample are similar. The *TIU Survey* contains information on model year and lifetime mileage, so that it is possible to control for the effects of these observable factors on maintenance. If these factors are controlled, the sample proportion will be an estimate of the probability of maintenance among trucks of that type.

Pickup trucks were selected for study because pickup trucks have the largest noncommercial demand of any trucks in the survey. In the sample, 50 percent of the pickups are used for personal transportation, 21 percent are in agriculture, and the remainder are in various commercial uses (primarily construction, services, and retail trade). It was felt that the large household demand would increase the likelihood of asymmetric information in secondhand markets, since one would expect that

Table 1. Summary statistics of the sample

| | | | Proportion requiring engine maintenance | |
| | Number in | Acquired | | |
Year	Sample	Used	New	Used
1976	2137	0.11	0.08	0.05
1975	1602	0.27	0.10	0.11
1974	2261	0.37	0.11	0.13
1973	2085	0.48	0.15	0.15
1972	1839	0.53	0.13	0.15

household purchasers have less expertise in evaluating used trucks than commercial purchasers.

In addition, several other bits of evidence suggest similarities with the automobile market. Pickup trucks are produced by the major automobile producers (both foreign and domestic) and are sold by many car dealers. The retail markup over dealer cost on a pickup is comparable to that of a full-size car. Finally, the frequency of trading of pickups is comparable to that of autos. Of the trucks purchased during 1976, 60 percent were purchased used. Although data for the same year are not available for automobiles, the 1972 survey of household durable purchases (Department of Commerce, 1973) indicates that 65 percent of automobiles purchased in that year were used.

One question that had to be addressed was the choice of model years to study. Enough time must be allowed for owners to become aware that their trucks are lemons, but if the model year studied is too old, many of the lemons may already have been scrapped.[2] Since the lemons model gives no guidance on this point, trucks that were from one- to five-years old in 1977 (model years 1972–76) were studied to give a fairly wide range of time for the lemons effect to occur.

Table 1 shows the number of pickups in the survey, the percentage acquired used, and the proportion of new and used trucks that required major engine maintenance for each model year. The proportion requiring maintenance is slightly higher for used trucks in three of the years. However, this comparison is biased against used trucks since used trucks had significantly higher lifetime mileage in each model year.

If the lemons hypothesis is true, the probability of maintenance should be higher for secondhand trucks than for trucks with similar characteristics that were acquired new. The effects of observable characteristics were controlled for by grouping trucks according to model year and lifetime mileage. Let P_{ijk}^n be the probability of maintenance of type i for trucks of model year j and mileage group k that were acquired new, and let P_{ijk}^u be the corresponding proportion for trucks acquired used. The first test of the lemons model was to test the null hypothesis of no difference in quality between trucks acquired new and trucks acquired used, $P_{ijk}^n = P_{ijk}^u$. If the number of observations is large enough, the difference in group means will be normally distributed. Due to the low frequencies of several types of maintenance and

Table 2. Tests of differences in proportions requiring maintenance

	Number of tests	Used inferior (10 percent level)	Used superior (10 percent level)
1976	19	1	2
1975	27	0	2
1974	44	2	3
1973	57	3	1
1972	67	2	1

the small number of used trucks in the 1975 and 1976 model years, larger mileage groupings had to be chosen to make the assumption of normality for those years.[3]

The advantage of the test for equality of individual group means is that it allows testing of the hypothesis that only some segments of the market operate inefficiently. For example, suppose that the unreliability of service and large amount of down time associated with operating a lemon precludes its being used very intensively. A buyer of a high mileage truck would then be certain that he was not getting a lemon. If lifetime mileage can be used as a signal for unobservable quality, some portions of the market might not contain lemons.

The results of the tests on group means are reported in Table 2, with the number of groups in which the used trucks were judged to be inferior at a 10 percent level of significance shown in column 2. The results indicate almost no support for the lemons model in any of the model years. In fact, equally strong support could be found for the hypothesis that trucks in the used market are superior (shown in column 3). There was no evidence that the cases where used trucks were inferior were concentrated in any particular segment of the market.

The data indicated that the probability of maintenance generally increased with the lifetime mileage of the truck, as one would expect.[4] Since maintenance is a dichotomous variable, the relationship between maintenance and mileage can be estimated using a logit model:

$$ln[P_i/(1 - P_i)] = \alpha_i + \beta_i x + \varepsilon, \qquad (1)$$

where P_i is the probability of maintenance of type i and x is lifetime mileage. A second test of the lemons model was performed by estimating (1) separately for both used and original owner trucks, and then testing whether the slope and constant terms were equal for the two equations. This provides an overall test of whether used trucks and original owner trucks have any difference in quality.

The presence of a market for lemons would be indicated by a constant term in the equation for used trucks that was significantly greater than that for trucks acquired new, or by a combination of differing slope and constant terms that indicate greater maintenance for used trucks over the relevant range. The model was estimated by grouping the data by mileage for both new and used trucks, and then using the group means to estimate (1) with the weighted least squares approximation to the logit discussed by D. R. Cox. Equations were estimated for all five types of maintenance for model years 1973 and 1975. In none of the equations were either the slopes or constant terms significantly different at the 5 percent level between original owner and used trucks. This test provides further support for the hypothesis that there is no dilution of quality in the used market.

CONCLUSION

The main finding of this note is that trucks that were purchased used required no more maintenance than trucks of similar age and lifetime mileage that had not been traded. This leads to a rejection of the hypothesis that the used pickup truckmarket is a market for lemons, which would have required used trucks to show significantly more maintenance. However, it should be noted that the failure to find an overabundance of lemons in the used market is not inconsistent with the commonly expressed notion that cars and trucks are traded when they become "too costly" to maintain. Suppose that there are two types of buyers in the market: one group with high maintenance costs and a second group of handymen with low maintenance costs. As trucks age and require more maintenance, high maintenance cost owners will prefer to sell to low maintenance cost buyers rather than to continue to operate the truck themselves.[5] While it might appear to members of the former group that used trucks are too costly to maintain, this results not from the existence of a market for lemons, but from the reallocation of the stock of assets to those individuals who value them most highly.

ACKNOWLEDGEMENTS

I thank Roger McCain, Richard Butler, Arnie Raphaelson and an anonymous referee for helpful comments on this paper. Wayne Morra and John Funk provided computational assistance.

NOTES

1. It would be preferable to have information on actual maintenance expenditures, since the quality depends not only on the probability of maintenance but also on the costliness of repairs. Unfortunately, expenditure data were not available. However, the costliness of repairs will be partially captured by the fact that the respondents are asked only to indicate major maintenance.
2. The median age of pickup trucks in the *IU Survey* was 7 years. By the time trucks were five years old, more than 50 percent had been traded at least once.
3. In order for the binomial distribution to be approximately normal, the expected frequency of maintenance should be at least 5 in each group (see R. Hogg and A. Craig). In order to satisfy this condition, it was necessary to expand the size of the mileage groups for the more recent model years (where relatively few trucks were used) and for transmission and rear axle maintenance (which were more rare events). For the 1972–74 data, the mileage groups

were in intervals of 10 000 miles for most maintenance tests. For the 1975–76 data, the groups had to be expanded to 15–20 000 miles intervals for all maintenance tests except the "other" category.

4. An exception to this was maintenance in the "other" category, which was negatively related to lifetime mileage.

REFERENCES

Akerlof, George A. The market for 'lemons': Quality uncertainty and the market mechanism, *Quarterly Journal of Economics*, August 1970, **84**: 488–500.

Akerlof, George A. The economics of caste and of the rat race and other woeful tales, *Quarterly Journal of Economics*, November 1976, **90**: 599–617.

Bond, Eric W. *A Theory of Trade-in Used Equipment*, *working paper* 1-81-2, Pennsylvania State University, 1981.

Cox, D. R. *Analysis of Binary Data*, London: Meuthen, 1970.

Hogg, R. and Craig, A. *Introduction to Mathematical Statistics*, New York: Macmillan, 1978.

US Department of Commerce, Bureau of the Census. *Current Population Reports: Consumer Buying Indicators*, P 65, No. 45, Washington: USGPO, 1973.

17b

Test of the Lemons Model: Comment

Michael D. Pratt and George E. Hoffer

In a recent article in *The American Economic Review*, Eric Bond (1982) provided an empirical test of the "lemons" model. Using the 1977 *Truck Inventory and Use (TIU) Survey*, Bond determined that there was not a significant difference between the maintenance records of pickup trucks which were purchased new and those purchased as used vehicles. He suggests several explanations for his findings. These include the counteracting institutions discussed by George Akerlof (1970), as well as the ability of consumers to obtain enough information to eliminate the buyer–seller informational asymmetry. While Bond's conclusions are interesting, we propose to provide a finer test of the lemons model in order to determine whether these conclusions accurately reflect conditions in the market for used pickup trucks. Our model introduces two refinements to Bond's analysis.

We believe that Bond was unable to verify the lemons model because of the lack of expenditure data in the *TIU Survey*. As he notes, the quality of a used vehicle depends "not only on the probability of maintenance but on the costliness of repairs" (p. 837). However, the relative cost of repairs cannot be captured to any significant degree in the maintenance categories of the *TIU Survey*. As shown in Table 1, the four defined maintenance categories range in average expenditure from \$100 to \$1200. Therefore, Bond's tests of differences in frequencies of repairs between vehicles acquired new and those acquired used are not as fine a test as necessary to verify the lemons model.[1] Not only does this test fail to capture the relative cost difference between repairs, it cannot account for vehicles that have more than one major repair during the year—perhaps the true lemon.

Moreover, the Bond model does not capture the complete character of a lemons market. As noted by Akerlof, it is more likely that the owner of a lemon will sell his vehicle than the owner of a "creampuff." For if a lemons market is presumed to exist, the owner of the creampuff vehicle will not be rewarded for the superior condition of his vehicle. Therefore a comparison of trucks acquired new versus trucks acquired used would identify only those vehicles for which the lemon characteristic is permanent.[2] One should compare trucks purchased used during a specific time period with those held during that time period, whether they had been acquired as

Reprinted with permission from *American Economic Review*, Vol. 72, No. 4, 1982, pp. 836–840.

Table 1. Relative reported maintenance costs for pickup trucks, 1977

Brakes	$ 100
Rear end—differential	200
Transmission	400
Engine	1200

Source: Automotive Service Council of Virginia (1983).

new or used vehicles, in order to capture both the "permanent lemon" as well as the "transitory lemon." The latter vehicle is the recently purchased used vehicle which is repaired by the new owner. In the model developed below, we test the lemons hypothesis using the *TIU Survey* data taking into account the two elements of a lemons market that should be included for a finer test of this hypothesis.

THE MODEL

To reflect the essential time element and market process described by a lemons model, the *TIU Survey* data were segmented into two transaction groups.[3] In the first group we concluded only pickup trucks that had been purchased used within one year of a state's survey date. These are the vehicles which would be more likely to include lemons. Our second group included pickup trucks which had been acquired either as new vehicles or used vehicles in some previous period and kept by that present owner. If there is a lemons market, this group should contain relatively more creampuffs. Excluded from both groups were vehicles that were reported to be leased, to be not in use, or to have been sold during the survey period.

Although Bond's test required that he control for vehicle age and total vehicle mileage, our test does not dictate this type of control. This is important, for to exclude some vehicles from the analysis because of their age and/or mileage characteristics precludes a full modeling of a lemons market.[4] At any given time, the market consists of a spectrum of trucks having various age and mileage characteristics. These characteristics provide information to a prospective buyer of a used vehicle but they do not effect the buyer–seller informational asymmetry.

To capture the relative cost of the reported maintenance categories we used the cost data presented in Table 1.[5] For example, as shown, in 1977 the average expenditure on transmission maintenance per year was four times that of the average expenditure on brake maintenance.

If the market for used vehicles is a lemons market, we would expect that the average yearly maintenance incurred for the four major repair categories reported in the *TIU Survey* to be significantly different between the two vehicle groups.[6] A priori, if the lemons hypothesis is true, we would expect that the average expenditure on vehicles purchased used within our observation period to be greater than the average maintenance expenditures on vehicles in the kept group. Under the null hypothesis

Table 2. Tests of the equality of mean maintenance expenditures[a]

	N	Mean	Standard deviation	Standard error
Recently transacted	2 395	$3.18	5.42	0.11
Not recently transacted	10 799	2.51	4.88	0.05

[a] Differences in the means are significant at the 0.01 level.

that the market for used vehicles is not a lemons market, there should be no difference in the mean repair expenditures between our transaction groups. Thus a test of the equality of the mean repair expenditures between these groups is performed to determine the acceptance of the null hypothesis.

The difference in the means reported in Table 2 is significant at the 1 percent level.[7] therefore we reject the null hypothesis, and given the ranking of the mean repair expenditures, we conclude that the market for used pickup trucks is a lemons market. Therefore arguments for the presence of Akerlof-type counteracting institutions, as well as explanations for a smaller difference in buyer–seller information, although possibly correct for some used markets, may not be significant factors in this market.[8]

ACKNOWLEDGEMENTS

We thank Eric Bond, Robert Reilly, and an anonymous referee for their helpful comments.

NOTES

1. We thank the referee for this interpretation.
2. We thank Bond for this clarification.
3. Bond's analysis involved pickup trucks aged 5 years or less. We have included all pickup trucks in our analysis.
4. Bond's tests require that he segment the market for used vehicles using age and mileage as a technical device. In the market, there is a segmentation of vehicles into sets that are considered by buyers and sellers to be nearly perfect substitutes. This need not correspond to a technical segmentation by age and lifetime mileage. Hence, although all trucks in Bond's sample are considered in his tests, this technical segmentation may not allow a proper test of the informational asymmetry between buyers and sellers within the same market segment.
5. Because of obvious ambiguity, the category used to report "other maintenance" was excluded from the analysis. We would expect that this category would include maintenance types whose expenditures would be lower than the average brake repair. Inclusion of this maintenance category does not affect the results.
6. There is not a significant difference between the average age or average lifetime mileage of these two transaction groups. Therefore, our test does not merely reflect differences in repair records that one might expect to exist due to significant differences in the average age or average lifetime mileage of vehicles in the two transaction groups.

7. A Sensitivity analysis shows that the results were invariant with respect to the actual dollar amounts reported in Table 1. The analysis is dependent on the relative ranking of the reported expenditure categories.
8. A direct test of the impact of counteracting institutions on the market for used vehicles is provided in our earlier paper (1983).

REFERENCES

Akerlof, George A. The market for 'lemons': Quality uncertainty and the market mechanism, *Quarterly Journal of Economics.* August 1970, **84**: 488–500.

Bond, Eric. W. A direct test of the 'lemons' model: The market for used pickup trucks, *American Economic Review*, September 1982, **72**: 836–840.

Pratt, Michael D. and Hoffer, George E. The Efficacy of Used Vehicle Disclosure Laws, *Working Paper* No. 83–01, Department of Economics, Virginia Commonwealth University, 1983.

US Department of Commerce, Bureau of the Census. *Truck Inventory and Use Survey, 1977,* Washington: USGPO, 1981.

Automotive Service Council of Virginia. Unpublished data, Richmond, Virginia, 1983.

17c

Test of the Lemons Model: Reply

Eric W. Bond

The purpose of my 1982 article was to test for differences in quality between original owner trucks and those that had been acquired used that could not be accounted for by differences in age and previous usage. Michael Pratt and George Hoffer (P–H) make several modifications of my tests by constructing a new measure of repair costs that is a linear combination of the frequency of repair information of different maintenance types and by choosing to compare recently traded trucks with those that were not traded recently. In introducing these changes, they argue that we should throw away information on age and lifetime mileage that is available to the buyer. I will show below that ignoring differences in previous use can lead to biases toward finding quality differences in a market where there is perfect information.

Adverse selection of the type described in George Akerlof's (1970) "lemons" model arises when products that are equivalent from the point of view of buyers are known to be different by the seller. If 3-year-old trucks with average usage vary widely in quality and the variations cannot be observed by potential buyers, then those of lower quality will obtain the same price as those of higher quality and adverse selection will result. However, the fact that a 4-year-old truck becomes too costly to operate and is sold by its owner, while a 3-year-old truck owned by the same owner is not, is not necessarily related to the market for lemons because the buyer can observe the difference in age and anticipate costlier repairs. The price paid for the truck can be adjusted for the expected difference in repair costs and the market price schedule for used trucks will be a hedonic price schedule with compensating differences for observable quality differences. Casual empiricism suggests that the market uses such information, since trucks decline in value with age and high mileage trucks sell for a discount. Trade takes place because the buyer's valuation on the truck exceeds that of the seller.

When differences in age and lifetime mileage are controlled for, I find no difference in maintenance between recently traded pickup trucks and those not traded for trucks less than 10 years old. For trucks more than 10 years old, which were not included in my earlier study, I find evidence of more frequent repairs among trucks that have been traded recently. Thus, the significant quality differences found by Pratt and Hoffer

Reprinted with permission from *American Economic Review*, Vol. 72, No. 4, 1982, pp. 836–840.

Table 1. Mean usage and repair cost by transaction group

Age (years)		Number of observations	Life mileage	Cost
1–5	Traded	1272	51.6[a]	2.16
	Not traded	7350	45.5	1.95
6–10	Traded	755	83.1	2.98
	Not traded	4154	82.0	2.80
> 10	Traded	1012	116.7	4.05[a]
	Not traded	4913	107.6	2.78

Notes: Not traded = not purchased within 12 months prior to sample. Traded = purchased used within 12 months prior to sample. Cost = average repair cost ($100) by P–H measure. Life mileage shown in 1000s.
[a]Mean significantly higher at 1 percent level than that for other transaction group of similar age.

arises from the inclusion of very old trucks in their sample, and from their failure to control for differences in characteristics that buyers can observe.

OBSERVABLE QUALITY DIFFERENCES

My 1983a article presents a model in which users with high utilization rates and high maintenance costs will have a comparative advantage in the operation of relatively new trucks when operating costs increase with age. In such a model, trucks will be passed from the highest intensity of use owners to the lowest intensity of use owners over their life, since the optimal trading ages occur earliest for those with the highest intensity of use.[1] Table 1 shows a comparison of lifetime mileage for trucks that have been recently traded (according to the P–H definition) against trucks that have not been traded. For trucks less than 5 years old, there is a significant difference in lifetime mileage between those trucks that were traded and those that were not traded, which is consistent with the model of trade based on comparative advantage. Tests that compare maintenance costs in this group without controlling for lifetime mileage differences would be biased toward finding higher maintenance costs for traded trucks. The mileage differences are not significant at the 10 percent level in the older groups, so that differences in characteristics are not likely to be a significant source of bias in these groups.[2]

The last column of Table 1 shows the mean repair cost according to the P–H measure for each group.[3] The difference between maintenance costs for trucks less than 5 years old is not significant at the 10 percent level, even though there is no adjustment for differences in lifetime mileage. The tests in my 1982 paper were limited to trucks less than 5 years old, so my findings of no difference in quality for this group is not sensitive to the alterations made by Pratt and Hoffer. If being a lemon is a permanent condition, then the first trucks to be scrapped should be the lemons and the tests should be done before significant scrapping has occurred. On the other hand, if major repairs must eventually be undertaken on all trucks, then the owner may be able to anticipate these events and sell the truck just before a major repair is needed. The remaining two rows of Table 1 show the mean repair costs for trucks 6 to 10 years old and greater than 10 years old. The difference in maintenance costs is not significant at the 10 percent level for trucks in the former group, but becomes significant at the 1 percent level for trucks more than 10 years old.

RECENTLY TRADED TRUCKS

The second change made by Pratt and Hoffer is to look for lemons among recently traded trucks rather than among trucks traded at least once. The issue involves where to place trucks that have been traded at least once, but not within the previous 12 months. If sellers of trucks fail to make repairs on trucks before they are traded, but these repairs are not an indication of permanently lower quality, then the P–H measure will be preferable. However, suppose that trading occurs when the owner obtains information (not available to buyers) that his truck is of permanently low quality. Then the stock of trucks that have been traded will be all those trucks for which unfavorable information has been received at least once in the past. In such a case, looking only among recently traded trucks for lemons would bias against finding quality differences unless unfavorable information is being received every year and the low quality trucks are traded every year. Thus, looking at recently traded trucks is an additional, although not necessarily preferable, way of examining the hypothesis.

To examine the sensitivity of my earlier results to the alternative definition of a used truck, I have reestimated my original model using the P–H definition of used trucks. Since maintenance is a dichotomous variable, the relationship between maintenance and observable characteristics can be estimated using a logit model:

$$\log(P_i/1 - P_i) = \beta_0 + \beta_1 AGE + \beta_2 LM + \beta_3 TRADED, \qquad i = 1, \ldots, 4;$$

where P_i = probability that maintenance of type i was performed, LM = log of lifetime mileage, and $TRADED$ is a dummy variable equal to 1 if the truck was purchased used within the last 12 months. The presence of a positive and significant value of β_3 indicates lower quality for used trucks that cannot be explained by observable quality differences. Equation (1) was estimated using maximum likelihood.

The results of these regressions are reported in Table 2. For trucks less than 5 years old, three of the estimated coefficients are negative (with one significant at the 1 percent level), indicating maintenance is less likely on recently traded trucks once the accumulated use differences are controlled. For trucks 6–10 years old, there are no significant coefficients and only two are positive. For trucks more than 10 years old, all are positive and two are significant at the 1 percent level. It should be noted that a similar result for trucks more than 10 years old is obtained if we compare original owner trucks with those that have been purchased used.

Use of the P–H maintenance cost variable in tests that control for differences in observable characteristics presents some econometric problems. The P–H variable is not dichotomous, but it is not a continuous variable either because it can take on only 16 values (resulting from the combinations of the 2 possible outcomes for each of the

Table 2. Effect of being traded on probability of maintenance

Age	Repair type			
	Engine	Transmission	Rear axle	Brakes
1–5	− .03	− .19	.02	.26[a]
	(.09)	(.11)	(.15)	(.09)
6–10	.12	− .09	− .18	.06
	(.10)	(.14)	(.10)	(.19)
> 10	.46[a]	.53[a]	.18	.13
	(.08)	(.11)	(.13)	(.08)

[a] Denotes significant at 1 percent level; standard errors are shown in parentheses.

4 maintenance categories). Thus, estimation of a maintenance cost relationship using ordinary least squares would suffer from problems of heteroskedasticity. The joint test of all maintenance cost variables is likely to lead to findings of lower quality among trucks where individual tests do not find lower quality in cases where the individual tests all yield positive but significant values of $\hat{\beta}_3$. An examination of the result of Table 2 for the 1–5 and 6–10-year-old groups, where the hypothesis of equal quality could not be rejected, do not indicate such a pattern. The joint test is therefore unlikely to yield results differing from those of the individual tests.

CONCLUSIONS

These results indicate that Pratt and Hoffer find used trucks to be of lower quality not because they have a "finer" test, but because they fail to adjust for observable quality differences and include trucks that are more than 10 years old. The failure to adjust for differences in age and previous use was shown to lead to biases toward accepting the hypothesis that trucks that have been recently traded are of lower quality than those not recently traded, with the bias strongest in trucks less than 5 years old.

The finding that trucks more than 10 years old that have been traded have significantly higher frequencies of maintenance than similar trucks not traded seems to support the hypothesis that counteracting institutions play an important role in assuring product quality. It is probably the case that most trucks sold by dealers fall into the category of trucks (1–10 years old) where there are no quality differences between those traded and those not traded. Trucks in the over 10-year-old age group account for approximately one-third of all pickup truck transactions, but account for less than 15 percent of annual mileage. Furthermore, the fact that a significant portion of trucks (presumably those of lowest quality) have been scrapped by that age indicates that this finding is not consistent with the interpretation of a lemon as a truck of permanently lower quality.

ACKNOWLEDGEMENTS

I thank J. Rodgers, M. Roberts, and H. Geerts for helpful discussions.

NOTES

1. This problem is treated in detail in my working article (1983b), which also estimates the impact of user characteristics on the age at sale.
2. As I found in my 1983a article for purchases of tractor trailers, the buyers of used pickup trucks in the older groups tend to be households or small firms. Both buyers and sellers in the oldest age group tend to be one-truck households that use pickups for personal transportation, so that comparative advantage does not explain trade in the oldest age group.
3. Letting P_i be the estimated frequency of maintenance of type i, my 1982 article used tests of the hypothesis $P_i^U - P_i^N = 0$, where the superscripts denote used and new trucks respectively. Letting α_i denote the maintenance cost of type i from the survey cited by P–H, their tests are of the hypothesis $\Sigma_i \alpha_i (P_i^U - P_i^N) = 0$. Clearly this cannot capture differences in the cost of a particular type of maintenance between different trucks (since the mean repair cost is assumed for all owners who report doing major maintenance), which is an important source of variation between trucks.

REFERENCES

Akerlof, George A. The market for 'lemons': Quality uncertainty and the market mechanism, *Quarterly Journal of Economics*, August 1970, **84**: 488–500.

Bond, Eric W. A direct test of the 'lemons' model: The market for used pickup trucks, *American Economic Review*, September 1982, **72**: 836–840.

Bond, Eric W. (1983a) Trade in used equipment with heterogeneous firms, *Journal of Political Economy*, August 1983, **91**, 688–705.

Bond, Eric W., (1983b) The Supply of Used Assets and Frequent Trading, Department of Economics *Working Paper*, Pennsylvania State University, 1983.

Pratt, Michael D. and Hoffer, George E. Test of the lemons model: Comment, *American Economic Review*, September 1984, **74**: 798–800.

18

The Causes and Consequences of The Dependence of Quality on Price

Joseph E. Stiglitz

If the legal rate ... was fixed so high ..., the greater part of the money which was to be lent, would be lent to prodigals and profectors, who alone would be willing to give this higher interest. Sober people, who will give for the use of money no more than a part of what they are likely to make by the use of it, would not venture into the competition. ... Adam Smith, *Wealth of Nations*, 1776.

A plentiful subsistence increases the bodily strength of the laborer and the comfortable hope of bettering his condition and ending his days perhaps in ease and plenty animates him to exert that strength to the utmost. Adam Smith, *Wealth of Nations*, 1776.

Low wages are by no means identical with cheap labour. From a purely quantitative point of view the efficiency of labour decreases with a wage which is physiologically insufficient ... the present-day average Silesian mows, when he exerts himself to the full, little more than two-thirds as much land as the better paid and nourished Pomeranian or Mecklenburger, and the Pole, the further East he comes from, accomplishes progressively less than the German. Low wages fail even from a purely business point of view wherever it is question of producing goods which require any sort of skilled labour, or the use of expensive machinery which is easily damaged, or in general wherever any greater amount of sharp attention of of initiative is required. Here low wages do not pay, and their effect is the opposite of what was intended. Max Weber, *The Protestant Ethic and the Spirit of Capitalism* (Schribner, New York, 1925, p. 61).

... highly paid labour is generally efficient and therefore not dear labour; a fact which though it is more full of hope for the future of the human race than any other that is known us, will be found to exercise a very complicating influence on the theory of distribution. Alfred Marshall, *Principles of Economics*, 1920.

... the landlord who attempted to exact more than his neighbour ... would render himself so odious, he would be so sure of not obtaining a metayer who was an honest man, that the contract of all the metayers may be considered as identical, at least in each province, and never gives rise to any competition among peasants in search of employment, or any offer to cultivate the soil on cheaper terms than one another. J. C. L. Simonde de Sismondi, *Political Economy*, 1814, cited in John Stuart Mill, *Principles of Political Economy*, 1848.

Reprinted with permission from *Journal of Economic Literature*, Vol. 25, No. 1, 1987, pp. 1–48

Conventional competitive economic theory begins with the hypothesis of price-taking firms and consumers buying and selling homogeneous commodities at well-defined marketplaces. In many situations, these assumptions are implausible: in insurance markets, firms know that some risks are greater than others (some individuals' life expectancy is greater than others'; some individuals are more likely to have an automobile accident than others), but cannot tell precisely who is the greater risk, even within fairly narrowly defined risk categories. In labor markets, firms know that some workers are better than others, but at the time they hire and train the worker, they cannot tell precisely who will turn out to be the more productive. In product markets, consumers know that some commodities are more durable than others, but at the time of purchase, they cannot ascertain precisely which are more durable. In capital markets, banks know that the probability of bankruptcy differs across loans, but cannot tell precisely which loans are better.

This heterogeneity has important consequences, some of which have long been recognized. There are strong incentives to sort, to distinguish the high risk from the low risk, the more able from the less able. This sorting can be done on the basis of observable characteristics (say, sex or age) or the (inferences made from) actions undertaken by individuals, e.g., the job for which the individual applies (George Akerlof, 1976), the wage structure chosen by the individual (Joanne Salop and Steven Salop, 1976), or the quantity of insurance purchased (Michael Rothschild and Joseph Stiglitz, 1976). In these models, the choices made convey information; individuals know this, and this affects their actions.

Willingness to trade may itself serve as a sorting device. In insurance markets, firms have recognized that as the price of insurance increases, the mix of applicants changes *adversely*. Akerlof (1970) has shown how such adverse selection effects may also arise in other markets, including the market for used cars (see Charles Wilson, 1979, 1980). His analysis has subsequently been applied to the labor market (Bruce Greenwald, 1986) and to capital markets (Greenwald, Stiglitz, and Andrew Weiss, 1984; Stewart Myers and Nicholas S. Majluf, 1984). In each of these instances, the uninformed party (the seller of insurance, the used car buyer, etc.) forms rational expectations concerning the quality mix of what is being offered on the market; the price serves as a signal or as a screening device. The fact that an employee is willing to work for $1 an hour suggests, that she knows of no better offers; others who have looked at her have evidently decided that she is worth no more than $1 an hour.

Insurance firms have also long recognized that the terms at which they write insurance contracts may affect the actions undertaken by individuals; that is, the likelihood of the insured against an event occurring is an *endogenous* variable which the insurance firm can hope to affect. The fact that individuals can undertake unobservable actions that affect the likelihood of an accident is referred to as the *moral hazard* problem. The term has come to be used to describe a wide range of incentive problems. In particular, employers know that the incentives workers have to work hard may be affected by the wage paid; and the incentives borrowers have to undertake risky projects may be affected by the interest rate charged on the bank's loan. Thus, the characteristics of what is being traded again depend on the price at which the trade is consummated, though now because of *incentive* effects rather than *selection* effects.

These are instances in which price serves a function in addition to that usually described to it in economic theory: it conveys information and affects behavior. Quality depends on price. Of course, in standard economic theory, higher-quality items will sell at higher prices: Prices depend on quality. But here, beliefs about quality, about what it is that is being traded, depend (rationally) on price.[1]

This dependence of beliefs about quality on price has some fundamental implications. Firstly, demand curves, may under quite plausible conditions, not be downward sloping. When the price of some security is higher, uninformed buyers may infer that the expected return is higher, and their demand may increase (Jerry Green 1973; Sanford Grossman and Stiglitz 1976, 1980). An increase in the wage may so increase the productivity of the workers that the demand for labor may actually increase. A decrease in the price of used cars results in a decrease in the average quality of those being offered and this may decrease demand (Akerlof 1970). In each of these instances, one can think of the change in the price as having two effects: a movement along a fixed-information demand curve, and a shift in the demand curve from the change in information (beliefs).

Secondly, one may not be able to separate out neatly the analysis of demand and supply. Individuals' demands are based on inferences they are making from prices, and these inferences are critically dependent on the nature of the supply responses. Thus, any alteration, say, in the probability distribution of supply characteristics will, in general, lead to an alteration in the demand functions.

Thirdly, markets may be thin. At the equilibrium price of insurance, some risk averse individuals choose not to purchase insurance, even though with perfect information, they would have. The marginal person buying insurance is, in effect, subsidizing other purchasers; he is not obtaining actuarially fair insurance, as he would in a (risk neutral) competitive market with full information.[2]

These models, while departing from the traditional paradigm in denying the validity of the hypothesis of homogeneous markets, retain the assumption of price-taking firms and consumers. In many situations, firms are not price or wage takers. Banks do not simply take the interest rate that they charge on loans as given.

This chapter is concerned with situations where firms not only recognize the dependence of quality on price (of productivity on wages, of default probability on the interest rate charged), but also attempt to use what control they have over price (wages, interest rates) to increase their profits. The recognition of this possibility has important implications for economic theory, which have recently been explored in a large number of articles in several disparate fields. The objective of this chapter is to survey these articles and to draw out the central themes of this literature.

This chapter is divided into four parts. In the first part, we discuss the most important implications of the dependence of quality on price for competitive equilibrium theory—the repeal of the law of supply and demand, the repeal of the law of the single price, the existence of discriminatory equilibria, the comparative static consequences, and the inefficiency of market equilibria. The second part discusses alternative explanations for the dependence of quality on price in labor, capital, and product markets. The third part explains more precisely how these models differ from standard competitive models and from other models with imperfect information. Finally, the fourth part discusses some of the more important applications of the theory, including those in macroeconomics and in development economics.

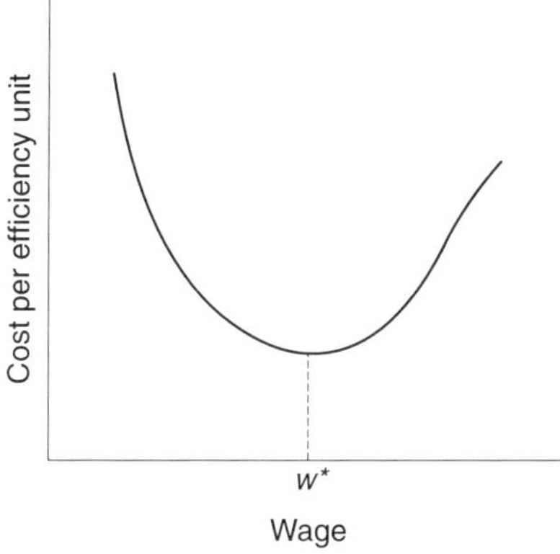

Figure 1. Cost per efficiency unit is minimized at wage w^*.

THE FUNDAMENTAL IMPLICATIONS OF THE DEPENDENCE OF QUALITY ON PRICE

Repeal of the law of supply and demand

No law in economics has such standing as the "Law of Supply and Demand". There is an old joke about being able to teach a parrot to be an economist—and a good economist at that—simply by teaching it to repeat the words "demand and supply". The law holds that competitive market equilibrium is characterized by demand equaling supply. It asserts that the way to analyze changes in market equilibrium is to isolate the changes in the demand function and in the supply function.

When quality depends on price, market equilibrium *may* be characterized by demand not equaling supply.[3]

Consider the labor market. Assume there is an excess supply of labor. The conventional story is that in the face of excess supply, unemployed workers go to potential employers and offer their services at lower wages. The wage is bid down. As the wage decreases, the demand for labor increases and the supply decreases. This process continues until the wage is bid down to the level where supply equals demand.

If, however, the firm believes that the workers who offer their services at a lower wage are less productive, then—if they are sufficiently less productive—it will not hire the lower-wage workers, for the cost per effective unit of labor service will actually be higher with the lower-wage worker.

Thus, in Figure 1 we have depicted the cost per effective unit of labor service as initially falling as the wage is increased. There is a wage, w^*, at which wage costs per effective unit of labor service are minimized. This is referred to as the *efficiency wage*. For this section, we assume the same costs per efficiency unit schedule faces all firms and characterizes all workers. (In the following sections we shall consider the consequences of differing costs per efficiency unit schedules.)

If, at the efficiency wage, there is an excess supply of laborers, no firm has an incentive to lower its wage, or to hire a worker who offers his services at a lower wage,

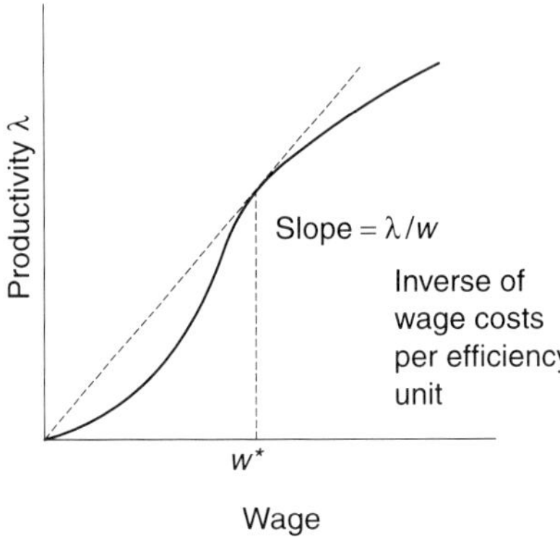

Figure 2. Wage productivity curve. λ/w increases as w increases to w^*, and then decreases.

for to do so simply increases labor costs. Thus, when at w^*, the supply of labor equals or exceeds the demand, w^* is the equilibrium wage.

This curve, giving the relationship between the cost per effective unit of labor and the wage rate, is derived from the more fundamental *wage productivity curve*, giving the productivity of the representative worker hired at a particular wage. The curve depicted in Figure 2 shows λ, the productivity of the worker, increasing with the wage; the essential feature of this productivity curve is that there is initially a region of increasing returns, where an increase in the wage leads to a more than proportionate increase in the productivity. Many of our results depend critically on the existence of some region for which this is true; in the models that we investigate in detail, we establish that this is in fact the case.

In Figure 2, the cost per efficiency unit (cost per effective unit of labor) is given by the (inverse of the) slope of a line through the origin to a point on the wage productivity curve. Because the slope is increasing as we increase the wage from 0 to w^*, the cost per effective unit of labor is decreasing. Beyond w^* the slope decreases and hence the cost per effective unit of labor increases. It is clear, then, that the wage productivity curve generates a cost per effective unit of labor curve of the form depicted in Figure 1.

The existence of a wage–productivity relationship has long been recognized, as the quotations at the beginning of this article indicate. The more recent revival of interest may be attributed to Harvey Leibenstein (1957) who discussed it in the context of less developed countries and the subsequent developments by James Mirrlees (1975) and Stiglitz (1976b). There, however, the relationship is based on nutritional considerations.[4] Near subsistence, workers are not very productive; increases in wages may lead to marked increases in efficiency. Though our analysis focuses on alternative explanations of the relationship, the consequences are very similar.

Exactly the same analysis applies to the capital market (Stiglitz and Weiss 1981). Assume that as the bank increases the interest rate, the "quality" of those who apply decreases; that is, those who apply have, on average, a higher probability of defaulting, of not repaying their loans. The safest borrowers are unwilling to borrow at high interest rates. Then, the expected return on a loan, ρ, may actually decrease as the

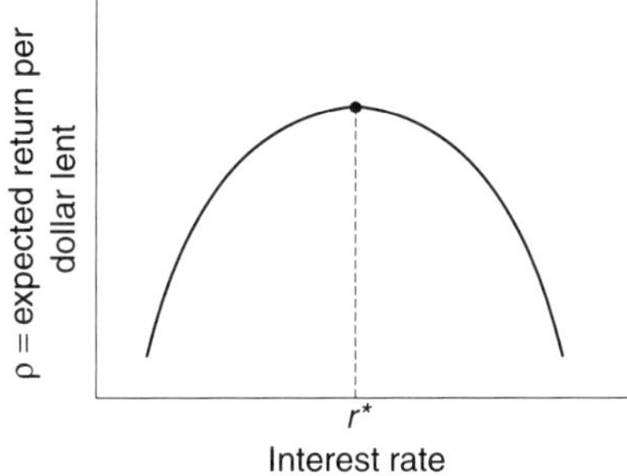

Figure 3. Expected return per dollar lent is maximized at r^*.

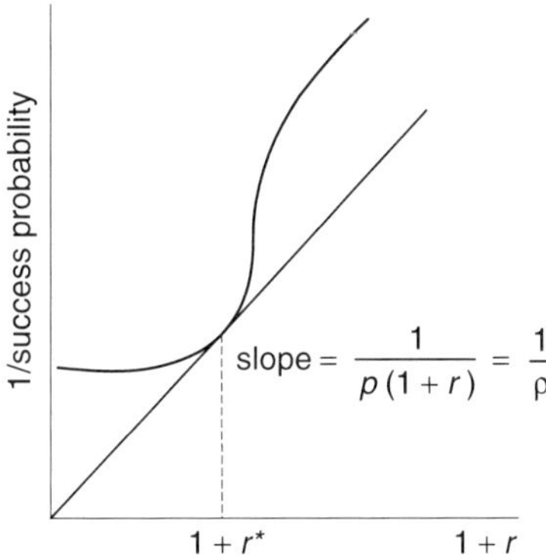

Figure 4. Default curve. $p(1 + r)$ increases as r increases to r^*, and then decreases.

interest rate, r, increases, as depicted in Figure 3; r^* is the efficiency interest rate. If, at r^*, there is an excess demand for loans (credit is rationed), r^* is still an equilibrium. The bank will refuse to lend to anyone offering to borrow at a higher interest rate; its expected return would be lower than what it obtains by lending at r^*.

The curve in Figure 3 may be derived from the default curve. The probability of a default is postulated to increase with the rate of interest charged. Let p = probability that the loan is repaid; we assume, for simplicity, that when the loan is not repaid the lender receives nothing. Thus, the expected return to a lender is

$$\rho = p(1 + r).$$

In Figure 4, we have plotted $1/p$ as a function of $1 + r$. Thus, the slope of any line from the origin to the default curve is $1/(1 + r)p$. The bank wishes to maximize $p(1 + r)$, i.e., find the point on the default curve with the lowest slope; this is clearly just the point of tangency of a line through the origin with the default curve. Note that the slope decreases as r increases up to $1 + r^*$ (i.e., ρ increases) and decreases thereafter (i.e., ρ decreases), just as depicted in Figure 3. (We postpone until later a justification for the shape of the default curve.)

Again, the conventional story for why there cannot be credit rationing in equilibrium is that those who are willing to borrow at the given interest but denied credit go to the bank and offer it a higher interest rate; this bids up the interest rate. As the interest rate is bid up, the supply of credit is increased and demand decreases. The process continues until equilibrium is reached at the point where the demand for loans equals the supply; there is no credit rationing. But now, the bank realizes that if it charges a higher interest rate, the probability of default increases; and it may increase so much that the expected return to the bank actually decreases. Thus, no bank will ever charge an interest rate above r^*.[5,6]

In each of these cases, the story is the same: Because quality (labor efficiency, bankruptcy probability) changes as the price (wage, interest rate) changes, excess supply or demand may persist without any tendency for price (wages, interest rates) to move to correct the market imbalance.

General Formulations.   In each of the instances described above, an individual (firm) sets the terms of the contract with another individual or firm to maximize its utility (profits), subject to offering terms that make the contract acceptable; under the circumstances described, the optimal contract will be such that the constraint on acceptability is not binding. That is, if $U[p, x, q(p, x)]$ is the utility of the buyer, paying a price p, and offering nonprice terms[7] of the contract x, where $q(p, x)$ represents a description of the (expected value of the) quality of the object (service) being purchased, a function of p and x, then the individual chooses p and x to

$$\underset{(p,\,x)}{Max\ U} \tag{1}$$

subject to the constraint of being able to obtain the item, i.e., if $V[p, x, q(p, x)]$ is the (expected) utility of an individual (firm) selling an item of quality q and V^* represents the reservation utility level,[8] then

$$V[p, x, q(p, x)] \geq V^*. \tag{2}$$

In a variety of circumstances, the solution to this problem may entail the constraint (2) not being binding, at least for some potential sellers.[9] When that happens, market equilibrium will be characterized by demand not equaling supply.[10]

Repeal of the law of the single price

The law of supply and demand is of course, only one of the fundamental "laws" of conventional economics. Another central aspect of the traditional paradigm is codified in the "Law of the Single Price". This law holds that all objects with the same observable charactcristics should sell at the same price. When there is a relationship between quality and price, the price itself becomes a relevant characteristic; market equilibrium may be characterized by a price distribution (or a wage distribution, or a

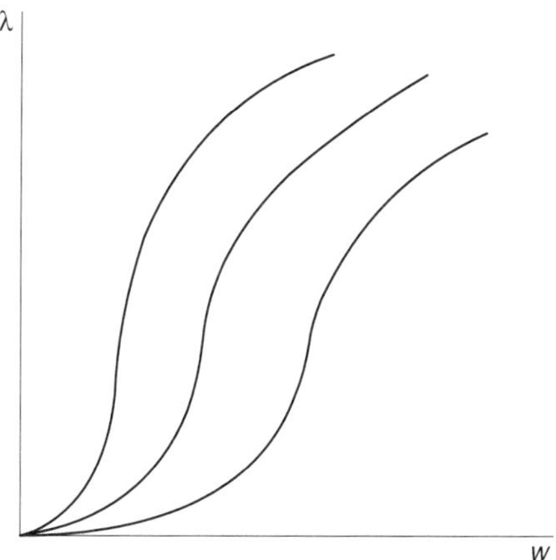

Figure 5. The wage–productivity relationship may differ across firms. Different firms may find it optimal to pay different wages.

distribution of interest rates) for objects that cannot be distinguished (before purchase) other than by price.

It has been widely observed that some firms have a high-wage policy; others pursue a low-wage policy. It is important to bear in mind that the differences we are concerned with here are not differences in whether the firm hires those with more education or less education, those with more work experience or those with less work experience. Rather, we are comparing the wages paid by firms for workers with a *given* set of observable qualifications.

There are several reasons that economies in which productivity depends on wages (or more generally quality on prices) may be characterized by a wage (price) distribution.

Differences in firms

If the wage–productivity relationship differs across firms, as in Figure 5, the efficiency wage may differ. More generally, firms where net productivity is more sensitive to wages (with higher turnover costs, higher monitoring costs, or where shirking workers can do more damage) will find it desirable to pay higher wages for workers of identical characteristics (Steven Salop 1973). This is consistent with the observation that more capital intensive firms tend to pay higher wages, because the "damage" a worker can do in such jobs may be higher. If monitoring costs are higher in firms employing large numbers of workers, one might expect to see such firms paying higher wages (other things being constant).

Wage distributions when costs per effective unit are not monotonic

Wage (price, or interest rate) distributions also arise when costs per effective unit are not monotone, as we suggested that they might not be.

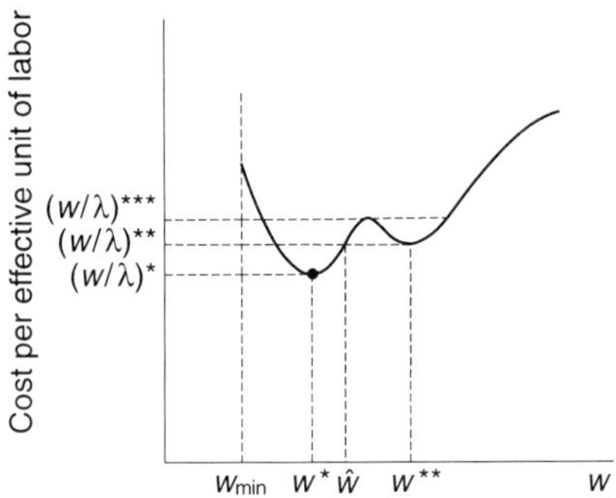

Figure 6. Wage distribution. Market equilibrium is characterized by excess supply of labor whenever Walrasian wage is lower than w^{*}. When Walrasian wage is between $\hat{w}$ and w^{**}, some workers are hired at w^{**}, and other workers are hired at $\hat{w}$.

Assume, in particular, that the reason that productivity increases with wage is nutritional;[11] though productivity always increases with wage, it may increase more or less than proportionately. When it increases more than proportionately, labor costs per efficiency unit decline with wage increases. Thus, if over some ranges, say, for very low wages and for an intermediate range of wages, productivity increases more than proportionately with wages, one would obtain a curve describing wage per efficiency unit as in Figure 6.

We define the Walrasian wage, $\tilde{w}$, as that wage at which demand for labor equals the supply. However, the Walrasian wage is not the equilibrium wage whenever there exists a wage higher than the Walrasian wage with a lower cost per efficiency unit. For it would pay any firm to increase its wage. Assume, in Figure 6, that the Walrasian equilibrium occurred at some wage between $\hat{w}$ and w^{**}. One might be tempted to suggest that w^{**}, the wage greater than the Walrasian wage at which costs per efficiency unit are minimized, is the market equilibrium; but at w^{**}, there is unemployment; and by lowering their wage enough (to any wage between $\hat{w}$ and w^{*}), workers can be hired with a cost per efficiency unit that is lower than at w^{**}. The equilibrium now entails full employment with a wage distribution; some workers are hired at w^{**} and others at $\hat{w}$. Costs per efficiency unit are exactly the same. If all workers were paid a wage of $\hat{w}$, there would be (by assumption) an excess demand for labor; that is why $\hat{w}$ is not an equilibrium. If all workers were paid w^{**}, there would be an excess supply of laborers. There is a particular proportion of workers hired at $\hat{w}$ and w^{**} at which demand is equal to supply for the low-wage jobs, though there is excess supply of labor at the high-wage firms.

Similar arguments apply to other markets.

Wage distributions when costs per effective unit are minimized at several different wages

The previous subsection considered a situation where the cost per effective unit was not monotonic. Equilibrium wage distributions also arise when the curve describing

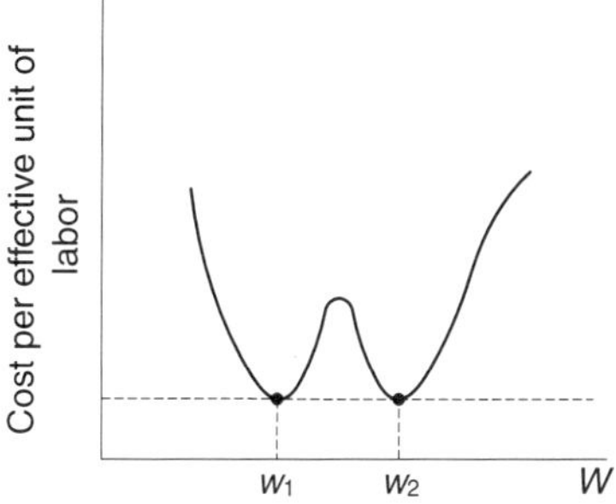

Figure 7. Wage distribution where cost per effective unit of labor is the same at w_1 and w_2.

the cost per effective unit of labor, depicted earlier, has several peaks, and all of the peaks generate exactly the same level of costs per effective unit of labor, as illustrated in Figure 7. Such a configuration would seem to be an anomaly. Even if there is no reason that the productivity curve has a single peak, why should the peaks occur at the same level? One can show that this may, in fact, occur quite easily. The curve that we have depicted is the curve facing a particular firm, *given* the wages paid by all other firms. Stiglitz (1974b, 1985) shows, in the context of the labor-turnover model, that there is a wages distribution (and in fact many such distributions) with the property that the productivity curve has many peaks, each of which yields exactly the same cost per effective unit of labor. The reason for this is that the turnover costs facing any firm are a function of the fraction of firms paying a higher wage, which itself is an endogenous variable. The low-wage firm faces a higher turnover. The fraction of high-wage firms is such that the total labor costs—wages plus turnover costs—are the same at low-wage firms and high-wage firms (see also Phillip Dybvig and Gerald Jaynes 1980).

Similar results can be obtained in the context of selection models. If different individuals have different costs associated with queuing, or with not selling their commodity (their labor), then high-wage firms may find that they face a longer queue and a higher quality of applicants. In these models, high-wage labor looks (in terms of observable characteristics) the same as low-wage labor, but in fact it is more productive with differences in productivity corresponding (in equilibrium) precisely to differences in wages. Wages together with queues are acting as self-selection devices.[12] (See Barry Nalebuff and Stiglitz 1982 and Stiglitz 1976a.)

Discrimination

It has long been noted that, in the absence of perfect information, there may be statistical discrimination: Members of a group will be paid the mean marginal product of the group, or will be charged an interest rate corresponding to the mean default probability of their group or charged an insurance premium corresponding to the mean probability of accident, illness, or death of their group. But the traditional theory of statistical discrimination (see, e.g., Dennis Aigner and Glen Cain 1977 or Rothschild and Stiglitz 1982) has not provided an explanation of job discrimination or

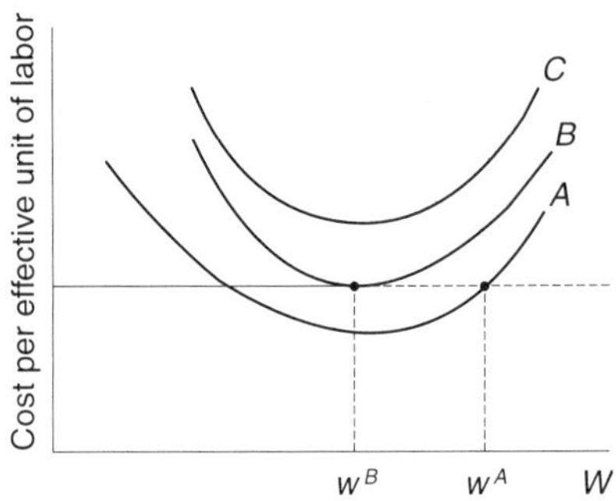

Figure 8. Group C is excluded from labor market.

red lining—differential access to certain jobs or credit of certain groups. The theories we are concerned with here do this.

Assume that in the labor market there are a number of different identifiable groups, each with its own "cost per effective unit of labor" curve, as depicted in Figure 8. Then, equilibrium will be characterized by all groups hired having the same cost per effective labor unit; those with lower costs per effective labor service at any wages are paid a higher wage. (There is, thus, wage discrimination.) But there are some groups, such as Group C in Figure 8, for whom the cost per labor service, at the optimum wage, and hence at any wage, exceeds that of the market equilibrium; such workers will not be hired. "Discrimination" takes the form not of paying the workers in group C a lower wage, but of refusing to hire them.

While all of those in category A will be hired, and none of those in category C, in general only some of those in category B will be hired. *Other apparently identical workers will not be employed.*

When productivity depends on the unemployment rate, there may be large differences in equilibrium in group specific unemployment rates as well as wage rates.[13]

The theory not only predicts that some groups may be rationed out of the market, but also suggests that the brunt of changes in the demand for labor (aggregate demand) will be felt by some groups in increased job rationing. Moreover, some versions of the theory predict which groups will be rationed out of the market. In particular, in the incentive version of the model (Carl Shapiro and Stiglitz 1984), the wage that must be paid to a worker to induce him not to shirk depends on the cost of being fired. This cost is likely to be lower for part-time workers, for those close to retirement, and for secondary participants in the labor force (e.g., low-wage workers with high-income spouses).

Exactly the same phenomenon can occur in credit markets. Assume that the function relating the expected return to the interest rate differs across individuals who differ in certain observable characteristics, as depicted in Figure 9. There will be an equilibrium rate of return on a loan; loans to all categories that are offered yield the same expected return.[14] The interest rate charged for categories of loans, such as A, whose maximal expected return exceeds ρ^*, are charged lower interest rates ($r_A < r_B$). On the other hand, loan category C is such that at no interest rate does it yield a return

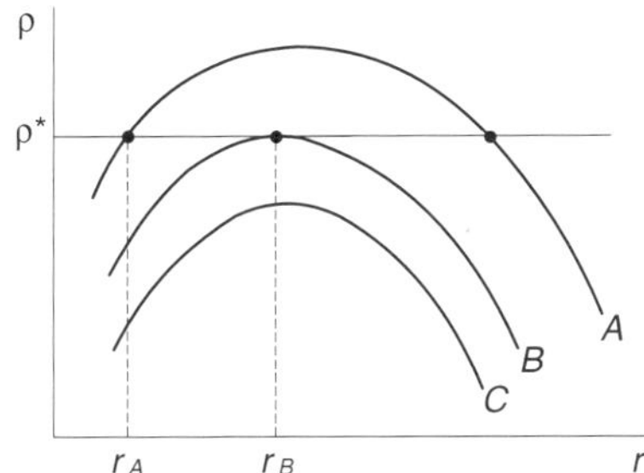

Figure 9. Group *C* is excluded from capital market.

equal to ρ^*; all those in this category are simply denied loans. The practice of denying credit to certain categories of potential borrowers is called red-lining. (Some of those in category B, where the maximal expected return is equal to ρ^*, receive loans, while others do not.)

Comparative statics

With "normally" shaped demand and supply curves, an increase in supply (that is, a shift in the supply curve such that at every price a greater quantity of the good is supplied) leads to an equilibrium with a lower price and a greater quantity traded. Similarly, a decrease in demand (that is, a shift in the demand curve such that at every price a smaller quantity of the good is demanded) leads to an equilibrium with a lower price and a lower quantity traded. Now, in the class of models being examined in this paper, the major effect of such a shift may be a change in the magnitude of rationing, with little effect on prices. Thus, in the labor market, when there is an equilibrium with excess supply of labor, a small increase in the demand for labor has no effect on the wage rate, but increases employment. An increase in the supply of credit available may have no effect on interest rates, but may simply lead to more loans (less credit rationing) at the old interest rates (Figure 10).

In markets where there are many groups in the population, a decrease in the demand for labor may result in some groups being completely excluded from the market, with only a slight lowering of the wage of those remaining. This is distinctly different from the conventional models, in which the wage for all workers would be reduced, and no group of workers would be excluded (though some groups of workers may decide to drop out of the labor market) (Figure 11a).

Similarly, in markets with credit rationing, a decrease in the supply of available credit may result in some groups being excluded from the credit market, with relatively small increases in the interest rates charged to those who are not excluded (Figure 11b).[15]

Shifts in the productivity curves

The other important source of changes in the equilibrium comes from changes in the productivity (or return) curves. In the labor market, a change in technology may result

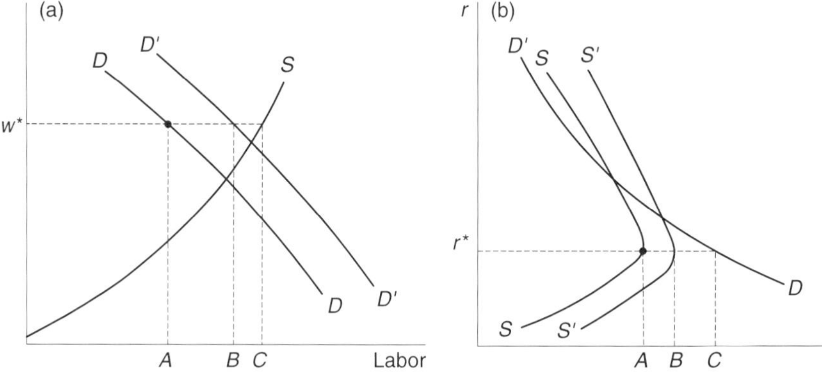

Figure 10. (a) An increase in the demand for labor may leave wage rate unchanged, but simply increase employment. (b) An increase in the supply of credit may leave interest rate unchanged, but simply decrease extent of credit rationing.

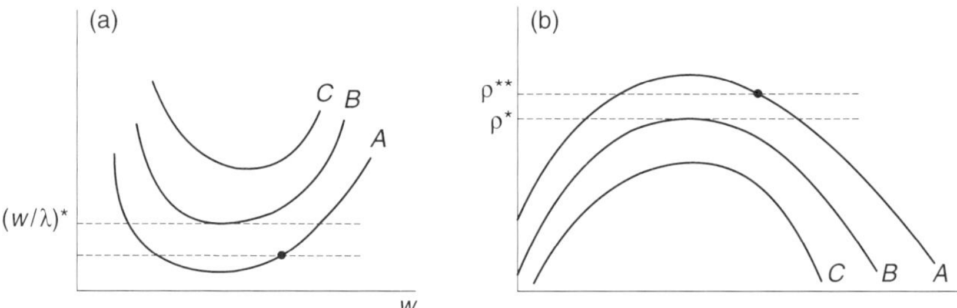

Figure 11 (a) A decrease in the demand for labor may lead to a decrease in the equilibrium cost per effective unit of labor, resulting in exclusion of some groups from the labor market. (When wage per efficiency unit falls from just above $(w/\lambda)^*$ to just below it, group B is excluded.) (b) A decrease in supply of credit may lead to an increase in the equilibrium return, resulting in the exclusion of some groups from the credit market.

in a change in the efficiency wage, as depicted in Figure 12a. If the efficiency wage increases markedly, but the cost per effective unit of labor decreases only slightly, as in Figure 12b, then the new equilibrium may be characterized by a lower level of employment and a higher wage.

Similarly, if banks' expectations of defaults increase, then the expected return, at any interest rate, will decrease. This will normally result in a decrease in the supply of credit; the effect on the extent of credit rationing will depend on how the changed expectations affect the demand for credit. But there are no clear implications for the interest rate charged by the bank; it may either increase or decrease (Figure 13).[16]

Implications for welfare economics

One of the crowning achievements of competitive equilibrium theory during the past half century has been the proof of the fundamental theorem of welfare economics

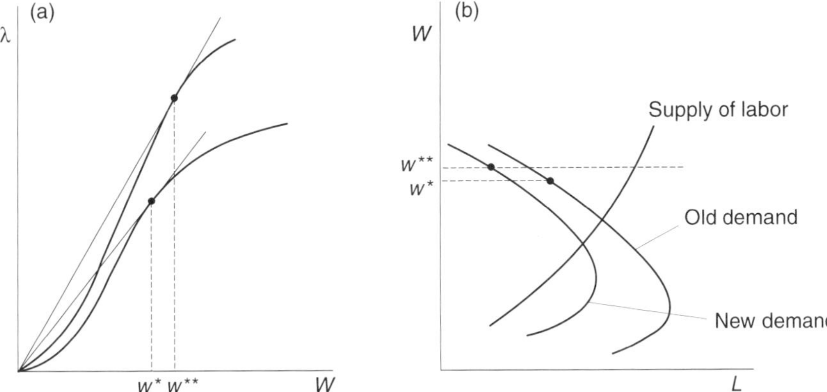

Figure 12(a) A change in technology may result in a large change in wages, but a relatively small change in the cost per efficiency unit of labor. (b) A technological change may lead to a higher wage and less employment.

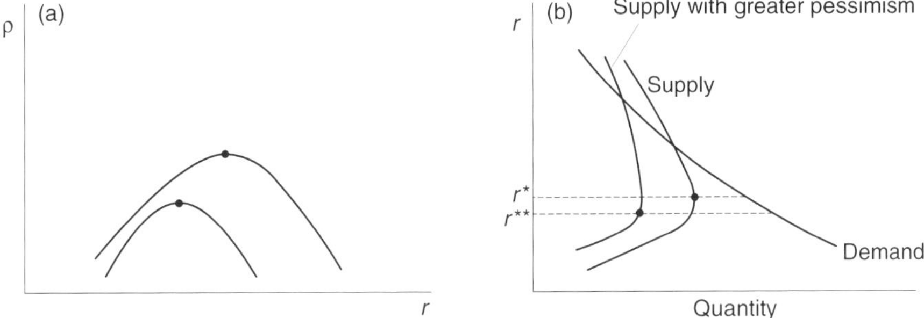

Figure 13(a) More pessimistic expectations may lower expected return and lower interest rate charged. (b) More pessimistic expectations may result in more credit rationing and lower interest rates.

—providing a precise statement of the meaning of Adam Smith's invisible hand conjecture.

An implicit assumption in the standard proofs of the Fundamental Theorem of Welfare Economics is that there is perfect information.[17] Obviously, economies with perfect information are likely to function better than economies with imperfect information:[18] That is an irrelevant comparison. The relevant question is, in a market characterized by incomplete information, are there interventions that can attain a Pareto improvement? Is the market, in other words, constrained Pareto efficient, taking into account the imperfections of information and costs of obtaining more information?

Greenwald and Stiglitz (1986a) have shown that competitive economies with incomplete markets and/or imperfect information are essentially never constrained Pareto efficient. These authors develop a general framework within which a variety of informational imperfections can be analyzed. They limit themselves to tax and subsidy interventions. They apply their analysis to one of the models that are the subject of discussion in this chapter, namely, the Akerlof adverse selection model, where the quality offered is a function of the price but markets clear. In the context of the labor market, they show that a welfare improvement can be attained by subsidizing commodities whose consumption increases the mean quality of labor sold on the market and by taxing commodities whose consumption decreases the mean quality. The mean quality of labor offered on the market resembles the mean quality of air: There is an important externality in each individual's decision.

Their earlier paper was limited to economies with market clearing. In a sequel (Greenwald and Stiglitz 1986b), they identify the inefficiencies that arise in economies in which quality is dependent on prices and markets do not clear. There are inefficiencies both in setting wages (interest rates) and determining the level of employment (the number of loans of different types).

A direct consequence of the Fundamental Theorem of Welfare Economics is the decentralizability of efficient resource allocations; and a direct consequence of the failure of the Fundamental Theorem—of the externalities we have noted—is that the scope for decentralization may be limited.[19]

Some rationing may be consistent with Pareto efficiency. Assume the government has no more information about the quality of workers or potential borrowers than do firms (or banks). It has to allocate workers to different jobs. It has to allocate capital among different firms. The wage at which workers are willing to work or the interest rate at which firms are willing to borrow conveys information to the government, just as it does to the employer or the bank, and it will, in general, wish to use this information, even though to use it necessitates rationing—unemployment or credit rationing. But the objectives of the government, what it wishes to glean from the information, are different from those of firms and banks in the private market equilibrium. The latter are simply concerned with maximizing their own profits. Thus, in choosing a wage, the government would be concerned with ascertaining that those with a comparative advantage in a job get assigned to that job; the firm is simply concerned with cost per efficiency unit. (Similarly, the bank is not concerned with how its actions affect the profitability of investors, only with how it affects the profitability of the bank.)

Private firms will not only set the wage incorrectly; they will also hire an incorrect number of workers. Because all workers whose opportunity cost is less than the wage offer themselves for work, the mean opportunity cost of an individual randomly hired by a firm is less than the wage. Thus firms will not hire workers up to the point where the wage equals the mean opportunity costs, as a government concerned with maximizing national income would.

The inefficiencies we noted above are not the only inefficiencies associated with private market allocations and there may be other grounds for government intervention. Taxes and subsidies may affect the consumption vector of individuals, and thus indirectly the effort exerted by the worker (or the wage required to induce the worker not to shirk). Such taxes and subsidies may thus be welfare enhancing (Arnott and Stiglitz 1985).

Shapiro and Stiglitz (1984) point out a variety of other inefficiencies that arise in their model where high wages are used to reduce shirking. These relate to the intensity of monitoring and policies that affect quits and shirking. For instance, if workers are very risk averse, unemployment insurance may be desirable even though in their model private firms will never supply unemployment insurance; if there is an excess supply of labor, firms can obtain the desired labor force at the going wage; any increase in unemployment compensation simply increase the wage that a firm must pay to induce workers not to shirk.[20]

These models also have some more basic implications for how we think about the welfare properties of market economies. One of the important consequences of the Fundamental Theorem of Welfare Economics was that it enabled a neat separation of efficiency and equity issues. In particular, whether the economy is or is not Pareto efficient did not depend on the distribution of wealth. In the models under examination, this is not true, for two reasons. First, the inefficiencies with which we have been concerned arise because of the asymmetric information between two parties to a transaction between landlord and worker, or between worker and capitalist. But whether these transactions arise is, at least partly, determined by the distribution of wealth. For instance, share-cropping arises largely because of the concentration of wealth. Secondly, the distribution of ownership of factors, determines whether it is, in fact, feasible to design Pareto improvements. In the Shapiro–Stiglitz model, for instance, national income can be increased by taxing capital and subsidizing wages; if wealth were equally distributed, the losses individuals would suffer qua capitalists would be more than offset by the gains that would be received qua workers. But if there are two distinct groups in the population, capitalists and workers, there may be no way of improving the welfare of the workers without simultaneously hurting the capitalists—the market equilibrium, while not maximizing net national product, is Pareto efficient (see Shapiro and Stiglitz 1984; Dasgupta and Ray 1986).

EXPLANATIONS FOR THE DEPENDENCE OF QUALITY ON PRICE

In the introduction, we described two broad classes of models giving rise to a dependence of quality on price based on incentive and selection effects. In the preceding sections, we showed that if the dependence of quality on price took on particular forms (e.g., the cost per effective unit had an interior minimum) then there might exist an equilibrium in which demand did not equal supply, or in which there might be, in equilibrium, a price (wage, interest rate) distribution. We now consider in more detail not only why quality may depend on price in certain situations, but why the dependence should take on a form that may give rise to nonmarket-clearing equilibria and/or wage/price/interest rate distributions.

The analysis is divided into three sections, describing selection models, incentive models, and nutritional models.

Selection models

Labor market

The reasons for the presence of adverse selection in the labor market are clear (Stiglitz 1976b; Weiss 1976, 1980; Greenwald 1979, 1986). One of the inferences I can make from the fact that a worker is willing to work for me for 50 cents an hour is that he does not have (know of) a better offer elsewhere.[21] If other firms are screening workers, keeping high-productivity workers and letting go of low-productivity workers, or adjusting their wages to reflect their lower productivity, the fact that no other firm has offered the worker a wage in excess of 50 cents an hour conveys a considerable amount of information. (Obviously, the inferences I make depend on a number of details of the surrounding circumstances; if the worker is a newly arrived worker to the United States, the fact that he is willing to accept a job at 50 cents an hour is more likely to reflect his limited opportunities for search and his lack of knowledge of the job market; if a job has a number of extremely attractive nonpecuniary advantages, the inferences I make should take that into account.)

More productive workers are likely to have better wage offers from other firms, but even if they are self-employed, they are likely to be more productive (that is, if those who are more able in one production task are more able, on average, in other production tasks as well).

In the simplest formulation of the adverse selection-labor model, a worker whose reservation wage is v has a productivity of $a(v)$; if all workers whose reservation wage v is less than or equal to w apply for a job with wage w,[22] then the mean productivity of the applicants is

$$\sum a(v) f(v)/F(v)$$

where $F(v)$ is the distribution function of the population by reservation wages, and $f(v)$ the density function. It is clear that if $a' > 0$, then mean productivity will increase with w. To see that it may have the shape depicted in Figure 1, consider a two group model; low-productivity individuals with productivity a_1 have a reservation wage of v_1 while high-productivity individuals with productivity a_2, have a reservation wage of v_2. $\bar{a}$ is the mean productivity; obviously, at high wages, when everyone is willing to work, $a = \bar{a}$. The resulting productivity curve is depicted in Figure 14a.

A variant of this model arises when there are job-specific skills, and positive search costs; the larger the applicant pool, the higher the expected productivity, simply because the firm can find a larger number of individuals that fit in well with the need of the firm.

Capital market

The intuitive reasons for the presence of adverse selection in the capital market follow along parallel lines to those in the labor market (Stiglitz and Weiss 1981). The fact that an individual is willing to borrow from a bank at a 24 percent interest rate implies that

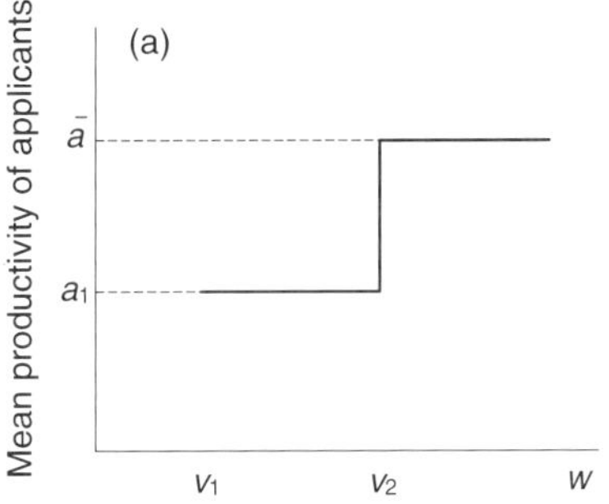
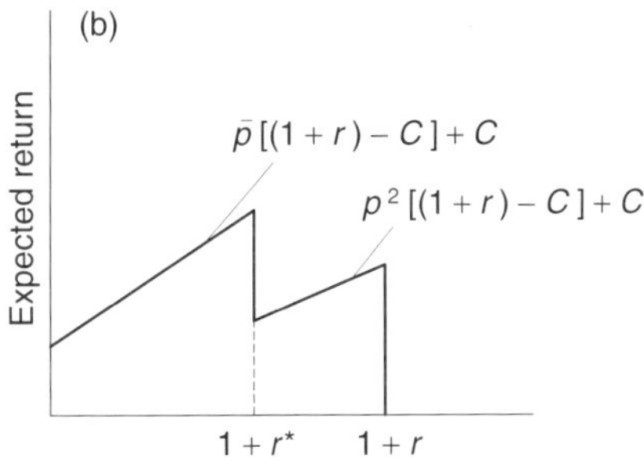

Figure 14(a) Wage productivity curve in two group model. (b) Expected return as function of interest rate change: two group model.

he has found no one else willing to lend to him at lower interest rate, and this fact conveys considerable information. Moreover, even if the individual had not been turned down by other banks, those who are undertaking very risky projects, with little prospect of repaying the loan, are likely to be less concerned about the interest rate they have promised to pay (when they do not default) than those who are undertaking safe projects and will always repay.

More formally, Stiglitz and Weiss (1981) consider a set of projects that the bank has identified as "similar." They all yield the same mean return, and require the same amount of bank finance. They show (*a*) the riskier projects[23] yield a lower return to the bank; (*b*) at any interest rate charged by the bank, firms with riskier projects apply, those with safer projects do not; and (*c*) as the bank increases the interest rate charged there is an adverse selection effect, with firms with the best projects (the least risky, i.e., those yielding the bank the highest expected return) no longer applying.[24] They show that the adverse selection effect may outweigh the direct gain from an increase in the interest rate. This may be seen most easily in the case where there are only two kinds of firms; each project costs B dollars, and is entirely bank financed. The firm is required to put up c dollars worth of collateral per dollar loaned, which it forfeits in the event of a default. The projects of type i firm yield a return of R^i if successful, and nothing otherwise; the probability of success is p^i. The expected return to the bank per dollar loaned from a loan to a firm of type i is just $p^i(1 + r) + (1 - p^i)c$, where r is the interest rate charged. Thus, if $p^1 > p^2$, *one* is the safe project and yields a higher return to the bank, provided $c < (1 + r)$, which it always would be (otherwise, the bank faces no risk).

The expected return to a firm of type i is $p^i[R^i - B(1 + r)] - cB(1 - p^i)$. It follows then that if the two projects have the same mean return, the riskier project yields the higher return to the firm. The safe firms no longer apply when

$$p^1[R^1 - (1 + r)B] - cB(1 - p^1) = 0.$$

Thus, for interest rates below $[p^1 R^1 - cB(1 - p^1)]/p^1 B - 1 = r^*$, both types of firm apply; for higher interest rates, only the risky firms apply. Even if at r^* there is an excess demand for funds, banks may not raise the interest rate (see Figure 14b).

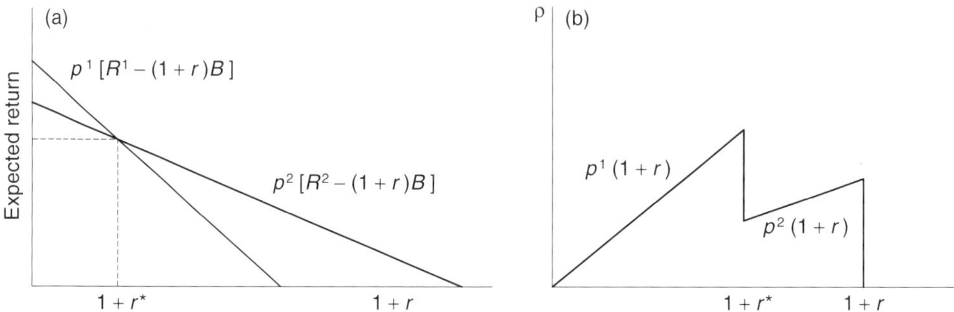

Figure 15. (a) Firm chooses safe project if and only if $r \leq r^*$. (b) Expected returns are maximized at r^*.

Incentive effects

We are concerned here with the variety of circumstances under which the quality of the product (the likelihood of bankruptcy, the productivity of a worker) is affected by actions of the seller (borrower, worker), and those actions are affected by the price (interest rate, wage). Two broad categories of models will be discussed, depending on whether there is or is not a long-term relationship. The latter are of particular interest; bad performance is (in these models) often punished by a termination of the relationship. For the threat of termination to be an effective incentive, the terms of the contract (relationship) must be such as to make that contract strictly better than that of the next best opportunity; e.g., price must be in excess of marginal cost or the wage paid must be higher than the minimum wage required to recruit the worker.

We now describe in greater detail the effects of wages, prices, or interest rates on economic incentives.

Capital markets

An increase in the interest rate charged on a loan may induce the borrower to undertake greater risks, lowering the expected return to the lender (William R. Keeton 1980; Stiglitz and Weiss 1981). This may be seen most simply in the case where the firm has two projects that it can undertake, each of which costs B. As before, project i has a return, if successful, of R^i, and the probability of success is p^i; if unsuccessful, the project yields no return. For simplicity, we ignore collateral. Then, the expected return to the firm of undertaking project i when the interest rate r is

$$p^i[R^i - (1+r)B].$$

As Figure 15 illustrates, the safe project 1 has a higher expected return to the form for $r \leq r^*$, where

$$(1+r^*)B = (p^1 R^1 - p^2 R^2)/(p^1 - p^2).$$

Thus, the bank will not raise the interest rate above r^*, even if there is an excess demand for funds at r^*, because to do so would induce firms to undertake the risky project, lowering the bank's return.

This is an example of what has come to be called a *principal-agent problem*.[25] The principal (here the bank) can exert only indirect control over the actions of the agent (the firm) and, he does so through the design of the payoff schedule. Changing the nominal price (here the interest rate) may have adverse (in terms of the interests of the principal) effects on the actions undertaken by the agent.

The discussion so far has focused on a single period model. Stiglitz and Weiss (1983) have extended the analysis to a multi (two) period model. They establish that the threat of *terminating* the credit relationship may have beneficial incentive effects and that terminations are a better incentive device than threats to charge higher interest rates (pay lower wages).

Their analysis is similar to the explanation of why the expected return may decrease with the rate of interest charged provided by the models of Jonathan Eaton and Mark Gersovitz (1980, 1981a, 1981b), Eaton (1985), and Franklin Allen (1980, 1981, 1983). They are concerned with situations where contracts are not enforceable. We might say that there are implicit contracts, which have to be designed to be self-enforcing. The terms of the contract determine whether, and under what circumstances, it will pay a borrower to refuse to repay a loan (for a sovereign to repudiate his debt).[26]

In these models, it is again the threat of termination of the relationship that induces the borrower to repay the loan. (In the Eaton–Gersovitz model, access to international capital markets enables the country to smooth out income variability). For any given amount loaned, the higher the rate of interest charged, the more likely it is that the loan will be repudiated.[27]

Labor markets

There are several different explanations for why the wage might affect the productivity of workers and the profitability of the firm.

Shirking.   (Walter J. Wessels 1979, 1985; Guillermo Calvo 1979; Calvo and Phelps 1977; Calvo and Stanislaw Wellisz 1979; Shapiro and Stiglitz 1984; Samuel Bowles 1985;[28] Stiglitz and Weiss 1983; Steve Stoft 1982). If there were no unemployment and if all firms paid the marketclearing wage, then the threat of being fired would not lead individuals to reduce their shirking: they would know that they could costlessly obtain another job. But if the firm pays wages in excess of that of other firms, or if there is unemployment (so that a fired worker must spend a period in the unemployment pool before he again obtains a job) then workers have an incentive not to shirk; there is a real cost to being fired.[29] One of the immediate consequences, then, of costly monitoring is that equilibrium must be characterized by unemployment and/or wage dispersion.

It also implies that the productivity of the worker hired by the ith firm, λ_i, is a function of the wage it pays, the wage paid by all other firms, w_{-i}, and the

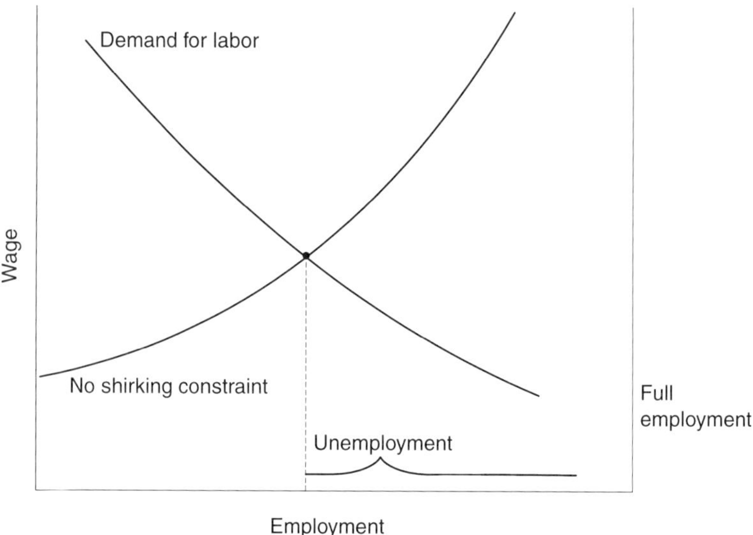

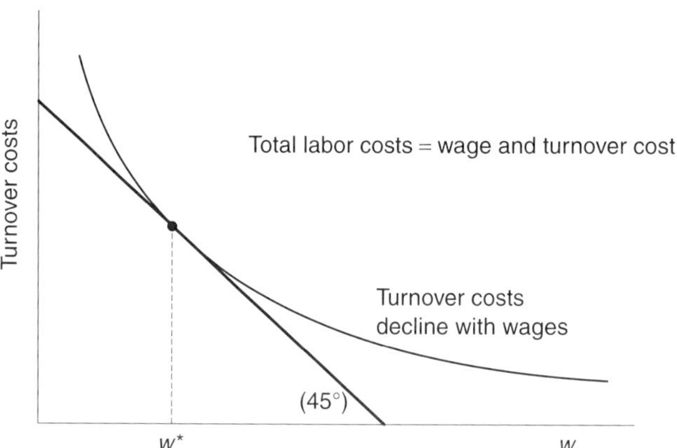

Figure 16. (a) Shirking Model. High wages and unemployment are necessary to induce workers not to shirk. (b) Labor turnover model. Total labor costs are minimized at w^*.

unemployment rate, U:

$$\lambda_i = \lambda_i(w_i, w_{-i}, U).$$

In the simplest version of the shirking model, workers either work or shirk; there is a critical wage below which the worker shirks. This critical wage is an increasing function of the employment level or of the wage differential between this firm and other firms. In the case where all firms pay the same wages, the so-called no-shirking constraint, giving the minimum wage below which shirking occurs, is depicted in Figure 16a. The demand for labor, given that workers do not shirk, is a decreasing function of the wage. Equilibrium, at the intersection of the demand curve and the no-shirking constraint, always entails unemployment.

Labor turnover.   (John Pencavel 1972; Wessels 1979; Stiglitz 1974b, 1974c, 1985; Robert Hall 1975; Salop 1973, 1979; Dybvig and Jaynes 1980; Ekkehart Schlicht 1978.) A second important way that workers' behavior affects the productivity of firms is through labor turnover.[30] In most jobs, there are costs to hiring and training that are specific to the firm. So long as individuals do not pay their full costs at the moment they are hired (recouping them later in the form of higher wages)[31] then the greater the quit rate, the greater the firm's expenditures on training and hiring costs. Increasing the wage rate (relative to wages paid by other firms) will, in general, lead to a reduction in the quit rate; there is a wage that minimizes total labor costs of the firm (Figure 16b). Moreover, the greater the unemployment rate, the less likely it is that the worker will find a better job. Because the effect of higher quit rates is to decrease the "net" productivity (net of turnover costs), we obtain a productivity wage relationship of the above form.

Morale effects.   (James E. Annable 1977, 1980, 1985; Stiglitz 1973, 1974a; Pencavel 1977; Akerlof 1984; Whiteside 1974.) Employers often allege that paying higher wage results in higher productivity, and not simply because of the greater penalty associated with being fired. A worker who believes he is being treated more than fairly may not only get more job satisfaction from his job, but also may put out more for his employer. And notions of fairness are closely related to how one *perceives* others of similar ability being treated. Thus, we can postulate than an individual's efforts depend not only on his own wage, but on the wage of others in his reference group, $\hat{w}$, the monitoring intensity, m, and the cost of being fired (the unemployment rate):[32]

$$e_i = e(w_i, \hat{w}, m, U).$$

The formal analysis of this model follows closely along the lines of that of the shirking model.[33] (It may, in fact, be possible to derive at least some variants of this morale model from a standard utility maximizing model, in which utility depends not only on effort and wages, but on relative wages.[34] Obviously, quit rates too depend on morale effects: Individuals may spend more resources searching for a better job if they believe that they are being unfairly treated on their present job.)

Sharecropping. (Stiglitz 1974d; David Newbery and Stiglitz 1979; Avishay Braverman and T. N. Srinivasan 1981; Braverman and Stiglitz 1982, 1986; Allen 1985a). It has long been recognized that increasing the share provided to the tenant worker could have beneficial effects on his work incentives, and thus could actually increase the receipts of the landlord.[35,36] It is possible that at the share at which the landlord's expected income is maximized, there is an excess supply of tenants.[37,38]

Product markets. (Joseph Farrell 1979, 1980; Shapiro 1983; Dybvig and Chester Spatt 1983; Allen 1984; Ben Klein and Keith B. Leffler 1981).

In the product market, incentive effects similar to those described earlier arise: Buyers often cannot ascertain the quality of a commodity before they purchase it. Earlier, we noted that the penalty associated with a worker caught shirking and who is thereupon fired depended on the wage relative to the wage paid by other firms and the cost of getting another job (which depends, in part, on the unemployment rate). Similarly, the penalty a customer levies on a firm that has cheated him is to terminate the relationship, and the penalty associated with this depends on how high the price is relative to the production costs (the profit the firm attains from the relationship) and how hard it is to recruit another, similar customer.

The essential insights are provided by the following simple model. Assume that the cost of production for a high-quality commodity is c^h, for a low-quality commodity is c^l, and the price is p. Assume that when a customer observes a bad-quality commodity, he infers that the seller will always continue to sell a bad quality. The bad quality commodity is worth nothing to the customer, so if he believes that the commodity is bad, he will terminate the relationship. Then, the value to the firm of continuing to product good-quality commodities is

$$(1 + r)(p - c^h)Q/r$$

where q is the quantity sold, r the rate of interest. The value of cheating and producing a bad quality commodity is

$$(p - c^l)Q.$$

Thus, for it to be worthwhile for the firm to produce good-quality commodities,

$$(1 + r)(p - c^h)/r > p - c^l$$

or

$$p > (1 + r)c^h - rc^l = p^*.$$

Accordingly, any individual who saw a firm attempting to sell a commodity for less than p^* would infer that that commodity was a low-quality commodity.[39]

Nutritional models

This paper focuses on the dependence of quality on price arising from imperfect information (adverse selection, moral hazard). But, as we noted, in one of the earliest sets of efficiency-wage models the quality of labor depended on the wage of nutritional reasons. How are these nutritional models related to the information models?

If the output of workers were perfectly observable, then presumably all workers would be paid on a piece rate basis. In equilibrium, some workers would be employed (at the efficiency wage), and other identical workers would be unemployed. Assume that workers get zero disutility from work, up to 40 hours per week, and infinite disutility thereafter (there is no disutility associated with effort up to a critical level λ, and infinite disutility thereafter) and that the output per unit time with the maximum effort level e is a function of nutrition. Then the number of labor units supplied will be a function of the wage rate. There is no way of obtaining any labor at a cost per efficiency unit of less than $w^*/\lambda(w^*)$. At wages in excess of w^* effective labor supply

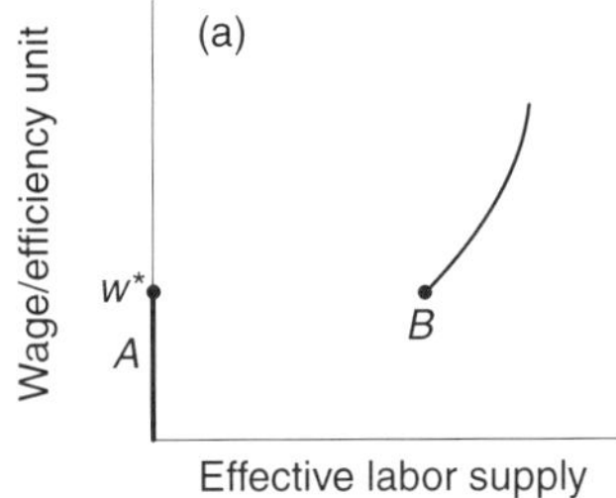

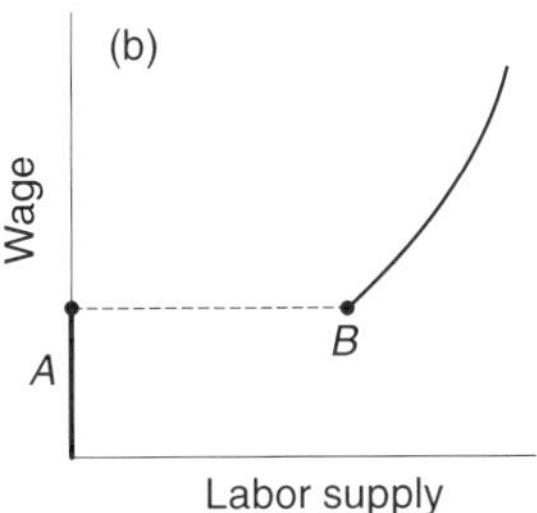

Figure 17(a) At wages below w^*, the effective labor supply is zero; at w^* it increases discontinuously. (b) With nonconvexities in preferences, labor supply may be discontinuous, but with continuum of individuals equilibrium exists.

increases, as depicted in Figure 17. Although, by assumption at w^*, each worker supplies either zero effective labor units or $\lambda(w^*)$, all workers strictly prefer to supply the latter; at w^* there is an excess supply of labor.

Although nutritional models can give rise to unemployment even if workers are paid on a piece rate basis, they obviously can also give rise to unemployment when piece rates are not feasible; thus, in the example given above, there are no incentive problems, whether workers are paid on a piece rate basis or not.[40]

Thus, the nutritional efficiency-wage models, while differing in fundamental ways from the informational efficiency-wage models in their microfoundations, yield similar conclusions: They generate similar reduced form relationships between productivity and the wage paid by the firm, wages paid by other firms, and the unemployment rate. It is worth noting, however, that in one polar form of the efficiency-wage model, where individuals do not share any of their income with others, productivity depends only on the absolute value of the wage paid by the firm; accordingly the equilibrium wage will be independent of the unemployment rate. (This stands in contrast with several versions of the informational efficiency-wage model, where relative wages and the unemployment rate are the primary determinants of productivity.)

THE IMPLICATIONS OF THE DEPENDENCE OF QUALITY ON PRICE FOR ECONOMIC THEORY

Differences between economies in which the law of supply and demand is repealed and those where it still holds

It is useful to clarify the differences between the assumptions in our analysis and those that are (often implicit) in the traditional competitive paradigm, e.g., of the model of Arrow and Debreu. Arrow and Debreu assume that each employer has perfect information concerning the quality of his labor, that each buyer of a commodity has perfect information concerning the quality of the commodities which he purchases, and that each lender has perfect information concerning the characteristics of those to whom he lends. Thus, when they speak of a market for a commodity, they have in mind a market for a collection of objects, all of which are identical, at least in all relevant aspects. The person buying a commodity or hiring on the market is completely indifferent about which commodity he obtains; the firm hiring a worker is indifferent about which worker he obtains, and no additional information would change his indifference.

This assumption of a competitive market for homogeneous commodities is neither plausible nor innocuous. Markets in which commodities are completely homogeneous—with respect to location and the date as well as other characteristics—are almost inherently sufficiently thin so that the postulate of perfect competition is inapplicable. Markets that are sufficiently "thick" to be competitive are almost always nonhomogeneous. Consider the market for labor. If we define a submarket, say, J. E. Stiglitz's labor, then it may be homogeneous, but hardly competitive; if we take a broader definition of the market, say, those with PhDs in economics, it may be fairly competitive, but it is hardly homogeneous.

The problems with which we are concerned are central in capital markets and insurance markets. Both markets are essentially intertemporal: In the capital market, the lender lends the borrower money today, in return for a promise to repay $\$(1 + r)$ next period, provided the borrower can; in the insurance market, the insurer agrees today to pay the insured a given amount next period if a particular event occurs. The lender cares about the likelihood that the borrower will default; the insurer cares about the likelihood that the insured against event will occur. Borrowers (the insured) differ, but lenders (insurers) cannot tell who is more likely to default (to have an accident).

Moreover, the probability of default (of an accident) can be affected by the actions of the borrower (insured).

The Arrow–Debreu model does not actually require perfect information. What it does require is that the nature of the "commodity" be fixed (i.e., that the average quality of labor be unaffected by prices or wages and that average default (accident) probability be unaffected by the terms of the loan (insurance policy)). There can be neither adverse selection or moral hazard effects; that is, if all individuals (commodities) are not identical, at least the mix of types is fixed *and* any actions which they might take that affect their productivity (or default, or accident, probabilities) are observable.

Many economic relationships involve an element of insurance and/or loan. This is the case, for instance, with most employment and rental arrangements.

There is one set of circumstances under which a firm does not care about the characteristics of those it hires. If the firm can perfectly and costlessly monitor the *actions*[41] of its employees, and pay the employee for the services performed, and there are no fixed costs associated with hiring a worker, then the firm is unconcerned whether the worker is a low-ability worker pulling out three medium sized weeds a day, or a high-productivity worker pulling out three hundred a day. It pays a fixed price per medium sized weed pulled out.

In fact, relatively few workers are paid even partially on a piece rate basis (which is not to say that performance goes unrewarded, either in terms of promotions or salary). The literature on compensation schemes details a number of reasons for this, all of which attest to the importance of the informational concerns that are the center of our analysis (Stiglitz 1975) but are completely ignored in the traditional competitive paradigm.[42]

Because most workers are not paid a piece rate equal to the value of their marginal product, and because there are costs associated with hiring workers, some of which are borne by the firm, firms are concerned both about the quality of the workers they hire, their productivity on the job, and their turnover rate.[43] The wage affects all of these variables. And so long as that is the case, the possibilities with which we have been concerned here—that equilibrium will be characterized by an excess supply of labor, and/or by a wage distribution—are real possibilities.[44]

It should be noted that most of the issues with which we have been concerned here would arise so long as individuals are not paid on a piece rate, regardless of the reason. Similarly, if the firm must pay a uniform wage to all workers, even though it knows which workers are more productive, it will worry about the adverse selection effects of lowering wages.

The conventional models assume not only that there is not imperfect information concerning what is being bought, but also, in trades which occur over time, that there are no *enforcement* problems. In fact, of course, there are important enforcement problems, arising both from the incompleteness of contracts and from the costs of enforcing the contract terms that are explicit.[45]

The nutritional efficiency wage models can give rise to unemployment even without informational problems, as we have already noted. These models differ from the conventional Arrow–Debreu model in two technical respects, which turn out to be important: There is a nonconvexity associated with the productivity wage relationship, and in equilibrium individuals are on the boundary of their feasible set.[46]

Alternative equilibrium concepts

In the first section we argued that when quality depends on price, equilibrium may be characterized by markets not clearing. In traditional economic theory, equilibrium is defined as market clearing. Clearly, different notions of equilibrium are being employed. Indeed, even within the literature recognizing the dependence of quality on price, more than one equilibrium notion has been employed, with contrasting results. In this section, we review and contrast several of the more important equilibrium concepts that have been used.

Walrasian versus rationing equilibria

In models where quality depends on price, there may exist a market-clearing price, for instance, a wage at which demand equals supply. We referred to this as the Walrasian equilibrium, but this may *not* be a market equilibrium. Whenever in the labor market there is a region where cost per effective labor unit decreases with an increase in the wage, or in the capital market there is a region where the expected return decreases with an increase in the interest rate, there *may* exist an equilibrium with excess supply of labor or excess demand for capital. Indeed, there always exists some level of demand for labor or supply of funds for which this is true.[47]

It is important to emphasize that we are not arguing here that equilibrium is *never* characterized by the equality of demand and supply, only that it may not be.[48]

The *Walrasian wage (interest rate)* is the market equilibrium if and only if there exists no higher wage (*lower interest rate*) at which costs per efficiency unit (*expected returns*) are lower (*higher*).[49]

The choice of appropriate equilibrium concepts

Our analysis thus differs from the standard Arrow–Debreu model not only in its informational assumptions, but also in its definition of equilibrium. Traditional theory has taken the equality of supply and demand to be part of the definition of equilibrium. This, I think, is wrong.

Equilibrium is defined, loosely, as a state where no economic agents have an incentive to change their behavior. Whether a particular configuration of the economy is an equilibrium depends, then, on agents' perceptions of the consequences of changes in their behavior. If employers believed that at a lower wage they would obtain exactly the same qualify of laborers as they obtained at a higher wage, then clearly, if a worker offered to work for a wage lower than that of existing workers, the firm would hire him (assuming there were no further repercussions of what might be viewed by other workers as antisocial behavior).[50] Under these circumstances, equilibrium would be characterized by demand equaling supply.

The fact that under these circumstances equilibrium is characterized by demand equaling supply is thus a theorem (admittedly trivial) to be proven; the equality of demand and supply should not be taken as a definition of equilibrium, but rather as a consequence following from more primitive behavioral postulates. What we have established in this paper is that, under plausible behavioral postulates, equilibrium may not be characterized by demand equaling supply. At the same time, it should be emphasized that our economy is competitive in the conventional sense in which that word is used: We are concerned with atomistic equilibria, in which all agents are small relative to the market though in spite of this they are not price takers.[51]

Passive versus active sellers and buyers

While the models presented here differ from the conventional competitive paradigm both in informational assumptions and in the equilibrium concept, these models differ from Akerlof's analysis of adverse selection only with respect to the equilibrium concept. In Akerlof's model, as in the traditional perfect information model, however, both buyers and sellers act completely passively. For instance, although firms know the statistical relationship between the wage paid and the productivity of the workers they hire, they do not try to use this knowledge to increase their profits, e.g., by setting wages at other than a market-clearing level. We would argue that there is, in most situations, no persuasive reason to limit out uninformed agents to the passive role that conventional theory has assigned to them.

Nonprice rationing

A number of writers have argued that when, in the capital market, interest rates cannot fall, there are other methods by which markets can be made to clear; similarly, in labor markets, when wages cannot fall, there are other methods by which markets can be made to clear. In markets with imperfect information, contractual arrangements involve more than a single term; and it must be shown that none of these can adjust in a way as to restore market clearing. There may be adverse selection and incentive effects from changes in each of the contract terms.

In the capital market, emphasis has been placed on the role of collateral. Increasing collateral does induce firms to undertake less risky projects, but may have adverse selection effects (Stiglitz and Weiss 1981; Hildegard Wette 1983; Gerhard E. Clemenz 1984, 1985; Chang-Ho Yoon 1984, 1985). Several authors (e.g., Helmut Bester 1985) have constructed models in which, if banks can design contracts with varying interest rates and collateral, there will be no credit rationing.

It is important to recall that our contention has been not that equilibrium would always be characterized by credit rationing, but that it may be, under plausible conditions. Indeed, it is easy to construct examples in which equilibrium is not characterized by credit rationing. Bester (1985) and David Besanko and Anjan Thakor (1984) provide examples with the peculiar property in that bankers can obtain, through offering a set of contracts, perfect information concerning their borrowers. By contrast, Stiglitz and Weiss (1986a, 1986b) argue that as long as there is a residual of imperfect information there may be scope for credit rationing.[52]

In the Stiglitz–Weiss models, each borrower borrows the same amount. Another term of the contract that can adjust is the amount lent. Under certain circumstances, reducing the amount lent reduces the risk faced by the bank. Thus, adjustments in the loan size can eliminate credit rationing (H. Milde and John Riley 1984). Again, the issue is not whether one can construct examples in which rationing does not occur, but rather, are there alternative, plausible structures under which it does. In a multiperiod context, Stiglitz and Weiss (1981) have shown that reducing the size of the loan may have an adverse effect on the risks undertaken by the borrower; they undertake projects that in effect, "force" the lender to ante up more money in subsequent periods, if they are to recover their initial loans (see also Martin Hellwig 1977).

In the labor market, discussions have focused on the role of bonding and "job" purchases. That is, a worker could put down a sum of money that he surrenders in the event of being caught shirking. Bonding, it is argued, can alleviate the incentive problems. B. Curtis Eaton and William White (1982), Shapiro and Stiglitz (1984, 1985a), Edward Lazear (1982), and Stoft (1985) have argued against this on several grounds: Firstly, they note that with young individuals having limited capital there is, at least for these workers, incomplete bonding, so that firms are, in fact, concerned with the relationship between wages and productivity. (Though they could borrow to put up the bond, this simply shifts who bears the risk that the worker fails to perform, from the firm to the lender. Though nonvested pensions can be viewed as a form of bonding, it takes individuals a number of years to accumulate enough within their pension fund to serve as a sufficiently effective bond to eliminate the need for firms to be concerned with whether their workers shirk.) Secondly, they note the "double moral hazard" problem, the incentive of the firm to declare that the worker has shirked when he has not. This may be alleviated by making the bond forfeiture go to a third party: again, the empirical relevance may be questioned; moreover such arrangements are sensitive to complicity by two of the parties against the third.[53] Thirdly, they note that many individuals may not have funds to post a bond; to borrow the funds would entail all the adverse effects noted earlier in our discussion of capital markets; and to restrict applicants to those who could finance the bond themselves would have the adverse selection effects noted earlier in connection with collateral.

Similar problems arise with job purchases (or, what is equivalent, in the context of labor turnover, with requiring individuals to pay for their full costs of training).[54]

Advocates of the efficiency wage models claim, in the end, that the central point is that firms do care about quit rates, they do care about the incentives of their workers, and they do use wage policies to affect the net profitability of their employees.

Other imperfect information models

The last two decades have seen a burgeoning in imperfect information models. It is worth noting the relationships between the models that are the center of discussion here and some of these other models.

Prices versus quantities

Earlier literature (Rothschild and Stiglitz 1976; Akerlof 1976; Michael Spence 1974) stressed the role of *quantities* in conveying information; the literature this chapter is concerned with stresses the role of prices on conveying information.

The quantity of education obtained by an individual conveys information because it is more costly for a less able individual to acquire education than for a more able individual. But it is no more costly for a less able individual to announce that he is willing to work only at a higher wage than a more able individual. How then can workers (informed sellers) use prices to convey information about themselves? There must be some cost to announcing a higher reservation price: The price is the lower probability of being employed (or selling one's commodity). Stiglitz (1976a) and Nalebuff and Stiglitz (1982) have constructed models in which higher-quality workers are willing to face a higher probability of not obtaining a job because their fallback wage is higher. (Wilson (1979, 1980) has constructed a similar model for the product market.)[55] Thus, if there are two types of workers, whose reduced form utility function can be represented by $U_i = U_i(w, g)$, where g is the probability of obtaining a job, then equilibrium may be characterized by both groups obtaining wages commensurate with their abilities (though employers cannot observe them directly), but with the low-ability individuals having a probability g^* just large enough to induce the low-ability not to apply, i.e., letting superscript 1 denote the low-ability workers

$$U^1(w^1, 1) = U^1(w^2, g^*)$$

(See Figure 18).[56,57]

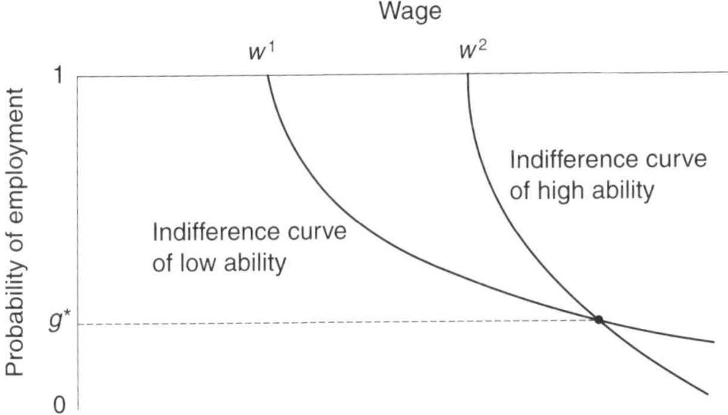

Figure 18. Wage and probability of employment acting as self-selection device.

In the simple models analyzing the dependence of quality on price, quantity variables are not observable. (There is no variable, like education, to reveal the individual's true ability.) But all that is required for wages/prices/interest rates to play a role in conveying quality information given whatever variables that are observable is that there remains some residual uncertainty of either the adverse selection or moral hazard sort.[58]

Information revealing prices in the capital market

There is a closely related literature to that discussed here, where prices also convey information. In capital markets, the price at which a security sells may convey information concerning the expected return of the security (or the likelihood of the occurrence of various states). (See Green 1973; Grossman and Stiglitz 1976, 1980; Margaret Bray 1981; Roy Radner 1979.) In structure, these models are most likely the Akerlof "Lemons" (1970) model, in which both sellers and buyers act nonstrategically: They take prices, and the information conveyed by the price, as given. They differ in that, while there is only one seller (and usually only one buyer) of any particular automobile, or any particular person's labor services, there are many potential buyers and sellers of any particular security. (Indeed, in the absence of transactions costs, with risk aversion and imperfectly correlated securities, virtually everyone is a buyer or seller.) Thus, while the price of a car sold at an auction reflects the valuation placed on it by those who value it most highly, in a security market, those who believe that a security is overpriced will sell it short, and their beliefs are, accordingly, reflected in the market equilibrium price.

APPLICATIONS

Implications for macroeconomics

These models have direct and important implications for macroeconomics.[59]

This section is divided into four subsections, dealing respectively with labor markets, capital markets, product markets, and the relationship of these theories to other recently advanced theories.

Labor markets

The fact that these theories have yielded competitive market equilibrium in which wages do not fall in the face of unemployment, in which there is an equilibrium level unemployment, immediately suggests the possibility that these theories may provide an important part of the explanation of involuntary unemployment. This is an area of active ongoing research and controversy. What I wish to do here is to explain why some economists find these models more persuasive than at least several of the competing theories, and to present what appear to be at the present time the major issues, both the criticism and the defenses, pointing to certain unsettled controversies.

The pattern and form of unemployment. A theory purporting to explain cyclical fluctuations in unemployment should not only show that it can generate unemployment, but also explain the pattern and form of unemployment. This efficiency-wage theories do.[60] Less productive workers—those for whom the minimum wage per efficiency unit is below some critical level—cannot get jobs, though they might at higher levels of effective demand. (These may include young workers, part-time workers, or others for whom the total surplus from work is small, so that the no-shirking wage, at any unemployment level, is high.)

Moreover, there is no work sharing, with the associated income reductions, for this would simply reduce the quality (productivity) of the labor force. In the incentive efficiency-wage model, it is the total surplus (the amount by which the value of wage payments exceeds the forgone leisure) that determines whether workers shirk; in the turnover model, it is the total surplus (relative to that offered by other firms) that determines whether a worker quits; in the selection models, it is again the total surplus that determines the individual's choice of one job over another. Work sharing reduces the surplus available to any individual, and thus adversely affects the effort (quality, labor turnover). See, for example, Arnott, Hosios, and Stiglitz (1983) or Michael Hoel and Bent Vale (1986).

Criticisms. Critics have raised several objections, concerning both the quantitative significance of the efficiency-wage effects and the consistency of the theory with certain observed macroeconomic phenomena.

1. *Can efficiency wage theory explain involuntary unemployment?* Perhaps the most widely cited criticism is that, unless efficiency wage considerations are important in all sectors, the theory cannot explain unemployment; that is, if there is some sector (such as agriculture) where workers can be paid on a piece rate basis, and the piece rate is flexible, then that sector should absorb all workers laid off from those sectors where efficiency-wage considerations are important. Thus, efficiency-wage theory might be able to explain wage differentials (the secondary labor market), but not unemployment. (Note that this objection can be raised against implicit contract theory explanations of unemployment as well.)[61]

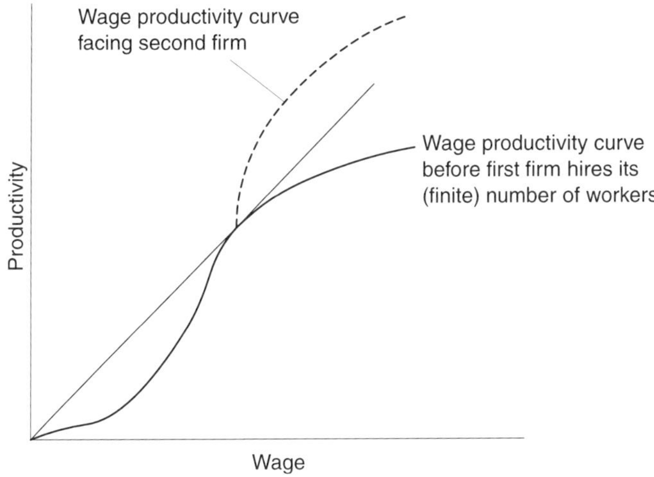

Figure 19. The advantages of being late.

Several of the efficiency-wage models have attempted to incorporate a flexible wage sector. In Stiglitz (1974c), for instance, the agricultural sector has flexible wages, while efficiency-wage considerations are important in the industrial sector. Individuals must choose in which sector to locate (mobility between the sectors is not costless and instantaneous). Unemployment in the urban sector is such as to equilibrate expected income (of the marginal migrant) in that sector to that in the rural sector.[62]

Jeremy Bulow and Larry Summers (1985) assume that individuals can search for a (high-wage) job only while unemployed, and thus even if individuals could have obtained a low-wage job, they choose not to do so.[63]

Greenwald has provided several alternative explanations for why individuals may not accept a low-wage job, based on information theoretic considerations: Accepting a low-wage job may convey information about the individual's ability; with high-ability individual's expecting to get a "good" job sooner than a low-ability individual, an individual who readily accepts a low-wage job signals that he thinks of himself as low-ability, and this signal will lower his future wages.[64] Moreover, accepting a job creates an information asymmetry—the firm's new employer will know more about the individual's ability than other prospective employers. Just as Akerlof showed that these information asymmetries lead to thin markets for used cars, Greenwald has shown that they result in thin markets for "used labor".[65] Finally, he has attempted to relate unemployment to capital market imperfections, which themselves can be explained by information theoretic concerns. There are, in general, some training costs that firms must bear when they hire a worker; moreover, hiring a worker represents a risky investment. With imperfect capital markets, firms cannot divest themselves of this risk; as a result, the implicit cost of capital may be very high in a recession, and hence it is possible that in a recession, firms are willing to hire workers only if the lifetime wages are lower than they would be if the worker were hired in a later period, when the risks faced by the firm are less.

Critics might say at this juncture, "Aha, so unemployment is really voluntary". We think little is gained from a semantic debate, over whether unemployment is, in this sense, voluntary or involuntary. What is critical is (a) in the market equilibrium, some individuals, with a given set of characteristics, have a distinctly higher level of (expected) utility than other similar individuals; (b) the equilibrium has, for one reason or another, some individuals in the unemployment pool who, under other circumstances, would be working; and (c) the market equilibrium is not (constrained) Pareto efficient.

2. *Are there alternative mechanisms for ensuring quality?* A second criticism is that if these efficiency-wage considerations were really important, alternative mechanisms would be found that would not be anywhere hear as socially costly as the unemployment to which it gives rise. There are several answers to this objection: Firstly, the fact of the matter is that firms are concerned about the quality of their labor force and their rates of turnover. Secondly, we have already detailed some reasons why at least some of the proposed alternatives that would eliminate unemployment (credit rationing) may be ineffective. Some of these arguments may hold with more force for some groups of workers or for some industries than for others. Thus, consider the argument that bonding is not employed because workers have insufficient capital. This argument seems more applicable to young workers and to low-wage (unskilled) workers than to older workers, and therefore might suggest that the effort-efficiency wage model is more relevant for these workers than for other groups of laborers.[66]

Finally, we note that because of the presence of the important externalities discussed earlier, the private costs of pursuing, say, high-wage policies (leading to unemployment) and of not employing alternative strategies of sorting and providing incentives may be much less than the social costs. This has been stressed by Akerlof and Janet Yellen (1985).[67] In particular, if firms are risk averse [68] then they may not revise their wages or may not change other policies even in the presence of some disturbance to the economy which leads to an excess supply of labor, even if were they to do so would be welfare enhancing.

3. *Can efficiency wage theory explain nominal as well as real wage rigidities?* Although the criticism that these models provide an explanation of real-wage rigidities, not of nominal-wage rigidities, is valid against most versions of the efficiency-wage models—as it is against most versions of implicit contract theory (where, in principle, contracts should be indexed)—it is worth noting that the labor-turnover efficiency-wage model is also consistent with money-wage rigidities: The turnover rate facing any firm depends on the wages set by other firms; if each firm believes that other firms will leave the wages unchanged in nominal terms, it pays it to leave its wage unchanged in nominal terms. The Akerlof (1984) morale model is also consistent with nominal-wage rigidities.

4. *Can efficiency wage theory explain rationing among several groups?* Simpler versions of the efficiency wage theory yielded rationing for only one group in the population. For all other groups, either no one was hired or there was full employment. But with more general specifications, with productivity depending on (each group's) unemployment rate then in equilibrium, there may be unemployment among several groups. And even if there were a continuum of groups, with only one group rationed the

discontinuity in utility (between similar groups) would remain. It is this discontinuity—with similar individuals being treated discretely differently—which is so much at odds with standard competitive theory.

5. *Can efficiency wage theory explain wage and employment dynamics?* The final criticism[69] is that while the efficiency-wage theory may provide an explanation of the "natural unemployment rate," it does not provide an explanation of cyclical movements in real wages. This criticism takes on two forms. First, it is observed, that in a recession, increases in unemployment (reductions in relevant opportunities, including self-employment income) should result in lower wages in the effort-efficiency wage models. Whether this is in fact the case is debatable; if the quality of workers laid off in a recession is, on average, lower than those retained (a pattern that itself is consistent with efficiency wage theory), then even if the average product wage does not fall much, the quality adjusted product wage may. Moreover, what is relevant for the incentive-based efficiency-wage theory is the lifetime return from holding a job; with low discount rates and long lifetimes, disturbances to the economy may leave this relatively unaffected. Though the value of alternative opportunities may decrease in a recession, thus enabling a myopic firm to lower its wage without inducing shirking, nonmyopic firms will realize that the value of the job is enhanced by the implicit insurance provided through income smoothing.[70,71] (On the other hand, because unemployment benefits are typically lengthened during recessions, and the stigma associated with being laid off is decreased, it may actually be worthwhile for firms to raise wages in recessions.)

Still, the criticism that the efficiency wage theories have yet to provide a dynamic theory is, for the most part, valid: The models constructed to date have been static. At a heuristic level, these models do provide an explanation for why when there is a sudden shift in, say, the demand for labor, it is not quickly reflected in a change in the wage, but rather is reflected in a decrease in employment; the new equilibrium may entail unemployment, but even if in the long run equilibrium entails full employment of labor, the adjustment process may entail unemployment as part of the transition.

The intuitive reason for this is easy to see. Under a variety of conditions, the quality of the workers obtained (or their productivity on the job) depends on the wage paid by the given firm relative to that of other firms. Thus, if the different firms in the economy do not simultaneously adjust their wages, given the high wages of other firms, it will not pay any single firm to lower its wage very much.[72]

Our analysis of dynamics stands in marked contrast to the standard kind of dynamics, which simply assumes slowness in the adjustment of wages and prices, and thus derives the transitional unemployment as a consequence of the ad hoc dynamic adjustment assumptions.

Consider, for instance, the staggered wage contract model (Taylor 1980). The *assumption* of nonsynchronous long-term contracts explains why wages at any particular firm do not fall instantaneously in the face of a decrease in the demand for labor, and why average wages fall only gradually. But in the absence of some kind of efficiency-wage story, staggered contracts cannot explain the persistence, even for a short while, of unemployment: At the first instance at which a contract comes up for renewal, the wage should fall to the market-clearing level.

Moreover, the explanation of the process by which wages change is markedly different from the conventional story. We have argued that in general the quality of the labor force (its productivity) depends on the unemployment rate as well as the wage. At higher unemployment levels, the efficiency wage may be lower. For a variety of reasons, firms may be slow to fire workers, and thus the unemployment rate increases only slowly in response to a decrease in the "long-run" demand for workers. In such circumstances, the fall in the wage rate can be viewed both as a consequence of the increased unemployment and as mitigating the extent to which unemployment increases. But in this theory the wage does not fall because of the "pressure" of excess supply directly on the labor market, but only because of the indirect effect, through the effect on the efficiency wage.

Capital markets

We have already noted how the theory we have presented provides a theory of credit rationing. Credit rationing, in turn, may provide both an explanation of why, and the mechanism by which, government policy affects the macroeconomic equilibrium (Alan Blinder and Stiglitz 1983), and a part of the explanation of why the effective cost of capital actually rises in the recession (Greenwald and Stiglitz 1986c, 1986d).[73]

Information concerning the nature of borrowers is firm-specific and not easily transferable. Accordingly, when the monetary authorities reduce the supply of high-power money, banks reduce the credit that they make available. Monetary policy, in this view, has effects not through the rate of interest (variations in real rates of interest until recently have been too small to account for much of the variability in investment or savings), but through its effects on the supply of credit. This theory agrees with the monetarists that the quantity of money may, as a result, play a more important role than the interest rate, but unlike the monetarists, provides a plausible mechanism by which these effects are realized.[74,75]

The increased uncertainty, for example, associated with recessionary periods, results in some groups being rationed out of the market who previously had not been. Moreover, other groups anticipate that the likelihood that they may be rationed out of the market sometime in the future has increased. Firms face, or anticipate facing, a liquidity crisis, one that may result in their bankruptcy; For them the effective cost of capital has increased. Thus, recessionary periods may be characterized by high effective interest rates (in contrast to low nominal interest rates, emphasized in the traditional literature); high effective interest rates can partly explain many of the anomolous features of the business cycle, including patterns of inventory accumulation (with a low shadow price on labor and low interest rates, there should be much more production smoothing than does in fact occur) and some aspects of pricing policies.[76]

Product markets

Allen (1985b) has emphasized an alternative explanation for why firms may not lower prices in the face of a downward shift in the demand for their products: To do so could be interpreted as a signal of a deterioration of quality.

Relationship to other macrotheories

We have already discussed briefly some of the contrasting implications of efficiency-wage theory and implicit contract theory.

Insider–Outsider theory.   Another important recent development is commonly called insider-outsider theory (Lindbeck and Snower 1984a, 1984b, 1986, 1987; Robert Solow 1985). This theory stresses the asymmetries between insiders (the firm's current employees) and outsiders (potential employees). These theories provide alternative explanations for why net profits of the firm might be reduced if a firm hired new workers at much lower wages; for example, the current workers, recognizing the threat that these workers pose to them, may refuse to provide them training. These theories are thus perfectly consistent with efficiency wage theories.[77]

Fixed price models and efficiency wage theories.   One of the reasons for interest in the efficiency wage theories is that they provide an explanation of wage and price rigidities, which play such a central role in the fixed wage-price models that have enjoyed such popularity during the past decade. Though the two approaches are, to that extent complementary,[78] the efficiency-wage models can also be seen as providing a critique of the fixed-wage models, or at least of the relevance of those models for policy purposes. Though wages do not fall to a market-clearing level, government policies can affect the level of wages and thus the equilibrium level of employment. (In contrast, the fixed-wage price models simply assume that wages and prices will remain unchanged.)

Multipliers.   Multipliers have had a long and noble history in macroeconomic analysis. It has not been widely recognized how difficult it is to obtain multipliers in conventional models: Usually price responses in stable systems dampen the effect of any initial disturbance. It is precisely because of price rigidities that traditional macroeconomic models yield multipliers. Our analysis provides the microfoundations of these price rigidities.[79]

Implications for development economics

We noted earlier that much of the recent interest in the unemployment consequences of the dependence of productivity on wages originated in the development literature, where the relationship was attributed to nutritional considerations. Since then a large literature has explored a variety of other causes and consequences of the wage-productivity nexus within LDCs.[80]

Mirrlees (1975) and Stiglitz (1976b) showed that wage-productivity relations of the form depicted in Figure 2 would give rise, even within utilitarian families (maximizing the sum of the utility of the members of the family) to inequality in consumption; some members would receive a low consumption level, others a high consumption level; those with a low consumption level would have a low productivity. What they consumed would exceed their marginal product, but be less than their marginal product plus a pro rata share of the rents. Conversely for the high consumers. Indeed, even if the family is Rawlsian (maximizes the welfare of the worst off individual) there may be consumption inequality.

Because productivity depends on consumption, individuals with landholdings will be more productive than landless workers, and will, accordingly, receive higher wages. Dasgupta and Ray (1986a, 1987) have explored the implications of inequality in land ownership for wages and output. In particular, they note that the very poor, those with very small landholdings, may be completely excluded from the market because their minimum wage costs per efficiency unit is too high. In their model, whether the economy is in an unemployment regime or a full employment regime will depend on the aggregate land supply (relative to the labor supply), in effect, on whether the Walrasian wage is below or above the efficiency wage; it may also depend on the distribution of land. A land reform may thus have a significant effect on national output.

The dependence of productivity on wages in the urban sector results in urban wages being set at levels in excess of the rural wage. This, by the familiar Harris–Todaro migration mechanism (Todaro 1968, 1969; Harris and Todaro 1970) and its generalizations (Stiglitz 1974c; Gary Fields 1975; Raaj Sah and Stiglitz 1984, 1985), results in urban unemployment. As noted earlier, the wage and employment levels set by private firms do not maximize national income (and are not Pareto efficient). On the other hand, even if the government could directly control the urban wage, it would not set it at the rural wage. Some level of unemployment is optimal. Moreover, policy prescriptions to reduce the real wage indirectly, through increasing the prices of commodities, are, at best, misguided. For private firms would respond, say, to an increase in the price of food by increasing the wage. Indeed, if productivity is more sensitive to the consumption of food than to the consumption of other commodities, government should subsidize the consumption of food.[81] In this context, specific and ad valorem wage subsidies have distinctly different effects on wage setting and employment policies. Because there are two objectives that the government wishes to achieve (the correct wage level and the correct urban employment level), it requires two instruments; the two forms of wage subsidies/taxes provide the requisite instruments.

The wage-productivity nexus also has important implications for the determination of the shadow wage of labor (particularly in the context of models with Harris–Todaro and related migration mechanisms). The opportunity cost of labor is not zero (in spite of the presence of unemployment) or even the rural wage. In some central cases, the shadow wage is the urban wage, independent of attitudes toward future generations; in other cases, it lies between the urban wage and the rural wage (see Stiglitz 1982a).

Further applications

The dependence of quality on price has a large number of other implications, two of which we briefly note here.

Technological change and competitive entry

The fact that a lower price is associated with lower quality has important implications for technological change. Normally, we argue that if a firm develops a cheaper way of making a mousetrap it will be able to undercut its rivals, and thus to capture the whole market for itself. When prices convey information, the firm may not be able to undercut its rivals; lowering the price may simply lead potential customers to believe that it is selling a lower-quality mousetrap. (Farrell 1984, 1985, has discussed the entry barriers that arise in these models.)

The consequences of the wage–quality relationship in noncompetitive markets

The analysis so far has been confined to competitive markets. But similar results apply to noncompetitive markets as well.

The standard theory maintains that a monopsonist would never ration. For at the given price, if there is an excess demand he can increase his profits simply by increasing his price. Similarly, a monopsonist in the labor market would never pay a wage in excess of the minimum wage required to hire the number of workers he wishes; there would never be an excess supply of workers (though the number of workers hired may be less than in a competitive market-clearing equilibrium). But if the firm recognizes that by raising the wage it increases the quality of its labor force, it may minimize its wage costs by paying a wage that is above the minimum required to obtain the amount of labor that it wishes to obtain. Similarly, in the capital market, a monopoly bank may charge an interest rate below the market-clearing level, recognizing that in doing so it increases its expected returns.

Earlier, we showed how, in a competition market, wages cum queues would screen individuals; more able individuals might be willing to take the risk of applying for a high-wage job, with a low probability of getting the job, when an (observationally identical) individual of lesser ability would not. The monopsonist would similarly attempt to use wages cum queues to differentiate among workers.

Still, it should be emphasized that the motives for differentiating among individuals (customers or workers) are markedly different under monopoly than under competition: Under competition, the motive is simply to identify workers who differ in productivity, while under monopoly, the motive is to discriminate, to capture as much of the consumer surplus from each worker/customer as possible.

CONCLUDING REMARKS

There is little doubt that the observation that quality may depend on price (productivity on wages; default probability on interest rates) has provided a rich mine for economic theorists: A simple modification of the basic assumptions results in a profound alteration of many of the basic conclusions of the standard paradigm. The Law of Supply and Demand has been repealed. The Law of the Single Price has been repealed. The Fundamental Theorem of Welfare Economics has been shown not to be valid.

More than that, the theories that we describe here provide the basis of progress toward a unification of macroeconomics and microeconomics. They provide an explanation of unemployment and credit rationing, derived from basic microeconomic principles. It is a theory in which the extensive idleness that periodically confronts society's resources, human and capital, is seen as but the most obvious example of market failures that pervasively and persistently distort the allocation of resources.

Several caveats should, however, be borne in mind. Firstly, the repeal of the Law of Supply and Demand (and the Law of the Single Price) is a selective repeal: We have not contended that equilibrium is never described by the equality of demand and supply, only that it need not be, and will not be in some important circumstances.

Secondly, though the basic outlines of the general theory appear now to be well established, there remain several important extensions and developments. We have referred to several of these within the text. The models presented here were, for the most part, static; it is imperative to develop an explicitly dynamic model if these theories are to provide part of the foundations of a theory explaining cyclical fluctuations in employment. Moreover, on several occasions we contrasted efficiency-wage theory with implicit contract theory, arguing that efficiency-wage theory provides a far better explanation of unemployment than does implicit contract theory. In fact, individuals do have long-term implicit contract relationships with their employers; these relationships are affected in fundamental ways by efficiency-wage considerations. The integration of implicit contract theory and efficiency-wage theory thus is a second important topic for a research agenda.

We have also noted that the problems with which we have been concerned are mitigated, but not eliminated, by monitoring and bonding (among other instruments that may be available to the firm). The limitations on monitoring and bonding have, however, received only limited theoretical scrutiny. Finally, we have, for the most part, analyzed incentive models and selection models in isolation from each other.[82] We have noted, however, that there may be important interactions between the two, and these require further study.

Thirdly, we have focused our attention on the burgeoning theoretical literature (but have made no pretense of being even complete within the scope of the topics covered). This is partly a consequence of the author's comparative advantage, but partly a consequence of the fact that the models presented here have not been the subject of extensive empirical testing.[83] We hope, in fact, that this survey will spur continuation of efforts in that direction.

This paper has, however, attempted to show how similar ideas have found application in the analysis of labor, capital, and product markets. These models provide an explanation of several phenomena within these markets that cannot be easily explained within the more conventional paradigm.

ACKNOWLEDGEMENTS

I am greatly indebted to my several coauthors, with whom I have worked on the analysis of the causes and consequences of the dependence of quality on price: Carl

Shapiro, Barry Nalebuff, Andy Weiss, and Bruce Greenwald. I am also indebted to helpful conversations with George Akerlof, Janet Yellen, Franklin Allen, Bill Rogerson, Mark Gersovitz, Jonathan Eaton, Partha Dasgupta, among others. Larry Summers and Gary Fields provided helpful comments on an earlier draft.

The opening quotations were supplied by Michael Perelman, Gavin Wright (second and fourth quotation), Graciela Chichilnisky, and Franklin Allen.

Gavin Wright has drawn my attention to the fact that there was a large literature in the eighteenth and nineteenth centuries arguing for a link between wages and productivity. For instance, he cites the former U.S. Secretary of State Thomas F. Bayard's "Introductory Letter" to Jacob Schoenhof (in *The Economy of High Wages*, New York, 1893) as saying, "The facts you have adduced and your deductions irresistibly establish the proposition that low wages do not mean cheap production, and that the best instructed and best paid labor proves itself to be the most productive. . . ." Similarly, Thomas Brassey, Jr., is quoted by John H. Habbakuk (*American and British Technology in the Nineteenth Century*, 1962) as saying, "The cheap labour at the command of our competitors seems to exercise the same enervating influence as the delights of Caphua on the soldiers of Hannibal" (*Work and Wages*, 1872, p. 142).

Some of this earlier literature is reviewed by Gregory Clark, in "Productivity Growth without Technical Change: European Agriculture before 1850" (1986), and by A. W. Coats, in "Changing Attitudes to Labour in the Mid-eighteenth Century," *Economic History Review* (August 1958, 2(11), 35–51). Coats traces the idea that high wages lead to high productivity back to Jacob Vanderlint, in *Money Answers All Things* (London, 1734).

Financial support from the Hoover Institution and the National Science Foundation is gratefully acknowledged.

NOTES

1. Some 40 years ago, Tibor Scitovsky (1945) wrote a brief but important paper discussing the consequences of the habit of judging quality by price. Another antecedent of the recent literature is Alvin Klevorick and Roger Alcaly (1970), who explore the implications for the traditional theory of consumers' behavior.
2. Akerlof (1970) investigated a case where equilibrium entailed no trade. As the price of cars decreased, supply decreased and demand decreased (the deterioration in car quality was so great that the quality-adjusted price actually increased): Intersection occurred only at zero trade. But this is a special case which arises primarily because of the limited incentives to trade in his model. The effect he noted in the used car market is the same as had long been recognized in insurance markets. As the price of insurance increases, the adverse selection effect implies that the mix of applicants changes adversely; thus the premium required for the insurance firms to break even must increase. None the less, there may exist insurance markets in which trade occurs.
3. And as we have already noted, because the inferences that can be drawn from observing a given price—and hence the demand at a given price—depend on the nature of supply, it may not be possible in some cases to isolate demand and supply disturbances.
4. For discussions of the validity of this relationship, see Christopher Bliss and Nicholas Stern (1978, 1981). See also P. H. Prasad (1970), G. B. Rodgers (1975), and Dasgupta and Ray (1986b).

5.   A cartoon appeared in several newspapers in the early eighties, when interest rates were soaring, in which a banker is seen leaning over his desk, asking the loan applicant, "What kind of person would be willing to borrow at the interest rates we charge?"

6.   Note too that in the circumstances with which we have just been concerned, where quality depends on price, the quantity demanded at any price depends on the quality supplied: Thus, for instance, a change in the mix of loan applicants will affect the supply of loans available at any interest rate; a change in the mix of job applicants will affect the demand for labor at any wage.

7.   Nonprice terms in credit markets include collateral requirements, specifications of circumstances under which credit is terminated, etc.

8.   The reservation utility level also may vary across sellers.

9.   In the incentive (moral hazard) versions, q is a result of an action taken by the individual; the action taken is a function of the terms of the contract. In the selection version, q is the average quality of those offering goods (services) at the price q and x; the constraint (2) is to be read as saying that at least one item is offered for sale at the given terms. In general, in adverse selection models, the constraint (2) is binding for only some individuals offering to sell the commodity.

10.   It is worth noting that while (2) may be viewed, from the perspective of the buyer, as what has come to be called the "individual rationality constraint," V^* is in general itself endogenously determined (it represents the individual's best alternative opportunity); and in the adverse selection models, (2) also can be viewed as a self-selection constraint, differentiating between those for whom the job (loan) is acceptable and those for whom it is not.

11.   We choose this example because in more general models, with adverse selection or incentive effects, the productivity of a worker at one firm depends on the wages paid at other firms and on the unemployment rate. We wish to avoid these complications in this simple exposition.

12.   Note, however, that the length of queue is not chosen by the firm, but is an endogenous property of the equilibrium. In this respect, these models differ in an important way from those in which the terms of the contract are determined either by the uninformed agent or the informed agent.

13.   If the productivity of group λ_i is a function of its wage w_i and its unemployment rate, U_i then in equilibrium, for all groups hired (for which $U_i < 1$)

$$\lambda_i(w_i, U_i)/w_i$$

is the same, and

$$\lambda_i(w_i, u_i)/w_i = \lambda_i(w_i, u_i)/w_i.$$

14.   Assuming that bankers are risk neutral, and thus care only about the expected return of the loan.

15.   Indeed, in some circumstances a decrease in supply may actually lead to a decrease in the weighted mean interest rate charged. See Stiglitz and Weiss (1986a, 1986b).

16.   In the simple models presented here, only one group in the population is rationed; those above the critical cutoff level receive all the credit they wish, or can sell all the labor they wish, while others are completely excluded from the market. But it is easy to construct models in which rationing is extended to many groups. See Barry Nalebuff and Stiglitz (1982) and Stiglitz and Weiss (1986a, 1986b, 1987).

17.   The analyses can be extended to situations where there is uncertainty, provided there is a complete set of risk markets, and provided that the nature of the commodity being traded (the quality of labor, the probability of bankruptcy, etc.) does not change as prices (wages, interest rates) change. It is the latter which concerns us here.

18.   This section focuses on the welfare economics of the imperfect information models. For a discussion of the welfare economics of the nutrition-based efficiency wage models, see Partha Dasgupta and Debraj Ray (1986a).

19. One should perhaps distinguish between two situations: that where the decentralized allocation *without* government intervention is inefficient, but government intervention, in the form of taxes and subsidies, can induce a decentralized efficient allocation; and those where even with this form of intervention, a decentralized allocation, cannot attain certain Pareto efficient allocations. Both problems may arise here.

20. This assumes that the firm cannot treat quits and fires differentially. There are good reasons for this: If quits are treated preferentially, a worker who knows he is about to be fired will quit. For a more extended discussion, see Shapiro and Stiglitz (1985a).

21. Unless a worker's productivity is completely firm-specific, then no information is conveyed to one firm by another firm's refusal to hire him.

22. More generally, the reservation wage of an individual will depend on his fallback (self-employment) income and the probability that he will obtain a higher wage, and this depends on the probability distribution of abilities and wage offers in the population, on the nature of the search technology, and on the costs of quitting a job once it has been accepted. See Nalebuff and Stiglitz (1982). Schlicht (1986) argues for a link between reservation wage and productivity based on the shorter expected duration of holding a job by less competent individuals.

23. A project is said to be riskier than another if its return is a mean preserving spread of that of the other.

24. The first result is a direct consequence of the concavity of the payoff function of the bank (in the absence of collateral, this is max $[R, (1 + r)B]$, where R is the return to the project, $(1 + r)B$ the amount the firm has promised to repay), the second result is a direct consequence of the convexity of the payoff function of the borrower (min $[R - (1 + r)B, 0]$ in the absence of collateral); the third result is an immediate consequence of the second.

25. A vast literature has developed on the principal agent problem since the early papers by Steve Ross (1973), Mirrlees (1974), and Stiglitz (1974d). We make note of only those papers that are directly relevant to the subject of this review, the dependence of quality on price.

26. In the Stiglitz and Weiss (1983) analysis, contracts are explicit, but enforceable only if it is in the interests of at least one party to the contract to do so. In the papers discussed in this paragraph, there is no legal enforcement mechanism. "Moral hazard" issues arise both in the compliance with the contract, and in the actions borrowers take which affect the likelihood they will wish to comply.

27. Repudiation could always be avoided if the repayments could be made state dependent, and if all states were perfectly observable and verifiable by both parties. For a more general discussion, see Eaton, Gersovitz, and Stiglitz (1986).

28. There is a large "radical" literature emphasizing the effect of the employment relationship on worker productivity. Other contributions to this literature include Herbert Gintis and Tsuneo Ishikawa (1985), Tom Weisskopf, Bowles, and David Gordon (1983), Gerry Oster (1980), and Geoff Hodgson (1982). The distinction between this literature and the nonradical literature is not always readily apparent. For instance, the Bowles (1985) and Shapiro and Stiglitz (1984) models appear to be essentially identical; some of the interpretations given to the model, and the lessons drawn, differ.

29. These models are thus long-term models. The "punishment" is provided "publicly" by the period of unemployment (rather than privately, through reduced wages or other means). Stiglitz and Weiss (1983) provide conditions showing that termination is in fact the optimal punishment. These models are constructed with identical individuals so there is no reputation effect associated with being fired. In any case, it is often hard to distinguish among voluntary and involuntary termination, in which case, the reputation effect of separations may be minimal (Shapiro and Stiglitz 1985a).

30. The importance of this had, of course, long been recognized by labor economists. See Sumner Slichter (1919).

31. Richard Arnott and Stiglitz (1985) and Shapiro and Stiglitz (1985a) provide explanations for why individuals do not bear the full costs of training; these have to do with worker risk aversion, incomplete insurance, and imperfect capital markets (though these market imperfections in turn, can be related to information imperfections).

32. These effects have, of course, long been discussed by labor economists. For an early formalization of the notion of interdependence, see Dan Hamermesh (1975).

33. The observation that it is individuals' perceptions of whether they are being treated fairly that affects behavior has one important consequence. The productivity curve of a group that believes it is being treated unfairly will (if our argument is correct) lie below that of groups of identical abilities that do not believe they are being treated unfairly. Such individuals either will not be hired, or will be hired at lower wages than someone of the *same* ability (let alone someone of the ability that they believe that they have). The fact that they are hired at lower wages reconfirms their belief they are not being treated fairly. The employer who pays the lower wage does not believe he is discriminating, only that he is paying wages that are in accord with productivity, which depends both on (statistical projections of) ability and effort.

34. Akerlof (1980, 1982) and Schlicht (1981a, 1981b) develop alternative theories of the employer–employee relationship in which psychological and sociological considerations lead to a dependence of productivity on wages. Akerlof (1984) describes some experiments in which different workers are assigned identical jobs and paid identical wages, but believe that they are either being under- or overpaid. These perceptions affect productivity.

35. Obviously, if the landlord could monitor the actions of the tenant, the share contract would specify the level of work required, and these incentive effects would not arise. See Steve Cheung (1969).

36. Braverman and Srinivasan (1981) have identified circumstances in which in equilibrium there *cannot* exist an excess supply of labor.

37. If part of the fixed payment is paid after the crop, then it is as if the landlord lent the funds to the worker; an increase in the amount to be paid has precisely the same effects as an increase in the rate of interest detailed earlier. An increase in the fixed fee can, accordingly, adversely affect the expected return of the landlord (-cum-lender) (D. Gale Johnson 1950). Allen (1985a) has shown that at low shares, tenants may have an incentive to "cheat" on the contract, absconding with the entire produce of the land.

38. The quotation from Sismondi in the introduction to this chapter makes it clear that selection effects may also arise in the context of sharecropping.

39. These beliefs are "rational"; given the beliefs of the individual, it would not pay the firm to produce a high-quality commodity, if it ever produced a low-quality commodity; and given that the firm indeed produces a low-quality commodity; the beliefs of individuals are consistent with firm behavior. More formally, the equilibrium can be shown to be a perfect equilibrium. See Dybvig and Spatt (1983).

   This is a "reputation" model based solely on incentive considerations. Other reputation models entail a mixture of incentive and adverse selection effects. There are good producers and bad producers. When a buyer purchases a commodity that turns out to be a low-quality commodity, then he infers that the seller must be a low-quality seller. It is their concern about being so labeled that induces good producers to produce high-quality commodities. One does not necessarily need many "bad" firms to induce good behavior on the part of the good firms, as David Kreps and Robert Wilson (1982) show in a rather different context.

40. It is straightforward to construct models that incorporate both incentive and nutritional effects.

41. Where "actions" are sufficiently precisely specified to imply a particular outcome in a particular situation, regardless of who performed the action.

42. The monitoring required by piece rate systems is costly; for it to be effective, there can be little variation in the quality of what is produced, or it needs to be easy to write a contract that specifies the relationship between quality and price, and then to observe and verify the quality of what is produced. Moreover, as technology changes, the piece rate needs to change; but this is often a contentious process. If, of course, there were no costs of labor mobility (no costs of hiring workers and no costs to the worker of moving to another firm) then if the firm offered too low a piece rate, resulting in an income below the worker's opportunity cost, then the worker would simply quit; exit would replace voice, to use Albert Hirschman's insightful terminology. But labor mobility is costly, and thus workers and firms

are concerned about how the piece rate is set; it determines the division of the "*ex post surplus*"—given that the workers are working for the firm, the difference between the worker's income and his opportunity cost; and the difference between the profits of the firm from the current employees and what the profits would be if the employer had to replace them.

43. To the extent that firms bear these turnover costs or pay workers not solely on the basis of their actions, firms can be thought of as providing insurance.

44. There is one other situation where moral hazard problems do not arise in labor markets: When workers are risk neutral (so there is no need for an insurance component in the relationship), then they can rent the machines on which they work (rent the land); because they receive all the residual, they will have "correct incentives"; and because what the capitalist (landlord) receives is independent of the action of the worker, he is indifferent to the actions they undertake. But even this is not correct if the worker cannot pay the rent ahead of time; then there is some probability that he will fail to pay the promised rent, and the likelihood of this is, in general, a function of the actions he undertakes: There is still a moral hazard problem. When rents are paid *ex post*, then it is as if the owner lent the money to the renter (see Johnson 1950; Stiglitz and Weiss 1981). Moreover, if how the worker uses the machine affects its future productivity and if it is difficult to verify whether the deterioration in the machine is due to misuse, there is a further moral hazard problem limiting the extent of rental markets. The contractual arrangements between the parties will try to limit these moral hazard problems, by stipulating restrictions on the use of the rented property. Thus, a landowner may stipulate what crops are to be planted, and he may impose restrictions on grazing. These moral hazard problems can be avoided by selling the machine, but this increases the risk of the worker; and it is even less likely that he will have the resources to pay for the purchase than to rent.

45. These enforcement problems are, of course, central both in international lending, in implicit contract theory, in sharecropping markets, and in product markets.

46. Thus what appears to be a technical assumption in Gerard Debreu's *Theory of Value* becomes of central importance in this analysis. Loosely speaking, to prove the existence of a market-clearing equilibrium, one must show that the supply correspondences are continuous, and to do this one must show that the budget sets are continuous functions of prices. To recast the nutritional efficiency-wage model in standard terms, we let $w\#$ denote the wage per efficiency unit. While at $w\# = w^*/\lambda^*$, the individual supplies λ^* efficiency units of labor, and at higher wages, the individual can supply, say, up to $\lambda(w)$ units of labor, at lower values of $w\#$ the feasible set shrinks to zero.

Note that while with nonconvex preferences, say, for leisure, the supply of labor correspondence might look as in Figure 17b, with the individual being indifferent between points A and B; with the efficiency wage model, the labor supply correspondence appears as in Figure 17a; the individual strictly prefers B to A. This explains why, with nonconvex preferences, an equilibrium exists with a continuum of individuals, but a market-clearing equilibrium does not exist in the efficiency-wage model. Moreover, while with standard nonconvexities those who supply labor and those who do not have the same level of utility, this is not true in our model. For a more extended discussion, see Dasgupta and Ray (1986a).

47. The demand curve is derived as follows. Assume the firm's production function is $Q = F[\lambda(w)L]$. It chooses w and L to maximize $Q - wL$ where we have chosen output as the numeraire. From the first-order conditions, $\lambda/\lambda' = w$ meaning that the wage is chosen to minimize labor costs per unit of effective labor (the efficiency wage). Employment is chosen so that, at the efficiency wage, the real wage equals the value of the marginal product of labor: $w = F'(w)\lambda$.

48. In particular, if the Walrasian wage exceeds the efficiency wage, the market equilibrium is the Walrasian wage, and the law of supply and demand holds. Any firm that attempted to lower the wage to the efficiency wage would not be able to obtain any labor.

49. In this example, the cost per effective unit of labor curve has taken on a simple shape: At wages below w^*, cost per effective labor unit is decreasing and at wages greater than w^*, it is increasing. There is no intrinsic reason why the cost per effective unit of labor curve should

take on such a simple shape as we have already noted (see Figure 6). Then, there will be an excess supply of labor if the Walrasian wage is below w^* or between $\hat{w}$ and w^{**}. It always pays the firms to pay the wage in excess of the Walrasian wage, which minimizes cost per effective unit of labor. Thus, for Walrasian wages in the interval between $\hat{w}$ and w^{**}, it pays the firm to increase the wage to w^{**}. (In these circumstances, equilibrium may be characterized by a wage distribution, as we noted earlier.)

50. These repercussions have been at the center of recent literature focusing on the distinction between insiders and outsiders. See Assar Lindbeck and Dennis Snower (1984a).

51. The concept of equilibrium employed by Dasgupta and Ray (1986a) in their analysis of the nutritional efficiency wage model corresponds to a quasi-equilibrium in Debreu (1959) and to the concept of a compensated equilibrium in Kenneth Arrow and Frank Hahn (1971).

52. They constructed a simple model in which they combine incentive and selection effects; there are two groups in the population, and each group has two activities (a safe and a risky project). Even though the bank is able to sort individuals perfectly, it cannot raise interest rates, because to do so would induce greater risk taking. Hence, they show that there may be credit rationing at one or both credit contracts. Credit rationing may also arise if individuals differ in more than one dimension, e.g., with respect to risk aversion and wealth.

53. These problems would also be ameliorated if firms could establish a reputation. Another mechanism for providing incentives for workers that does not suffer from the "double moral hazard" problem are contests (Lazear and Sherwin Rosen 1981; Green and Nancy Stokey 1983; Nalebuff and Stiglitz 1983b; Sudipto Bhattacharya 1983). They do impose some risk for workers, and workers have to believe that the contests are fairly administered, and that they are evenly matched with their competitors. Intrafirm contests may also have deleterious morale effects.

54. Some of the "problems" with job purchases explain why the price for jobs would be low (e.g., workers' risk aversion, limitations on workers' access to the capital market), but not why the market for jobs does not clear.

55. Similarly the probability of consummating a deal may serve as a self-selection device within a bargaining model.

56. Technically, this analysis should be contrasted with that of Rothschild and Stiglitz (1976), where each firm (uninformed agent) sets the price and quantity; here firms set only the price; the unemployment rate is determined as part of the equilibrium. This is also true of the Stiglitz–Weiss (1986a) model of the capital market. Some questions have been raised about the relevance of this particular model for the description of labor markets; it may have more to do with the number of hours worked by a Harley Street doctor than it does with unemployment among the low skilled. It is important to note, however, that in this model "unemployment" does not have the same interpretation that it does in the national income statistics: It means that the individual is not employed by others. For the low skilled, this may indeed correspond to unemployment; for the high skilled, it may correspond to self-employment.

57. This model has been extended by Nalebuff and Stiglitz (1982) to the case where individuals can apply for several jobs. In that case, the nature of the equilibrium depends critically on whether contracts are binding—whether once a job has been accepted, the worker can quit when he is offered a better job. If contracts are binding, the opportunity cost of accepting a low-wage job is the foregone possibility of a high-wage job, the likelihood of which depends on both the job offers of different firms and the behavior of other individuals (how high they set their reservation wages). They show that there exists a particular wage distribution, such that when all workers rationally set their reservation wages, the cost-per-efficiency unit of the firm is the same for all firms. (In their equilibrium, while the quality of those who apply at each wage are, in fact, different, it is only the wage-cum-unemployment rate that distinguishes them: in all other respects the workers look the same. Moreover, at each wage, except the lowest, there is an excess supply of applicants.)

By contrast, if the first firm to enter the market had simply hired at what it thought was the efficiency wage, because it would have hired only lower-ability workers, those with reservation wages below the efficiency wages, the "new" efficiency-wage schedule facing the later entrant would lie above the old one, for $w > w^*$, and hence there would be an advantage to being late. See Lewis Guasch and Weiss (1980).

58. Thus, models in which there are only limited sources of imperfect information may be very misleading. For instance, if individuals differ only in one dimension, then education may serve to sort individuals perfectly: There will be no residual imperfect information, and hence no need to lower wages to improve the mix of laborers. But if individuals differ in several dimensions, then education alone will not suffice to provide complete information. Similarly, in the capital market, if borrowers differ only in one dimension, and there is no moral hazard problem, there may exist a fully revealing self-selection equilibrium, and there will be, as a consequence, no role for credit rationing. But if borrowers differ in several dimensions and/or there are moral hazard problems, there may exist credit rationing. Though self-selection devices may reveal some information, they will not be perfectly revealing.

59. It is important to emphasize that although we believe that these models provide an important part of the microfoundations for macroeconomics, they do not provide the whole story: Other models (many of them also based on considerations of imperfect information) are required. This section owes much to the comments of Bruce Greenwald and Larry Summers.

60. This should be contrasted with the standard implicit contract theories (e.g., Costas Azariadis 1983; Grossman and Oliver Hart 1981; for recent surveys, see Azariadis and Stiglitz 1983; and Hart 1983) which, at best, provide an explanation of work sharing (see Stiglitz 1986). Arnott, Arthur Hosios, and Stiglitz (1983) incorporate some aspects of efficiency-wage theory in their analysis of labor contracts with costly labor mobility.

61. Including theories of staggered contracts (Taylor 1980), which need to explain why labor is not absorbed into those sectors whose contracts are up for negotiation.

62. John Harris and Michael Todaro (1970) have developed a similar analysis to explain urban unemployment in LDCs. The major difference between the Harris–Todaro model and the Stiglitz model is that in the former, the wage is exogenous and in the latter—as in all the work under examination here—it is endogenous. Robert Hall (1975) has used a similar model to explain differences in unemployment rates in different urban areas.

63. Similarly, Arnott, Hosios and Stiglitz (1985) assume that the costs of search for the unemployed and the employed may be different and show that optimal contracts may then entail some individuals being layed off even if it means a finite probability of being unemployed for a period.

64. As is often the case, there may be another equilibrium in which accepting a low-wage job does not signal one's ability: When there are significant transactions costs, it is more plausible that the acceptance of a low-wage job will serve as a signal. Alternatively, the argument to be given next serves to explain why accepting a job would lower one's lifetime wage prospects quite apart from signaling considerations: Signaling considerations would then serve to strengthen the magnitude of the effect of the acceptance of a low-wage job on lifetime income.

65. This result depends, in part, on the firm's not being able to commit itself to paying higher wages in the future. Those commitments themselves are, at best conditional on the firm's surviving. Thus, a worker who accepts a low wage now from a firm in bad financial straits with the promise of a high wage in the future takes, in effect, an equity position in the firm. The reasons why workers may not be willing to do so have been set forth in Greenwald, Stiglitz and Weiss (1984).

66. This argument was put forward by Robert Hall in his discussion of Yellen's survey of efficiency-wage models at the San Francisco meetings of the American Economic Association, December 1984.

67. This is in fact a general property of economies that are not (constrained) Pareto efficient. There then exist large classes of perturbations to the economy that effect pareto improvements. If the firm sets its wage in a privately optimal way, there exist some perturbations of this wage that have a second order effect on the profits of the firm but have a first order effect on the welfare of other agents in the economy. See Greenwald and Stiglitz (1986a).

68. Again, the fact that firms behave in a risk averse manner can be explained in terms of certain capital market imperfections which, in turn, can be related to imperfect information.
69. This list of criticisms is not meant to be exhaustive. Another objections is that these models require not only that productivity increase with wages, but also that there be a range of wages over which increases in wages lead to more than proportionate increases in productivity. This objection has been dealt with where we showed how several simple models exhibiting these properties can be constructed. It then becomes an empirical question whether in practice the wage-productivity relationship has the required shape. Unfortunately, there is insufficient empirical evidence to date to provide a convincing answer.
70. This formulation entails, in effect, a synthesis of implicit contract theory with efficiency wage theory. A firm that cheats on the implicit contract will find that their workers leave later, when job opportunities become better. In this view, the appropriate time unit for the analysis of the worker–employer relationship is longer than just a month or even a year.
    Moreover, selection (quality-efficiency wage) considerations may strengthen these concerns, because it is likely to be the better workers who will have the easiest time finding alternative opportunities and will have the highest propensity to quit.
71. Moreover, wages are affected not only by demand disturbances but also by any shock that affects the no-shirking constraint. Thus, the expectation of an upturn in the economy would shift the no-shirking constraint upward, necessitating an increase in today's wage and a decrease in current employment.
72. The analysis is somewhat more subtle than this suggests: each firm's wage is dependent not only on other firm's wages, but also on the unemployment rate; nevertheless, in at least some versions of the efficiency-wage model, the unemployment effect is dominated by the wage effect, and wages do not fall, or fall only slowly in the face of a downward shift in the demand curve for labor.
73. This analysis can also be related to the recent studies (Robert Barro 1974; Stiglitz 1982c, 1983; Neil Wallace 1981) arguing for the irrelevance of public financial policies. A critical assumption in these analyses is that public and private borrowing are perfect substitutes for each other; in particular, individuals are assumed to have unlimited access to the capital market. If they do not (and the theories presented here explain why they do not), then public financial policies are not irrelevant.
74. For this to be a cogent explanation of the cyclical variability in investment, one must explain why firms do not turn to other sources of funds. The explanation for this is provided in Greenwald, Stiglitz, and Weiss (1984), where they argue that asymmetries of information make the cost of raising capital on the equity market very high, prohibitively high for many firms. (Their model is essentially a direct application of the Akerlof Lemons model to the equity market; their result on the thinness of equity markets corresponds to Akerlof's results on the thinness of used car markets.)
    Equity rationing can give rise to investment fluctuations, even without credit rationing; for the absence of futures markets combined with limitations on the ability to sell equity imply that a decision to produce forces managers/owners to absorb risk. A reduction in their working capital will thus lead to a reduction in their equilibrium production levels. If, as is in fact the case, debt is not indexed, monetary shocks can have real effects through their effects on working capital.
75. For other studies of monetary policy in the presence of credit rationing, see Jackman and John Sutton (1982), Smith (1983), Vale (1986), and Lindbeck (1963).
76. As Edmund Phelps and Sidney Winter (1970) emphasized, there may be a trade-off involved in recruiting customers today by lowering prices, with higher future profits, but lower current profits. An increase in the effective cost of capital tilts the trade-off toward higher current profits, i.e., higher prices today.
77. They emphasize, however, at least one important aspect to which efficiency-wage theory has paid insufficient attention: The worker may not be able to commit himself to receiving low wages in the future; after he is trained he may be in a position to extract a high wage. What is relevant, of course, for the firm's decision is the relationship between lifetime wages and

productivity. (Notice that while Greenwald has emphasized the consequences of the inability of firms to commit themselves to pay high wages in the future, insider-outsider theory has emphasized the consequences of the inability of workers to commit themselves to accepting low wages in the future.)

78. For an explicit attempt to integrate the two approaches, see Karl Moene (1985).

79. The externalities associated with incomplete markets and imperfect information also give rise to multipliers. These multipliers should not be confused with the welfare multipliers that arise whenever the economy is not (constrained) Pareto efficient. Then there always exist some perturbations to some individual or firm that have a second order effect on the welfare of the individual or firm but a first order effect on social welfare (see Greenwald and Stiglitz 1986b).

80. In this section, we focus our discussion on the consequences of the nutritional-wage productivity nexus for LDCs. For a discussion of alternative explanations, see Stiglitz (1982b, 1974c).

81. Firms would, in such circumstances, find it in their interests to subsidize the consumption of food; but unless the subsidy is provided for on-premise consumption, workers could resell the subsidized food, and the firm would thus not directly gain from the food subsidy.

    For an analysis of optimal taxation and subsidies in the presence of productivity effects, see Sah and Stiglitz (1984).

82. An exception is the Stiglitz and Weiss (1986a, 1986b) studies.

83. There have, however, been numerous studies addressing particular aspects of the theories described in this paper. For an early investigation of the price-quality relationship, see Gabor and Granger (1966). For a recent examination of the empirical evidence on whether the labor market clears, see Thomas Kniesner and Arthur Goldsmith (1986). For a recent discussion of the relationship between productivity and wages, see, for example, James Medoff and Katharine Abraham (1981). Macroeconomic analyses of the relationship between unemployment and productivity include James Rebitzeer (1985), and Weisskopf, Bowles, and Gordon (1983).

    There is a growing literature attempting to test the credit-rationing models. See, for instance, Charles Calomiris and R. Glenn Hubbard (1985), Leonard Nakamura (1985), and P. Kugler (1985).

REFERENCES

Aigner, Dennis and Cain, Glen. Statistical theories of discrimination in labor markets, *Ind. Lab. Relat. Rev.*, Jan. 1977, **30**(2): 175–187.

Akerlof, George A. The market for 'lemons': Qualitative uncertainty and the market mechanism, *Quarterly Journal of Economics*, Aug. 1970, **84**(3): 488–500.

Akerlof, George A. The Economics of caste and of the rat race and other woeful tales, *Quarterly Journal of Economics*, Nov. 1976, **90**(4): 599–617.

Akerlof, George A. A Theory of social custom, of which unemployment may be one consequence, *Quarterly Journal of Economics*, June 1980: **94**, 749–775.

Akerlof, George A. Labor contracts as partial gift exchange, *Quarterly Journal of Economics*, Nov. 1982, **97**(4): 543–569.

Akerlof, George A. Gift Exchange and Efficiency Wage Theory: Four Views, *American Economic Review*, May 1984, **74**(2): 79–83.

Akerlof, George A. and Stiglitz, Joseph. Capital, wages and structural unemployment, *Economic Journal*, June 1969, **79**(314): 269–281.

Akerlof, George A. and Yellen, Janet. *The Macroeconomic Consequences of Near Rational Rule of Thumb Behavior.* Mimeo, U.C. Berkeley, 1983.

Akerlof, George A. and Yellen, Janet. A near-rational model of the business cycle, with wage and Price Inertia, *Quarterly Journal of Economics*, Supp. 1985, **100**(5): 823–838.

Allen, Franklin. *Loans, Bequests and Taxes Where Abilities Differ: A Theoretical Analysis Using a Two-ability Model.* D. Phil. thesis, Oxford, 1980.

Allen, Franklin. The prevention of default, *Journal of Finance,* May 1981, **36**(2): 271–276.

Allen, Franklin. Credit rationing and payment incentives, *Review Economic Studies,* Oct. 1983, **50**(4): 639–646.

Allen, Franklin. Reputation and product quality, *Rand J. Econ.,* 1984, **15**(3): 311–327.

Allen, Franklin. On the fixed nature of sharecropping contrasts, *Economic Journal,* Mar. 1985a, **95**(377): 30–48.

Allen, Franklin. A Theory of Price Rigidities When Quality Is Unobservable. Mimeo, U. of Pennsylvania, 1985b.

Annable, James E., Jr. A theory of downward-rigid wages and cyclical unemployment, *Economic Inquiry,* July 1977, **15**(3): 326–44.

Annable, James E., Jr. Money wage determination in post Keynesian economics, *Journal Post Keynesian Economics.,* Spring 1980, **2**(3): 405–419.

Annable, James, E., Jr. *Another auctioneer is missing.* Mimeo, Economics Department, The First National Bank of Chicago, 1985 (earlier version presented at meetings of the International Atlantic Economic Association, Rome, 1985).

Arnott, R., Hosios, A. and Stiglitz, J. Implicit Contracts, Labor Mobility and Unemployment. Mimeo, Princeton U., 1983 (revised version of a paper presented at NBER-NSF conference, Dec. 1980).

Arnott, R. and Stiglitz, J. Labor turnover, wage structures and moral hazard, *Journal of Labour Economics,* 1985, **3**(4): 434–462.

Arnott, R. and Stiglitz, J. Moral hazard and Optimal commodity taxation, *Journal Public Economics,* Feb 1986, **29**: 1–24.

Arrow, Kenneth J. and Hahn, F.H. *General competitive analysis.* Edinburgh: Oliver and Boyd, 1971.

Azariadis, C. Employment with asymmetric information, *Quarterly Journal of Economics.* Supplement 1983, **98**(3): 157–172.

Azariadis, C. and Stiglitz, J.E. Implicit contracts and fixed price equilibria, *Quarterly Journal of Economics.* Supplement, 1983, **98**(3): 1–22.

Baltensperger, Ernst and Milde, Hellmuth. Loan rate flexibility and asymmetric default information, *Geld, Banken und Versicherungen,* 1982, 1165–1178.

Barro, Robert. Are Government Bonds net wealth? *Journal of Political Economy,* Nov./Dec. 1974, **82**(6): 1095–1117.

Becker, Gary S. and Stigler, George J. Law enforcement, malfeasance, and compensation of enforcers, *Journal of Legal Studies,* Jan. 1974, **3**(1): 1–18.

Besanko, David and Thakor, Anjan. Collateral and Rationing: Sorting Equilibria in Monopolistic and Competitive Markets. Northwestern University Discussion Paper, 1984.

Bester, Helmut. Screening vs. rationing in credit markets with imperfect information, *American Economic Review,* Sept. 1985, **75**(4): 850–855.

Bhattacharya, Sudipto. Tournaments, Termination Schemes and Forcing Contracts. Mimeo, U. of California, Berkeley, June 1985.

Blinder, A. and Stiglitz, J.E. Money, Credit Constraints and Economic Activity, *American Economic Review.,* May 1983, **73**(2): 297–302.

Bliss, Christopher J. and Stern, Nicholas. Productivity, Wages and Nutrition, *Journal of Development Economics,* Dec. 1978, **5**(4): 331–397.

Bliss, Christopher J. *Palanpur-studies in the economy of a North Indian village.* New Delhi: Oxford U. Press, 1981.

Bowles, Samuel. The production process in a competitive economy: Walrasian, Neo-Hobbesian, and Marxian models, *American Economic Review.,* Mar 1985, **75**(1): 16–36.

Braverman, Avishay and Srinivasan, T.N. Credit and Sharecropping in Agrarian Societies, *Journal of Development Economics,* Dec. 1981, **9**(3): 289–312.

Braverman, Avishay and Stiglitz, Joseph E. Sharecropping and the interlinking of agrarian markets, *American Economic Review,* Sept. 1982, **72**(4): 695–715.

Braverman, Avishay and Stiglitz, Joseph E. Landlords, tenants and technological innovations, *Journal of Development Economics,* 1986.

Bray, Margaret. Futures trading, Rational Expectations, and the Efficient Markets hypothesis, *Econometrica*, May 1981, **49**(3): 575–596.

Bulow, Jeremy I. and Summers, Lawrence H. A Theory of Dual Labor Markets with Application to Industrial Policy, Discrimination and Keynesian Unemployment. NBER Working Paper No. 1666, July 1985.

Calomiris, Charles and Hubbard, Robert Glenn. *Price Flexibility, Credit Rationing and Economic Fluctuations: Evidence from the U.S., 1979–1914.* Mimeo, Northwestern U., Oct. 1985.

Calvo, Guillermo. Quasi-Walrasian theories of unemployment, *American Economic Review*, May 1979, **69**(2): 102–107.

Calvo, Guillermo and Phelps, Edmund. Indexation issues: Appendix: Employment contingent wage contracts, *Journal Monetary Economics*, Suppl., Series 1977, **5**: 160–68.

Calvo, Guillermo and Wellisz, Stanislaw. Hierarchy, Ability and income distribution, *Journal of Political Economy*, Part 1, Oct. 1979, **87**(5): 991–1010.

Cheung, S.N.S. *The theory of share tenancy.* Chicago: U. of Chicago Press, 1969.

Clark, Gregory. *Productivity Growth without Technical Change: European Agriculture before 1850.* Unpub. ms., 1986.

Clark, Kim and Summers, Laurence. Labor market dynamics and unemployment: A reconsideration, *Brookings Papers on Economic Activity*: 1979, **1**: 13–60.

Clemenz, G. *Credit Rationing in the Absence of Direct Observability of Efforts and Abilities of Borrowers* Institut für Wirtschaftswissenschaften der Universität Wien, Working Paper No. 8405, June 1984.

Clemenz, G. *Credit Markets with Asymmetric Information and the Role of Collateral.* Mimeo, U. Wien, 1985.

Dasgupta, Partha and Ray, Debraj. Inequality as a determinant of malnutrition and unemployment: Theory, *Economic Journal*, Dec. 1986a, **96**(384): 1011–1034.

Dasgupta, Partha and Ray, Debraj. *Adapting to Undernourishment: The Clinical Evidence and Its Implications.* Mimeo, U. of Cambridge, 1986b.

Dasgupta, Partha and Ray, Debraj. Inequality as a determinant of malnutrition and unemployment: Policy, *Economic Journal*, 1987, **97**(385): 177–188.

Debreu, Gerard. *Theory of value.* NY: John Wiley, 1959.

Devinney, Timothy M. Incentives and multi-period rationing in loan contracts. In: Goppl, Hermann and Henn, Rudof, eds., *Geld, Banken und Versicherungen*, VVW Karlsruhe, 629–646.

Dybvig, Philip H. and Jaynes, G. Output-supply, Employment and Intra-Industry Wage Dispersion, Cowles Foundation Discussion Paper No. 546, 1980.

Dybvig, Philip H. and Spatt, Chester S. Does it pay to maintain a reputation? Consumer information and product quality. Working paper, 1983.

Eaton, B. Curtis and White, William D. Agent compensation and the limits of bonding, *Economic Inquiry*, July 1982, *20*(3): 330–343.

Eaton, Jonathan. Lending with costly enforcement of repayment and potential fraud. *Journal Banking and Finance*, 1986, **10**: 281–93.

Eaton, Jonathan and Gersovitz, Mark. LDC participation in international financial markets: Debt and reserves, *Journal of Development Economics*, Mar. 1980, **7**(1): 3–21.

Eaton, Jonathan and Gersovitz, Mark. Debt with potential repudiation: Theoretical and empirical analysis, *Review of Economic Studies*, Apr. 1981a, **48**(2): 289–309.

Eaton, Jonathan and Gersovitz, Mark. Poor Country Borrowing and the Repudiation Issue. Princeton Studies in International Finance No. 47, Princeton, NJ, June 1981b.

Eaton, Jonathan, Gersovitz, Mark and Stiglitz, J.E. The pure theory of country risk, *European Economic Review*, 1986, **30**(3): 481–513.

Farrell, Joseph. *Prices as Signals of Quality.* M. Phil. dissertation, Oxford, 1979.

Farrell, Joseph. *Repeat Sales, Quality and Prices.* Mimeo, M.I.T., Dec. 1980.

Farrell, Joseph. Moral Hazard in Quality, Entry Barriers, and Introductory Offers, M.I.T. Working Paper, May 1984.

Farrell, Joseph. Moral hazard as an entry barrier. *Rand Journal of Economics*, Fall 1986, **17**: 440–449.

Fields, Gary. Rural-urban migration, urban unemployment and underemployment, and job search activity in LDCs," *Journal of Development Economics.*, June 1975, **2**(2): 165–187.

Fitzroy, F. *Contests.* Mimeo, International Institute of management, West Berlin, 1981.

Freimer, Marshall and Gordon, M.J. Why Bankers Ration Credit, *Quarterly Journal of Economics*, Aug. 1965, **79**: 397–416.

Friedman, Benjamin M. The Roles of Money and Credit in Macroeconomic Analysis. in *Macroeconomics, prices, and quantities: Essays in memory of Arthur M. Okun.* Ed.: James Tobin. Washington, DC: Brookings Inst., 1983: 161–89.

Gabor, Andrè and Granger C.W.J. Price as an indicator of quality: Report of an inquiry, *Economica*, Feb. 1966, **33**: 43–70.

Gintis, Herbert and Ishikawa, Tsuneo. Wages, work intensity and unemployment, in *Journal of the Japanese and International Economies*, June 1987, **1**(2): 195–228.

Gintis, Herbert and Ishikawa, Tsuneo. *The Theory of Production and Price in Contingent Renewal Markets.* Mimeo, U. of Massachusetts, Nov. 1985.

Green, Jerry. *Information, Efficiency and Equilibrium.* Harvard Institute of Economic Research, Discussion Paper No. 284, Mar. 1973.

Green, Jerry and Stokey, Nancy. A comparison of tournaments and contracts, *Journal of Political Economy*, June 1983, **91**(3): 349–364.

Greenwald, Bruce. *Adverse selection in the labor market.* NY: Garland, 1979.

Greenwald, Bruce. Adverse selection in the labour market, *Review of Economic Studies*, July 1986, **53**(3): 325–347.

Greenwald, Bruce and Stiglitz Joseph. Externalities in economics with imperfect information and incomplete markets, *Quarterly Journal of Economics*, May 1986a, **101**(2): 229-264.

Greenwald, Bruce and Stiglitz, J. Externalities in economics with information, *Quarterly Journal of Economics*, Feb. 1986a, **101**(2): 229–264.

Greenwald, Bruce and Stiglitz, J. *The Inefficiency of Competitive Equilibria with Rationing.* Mimeo, 1986b.

Greenwald, Bruce and Stiglitz, J. *Information, Finance Constraints and Business Fluctuations.* Paper prepared for the Seminar on Monetary Theory, Taipei, Jan. 3–8, 1986c.

Greenwald, Bruce and Stiglitz, J. *Money, Imperfect Information, and Economic Fluctuations.* Paper prepared for the Seminar on Monetary Theory, Taipei, Jan. 3–8, 1986d.

Greenwald, Bruce, Stiglitz, Joseph and Weiss, Andrew. Informational imperfections and macroeconomic fluctuations, *American Economic Review*, May 1984, **74**(2): 194–199.

Grossman, Sanford and Hart, Oliver. Implicit contracts, moral hazard, and unemployment, *American Economic Review*, May 1981, **71**(2): 301–307.

Grossman, Sanford and Stiglitz, Joseph E. Information and competitive price systems, *American Economic Review*, May 1976, **66**(2): 246-253.

Grossman, Sanford and Stiglitz, Joseph E. On the impossibility of informationally efficient markets, *American Economic Review*, June 1980, **70**(3): 393–408.

Guasch, Luis and Weiss, Andrew. Adverse selection by markets and the advantage of being late, *Quarterly Journal of Economics*, May 1980, **94**(3): 453–466.

Hall, Robert. The rigidity of wages and the persistence of unemployment, *Brookings Papers on Economic Activity*, 1975, **2**: 301–349.

Hall, Robert. Employment Fluctuations and Wage Rigidity, *Brookings Papers on Economic Activity*, 1980, **1**: 91–123.

Hamermesh, Daniel S. Interdependence in the Labour Market, *Economica*, Nov. 1975, **42**(168): 420–429.

Harberger, A.C. On measuring the social opportunity cost of labour, *International Labour Review*, June 1971, **103**(6): 559–579.

Harris, John R. and Todaro, Michael P. Migration, unemployment & development: A two-sector analysis, *American Economic Review*, Mar. 1970, **60**(1): 126–142.

Hart, Oliver. Optimal labour contracts under asymmetric information: An introduction, *Review of Economic Studies*, Jan. 1983, **50**(1): 3–35.

Heal, Geoffrey. Do bad products drive out good? *Quarterly Journal of Economics*, Aug. 1976, **90**(32): 499–502.

Hellwig, Martin F. A model of borrowing and lending with bankruptcy, *Econometrica*, Nov. 1977, **45**: 1879–1906.

Hodgson, Geoff. Theoretical and political implications of variable productivity, *Cambridge Journal of Economics*, Sept. 1982, **6**(3): 213–226.

Hoel, M. and Vale, Bent. Effects of reduced working time in an economy where firms set wages, *European Economic Review*, 1986, **30**: 1097–1104.

Holmström, Bengt. Equilibrium long-term labor contracts, *Quarterly Journal of Economics*, 1983, **98**(5): 23–54.

Jackman, R., Layard, R. and Pissarides, C. Policies for reducing the natural rate of unemployment. In: Butkiewicz, J. L., Koford, K. J. and Miller, J. B., eds., *Keynes Economic Legacy*. Praeger, 1986: 111–152.

Jackman, Richard and Sutton, John. Imperfect capital markets and the monetarist black-box: Liquidity constraints. inflation, and the asymmetric effects of interest rate policy, *Economic Journal*, Mar. 1982, **92**(365): 108–128.

Jaffee, Dwight and Russell, Thomas. Imperfect information, uncertainty, and credit rationing, *Quarterly Journal of Economics*. Nov. 1976, **90**(4): 651–666.

Johnson, D. Gale. Resource allocation under share contracts, *Journal of Political Economy.*, Apr. 1950, **58**: 111–123.

Keeton, William R. *Equilibrium credit rationing*. NY: Garland, 1980.

Klein, Benjamin and Leffler, Keith B. The role of market forces in assuring contractural performance, *Journal of Political Economy*, Aug. 1981, **89**(4): 615–641.

Klevorick, Alvin K. and Alcaly, Roger E. Judging quality by price, snob appeal, and the new consumer theory, *Z. Nationalökon.*, 1970, **30**(1–2): 53–64.

Kniesner, Thomas and Goldsmith, Arthur H. Does the labor market clear? A survey of the evidence for the US, *Res. Labor Econ.* Forthcoming.

Kreps, David M. and Wilson, Robert. Reputation and imperfect information, *Journal of Economic Theory*, Aug. 1982, **27**(2): 253–279.

Kugler, P. Credit Rationing: Evidence from Disequilibrium Interest Rate Equations. U. Basel Working Paper No. 32, 1985.

Lazear, Edward P. Agency, earnings profiles, productivity and hours restrictions, *American Economic Review*, Sept. 1982, **71**(4): 606–620.

Lazer, Edward P. and Rosen, Sherwin. Rank order tournaments as optimum labor contracts, *Journal of Political Economy*, Oct. 1981, **89**(5): 841–864.

Leibenstein, Harvey. *Economic backwardness and economic growth*. NY: Wiley, 1957.

Lindbeck, Assar. *A study in monetary analysis*. Stockholm: Almquist and Wiksell, 1963.

Lindbeck, Assar and Snower, Dennis. Involuntary unemployment as an insider-outsider dilemma. Seminar Paper No. 282, Institute for International Economic Studies, U. of Stockholm, 1984a, Revised as Wage rigidity, union activity and unemployment. In: Beckerman, Wilfred, ed., *Wage rigidity and unemployment*. Duckworth and Johns Hopkins U. Press, 1986, ch. 5.

Lindbeck, Assar and Snower, Dennis. *Labor Turnover, Insider Morale and Involuntary Unemployment*. Seminar Paper No. 310, Institute for International Economic Studies. U. of Stockholm, 1984b.

Lindbeck, Assar and Snower, Dennis. Explanations of unemployment, *Oxford Review of Economic Policy*, 1986, **1**(2): 34–59.

Lindbeck, Assar and Snower, Dennis. Efficiency wages versus insiders and outsiders, *European Economic Review*, 1987.

Malcolmson, James. Unemployment and the efficiency wage hypothesis, *Economic Journal*, Dec. 1981, **91**(364): 848–866.

Manove, Michael. *Job Responsibility and Promotion: An Efficiency-Wage Analysis*. Mimeo, Dept. of Economics, Boston U., Boston, MA, Apr. 2, 1986.

Marshall, Alfred. *Principles of economics*, 8th ed. London: Macmillan, 1920.

Mcdoff, James L. and Abraham, Katharine. Are those paid more really more productive? *Journal of Human Resources*, Spring 1981, **16**(2): 186–216.

Melnik, A. and Plaut, S. Loan commitment contracts, terms of lending, and credit allocation, *Journal of Finance*, June 1986, **41**: 425–435.

Milde, Hellmuth and Riley, John. *Signaling in Credit Markets*, UCLA Working Paper 334, 1984.

Mill, J.S. *Principles of political economy*. London: J.W. Parker, 1848.

Mirrlees, James. Notes on welfare economics, information, and uncertainty. In: Balch, M. S., McFadden, D. L. and Wu, S. Y., eds., *Contributions to economic analysis*. Amsterdam: North-Holland, 1974.

Mirrlees, James. A pure theory of underdeveloped economies. In: Reynolds, L. A., ed., *Agriculture in Development Theory*, New Haven: Yale U. Press, 1975, 84–106.

Miyazaki, Hajime. Work norms and involuntary unemployment. *Quarterly Journal of Economics*, May 1984, 297–311.

Moene, Karl O. A note on Keynesian unemployment as a worker discipline device, *Economics Letters*, 1985, **18**(1): 17–19.

Mookherjee, Dilip. *Involuntary Unemployment and Worker Moral Hazard*. Stanford U. Graduate School of Business, May 1985.

Myers, Stewart C. and Majluf, Nicholas S. Corporate financing and investment decisions when firms have information that investors do not have, *Journal of Financial Economics*, June 1984, **13**(2): 187–221.

Nakamura, Leonard Usamu. *Customer Credit, Financial Intermediaries and Real Income: Preliminary Evidence That Credit Matters*, Mimeo, Dept. of Economics, Rutgers, Oct. 1985.

Nalebuff, Barry T. and Stiglitz, Joseph E. *Quality and Prices*. Econometric Research Program Memorandum No. 297, Princeton U., May 1982.

Nalebuff, Barry T. and Stiglitz, Joseph E. Information, competition and markets, *American Economic Review*, May 1983, **73**(2): 278–283.

Nalebuff, Barry T. and Stiglitz, Joseph E. Prizes and contests: Towards a general theory of compensation and competition, *Bell Journal of Economics.*, Spring 1983b, **14**: 21–43.

Newbery, David and Stiglitz, Joseph E. Share-cropping, risk sharing and the importance of imperfect information. In: Roumasset, J. A., Boussard, J. M. and Singh, I., eds., *Risk, uncertainty and agricultural development*. SEARCA, A/D/C, 1979, 311–341.

Newbery, David and Stiglitz, Joseph E. *The theory of commodity price stabilization: A study in the economics of risk*. Oxford: Clarendon Press, 1981.

Oster, Gerry. Labour relations and demand relations: A case study of the 'Unemployment Effect,' *Cambridge Journal of Economics*, Dec. 1980, **4**(4): 337–348.

Pencavel, J.H. Wages, specific training, and labor turnover in U.S. manufacturing industries, *International Economics Review*, Feb. 1972, **13**(1): 53–64.

Pencavel, J.H. Industrial morale. In: Ashenfelter, O. and Oates, Wallace E., eds., *Essays in labor market analysis in memory of Yochanan Peter Comay*. NY: Wiley, 1977, 129–146.

Phelps, Edmund S. and Winter, Sidney G. Optimal price policy under atomistic competition. In: Phelps, Edmund S., ed., *Microeconomic foundations of employment and inflation theory*. NY: Norton, 1970, 309–337.

Prasad, P.H. *Growth with full employment*. Bombay: Allied Publishers, 1970.

Radner, Roy. Rational expectations equilibrium: Generic existence and the information revealed by prices,'' *Econometrica*, May 1979, **47**(3): 655–678.

Rebitzer, James B. Unemployment, Long-term Employment Relations, and Labor Productivity Growth. Mimeo, U. of Texas, Nov. 1985.

Repullo, Rafael. A Simple Model of Interest Rate Deregulation. Mimeo, London School of Economics and Bank of Spain, Nov. 1985.

Riley, J. and Zeckhauser, R. Optimal selling strategies: when to haggle, when to hold firm, *Quarterly Journal of Economics*, May 1983, **98**(2): 267–289.

Rodgers, G.B. Nutritionally based wage determination in the low income labour market, *Oxford Economic Papers*, Mar. 1975, **27**(1): 61–81.

Ross, Stephen A. The economic theory of agency: The principal's problem, *American Economic Review*, May 1973, **63**(2): 134–139.

Rothschild, Michael and Stiglitz, J.E. Equilibrium in competitive insurance markets: An essay on the economics of imperfect information, *Quarterly Journal of Economics*, Nov. 1976, **90**(4): 630–649.

Rothschild, Michael and Stiglitz, J.E. A model of employment outcomes illustrating the effect of the structure of information on the level and distribution of income, *Economics Letters*, 1982, **10**: 231–236.

Sah, Raaj Kumar and Stiglitz, Joseph. The Taxation and Pricing of Agricultural and Industrial Goods. In: *Developing Economics*, Newbery, D. and Stern, N., eds., *Modern Tax Theory for Developing Countries*. Oxford U. Press, 1987.

Sah, Raaj Kumar and Stiglitz Joseph. The social cost of labor and project evaluation: A general approach, *Journal of Public Economics*, Nov. 1985, **28**(2): 135–163.

Salop, Joanne and Salop, Steven. Self-selection and turnover in the labor market, *Quarterly Journal of Economics*, Nov. 1976, **90**(4): 619–627.

Salop, Steven C. Wage differentials in a dynamic theory of the firm. *Journal of Economic Theory*, Aug. 1973, **6**(4): 321–344.

Salop, Steven C. A model of the natural rate of unemployment, *American Economic Review*, Mar. 1979, **69**(1): 117–125.

Schlicht, Ekkerhart. Labour turnover, wage structure and natural unemployment, *Zeitschrift für die Gesamte Staatswissenschaft*, June 1978, **134**(2): 337–346.

Schlicht, Ekkerhart. Reference group behaviour and economic incentives: A remark, *Zeitschrift für die Gesamte Staatswissenschaft.*, Mar. 1981a, **137**: 125–127.

Schlicht, Ekkerhart. Reference group behaviour and economic incentives: A further remark, *Zeitschrift für die Gesamte Staatswissenschaft.*, Dec. 1981b, **137**(4): 733–736.

Schlicht, Ekkerhart. Dismissal vs. fines as a discipline device: Comment on Shapiro-Stiglitz. Mimeo, Institute for Advanced Study, Princeton, NJ, Dec. 1985.

Schlicht, Ekkerhart. A Link Between Reservation Wage and Productivity. Mimeo, Institute for Advanced Study, Princeton, NJ, Feb. 1986.

Scitovsky, Tibor. Some consequences of the habit of judging quality by price, *Review of Economic Studies*, 1945, **12**(2): 100–105.

Shapiro, Carl. Premiums for high quality products as returns to reputations, *Quarterly Journal of Economics*, Nov. 1983, **98**(4): 659–679.

Shapiro, Carl and Stiglitz, Joseph E. Equilibrium unemployment as a worker discipline device, *American Economic Review*, June 1984, **74**(3): 433–444.

Shapiro, Carl and Stiglitz, Joseph E. Equilibrium unemployment as a worker discipline device: A reply, *American Economic Review*, Sept. 1985a, **75**(4): 892–893.

Shapiro, Carl and Stiglitz, Joseph E. Can unemployment be involuntary?: Reply, *American Economic Review*, Dec. 1985b, **75**(5): 1215–1217.

Simonde de Sismondi, J. C. L. *Political Economy*. NY: Kelley, [1814] 1966.

Slichter, Sumner H. *The Turnover of Factory Labor*. NY: Appleton, 1919.

Smith, Bruce. Limited information, credit rationing, and optimal government lending, *American Economic Review*, June 1983, **73**(3): 305–318.

Solow, Robert. Another possible source of wage stickiness, *Journal of Macroeconomics.*, Winter 1979, **1**(1): 79–82.

Solow, Robert. On theories of unemployment, *American Economic Review*, Mar. 1980, **70**(1): 1–11.

Solow, Robert. Insiders and outsiders in wage determination, *Scandinavian Journal of Economics*, 1985, **87**(2): 411–428.

Spence, A. Michael. *Market Signaling: Informational Transfer in Hiring and Related Processes*. Cambridge, ME: Harvard U. Press, 1974.

Stiglitz, Joseph E. Approaches to the economics of discrimination, *American Economic Review*, May 1973, **3**(2): 287–295.

Stiglitz, Joseph E. Theories of Discrimination and Economic Policy. In: von Furstenberg, ed., *Patterns of Racial Discrimination*. Lexington, MA: Lexington, 1974a, 5–26.

Stiglitz, Joseph E. Equilibrium Wage Distribution. *Economic Journal*, Sept. 1985, **95**(379): 595–618.

Stiglitz, Joseph E. Alternative theories of wage determination and unemployment in L.D.C.'s: The labor turnover model, *Quarterly Journal of Economics*, May 1974c, **88**(2): 194–227.

Stiglitz, Joseph E. Incentives and risk sharing in sharecropping, *Review of Economic Studies*, Apr. 1974d, **41**(2): 219–255.

Stiglitz, Joseph E. Incentives, risk and information: Notes towards a theory of hierarchy, *Bell Journal of Economic Management Science*, Autumn 1975, **6**(2): 552–579.

Stiglitz, Joseph E. Prices and Queues as Screening Devices in Competitive Markets. IMSSS Technical Report No. 212, Stanford U. Aug. 1976a.

Stiglitz, Joseph E. The efficiency wage hypothesis, surplus labour and the distribution of income in L.D.C.s, *Oxford Economic Papers*, July 1976b, **28**(2): 185–207.

Stiglitz, Joseph E. Lectures in Macro-economics. Mimeo, Oxford U., 1978.

Stiglitz, Joseph E. The Wage-Productivity Hypothesis: Its Economic Consequences and Policy Implications. Paper presented at the New York Meetings of the American Economic Association, 1982a, *Modern Developments in Public Finance: Essays in Honor of Arnold Harberger.* Ed.: M. Boskin. Basil Blackwell, Forthcoming.

Stiglitz, Joseph E. Alternative theories of wage determination and unemployment: The efficiency wage model. In: Gersovitz, Mark et al., eds., *The theory and experience of economic development's essays in honor of Sir W. Arthur Lewis.* London: Allen & Unwin, 1982b, 78–106.

Stiglitz, Joseph E. *On the Relevance or Irrelevance of Public Financial Policy.* Paper presented to a conference at Rice University, NBER Working Paper No. 1057, Apr. 1982c.

Stiglitz, Joseph E. On the relevance of irrelevance of public financial policy: Indexation, price rigidities and optimal monetary policy. In: Dornbusch, Rudiger and Simonsen, Mario, eds., *Inflation, Debt and Indexation.* Papers presented to a conference at Rio de Janeiro, Dec. 1981. Cambridge, MA: MIT Press, 1983, 183–222.

Stiglitz, Joseph E. Theories of wage rigidity. In: Butkiewicz, J., Koford, K. and Miller, J., eds., *Keynes' economic legacy.* NY: Prager, 1986, 153–221 (also available as NBER Working Paper No. 1442).

Stiglitz, Joseph E. and Weiss, Andrew. Credit rationing in markets with imperfect information, *American Economic Review,* June 1981, **71**(3): 393–410.

Stiglitz, Joseph E. and Weiss, Andrew. Incentive effects of terminations: Applications to the credit and labor markets, *American Economic Review,* Dec. 1983, **73**(5): 912–927.

Stiglitz, Joseph E. and Weiss, Andrew. Credit rationing and collateral. In: Edwards, Jeremy, Franks, Julian, Mayer, Colin and Schaefer, Stephen, eds., *Recent Developments in Corporate Finance.* NY: Cambridge U. Press, 1986a, 101–135.

Stiglitz, Joseph E. and Weiss, Andrew. Macroeconomic Equilibrium and Credit Rationing. Mimeo, Bellcore, 1986b.

Stiglitz, Joseph E. and Weiss, Andrew. Credit rationing: Reply, *American Economic Review,* Mar. 1987, **77**(1).

Stoft, Steven. Cheat Threat Theory: An Explanation of Involuntary Unemployment. Mimeo, Boston U., 1982.

Stoft, Steven. Wages, Unemployment and Piece Rate: Double Asymmetric Information. Boston U. Discussion Paper No. 113, July 1985.

Strand, Jon. Efficiency Wages, Implicit Contracts and Dual Labor Markets: A Theory of Work Habit Formation. Mimeo, Dept. of Economics, U. of Oslo, 1986.

Tan, Tommy Chin-Chiu and Da Costa Werlang, Sergio Ribeiro. *Life Cycle Credit Rationing.* Mimeo, U. of Chicago, June, 1985.

Taylor, John B. Aggregate dynamics and staggered contracts, *Journal of Political Economy,* Feb. 1980, **88**(1): 1–23.

Todaro, Michael. The urban employment problem in less developed countries: An analysis of demand and supply, *Yale Economics Essays,* 1968, **8**(2): 331–402.

Todaro, Michael, A model for labor migration and urban unemployment in less developed countries, *American Economic Review,* Mar. 1969, **59**(1): 138–148.

Vale, B. Effects of Bank Reserve Requirements with 'Grey' Credit Markets Under Asymmetric Information. Mimeo No. 15, U. of Oslo, Aug. 19, 1986.

Wallace, Neil. A Modigliani-Miller theorem for open market operations, *American Economic Review,* June 1981, **71**(3): 267–274.

Weiss, Andrew. *A Theory of Limited Labor Markets.* Ph.D. dissertation, Stanford U., 1976.

Weiss, Andrew. Job queues and layoffs in labor markets with flexible wages, *Journal of Political Economy,* June 1980, **88**(3): 526–538.

Weisskopf, Thomas E. Bowles, Sumner and Gordon, David M. Hearts and minds: A social model of U.S. productivity growth, *Brookings Papers Economic Activity,* 1983, **2**: 381–450.

Wessels, Walter J. The contribution by firms to unemployment: A dynamic model, *Southern Economic Journal,* Apr. 1979, **45**(4): 1130–1150.

Wessels, Walter J. The Uses and Limits of Unemployment as a Disciplining Device in the Efficiency Wage Model. Mimeo. North Carolina State U., Nov. 1986.

Wette, Hildegard. Collateral in credit rationing in markets with imperfect information: Note, *American Economic Review,* June 1983, **73**(3): 442–445.

Whiteside, Harold D. Wages: An equity approach, *Journal of Behavioral Economics*, 1974, **3**(1): 64–84.

Wilson, Charles A. Equilibrium and adverse selection, *American Economic Review*, May 1979, **69**(2): 313–317.

Wilson, Charles A. The nature of equilibrium in markets with adverse selection, *Bell Journal of Economics*, 1980, **11**(1): 108–130.

Yellen, Janet. Efficiency wage models of unemployment, *American Economic Review*, May 1984, **74**(2): 200–205.

Yoon, Chang-Ho. A Reexamination of the Theory of Credit Rationing. Mimeo, Stanford U., 1984a.

Yoon, Chang-Ho. On the Theory of Credit Rationing: Further Analysis. Mimeo, Stanford U., 1984b.

Part VII

Oligopoly: Theory and an Application

CONTENTS

19

Oligopoly Theory Made Simple

Huw Dixon

Oligopoly theory lies at the heart of industrial organisation (IO) since its object of study is the interdependence of firms. Much of traditional micro-economics presumes that firms act as passive price-takers, and thus avoids the complex issues involved in understanding firms' behaviour in an interdependent environment. As such, recent developments in oligopoly theory cover most or all areas of theoretical IO, and particularly the "new" IO. This survey is therefore very selective in the material it surveys: the goal is to present some of the basic or "core" results of oligopoly theory that have a general relevance to IO.

The recent development of oligopoly theory is inextricably bound up with developments in abstract game theory. New results in game theory have often been applied first in the area of oligopoly (for example, the application of mixed strategies in the 1950s—see Shubik 1959, and more recently the use of subgame perfection to model credibility). the flow is often in the opposite direction: most recently, the development of sequential equilibria by Kreps, Milgrom, Roberts, and Wilson arose out of modelling reputational effects in oligopoly markets. Over recent years, with the new IO, the relationship with game theory has become closer. This chapter therefore opens with a review of the basic equilibrium concepts employed in the IO—Nash equilibrium, perfect equilibrium, and sequential equilibrium.

The basic methodology of the new IO is neo-classical: oligopolistic rivalry is studied from an equilibrium perspective, with maximising firms, and uncertainty is dealt with by expected profit or payoff maximisation. However, the subject matter of the new IO differs significantly from the neo-classical micro-economics of the standard textbook. Most importantly, much of the new IO focuses on the process of competition over time, and on the effects of imperfect information and uncertainty. As such, it has expanded its vision from static models to consider aspects of phenomena which Austrian economists have long been emphasising, albeit with a rather different methodology.

The outline of the chapter is as follows. After describing the basic equilibrium concepts in an abstract manner in the first section, the subsequent two sections

Reprinted by permission of Addison Wesley Longman Ltd from *Economics of Industrial Organisation*, Davies, S. and Lyons, B. (eds.), pp. 127–165
© 1989 Addison Wesley Longman Ltd

explore and contrast the two basic static equilibria employed by oligopoly theory to model product market competition—Bertrand (price) competition, and Cournot (quantity) competition. These two approaches yield very different results in terms of the degree of competition, the nature of the first-mover advantage, and the relationship between market structure (concentration) and the price-cost margin.

The fourth section moves on to consider the incentive of firms to precommit themselves in sequential models; how firms can use irreversible decisions such as investment or choice of managers to influence the market outcome in their favour. This approach employs the notion of subgame perfect equilibria, and can shed light on such issues as whether or not oligopolists will overinvest, and why non-profit maximising managers might be more profitable for their firm than profit maximisers. The fifth section explores competition over time, and focuses on the results that have been obtained in game-theoretic literature on repeated games with perfect and imperfect information. This analysis centres on the extent to which collusive outcomes can be supported over time by credible threats, and the influence of imperfect information on firm's behaviour in such a situation. Alas, many areas of equal interest have had to be omitted—notably the literature on product differentiation, advertising, information transmission, and price wars. References are given for these in the final section.

Lastly, a word on style. I have made the exposition of this chapter as simple as possible. Throughout the chapter I employ a simple linearised model as an example to illustrate the mechanics of the ideas introduced. I hope that readers will find this useful, and I believe that it is a vital complement to general conceptual understanding. For those readers who appreciate a more rigorous and general mathematical exposition, I apologise in advance for what may seem sloppy in places. I believe, however, that many of the basic concepts of oligopoly theory are sufficiently clear to be understood without a general analysis, and that they deserve a wider audience than a more formal exposition would receive.

NON-COOPERATIVE EQUILIBRIUM

The basic equilibrium concept employed most commonly in oligopoly theory is that of the *Nash equilibrium*, which originated in Cournot's analysis of duopoly (1838). The Nash equilibrium applies best in situations of a one-off game with perfect information. However, if firms compete repeatedly over time, or have imperfect information, then the basic equilibrium concept needs to be refined. Two commonly used equilibrium concepts in repeated games are those of *subgame perfection* (Selten 1965), and if information is imperfect, *sequential equilibria* (Kreps *et al.* 1982).

We shall first introduce the idea of a Nash equilibrium formally, using some of the terminology of game theory. There are n firms, $i = 1 \ldots, n$, who each choose some strategy a_i from a set of feasible actions A_i. The firm's strategy might be one variable (price/quantity/R&D) or a *vector* of variables. For simplicity, we will take the case where each firm chooses one variable only. We can summarise what each and every firm does by the n-vector $(a_1, a_2 \ldots, a_n)$. The "payoff" function shows the firm's profits π_i as a function of the strategies of each firm:

$$\pi_i = \pi_i(a_1, a_2, \ldots, a_n) \tag{1}$$

The payoff function essentially describes the market environment in which the firms operate, and will embody all the relevant information about demand, costs, and so on. What will happen in this market? A Nash equilibrium is one possibility, and is based on the idea that firms choose their strategies non-cooperatively. A Nash equilibrium occurs when each firm is choosing its strategy optimally, given the strategies of the other firms. Formally, the Nash equilibrium is an n-vector of strategies $(a_1^*, a_2^* \ldots, a_n^*)$ such that for each firm i, a_i^* yields maximum profits given the strategies of the $n-1$ other firms a_{-i}^*.[1] That is, for each firm:

$$\pi_i(a_i^*, a_{-i}^*) \geq \pi_i(a_i, a_{-i}^*) \tag{2}$$

for all feasible strategies $a_i \in A_i$. The Nash equilibrium is often defined using the concept of a *reaction function*. A reaction function for firm i gives its best response given what the other firms are doing. In a Nash equilibrium, each firm will be on its reaction function.

Why is the Nash equilibrium so commonly employed in oligopoly theory? Firstly, because no firm acting on its own has any incentive to deviate from the equilibrium. Secondly, if all firms expect a Nash equilibrium to occur, they will choose their Nash equilibrium strategy, since this is their best response to what they expect the other firms to do. Only a Nash equilibrium can be consistent with this rational anticipation on the part of firms. Of course, a Nash equilibrium may not exist, and there may be multiple equilibria. There are many results in game theory relating to the existence of Nash equilibrium. For the purpose of industrial economics, however, perhaps the most relevant is that if the payoff functions are continuous and strictly concave in each firm's own strategy then at least one equilibrium exists.[2] Uniqueness is rather harder to ensure, although industrial economists usually make strong enough assumptions to ensure uniqueness.[3]

If market competition is seen as occurring over time, it may be inappropriate to employ a one-shot model as above. In a *repeated game* the one-shot *constituent* game is repeated over T periods (where T may be finite or infinite). Rather than simply choosing a one-off action, firms will choose an action a_{it} in each period $t = 1 \ldots, T$. For repeated games, the most commonly used equilibrium concept in recent oligopoly theory literature is that of subgame perfection which was first formalised by Selten (1965), although the idea had been used informally (e.g. Cyert and De Groot 1970). At each time t, the firm will decide on its action a_{it} given the past history of the market h_t, which will include the previous moves by all firms in the market.

A firm's "strategy" in the repeated game[4] is simply a rule σ_i which the firm adopts to choose its action a_{it} at each period given the history of the market up to then, h_t:

$$a_{it} = \sigma_i(h_t)$$

If we employ the standard Nash equilibrium approach, an equilibrium in the repeated game is simply n strategies $(\sigma_1^*, \sigma_2^* \ldots, \sigma_n^*)$ such that each firm's strategy σ_i^* is optimal given the other firms' strategies σ_{-i}^*. Thus no firm can improve its payoff by choosing a different strategy, given the strategies of the other firms.

However, a major criticism of using the standard Nash equilibrium in repeated games is that it allows firms to make "threats" which are not *credible*, in the sense that it would not be in their interest to carry out the threat. For example, consider the example of entry deterrence, with two periods. In the first period, the entrant decides whether or not to enter. In the second period, the entrant and incumbent choose outputs. The incumbent could adopt the following strategy: if entry does not occur, produce the monopoly output. If entry does occur, produce a very large output which drives down the price below costs at whatever output is chosen by the entrant. In effect, the entrant is posed with a powerful threat by the incumbent: "if you enter, I'll flood the market and we'll both lose money". Clearly, with this powerful threat, the incumbent will be able to deter entry. However, it is not a *credible* threat: if entry *were* to occur, then the incumbent would not wish to carry out this potent threat. Thus the incumbent's strategy is not credible, since he would be making unnecessary losses.

Subgame perfection was formulated to restrict firms to *credible* strategies. The basic idea of subgame perfection is quite simple. In a Nash equilibrium the firm chooses its strategy σ_i "once and for all" at the beginning of the game, and is committed to it throughout the play (as in the above example). To rule out non-credible threats, however, in a subgame-perfect equilibrium at each point in time firms choose their strategy for the rest of the game. The "subgame" at any time t is simply the remainder of the game from t through to the last period T. Subgame perfection requires that the strategies chosen are Nash equilibria in each subgame. This rules out non-credible threats, since in effect it requires a firm to choose its strategy optimally at each stage in the game. In our example, the incumbent's threat to expand output is not "credible": in the subgame consisting of the second period, it is not a Nash equilibrium. Indeed, if the market is Cournot, and there is a unique Cournot equilibrium, then the unique subgame-perfect strategy for the incumbent involves producing the Cournot output if entry has occurred. One of the major attractions of subgame perfection is that it narrows down the number of equilibria: there are often multiple Nash equilibria in repeated games and imposing "credibility" on strategies can reduce the number considerably, at least in finitely repeated games.

With imperfect information, a commonly used equilibrium concept is that of a "sequential" equilibrium (Kreps *et al.* 1982). This is formally a rather complex concept, but we shall provide a simple example in the section "competition over time". The basic idea of subgame perfection is employed, with the added ingredient of Bayesian updating of information.[5] Firms may be uncertain about each other's payoff functions (e.g. they do not know each other's costs or each other's objectives). At the start of the game, firms have certain prior beliefs, which they then update through the game. Firms may be able to learn something about each other from each other's actions. In such a situation, firms of a certain type may be able to build a "reputation" by taking actions which distinguish themselves from firms of another type. For example, in Milgrom and Roberts' (1982b) paper on entry deterrence, low-cost incumbents are able to distinguish themselves from high-cost incumbents by following a "limit pricing" strategy which it is unprofitable for high-cost firms to pursue. These reputational equilibria are very important, since they can explain how firms might behave against their short-run interest in order to preserve their reputation intact, for example as a low-cost firm or as an aggressive competitor.

COURNOT AND BERTRAND EQUILIBRIA WITH HOMOGENEOUS PRODUCTS

The previous section considered the concept of a Nash equilibrium in purely abstract terms. To make the concept concrete, we need to specify the exact nature of the strategies chosen, and define the payoff function. Corporate strategy is of course very broad, embracing all the activities of the firm—price, output, investment, advertising, R&D, and so on. In practice, oligopoly theory abstracts from the complexity of real-life corporate strategy, and concentrates on just on or two strategic variables. There are two basic ways of modelling how firms compete in the market. The first takes the view that the firm's strategic variable is its output, and originates in Cournot (1838). the second takes the view that the firm's basic strategic variable is price, and originates in the work of Bertrand (1883), Edgeworth (1925) and more recently in models of imperfect competition with product differentiation (e.g. Chamberlin 1933; Dixit and Stiglitz 1977).

As we shall see, whether price or output is the strategy makes a difference to the equilibrium outcome. For example, one of the basic issues of interest to industrial economists is the relationship between concentration and the price–cost margin. The standard notion that higher concentration leads to a higher price-cost margin is based on the Cournot view, and does not hold in the Bertrand framework, where there can be a perfectly competitive outcome with two or more firms. The distinction between price and quantity setting in the context of oligopoly is not present in monopoly, where it makes no difference whether the monopolist chooses a price or quantity (the monopolist simply chooses a point on its demand curve). In order to capture the distinction between the Cournot and Bertrand framework in its starkest form, we will first consider the simplest case of homogeneous goods. We will then discuss what arguments there are for choosing between the two competing approaches to modelling product market competition. In the next section, we will pursue this fundamental dichotomy further in the context of the more realistic case of differentiated commodities.

Cournot–Nash equilibrium with homogeneous goods

The basic view of the market taken by Cournot was that firms choose their outputs, and that the market then "clears" given the total output of firms. There are n firms $i = 1\ldots, n$, which produce outputs x_i, industry output being $x = \sum_{i=1}^{n} x_i$. We will make the simplest possible assumption about demand and costs:

A1   *Industry demand*
$$P = 1 - \sum_{i=1}^{n} x_i \tag{3}$$

A2   *Firm's costs*
$$c(x_i) = c\,x_i$$

Equation (3) is called the *inverse industry demand function*. Normally, the industry demand curve is seen as arising from the utility-maximising behaviour of consumers—

the market demand curve tells us how much households wish to buy at a given price. The mathematical operation of taking the inverse, as in (3), has important economic implications: it assumes that there can only be one "market" price. Thus firms have no direct control over the price of their output, only an indirect control via the effect that changes in their own output have on the total industry output.

Given A1–A2, we can define the firm's payoff function which gives firm i's profits as a function of the outputs chosen:

$$\pi_i(x_1, x_2, \ldots, x_n) = x_i\left(1 - \sum_{j=1}^{n} x_j\right) - c\,x_i$$
$$= x_i - x_i^2 - x_i \sum_{j \neq i} x_j - cx_i \tag{4}$$

Each firm has a reaction function, which gives its profit-maximising output as a function of the outputs chosen by the other firms. Since firm i treats the output of the other firm $j \neq i$ as fixed, the first-order condition for maximising (4) with respect to x_i is[6]:

$$\frac{\partial \pi_i}{\partial x_i} = 1 - \sum_{j \neq i} x_j - 2x_i - c = 0$$

Solving this defines the reaction function for firm i:

$$x_i = \frac{1 - \sum_{j \neq i}^{n} x_j - c}{2} \qquad i = 1, \ldots, n \tag{5}$$

Each firm has a similar reaction function, and the Nash equilibrium occurs when each firm is on its reaction function (i.e. choosing its optimal output given the output of the other firms). There will be a symmetric and unique Cournot–Nash equilibrium which is obtained by solving the n equations (5) for outputs (which are all equal by symmetry),

$$x_i^* = x^c = \frac{1 - c}{n + 1} \qquad \textit{Cournot–Nash equilibrium output} \tag{6}$$

which results in equilibrium price:

$$p^c = \frac{1}{n + 1} + \frac{n}{n + 1}\,c \tag{7}$$

For example, if $n = 1$ (monopoly) we get the standard monopoly solution. For $n = 2$, $x^c = (1 - c)/3$, $p^c = 1/3 + (2/3)c$. The price cost margin for each firm is:

$$\mu^c = \frac{p^c - c}{p^c} = \frac{1 - c}{1 + nc} \tag{8}$$

There is a clear inverse relationship between the equilibrium price–cost margin and the number of firms. As the number of firms become infinite ($n \to \infty$), the price–cost margin tends to its competitive level of 0: as the number falls to one, it tends to its monopoly level $(1 - c)/(1 + c)$, as predicted in Figure 1.

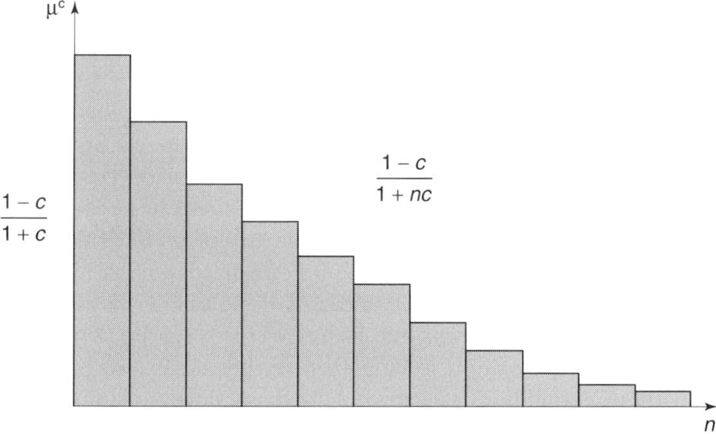

Figure 1. The price–cost margin and the number of firms in the Cournot–Nash equilibrium.

What is the intuition behind this relationship between number of firms and the price–cost margin? Very simply, with more firms, each firm's own demand becomes more elastic. With an infinite number of firms, the firm's elasticity becomes infinite, and hence the firms behave as competitive price-takers. The representative firm's elasticity η_i can be related to the industry elasticity η:

$$\eta = \frac{p}{x}\frac{\mathrm{d}x}{\mathrm{d}p} \tag{9a}$$

$$\eta_i = \frac{p}{x_i}\frac{\mathrm{d}x_i}{\mathrm{d}p} = \frac{x}{x_i}\left(\frac{p}{x}\frac{\mathrm{d}x_i}{\mathrm{d}p}\right) \tag{9b}$$

Under the Nash assumption firms treat the other firms' outputs as given, and the change in industry output x equals the change in firm i's output. Hence $\mathrm{d}x_i/\mathrm{d}p = \mathrm{d}x/\mathrm{d}p$. Of course, x_i/x is the ith firm's market share, which for our example is in equilibrium $1/n$. Hence (9b) becomes:

$$\eta_i = n \cdot \eta \tag{10}$$

In equilibrium, each firm's elasticity is equal to n times the industry elasticity of demand. As n gets large, so does η_i, leading to approximately "price-taking" behaviour.

Bertrand competition with homogeneous products

In his famous review, Bertrand criticised Cournot's model on several counts. One of these was the reasonable one that firms set prices, not quantities: the output sold by the firm is determined by the demand it faces at the price it sets. What is the equilibrium in the market when firms set prices, the Bertrand–Nash equilibrium?

If firms set prices, the model is rather more complicated than in the Cournot framework, since there can be as many prices in the market as there are firms. In the Cournot framework, the inverse industry demand curve implies a single "market" price. In the Bertrand framework each firm directly controls the price at which it sells its output, and in general, the demand for its output will depend on the price set by each firm and the amount that they wish to sell at that price (see Dixon 1987b). However, in the case of a homogeneous product where firms have constant returns to scale, the demand facing each firm is very simple to calculate. Taking the case of duopoly, if both firms set *different* prices, then all households will wish to buy from the lower-prices firm, which will want to meet all demand (so long as its price covers cost), and the higher-priced firm will sell nothing. If the two firms set the *same* price, then the households are indifferent between buying from either seller, and demand will be divided between them (equally, for example). If firms have constant marginal cost, there exists a unique Bertrand–Nash equilibrium with two or more firms, where each firm sets its price p_i equal to marginal cost—the competitive equilibrium. This can be shown in three steps:

Step 1. If both firms set different prices, then that cannot be an equilibrium. The higher-priced firm will face no demand, and hence can increase profits by undercutting the lower-priced firm, so long as the lower-priced firm charges in excess of c. If the *lower*-price firm charged c, it could increase profits from 0 by raising its price slightly while undercutting the higher-priced firm. Hence any Bertrand–Nash equilibrium must be a single-price equilibrium (SPE).

Step 2. The only SPE is where all firms set the competitive price. If both firms set a price *above* c, then either firm can gain by undercutting the other by a small amount. By undercutting, it can capture the whole market, and hence by choosing a small enough price reduction it can increase its profits.

Step 3. The competitive price is a Nash equilibrium. If both firms set the competitive price, then neither can gain by raising its price. If one firm raises its price while the other continues to set $p_i = c$, the lower-priced firm will face the industry demand, leaving the firm which has raised its price with no demand.

The Bertrand–Nash framework yields a very different relationship between structure and conduct from the Cournot–Nash equilibrium: with one firm, the monopoly outcome occurs; with two or more firms the competitive outcome occurs. Large numbers are not necessary to obtain the competitive outcome, and in general price-setting firms will set the competitive "price-taking" price.

Clearly, it makes a difference whether firms choose prices or quantities. What grounds do we have for choosing between them? First, and perhaps most importantly, there is the question of the *type* of market. In some markets (for primary products, stocks and shares) the people who set prices (brokers) are different to the producers. There exists what is essentially an *auction* market: producers/suppliers release a certain quantity into the market, and then brokers will sell this for the highest price possible (the market clearing price). The Cournot framework would thus seem natural where there are *auction* markets. While there are auction markets, there are also many industrial markets without "brokers", where the producers directly set the price at which they sell their produce. Clearly, the "typical" sort of market which concerns industrial economists is not an auction market, but a market with price-setting firms. How can the use of the Cournot framework be justified in markets with price-setting firms?

It is often argued that the choice of Bertrand or Cournot competition rests on the *relative* flexibility of prices and output. In the Bertrand framework, firms set prices and then produce to order. Thus, once set, prices are fixed, while output is perfectly flexible. In the Cournot framework, however, once chosen, outputs are fixed, while the price is flexible in the sense that it clears the market. Thus the choice between the two frameworks rests on the relative flexibility of price and output. This is of course an empirical question, but many would argue that prices are more flexible than quantities (e.g., Hart 1985), and hence the Cournot equilibrium is more appropriate.

A very influential paper which explores this view is Kreps and Scheinkman (1983). They consider the subgame perfect equilibrium in a two-stage model. In the first stage, firms choose capacities; in the second stage firms compete with price as in the Bertrand model, and can produce up to the capacity installed. The resultant subgame-perfect equilibrium of the two-stage model turns out to be equivalent to the standard Cournot outcome. This result, however, is not general, and rests crucially on an assumption about contingent demand (the demand for a higher-priced firm given that the lower-priced firm does not completely satisfy its demand)—see Dixon (1987a). An alternative approach is to allow for the flexibility of production to be endogenous (Dixon 1985; Vives 1986). The Bertrand and Cournot equilibria then come out as limiting cases corresponding to when production is perfectly flexible (a horizontal marginal cost curve) or totally inflexible (a vertical marginal cost curve at capacity).

Another reason that the Cournot framework is preferred to the Bertrand is purely technical: there is a fundamental problem of the non-existence of equilibrium in the Bertrand model (see Edgeworth 1925; Dixon 1987a). In our simple example, firms have constant average/marginal costs. If this assumption is generalised—for example, to allow for rising marginal cost—non-existence of equilibrium is a problem.[7]

A common argument for the Cournot framework is its "plausibility" relative to the Bertrand framework. Many economists believe that "numbers matter": it makes a difference whether there are two firms or two thousand. Thus the prediction of the Bertrand model—a zero price-cost margin with two or more firms—is implausible (see, for example, Hart 1979; Allen and Hellwigg 1986). The Cournot equilibrium captures the "intuition" that competition decreases with fewer firms. There are two points to be raised here: one empirical, one theoretical. Firstly, on the empirical level, there exists little or no evidence that there is a smooth monotonic relationship between the level of concentration and the price-cost margin. Secondly, on the theoretical level, the stark contrast in the Bertrand and Cournot formulations has been exhibited here only in the case of a simple one-shot game. In a repeated game, numbers may well matter. For example, Brock and Scheinkman (1985) consider a price-setting super-game, and show that there is a relationship between numbers and the prices that can be sustained in the industry (although the relationship is not a simple monotonic one). A related point is that the Nash equilibrium is a non-cooperative equilibrium. Numbers may well matter when it comes to maintaining and enforcing collusion, and one of Bertrand's criticisms of Cournot was that collusion was a likely outcome with only two firms.

COURNOT AND BERTRAND EQUILIBRIA WITH DIFFERENTIATED COMMODITIES

In this section, we will explore and contrast the Bertrand and Cournot approaches within a common framework of differentiated products with symmetric linear demands. As we shall see, there are again significant contrasts between markets where firms compete with prices and quantities. Firstly, we will compare the equilibrium prices and show that the Cournot equilibrium yields a higher price than the Bertrand equilibrium. Thus, as in the case of homogeneous products, Cournot competition is less competitive than Bertrand competition, although the contrast is less.

Secondly, we contrast the "Stackelberg" equilibrium (where one firm moves before the other) and the corresponding "first-mover" advantage. In the Cournot framework, the leader increases his own output and profits at the expense of the follower, and total output increases, reflecting a more competitive outcome than the standard Nash equilibrium. In the Bertrand framework the Stackelberg leader will raise his price and increase his profits. The follower will also raise his prices, and indeed his profits will increase by more than the leaders. Unlike the Cournot case, there is then a "second-mover advantage" in the Bertrand case. Overall, with price competition the Stackelberg equilibrium leads to higher prices and profits, and a contraction in total output. These differences between the behaviour of markets with price and quantity competition have important policy implications, which will be discussed at the end of this section in the context of the recent literature on strategic trade policy.

We continue to assume that firms have constant average/marginal cost, A2. However, we will drop A1 and assume that there is a symmetric linear demand system; in the case of two firms with differentiated products we have:

$A3$ For $0 < \alpha < 1$

$$x_i = 1 - p_1 + \alpha p_2 \tag{11a}$$

$$x_2 = 1 - p_2 + \alpha p_1 \tag{11b}$$

where $\alpha > 0$ implies the two outputs are *substitutes* (e.g. margarine and butter): if α were negative then they would be *complements* (e.g. personal computers and software). In the exposition, we will assume throughout that the firms produce *substitutes*, and for technical reasons that $\alpha < 1$ (i.e. quite plausibly the firm's own price has a greater absolute effect on its demand than the other firm's price).

The above equations express outputs (or, more precisely, demands) as a function of prices.[8] If we want to explore the Cournot framework with differentiated products, we need to invert (11) to give the prices that will "clear" the markets for chosen outputs.

Inverting (11) we have:

$$p_1 = a_0 - a_1 x_1 - a_2 x_2 \tag{12a}$$

$$p_2 = a_0 - a_1 x_2 - a_2 x_1 \qquad (12b)$$

where $\quad a_0 = \dfrac{1+\alpha}{1-\alpha^2}; \qquad a_1 = \dfrac{1}{1-\alpha^2}; \qquad a_2 = \dfrac{\alpha}{1-\alpha^2}$

Since $\alpha > 0$, both prices are decreasing in both outputs. Thus an increase in x_1 by one unit will decrease p_1 by a_1, and p_2 by a_2 (of course $a_1 > a_2$ for $\alpha < 1$).

Cournot–Nash equilibrium

There are two firms which choose outputs, the resultant prices given by the inverse demand system (12). Firm 1's "payoff" function is:

$$\pi_1 = x_1[(a_0 - a_1 x_1 - a_2 x_2) - c]$$

To obtain firm 1's reaction function, x_1 is chosen optimally given x_2:

$$\frac{\partial \pi_1}{\partial x_1} = a_0 - 2a_1 x_1 - a_2 x_2 - c = 0$$

Solving for x_1 this yields:

$$x_1 = r_1(x_2) = \frac{a_0 - c - a_2 x_2}{2a_1} \qquad (13)$$

The slope of the reaction function is given by:

$$\left.\frac{\mathrm{d}x_1}{\mathrm{d}x_2}\right|_{r_1} = \frac{-a_2}{2a_1} = -\frac{\alpha}{2} < 0$$

With substitutes, each firm's reaction function is downward sloping in output space, as in Figure 2.

The firms are identical, and there is a unique symmetric equilibrium at N with $x_1 = x_2 = x^c$:

$$x^c = \frac{a_0 - c}{2a_1 + a_2} = \frac{1 + \alpha - c(1 - \alpha^2)}{2 + \alpha} \qquad (14)$$

with resultant price:

$$p^c = \frac{1 + c(1 - \alpha)}{(2 + \alpha)(1 - \alpha)} \qquad (15)$$

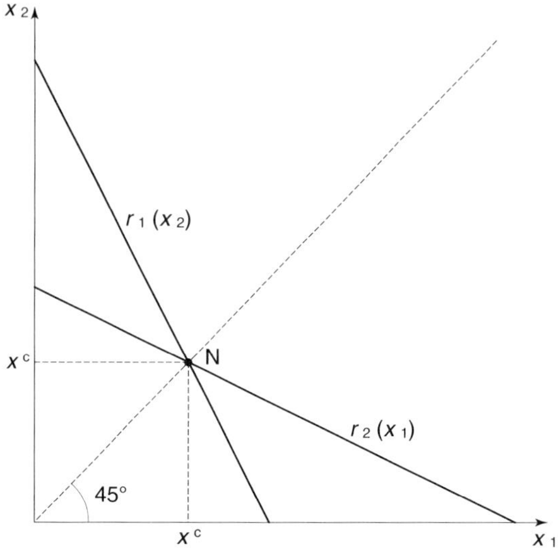

Figure 2. Cournot reaction functions.

Bertrand–Nash equilibrium

Turning now to the Bertrand case, firms choose *prices*, so that we use the direct demand system (11). Firm 1's profits are:

$$\pi_1 = p_1(1 - p_1 + \alpha p_2) - c(1 - p_1 + \alpha p_2) \tag{16}$$

$$\frac{\partial \pi_1}{\partial p_1} = 1 - 2p_1 + \alpha p_2 + c = 0$$

Hence firm 1's reaction function in price space is:

$$p_1 = s_1(p_2) = \frac{1 + c + \alpha p_2}{2} \tag{17}$$

The slope is:

$$\left. \frac{\mathrm{d}p_1}{\mathrm{d}p_2} \right|_{s_1} = \frac{\alpha}{2} > 0$$

Thus, the two firms' reaction functions are upward sloping in price space as depicted in Figure 3.

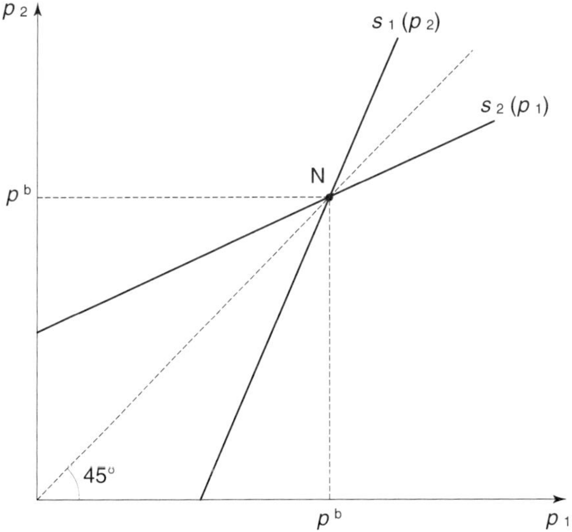

Figure 3. Bertrand–Nash equilibrium.

There is a unique symmetric equilibrium price $p_1 = p_2 = p^b$, with corresponding output, price, and price-cost margins:

$$p^{\mathrm{b}} = \frac{1 + c}{2 - \alpha} \tag{18}$$

$$x^{\mathrm{b}} = \frac{1 - c(1 - \alpha)}{2 - \alpha} \tag{19}$$

$$\mu^{\mathrm{b}} = \frac{1 - c(2 - \alpha)}{1 + c} \tag{20}$$

How do the Cournot and Bertrand equilibria compare? Direct comparison of (18) with (15) shows that $p^b < p^c$: i.e. the Bertrand equilibrium prices are *lower* than Cournot prices. We formulate this in the following observation:

Observation.   If firms demands are interdependent, $\alpha \neq 0$, then:

$$p^c > p^b; \quad x^c < x^b; \quad \mu^c > \mu^b$$

If $\alpha = 0$, then each firm is in effect a monopolist, since there are no cross-price effects, and the two outcomes are of course the same. It should be noted that the above observation remains true when the goods are complements $(-1 < \alpha < 0)$.

With differentiated products, then, Bertrand competition will be more competitive than Cournot competition, although the difference is less stark than in the case of homogeneous products. With product differentiation, firms have some monopoly power even with price competition, and do not have the same incentives for undercutting their competition as in the homogeneous goods case.

What is the intuition behind the above observation, that price competition is more competitive than quantity competition? Clearly, for a monopoly, it makes no difference whether price or quantity is chosen; it simply chooses the profit-maximising price–output point on its demand curve. There is a sense in which this is also true for the oligopolist: *given* what the other firm is doing, it faces a demand curve, and chooses a point on that demand curve. However, the demand curve facing firm 1 will be different if firm 2 keeps x_2 constant (and hence allows p_2 to vary) from when firm 2 keeps p_2 constant (and hence allows x_2 to vary). From (11), if firm 2 has price as its strategy, and holds p_2 constant, firm 1's demand is:

$$x_1 = (1 + \alpha p_2) - p_1 \tag{21}$$

with slope

$$\left. \frac{\mathrm{d}x_1}{\mathrm{d}p_1} \right|_{p_2} = -1 \tag{22a}$$

and elasticity

$$\left. \eta_1 \right|_{p_2} = \frac{p_1}{x_1} \tag{22b}$$

If, on the contrary, firm 2 has output as its strategy, it allows its price p_2 to vary as p_1 varies (to keep x_1 constant):

$$p_2 = 1 - x_2 + \alpha p_1 \tag{23}$$

Substituting (23) into (11a) we obtain firm 1's demand when x_2 is held constant:

$$x_1 = (1 + \alpha) - (1 - \alpha^2)p_1 - \alpha x_2 \tag{24}$$

with slope and elasticity:

$$\left. \frac{\mathrm{d}x_1}{\mathrm{d}p_1} \right|_{x_2} = -(1 - \alpha^2); \qquad \left. \eta_1 \right|_{x_2} = -\frac{p_1}{x_1}(1 - \alpha^2) \tag{25}$$

Clearly, comparing elasticities (22) and (25):

$$\left. \eta_1 \right|_{p_2} < \left. \eta_1 \right|_{x_2} < 0$$

Thus the demand facing firm 1 is *more* elastic when firm 2 holds p_2 constant (and allows x_2 to vary) than when x_2 is held constant (and p_2 allowed to vary). For example, suppose that firm 1 considers moving up its demand curve to sell one less unit of x_1, with substitutes ($\alpha > 0$). If firm 2 holds x_2 constant, then as firm 1 reduces its output and raises its price, the price for x_2 will rise (via (11b)). Clearly, the demand for firm 1 will be more elastic in the case where firm 2 does not raise its price and expands output.

We have derived the above observation under very special assumptions A1, A3: how far can we generalise this comparison of Cournot and Bertrand prices? This has been the subject of much recent research—see for example Cheng (1984), Hathaway and Rickard (1979), Okuguchi (1987), Singh and Vives (1984), Vives (1985a,b). Vives (1985a) considers a more general differentiated demand system, which need not be linear or symmetric (*ibid.* 168) and derives fairly general conditions for which the Bertrand price is less than the Cournot price. Of course, there need not be unique Cournot or Bertrand equilibria: with multiple equilibria, the comparison becomes conceptually more complex. Vives (1985b) has established a result that for very general conditions, there exists a Bertrand equilibrium which involves a lower price than any Cournot equilibrium.

Of course, there are other contrasts to be drawn between Cournot and Bertrand–Nash equilibria. For example, there is the question of welfare analysis employing standard consumer surplus. A simple example employing the linear demand system (11), (12) is provided by Singh and Vives (1984: 76) which shows that the sum of consumer and producer surplus is larger in Bertrand than in Cournot–Nash equilibrium, both when goods are substitutes and complements.

Stackelberg leadership and the advantages of moving first

The difference between Cournot and Bertrand competition go deeper than the simple comparisons of the previous section. To illustrate this, we will examine the advantages of moving first in the two frameworks. The standard Nash equilibrium assumes that firms move simultaneously. However, Heinrich von Stackelberg (1934) suggested an alternative in which one firm (the leader) moves first, the other (the follower) moves second. Thus, when the follower chooses its strategy it treats the leader's choice as given. However, the leader will be able to infer the follower's choice and take this into account in its decision. The explicit algebraic analysis of the Stackelberg equilibrium is rather complicated, and we will rather employ the familiar iso-profit loci.[9] In the following analysis, it is important to note that under A1, A3 the model is perfectly symmetric; thus whether in price or quantity space, the firms' reactions functions are "symmetric" in the sense that firm 1's reaction function is a reflection of firm 2's in the 45° line (see Figures 2, 3). Similarly, firm 1's iso-profit loci are simply reflections of firm 2's in the 45° line, and vice versa.

Firstly we analyse the Stackelberg equilibrium in the Cournot case. The follower (firm 2) will simply choose its output to maximise its profits given x_1, so that $x_2 = r_2(x_1)$. The leader, however, will choose x_1 to maximise its profits given that x_2 depends on x_1 via r_2. Thus, by moving first, the leader can pick the point on firm 2's

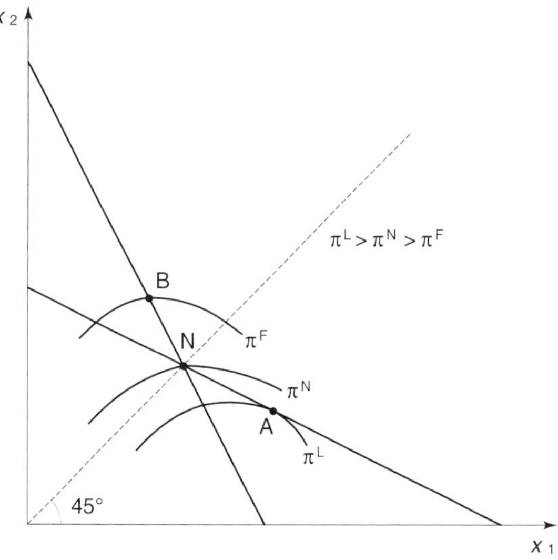

Figure 4. First-mover advantage in Cournot model.

reaction function that yields it the highest profits: this is represented in Figure 4 by the tangency of iso-profit loci π^L to r_2 at point A.

If firm 2 were the leader, and firm 1 the follower, then by symmetry firm 2's Stackelberg point would be at point B—the reflection of A in the 45° line (at this point firm 2's iso-profit locus is tangential to firm 1's reaction function). Comparing points A, B and the Nash equilibrium at point N, we can see that if firm 1 is the leader it earns, π^L, which is greater than in the Nash equilibrium π^N. If firm 1 is a follower, it will end up at point B, and earn only π^F which is *less* than π^N. Hence, in the Cournot framework, we have:

$$\pi^L \quad > \quad \pi^N \quad > \quad \pi^F \qquad (Cournot)$$

<table>
<tr><td>profits
of
leader</td><td>Nash
profits</td><td>profits
of
follower</td></tr>
</table>

There is thus a first-move advantage in two senses: the leader earns more than in the simultaneous-move case ($\pi^L > \pi^N$); the leader earns more than the follow ($\pi^L > \pi^F$). The leader increases his output and profits at the expense of the follower (in fact, the decline in the follower's profits from π^N to π^F is *larger* than the increase in the leaders from π^N to π^L: industry profits fall).

In the Bertrand case, the story is rather different: there is a "second-mover" advantage. The reaction functions and iso-profit loci of firm 1 depicted in price space are shown in Figure 5, and again are symmetric. The iso-profit loci for firm 1 are higher, the further away they are positioned from the x-axis (firm 1 will earn higher profits, the higher p_2 is). N is the Nash equilibrium, A occurs if 1 is the leader, B if 2 is the leader.

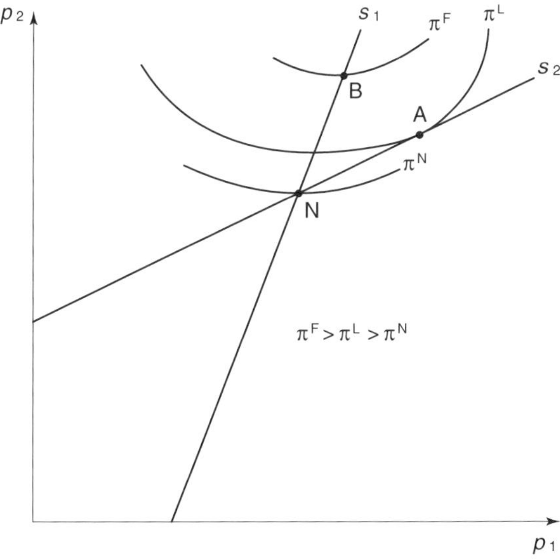

Figure 5. Second-mover advantage in Bertrand model.

If firm 1 is the leader, it will choose to raise its price, moving along firm 2's reaction function S_2 from N to A and profits will increase from π^N to π^L. However, if firm 1 is the follower, it will end up at B with profits π^F. Note that the follower raises his price by less than the leader, and that $\pi^F > \pi^L$. Thus the leader will set a higher price than the follower, produce a lower output and earn *less* profits:

$$\pi^F > \pi^L > \pi^N \qquad (Bertrand)$$

There is an advantage to moving "second". The second-mover advantage goes beyond Bertrand equilibria, and extends to any game with upward-sloping reaction functions (Gal-Or 1986). There is still a first-mover advantage in the sense that the leader earns more than in the simultaneous move case ($\pi^L > \pi^N$). In contrast to the Cournot case, in the Bertrand case Stackelberg leadership leads to higher prices, profits and lower outputs.

Prices vs. quantities

Price and quantity competition have very different implications for the nature of product market competition between firms. Most importantly, from the firms' point of view, price competition leads to lower profits than does quantity competition in Nash equilibrium. As was discussed earlier, whether firms should be viewed as competing with price or quantity can be seen as depending on structural or institutional characteristics of the market—the flexibility of production, whether the market is an auction market, etc.

An alternative approach is to treat the firm's decision to choose price or quantity as itself a strategic decision (Klemperer and Meyer 1986; Singh and Vives 1984). While it is perhaps not quite clear how firms might achieve this, it is at least a useful "experiment" and will reveal the incentives which firms have to achieve one or the other type of competition.

Without uncertainty, this "experiment" is not fruitful: firms are *indifferent* between choosing price or quantity. The reason is that from the individual firm's perspective, it simply faces a demand curve, and—like a monopolist—chooses a point on that demand curve. It can achieve any point on the demand curve by choosing either price or quantity. The firm's own price/quantity decision does not affect this demand curve, which is rather determined by the *other* firm's choice. Firm 1's choice has a pure externality effect on the demand faced by firm 2: if 1 chooses price, 2's demand is more elastic than if firm 1 had chosen quantity. However, in the Nash framework, each firm will ignore this externality: given the other firm's choice, each firm will face a particular demand curve, and will be indifferent between setting price or quantity itself. In the case of duopoly, there will be four Nash equilibria in this strategic game: one where both set quantities (Cournot); one where both set prices (Bertrand); and two asymmetric equilibria where one sets price, the other quantity. With certainty, then, allowing firms to choose price or quantity tells us nothing about which may be more appropriate.

The presence of uncertainty (adding a stochastic term to A3, for example) can mean that firms have a strict preference between price and quantity setting. The results depend very much on the exact assumptions made (is demand uncertainty additive or multiplicative; is demand linear in prices?). For the simple linear demand system A3 with an additive stochastic term, firms will prefer quantity setting if marginal costs are increasing; they will be indifferent if marginal costs are constant (as in A1); they prefer price setting if marginal costs are decreasing (Klemperer and Meyer 1986; proposition 1). While this and related results are at present rather specific, they do suggest that the presence and nature of uncertainty provide some insights into how firms view the alternatives of price and quantity setting.

PRECOMMITMENT: STRATEGIC INVESTMENT AND DELEGATION

In the previous section, we explored the nature of the first-mover advantage in the Cournot and Bertrand framework. Clearly, if we start from the Nash equilibrium, there is an incentive for the firm to precommit its output/price to obtain this first-mover advantage. By "precommitment" it is meant that the firm takes some action prior to competing in the product market which commits it to a certain course of action. In the standard Cournot model, it is not credible for one firm to produce the Stackelberg output in the simultaneous move game. For example, in terms of Figure 6, firm 1's Stackelberg point A is not on its reaction function—so that given firm 2's output x_{2A}, firm 1 would like to produce x'_1. The only credible equilibrium is the Nash equilibrium at N. In order to move towards its Stackelberg point, the firm must be able to precommit its output in some way. In the previous section we simply assumed that the leader was able to move first. In some situations it is natural to assume a particular sequence of moves (e.g. entrant/incumbent, dominant firm). However, in the case of

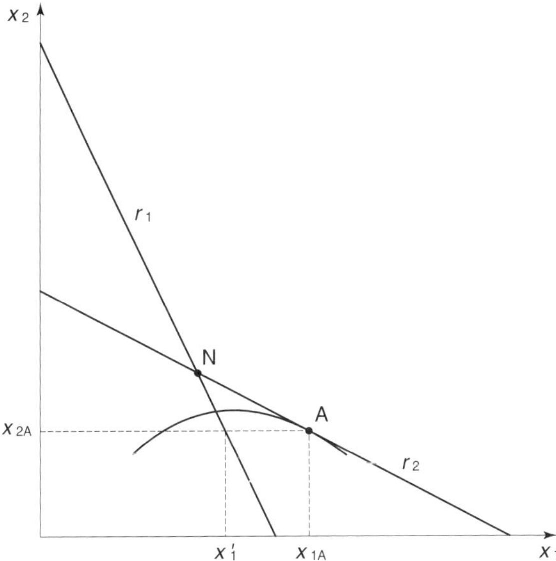

Figure 6. Non-credibility of Stackelberg point.

active incumbents which are competing on even terms, simultaneous moves seem more natural.

Given that there is an incentive for the firm to precommit, how can this be achieved? This section will look at two methods of precommitment which have received much recent attention—precommitment through investment, and precommitment through delegation. The basic idea is simple: the firm can take actions prior to competing in the market, which will alter the Nash equilibrium in the market. Firms can take actions, such as investment decisions,[10] choice of managers, that are irreversible (in the sense of being "fixed" over the market period), and which alter the firm's reaction function, thus shifting the Nash equilibrium in the market. We will first consider how investment by firms can be used strategically to alter the market outcome.

For a wide range of industrial processes, economists since Marshall have taken the view that it is appropriate to treat the capital stock decision as being taken on a different time scale (the "long run") to price/output decisions (the "short-run"). When firms compete in the product market, it follows that they treat their capital stock as fixed. The capital stock chosen by the firm will influence its *costs* when it competes in the market. The fact that capital is committed "before" output/price decisions means that it can use investment strategically, to influence the market outcome. In essence, through its choice of capital stock, the firm will determine the short-run costs which it will have when it chooses output/price; the firm's marginal costs will determine its reaction function, and hence the Nash equilibrium in the product market. Schematically:

$$\text{investment} \xrightarrow{} \begin{array}{c}\text{short-run}\\ \text{marginal cost}\end{array} \xrightarrow{} \begin{array}{c}\text{reaction}\\ \text{function}\end{array} \xrightarrow{} \begin{array}{c}\text{market}\\ \text{equilibrium}\end{array}$$

For example, in the Cournot case, the firm can increase its investment, reduce its marginal cost, and hence shift its reaction function out, so that the product market equilibrium moves towards the Stackelberg point. Of course, this precommitment is not costless: capital costs money, and as we shall see, such use of capital leads to productive inefficiency. Again, there is an important dichotomy between the Cournot and Bertrand approaches: if the product market is Cournot, then the firm will want to overinvest; if the product market is Bertrand, then the firms will want to underinvest. We will briefly illustrate both situations.

The structure of strategic investment models is very simple: there are two stages to capture the distinction between the short and the long run. In the first "strategic" stage, the firms choose their capital stock; in the second "market" stage, firms choose output/price. The choice of capital stock in the first stage will determine the cost function which the firm has. In the previous two sections we assumed constant average/marginal cost at c (A2). This can be conceived of as the long-run cost function. In order to keep the exposition consistent, we will assume that firms have a production function of the form:

$$A4 \qquad\qquad x_i = k_i^{1/2} L_i^{1/2}$$

where L_i is labour input. If capital costs r, and labour's wage is normalised to unity, the resultant short-run cost function given investment is:

$$c(x_i, k_i) = rk_i + \frac{x_i^2}{k_i} \tag{26}$$

where linear increasing marginal cost:

$$\frac{\partial c}{\partial x_i} = \frac{2}{k_i} x_i \tag{27}$$

Thus an increase in investment lowers the marginal cost of producing output. The production function A4 displays constant returns to scale, and hence the long-run cost function has constant average/marginal cost in terms of A2,[11] minimum average cost $c = 2\sqrt{r}$.

We will first outline the strategic investment model with Cournot competition in the product market, a simple version of Brander and Spencer's (1983) article. If investment is used non-strategically, then the firm simply operates on its long run cost function given by A2: capital and labour are chosen to minimise production costs. In the strategic investment framework, however, the firm's costs will be given by its short-run cost function (26). Turning to the market stage, the firm's profits are:

$$\pi_i = x_i(a_0 - a_1 x_i - a_2 x_j) - rk_i - \frac{x_i^2}{k_i} \tag{28}$$

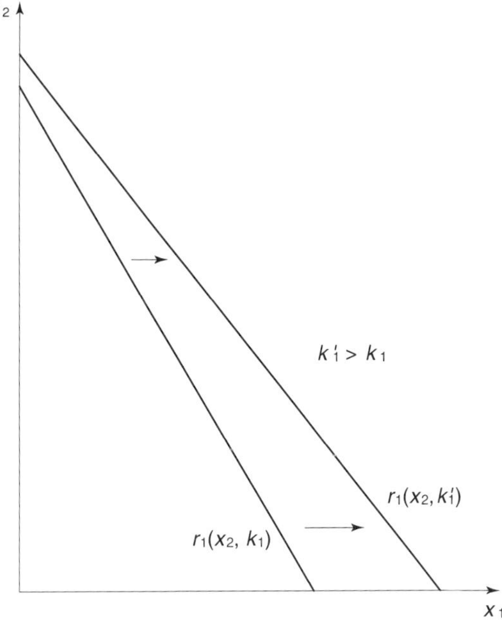

Figure 7. Investment shifts from 1's reaction function out.

The reaction function which the firm has in the market stage, conditional on k_i, is derived by setting $\partial \pi_i / \partial x_i = 0$:

$$x_i = r_i(x_j, k_i) = \frac{a_0 - a_2 x_j}{2a_1 + (2/k_i)} \tag{29}$$

By increasing its investment, firm i will reduce its marginal costs, and from (29) it will shift its reaction function out, as in Figure 7. Given the level of investment by the two firms (k_1, k_2) the Cournot–Nash equilibrium in the market stage is given by solving for the intersection of the two firms' reaction functions, as in Figure 8. Thus the equilibrium outputs conditional on (k_1, k_2) are obtained by solving (29) for x_1 and x_2 (we leave this as an exercise for the reader). In general form:

$$x_i = x_i(k_i, k_j) \tag{30}$$
$${\scriptstyle(+)\ (-)}$$

This notation signifies that firm i's equilibrium output in the market stage depends positively on its own investment, and negatively on investment by the other firm. Suppose we start off at point A in Figure 9: an increase in k_1 to k_1' shift out r_1, so that the market equilibrium goes from A to B, x_i rising and x_2 falling. Conversely, an increase in k_2 shifts the equilibrium from A to C. Thus by altering their investment, the firms can alter their reaction functions, and hence the market stage equilibrium.

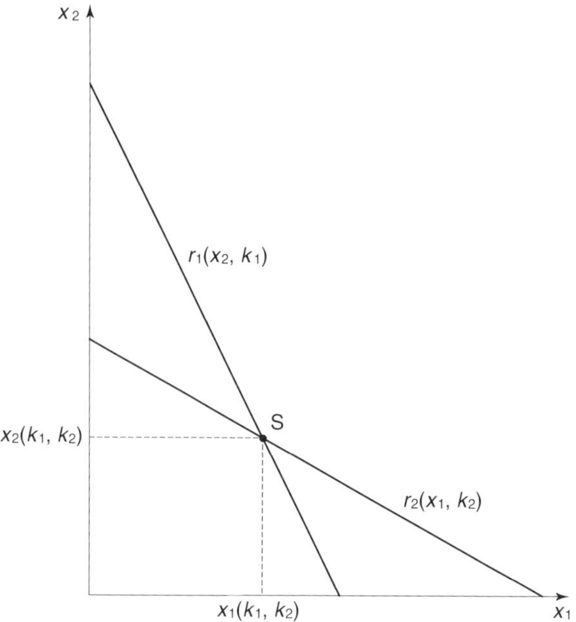

Figure 8. Market stage equilibrium given investment k_1, k_2.

How is the optimal level of investment in the first strategic stage determined? Firms choose investment levels k_i, *given* that the second-stage outputs will be as in (30). We can see their profits as a function of capital stocks. For firm 1 we have profits:

$$u_i(k_1, k_2) = x_1(k_1, k_2)[a_0 - a_1 x_1(k_1, k_2) - a_2 x_2(k_1, k_2)] - c(x_i(k_1, k_2), k_1) \qquad (31)$$

The RHS term in square brackets is the price, which is multiplied by output to obtain revenue, from which are subtracted costs.

The firm will choose k_1 to maximise its profits (31), hence:

$$\frac{\partial \pi_1}{\partial k_1} = \frac{\partial x_1}{\partial k_1}\left[a_0 - 2a_1 x_1 - a_2 x_2 - \frac{\partial c}{\partial x_1}\right] - a_2 x_1 \frac{\partial x_2}{\partial k_1} - \frac{\partial c}{\partial k_1} = 0 \qquad (32)$$

Since firm 1 chooses x_1 to maximise profits given x_2 and k_1 in the second stage, the bracket on the right-hand side of (32) is zero (it is simply its reaction function (29)). Hence (32) becomes:

$$\frac{\partial c}{\partial k_1} = -a_2 \frac{\partial x_2}{\partial k_1} x_1 > 0 \qquad (33)$$

What does (33) tell us? $\partial c/\partial k_1$ gives the effect of investment on the total costs of producing x_1. If $\partial c/\partial k_1 = 0$, as in the standard non-strategic case, then k_1 *minimises* the

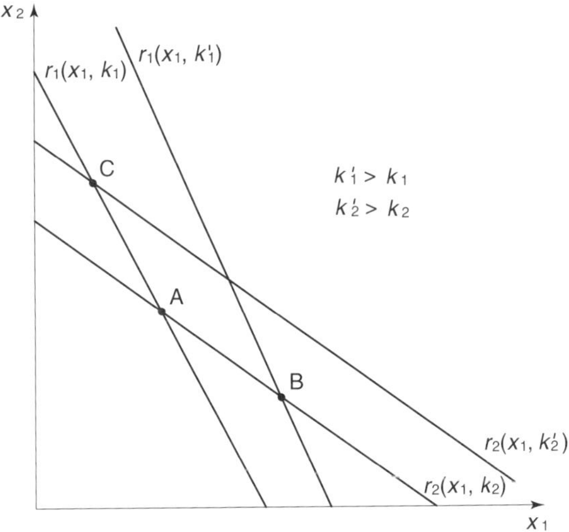

Figure 9. Market stage equilibrium and changes in investment.

cost of producing x_1. If $\partial c/\partial k_1 > 0$, as in (33), then there is "overcapitalisation", more investment than would minimise costs (a reduction in k_1 would reduce average costs). If $\partial c/\partial k_i < 0$, then there is "undercapitalisation": less investment than would minimise costs.

With a Cournot market stage, then, there is overcapitalisation of production in the market stage. The intuitive reason is quite simple. Given the other firm's reaction function, each firm can shift its own reaction function out towards its Stackelberg point. Of course, there is a cost to this: more investment leads to higher capital costs and inefficient production. The firms will shift out their reaction functions beyond their "innocent" level, and the final product market equilibrium will be at a point such as S in Figure 10. At the equilibrium level of investment, the additional cost of investment equals the additional gains from moving out the reaction function further. In the strategic investment equilibrium S then, both firms produce a larger output than in the non-strategic equilibrium N.

In the Bertrand case, an exactly analogous argument applies for strategic investment: however, there is the opposite result of *undercapitalisation*. The Stackelberg equilibrium results in higher prices and lower outputs than in the Bertrand case. Thus firms will *restrict* investment relative to the innocent Bertrand equilibrium, in order to shift their reaction function *out* in price space, as in Figure 11. Starting from the "innocent" Bertrand equilibrium at N, if firm 1 restrict its investment, its marginal costs *rise*, and its reaction function shifts outwards to s_1' (an outward shift because with higher marginal costs, it will wish to set a higher price and produce a smaller quantity given the price chosen by the other firm). If both firms underinvest strategically, the resultant equilibrium will be at S, with higher prices and lower output.

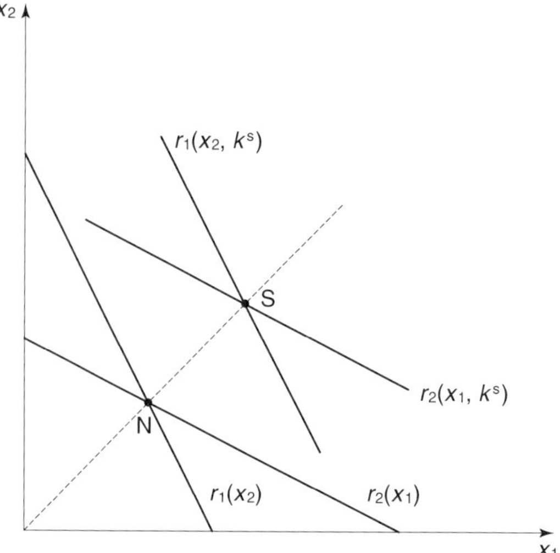

Figure 10. Strategic investment equilibrium—the Cournot case.

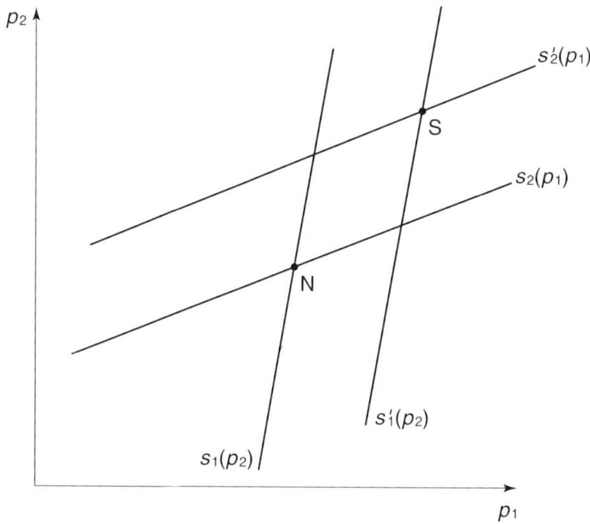

Figure 11. Underinvestment raises prices.

We will briefly sketch the algebra underlying this result. Under A1, A4, the firm's profits are:

$$\pi_i = p_i - p_i^2 - \alpha p_i p_j - \frac{1}{k_i}(1 - p_i - \alpha p_i p_j)^2 - rk_i \tag{34}$$

Setting $\partial \pi_i / \partial p_i = 0$, firm i's reaction function $p_i = s_i(p_j)$ is:

$$P_i = \frac{1 + 2/k_i}{2 + 2/k_i} + \frac{\alpha(1 + 2/k_i)}{(2 + 2/k_i)}\, p_j \tag{35}$$

Solving for p_i to p_j given k_i and k_j, in general terms we have:

$$P_i = p_i(k_i,\ k_j) \qquad i, j = 1, 2, i \neq j \tag{36}$$
$${}_{(+)}\ {}_{(-)}$$

The firms choose k_i to maximise (34) given that in the market subgame firms' prices are given by (36) (i.e. a Bertrand–Nash equilibrium occurs).

$$\frac{d\pi_i}{dk_i} = \frac{\partial \pi_i}{\partial p_i} \cdot \frac{dp_j}{dk_i} + \frac{\partial \pi_j}{\partial p_j} \cdot \frac{dp_j}{dk_j} + \frac{\partial \pi_i}{\partial k_i} = 0 \tag{37}$$
$${}_{(0)}{}_{(-)}{}_{(+)}{}_{(-)}{}_{(+)}$$

Note that $\partial \pi_i / \partial p_i = 0$, since firms are in their market stage reaction function (35), and further that $\partial \pi_i / \partial k_i = -\partial c_i / \partial k_i$. Hence (37) can be expressed as:

$$\frac{\partial c}{\partial k_i} = \frac{\partial \pi_i}{\partial p_j}\,\frac{dp_j}{dk_i} < 0 \tag{38}$$
$$\phantom{\frac{\partial c}{\partial k_i} = }{}_{(+)}\ {}_{(-)}$$

That is, *undercapitalisation* of production results from the strategic use of investment with Bertrand product market competition.

Clearly, the result of strategic investment models depends on the nature of product market competition. Other papers have made different assumptions than the simple Cournot–Nash and Bertrand–Nash equilibria. Dixon (1985) considers the case of a *competitive* product market; Eaton and Grossman (1984) and Yarrow (1985) a *conjectural* Cournot equilibrium; Dixon (1986b) a *consistent conjectural* variation equilibrium in the product market.

Since production will generally be inefficient in a strategic investment equilibrium, firms have an incentive to try and precommit their labour input at the same time as their capital. By so doing, firms will be able to produce any output efficiently, while being free to precommit themselves to a wide range of outputs. In Dixon (1986a), precommitment is treated as a strategic choice by the firm: the firm can precommit either, neither, or both capital and labour in the strategic stage. Because of the strategic inefficiency in production that occurs when only capital is precommited, under almost any assumption about the nature of product market competition, firms would prefer to precommit both factors of production (Dixon 1986a; Theorem and p. 67). If firms precommit both factors of production in the strategic stage, then in effect they have chosen their output for the market stage, and the resultant equilibrium is equivalent to the standard Cournot equilibrium. How might firms be able to precommit their output in this manner? One important method that may be available is choice of technology. More specifically, the firm may have a choice between a putty–putty technology that allows for smooth substitution of capital for labour in the market stage, or an otherwise equivalent putty–clay technology that is Leontief in the market stage. If the firm chooses a putty–clay technology, then its choice of investment and technique in the strategic stage effectively ties down its output and employment in the market stage. If possible, then, firms would prefer to have totally inflexible production in the market stage. This strong result ignores uncertainty, of course. If demand or factor prices are uncertain, there will be a countervailing incentive to retain flexibility.

In strategic investment models it is firms themselves which precommit. Governments, however, can undertake precommitments which firms themselves cannot make. In the context of trade policy, there has been much recent research on how governments can improve the position of their own firms competing in international markets (see Venables 1985, for excellent surveys). If domestic firms are competing in foreign markets, the net benefit to the home country in terms of consumer surplus is the repatriated profits—total revenue less the production costs (with competitive factors markets, production costs represent a real social cost to the exporting country). Government trade policy may therefore be motivated by what is called "rent extraction", that is, helping their own firms to make larger profits which are then repatriated. Trade policy, usually in the form of an export subsidy or tax, is a form of precommitment by the government which enables domestic firms to improve their position in foreign markets. Brander and Spencer (1984) presented the first model based on the rent-extraction principle, and argued for the use of export subsidies in the context of a Cournot–Nash product market. Subsidies have the effect of *reducing* the marginal costs faced by exporters, and can thus be used to shift out their reaction functions to the Stackelberg point (the cost subsidies "cost" nothing from the point of view of the exporting country, since they merely redistribute money from the taxpayers to shareholders). As Eaton and Grossman (1983) argued, the exact form of the trade policy will be sensitive to the nature of product market competition. With a Bertrand product market, of course, rent extraction arguments lead to the imposition of an export *tax*, since this will shift the Bertrand competitor's reaction function outwards in price space towards its Stackelberg point.

The incentive to precommit in oligopolistic markets also sheds light on one of the perennial issues of industrial economics—what are the objectives of firms? The divorce of ownership from control can be viewed as an act of delegation by shareholders. This act of delegation can be employed as a form of precommitment by shareholders. What sort of Managers do shareholders want to manage their firms? There is an obvious answer to this question, which underlies the managerialist view of Marris (1964): shareholders want managers who maximise profits (share valuation) and work hard. This may be true in the context of monopoly: in an imperfectly competitive framework, matters are rather different. Several recent papers (Fershtman 1985; Lyons 1986; Vickers 1985a) have shown how higher profits for shareholders can be obtained when they have non-profit maximising shareholders. The reaction functions of firms in the standard Cournot and Bertrand models are based on the assumption of profit maximisation. By choosing managers with different objectives (e.g. a preference for sales, or an aversion to work) the firms' reaction functions will be shifted. We will illustrate this with a very simple example adapted from Lyons (1986). Managers maximise utility, which depends on profits (remuneration) and sales R (power, prestige, and so on). The utility is a convex combination of

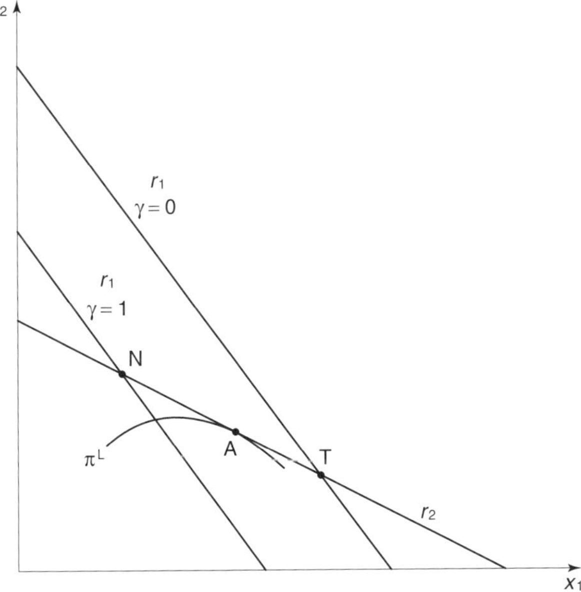

Figure 12. Equilibrium outcome and managerial preferences.

the two:

$$u = \gamma\pi + (1-\gamma)R \qquad 0 \le \gamma \le 1$$
$$= R - \gamma c$$

since $\pi = R - c$. The coefficient γ represents the weight put on *profits*: $\gamma = 1$ is profit maximisation, $\gamma = 0$ yields sales maximisation.

Using the common framework A1, A2, assuming that managers choose outputs to maximise utility, we can derive the firm's reaction functions:

$$u_1 = x_1(a_0 - a_1 x_1 - a_2 x_2) - \gamma c x_1$$

$$\frac{\partial u_1}{\partial x_1} = a_0 - 2a_1 x_1 - a_2 x_2 - \gamma c = 0$$

which yields the reaction function:

$$x_1 = r_1(x_2,\, \gamma_1) = \frac{a_0 - \gamma c - a_2 x_2}{2a_1}$$
$$(-)\,(-)$$

By choosing managers with a preference for sales (i.e. γ smaller than unity), shareholders can push out their firm's reaction function. In Figure 12 we depict the two extreme reaction functions: the one nearest the origin corresponding to profit maximisation $\gamma = 1$, the other to sales maximisation $\gamma = 0$. Given firm 2's reaction function, firm 1 can move to any point between N and T by choosing the appropriate value of γ. If, as depicted, the Stackelberg point A lies between N and T, then firms will be able to attain their Stackelberg point—note that since A will lie to the left of N, the choice of γ will surely be less than unity, reflecting non-maximisation of profits due to some sales preference. In such a market, if one firm is a profit maximiser with $\gamma = 1$ and the other has management with $\gamma < 1$, the nonprofit maximising firm will earn *more* than the profit-maximising firm! Of course, in a Bertrand market, the shareholders would wish to choose managers who would restrict output and raise prices—perhaps lazy managers with an aversion to work (see Dixon and Manning 1986, for an example). While we have talked about different "types" of managers, the precommitment made by shareholders can be seen as taking the form of different types of remuneration packages which elicit the desired behaviour from managers.

In an imperfectly competitive market then, it can pay shareholders to have non-profit maximising managers. There need not be the conflict of interest between owners and managers that is central to managerialist theories of the firm. Also, "natural selection" processes need not favour profit maximisers in oligopolistic markets, since (for example) sales-orientated managers can earn larger profits than their more profit-orientated competitors. This is a comforting result given the apparent prevalence of motives other than profits in managerial decisions.

The presence of a first-mover advantage means that firms competing in an oligopolistic environment have an incentive to precommit themselves in some way. We have explored *two* methods of precommitment: through investment, and through delegation. Strategic investment leads to productive inefficiency, and from the point of view of the firm, it may be cheaper to make its precommitment through its choice of managers rather than its choice of capital stock.

COMPETITION OVER TIME

In general, Nash equilibria are "inefficient" in the sense that in equilibrium, profits of all the firms can be increased. The fundamental reason is that firms' profits are interdependent (via the payoff function): each firm's profits depend partly on what the other firms are doing. There is thus an "externality" involved when each firm chooses its strategy. For example, in the Cournot framework, if one firm raises its output, it reduces the prices obtained by the other firms, thus reducing their profits (a negative externality). In the Bertrand case, a rise in price by one firm is a positive externality, since it raises the demand for other firms. Under the Nash assumption, each firm chooses its own strategy taking into account only the impact on its *own* profits, ignoring the externality.

The inefficiency of Nash equilibria can easily be demonstrated using the abstract notation of the section "Non-cooperative equilibrium". For simplicity we will take the case of duopoly. To obtain an *efficient* (Pareto optimal) outcome between the two firms, simply maximise a weighted sum of firms' profits:

$$\max_{a_1,a_2} \lambda\pi_1(a_1,a_2) + (1-\lambda)\pi_2(a_1,a_2) \tag{39}$$

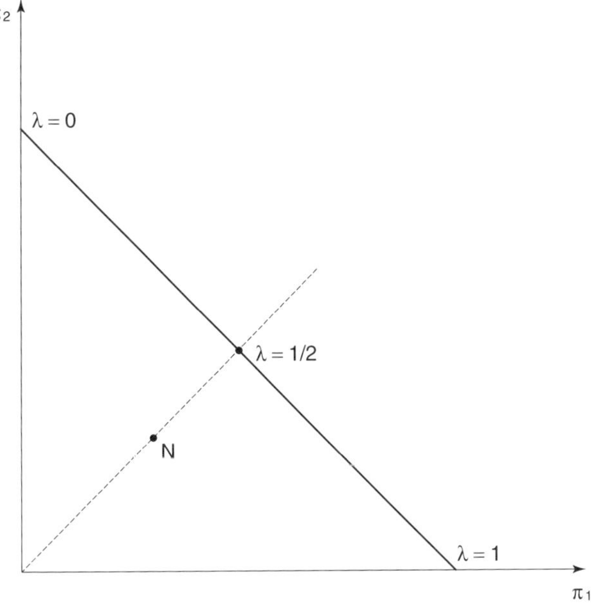

Figure 13. The profit frontier.

where $0 \leq \lambda \leq 1$. The first-order conditions for (39) are:

$$\lambda \frac{\partial \pi_1}{\partial a_1} + (1 - \lambda) \frac{\partial \pi_2}{\partial a_1} = 0 \tag{40a}$$

$$\lambda \frac{\partial \pi_1}{\partial a_2} + (1 - \lambda) \frac{\partial \pi_2}{\partial a_2} = 0 \tag{40b}$$

The leading diagonal terms represent the effect of a_i on π_i, the firm's strategy on its own profits. The off-diagonal terms reflect the "externality", the effect of a firm's strategy on the other firm's profits. Depending on the weight λ, a whole range of Pareto-optimal outcomes is possible (corresponding to the contract curve of the Edgeworth box). These outcomes can be represented as the profit frontier in payoff space, as in Figure 13. On the frontier, each firm's profits are maximised given the other firm's profits. As λ moves from 0 to 1, more weight is put on firm 1's profits and we move down the profit frontier.[12]

The Nash equilibrium profits are not Pareto optimal, and lay *inside* the profit frontier at point N, for example. To see why, note that for a Nash equilibrium to occur, both firms choose a_i to maximise their own profits (they are both on their reaction functions). Thus the first-order equations defining the Nash equilibrium are:

$$\frac{\partial \pi_1}{\partial a_1} = \frac{\partial \pi_2}{\partial a_2} = 0 \tag{41}$$

If we compare (41) with (40), we can immediately see that if there is some interdependence captured by a non-zero cross-effect ($\partial \pi_i / \partial a_j \neq 0$), then (41) will not be efficient. If there is a *negative* cross-effect, then at the Nash equilibrium N:

$$\frac{\lambda \partial \pi_1}{\partial a_1}\bigg|_{\text{N}} + (1 - \lambda)\,\frac{\partial \pi_2}{\partial a_1}\bigg|_{\text{N}} < 0 \qquad (42)$$
$$\underset{(0)}{} \qquad\qquad \underset{(-)}{}$$

The marginal effect of a_i on the weighted sum of industry profits is *negative*: there is too much output chosen. Conversely, in the Bertrand case, at the Nash equilibrium, the marginal effect of a price rise on the weighted sum of industry profits is *positive*.

This inefficiency of Nash equilibria means that there is an incentive for firms to collude—to choose their strategies (a_1, a_2) *jointly*, and move from N towards the profit frontier. Of course, if the two firms could merge, or write legally binding contracts, it would be possible for them to do this directly. However, anti-trust law prevents them from doing so: firms have to behave non-cooperatively. However, since the efficient outcomes are not Nash equilibria, each firm will have an incentive to *deviate* from the efficient outcome: it will be able to increase its profits, e.g. from (40) at an efficient outcome where partial $\partial \pi_i / \partial a_j$ is positive (negative), then $\partial \pi_i / \partial a_i$ will be negative (positive), so that a slight reduction (increase) in a_i will increase i's profits.

Given that firms have an incentive to cooperate, how can they enforce cooperative behaviour if there is also an incentive for firms to deviate from it? One response is to argue that firms compete over time: firms can enforce cooperative behaviour by punishing deviation from a collusive outcome. Since firms are involved in a repeated game, if one firm deviates at time t, then it can be "punished" at subsequent periods. In a repeated game, might not such "threats" enable firms to enforce a collusive outcome over time? This question has provided the impetus for much research in recent years.

In a finitely repeated game with perfect information, it turns out that the unique subgame-perfect equilibrium will be to have the Nash equilibrium in each period (assuming that there is a unique Nash equilibrium in the constituent game). That is, if we restrict firms to *credible* punishment threats, then those credible threats will not enable the firms to do better than their Nash equilibrium profits in each period. The argument is a standard backwards induction argument. Consider the subgame consisting of the last period. There is a unique Nash equilibrium for this subgame, which is that the firms play their Nash strategies. Any other strategy in the last period would not be "credible", would not involve all firms adopting their best response to each other. Consider the subgame consisting of the last two periods. Firms know that whatever they do in the penultimate period, the standard Nash equilibrium will occur next period. Therefore, they will want to choose their action to maximise their profits in the penultimate period, given what the other firms do. If all firms do this, the standard Nash equilibrium will occur in the penultimate period. By similar arguments, as we go backwards, for any period t, given that in subsequent periods the Nash equilibrium will occur, the Nash equilibrium will occur in period t as well. Hence finite repetition of the game yields the standard Nash outcome in each stage of the history of the market. This backwards induction argument goes back to Luce and Raiffa's analysis of the repeated prisoner's dilemma (1957).

In finitely repeated games, then, there is no scope for threats/punishments to move firms' profits above their Nash level. The argument relied upon a known terminal period, "the end of the world". An alternative approach is to analyse *infinitely* repeated games, reflecting the view that market competition is interminable. This raises a different problem: there are generally many subgame perfect equilibria in infinitely repeated games. Clearly, the above backwards induction argument cannot be employed in infinitely repeated games, because there is no last period to start from! It has proven mathematically quite complex to characterise the set of subgame perfect equilibria in infinitely repeated games. There are two types of results (commonly called "Folk theorems") corresponding to two different views of how to evaluate the firm's payoffs over an infinitely repeated game. One approach is to view the firm maximising its discounted profits for the rest of the game at each period (Lockwood 1984; Abreu 1985; Radner 1986). The other is to view that the firm does not discount but maximises its average per-period payoff.

Let us first look at the "Folk theorem" for infinitely repeated games without discounting, which is based on work by Rubinstein (1979). The key reference point is the "*security level*" of firms: this represents the worst punishment that can be inflicted on them in the one-shot constituent game. This is the "minimax" payoff of the firm, the worst payoff that can be imposed on the firm given that it responds optimally to the other firm(s). For example, take the simple Cournot model: the lowest level to which firm 1 can drive firm 2 is zero—this corresponds to where firm 2's reaction function cuts the *x*-axis, and firm 2's output and profits are driven to zero. In the framework we have employed each firms' security level corresponding to the worst possible punishment it can receive is equal to zero. An individually rational payoff in the constituent game is defined as a payoff which yields both firms their security level. The basic result is that *any* individually rational payoff in the constituent game can be "sustained" as a perfect equilibrium in an infinitely repeated game without discounting. By "sustained" it is meant that there corresponds equilibrium strategies that yield those payoffs for each firm. In our example, this means that *any* combination of non-negative profits is possible! This will include the outcomes on the profit frontier, of course, but also outcomes that are far worse than the standard Cournot–Nash equilibrium! In terms of Figure 13, the whole of the area between the axes and the profit frontier (inclusive) represents possible payoffs of some subgame perfect equilibrium!

With discounting, the range of possible equilibria depends on the discount rate δ. At period t, the future discounted profits for the rest of the game are:

$$\sum_{s=0}^{\infty} \delta^s \pi_{it+s}$$

where $0 \leq \delta < 1$ (if the interest rate is r, then $\delta = 1/(1 + r)$). The larger is δ, the more weight is put on the future: as δ tends to one, we reach the no-discounting case (since equal weight is put on profits in each period); with δ equal to zero, the future is very heavily discounted, and the firm concentrates only on the current period. The analysis of infinitely repeated games with discounting is rather more complex than the no-discounting case, not least because it is more difficult to define the firm's security level which itself varies with δ (see Fudenberg and Maskin 1986). The basic Folk theorem is that: (a) as $\delta \to 0$, then the set of perfect equilibrium payoffs shrink to the one-shot Nash payoffs; (b) as $\delta \to 1$, then any individually rational payoff is an equilibrium payoff. Again, the analysis is rather complicated here, and the reader is referred to Lockwood (1987) for an excellent analysis of the issues. The basic message for games with discounting is that the set of perfect equilibria depends on the discount rate, and may be very large.

From the point of view of industrial economics, the game-theoretic results for repeated games are far from satisfactory. With finite repetition, the equilibrium is the same as in the one-shot case: with infinite repetition there are far too many equilibria—almost anything goes! There seems to be little middle ground.

However, recent advances involving games of imperfect information may provide some answer to this dilemma (Kreps *et al.* 1982). The basic idea is very simple. Suppose that the firms are uncertain about each other's objectives. In a repeated game, firms can learn about each other's "character" from observing their actions through time. In this circumstance, firms are able to build up reputations. Let us take a very simple example: there are two firms A and B with two strategies, cooperate (c) or defect (d). The resultant profits of the two firms are of the familiar prisoner's dilemma structure:

$$
\begin{array}{cccc}
 & & \multicolumn{2}{c}{\text{B}} \\
 & & c & d \\
\text{A} \quad c & 1 \quad\ 1 & -1, \quad 2 \\
\qquad\ d & 2, \ -1 & 0 \quad\ 0
\end{array}
$$

Defection is the "dominant" strategy: whatever the other firm does, defection yields the highest profits, hence the unique Nash equilibrium is for both firms to defect. This outcome is Pareto-dominated by the outcome where both firms cooperate. If there is perfect information, and the game is repeated over time, then the unique subgame-perfect equilibrium is for both firms to defect throughout (by the standard backwards induction argument).

Now, following Kreps *et al.* (1982), introduce some uncertainty. We will take the case where firms are uncertain about each other's motivation. In general, firms are of two types: a proportion α are "Rats" and play rationally; proportion $(1 - \alpha)$ are "Triggers" and play "trigger" strategies. A trigger strategy means that the firm will play cooperatively until the other firm defects, after which it will punish the defector by playing non-cooperatively for the rest of the game.

In a multi-period game like this where there is imperfect information, each firm may be able to infer the other firm's type from its past actions. For example, if one firm defects when they have previously both been cooperative, then the other firm can infer that the other firm is a Rat (since a Trigger only defects in response to an earlier defection). By playing cooperatively, then, a Rat can leave the other firm guessing as to his true type; if a Rat defects, he knows he will lose his reputation and "reveal" his true nature.

To illustrate this as simply as possible, we will consider what happens when the above game is repeated for three periods, and firms have discount rates δ. For certain values of α and δ, it will be an equilibrium for both firms to cooperate for the first two periods, and defect in the last period. Consider the following strategy from a Rat's point of view (a Trigger will of course follow a trigger strategy).

Period 1:   Cooperate
Period 2:   Cooperate if the other firm cooperated in period 1, defect otherwise.
Period 3:   Defect.

We will now show that this can be a perfect-equilibrium strategy for a Rat. Recall that the Rat does not know whether his opponent is a Trigger, or a Rat following the same strategy.

In period 3, it is clearly subgame perfect to defect—whatever the type of the opponent, be he Rat or Trigger, defection is the dominant strategy and yields the highest payoff. In period 2, the decision is a little more complex. If the other firm (B, say) defected in period 1, then of course he has revealed himself to be a Rat, and so defection is the best response for A for period 2. If firm B did not defect in period 1, then he may be a Trigger or a Rat (with probability $(1 - \alpha)$ and α respectively). If firm A defects in period 2, then whatever the type of firm B, it will earn two units in period 2, and nothing in period 3 (since firm B will retaliate whether a Rat or a Trigger). Its expected discounted profits are 2. If, however, firm A cooperates in period 2, it will earn 1 unit of profit in that period: in period 3 its profit will depend on firm A's type— with probability α the other firm is a Rat and will defect anyway: with probability $(1 - \alpha)$ the other firm is a Trigger, and will cooperate in the last period. Thus, if A cooperates in period 2, its expected period 3 profits are $\alpha 0 + (1 - \alpha)2$. In period 2, firm A's expected discounted profits if it cooperates will be $1 + \delta(1 - \alpha)2$. Clearly, firm A will cooperate in period 2 if the expected discounted profits doing so exceed those from defection, i.e.

$$\begin{array}{ccc} \text{defect in} & 2 < 1 + \delta(1 - \alpha)2 & \text{cooperate in} \\ \text{period 2} & & \text{period 2} \end{array}$$

This is satisfied for $\delta(1 - \alpha) > 1/2$. In period 1 the decision is similar. If it defects in period 1, it earns 2, then nothing thereafter. If it cooperates, then it expects to earn 1 in period 1, 1 in period 2 (from the foregoing argument), and $(1 - \alpha)2$ in period 3. The expected discounted profits from cooperation in period 1 are thus $1 + \delta + \delta(1 - \alpha)2$. If $\delta(1 - \alpha) > 1/2$, then again cooperation in period 1 yields higher expected profits than defection. Thus the above strategy us subgame perfect if the proportion of Triggers is high enough $(1 - \alpha) > 1/2\delta$.

With uncertainty then, it can be an equilibrium to have both firms cooperating initially during the game, and only to defect towards the end of the game (the last period in the above example). The intuition is simple enough: by playing cooperatively in the first two periods, the Rat hides his true nature from his competitors. There is a "pooling" equilibrium early on: both Rats and Triggers cooperate, so that cooperation yields no additional information about the firm's type to alter the "priors" based on population proportions $\alpha, (1 - \alpha)$. One problem with this account—for neo-classical economists at least—is the need to assume the existence of non-rational players to sustain the collusive outcome. This is a problem in two senses. Firstly, there are an indefinite number of ways to be non-rational: alongside the Trigger, the bestiary of the non-rational includes the "Tit-for-Tats" (Kreps *et al.* 1982), and many other fantastical possibilities. Secondly, the methodology of most economics is based on an axiom that all agents are rational maximisers: yet here we have an explanation which presumes that only some are rational maximisers. It might be said that all that is required for such equilibria is the *belief* that there are some non-rational players. While this may be so, it would seem less than satisfactory if the belief were not justified by the existence of the required proportion α of Triggers.

This sort of equilibrium with imperfect information is called a *sequential equilibrium*, and has the added ingredient that firms use the history of the game to learn about each other's type, by Bayesian updating. The equilibrium strategies in the example need not be unique: for some values of δ and α, it is also an equilibrium for Rats to defect throughout the game, as in the full-information case. However, there exists the possibility of sustaining cooperative behaviour for some part of the game even with a limited period of play. The use of sequential equilibria has been applied to several areas of interest and industrial economists—most notably entry deterrence (Milgrom and Roberts 1982a,b).

CONCLUSIONS

This chapter has tried to present some of the basic results in the recent literature on oligopoly theory in relation to product market competition. Given the vastness of the oligopoly literature past and present, the coverage has been limited. For those interested in a more formal game-theoretic approach, Lockwood (1987) is excellent (particularly on repeated games and optimal punishment strategies). On the growing literature on product differentiation, Ireland (1986) is comprehensive. Vickers (1985b) provides an excellent survey of the new industrial economics, with particular emphasis on its policy implications.

ACKNOWLEDGEMENTS

The material of this chapter is based on MSc lectures given at Birkbeck over the period 1985–86. I would like to thank students for their comments and reactions, from which I learned a lot. I would also like to thank Ben Lockwood for invaluable comments, as well as Bruce Lyons, Steve Davies and the editors. Errors, alas, remain my own.

NOTES

1. a^*_{-i} is the n-1 vector of all firms' strategies excepting i's.
2. See Debreu (1952), Glicksberg (1952), and Fan (1952). Strict concavity is a stronger condition than we need—it can be relaxed to quasiconcavity.
3. A sufficient condition for uniqueness is that each firm's reaction function is a "contraction mapping"—see Friedman (1978) for a formal definition.

4. Note the change in the use of the word "strategy". In a one-shot game, the firm's strategy is simply the action it pursues. In a repeated game "action" and "strategy" cease to be equivalent, "strategy" being its "game plan", the rule by which the firm chooses its action in each period.

5. Bayesian updating means that firms have subjective probabilities which they update according to Bayes rule. Firms start the game with "prior" beliefs, and revise these to take into account what happens. This is a common way to model learning in neoclassical models.

6. This simply states that x_i is chosen to equate marginal revenue with marginal cost.

7. The reason for this non-existence is quite simple—step 3 of our intuitive proof breaks down, and the competitive price need not be an equilibrium. The competitive price is an equilibrium with constant returns because when one firm raises its price, the other is willing and able to expand its output to meet all demand. However, if firms have rising marginal cost curves, they are supplying as much as they want to at the competitive price (they are on their supply functions). If one firm raises its price, there will be excess demand for the firm(s) still setting the competitive price. The firm raising its price will thus face this unsatisfied residual demand, and in general will be able to raise its profits by so doing (see Dixon 1987a: Theorem 1). One response to this non existence problem is to allow for *mixed* strategies (rather than firms setting a particular price with probability one, they can set a range of prices each with a particular probability). Mixed-strategy equilibria exist under very general assumptions indeed (Dasgupta and Maskin 1986a,b) and certainly exist under a wide range of assumptions in the Bertrand framework (Dasgupta and Maskin 1986a; Dixon 1984; Dixon and Maskin 1985; Maskin 1986). However, the analysis of mixed-strategy equilibria is relatively complex, and it has yet to be seen how useful it really is. It can be argued that it is difficult to see that mixed strategies reflect a genuine aspect of corporate policy.

8. The standard models of Bertrand competition assume that outputs are demand-determined (see 11): each firm's output is equal to the demand for it. This was the assumption made by Chamberlin (1933) in his analysis of monopolistic competition. This is appropriate with constant costs, since firms will be willing to supply any quantity at the price they have set (for $p_i \geq c$, profits are increasing in output). More generally, however, it is very strong. Surely firms will only meet demand insofar as it raises the firm's profits. With rising marginal cost, the output that the firm wishes to produce given the price it has set is given by its supply function (the output that the firm wishes to produce given the price it has set is given by its supply function). If demand exceeds this quantity, and there is *voluntary trading*, then the firm will turn customers away (otherwise marginal cost would exceed price). This approach is similar to Edgeworth's (1925) analysis of the homogeneous case—see Dixon (1987b), Benassy (1986). Benassy (1986) has analysed the implications of including an Edgeworthian voluntary trading constraint on price-setting equilibria. While the Nash equilibrium prices will be the same there is, however, an existence problem: if demand is highly cross-elastic between firms, then no equilibrium may exist.

9. The formula can be obtained by total differentiation of the implicit function $\pi_i(a_i, a_j) = 0$.

10. "Investment" can be taken as any fixed factor—(capital, R&D, firm-specific human capital, and so on).

11. Long-run average cost is derived as follows. Minimise total costs $rK + L$ with respect to the production function constraint A4. Since the production function displays constant returns, long-run average and marginal cost are equal.

12. The profit frontier in Figure 13 is derived under the common framework A1 2. Linearity comes from constant returns with a homogeneous product. The actual solution is that *total* output on the frontier equals the monopoly output M, with total profits at their monopoly level μ. L determines the firms' share of output and profit:

$$x_1 = \lambda M;\ \pi_1 = \lambda\mu;\ x_2 = (1 - \lambda)M;\ \pi_2 = (1 - \lambda)\mu$$

With diminishing returns, i.e. a strictly convex function, the profit frontier will have a concave shape.

REFERENCES

Abreu, D. Extremal equilibria of oligopolistic supergames, *Journal of Economic Theory*, 1986, **39**(1): 191–225.

Allen, B. and Hellwig, M. Bertrand–Edgeworth oligopoly in large markets. *Review of Economic Studies*, 1986, **53**: 175–204.

Benassy, J. P. On the role of market size in imperfect competition: A Bertrand–Edgeworth–Chamberlin synthesis, 1986, *CEPREMAP No. 8610*.

Bertrand, J. Review of Cournot's 'recherches sur la theorie mathematique de la Richess', *Journal des Savants*, 1983, pp. 449–450.

Brander, J. and Spencer, B. Strategic commitment with R & D: the symmetric case, *Bell Journal of Economics*, 1983, **14**: 225–235.

Brander, J. and Spencer, B. Export subsidies and international market share rivalry, *NBER Working Paper*, 1984, 1404.

Brock, W. and Scheinkman, J. Price-setting supergames with capacity constraints, *Review of Economic Studies*, 1985, **52**: 371–382.

Chamberlin, E. *The Theory of Monopolistic Competition*, 1933: Harvard University Press: Cambridge, MA.

Cheng, L. Bertrand equilibrium is more efficient than the Cournot equilibrium: the case of differentiated products, 1984, Mimeo, Florida.

Cournot, A. *Recherches sur la theorie mathematique de la Richesse*, 1938.

Cyert, R. and De Groot, M. Multiperiod decision models with alternating choices as a solution to the duopoly problem. *Quarterly Journal of Economics*, 1970, **84**: 410–429.

Dasgupta, P. and Maskin, E. The existence of equilibrium in discontinuous economic games, I: Theory, *Review of Economic Studies*, 1986a, **53**: 1–26.

Dasgupta, P. and Maskin, E. The existence of equilibrium in discontinuous economic games, II: Applications, *Review of Economic Studies*, 1986b, **53**: 27–42.

Debreu, G. A social equilibrium existence theorem, *Proceedings of the National Academy of Sciences*, 1952, **38**: 886–893.

Dixit, A. and Stiglitz, J. Monopolistic competition and optimum product diversity, *American Economic Review*, 1977, **67**: 297–308.

Dixon, H. The existence of mixed-strategy equilibria in a price-setting oligopoly with convex costs, *Economics Letters*, 1984, **16**: 205–12.

Dixon, H. Strategic investment in a competitive industry, *Journal of Industrial Economics*, 1985 **33**: 205–212.

Dixon, H. Cournot and Bertrand outcomes as equilibria in a strategic metagame, 1986a, *Economic Journal*, Conference Supplement, **96**: 59–70.

Dixon, H. Strategic investment and consistent conjectures, 1986b, *Oxford Economic Papers*, **38**: 111-128.

Dixon, H. Approximate Bertrand equilibria in a replicated industry, *Review of Economic Studies*, 1987a, **54**: 47–62.

Dixon, H. The general theory of household and market contingent demand, *The Manchester School*, 1987b, **55**: 287–304.

Dixon, H. and Manning, A. Competition and efficiency, 1986, Mimeo, Birkbeck College.

Dixon, H. and Maskin, E. The existence of equilibrium with price-setting firms, 1985, Mimeo, Harvard University.

Eaton, J. and Grossman, G. Optimal trade and industrial policy under oligopoly, 1983, *NEBR Working Paper 1236*.

Eaton, J. and Grossman, G. Strategic capacity investment and product market competition, *Woodrow Wilson School Discussion Paper 80*, 1984, Princeton.

Edgeworth, F. The pure theory of monopoly, collected in *Papers Relating to Political Economy*, Vol. I, 1925, Macmillan.

Fan, K. Fixed point and minimax theories in locally convex topological spaces, *Proceedings of the National Academy of Sciences*, 1952, **38**: 121–6.

Fershtman, C. Managerial incentives as a strategic variable in a duopolistic environment, *International Journal of Industrial Organisation*, 1985, **3**: 245–53.

Friedman, J. W. *Oligopoly and the Theory of Games*, 1978, N.H.P.C.

Fudenberg, D. and Maskin, E. (1986) The Folk theorem for repeated games with discounting and incomplete information, *Econometrica*, **54**, 533–44.

Gal-Or, E. First and second mover advantages. *International Economic Review* 1985, 1986, **26**: 649–653.

Glicksberg, I. A further generalisation of the Kakutani fixed point theorem with application to Nash-equilibrium points, *Proceedings of the National Academy of Sciences*, 1952, **38**: 170–174.

Hart, O. Monopolistic competition in a large economy with differentiated commodities, *Review of Economic Studies*, 1979, **46**: 1–30.

Hart, O. Perfect competition and optimal product differentiation, in A. Mas-Collel (ed) *The Non-cooperative Foundations of Perfect Competition*, 1982, Academic Press.

Hathaway, N. and Rickard, J. Equilibria of price-setting and quantity setting duopolies, *Economic Letters*, 1979, **3**: 133–137.

Ireland, N. *Product Differentiation and the Non-Price Decisions of Firms*, 1986, Blackwell: Oxford.

Klemperer, P. and Meyer, M. Price competition vs quantity competition: the role of uncertainty, *Rand Journal of Economics*, 1986, **17**: No. 4.

Kreps, D. and Scheinkman, J. Quantity pre-commitment and Bertrand competition yield Cournot outcomes, *Bell Journal of Economics*, 1983, **4**: 326–337.

Kreps, D. and Wilson, R. Sequential equilibria, *Econometrica*, 1982a, **50**: 863–894.

Kreps, D. and Wilson, R. Reputation and imperfect information, *Journal of Economic Theory*, 1982b, **27**: 253–259.

Kreps, D., Milgrom, P. and Wilson, R. Rational cooperation in the finitely repeated prisoner's dilemma, *Journal of Economic Theory*, 1982, **27**: 245–252.

Lockwood, B. Perfect equilibria in repeated games with discounting, 1984, Cambridge University Economic Theory *Discussion Paper* 65.

Lockwood, B. Some recent developments in the theory of non-cooperative games and its economic applications, in Pearce and Rau (eds), 1987, *Economic Perspectives*.

Luce, R. and Raiffa, H. *Games and Decisions*, 1957, Wiley.

Lyons, B. Mixed-motive duopoly, Mimeo, 1986, UEA.

Marris, R. *Managerial Capitalism*, 1964, Macmillan.

Milgrom, P. and Roberts, J. Predation, reputation and entry deterrence, *Journal of Economic Theory*, 1982a, **27**: 280–312.

Milgrom, P. and Roberts, J. Limit pricing and entry under incomplete information: an equilibrium analysis, *Econometrica*, 1982b, **50**: 443–455.

Okuguchi, K. Equilibrium prices in the Bertrand and Cournot oligopolies, *Journal of Economic Theory*, 1987, **42**(1): 128–139.

Radner, R. Repeated principal agent games with discounting, *Econometrica*, 1986, **53**: 1173–1197.

Rubinstein, A. Equilibrium in supergames with the overtaking criterion, *Journal of Economic Theory*, 1979, **21**: 1–9.

Selten, R. Spieltheoretic Behandlung eines Oligopolmodells mit Nachtragetrgheit, 1965, *Zeitschrift fur die Gesamte Staatswissenschaft*, **121**: 301–324, 667–689.

Shubik, M. *Strategy and Market Structure*, 1959, John Wiley and Sons: New York.

Singh, N. and Vives, X. Price and quantity competition in a differentiated duopoly, *Rand Journal of Economics*, 1984, **15**: 540–554.

Venables, A. International trade, industrial policy, and imperfect competition, 1985, *CEPR Discussion Paper 74*.

Vickers, J. Delegation and the theory of the firm, *Economic Journal*, 1985a **95**, 138–147.

Vickers, J. Strategic competition among the few in the economics of industry—some recent developments, 1985b, *Oxford Review of Economic Policy*, **1**(3): 39–62.

Vives, X. On the efficiency of Cournot and Bertrand equilibria with product differentiation, *Journal of Economic Theory*, 1985a, **36**: 166–175.

Vives, X. Nash equilibrium with monotone best responses, 1985b, Mimeo, University of Pennsylvania.

Vives, X. Commitment, flexibility, and market outcome, *International Journal of Industrial Organisation*, 1986, **2**, 217–230.

von Stackelberg, H. *Marketform und Gleichgewicht*, 1934, Vienna and Berlin.

Yarrow, G. Measures of monopoly welfare loss in markets with differentiated products, *Journal of Industrial Economics*, 1985, **33**: 515–530.

20

Equilibrium Incentives in Oligopoly

Chaim Fershtman and Kenneth L. Judd

We examine the incentives that owners of competing firms give their managers. We show that, in equilibrium, each manager will be paid in excess of his decision's marginal profit in a Cournot-quantity game, but paid less than the marginal profit in a price game. In the Cournot case, deviations from profit maximization are reduced by ex ante cost uncertainty and increased by correlation in the firms' costs.

Orthodox economic theory treats firms as economic agents with the sole objective of profit maximization. Some have criticized this view of the firm as being simplistic, arguing that real firms may consistently strive toward a different goal. For example, William Baumol (1958) suggested sales maximization as a possible objective function of firms. Later, when economists more seriously considered the fact that the modern corporation is characterized by a separation of ownership and management, their attention focused on managerial objectives (see Herbert Simon, 1964; Oliver Williamson, 1964; Michael Jensen and William Meckling 1976; and the principal-agent literature, such as Stephen Ross, 1973).

It is generally argued that a proper analysis of the firm's objective function should be based on the analysis of the owner–manager relationship. A manager's objective depends on the structure of the incentives that his owner designs to motivate him. Owners often index managerial compensation to profits, sales, output, quality, and many other variables. Even if we accept the traditional view that owners want to maximize profits, the incentive scheme they design may imply managerial incentives different from profit maximization. For a monopolistic firm, the owner–manager relationship can be described as a standard principal-agent problem. Such analysis have yielded rich insights into the structure of agents' incentives.[1] For example, Bengt Holmstrom (1977) showed that compensation in optimal contracts would likely use information other than final profits.

However, when we discuss oligopolistic markets, the individual owner–manager relationships must be examined within the context of *rivalrous* owner–manager pairings. More generally, whenever the profit accruing to a principal-agent pair

Reprinted with permission from *American Economic Review*, Vol. 77, No. 5, 1987, pp. 927–940

depends on decisions that other rational agents make, the potential interactions must be considered. In this paper we examine the incentive contracts that principals (owners) will choose for their agents (managers) in an oligopolistic context, focusing on how competing owners may strategically manipulate these incentive contracts and the resulting impact on the oligopoly outcome. This analysis will yield different insights as to why managerial compensation contracts may not depend solely on realized profits, and also examine interactions between the structure of internal incentives within a firm and market structure elements external to the firm.

Even though it comes as no surprise that the strategic use of incentives can be important, little work has been done on the problem. Once one begins to think of incentives as strategic tools, it is clear that there may be value to the owner of distorting his manager's incentives away from maximizing the owner's welfare if the reaction of the owner's competitors is beneficial. In the case of a monopoly firm, the optimal incentive structure is obviously the regular principal-agent problem since there are no opponents and in the absence of risk-sharing and asymmetric information considerations, such an owner will motivate his manager to maximize profits. In the case of an oligopolistic market, the optimal incentive structure is not so clear a priori. For example, Chaim Fershtman (1985) showed that nonprofit-maximizing firms may enjoy more profits than profit-maximizing firms in a duopoly. The strategic trade analysis of James Brander and Barbara Spencer (1983, 1985) is also an example of a "principal," in their case a government, distorting the incentives faced by an "agent," the local firms, in order to change the behavior of a competing "principal-agent" pair, a foreign government and its firms, in a fashion that advances the principal's objectives. Our analysis also expands on their insights on international trade policy by allowing uncertainty in critical parameters. More recent work by Brander and Tracy Lewis (1986) and Vojislav Maksimovic (1986) showed that a firm's owners may alter its capital structure in order to alter their incentives and the competitors' behavior.

In this chapter we examine equilibrium incentive contracts in an oligopoly. We show that profit-maximizing owners will almost never tell their managers to maximize profits when each firm's managers are aware of other managers' incentives since each manager will react to the incentives given to competing managers. For example, if one firm's manager is told to maximize sales revenue instead of profit, he will become a very aggressive seller. Since his payoff is thereby affected, there will be a different equilibrium outcome in the competition among the managers. Also, the other managers' equilibrium behavior will be affected if they are aware of the firm's new incentive for sales maximization or learn of it through repeated play. This reaction in the competing firms' managers' behavior gives each owner an opportunity to be a Stackelberg leader vis-à-vis the other firm's managers when he determines his managers' incentives. We find that this interaction causes owners to twist their managers away from profit maximization even though the owners care only about profits.

We find, however, that the nature of the desired distortion critically depends on the nature of oligopolistic competition. In the case of Cournot-quantity competition, we prove that each owner wants to motivate his manager toward high production in order to get competing managers, who are aware of these incentives, to reduce their output. Therefore, in equilibrium owners will give a positive incentive for sales. On the other hand. if firms are selling differentiated products and compete in price, each owner will want his manager to set a high price, thereby encouraging competing managers to also raise their prices. Therefore, with price competition owners will pay managers to keep sales low.

This chapter also determines the impact of uncertainty and heterogeneity on the oligopoly outcome. In the Cournot-quantity game, we find that the equilibrium outcome with incentive contracts is more efficient than the simple Cournot outcome not only because of the increase in output but also because the low-cost firm's share of output is greater. Furthermore, if the firms' costs are uncorrelated, *ex ante* uncertainty at the time the incentive contracts are written will reduce the deviation from profit maximization.

Even though our models will be specific, it will be clear that the idea of strategic manipulation of agents' incentives is of general interest. For example, we could similarly analyze a sales manager's decisions when he establishes incentives for his salespeople, and show that he overcompensates his salespeople at the margin if that will cause competing salespeople to work less. Also, many of our results continue to hold when incomplete information and a moral hazard manager determine the information available for contracting purposes (see Fershtman and Kenneth Judd, 1987).

The first section describes the general framework we examine. The second section examines the results for a Cournot industry with random demand, whereas the third section examines the case of random costs. The fourth section studies the case of n Cournot firms. The fifth section examines price competition in a differentiated product market. The final section summarizes this study's results.

THE BASIC MODEL

Our model assumes two firms, each with an owner and a manager. When we say "owner", we mean a decision maker whose objective is to maximize the expected profits of the firm. This could be the actual owner, a board of directors, or a chief executive officer. "Manager" refers to an agent that the owner hires to observe demand and cost conditions and make the real-time decisions concerning output and/or price. While we will refer to the profit-maximizing agent as the owner, he in turn could be an employee who has been given incentives to maximize firm profits.

We examine a two-stage game. In the first stage, the owners of each firm simultaneously determine the incentive structure for its manager, knowing the true probability distributions governing demand and costs. Each owner must offer his manager a contract under which the manager expects to receive his opportunity cost of participation; at this stage the manager shares his employer's uncertainty about demand and costs and the belief about the incentives under which the opposing manager will work. In the second stage, the competing managers play an oligopoly game, with each firm's manager knowing his incentive contract and those of competing managers. In the second stage, the realized nature of demand and costs facing all firms will be perfectly known and common knowledge among the managers.

After all sales have been made, each owner observes the costs and sales, and hence profits, of his firm.

Before continuing, we should note that our analysis is equivalent to another view of the market for managers.[2] Some will argue that instead of shareholders hiring managers, it is managers who propose incentive structures to the capital market, which then chooses among the competing managerial proposals. Even if one views the managers as making the first move, the resulting game is equivalent to our game as long as any contract which the managers can propose can also be proposed to the managers in our game, and vice versa. The order of who proposes the incentive contract, firm or potential managers, is not important. The crucial assumption is that the firm gets all the rent from the relationship, an outcome that will occur in either situation as long as there are a large number of potential managers per firm: if the firm proposes an incentive scheme in a take-it-or-leave-it fashion, it need offer a manager only his opportunity cost; whereas if there are many managers with similar opportunity costs making proposals to the shareholders, competition among them will leave the winner only with his opportunity cost, and in both cases an optimal scheme from each firm's point of view will be proposed and accepted. In some respects, this alternative formulation is attractive since a crucial assumption of our analysis is that the "owners" observe only profits and sales, and do not bother learning about the day-to-day details of the firm's operation, an assumption which is a plausible description of shareholders. In any case, we will stick with the more common theoretical structure of an owner proposing a contract and the manager responding.

The assumption that each firm's manager in stage two knows the other firm's manager's incentive contract and costs is a natural one in this context. We view the manager's contracts as being infrequently altered and in force for a substantial amount of time. Repeated play would presumably cause managers eventually to learn one another's true incentives even if they were not initially common knowledge. However, despite this appeal to repeated play, we are assuming a single-shot game with common knowledge in stage two among managers about their incentives. A true repeated play specification of the managers' game would clearly generate many interesting new possibilities, but because of the intractable inference problems and the multiple-equilibria problems that arise in repeated games, it is beyond the scope of this paper to move beyond our two-period specification. Moreover, it will be clear in this two-stage game that each owner will want its manager's incentives to be common knowledge. For these reasons, we regard this critical information specification as appropriate and the two-period specification a reasonable one in which to study the issues on which we want to focus.

We assume that the incentive structure takes a particular form: risk-neutral managers are paid at the margin in proportion to a linear combination of profits and sales. More formally, firm i's managers will be given incentive to maximize

$$O_i = \alpha_i \pi_i + (1 - \alpha_i) S_i,$$

where π_i and S_i are firm i's profits and sales.[3] This formulation is moderately general in that it is equivalent to maximizing linear combinations of profits and costs or sales and costs. We make no restrictions on α_i, allowing even negative values. We are assuming that, after the managers have acted and sales and production have been realized, the firms' owners can (or choose to) observe only profits and sales figures, not realizations of demand parameters or number of units sold. We allow managers to do whatever is in their best interest given their options and incentives, making the owner-manager relationship a delegation relationship, not a team relationship. The linearity restriction is not descriptively unreasonable. Furthermore, tractability demands that some restriction be put on the space of contracts since in similar generalized principal-agent problems it is known that equilibrium may not exist in unrestricted contracts (see Roger Myerson, 1982). While this is an unfortunate limitation of our analysis, it will be clear that it is not the reason for the qualitative nature of our results.[4]

Another crucial element of our model will be the assumption that there is uncertainty about crucial market parameters describing demand and costs at the time the incentives are determined. Such uncertainty from the owners' perspective is natural and also gives the managers a role as observers of these random variables. Uncertainty is also crucial to our focus on equilibria in which incentives are distorted away from profit maximization. We will argue that if we had no uncertainty about the *ex post* state of the market, then our analysis would be unconvincing since there would be no justification for ignoring quantity- or price-indexed contracts that would force the usual Cournot and Bertrand outcomes. However, simple deterministic forcing contracts will not be desired by owners when they face nontrivial uncertainty since each owner will want his manager to react to the eventual environment. Therefore, uncertainty is necessary to make the use of linear contracts in profits and sales reasonable and superior to contracts which yield the usual oligopoly outcomes.

The implicit restriction that i's manager's compensation depends on only firm i's sales and profits, not its competitor's, is motivated by a couple of realistic considerations. First, a firm has much better information about its profits and sales than about its competitor's. Second, giving one's manager any incentive to increase a competitor's profits could possibly be illegal because of its clear role as a device to facilitate collusion. Third, even if we did allow cross effects in compensation, it will be clear that our main result of incentive manipulation would continue to hold true since each firm wants the other manager to operate in a cooperative fashion, but not its own manager.[5]

We examine the subgame-perfect Nash equilibrium of our two-stage game. In the second stage, we compute the Nash equilibrium that results when the firm's managers make simultaneous choices of their strategic variables, knowing one another's incentive contract and the realized nature of demand and costs. Below, we will examine cases in which the strategic variable is either price or quantity and make various assumptions concerning the information each firm has in the contract-writing stage about the eventual costs and demand. In the first stage, each owner simultaneously chooses its α_i, the relative weight it forces the manager to give to profits, with Nash equilibrium describing the outcome. In this game among the owners, each knows the payoff structure of each possible second-stage game as a function of the α's. We will refer to the stage-one equilibrium choice of the α_i and the resulting probability distribution of output and prices as the *incentive equilibrium*. We now move to the determination of incentive equilibria in several contexts.

INCENTIVE EQUILIBRIUM WITH COURNOT COMPETITION AND RANDOM DEMAND

We first examine the issue of oligopolistic incentive structures for managers in a model of duopoly Cournot competition in a homogeneous good market. For reasons of tractability, demand is assumed to be linear:

$$p = a - bQ, \qquad a, b > 0, \tag{1}$$

where p is market price and Q is total output. q_i denotes the output of firm i, $i = 1, 2$. Firm i will have constant unit cost $c_i \geq 0$, $i = 1, 2$. Both a or b are possibly unknown to all in stage one, but revealed to the managers at the beginning of stage two. We will make no special assumptions about the distribution of a and b other than assumptions on the support of their distributions necessary to assure that each firm's output will be positive in equilibrium. We see no reason to burden the reader with the extra algebra that would be needed when zero output is a possible equilibrium outcome, particularly since our interest is in the study of active oligopolies. The exact nature of such assumptions will be made explicit in the statements of the theorems below. In this section c_1 and c_2 are known perfectly by all in both stages.

We solve for the incentive equilibrium in the standard backward fashion. In stage two, the manager of each firm observes a, b, c_1, c_2, α_1, and α_2, and chooses q_1 to maximize O_i. In this case, O_i becomes

$$O_i = \alpha_i(a - bQ - c_i)q_i + (1 - \alpha_i)(a - bQ)q_i. \tag{2}$$

Given α_1 and α_2, the Cournot reaction functions in quantity are

$$q_i = \frac{a - bq_2}{2b} - \frac{\alpha_1 c_1}{2b}, \tag{3}$$

and symmetrically for firm two. Note that α_1 just affects the manager's perspective on costs. If $\alpha_1 < 1$, that is, firm one's manager moves away from strict profit maximization toward including consideration of sales, then firm one's reaction function moves out in a parallel fashion since the managers view $\alpha_1 c_1$ as the marginal cost of production. Therefore, as the owner of firm one changes α_1, he essentially changes his manager's reaction function. Symmetric results hold for firm two. These facts play the crucial role in the results below.

For values of $\alpha_i, i = 1, 2$, inherited from the outcome of stage one, stage-two equilibrium in terms of demand, cost, and incentive parameters is

$$p = (a + \alpha_1 c_1 + \alpha_2 c_2)/3, \tag{4a}$$

$$q_1 = (a - 2\alpha_1 c_1 + \alpha_2 c_2)/3b, \tag{4b}$$

$$\pi_1 = (a + \alpha_1 c_1 + \alpha_2 c_2 - 3c_1) \times (a - 2\alpha_1 c_1 + \alpha_2 c_2)/9b, \tag{4c}$$

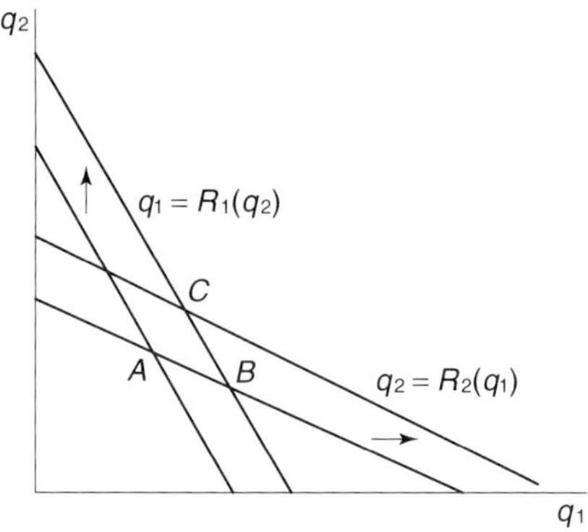

Figure 1.

and similarly for q_2. Note that as α_1 and α_2 are smaller, p is smaller, reflecting the fact that providing incentives for sales results in output beyond the profit-maximizing level.

Given the outcomes in stage two, firm one's owner chooses α_i in stage one so as to maximize his expected profits net of his manager's opportunity costs. Since the cost of hiring a manager is fixed and unaffected by risk, this is equivalent to maximizing expected profits.[6] We first address the case in which only b is unknown *ex ante*. In this case, the reaction function for firm one's owner's choice of α_1 as a function of α_2 is

$$\alpha_1 = \frac{3}{2} - \frac{a}{4c_1} - \frac{\alpha_2}{4}\frac{c_2}{c_1}, \tag{5}$$

and similarly for firm two's owner's choice of α_2.

The case of uncertain b is particularly easy to examine since b is simply a parameter for the scale of the market and, as seen in (5), does not enter into the owners' choice of α_1 and α_2. Note that if firm two's manager maximizes profits, that is, $\alpha_2 = 1$, and costs are equal, then firm one's owner will choose $\alpha_1 < 1$. Therefore, profit-maximizing contracts generally do not arise in equilibrium. In fact, the final outcome is

$$\alpha_1 = 1 - \frac{a + 2c_2 - 3c_1}{5c_1}, \tag{6a}$$

$$q_1 = (2a - 6c_1 + 4c_2)/5b, \tag{6b}$$

and similarly for firm two. Since $\alpha_1 < 1$, if and only if $q_1 > 0$, we find that if both firms produce output, both will twist their manager's incentives away from strict profit maximization toward sales incentives as well.

The intuitive explanation for these results is given in Figure 1. For a particular b, R_i is firm i's reaction function, yielding q_i as a function of q_{3-i}. First, take the point of the owner of firm one. His choosing $\alpha_1 < 1$ pushes R_1 out and pushes the Nash equilibrium down firm two's manager's reaction function from A to B. The fact that α_1 is communicated to the manager of firm two means that firm one's owner acts as a Stackelberg leader with respect to firm two's manager. Here, however, each owner is a leader vis-à-vis his opponent's management. This dual leadership causes both owners to make their managers more aggressive sellers, leading both owners to choose an α_i less than unity, pushing both reaction curves out, and finally causing the stage-two Cournot equilibrium to shift from A to C. Theorem 1 summarizes.

Theorem 1. In a Cournot market, if a, c_1, and c_2 are known in stage one and both firms always produce positive quantities in equilibrium for any value in the support of b, then, for $i, j = 1, 2$.

$$\alpha_i = 1 - \frac{a + 2c_j - 3c_i}{5c_i}, \quad i \neq j \tag{7a}$$

$$q_i = (2a - 6c_i + 4c_j)/5b, \quad i \neq j \tag{7b}$$

$$p = (a + 2(c_1 + c_2))/5, \tag{7c}$$

implying that owners always give incentives for sales and may even penalize for profits if costs are sufficiently low.

There are several interesting comparisons between our incentive equilibrium outcome and the Cournot outcome. Total output in the incentive equilibrium always exceeds Cournot output, and profits and prices are lower. For example, if $c_1 = c_2 = c$, then Cournot price is $(a + 2c)/3$, whereas the incentive equilibrium price is lower and equal to $(a + 4c)/5$. Similarly, Cournot profits equal $(a - c)^2/9b$, whereas in our incentive equilibrium they are $2(a - c)^2/25b$, a lesser amount.

The incentive equilibrium outcome also has strong performance implications relative to the usual Cournot-quantity analysis. Since output is increased and oligopoly rents are lower, efficiency is improved. However, the incentive equilibria are more efficient not only because price is closer to marginal cost but also because production rises relatively more at the low-cost firm. If firm one is the low-cost firm, straightforward calculations show that its market share is $1 + (c_2 - c_1)/(a - 2c_1 + c_2)$ times greater in the incentive equilibrium than in the Cournot equilibrium. Corollary 1 summarizes.

Corollary 1. Under the assumptions of Theorem 1, incentive equilibria in the quantity game generates greater output, lower rents, lower prices, and a more efficient allocation of production than the usual Cournot equilibria.

The case of uncertain a is similarly examined. Let $\bar{a}$ denote the mean of a. Proceeding as above, we find Theorem 2.

Theorem 2. If b, c_1, and c_2 are known in stage one and if the minimum value of a with nonzero probability exceeds $2c_2 - c$ and $2c_1 - c_2$, then in the incentive equilibrium

$$\alpha_1 = 1 - (\bar{a} + 2c_2 - 3c)/5c, \tag{8a}$$

$$q_1 = (2a - 6c_1 + 4c_2)/5b, \tag{8b}$$

and similarly for firm two.

Before continuing, we should discuss one alternative formulation and its relationship to our game, particularly since it will give an argument as to why the addition of uncertainty was important to our analysis. Suppose that owners could write only contracts that force managers to produce a certain level of output and that there were no uncertainty in the level of demand. Such a word is equivalent to the usual Cournot game. Now suppose that the firms could write both these forcing contracts and the linear contracts we studied above. If firm one wrote a contract forcing its Cournot level of output, the best firm two could do would also be to write a contract that specifies its Cournot output since it could not manipulate the performance of firm one's manager. In Figure 1, such a forcing contract would cause R_1 to be vertical, a graphical representation of its nonmanipulability. Of course, the same argument applies to firm one. Therefore, the usual Cournot outcome is also an equilibrium if we assume no uncertainty and allow quantity-forcing contracts.

This observation does not, however, immediately eliminate the incentive equilibrium we computed above since it also remains an equilibrium in this extended game. The crucial fact is that, without uncertainty, a firm can choose any point along its opposing manager's reaction curve by choosing a quantity-forcing contract or a linear contract. If firm one believed that firm two was going to write the incentive equilibrium contract with its manager, then firm one is indifferent between writing a contract that forces its manager to produce the best point along firm two's manager's reaction curve and giving its manager the incentive equilibrium contract that will also produce that outcome. Similarly, if firm two's owner believed that one's manager was going to write the incentive equilibrium contract, it could do no better than to write its incentive equilibrium contract. Therefore, multiple equilibria often result if both forcing and linear incentive contracts were possible.

In many cases of multiple equilibria, there is no reason to choose one over the other. However, the incentive equilibria would not be the natural one to focus on here in the absence of uncertainty. To argue this, we appeal to focal point considerations. Since our incentive equilibrium often results in less profit for both firms (and surely will if costs are identical), the incentive equilibrium would often be strictly Pareto inferior. In such cases, focal point considerations argue that the owners would realize that it is in their mutual interest to act according to the simple Cournot allocation implemented by forcing contracts. Therefore, the incentive equilibria lose much of their appeal in deterministic versions of our model.

However, if there are nontrivial levels of uncertainty, then such *noncontingent* quantity-forcing contracts would not be desirable since the owner would want the manager to be able to respond to contingencies that the owner does not observe, but which do affect his profits. Such flexibility could be partially attained in this context by a profit-maximizing contract. If both firms chose profit maximizing contracts, then the state-contingent Cournot outcomes would result. However, once firms chose such contracts for their managers, each manager will react to deviations in the other's incentive contract. Therefore, by assuming uncertainty, we have both given a function to the manager and also increased the plausibility of our incentive equilibrium relative to one important perturbation of our game.

These comments also apply to the trade policy analyses in the papers by Brander and Spencer (1983, 1985). Their models will also have additional equilibria in similarly extended strategy spaces, with the extra equilibria being mutually preferable to both nations; however, uncertainty about the underlying profit opportunities will again make the linear contract equilibria the more plausible ones. The nature of our results also generalizes, implying that the strategic trade interventions will tend to be less valuable in the presence of uncertainty.

This section has demonstrated the basic insight in our analysis: profit-maximizing owners may not want to give profit-maximizing incentives to their managers because an owner can influence the outcome of the competition between the managers in his favor by distorting his manager's incentives. This result does not rely on asymmetric information considerations as in Holmstrom, since a firm in this model will choose profit-maximizing contracts if it faces no competition. This result shows that internal relationships and incentives can be distorted and manipulated for interfirm strategic reasons, giving a new and fundamentally different role for internal contracts. In the following sections we elaborate on this theme for the cases of random costs, multiple-firm oligopoly, and price competition in differentiated markets.

INCENTIVE EQUILIBRIUM WITH COURNOT COMPETITION AND RANDOM COSTS

The case of random costs is substantially different. We examine it because new results concerning the impact of inter-firm heterogeneity are obtained.

Suppose that c_1 and c_2 are identically distributed with mean μ, variance σ^2, and correlation coefficient r. Let $v = \sigma/\mu$ be the coefficient of variation. Again, we will assume that the cost randomness is obtained so that output for each firm is positive in each state of the world. We assume that each manager knows the other's costs in stage two. In this section, we assume that a and b, the demand parameters, are known perfectly in both stages. Therefore, the stage-two reaction functions are given by (3). In stage one, owner i chooses α_i to maximize expected profits given his expectation of α_{3-i}. Expected profits are given by *ex ante* expectation of (4c). Stage-one reaction functions are

$$\alpha_i = \frac{3}{2} - \frac{a}{4\mu}\frac{1}{v^2+1} - \frac{\alpha_{3-i}}{4}\frac{1+rv^2}{1+v^2}, \quad i-1,2. \tag{9}$$

Understanding the dependence of this reaction function on r, v, and μ is crucial to understanding the equilibrium results. If there were no reaction by firm two's manager to firm one's incentive structure, there would be no gain to the owner from distorting his manager's incentives. The marginal gain to firm one's owner of increasing α_i by

$d\alpha_1$, assuming firm two's manager does *not* react to this change in his opponent's incentives, is

$$2(1 - \alpha_1)(3b)^{-1}E\{c\}^2 d\alpha_1,$$

which is zero at $\alpha_1 = 1$, the profit-maximizing contract. However, since the manager of firm two will react in the stage-two equilibrium by increasing output as α_1 is increased, the marginal loss of increasing α_1 arising from this reaction is

$$(a\mu + \alpha_2 r\sigma^2 - 2\alpha_1(\mu^2 + \sigma^2))(3b)^{-1} d\alpha_1,$$

which is positive if q_1 is positive for all c_1, c_2 realizations. The reaction function chooses α_1, which equates the marginal gain and loss of an increase in α_1. As the variance, σ^2, increases, marginal losses due to deviations from profit-maximizing incentives increase, pushing the optimal α_1 toward 1. Also, if α_1 is near its optimal value given α_2, the gains from such deviations fall as σ^2 rises. Hence, we see that as σ^2 rises, firms move toward a profit maximization. Similarly, as costs are more correlated, the benefits of deviations from profit-maximizing incentives rise, implying that the optimal α_1 falls. Also, as a/μ rises, that is, the choke price rises relative to mean cost, the profit margin is greater and firms move away from profit-maximization incentives, as was the case for deterministic c.

Theorem 3 follows directly from an examination of the reaction functions.

Theorem 3.   With ex ante uncertain and identically distributed costs, if q_1 and q_2 are nonnegative in equilibrium for all realizations of (c_1, c_2), then in equilibrium,

$$\alpha_1 = \alpha_2 = \alpha = \frac{6(v^2 + 1) - a/\mu}{(4 + r)v^2 + 5}. \tag{10}$$

Therefore: (*i*) α rises as a/μ falls and as v and r rise, and (*ii*) $\alpha < 1$ for r sufficiently close to 1 and v sufficiently close to zero.

The case of random costs is somewhat richer but more difficult to analyze completely. If the equilibrium α is less than unity, then an increase in the uncertainty of costs and their correlation will cause firms to move closer to profit maximization because it is more difficult to choose the right α conditional on the realized costs. We are not able to prove that α is always less than 1, but we know of no case in which it is not. The formula for α would seem to indicate that α could exceed one, but only if the variance of costs is large and costs are not perfectly correlated. This situation could possibly lead to negative output according to (6b) and violating the nonnegativity condition on output. To determine whether this occurs, one would have to impose specific distributions on the random variables. We want to confine the analysis in this study to cases in which examination of the random variables' first and second moments and weak conditions on their support is sufficient. Since the nonnegativity constraints on output are satisfied for r close to one or when the support for costs is small, yielding a v nearly zero, the formula for α in Theorem 3 is valid in these cases and (*ii*) of Theorem 3 holds, showing that Theorem 3 applies for a nontrivial set of cases.

This section shows how cost shocks affect the equilibrium nature of incentives. If cost shocks are commonly experienced, as in the case of an uncertain price for a common input, then the owners decide to distort incentives. However, if shocks are not commonly experienced, then deviations from profit maximization are reduced. Similarly, if there is too much variance in costs, then owners are not as willing to distort incentives away from profit maximization.

EQUILIBRIUM WITH MANY FIRMS

We saw above in a duopoly that owners may distort their managers' incentives if each firm's manager reacts to distortions in the competing managers' incentives. It is natural to ask next if these distortions of owners' incentives disappear as the industry is less concentrated. We establish this formally in the case of perfectly correlated uniform costs. The same results for the cases of uncertain a and b are easily proven.

Theorem 4.   As n approaches infinity, the firms' managers become profit maximizers, that is, $\alpha_i \to 1$, if a is uncertain, b is uncertain, or costs are equal but uncertain in stage one.

Proof.   *Firm i*'s objective function is

$$\alpha_i(a - bQ - c)q_i + (1 - \alpha_i)q_i(a - bQ). \tag{11}$$

The first-order condition for choosing q_i is

$$(a - 2bq_i - b\bar{Q}_i) - \alpha_i c = 0, \tag{12}$$

where $\bar{Q}_i = Q - q_i$. The second-order conditions are clearly satisfied. Thus, the *i*th firm's reaction function is

$$q_i = \frac{a - b\bar{Q}_i - \alpha_i c}{2b}, \quad Si = 1, \ldots, n. \tag{13}$$

Summing (13) yields

$$\sum_{j=1}^{n} q_j = \frac{1}{2b}\left(na - b(n - 1)Q - \sum_{j=1}^{n} \alpha_j c\right).$$

Since $\Sigma q_i = Q$, then $b(n+1)Q = na - \Sigma\alpha_j c$. Therefore,

$$Q = \frac{1}{b(n+1)}\left(na - c\sum\alpha_j\right). \tag{14}$$

Substituting (14) into (13) $(\bar{Q}_i = Q - q_i)$ yields

$$2bq_i = a - \alpha_i c - \frac{n}{n+1}\,a + \frac{c\Sigma\alpha_j}{n+1} + bq_i, \quad q_i = \frac{1}{b(n+1)}\left(a + c\sum_{j\neq 1}\alpha_j - nc\alpha_i\right).$$

From (14) we can calculate the price

$$p = a - \frac{1}{n+1}\left(na - c\sum_{j=1}^{n}\alpha_j\right) = \frac{1}{n+1}\left(a + c\sum_{j=1}^{n}\alpha_j\right).$$

The ith firm's expected profit when c is unknown in stage one is

$$\pi_i = \frac{1}{b(n+1)^2} \times E\left\{\left(a - c\sum_{j\neq i}\alpha_j - nc\alpha_i\right) \times \left(a + c\sum_{j=1}^{n}\alpha_j - (n+1)c\right)\right\}. \tag{15}$$

Maximizing the above profit functions for each i yields

$$E\left\{c\left(a + c\sum_{j\neq i}\alpha_j - nc\alpha_i\right) - nc\left(a + c\sum_{j=1}^{n}\alpha_j - (n+1)c\right)\right\} = 0. \tag{16}$$

Since at the symmetric equilibrium $\alpha_i = \alpha$ for all i,

$$\alpha = 1 - \frac{n-1}{n^2+1}\left(\frac{a\mu - \sigma^2 - \mu^2}{1 + \sigma^2 + \mu^2}\right), \tag{17}$$

where $\mu = E\{c\}$ and σ^2 is the variance of c. Thus $\lim_{n\to\infty}\alpha = 1$. This proves Theorem 4.

This result is intuitively appealing because it coincides with our understanding of the perfectly competitive market. In the traditional theory of perfect competition with free entry, firms cannot afford to do anything other than be profit maximizers. If all firms have the same technology, the long-run equilibrium price is identical to minimum average cost. If one firm deviates from its profit-maximizing output, its average cost is going to increase above the market price, implying that the firm loses money.

Since monopolists want their managers to maximize profits, we find that managers in both monopolized and competitive sectors will be told to maximize profits. Nonprofit-maximizing incentives will be given only in oligopolistic industries, showing that the relationship between market structure and managerial incentives will likely not be monotonic.

PRICE COMPETITION AND INCENTIVE EQUILIBRIUM IN A DIFFERENTIATED PRODUCT DUOPOLY

The analysis of incentive equilibrium in a differentiated market is similar to the analysis in the previous section with one exception—now we assume price competition between firms selling differentiated products instead of Cournot-quantity competition. We assume that the demand is given by

$$q_i = A\tilde{\varepsilon} - bp_i + ap_{3-i}, \qquad i = 1, 2, \tag{18}$$

where $\tilde{\varepsilon}$ is a common shock to demand. We assume $\tilde{\varepsilon} = 1$. Also $b > a$, implying that the effect of a firm's own price on sales is greater than the effect of its rival's price. This is equivalent to concavity in the implicit linear-quadratic consumer utility function.

Owners know that the strategic variable in the competition between managers in the second stage is price. Thus, given an incentive structure which is a linear combination of profits and sales, firm i's manager will act so as to maximize

$$Q_i = \alpha_i(p_i - c)(A\tilde{\varepsilon} - bp_i + ap_j) + (1 - \alpha_i)p_i(A\tilde{\varepsilon} - bp_i + ap_j). \tag{19}$$

Theorem 5.   When price is the strategic variable in the second stage of the competition among differentiated producers facing linear demand, $\alpha_i > 1$, that is, the incentive equilibrium is such that managers are overcompensated at the margin for profits.

Proof.   The reaction function of firm i's managers is given by

$$p_i = \frac{A + ap_j + \alpha_i cb}{2b}, \qquad i \neq j, i, j = 1, 2, \tag{20}$$

and the stage-two equilibrium prices, as a function of incentive and demand parameters, are

$$P_i(\alpha_i, \alpha_j, \tilde{\varepsilon}) = \frac{2bA\tilde{\varepsilon} + aA\tilde{\varepsilon} + a\alpha_j cb}{4b^2 - a^2} + \frac{2b^2\alpha_i c}{4b^2 - a^2}, \qquad j \neq i, \ i, j = 1, 2. \tag{21}$$

Given the equilibrium in the second stage, the owners can compute their expected profits, π_i, $i = 1, 2$, as a function of the incentive structures in their own firm as well as in the rival's firm:

$$\pi_i = E\left\{ \frac{2bA\tilde{\varepsilon} + aA\tilde{\varepsilon} + a\alpha_j cb - 4b^2 c + a^2 c + 2b^2\alpha_i c}{4b^2 - a^2} \times [A\tilde{\varepsilon} - bP_i(\alpha_i, \alpha_j, \tilde{\varepsilon}) + aP_j(\alpha_i, \alpha_j, \tilde{\varepsilon})] \right\}. \tag{22}$$

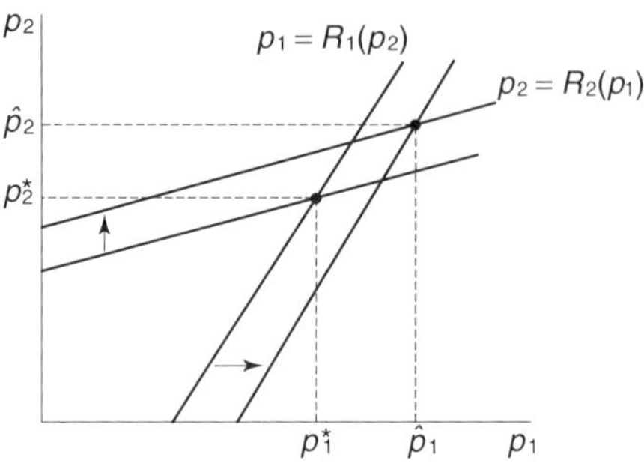

Figure 2.

By differentiating (22) with respect to α_i and equating it to zero, we find the reaction function of firm i's owner to firm $j = 3 - i$ to be

$$\alpha_i = m + \beta\alpha_j, \tag{23}$$

where

$$m = \frac{2ba^2A + a^3A - 6a^2b^2c + a^4c + 8b^4c}{4b^2(2b^2 - a^2)c},$$

$$\beta = \frac{a^3}{4b(2b^2 - a^2)}.$$

The equilibrium in the first stage of the game is a pair (α_1^*, α_2^*) such that (23) is satisfied for $i = 1, 2$. Substituting (22) into (23) and solving for α_i yields

$$\alpha_i^* = 1 + \frac{(A - (a - b)c)(a^3 + 2a^2b)}{bc(8b^3 - 4a^2b - a^3)} > 1, \qquad i = 1, 2 \tag{24}$$

since $a < b$. The overcompensation for profits can also be interpreted as an owner's tax on the manager for his input expenditures. This tax disciplines the manager and prevents him from being too aggressive in his pricing strategy.

An immediate corollary of Theorem 5 is that the price in the incentive equilibrium is above the equilibrium price in an industry in which managers maximize profit, the usual specification of behavior in a differentiated market. This can be illustrated by a reaction function analysis. The crucial difference between this case and the Cournot-quantity case is that here the reaction curves in prices slope upward, that is, the greater a firm's expectation about its opponent's price, the greater will be the price he chooses. Under the profit-maximization hypothesis the equilibrium prices are (p_1^*, p_2^*) in Figure 2. By penalizing managers on sales at the margin, as occurs here since the equilibrium of the owner's game implies that $\alpha > 1$ for both forms, managers will price less aggressively than under the regular profit-maximization hypothesis. This pushes their reaction functions upward, a shift evident from (20) which describes i's reaction function. This mutual restraint results in equilibrium moving outward, a direction favorable to both, and leading to prices of $(\hat{p}_1, \hat{p}_2)$, which are higher than the equilibrium prices under the profit-maximization hypothesis.

Comparing the above result with the equilibrium in the quantity competition case[7] demonstrates that the equilibrium incentive structure depends on the way firms compete in the market. In the quantity competition case, $\alpha < 1$ and owners motivate managers to behave aggressively and to produce beyond the profit-maximization level, whereas in the price competition case $\alpha > 1$ and managers behave nonaggressively. In the quantity competition case each owner, acting as a Stackelberg leader with respect to the opposing manager, recognizes the negative slope of its rival manager's reaction function and therefore wants his manager to expand output. In the price competition case, each owner knows that any credible increase in its own price will be followed by an increase in its rival's price, therefore motivating its manager to be less aggressive and charge a price above the profit-maximizing price.

Moreover, the performance implications of incentive equilibrium differ in the two cases. In the quantity competition case, the incentive equilibrium increases efficiency and reduces oligopoly rents since the outcome is closer to perfect competition than the outcome in the regular Cournot competition. However, in the price competition case, incentive equilibrium essentially pushes the price toward the monopolistic price. The structure of our incentive contract game would therefore be one of the mutual advantage to the firms and hence one toward which they would like to move instead of the decision-making structure implicit in the usual Bertrand analysis.

Finally, the argument that incentive equilibria in the deterministic quantity competition case with no uncertainty were not plausible for focal point reasons when we expand the space of possible contracts does *not* apply here. Since firm profits are increased by incentive contracts, such considerations argue in favor of the incentive contracts over forcing contracts (which here would be interpreted to force the manager to choose a certain price) even when both were equilibria in the expanded contract space. These arguments indicate that our theory of incentive equilibria may be more relevant for the case of differentiated markets.

CONCLUDING COMMENTS

This chapter has examined the interactions of internal contracting and external strategic considerations. We found a principal (firm owner) will want to distort the incentives of his agents (firm managers) in order to affect the outcome of the competition between his agent and competing agents. The general implications of our analysis are clear. In general, the owner of a firm will alter his managers' incentives in that direction which will cause opposing agents to change their behavior in beneficial directions. For example, if advertising will cause opposing firms to reduce their advertising, then a firm's owner will give his managers extra incentive to advertise. This can be implemented by explicit incentives or by hiring agents who are known to be inclined to aggressively advertise. In some cases, various asymmetries may cause the owners to distort their managers' behavior in opposing directions. For example, if in the differentiated products case firm one is a price setter, but firm two, for some technical reason, fixes his quantity, then firm one's manager will be paid to overproduce in order to get firm two's manager to reduce his output, but firm two's manager may be paid to keep his price high and output low in order to encourage firm one's manager to allow the market prices to be high. The variety of problems that can be analyzed by focusing on this joint determination of internal incentives and external environment is obvious.

There are a variety of directions which further research should pursue. The major weakness of the analysis above is the assumption of linear contracts and the absence of a detailed asymmetric information structure which motivates the existence of contracts in the first place. This study is offered as an imperfect but intuitive and suggestive analysis of the possibilities that arise when we jointly examine managerial incentives and market structure. A more recent paper by the authors (Fershtman and Judd, 1986) examines a model with a more standard incomplete information and moral hazard structure, which demonstrates that the intuitive results derived above continue to hold within a more standard principal-agent structure.

We also assumed that the managers play a simple Nash noncooperative equilibrium when they compete. An alternative theory of their behavior would be to have them bargain toward some outcome that is cooperative from their point of view. While this may substantially affect the outcome of the managers' game for any given set of managerial incentives, the owners would still take into account the impact their decisions have on the outcome of the managers' decision-making process. For example, if the managers were known by the owners to bargain in accordance with a "split the gains from trade" rule, then each owner will strive to increase his profits by demanding a large bond from the manager and then contract to give a large portion of it back whether bargaining succeeds. This will raise the manager's threat point, making the agreement point more favorable to his firm, and increase the owner's profits. In any case, strategic manipulation of managerial incentives will be valuable to owners as long as the manager's incentives affect the joint allocation of profits in the manager's game, a feature which appears in most cooperative modes of interaction as well as noncooperative.

This paper has demonstrated that competing firms' owners will often distort their managers' objectives away from strict profit maximization for *strategic* reasons. This initial analysis made several simplifying assumptions including linear payoffs to managers, absence of the usual moral hazard problems, and linear demand. Further research should generalize our analysis. However, it is clear from the basic intuition that distortions of managers' incentives are potentially important strategic instruments for owners of competing firms and point to the importance of external competitive conditions for the determination of internal relationships.

ACKNOWLEDGEMENTS

The authors would like to thank Steve Matthews, John Panzar, and Mark Satterthwaite for their comments. Professor Judd also gratefully acknowledges the financial support of National Science Foundation grant nos. SES-8409786 and SES-8606581, the Sloan Foundation, the Hoover Institution, and the Kellogg Graduate School of Management.

NOTES

1. The principal-agent approach (Ross, 1973; James Mirrlees, 1976; Bengt Holmstrom, 1977; Milton Harris and Artur Raviv, 1979; Roger Myerson, 1982; and many others) assumes that a principal chooses an incentive structure for agents which maximizes his welfare subject to information constraints and adequate compensation for the agents.
2. We thank an anonymous referee for pointing out this alternative view of the interaction between the capital and managerial markets.
3. O_i will not be a manager's reward in general. Since his reward is linear in profits and sales, he is paid $A_i + B_i Q_i$ for some constants, A_i, B_i, with $B_i > 0$. Since he is risk-neutral, he acts to maximize O_i and the values of A_i and B_i are irrelevant.
4. Recent work has indicated that the restriction to linear contracts is reasonable and does not mislead us. Bengt Holmstrom and Paul Milgrom (1987) show that linear contracts are optimal in some realistic continuous-time principal-agent problems. Fershtman and Judd (1987) showed that the basic insights of this paper continue to hold when moral hazard considerations also enter into the contracting problems of a duopolist. The focus on linear contracts here allows us to address questions that are intractable when we combine shirking by agents with a more complex dynamic structure.
5. Fershtman and Judd (1987) demonstrate this in a simple model.
6. Recall, from note 3, that i's manager is paid $A_i + B_i O_i$. Since managers are risk neutral, the owners can first set the optimal α's, yielding the O_i, and then promise A_i's, which set the means of $A_i + B_i O_i$ equal to the manager's opportunity cost. Hence, owners' profits equal expected profits minus managerial opportunity costs.
7. Had we assumed our differentiated producers completed in quantities, then the results would have resembled those of the nondifferentiated Cournot analysis. Therefore the comparisons we make here result from the mode of competition, not from product differentiation. The product differentiation feature was added to the analysis of the preceding section in order to keep price competition from always resulting in marginal cost pricing.

REFERENCES

Baumol, William. On the theory of oligopoly, *Economica*, August 1958, **25**: 187–198.

Brander, James A. and Lewis, Tracy R. Oligopoly and financial structure: The limited liability effect, *American Economic Review*, December 1986, **76**: 956–970.

Brander, James A. and Spencer, Barbara J. Export subsidies and international market share rivalry, *Journal of International Economics*, February 1985, **18**: 83–100.

Fershtman, Chaim. Internal organizations and managerial incentives as strategic variables in competitive environment, *International Journal of Industrial Organization*, 1985, **3**: 245–53.

Fershtman, Chaim and Judd, Kenneth L. Strategic Incentive Manipulation in Rivalrous Agency, Hoover Institution *Working Papers in Economics* E-87-11, 1987.

Holmstrom, Bengt. *On Incentives and Control in Organizations*, unpublished doctoral dissertation, Stanford University, 1977.

Holmstrom, Bengt and Milgrom, Paul. Aggregation and linearity in the provision of intertemporal incentives, *Econometrica*, March 1987, **55**: 303–328.

Harris, Milton and Raviv, Artur. Optimal incentive contracts with imperfect information, *Journal of Economic Theory*, April 1979, **20**: 231–259.

Jensen, Michael C. and Meckling, William H. Theory of the firm: Managerial behavior, agency costs and ownership structure, *Journal of Financial Economics*, October 1976, **3**: 305–360.

Maksimovic, Vojislav. *Optimal Capital Structure in Oligopolies*, unpublished doctoral dissertation, Harvard University, 1986.

McGuire, J., Chiu, J. and Elbing, A. Executive income, sales, and profits, *American Economic Review*, September 1962, **52**: 753–761.

Mirrlees, James. The optimal structure of incentives and authority within an organization, *Bell Journal of Economics*, Spring 1976, **7**: 165–181.

Myerson, Roger. Optimal coordination mechanisms in generalized principal–agent problems, *Journal of Mathematical Economics*, June 1982, **10**: 67–81.

Ross, Stephen. The economic theory of agency: The principal's problem, *American Economic Review*, May 1973, **63**: 134–139.

Simon, Herbert. On the concept of organizational goal, *Administrative Science Quarterly*, June 1964, **9**, 1–21.

Spencer, Barbara J. and Brander, James A. International R&D rivalry and industrial strategy, *Review of Economic Studies*, October 1983, **50**: 707–722.

Williamson, Oliver E. *The Economics of Discretionary Behavior: Managerial Objectives in a Theory of the Firm*, Englewood Cliffs: Prentice-Hall, 1964.

Part VIII

Social Choice

CONTENTS

21

The Impossibility of a Paretian Liberal

Amartya Sen

INTRODUCTION

The purpose of this chapter is to present an impossibility result that seems to have some disturbing consequences for principles of social choice. A common objection to the method of majority decision is that it is illiberal. The argument takes the following form: Given other things in the society, if you prefer to have pink walls rather than white, then society should permit you to have this, even if a majority of the community would like to see your walls white. Similarly, whether you should sleep on your back or on your belly is a matter in which the society should permit you absolute freedom, even if a majority of the community is nosey enough to feel that you must sleep on your back. We formalize this concept of individual liberty in an extremely weak form and examine its consequences.

THE THEOREM

Let R_i be the ordering of the ith individual over the set X of all possible social states, each social state being a complete description of society including every individual's position in it. There are n individuals. Let R be the social preference relation that is to be determined.

Definition 1.   *A collective choice rule* is a functional relationship that specifies one and only one social preference relation R for any set of n individual orderings (one ordering for each individual).

A special case of a collective choice rule is one that Arrow (1951) calls a social welfare function, namely, a rule such that R must be an ordering.

Definition 2.   A social welfare function is a collective choice rule, the range of which is restricted to orderings.

A weaker requirement is that each R should generate a "choice function", that is, in every subset of alternatives there must be a "best" alternative, or, in other words, there must be some (but not necessarily only one) alternative that is at least as good as all the other alternatives in that subset. This may be called a "social decision function".

Definition 3.   A social decision function is a collective choice rule, the range of which is restricted to social preference relations that generate a choice function.

It was shown in Sen (1969) that the conditions that were proven to be inconsistent by Arrow (1951, 1963) in his justly famous "impossibility theorem" in the context of a social welfare function are in fact perfectly consistent if imposed on a social decision function. The impossibility theorem to be presented here holds, however, for social decision functions as well.

Arrow's condition of collective rationality (Condition 1′) can be seen to be merely a requirement that the domain of the collective choice rule should not be arbitrarily restricted.

Condition U (Unrestricted Domain).   Every logically possible set of individual orderings is included in the domain of the collective choice rule.

Arrow used a weak version of the Pareto principle.

Condition P.   If every individual prefers any alternative x to another alternative y, then society must prefer x to y.

Finally, we introduce the condition of individual liberty in a very weak form.

Condition L (Liberalism).   For each individual i, there is at least one pair of alternatives, say (x, y), such that if this individual prefers x to y, then society should prefer x to y, and if this individual prefers y to x, then society should prefer y to x.[1]

The intention is to permit each individual the freedom to determine at least one social choice, for example, having his own walls pink rather than white, other things remaining the same for him and the rest of the society.[2]

The following impossibility theorem holds.

Theorem I.   There is no social decision function that can simultaneously satisfy Conditions U, P, and L.

In fact, we can weaken the condition of liberalism further. Such freedom may not be given to all, but to a proper subset of individuals. However, to make sense the subset must have more than one member, since if it includes only one then we might have a dictatorship. Hence, we demand such freedom for at least two individuals.

Condition L (Minimal Liberalism).*   There are at least two individuals such that for each of them there is at least one pair of alternatives over which he is decisive, that is, there is a pair of *x, y*, such that if he prefers *x* (respectively *y*) to *y* (respectively *x*), then society should prefer *x* (respectively *y*) to *y* (respectively *x*).

The following theorem is stronger than Theorem I and subsumes it.

Theorem II.   There is no social decision function that can simultaneously satisfy Conditions *U, P,* and *L**.

Proof.   Let the two individuals referred to in Condition *L** be 1 and 2, respectively, and the two pairs of alternatives referred to be (*x, y*) and (*z, w*), respectively. If (*x, y*) and (*z, w*) are the same pair of alternatives, then there is a contradiction. They have, therefore, at most one alternative in common, say *x = z*. Assume now that person 1 prefers *x* to *y*, and person 2 prefers *w* to *z* (= *x*). And let everyone in the community including 1 and 2 prefer *y* to *w*. There is in this no inconsistency for anyone, not even for 1 and 2, and their respective orderings are: 1 prefers *x* to *y* and *y* to *w*, while 2 prefers *y* to *w* and *w* to *x*. By Condition *U* this should be in the domain of the social decision mechanism. But by Condition *L**, *x* must be preferred to *y*, and *w* must be preferred to *x* (= *z*), while by the Pareto principle, *y* must be preferred to *w*. Thus, there is no best element in the set (*x = z, y, w*) in terms of social preference, and every alternative is worse than some other. A choice function for the society does not therefore exist.

Next, let *x, y, z,* and *w*, be all distinct. Let 1 prefer *x* to *y*, and 2 prefer *z* to *w*. And let everyone in the community including 1 and 2 prefer *w* to *x* and *y* to *z*. There is no contradiction for 1 or 2, for 1 simply prefers *w* to *x, x* to *y*, and *y* to *z*, while 2 prefers *y* to *z, z* to *w*, and *w* to *x*. By Condition *U* this configuration of individual preferences must yield a social choice function. But by Condition *L** society should prefer *x* to *y* and *z* to *w*, while by the Pareto principle society must prefer *w* to *x*, and *y* to *z*. This means that there is no best alternative for this set, and a choice function does not exist for any set that includes these four alternatives. Thus, there is no social decision function satisfying Conditions *U, P,* and *L**, and the proof is complete.[3]

AN EXAMPLE

We give now a simple example of the type of impossibility that is involved in Theorem II by taking a special case of two individuals and three alternatives. There is one copy of a certain book, say *Lady Chatterley's Lover*, which is viewed differently by 1 and 2. The three alternatives are: that individual 1 reads it (*x*), that individual 2 reads it (*y*), and that no one reads it (*z*). Person 1, who is a prude, prefers most that no one reads it, but given the choice between either of the two reading it, he would prefer that he read it himself rather than exposing gullible Mr 2 to the influences of Lawrence. (Prudes, I am told, tend to prefer to be censors rather than being censored). In decreasing order of preference, his ranking is *z, x, y*. Person 2, however, prefers that either of them should read it rather than neither. Furthermore, he takes delight in the thought that prudish Mr 1 may have to read Lawrence, and his first preference is that person 1 should read it, next best that he himself should read it, and worst that neither should. His ranking is, therefore, *x, y, z*.

Now if the choice is precisely between the pair (x, z), i.e., between person 1 reading the book and no one reading it, someone with liberal values may argue that it is person 1's preference that should count; since the prude would not like to read it, he should not be forced to. Thus, the society should prefer z to x. Similarly, in the choice exactly between person 2 reading the book (y) and no one reading it (z), liberal values require that person 2's preference should be decisive, and since he is clearly anxious to read the book he should be permitted to do this. Hence y should be judged socially better than z. thus, in terms of liberal values it is better that no one reads it rather than person 1 being forced to read it, and it is still better that person 2 is permitted to read the book rather than no one reading it. That is, the society should prefer y to z, and z to x. This discourse could end happily with the book being handed over to person 2 but for the fact that it is a Pareto inferior alternative, being worse than person 1 reading it, in the view of both persons, i.e., x is Pareto superior to y.

Every solution that we can think of is bettered by some other solution, given the Pareto principle and the principle of liberalism, and we seem to have an inconsistency of choice. This is an example of the type of problem that is involved in Theorems I and II.

RELEVANCE

The dilemma posed here may appear to be somewhat disturbing. It is, of course, not necessarily disturbing for every conceivable society, since the conflict arises with only particular configurations of individual preferences. The ultimate guarantee for individual liberty may rest not on rules for social choice but on developing individual values that respect each other's personal choices. The conflict posed here is concerned with societies where such a condition does not hold and where pairwise choice based on liberal values may conflict with those based on the Pareto principle. Like Arrow's "General Possibility Theorem," here also the Condition of Unrestricted Domain is used.

However, unlike in the theorem of Arrow, we have not required transitivity of social preference. We have required neither transitivity of strict preference, nor transitivity of indifference, but merely the existence of a best alternative in each choice situation.[4] Suppose society prefers x to y, and y to z, and is indifferent between z and x. Arrow would rule this out, since there is an intransitivity; but we do not, for here alternative x is "best" in the sense of being at least as good as both the other alternatives. Our requirements are, in this respect, very mild, and we still have an impossibility.

Second, we have not imposed Arrow's much debated condition of "the independence of irrelevant alternatives".[5] Many people find the relaxation of this condition to be an appealing way of escaping the Arrow dilemma. This way out is not open here, for the theorem holds without imposing this condition.

The Pareto principle is used here in a very weak version, as in Arrow. We do not necessarily require that if someone prefers x to y and everyone regards x to be at least as good as y, then x is socially better. We permit the possibility of having collective choice rules that will violate this provided everyone strictly preferring x to y must make x socially better than y. Nevertheless it turns out that a principle reflecting liberal values even in a very mild form cannot possibly be combined with the weak Pareto principle, given an unrestricted domain. If we do believe in these other conditions, then the society cannot permit even minimal liberalizm. Society cannot then let more than one individual be free to read what they like, sleep the way they prefer, dress as they care to, etc., *irrespective* of the preferences of others in the community.

What is the moral? It is that in a very basic sense liberal values conflict with the Pareto principle. If someone takes the Pareto principle seriously, as economists seem to do, then he has to face problems of consistency in cherishing liberal values, even very mild ones.[6] Or, to look at it in another way, if someone does have certain liberal values, then he may have to eschew his adherence to Pareto optimality. While the Pareto criterion has been thought to be an expression of individual liberty, it appears that in choices involving more than two alternatives it can have consequences that are, in fact, deeply illiberal.

ACKNOWLEDGEMENTS

For comments and criticisms I am grateful to Kenneth Arrow, Peter Diamond, Milton Friedman, Tapas Majumdar, Stephen Marglin, and Thomas Schelling.

NOTES

1. The term "liberalism" is elusive and is open to alternative interpretations. Some uses of the term may not embrace the condition defined here, while many uses will. I do not wish to engage in a debate on the right use of the term. What is relevant is that Condition L represents a value involving individual liberty that many people would subscribe to. Whether such people are best described as liberals is a question that is not crucial to the point of this paper.
2. Even this informal statement, which sounds mild, is much more demanding than Condition L. If the individual's preference over a personal choice (like choosing the color of his wall) is to be accepted by the society, other things remaining the same, then this gives the individual rights not only over one pair, which is all that is required by Condition L, but over many pairs (possibly an infinite number of pairs) varying with the "other things". If it is socially all right for me to have my walls either pink or white as I like in a social state where you smoke cigars, it should be socially all right for me to do the same where you indulge yourself in ways other than smoking cigars. Even this is not required by Condition L, which seems to demand very little.
3. We can strengthen this theorem further by weakening Condition L^* by demanding only that 1 be decisive for x against y, but not vice versa, and 2 be decisive for z against w, but not vice versa, and require that $x \neq z$, and $y \neq w$. This condition, too, can be shown to be inconsistent with Condition U and P, but the logical gain involved in this extension does not, alas, seem to be associated with any significant increase of relevance that I can think of.
4. It may appear that one way of solving the dilemma is to dispense with the social choice function based on a binary relation, that is, to relax not merely transitivity but also *acyclicity*. A choice function that need not correspond to any binary relation has undoubtedly a wider scope. But then Condition P and Condition L would have to be redefined, for example: (1) x should not be chosen when y is available, if everyone prefers y to x, and (2) for each individual there is a pair (x_i, y_i) such that if he prefers x_i (respectively y_i) to y_i (respectively

x_i), then y_i (respectively x_i) should not be chosen if x_i (respectively y_i) is available. Thus redefined, the choice set for the set of alternatives may be rendered empty even without bringing in acyclicity, and the contradiction will reappear. This and other possible "ways out" are discussed more fully in my book (Sen, 1970, chap. 6).

5. Using the condition of the independence of irrelevant alternatives, A. Gibbard, in an unpublished paper, has recently proved the following important theorem: Any social decision function that must generate social preferences that are all transitive in the strict relation (quasi-transitive) and which must satisfy Conditions U, P, nondictatorship, and the independence of irrelevant alternatives, must be an oligarchy in the sense that there is a unique group of individuals each of whom, by preferring x to y, can make the society regard x to be at least as good as y, and by all preferring x to y can make the society prefer x to y, irrespective of the preferences of those who are not in this group, Gibbard's Theorem is disturbing, for the conditions look appealing but the resultant oligarchy seems revolting, and it is a major extension of the problem posed by Arrow (1951, 1963). Gibbard argues against the simultaneous insistence on a binary relation of social preference generating a choice function and on the condition of the independence of irrelevant alternatives. We have not imposed the latter.

6. The difficulties of *achieving* Pareto optimality in the presence of externalities are well known. What is at issue here is the *acceptability* of Pareto optimality as an objective in the contex of liberal values, given certain types of externalities.

REFERENCES

Arrow, K. J. *Individual Values and Social Choice.* New York: Wiley, 1951; 2d ed., 1963.

Sen, A. K. Quasi-transitivity, Rational Choice and Collective Decisions. *Review of Economic Studies,* July 1969, **36**(3): 381–393.

Sen, A. K. *Collective Choice and Social Welfare.* San Francisco: Holden-Day; and Edinburgh: Oliver & Boyd, 1970.

22

Rationality and Social Choice

Amartya Sen

While Aristotle agreed with Agathon that even God could not change the past, he did think that the future was ours to make—by basing our choices on reasoning. The idea of using reason to identify and promote better—or more acceptable—societies, and to eliminate intolerable deprivations of different kinds, has powerfully moved people in the past and continues to do so now. In this chapter I would like to discuss some aspects of this question which have received attention in the recent literature in social-choice and public-choice theories. The contemporary world suffers from many new as well as old economic problems, including, among others, the persistence of poverty and deprivation despite general economic progress, the occurrence of famines and more widespread hunger, and threats to our environment and to the sustainability of the world in which we live. Rational use of the opportunities offered by modern science and technology, in line with our values and ends, is a powerful challenge today.

PROBLEMS AND DIFFICULTIES

How are we to view the demands of rationality in social decisions? How much guidance do we get from Aristotle's general recommendation that choice should be governed by "desire and reasoning directed to some end"? There are several deep-seated difficulties here

The first problem relates to the question: *whose* desires, *whose* ends? Different persons have disparate objects and interests, and as Horace put it, "there are as many preferences as there are people". Kenneth Arrow (1951) has shown, through his famous "General Possibility Theorem" (an oddly optimistic name for what is more commonly—and more revealingly—called Arrow's "impossibility theorem"), that in trying to obtain an integrated social preference from diverse individual preferences, it is not in general possible to satisfy even some mild-looking conditions that would seem to reflect elementary demands of reasonableness.[1] Other impossibility results have also

Reprinted with permission from *American Economic Review*, Vol. 85, No. 1, 1995, pp. 1–24

emerged, even without using some of Arrow's conditions, but involving other elementary criteria, such as the priority of individual liberty.[2] We have to discuss why these difficulties arise, and how we can deal with them. Are the pessimistic conclusions that some have drawn from them justified? Can we sensibly make aggregative social-welfare judgements? Do procedures for social decision-making exist that reasonably respect individual values and preferences?

Second, another set of problems relates to questions raised by James Buchanan (1954a,b), which were partly a response to Arrow's results, but they are momentous in their own right.[3] Pointing to "the fundamental philosophical issues" involved in "the idea of social rationality", Buchanan (1954a) argued that "rationality or irrationality as an attribute of the social group implies the imputation to that group of an organic existence apart from that of its individual components" (p. 116). Buchanan was perhaps "the first commentator to interpret Arrow's impossibility theorem as the result of a mistaken attempt to impose the logic of welfare maximization on the procedures of collective choice" (Robert Sugden, 1993 p. 1948). But in addition, he was arguing that there was a deep "confusion surrounding the Arrow analysis" (not just the impossibility theorem but the entire framework used by Arrow and his followers) which ensued from the mistaken idea of "social or collective rationality in terms of producing results indicated by a social ordering" (Buchanan, 1960 pp. 88–89). We certainly have to examine whether Buchanan's critique negates the impossibility results, but we must also investigate the more general issues raised by Buchanan.[4]

Third, Buchanan's reasoned questioning of the idea of "social preference" suggests, at the very least, a need for caution in imposing strong "consistency properties" in social choice, but his emphasis on procedural judgements may be taken to suggest, much more ambitiously, that we should abandon altogether consequence-based evaluation of social happenings, opting instead for a procedural approach. In its pure form, such an approach would look for "right" institutions rather than "good" outcomes and would demand the priority of appropriate procedures (including the acceptance of what follows from these procedures). This approach, which is the polar opposite of the welfare-economic tradition based on classical utilitarianism of founding every decision on an ordering of different states of affairs (treating procedures just as instruments to generate good states), has not been fully endorsed by Buchanan himself, but significant work in that direction has occurred in public choice theory and in other writings influenced by Buchanan's work (most notably, in the important contributions of Robert Sugden (1981, 1986)).

This contrast is particularly important in characterizing rights in general and liberties in particular. In the social choice literature, these characterizations have typically been in terms of states of affairs, concentrating on what happens vis-à-vis what the person wanted or chose to do. In contrast, in the libertarian literature, inspired by the pioneering work of Robert Nozick (1974), and in related contributions using "game-form" formulations (most notably, by Wulf Gaertner, Pattanaik, and Suzumura (1992)), rights have been characterized in procedural terms, without referring to states of affairs. We have to examine how deep the differences between the disparate formulations are, and we must also scrutinize their respective adequacies.

Fourth, the prospects of rationality in social decisions must be fundamentally conditional on the nature of *individual* rationality. There are many different conceptions of rational behavior of the individual. There is, for example, the view of rationality as canny maximization of self-interest (the presumption of human beings as "*homo economicus*", used in public choice theory, fits into this framework). Arrow's (1951) formulation is more permissive; it allows social considerations to influence the choices people make. Individual preferences, in this interpretation reflect "values" in general, rather than being based only on what Arrow calls "tastes" (p. 23). How adequate are the respective characterizations of individual rationality, and through the presumption of rational behavior (shared by most economic models), the depiction of actual conduct and choices?

Another issue, related to individual behavior and rationality, concerns the role of social interactions in the development of values, and also the connection between value formation and the decision-making processes. Social choice theory has tended to avoid this use, following Arrow's own abstinence: "We will also assume in the present study that individual values are taken as data and are not capable of being altered by the nature of the decision process itself" (Arrow, 1951 p. 7).[5] On this subject, Buchanan has taken a more permissive position—indeed emphatically so: "The definition of democracy as 'government by discussion' implies that individual values can and do change in the process of decision-making" (Buchanan, 1954a p. 120).[6] We have to scrutinize the importance of this difference as well.

This is a long and somewhat exacting list, but the different issues relate to each other, and I shall try to examine them briefly and also comment on some of their practical implications.

SOCIAL WELFARE JUDGEMENTS AND ARROW'S IMPOSSIBILITY THEOREM

The subject of welfare economics was dominated for a long time by the utilitarian tradition, which performs interpersonal aggregation through the device of looking at the sum-total of the utilities of all the people involved. By the 1930s, however, economists came to be persuaded by arguments presented by Lionel Robbins (1938) and others (influenced by the philosophy of "logical positivism") that interpersonal comparisons of utility had no scientific basis.[7] Thus, the epistemic foundations of utilitarian welfare economics were seen as incurably defective.

Because of the eschewal of interpersonal comparability of individual utilities, the "new welfare economics" that emerged tried to rely only on one basic criterion of social improvement, the Pareto criterion. Since this confines the recognition of a social improvement only to the case in which everyone's utility goes up (or someone's goes up and no one's goes down), it does not require any interpersonal comparison, nor for that matter, any cardinality of individual utilities. However, Pareto efficiency can scarcely be an adequate condition for a good society. It is quite insensitive to the *distribution* of utilities (including inequalities of happiness and miseries), and it takes no direct note of anything *other than* utilities (such as rights or freedoms) beyond their indirect role in generating utilities. There is a need, certainly, for *further* criteria for social welfare judgements.

The demands of orderly, overall judgements of "social welfare" (or the general goodness of states of affairs) were clarified by Abram Bergson (1938, 1966) and extensively explored by Paul Samuelson (1947). The concentration was on the need for a real-valued function W of "social welfare" defined over all the alternative social states, or at least an aggregate ordering R over them, the so-called "social preference". In the reexamination that followed the Bergson–Samuelson initiative (including the development of social choice theory as a discipline), the search for principles underlying a social welfare function played a prominent part.

Arrow (1951) defined a "social welfare function" as a functional relation that specifies a social ordering R over all the social states for every set of individual preference orderings. In addition to assuming—not especially controversially—that there are at least three distinct social states and at least two (but not infinitely many) individuals, Arrow also wanted a social welfare function to yield a social ordering for every possible combination of individual preferences; that is, it must have a *universal domain*. A second condition is called *the independence of irrelevant alternatives*. This can be defined in different ways, and I shall choose an extremely simple form. The way a society ranks a pair of alternative social states x and y should depend on the individual preferences only over *that* pair—in particular, *not* on how the other ("irrelevant") alternatives are ranked.

Now consider the idea of some people being "decisive": a set G of people—I shall call them a group G—having their way no matter what others prefer. In ranking a pair x and y, if it turns out that x gets socially ranked above y *whenever* everyone in group G prefers x to y (no matter what preferences those not in G have), then G is decisive over that ordered pair (x, y). When a group G is decisive over all ordered pairs, it is simply "decisive".

Arrow required that no individual (formally, no single-member group) should be decisive (*nondictatorship*), but—following the Paretian tradition—also demanded that the group of all individuals taken together should be decisive (the *Pareto principle*). The "impossibility theorem", in this version (presented in Arrow (1963)), shows that it is impossible to have a social welfare function with *universal domain*, satisfying *independence*, the *Pareto principle*, and *nondictatorship*.

The theorem can be proved in three simple steps.[8] The first two steps are the following (with the second lemma drawing on the first).

Field-expansion lemma.   If a group is decisive over any pair of states, it is decisive.[9]

Group-contraction lemma.   If a group (of more than one person) is decisive, then so is some smaller group contained in it.[10]

The final step uses the group-contraction lemma to prove the theorem. By the Pareto principle, the group of all individuals is decisive. Since it is finite, by successive partitioning (and each time picking the decisive part), we arrive at a decisive individual, who must, thus, be a dictator. Hence the impossibility.

SOCIAL PREFERENCE, SOCIAL CHOICE, AND IMPOSSIBILITY

The preceding discussion makes abundant use of the idea of "social preference". Should it be dropped, as suggested by Buchanan? And if so, what would remain of Arrow's impossibility theorem?

We have to distinguish between two quite different uses of the notion of "social preference", related respectively to (i) the operation of *decision mechanisms*, and (ii) the making of *social welfare judgements*. The first notion of "social preference" is something like the "underlying preference" on which *choices* actually made for the society by prevailing mechanisms are implicitly based—a kind of "revealed preference" of the society.[11] This "derivative" view of social preference would be, formally, a binary representation of the choices emerging from decision mechanisms.

The second idea of "social preference"—as social welfare judgements—reflects a view of the social good: some ranking of what would be better or worse for the society. Such judgements would be typically made by a given person or agency. Here too an aggregation is involved, since an individual who is making judgements about social welfare, or about the relative goodness of distinct social states, must somehow combine the diverse interests and preferences of different people.

Buchanan's objection is quite persuasive for the first interpretation (involving decision mechanisms), especially since there is no a priori presumption that the mechanisms used *must*—or even *should*—necessarily lead to choices that satisfy the requirements of binary representation (not to mention the more exacting demands of an ordering representation).[12] On the other hand, the second interpretation does not involve this problem, and even an individual when expressing a view about social welfare needs a concept of this kind.[13] When applied to the making of social welfare judgements by an individual or an agency, Arrow's impossibility theorem thus cannot be disputed on the ground that some organic existence is being imputed to the society. The amelioration of impossibility must be sought elsewhere (see the next section). However, Buchanan's critique of Arrow's theorem would apply to *mechanisms* of social decision (such as voting procedures).

Would the dropping of the requirement that social choices be based on a binary relation—in particular a transitive ordering—negate the result in the case of social decision mechanisms? A large literature has already established that the arbitrariness of power, of which Arrow's case of dictatorship is an extreme example, lingers in one form or another even when transitivity is dropped, so long as *some* regularity is demanded (such as the absence of cycles).[14] There is, however, cause for going further, precisely for the reasons identified by Buchanan, and to eschew not just the transitivity of social preference, but the idea of social preference itself. All that is needed from the point of view of choice is that the decision mechanisms determine a "choice function" for the society, which identifies what is picked from each alternative "menu" (or opportunity set).[15]

However, provided some conditions are imposed on the "internal consistency" of the choice function (relating decisions over one menu in a "consistent" way to decisions over other—related—menus), it can be shown that some arbitrariness of power would still survive.[16] But the methodological critique of James Buchanan would still apply forcefully, as reformulated in the following way: why should *any* restriction whatever be placed a priori on the choice function for the society? Why should not the decisions emerging from agreed social mechanisms be acceptable without having to check them against some preconceived idea of how choices made in different situations should relate to each other?

What happens, then, to Arrow's impossibility problem if no restrictions whatever are placed on the so-called "internal consistency" of the choice function for the society?

Would the conditions relating individual preferences to social choice (i.e., the Pareto principle, nondictatorship, and independence) then be consistent with each other? The answer, in fact, is no, not so. If the Pareto principle and the conditions of nondictatorship and independence are redefined to take full note of the fact that they must relate to social *choices*, not to any prior notion of social *preference*, then a very similar impossibility reemerges (see Theorem 3 in Sen (1993)).

How does this "general choice-functional impossibility theorem" work? The underlying intuition is this. Each of the conditions relating individual preferences to social decisions eliminates—either on its own or in the presence of the other conditions—the possibility of choosing *some* alternatives. And the conjunction of these conditions can lead to an empty choice set, making it "impossible" to choose anything.

For example, the Pareto principle is just such a condition, and the object of this condition in a choice context, surely, is to avoid the selection of a Pareto-inferior alternative. Therefore this condition can be sensibly redefined to demand that if everyone prefers x to y, then the social decision mechanism should be such that y should not get chosen if x is available.[17] Indeed, to eliminate any possibility that we are implicitly or indirectly using any intermenu consistency condition for social choice, we can define all the conditions for only *one given menu* (or opportunity set) S; that is, we can consider the choice problem exclusively over a given set of alternative states. The Pareto principle for that set S then only demands that if everyone prefers some x to some y in that set, then y must not be chosen from that set.

Similarly, nondictatorship would demand that there be no person such that whenever she prefers any x to any y in that set S, then y cannot be chosen from that set. What about independence? We have to modify the idea of decisiveness of a group in this choice context, related to choices over this given set S. A group would be decisive for x against y if and only if, whenever all members of this group prefer any x to any y in this set S, then y is not to be chosen from S. Independence would now demand that any group's power of decisiveness over a pair (x, y) be completely independent of individual preferences over pairs other than (x, y). It can be shown that there is no way of going from individual preferences to social choice satisfying these choice-oriented conditions of independence, the Pareto principle, nondictatorship, and unrestricted domain, even without invoking any "social preference", and without imposing any demand of "collective rationality", or any intermenu consistency condition on social choice.[18]

The morals to be drawn from all this for Buchanan's questioning of "social preference" would appear to be the following. The "impossibility" result identified in a particular form by Arrow can be extended and shown to hold even when the idea of "social preference" is totally dropped and even when no conditions are imposed on "internal consistency" of social choice. This does not, however, annul the importance of Buchanan's criticism of the idea of social preference (in the context of choices emerging from *decision mechanisms* for the society), since it is a valid criticism on its own right. But the "impossibility" problem identified by Arrow cannot be escaped by this move.

ON REASONED SOCIAL WELFARE JUDGEMENTS

How might we then avoid that impossibility? It is important to distinguish the bearing of the problem in the making of aggregative social welfare judgements, as opposed to the operation of social decision mechanisms. I start with the former.

It may be recalled that the Bergson–Samuelson analysis and Arrow's impossibility theorem followed a turn in welfare economics that had involved the dropping of interpersonal comparisons of utility. As it happens, because of its utilitarian form, traditional welfare economics had informational exclusions of its own, and it had been opposed to any basic use of nonutility information, since everything had to be judged ultimately by utility sum-totals in consequent states of affairs. To this was now added the exclusions of interpersonal comparisons of utilities, without removing the exclusion of nonutility information. This barren informational landscape makes it hard to arrive at systematic judgements of social welfare. Arrow's theorem can be interpreted, in this context, as a demonstration that even some very weak conditions relating individual preferences to social welfare judgements cannot be simultaneously satisfied given this informational privation.[19]

The problem is not just one of impossibility. Consider the field-expansion lemma: decisiveness over *any* pair of alternatives entails decisiveness over *every* pair of alternatives, *irrespective of the nature of the states involved.* Consider three divisions of a given cake between two persons: (99,1), (50,50), and (1,99). Let us begin with the assumption that each person—as *homo economicus*—prefers a larger personal share of the cake. So they happen to have opposite preferences. Consider now the ranking of (99,1) and (50,50). If it is decided that (50,50) is better for the society than (99,1), then in terms of preference-based information, person 2's preference is getting priority over person 1's.

A variant of the field-expansion lemma would then claim that person 2's preference must get priority over all other pairs as well, so that even (1,99) must be preferred to (50,50).[20] Indeed, it is not possible, given the assumptions, to regard (50,50) as best of the three; we could either have (99,1), giving priority to person 1's preference, or (1,99), giving priority to 2's preference. But *not* (50,50). I am not arguing here that (50,50) must necessarily be taken to be the best, but it is absurd that we are not even permitted to consider (50,50) as a claimant to being the best element in this cake-division problem.

It is useful to consider what arguments there might be for considering (50,50) as a good possibility, and why we cannot use any of these arguments in the information framework resulting from Arrow's conditions. First, it might seem good to divide the cake equally on some general *non-welfarist* ground, without even going into preferences or utilities. This is not permitted because of the exclusion of evaluative use of nonutility information, and this is what the field-expansion lemma is formalizing. Second, presuming that everyone has the same strictly concave utility function, we might think that the sum-total of utilities would be maximized by an equal division of the cake. But this utilitarian argument involves comparability of cardinal utilities, which is ruled out. Third, we might think that equal division of the cake will equate utilities, and there are arguments for utility-centered egalitarianism (see James Meade, 1976). But that involves interpersonal comparison of ordinal utilities, which too is ruled out. None of the standard ways of discriminating between the alternative states is viable in this informational framework, and the only way to choose between them is to go by the preference of one person or another (since they have opposite preferences).

To try to make social welfare judgements *without* using any interpersonal comparison of utilities, and *without* using any nonutility information, is not a fruitful enterprise. We do care about the size and distribution of the overall achievements; we have reasons to want to reduce deprivations, poverty, and inequality; and all these call for interpersonal comparisons—either of utilities or of other indicators of individual advantages, such as real incomes, opportunities, primary goods, or capabilities.[21] Once interpersonal comparisons are introduced, the impossibility problem, in the appropriately redefined framework, vanishes.[22] The comparisons may have to be rough and ready and often open to disputation, but such comparisons are staple elements of systematic social welfare judgements. Even without any cardinality, ordinal interpersonal comparisons permit the use of such rules of social judgement as maximin, or lexicographic maximin.[23] This satisfies all of Arrow's conditions (and many others), though the class of permissible social welfare rules that do this is quite limited, unless cardinality is also admitted, along with interpersonal comparisons (see Louis Gevers, 1979; Kevin Roberts, 1980a). With the possibility of using interpersonal comparisons, other classes of possible rules for social welfare judgements (including inter alia, utilitarianism) become usable.[24]

While the axiomatic derivations of different social-welfare rules in this literature are based on applying interpersonal comparisons to utilities only, the analytical problems are, in many respects, rather similar when people are compared in terms of some other feature, such as real income, holdings of primary goods, or capabilities to function. There are, thus, whole varieties of ways in which social welfare judgements can be made using richer information than in the Arrow framework.

This applies also to *procedures* specifically aimed at making social welfare judgements and other aggregative evaluations, based on institutionally accepted ways of making interpersonal comparisons; for example, in using indexes of income inequality (see Serge Kolm's (1969) and Anthony Atkinson's (1970) pioneering work on this), or in aggregate measures of distribution-corrected real national income (Sen, 1976a), or of aggregate poverty (Sen, 1976b).[25] This links the theory of social choice to some of the most intensely practical debates on economic policy.[26] While Arrow's impossibility theorem is a negative result, the challenge it provided has led, dialectically, to a great many constructive developments.

ON SOCIAL DECISION MECHANISMS

Moving from the exercise of making social judgements to that of choosing social decision mechanisms, there are other difficulties to be faced. While systematic interpersonal comparisons of utilities (and other ways of seeing individual advantage) can be used by a person making social welfare judgement, or in agreed *procedures* for social judgements (based on interpreting available statistics to arrive at, say, orderings of aggregate poverty or inequality or distribution-corrected real national income), this is not an easy thing to do in social-decision mechanisms which must rely on some standard expressions of individual preference (such as voting), which do not readily lend themselves to interpersonal comparisons.

The impossibility problem, thus, has greater resilience here. While it is also the case that the critique of James Buchanan (and others) of the idea of "social rationality" and the concept of "social preference" applies particularly in this case (that of judging social *decision mechanisms*), the impossibility problem does indeed survive, as we have seen, even when the concept of social preference is eschewed and the idea of social rationality in the Arrovian form is dropped altogether. How, then, can we respond to the challenge in this case?

We may begin by noting that the conditions formulated and used by Arrow, while appealing enough, are not beyond criticism. First, not every conceivable combination of individual preferences need be considered in devising a social decision procedure, since only some would come up in practice. As Arrow had himself noted, if the condition of unrestricted domain is relaxed, we can find decision rules that satisfy all the other conditions (and many other demands) over substantial domains of individual preference profiles. Arrow (1951), along with Duncan Black, had particularly explored the case of "single-peaked preferences", but it can be shown (Sen, 1966) that this condition can be far extended and generalized to a much less demanding restriction called "value restriction".[27]

The plausibility of different profiles of individual preferences depends on the nature of the problem and on the characteristics of individual motivations. It is readily checked that with three or more people, if everyone acts as *homo economicus* in a cake-division problem (always preferring more cake to oneself over all else), then value restriction and the related conditions would all be violated, and majority rule would standardly lead to intransitivities. It is also easy to show that in the commodity space, with each concentrating on her own commodity basket, the Arrow conditions could not be all satisfied by any decision mechanism over that domain. Majority rule and other voting procedures of this kind do cause cycles in general in what is called "the economic domain" (of interpersonal commodity space), if everyone votes in a narrowly self-interested way.

However, majority rule would be a terrible decision procedure in this case, and its intransitivity is hardly the main problem here. For example, taking the most deprived person in a community and passing on half her share of the cake divided between two richer persons would be a majority improvement, but scarcely a great welfare-economic triumph. In view of this, it is perhaps just as well that the majority rule is not only nasty and brutish, but also short in consistency.[28] The tension between social welfare judgements (of different kinds explored, for example, by Meade (1976), Arrow (1977), Mirrlees (1982), William J. Baumol (1986) or John Broome (1991)) and mechanical decision rules (like majority decision) with inward-looking, self-centered individuals is most obvious here. Also, as Buchanan (1994a,b) has argued, the acceptability of majority rule is, in fact, related to its tendency to generate cycles, and the endemic cyclicity of majority decisions is inescapable, given that endogeneity of alternative proposals that can be presented for consideration.

In practice, in facing political decisions, the choices may not come in these stark forms (there are many issues that are mixed together in political programs and proposals), and also individuals do not necessarily only look at their "own share of the cake" in taking up political positions and attitudes.[29] The "public choice" school has tended to emphasize the role of logrolling in political compromises and social decisions. While that school has also been rather wedded to the presumption of each person being *homo economicus* even in these exercises (see Buchanan and Tullock, 1962), there is a more general social process here (involving a variety of motivations) that can be fruitfully considered in examining decision mechanisms. Central to this is the role of public discussion in the formation of preferences and values, which has been emphasized by Buchanan (1954a,b).

The condition of independence of irrelevant alternatives is also not beyond disputation, and, indeed, has led to debates—explicitly or by implication—for a very long time. It was one of the issues that divided J.C. Borda (1781) and Marquis de Condorcet (1785), the two French mathematicians, who had pioneered the systematic theory of voting and group decision procedures in the 18th century. One version of the rule proposed by Borda, based on adding the rank-order numbers of candidates in each voter's preference list, violates the independence condition rather robustly, but it is not devoid of other merits (and is frequently used in practice).[30] Other types of voting rules have also been shown to have different desirable properties.

In examining social decision mechanisms, we have to take the Arrow conditions seriously, but not as inescapable commandments. Our intuitions vary on these matters, and Arrow's own theorem shows that not everything that appeals to us initially would really be simultaneously sustainable. There is a need for some de-escalation in the grim "fight for basic principles". The issue is not the likely absence of rationally defendable procedures for social decisions, but the relative importance of disparate considerations that pull us in different directions in evaluating diverse procedures. We are not at the edge of a precipice, trying to determine whether it is at all "possible" for us to hang on.

PROCEDURES AND CONSEQUENCES

I turn now to the general issue, identified earlier, of the contrast between relying respectively on (i) the "rightness" of procedures, and (ii) the "goodness" of outcomes. Social choice theory, in its traditional form, would seem to belong to the latter part of the dichotomy, with the states of affairs judged first (the subject matter of "social preference" or "social welfare judgements"), followed by identification of procedures that generate the "best" or "maximal" or "satisficing" states. There are two issues here. First, can consequences really be judged adequately without any notion of the process through which they are brought about? I shall also presently question whether this presumption of *process-independence* is the right way of seeing the claims of social choice theory. Second, can we do the converse of this, and judge procedures adequately in a *consequence-independent* way? This issue I take up first.

Sugden (1981, 1986), who has extensively analyzed this dichotomy (between procedural and consequence-based views), explains that in the public choice approach, which he supports, "the primary role of the government is not to maximize the social good, but rather to maintain a framework of rules within which individuals are left free to pursue their own ends" (Sugden, 1993 p. 1948). This is indeed so, but even in judging a "framework of rules" in this way, we do need some consequential analysis, dealing with the *effectiveness* of these frameworks in letting individuals be *actually* "free to pursue their own ends". In an interdependent world, examples of permissive rules that fail to generate the freedom to pursue the respective individual ends are not hard to find (see Sen, 1982b).

Indeed, it is not easy to believe that the public-choice approach is—or can be—really consequence-independent. For example, Buchanan's support of market systems is based on a reading of the consequences that the market mechanism tends to produce, and consequences certainly do enter substantially in Buchanan's evaluation of procedures: "To the extent that voluntary exchange among persons is valued positively while coercion is valued negatively, there emerges the implication that substitution of the former for the latter is desired, on the presumption, of course, that such substitution is technologically feasible and is not prohibitively costly in resources" (Buchanan, 1986 p. 22). While this is not in serious conflict with Buchanan's rejection of any "transcendental" evaluation of the outcomes (p. 22), nevertheless the assessment of outcomes must, in *some* form, enter this evaluative exercise.[32]

There are, however, other—more purely procedural—systems to be found in this literature. If the utilitarian tradition of judging everything by the consequent utilities is one extreme in the contrast (focusing only on a limited class of consequences), Nozick's (1974) elegant exploration of libertarian "entitlement theory" comes close to the other end (focusing on the right rules that cover personal liberties as well as rights of holding, using, exchanging, and bequeathing legitimately owned property). But the possibility of having unacceptable consequences has to be addressed by any such procedural system. What if the results are dreadful for many, or even all?

Indeed, it can be shown that even gigantic famines can actually take place in an economy that fulfills all the libertarian rights and entitlements specified in the Nozick system.[33] It is, thus, particularly appropriate that Nozick (1974) makes exceptions to consequence-independence in cases where the exercise of these rights would lead to "catastrophic moral horrors".[34] Because of this qualification, consequences are made to matter after all, and underlying this concession is Nozick's good sense (similar to Buchanan's) that a procedural system of entitlements that happens to yield catastrophic moral horrors (we have to have some consensus on what these are) would be—and should be—ethically unacceptable. However, once consequences are brought into the story, not only is the purity of a consequence-independent system lost, but also the issue of deciding on the relative importance of "right rules" and "good consequences" is forcefully reestablished.

I turn now to the other side of the dichotomy: can we have sensible outcome judgements in a totally procedure-independent way? Classical utilitarianism does indeed propose such a system, but it is hard to be convinced that we can plausibly judge any given utility distribution ignoring *altogether* the process that led to that distribution (attaching, for example, no intrinsic importance whatever to whether a particular utility redistribution is caused by charity, or taxation, or torture).[35]

This recognition of the role of processes is not, in fact, hostile to social choice theory, since there is nothing to prevent us from seeing the description of processes as a part of the consequent states generated by them.[36] If action *A* is performed, then "action *A* has been done" must be one—indeed, the most elementary—consequence of that event. If Mr John Major were to wish not merely that he should be reelected as Prime Minister, but that he should be "reelected fairly" (I am not, of course, insinuating that any such preference has been expressed by Mr Major), the consequence that he would be seeking would have procedural requirements incorporated within it.

This is not to claim that every process can be comfortably placed within the description of states of affairs without changing anything in social choice theory. Parts of the literature that deal with comparisons of decision mechanisms in arriving at *given* states would need modification. If, in general, processes leading to the emergence of a social state were standardly included in the characterization of that state, then we have to construct "equivalence classes" to *ignore* some differences (in this case, between some antecedent processes) to be able to discuss cogently the "same state" being brought about by different decision mechanisms. To make sense of such ideas as, say, "path independence" (on which see Plott (1973)), so that they are not rendered vacuous, equivalence classes of this type would certainly have to be constructed (on the concepts of equivalence classes and invariance conditions, see Sen (1986b)).

The contrast between the procedural and consequential approaches is, thus, somewhat overdrawn, and it may be possible to combine them, to a considerable extent, in an adequately rich characterization of states of affairs. The dichotomy is far from pure, and it is mainly a question of relative concentration.

LIBERTIES, RIGHTS, AND PREFERENCES

The need to integrate procedural considerations in consequential analysis is especially important in the field of rights and liberties. The violation or fulfillment of basic liberties or rights tends to be ignored in traditional utilitarian welfare economics not just because of its consequentialist focus, but particularly because of its "welfarism", whereby consequent states of affairs are judged exclusively by the utilities generated in the respective states.[37] While processes may end up getting some *indirect* attention insofar as they influence people's utilities, nevertheless no direct and basic importance is attached in the utilitarian framework to rights and liberties in the evaluation of states of affairs.

The initial formulation of social choice did not depart in this respect from the utilitarian heritage, but it is possible to change this within a broadly Arrovian framework (see Sen, 1970, 1982a), and a good deal of work has been done in later social choice theory to accommodate the basic relevance of rights and liberties in assessing states of affairs, and thus to evaluate economic, political, and social arrangements. If a person is prevented from doing some preferred thing even though that choice is sensibly seen to be in her "personal domain," then the state of affairs can be seen to have been worsened by this failure. The extent of worsening is not to be judged only by the magnitude of the utility loss resulting from this (to be compared with utility gains of others, if any), since something more is also at stake. As John Stuart Mill (1859 p. 140) noted, "there is no parity between the feeling of a person for his own opinion, and the feeling of another who is offended at his holding it".[38] The need to guarantee some "minimal liberties" on a priority basis can be incorporated in social choice formulations.

It turns out, however, that such unconditional priority being given even to minimal liberty can conflict with other principles of social choice, including the redoubtable Pareto principle. The "impossibility of the Paretian liberal" captures the conflict between (i) the special importance of a person's preferences over her own personal sphere, and (ii) the general importance of people's preferences over any choice, irrespective of field. This impossibility theorem has led to a large literature extending, explaining, disputing, and ameliorating the result.[39] The "ways out" that have been sought have varied between: (i) weakening the priority of liberties (thereby qualifying the minimal liberty condition); (ii) constraining the field-independent general force of preferences (thereby qualifying the Pareto principle), and (iii) restricting the domain of permissible individual-preference profiles. As in the case of the Arrow impossibility problem, the different ways of resolving this conflict have variable relevance depending on the exact nature of the social choice exercise involved.

There have also been attempts to redefine liberty in purely *procedural* terms. The last is an important subject on its own (quite independently of any use it might have as an attempt to resolve the impossibility), and I shall presently consider it. But as has been noted by Gaertner, Pattanaik, and Suzumura (1992), who have recently provided the most extensive recharacterization of liberty (in terms of "game forms"), the impossibility problem "persists under virtually every plausible concept of individual rights" (p. 161).[40]

The decisive move in the direction of a purely procedural view of liberty was made by Nozick (1974), responding to my social choice formulation and to the impossibility of the Paretian liberal (Sen, 1970). This has been followed by important constructive contributions by Gärdenfors (1981) and Sugden (1981), and the approach has been extended and developed into game-form formulations by Gaertner *et al.* (1992). In the game-form view, each of the players has a set of permissible strategies, and the outcome is a function of the combination of strategies chosen by each of the players (perhaps qualified by an additional "move" by "nature"). The liberties and rights of the different persons are defined by specifying a permissible subset from the product of the strategy sets of the different individuals. A person can exercise his rights as he likes, subject to the strategy combination belonging to the permissible set.

In defining what rights a person has, or in checking whether his rights were respected, there is, on this account, no need to examine or evaluate the resulting state of affairs, and no necessity to examine what states the individuals involved prefer. In contrasting this characterization of preference-independent, consequence-detached rights with the social choice approach to rights, perhaps the central question that is raised is the plausibility of making people's putative rights, in general, so dissociated from the effects of exercising them. This is a general issue that was already discussed at a broader level in the previous section.

In some contexts, the idea of seeing rights in the form of permission to act can be quite inadequate, particularly because of "choice inhibition" that might arise from a variety of causes. The long British discussion on the failure of millions of potential welfare recipients from making legitimate claims (apparently due to the shame and stigma of having one's penury publicized and recorded) illustrate's a kind of nonrealization of rights in which permission is not the main issue at all.[41] Similarly, the inability of women in traditionally sexist societies to use even those rights that have not been formally denied to them also illustrates a type of rights failure that is not helpfully seen in terms of game forms (see Sen, 1992b pp. 148–50). Even the questions that standardly come up in this country in determining whether a rape has occurred have to go well beyond checking whether the victim in question was "free" to defy.

Leaving out such cases, it might well be plausible to argue that rights can be nicely characterized by game forms in many situations. However, even when that is the case, in deciding on what rights to protect and codify, and in determining how the underlying purpose might be most effectively achieved, there is a need to look at the likely consequences of different game-form specifications and to relate them to what people value and desire. If, for example, it appears that not banning smoking in certain gatherings (leaving the matter to the discretion of the people involved) would actually lead to unwilling victims having to inhale other people's smoke, then there would be a case for considering that the game-form be so modified that smoking is simply banned in those gatherings. Whether or not to make this move must depend crucially on consequential analysis. The object, in this case, is the prevention of the state of affairs in which nonsmokers have to inhale unwillingly other people's smoke: a situation they resent and which—it is assumed—they have a right to avoid. We proceed from there, through consequential analysis (in an "inverse" form: from consequences to antecedents), to the particular game-form formulation that would not achieve an acceptable result. The fact that the *articulation* of the game-form would be consequence-independent and preference-independent is not a terribly profound assertion and is quite consistent with the fundamental relevance of consequences and preferences.

The contrast between game-form formulations and social-choice conceptions of rights is, thus, less deep than it might first appear (see Sen, 1992b).[42] As in other fields considered earlier, in this area too, the need to combine procedural concerns with those of actual events and outcomes is quite strong.

VALUES AND INDIVIDUAL CHOICES

I have so far postponed discussing individual behavior and rationality, though the issue has indirectly figured in the preceding discussions (for example, in dealing with norms for social choice, individual interest in social welfare judgements, and determination of voting behavior). The public choice tradition has tended to rely a good deal on the presumption that people behave in a rather narrowly self-centered way—as *homo economicus* in particular, even though Buchanan (1986 p. 26) himself notes some "tension" on this issue (see also Geoffrey Brennan and Loren Lomarsky, 1993). Public servants *inter alia* are to be seen as working for their own well-being and success.

Adam Smith is sometimes described as the original proponent of the ubiquity and ethical adequacy of "the economic man", but that would be fairly sloppy history. In fact, Smith (1776, 1790) had examined the distinct disciplines of "self-love", "prudence", "sympathy", "generosity", and "public spirit", among others, and had discussed not only their intrinsic importance, but also their instrumental roles in the success of a society, and also their practical influence on actual behavior. The demands of rationality need not be geared entirely to the use of only one of these motivations (such as self-love), and there is plenty of empirical evidence to indicate that the presumption of uncompromising pursuit of narrowly defined self-interest is as mistaken today as it was in Smith's time.[43] Just as it is necessary to avoid the high-minded sentimentalism of assuming that all human beings (and public servants, in particular) try constantly to promote some selfless "social good", it is also important to escape what may be called the "low-minded sentimentalism" of assuming that everyone is constantly motivated entirely by personal self-interest.[44]

This does not, however, negate an important implication of the question raised by Buchanan and others that public servants would tend to have their own objective functions; I would dissociate that point from the further claim, with which it has come mixed, that these objective functions are narrowly confined to the officials' own self-interest. The important issue to emerge is that there is something missing in a large part of the resource-allocation literature (for example, in proposals of algorithms for decentralized resource allocation, from Oscar Lange and Abba Lerner onward) which make do without any independent objective function of the agents of public action. The additional assumption of *homo economicus* is not needed to point to this general lacuna.

While this has been a somewhat neglected question in social choice theory (though partially dealt with in the related literature on implementation), there is no particular reason why such plurality of motivations cannot be accommodated within a social choice framework with more richly described social states and more articulated characterization of individual choices and behavior. In the formulation of individual preference used by Arrow (1951) and in traditional social choice theory, the nature of the objective function of each individual is left unspecified. While there is need for supplementary work here, this is a helpfully permissive framework—not tied either to ceaseless do-gooding, or to uncompromising self-centeredness.

Even with this extended framework, taking us well beyond the *homo economicus*, there remain some difficulties with the notion of individual rationality used here. There is a problem of "insufficiency" shared by this approach to rationality with other "instrumental" approaches to rationality, since it does not have any condition of critical scrutiny of the objectives themselves. Socrates might have overstated matters a bit when he proclaimed that "the unexamined life is not worth living", but an examination of what kind of life one should sensibly choose cannot really be completely irrelevant to rational choice.[34] An "instrumental rationalist"; is a decision expert whose response to seeing a man engaged in slicing his toes with a blunt knife is to rush to advise him that he should use a sharper knife to better serve his evident objective.

This is perhaps more of a limitation in the normative context than in using the presumption of rationality as a device for predicting behavior, since such critical scrutiny might not be very widely practised. However, the last is not altogether clear, since discussions and exchange, and even political arguments, contribute to the formation and revision of values. As Frank Knight (1947 p. 280) noted, "Values are established or validated and recognized through *discussion,* an activity which is at once social, intellectual, and creative." There is, in fact, much force in Buchanan's (1954a p. 120) assertion that this is a central component of democracy ("government by discussion") and that "individual values can and do change in the process of decision-making".

This issue has some real practical importance. To illustrate, in studying the fact that famines occur in some countries but not in others. I have tried to point to the phenomenon that no major famine has ever taken place in any country with a multiparty democracy with regular elections and with a reasonably free press (Sen, 1984).[46] This applies as much to the poorer democratic countries (such as India, Zimbabwe, or Botswana) as to the richer ones.[47] This is largely because famines, while killing millions, do not much affect the direct well-being of the ruling classes and dictators, who have little political incentive to prevent famines unless their rule is threatened by them. The economic analysis of famines across the world indicates that only a small proportion of the population tends to be stricken—rarely more than 5 percent or so. Since the shares of income and food of these poor groups tend normally to be no more than 3 percent of the total for the nation, it is not hard to rebuild their lost share of income and food, even in very poor countries, if a serious effort is made in that direction (see Sen, 1981; Drèze and Sen, 1989). Famines are thus easily preventable, and the need to face public criticism and to encounter the electorate provides the government with the political incentive to take preventive action with some urgency.

The question that remains is this. Since only a very small proportion of the population is struck by a famine (typically 5 percent or less), how does it become such a potent force in elections and in public criticism? This is in some tension with the assumption of universal self-centeredness, and presumably we do have the capacity— and often the inclination—to understand and respond to the predicament of others.[48] There is a particular need in this context to examine value formation that results from public discussion of miserable events, in generating sympathy and commitment on the part of citizens to do something to prevent their occurrence.

Even the idea of "basic needs", fruitfully used in the development literature, has to be related to the fact that what is taken as a "need" is not determined only by biological and uninfluencible factors. For example, in those parts of the so-called Third World in which there has been increased and extensive public discussion of the consequences of frequent childbearing on the well-being and freedom of mothers, the perception that a smaller family is a "basic need" of women (and men too) has grown, and in this value formation a combination of democracy, free public media, and basic education (especially female education) has been very potent. The implications of this finding are particularly important for rational consideration of the so-called "world population problem".[49]

Similar issues arise in dealing with environmental problems. The threats that we face call for organized international action as well as changes in national policies, particularly for better reflecting social costs in prices and incentives. But they are also dependent on value formation, related to public discussions, both for their influence on individual behavior and for bringing about policy changes through the political process. There are plenty of "social choice problems" in all this, but in analyzing them, we have to go beyond looking only for the best reflection of *given* individual preferences, or the most acceptable procedures for choices based on those preferences. We need to depart both from the assumption of given preferences (as in traditional social choice theory) and from the presumption that people are narrowly self-interested *homo economicus* (as in traditional public choice theory).

CONCLUDING REMARKS

Perhaps I could end by briefly returning to the questions with which I began. Arrow's impossibility theorem does indeed identify a profound difficulty in combining individual preference orderings into aggregative social welfare judgements. But the result must not be seen as mainly a negative one, since it directly leads on to questions about how to overcome these problems. In the context of social welfare judgements, the natural resolution of these problems lies in enriching the informational base, and there are several distinct ways of doing this. These approaches are used in practice for aggregative judgements made by individuals, but they can also be used for organized procedures for arriving at social measures of poverty, inequality, distribution-adjusted real national incomes, and other such aggregative indicators.

Second, Buchanan's questioning of the concept of social preference (and of its use as an ordering to make—or explain—social choices) is indeed appropriate in the case of social decision *mechanisms*, though less so for social welfare *judgements*. The Arrow theorem, in its original form, does not apply once social decision-making is characterized in terms of choice functions *without* any imposed requirement of intermenu consistency. However, when the natural implications of taking a choice-functional view of social decisions are worked out, Arrow's conditions have to be correspondingly restated, and then the impossibility result returns in its entirety once again. The idea of social preference or internal consistency of social choice is basically redundant for this impossibility result. So Buchanan's move does not negate Arrow's impossibility. On the other hand, it is an important departure in its own right.

Coming to terms with the impossibility problem in the case of social decision mechanisms is largely a matter of give and take between different principles with respective appeals. This calls for a less rigid interpretation of the role of axiomatic demands on permissible social decision rules.

Third, Buchanan's argument for a more procedural view of social decisions has much merit. Nevertheless, there are good reasons to doubt the adequacy of a purely procedural view (independent of consequences), just as there are serious defects in narrowly consequentialist views (independent of procedures). Procedural concerns can, however, be amalgamated with consequential ones by recharacterizing states of affairs appropriately, and the evaluation of states can then take note of the two aspects together. This combination is especially important in accommodating liberty and rights in social judgements as well as social decision mechanisms.

Finally, there is room for paying more attention to the rationality of individual behavior as an integral component of rational social decisions. In particular, the practical reach of social choice theory, in its traditional form, is considerably reduced by its tendency to ignore value formation through social interactions. Buchanan is right to emphasize the role of public discussion in the development of preferences (as an important part of democracy). However, traditional public choice theory is made unduly narrow by the insistence that individuals invariably behave as *homo economicus* (a subject on which social choice theory is much more permissive). This uncompromising restriction can significantly misrepresent the nature of social concerns and values. But aside from this descriptive limitation, there is also an important issue of "practical reason" here. Many of the more exacting problems of the contemporary world—

varying from famine prevention to environmental preservation—actually call for value formation through public discussion.

On the rationality of social decisions, many important lessons have emerged from the discipline of social choice theory as well as the public choice approach. In fact, we can get quite a bit more by *combining* these lessons. As a social choice theorist, I had not, in fact, planned to be particularly evenhanded in this paper, but need not, I suppose, apologize for ending up with rather even hands.

ACKNOWLEDGEMENTS

For helpful discussions I am most grateful to Eric Maskin and to Sudhir Anand, Kenneth Arrow, Nick Baigent, Kaushik Basu, Anthony de Jasay, Frank Hahn, Pia Malaney, Dennis Mueller, Robert Nozick, Mancur Olson, Ben Polak, Louis Putterman, Emma Rothschild, Kotaro Suzumura, Vivian Walsh, and Stefano Zamagni.

NOTES

1. For discussions of the axioms involved and alternative formulations and proofs, see Arrow (1951, 1963), Sen (1970, 1986b), Peter C. Fishburn (1973), Robert Wilson (1975), Bengt Hansson (1976), Jerry S. Kelly (1978), Graciela Chichilnisky (1982), Chichilnisky and Geoffrey Heal (1983), Prasanta Pattanaik and Maurice Salles (1983), Kotaro Suzumura (1983), Charles Blackorby *et al.* (1984), and Ken Binmore (1994), among others.
2. On "the impossibility of the Paretian liberal", see Sen (1970, 1983), Kelly (1978), Suzumura (1983), John Wriglesworth (1985), and Jonathan Riley (1987), among other contributions. Other results related to Arrow's theorem include the demonstration by Allan F. Gibbard (1973) and Mark A. Satterthwaite (1975) that "manipulability" is a ubiquitous characteristic of voting schemes; on related issues see Pattanaik (1978), Jean-Jacques Laffont (1979), Hervé Moulin (1983), Bazalel Peleg (1984), and Salvador Barberá and Bhaskar Dutta (1986), among others.
3. Dennis C. Mueller (1989) provides an excellent introduction to public choice theory and its relation to social choice theory. See also Atkinson (1987) and Sandmo (1990) on Buchanan's contributions.
4. The canonical treatise on the "public choice" approach is Buchanan and Tullock (1962), but it is important to note the differences in emphases between the appendix by Buchanan and that by Tullock.
5. Arrow (1951) himself points out "the unreality of this assumption" (p. 8).
6. The importance of politics as discussion has also been stressed in the Habermasian tradition; on this see Jon Elster and Aanund Hylland (1986) and Jürgen Habermas (1994). See also Albert Hirschman (1970) and the works inspired by his writings.
7. Robbins (1938) himself was opposed not so much to making interpersonal comparisons, but to claiming them to be "scientific".
8. The strategy of proof employed here (as in Sen (1986b)) is more direct and simpler than the versions used in Arrow (1963) and Sen (1970) and does not require defining additional concepts (such as "almost decisiveness").
9. For proof, take two pairs of alternative states (x, y) and (a, b), all distinct (the proof when they are not all distinct is quite similar). Group G is decisive over (x, y); we have to show that it is decisive over (a, b) as well. By unrestricted domain, let everyone in G prefer a to x to y to b, while all others prefer a to x, and y to b, but rank the other pairs in any way

whatever. By the decisiveness of G over (x, y), x is socially preferred to y. By the Pareto principle, a is socially preferred to x, and y to b. Therefore, by transitivity, a is socially preferred to b. If this result is influenced by individual preferences over any pair other than (a, b), then the condition of independence would be violated. Thus, a must be ranked above b simply by virtue of everyone in G preferring a to b (since others can have any preference whatever over this pair). So G is indeed decisive over (a, b).

10. For proof, take a decisive group G and partition it into G_1 and G_2. Let everyone in G_1 prefer x to y and x to z, with any possible ranking of (y, z), and let everyone in group G_2 prefer x to y and z to y, with any possible ranking of (x, z). It does not matter what those not in G prefer. If, now, x is socially preferred to z then the members of group G_1 would be decisive over this pair, since they alone definitely prefer x to z (the others can rank this pair in any way). If G_1 is not to be decisive, we must have z at least as good as x for some individual preferences over (x, z) of nonmembers of G_1. Take that case, and combine this social ranking (that z is at least as good as x) with the social preference for x over y (a consequence of the decisiveness of G and the fact that everyone in G prefers x to y). By transitivity, z is socially preferred to y. But only G_2 members definitely prefer z to y. Thus G_2 is decisive over this pair (z, y). Thus, from the field-expansion lemma, G_2 is decisive. So either G_1 or G_2 must be decisive—proving the lemma.

11. On some analytical problems involved in deriving "the revealed preference of a government" by observing its choices, see Kaushik Basu (1980).

12. Binariness requires a combination of two types of choice consistency: basic "contraction consistency" (α) and basic "expansion consistency" (γ). These conditions are quite exacting, and they have to be further strengthened to get transitivity and other additional properties (on this, see Sen (1971, 1977a), Rajat Deb (1983), and Isaac Levi (1986)).

13. On this, see Harsanyi (1955, p. 310): "Of course, when I speak of preferences 'from a social standpoint,' often abbreviated to 'social' preferences and the like, I always mean preferences based on a given individual's value judgments concerning 'social welfare'."

14. This has been established in a sequence of results, presented by Gibbard, Hansson, Andreu Mas-Colell, Hugo Sonnenschein, Donald Brown, Georges Bordes, Kelly, Suzumura, Douglas Blair, Robert Pollak, Julian Blau, Deb, David Kelsey, and others; for critical overviews, see Blair and Pollak (1982), Suzumura (1983), and Sen (1986a).

15. The pioneering work on choice-functional formulations came from Hansson (1968, 1969), Thomas Schwartz (1972, 1985), Fishburn (1973), and Plott (1973). Mark Aizerman and his colleagues at the Institute of Control Sciences in Moscow provided a series of penetrating investigations of the general choice-functional features of moving from individual-choice functions to social-choice functions (see Aizerman, 1985; Aizerman and Fuad Aleskerov, 1986). On related matters see also Aizerman and A. V. Malishevski (1981).

16. A sequence of contributions on this and related issues has come from Plott, Fishburn, Hansson, Donald Campbell, Bordes, Blair, Kelly, Suzumura, Deb, R. R. Parks, John Ferejohn, D. M. Grether, Kelsey, V. Denicolo, and Yasumi Matsumoto, among others. For general overviews and critiques, see Blair *et al.* (1976), Suzumura (1983), and Sen (1986a).

17. See also Buchanan and Tullock (1962).

18. For exact statements of the conditions and a proof of the theorem, see Sen (1993).

19. On this issue, see Sen (1977b, 1982a).

20. Formally, person 2 is "almost decisive" over the first pair (in the sense of winning against opposition by all others—in this case, person 1), and an alternative version of the field-expansion lemma shows that he will be almost decisive (indeed fully decisive) over all other pairs as well (see Lemma 3a in Sen (1970 pp. 43–44)). Note that "field expansion" is based inter alia on the use of the condition of "unrestricted domain", allowing the possibility that the individuals involved *could have* had other preferences as well.

21. On different types of interpersonal comparisons, and the relevance of distinct "spaces" in making efficiency and equity judgements, see Sen (1982a, 1992a), John Roemer (1986), Martha Nussbaum (1988), Richard Arneson (1989), G. A. Cohen (1989), Arrow (1991), Elster and Roemer (1991), and Nussbaum and Sen (1993).

22. On the other hand, Arrow's impossibility theorem can be generalized to accommodate cardinality of utilities without interpersonal comparisons; see Theorem 8.2 in Sen (1970).

23. Maximin gives complete priority to the interest of the worst off. It was proposed by John Rawls (1963), as a part of his "difference principle" (though the comparisons that he uses are not of utilities, but of holdings of primary goods). Lexicographic maximin, sometimes called "leximin," was proposed in Sen (1970) to make the Rawlsian approach consistent with the strong Pareto principle, and it has been endorsed and used in his *Theory of Justice* by Rawls (1971). Axiomatic derivations of leximin were pioneered by Peter J. Hammond (1976), and Claude d'Aspremont and Gevers (1977), among others. See also Edmund Phelps (1973).

24. See Harsanyi (1955), Patrick Suppes (1966), Sen (1970, 1977b), Phelps (1973), Hammond (1976, 1985), Arrow (1977), d'Aspremont and Gevers (1977), Gevers (1979), Eric Maskin (1978, 1979), Roberts (1980a,b), Roger B. Myerson (1981), James Mirrlees (1982), Suzumura (1983), Blackorby *et al.* (1984), d'Aspremont (1985), and Kelsey (1987), among others.

25. The literature on such measures is now quite large. Different types of exercises are illustrated by Sen (1973), Frank Cowell (1977), Blackorby and Donaldson (1978, 1980), Siddiq Osmani (1982), Sudhir Anand (1983), Atkinson (1983, 1989), S. R. Chakravarty (1983), Anthony Shorrocks (1983), Suzumura (1983), James E. Foster (1984, 1985), Ravi Kanbur (1984), Michel Le Breton and Alain Trannoy (1987), W. Eichhorn (1988), Peter J. Lambert (1989), and Martin Ravallion (1994), among many other contributions.

26. The policy discussions include those surrounding the influential *Human Development Reports*, produced by the United Nations Development Programme. Another strong force in that direction has been the sequence of UNICEF reports on *The State of the World's Children*. Policy issues related to such social judgements have been discussed by Paul Streeten *et al.* (1981), Nanak Kakwani (1986), Jean Drèze and Sen (1989), Alan Hamlin and Philip Pettit (1989), Keith Griffin and John Knight (1990), Anand and Ravallion (1993), Partha Dasgupta (1993), and Meghnad Desai (1995).

27. "Value restriction" turns out to be necessary and sufficient for this class of domain conditions for consistent majority rule when individual preferences are linear orderings, though the conditions are more complex in the general case of weak orderings (see Sen and Prasanta Pattanaik, 1969; see also Ken-ichi Inada, 1969, 1970). These relations can be generalized to all Arrovian social welfare functions and for nonmanipulable voting procedures (on which see Maskin (1976) and E. Kalai and E. Muller (1977)). Other types of conditions have been proposed by Tullock (1967) (with a somewhat exaggerated title: "The General Irrelevance of the General Possibility Theorem") and in a definitive paper by Jean-Michel Grandmont (1978). Fine discussions of the issues involved in the different types of domain conditions can be found in Gaertner (1979) and Arrow and Hervé Raynaud (1986).

28. The ubiquitous presence of voting cycles in majority rule has been extensively studied by R. D. McKelvey (1979) and Norman Schofield (1983).

29. Even individual social welfare judgements (and more generally, individual views of social appropriateness) presumably have some influence on political preferences.

30. Positional rules of other kinds have been studied extensively by Peter Gärdenfors (1973) and Ben Fine and Kit Fine (1974a,b). On different versions of the Borda rule, see Sen (1977a, 1982a, pp. 186–87).

31. For example, Andrew Caplin and Barry Nalebuff (1988) provide a case for 64 percent majority rule. Also see the symposium on voting procedures led by Jonathan Levin and Nalebuff (1995).

32. Buchanan (1986) expresses some basic sympathy for "libertarian socialists" (as opposed to *antilibertarian* socialists) but attributes what he sees as their well-intentioned but mistaken opposition to markets to their not having "the foggiest notion of the way the market works" and to their being "blissfully ignorant of economic theory" (pp. 4–5). *Consequential* analysis incorporated in economic theory is precisely what Buchanan is evoking here to dispute the libertarian socialist position.

33. On this see Sen (1981), linking starvation on unequal entitlements, with actual case studies of four famines. See also Ravallion (1987), Drèze and Sen (1989), and Desai (1995).

34. See also Nozick's (1974) discussion of "Locke's proviso".

35. On this question, see Sen (1982a,b).
36. On this question, see Sen (1982b), Hammond (1986), and Levi (1986).
37. Utilities can be defined in terms of choices made, desires entertained, or satisfactions received, but the point at issue applies to each of these interpretations. Utilitarian welfare economics has tended traditionally to focus on satisfactions, partly because individual choices do not immediately yield any basis for interpersonal comparisons unless some elaborately hypothetical choices are considered, on which see Harsanyi (1955), but also because "satisfaction" had appeared to utilitarian economists as providing a more solid basis for judging individual welfare. For example, this was the reason given by A. C. Pigou (1951 pp. 288–89):

    > Some economists ... have employed the term 'utility' indifferently for satisfactions and for desiredness. I shall employ it here to mean satisfactions, so that we may say that a man's economic welfare is made up of his utilities.

38. The idea of "personal domains" and "protected spheres" goes back to Mill (see Riley, 1987), and more recently has found strong and eloquent expression in the writings of Friedrich Hayek (1960).
39. For general accounts of the literature, see Kelly (1978), Suzumura (1983, 1991), Wriglesworth (1985), Paul Seabright (1989), and Pattanaik and Suzumura (1994a,b). For public-choice critiques, see Sugden (1981, 1993) and Rowley (1993).
40. The belief that the problem can be resolved through Pareto-improving contracts, which has been suggested by some authors, overlooks the incentive-incompatibility of the touted solution and, perhaps more importantly, confounds the nature of the conflict itself, since the conflict in values keeps open the question as to what contracts would be offered or accepted by the persons involved. For example, in the (rather overdiscussed) case of whether the prude or the lewd should read *Lady Chatterley's Lover*, it is not at all clear that the prude, if he has any libertarian inclinations, would actually offer a contract by which he agrees to read a book that he hates to make the lewd refrain from reading a book he loves. In fact, while the prude may prefer that the lewd does not read that book, consistent with that he may not want to bring this about through an enforceable contract, and the "dilemma of the Paretian liberal" could be his dilemma too. The lewd too faces a decision problem about whether to try to alter the prude's personal life rather than minding his own business. On these issues, see (Sen (1983, 1992b), Basu (1984), and Elster and Hylland (1986).
41. Stig Kanger (1985) has illuminatingly discussed "nonrealization" of rights, and the variety of ways this can occur.
42. On related matters, see also Pattanaik and Suzumura (1994a,b).
43. A set of studies on this and related issues is presented in Jane Mansbridge (1990).
44. Efforts to explain every socially motivated action as some kind of a cunning attempt at maximization of purely private gain are frequent in part of modern economics. There is an interesting question as to whether the presumption of exclusive self-interestedness is a more common general belief in America than in Europe, without being a general characteristic of *actual* behavior. Alexis de Tocqueville thought so:

    > The Americans ... are fond of explaining almost all the actions of their lives by the principle of self-interest rightly understood; they show with complacency how an enlightened regard for themselves constantly prompts them to assist one another and inclines them willingly to sacrifice a portion of their time and property to the welfare of the state. In this respect, they frequently fail to do themselves justice; for in the United States as well as elsewhere people are sometimes seen to give way to those disinterested and spontaneous impulses that are natural to man; but the Americans seldom admit that they yield to emotions of this kind; they are more anxious to do honor to their philosophy than to themselves.

    (Tocqueville, 1840 (Book II, Chapter VIII; in the 1945 edition, p. 122)).

45. On this subject, see Nozick (1989).
46. See also Drèze and Sen (1989) and *World Disasters Report* (1994 pp. 33–37).
47. In contrast, China—despite its fine record of public health and education even before the reforms—managed to have perhaps the largest famine in recorded history, during 1959–

1962, in which 23–30 million people died, while the mistaken public policies were not revised for three years through the famine. In India, on the other hand, despite its bungling ways, large famines stopped abruptly with independence in 1947 and the installing of a multiparty democracy (the last such famine, "the great Bengal famine", had occurred in 1943).

48. On this general question, see Rawls (1971) and Thomas Scanlon (1982). See also Daniel Hausman and Michael McPherson (1993).

49. See the discussion and the literature cited in Sen (1994 pp. 62–71), particularly Dasgupta (1993). See also Adam Przeworski and Fernando Limongi's (1994) international comparisons, which indicate a fairly strong association between democracy and fertility reduction. In the rapid reduction of the total fertility rate in the Indian state of Kerala from 4.4 in the 1950s to the present figure of 1.8 (a level similar to that in Britain and France and lower than in the United States), value formation related to education, democracy, and public discussion has played a major part. While the fertility rate has also come down in China (though not as much as in Kerala), China's use of compulsion rather than consensual progress has resulted in relatively high infant-mortality rates (28 per thousand for boys and 33 per thousand for girls, compared with Kerala's 17 per thousand for boys and 16 per thousand for girls in 1991). Such public dialogues are, however, hard to achieve in many other parts of India, despite democracy, because of the low level of elementary education, especially for women. These and related issues are discussed in Drèze and Sen (1995).

REFERENCES

Aizerman, M.A. New Problems in the General Choice Theory. *Social Choice and Welfare*, December 1985, **2**(4): 235–82.

Aizerman, Mark A. and Aleskerov, Fuad. Voting Operators in the Space of Choice Functions. *Mathematical Social Sciences*, June 1986, **11**(3): 201–242; *corrigendum*, June 1988, **13**(3): 305.

Aizerman, Mark A. and Malishevski, A.V. General Theory of Best Variants Choice: Some Aspects. *IEEE Transactions on Automatic Control*, 1981, AC-26, 1031–41.

Anand, Sudhir. *Inequality and poverty in Malaysia: Measurement and decomposition*. New York: Oxford University Press, 1983.

Anand, Sudhir and Ravallion, Martin. Human Development in Poor Countries: On the Role of Private Incomes and Public Services. *Journal of Economic Perspectives*, Winter 1993, **7**(1): 133–50.

Arneson, Richard J. Equality and Equal Opportunity for Welfare. *Philosophical Studies*, May 1989, **56**(1): 77–93.

Arrow, Kenneth J. *Social choice and individual values*. New York: Wiley, 1951; 2nd Ed., 1963.

Arrow, Kenneth J. Extended Sympathy and the Possibility of Social Choice. *American Economic Review*, February 1977, **67**(1): 219–25.

Arrow, Kenneth J., ed. *Markets and welfare*. London: Macmillan, 1991.

Arrow, Kenneth J. and Raynaud, Hervé. *Social choice and multicriterion decision-making*. Cambridge, MA: MIT Press, 1986.

Atkinson, Anthony B. On the Measurement of Inequality. *Journal of Economic Theory*. September 1970, **2**(3): 244–63.

Atkinson, Anthony B. *Social justice and public policy*. Cambridge, MA: MIT Press, 1983.

Atkinson, Anthony B. James M. Buchanan's Contributions to Economics. *Scandinavian Journal of Economics*, 1987, **89**(1): 5–15.

Atkinson, Anthony B. *Poverty and social security*. New York: Harvester Wheatsheaf, 1989.

Barberá, Salvador and Dutta, Bhaskar. General, Direct and Self-Implementation of Social Choice Functions via Protective Equilibria. *Mathematical Social Sciences*, April 1986, **11**(2): 109–27.

Basu, Kaushik. *Revealed preference of government.* Cambridge: Cambridge University Press, 1980.

Basu, Kaushik. The Right To Give Up Rights. *Economica*, November 1984, **51**(204): 413–22.

Baumol, William J. *Superfairness*, Cambridge, MA: MIT Press, 1986.

Bergson, Abram. A Reformulation of Certain Aspects of Welfare Economics. *Quarterly Journal of Economics*, February 1938, **52**(1): 310–34.

Bergson, Abram. *Essays in normative economics.* Cambridge, MA: Harvard University Press, 1966.

Binmore, Ken. *Playing fair: Game theory and the social contract*, Vol. I. London: MIT Press, 1994.

Blackorby, Charles and Donaldson, David. Measures of Relative Equality and Their Meaning in Terms of Social Welfare. *Journal of Economic Theory*, June 1978, **18**(1): 59–80.

Blackorby, Charles and Donaldson, David. Ethical Indices for the Measurement of Poverty. *Econometrica*, May 1980, **48**(4): 1053–60.

Blackorby, Charles, Donaldson, David and Weymark, John. Social Choice with Interpersonal Utility Comparisons: A Diagrammatic Introduction. *International Economic Review*, June 1984, **25**(2): 325–56.

Blair, Douglas H., Bordes, Georges A., Kelly, Jerry S. and Suzumura, Kotaro. Impossibility Theorems without Collective Rationality. *Journal of Economic Theory*, December 1976, **13**(3): 361–79.

Blair, Douglas H. and Pollak, Robert A. Acyclic Collective Choice Rules. *Econometrica*, July 1982, **50**(4): 931–44.

Borda, J.C. Mémoire sur les Élections au Scrutin. *Mémoires de l'Académie Royale des Sciences* (Paris), 1781.

Brennan, Geoffrey and Lomasky, Loiren. *Democracy and decision: The pure theory of electoral preference.* Cambridge: Cambridge University Press, 1993.

Broome, John. *Weighing goods.* Oxford: Blackwell, 1991.

Buchanan, James M. Social Choice, Democracy, and Free Markets. *Journal of Political Economy*, April 1954a, **62**(2): 114–23.

Buchanan, James M. Individual Choice in Voting and the Market. *Journal of Political Economy*, August 1954b, **62**(3): 334–43.

Buchanan, James M. *Fiscal theory and political economy.* Chapel Hill, NC: University of North Carolina Press, 1960.

Buchanan, James M. *Liberty, market and the state.* Brighton, UK: Wheatsheaf, 1986.

Buchanan, James M. Foundational Concerns: A criticism of Public Choice Theory. Unpublished manuscript presented at the European Public Choice Meeting, Valencia, Spain, April 1994a.

Buchanan, James M. Dimensionality, Rights and Choices among Relevant Alternatives. Unpublished manuscript presented at a meeting honoring Peter Bernholz, Basel, Switzerland, April 1994b.

Buchanan, James M. and Tullock, Gordon. *The calculus of consent.* Ann Arbor: University of Michigan Press, 1962.

Caplin, Andrew and Nalebuff, Barry. On 64% Majority Rule. *Econometrica*, July 1988, **56**(4): 787–814.

Chakravarty, S.R. Ethically Flexible Measures of Poverty. *Canadian Journal of Economics*, February 1983, **16**(1): 74–85.

Chichilnisky, Graciela. Social Aggregation Rules and Continuity. *Quarterly Journal of Economics*, May 1982, *97*(2): 337–52.

Chichilnisky, Graciela and Heal, Geoffrey M. Necessary and Sufficient Conditions for a Resolution of the Social Choice Paradox. *Journal of Economic Theory*, October 1983, **31**(1): 68–87.

Cohen, G.A. On the Currency of Egalitarian Justice. *Ethics*, July 1989, **99**(4): 906–44.

Condorcet, Marquis de. *Essai sur l'application de l'analyse à la probabilité des décisions rendues à la pluralité des voix.* Paris: L'Imprimerie Royale, 1785.

Cowell, Frank A. *Measuring inequality*. New York: Wiley, 1977.

Dasgupta, Partha. *An inquiry into well-being and destitution*. Oxford: Oxford University Press, 1993.

d'Aspremont, Claude. Axioms for Social Welfare Ordering, in Leonid Hurwicz, David Schmeidler, and Hugo Sonnenschein, eds., *Social goals and social organization*. Cambridge: Cambridge University Press, 1985, 19–76.

d'Aspremont, Claude and Gevers, Louis. Equity and the Informational Basis of Collective Choice. *Review of Economic Studies*, June 1977, **44**(2): 199–209.

Deb, Rajat. Binariness and Rational Choice. *Mathematical Social Sciences*, August 1983, **5**(1): 97–106.

Desai, Meghnad. *Poverty, famine and economic development*, Aldershot, UK: Elgar, 1995.

Drèze, Jean and Sen, Amartya. *Hunger and public action*. Oxford: Oxford University Press, 1989.

Drèze, Jean and Sen, Amartya. *India: Economic development and social opportunity*. Oxford: Oxford University Press, 1995.

Eichhorn, W. *Measurement in economics*. New York: Physica-Verlag, 1988.

Elster, Jon and Hylland, Aanund, eds. *Foundations of social choice theory*. Cambridge: Cambridge University Press, 1986.

Elster, Jon and Roemer, John, eds. *Interpersonal comparisons of well-being*. Cambridge: Cambridge University Press, 1991.

Fine, Ben and Fine, Kit. Social Choice and Individual Ranking I. *Review of Economic Studies*, July 1974, **41**(3): 303–22.

Fine, Ben and Fine, Kit. Social Choice and Individual Rankings II. October 1974, **41**(4): 459–85.

Fishburn, Peter C. *The theory of social choice*. Princeton, NJ: Princeton University Press, 1973.

Foster, James E. On Economic Poverty: A Survey of Aggregate Measures. *Advances in Econometrics*, 1984, **3: 215–51.**

Foster, James E. Inequality Measurement, in H. Peyton Young, ed., *Fair allocation*. Providence, RI: American Mathematical Society, 1985, 31–68.

Gaertner, Wulf. An Analysis and Comparison of Several Necessary and Sufficient Conditions for Transitivity of Majority Decision Rule, in Jean-Jacques Laffont, eds., *Aggregation and revelation of preferences*. Amsterdam: North-Holland, 1979, pp. 91–112.

Gaertner, Wulf, Pattanaik, Prasanta K. and Suzumura, Kotaro. Individual Rights Revisited. *Economica*, May 1992, **59**(234): 161–78.

Gärdenfors, Peter. Positional Voting Functions. *Theory and Decision*, September 1973 **4**(1): 1–24.

Gärdenfors, Peter. Rights, Games and Social Choice. *Nous*, September 1981, **15**(3): 341–56.

Gevers, Louis. On Interpersonal Comparability and Social Welfare Orderings. *Econometrica*, January 1979, **47**(1): 75–89.

Gibbard, Allan F. Manipulation of Voting Schemes: A General Result. *Econometrica*, July 1973, **41**(4): 587–601.

Grandmont, Jean-Michel. Intermediate Preferences and the Majority Rule. *Econometrica*, March 1978, **46**(2): 317–30.

Griffin, Keith and Knight, John, eds. *Human development and the international development strategy for the 1990s*. London: Macmillan, 1990.

Habermas, J. Three Models of Democracy. *Constellations*, April 1994, **1**(1): 1–10.

Hamlin, Alan and Pettit, Philip, eds. *The good polity*. Oxford: Blackwell, 1989.

Hammond, Peter J. Equity, Arrow's Conditions, and Rawls' Difference Principle. *Econometrica*, July 1976, **44**(4): 793–804.

Hammond, Peter J. Welfare Economics, in G. Feiwel, eds., *Issues in contemporary microeconomics and welfare*. Albany: State University of New York Press, 1985, 405–34.

Hammond, Peter J. Consequentialist Social Norms of Public Decisions, in Walter P. Heller, Ross M. Starr, and David A. Starrett, eds., *Social choice and public decision-making*, Vol. 1. *Essays in honor of Kenneth J. Arrow*, Cambridge: Cambridge University Press, 1986, 3–27.

Hansson, Bengt. Choice Structures and Preference Relations. *Synthese*, October 1968, **18**(4): 443–58.

Hansson, Bengt. Voting and Group Decision Functions. *Synthese,* December 1969, **20**(4): 526–37.

Hansson, Bengt. The Existence of Group Preference. *Public Choice,* Winter 1976, **28: 89–98.**

Harsanyi, John C. Cardinal Welfare, Individualistic Ethics, and Interpersonal Comparisons of Utility. *Journal of Political Economy,* August 1955, **63**(3): 309–21.

Hausman, Daniel M. and McPherson, Michael S. Taking Ethics Seriously: Economics and Contemporary Moral Philosophy. *Journal of Economic Literature,* June 1993, **31**(2): 671–731.

Hayek, Friedrich A. *The constitution of liberty.* London: Routledge and Kegan Paul, 1960.

Heller, Walter P., Starr, Ross M. and Starrett, David A., eds. *Social choice and public decision-making, Vol. 1. Essays in honor of Kenneth J. Arrow,* Cambridge: Cambridge University Press, 1986.

Hirschman, Albert. *Exit, voice and loyalty.* Cambridge, MA: Harvard University Press, 1970.

Inada, Ken-ichi. On the Simple Majority Decision Rule. *Econometrica,* July 1969, **37**(3): 490–506.

Inada, Ken-ichi. Majority Rule and Rationality. *Journal of Economic Theory,* March 1970, **2**(1): 27–40.

Kakwani, Nanak. *Analyzing redistribution policies.* Cambridge: Cambridge University Press, 1986.

Kalai, E. and Muller E. Characterization of Domains Admitting Nondictatorial Social Welfare Functions and Nonmanipulable Voting Procedures. *Journal of Economic Theory,* December 1977, **16**(2): 457–69.

Kanbur, S.M. (Ravi). The Measurement and Decomposition of Inequality and Poverty, in F. van der Ploeg, ed., *Mathematical methods in economics.* New York: Wiley, 1984, 403–32.

Kanger, Stig. On Realization of Human Rights, *Acta Philosophica Fennica,* May 1985, **38**: 71–78.

Kelly, Jerry S. *Arrow impossibility theorems.* New York: Academic Press, 1978.

Kelsey, David. The Role of Information in Social Welfare Judgments. *Oxford Economic Papers,* June 1987, **39**(2): 301–17.

Knight, Frank. *Freedom and reform: Essays in economic and social philosophy.* New York: Harper, 1947; republished, Indianapolis: Liberty, 1982.

Kolm, Serge Ch. The Optimal Production of Social Justice, in J. Margolis and H. Guitton, eds., *Public economics.* London: Macmillan, 1969, 145–200.

Laffont, Jean-Jacques, ed. *Aggregation and revelation of preferences.* Amsterdam: North-Holland, 1979.

Lambert, Peter J. *The distribution and redistribution of income: A mathematical analysis.* Oxford: Blackwell, 1989.

Le Breton, Michel and Trannoy, Alain. Measures of Inequalities as an Aggregation of Individual Preferences About Income Distribution: The Arrovian Case. *Journal of Economic Theory,* April 1987, **41**(2): 248–69.

Levi, Isaac. *Hard choices.* Cambridge: Cambridge University Press, 1986.

Levin, Jonathan and Nalebuff, Barry. An Introduction to Vote-Counting Schemes. *Journal of Economic Perspectives,* 1995, **9**(1): 3–26.

Mansbridge, Jane J., eds. *Beyond self-interest.* Chicago: University of Chicago Press, 1990.

Maskin, Eric. Social Welfare Functions on Restricted Domain. Mimeo, Harvard University, 1976.

Maskin, Eric. A Theorem on Utilitarianism. *Review of Economic Studies,* February 1978, **45**(1): 93–96.

Maskin, Eric. Decision-making under Ignorance with Implications for Social Choice. Theory and Decision, September 1979, **11**(3): 319–37.

McKelvey, R.D. General Conditions for Global Intransitivities in Formal Voting Models. *Econometrica,* September 1979, **47**(5): 1085–1112.

Mcade, James E. *The just economy.* London: Allen and Unwin, 1976.

Mill, John Stuart. *On liberty.* London: Parker, 1859; republished, in *Utilitarianism; On liberty; Representative government.* London: Everyman's Library, 1910.

Mirrlees, James A. The Economic Uses of Utilitarianism, in Amartya Sen and Bernard Williams, eds., *Utilitarianism and Beyond.* Cambridge: Cambridge University Press, 1982, 63–84.

Moulin, Hervé. *The strategy of social choice.* Amsterdam: North-Holland, 1983.

Mueller, Dennis C. *Public choice II*. Cambridge: Cambridge University Press, 1989.

Myerson, Roger B. Utilitarianism, Egalitarianism, and the Timing Effect in Social Choice Problems. Econometrica, July 1981, **49**(4): 883-97.

Nozick, Robert. *Anarchy, state, and utopia*. New York: Basic Books, 1974.

Nozick, Robert. *The examined life*. New York: Simon and Schuster, 1989.

Nussbaum, Martha. Nature, Function and Capability: Aristotle on Political Distribution. Oxford Studies in Ancient Philosophy, Supplementary volume, 1988, 145–84.

Nussbaum, Martha and Sen, Amartya, eds. *The quality of life*. Oxford: Oxford University Press, 1993.

Osmani, Siddiq R. *Economic inequality and group welfare*. Oxford: Oxford University Press, 1982.

Pattanaik, Prasanta K. *Strategy and group choice*. Amsterdam: North-Holland, 1978.

Pattanaik, Prasanta K. and Salles, Maurice, eds. *Social choice and welfare*. Amsterdam: North-Holland, 1983.

Pattanaik, Prasanta K. and Suzumura, Kotaro. Rights, Welfarism and Social Choice. *American Economic Review*, May 1994a (*Papers and Proceedings*), **84**(2): 435–39.

Pattanaik, Prasanta K. and Suzumura, Kotaro. Individual Rights and Social Evaluation: A Conceptual Framework. Mimeo, University of California, Riverside, 1994b.

Peleg, Bazalel. *Game theoretic analysis of voting in committees*. Cambridge: Cambridge University Press, 1984.

Phelps, Edmund S., ed. *Economic justice*. Harmondsworth, UK: Penguin, 1973.

Pigou, Arthur C. Some Aspects of Welfare Economics. *American Economic Review*, June 1951, **41**(3): 287–302.

Plott, Charles. Path Independence, Rationality and Social Choice. *Econometrica*, November 1973, **41**(6): 1075–91.

Przeworski, Adam and Limongi, Fernando. Democracy and Development. Mimeo, University of Chicago, 1994.

Ravallion, Martin. *Markets and famines*. Oxford: Oxford University Press, 1987.

Ravallion, Martin. *Poverty comparisons*. Chur, Switzerland: Harwood, 1994.

Rawls, John. The Sense of Justice. *Philosophical Review*, July 1963, **72**(3): 281–305.

Rawls, John. *A theory of justice*. Cambridge, MA: Harvard University Press, 1971.

Riley, Jonathan. *Liberal utilitarianism: Social choice theory and J.S. Mill's philosophy*. Cambridge: Cambridge University Press, 1987.

Robbins, Lionel. Interpersonal Comparisons of Utility: A Comment. *Economic Journal*, December 1938, **48**(192): 635–41.

Roberts, Kevin W.S. Possibility Theorems with Interpersonally Comparable Welfare Levels. *Review of Economic Studies*, January 1980a, **47**(2): 409–20.

Roberts, Kevin W.S. Interpersonal Comparability and Social Choice Theory. *Review of Economic Studies*, January 1980b, **47**(2): 421–39.

Roemer, John. An Historical Materialist Alternative to Welfarism, in Jon Elster and Aanund Hylland, eds., *Foundations of social choice theory*. Cambridge: Cambridge University Press, 1986, 133–64.

Rowley, Charles K. *Liberty and the state*, Aldershot, UK: Elgar, 1993.

Samuelson, Paul A. *Foundations of economic analysis*. Cambridge, MA: Harvard University Press, 1947.

Sandmo, Agnar. Buchanan on Political Economy: A Review Article. *Journal of Economic Literature*, March 1990, **28**(1): 50–65.

Satterthwaite, Mark A. Strategy-proofness and Arrow's Conditions: Existence and Correspondence Theorems for Voting Procedures and Social Welfare Functions. *Journal of Economic Theory*, April 1975, **10**(2): 187–217.

Scanlon, Thomas M. Contractualism and Utilitarianism. in Amartya Sen and Bernard Williams, eds., *Utilitarianism and beyond*. Cambridge: Cambridge University Press, 1982, 103–28.

Schofield, Norman J. Generic Instability of Majority Rule. *Review of Economic Studies*, October 1983, **50**(4): 695–705.

Schwartz, Thomas. Rationality and the Myth of the Maximum. *Nous*, May 1972, **6**(2): 97–117.

Schwartz, Thomas. *The logic of collective choice*. New York: Columbia University Press, 1985.

Seabright, Paul. Social Choice and Social theories. *Philosophy and Public Affairs*, Fall 1989, **18**(4): 365–87.

Sen, Amartya K. A Possibility Theorem on Majority Decisions. *Econometrica*, April 1966, **34**(2): 491–99.

Sen, Amartya K. Choice Functions and Revealed Preference. *Review of Economic Studies*, July 1971, **38**(3): 307–17; reprinted in Sen (1982a).

Sen, Amartya K. *Collective choice and social welfare*. San Francisco: Holden-Day, 1970; reprinted, Amsterdam: North-Holland, 1979.

Sen, Amartya K. *On economic inequality*. Oxford: Oxford University Press, 1973.

Sen, Amartya K. Real National Income. *Review of Economic Studies*, February 1976a, **43**(1): 19–39; reprinted in Sen (1982a).

Sen, Amartya K. Poverty: An Ordinal Approach to Measurement. *Econometrica*, March 1976b, **44**(2): 219–31; reprinted in Sen (1982a).

Sen, Amartya K. Social Choice Theory: A Reexamination. *Econometrica*, January 1977a, **45**(1): 53–89; reprinted in Sen (1982a).

Sen, Amartya K. On Weights and Measures: Informational Constraints in Social Welfare Analysis. *Econometrica*, October 1977b, **45**(7): 1539–72; reprinted in Sen (1982a).

Sen, Amartya K. *Poverty and famines: An essay on entitlement and deprivation*. Oxford: Oxford University Press, 1981.

Sen, Amartya K. *Choice, welfare and measurement*. Oxford: Blackwell, 1982a.

Sen, Amartya K. Rights and Agency. *Philosophy and Public Affairs*, Spring 1982b, **11**(2): 113–32.

Sen, Amartya K. Liberty and Social Choice. *Journal of Philosophy*, January 1983, **80**(1): 5–28.

Sen, Amartya K. *Resources, Values and Development*. Oxford: Blackwell, 1984.

Sen, Amartya K. Social Choice Theory, in Kenneth J. Arrow and Michael Intriligator, eds., *Handbook of mathematical economics*, Vol. III. Amsterdam: North-Holland, 1986a, 1073–1181.

Sen, Amartya K. Information and Invariance in Normative Choice, in Walter P. Heller, Ross M. Starr, and David A. Starrett, eds., *Social choice and public decision-making, Vol. 1. Essays in honor of Kenneth J. Arrow*. Cambridge: Cambridge University Press, 1986b, 29–55.

Sen, Amartya K. *Inequality reexamined*. Oxford: Oxford University Press, 1992a.

Sen, Amartya K. Minimal Liberty. *Economica*, May 1992b, **59**(234): 139–60.

Sen, Amartya K. Internal Consistency of Choice. *Econometrica*, May 1993, **61**(3): 495–521.

Sen, Amartya K. Population: Delusion and Reality. *New York Review of Books*, 22 September 1994, **41**(15): 62–71.

Sen, Amartya K. and Pattanaik, Prasanta K. Necessary and Sufficient Conditions for Rational Choice under Majority Decision. *Journal of Economic Theory*, August 1969, **1**(2): 178–202.

Shorrocks, Anthony F. Ranking Income Distributions. *Economica*, February 1983, **50**(197): 3–17.

Smith, Adam. *An inquiry into the nature and causes of the wealth of nations*. London: W. Strahan and T. Cadell, 1776; republished, Oxford: Oxford University Press, 1976.

Smith, Adam. *The theory of moral sentiments*, Revised Edition. London: T. Cadell, 1790; republished, Oxford: Oxford University Press, 1975.

Streeten, Paul, Burki, S.J., Haq, Mahbub ul, Hicks, Norman and Stewart, Frances. *First things first: Meeting basic human needs in developing countries*. London: Oxford University Press, 1981.Sugden, Robert. *The political economy of public choice*. Oxford: Martin Robertson, 1981.

Sugden, Robert. *The economics of rights, co-operation and welfare*. Oxford: Blackwell, 1986.

Sugden, Robert. Welfare, Resources, and Capabilities: A Review of *Inequality Reexamined* by Amartya Sen. *Journal of Economic Literature*, December 1993, **31**(4): 1947–62.

Suppes, Patrick. Some Formal Models of Grading Principles. *Synthese*, December 1966, **16**(3/4): 284–306.

Suzumura, Kotaro. *Rational choice, collective decisions and social welfare*. Cambridge: Cambridge University Press, 1983.

Suzumura, Kotaro. Alternative Approaches to Libertarian Rights, in Kenneth J. Arrow, eds., *Markets and welfare*. London: Macmillan, 1991, 215–42.

Tocqueville, Alexis de. *Democracy in America*. New York: Langley, 1840; republished, New York: Knopf, 1945.

Tullock, Gordon, The General Irrelevance of the General Possibility Theorem. *Quarterly Journal of Economics*, May 1967, **81**(2): 256–70.

Wilson, Robert. On the Theory of Aggregation. *Journal of Economic Theory*, February 1975, **10**(1): 89–99.

World disasters report. Geneva: International Federation of Red Cross and Red Crescent Societies, 1994.

Wrigglesworth, John. *Libertarian conflicts in social choice.* Cambridge: Cambridge University Press, 1985.

Young, H. Peyton. ed. *Fair allocation.* Providence, RI: American Mathematical Society, 1985.

23

An Introduction to Vote-counting Schemes

Jonathan Levin and Barry Nalebuff

The design of an electoral system is fundamental to any democracy. Motivation for understanding how electoral system design matters comes from many directions: the creation of new constitutions in eastern Europe; the recent trauma of a three-way presidential election in the United States; the ongoing debate over US redistricting and gerrymandering; the furor caused by Lani Guinier's call for a more representative voting system. The status quo adds another incentive. Plurality rule is pervasive even though it is a flawed system. Fortunately, there is no lack of suitable alternatives. One of the purposes of this symposium—and this chapter in particular—is to help illustrate and motivate the remarkable variety of alternative mechanisms that aggregate individual preferences to decide an election. This overview offers a summary of sixteen distinct methods and demonstrates by example how some of the more complex systems work. The shorter papers that follow focus on some of the more popular alternatives, including approval voting, single transferable vote, the maximum likelihood rule, and more.

One can speculate on why alternatives to plurality rule have had such a difficult time being adopted. Part of the cause may be Arrow's general possibility theorem. Arrow (1951) demonstrates that any voting system applied to an unrestricted collection of voter preferences must have some serious defect; we must always choose between flawed alternatives. With conflicting theoretical guidance to help select the least-flawed option, people evaluate a system by its likely effect on the status quo outcome. Since those in power tend to want to preserve the status quo—the status quo electoral system is what brought them into power—we should not be surprised by the difficulty of implementing electoral reform.

An electoral system has to balance multiple objectives: establishing legitimacy, encouraging participation, discouraging factionalization. We focus on the goal of representativeness. How do we go about choosing a representative outcome? What is meant by representation?[1] Should we examine the position of the elected representatives or the position of the policies that they pass? How do we trade off

Reprinted with permission from *Journal of Economic Perspectives* Vol. 9, No. 1, 1995, pp. 3–26 these objectives? We do not believe that there is any one right answer (although there are certainly many wrong ones).

The point of this paper is to move away from theoretical discussions of various properties; our aim is to provide the motivation behind different counting schemes. Are they better suited for choosing a single winner or for ranking the candidates? Do they tend to favor candidates with loyal minorities or candidates who are acceptable to all and the favorite of none? Are they simple enough to be used for a general political election where voters may only be familiar with one or two candidates, or are they more applicable in a board of directors situation where each voter possesses more detailed information? We try to give some examples of how and why they work and where they fail. We have also taken several of the methods and applied them to voting data gathered from British Union elections (data collected separately by N. Tideman and I.D. Hill). An interesting feature of these British elections is that voters are required to rank the candidates. As a result, knowing the voter ranking, we can simulate elections under a variety of electoral systems. It is perhaps remarkable that among the 30 elections we examined, with the exception of plurality rule and single transferable vote, none of the other seven alternatives considered gave a different top choice (see later section). The systems differed in the rankings of the lower candidates. This empirical regularity suggests a connection to some recent theoretical work (Caplin and Nalebuff, 1988, 1991): when voter preferences are sufficiently similar, a variety of voting systems lead to similar choices, and these choices have desirable properties. The difficulties in aggregating preferences arise in the case of a population with a lack of a consensus; this is the situation where the choice of electoral system can make the greatest difference and where apparently minor differences can directly influence the outcome.

The next section of our paper describes the basis information on which most vote-counting schemes rely: voter rankings and paired comparisons. We then described five voting rules scored directly from the voter rankings, six paired-comparisons rules, and two additional rules derived from sports rankings. An Appendix then offers a few additional rules. We then attempt to point out how differences between rules might affect candidates' strategies and the outcome of a real election. In the final section, we address different factors that distinguish the methods and attempt to provide a basis to choose between methods. In our description of the various vote-counting rules, we have benefited greatly from the excellent surveys done by Lowell Anderson (1990, 1994) and Nicolaus Tideman (1993).

VOTER RANKINGS AND PAIRED COMPARISONS

Before describing the various counting rules, we need to consider their general structure and the information they rely on. Even if we actually had knowledge of all the voters' utility functions, there is the quandary of trying to make interpersonal comparisons of utility. This leads us to take as data a voter's ordinal ranking of the various candidates. However, there is a fundamental problem of getting people to reveal their true preferences accurately, since all voting systems encourage strategizing. Even if we had truthful rankings, there remains the issue of how to take averages over these rankings. Our focus is on this last step. Most of the variety in electoral schemes comes from the choice of different metrics for measuring the distance between one ranking and another.

From the start we should note that in a multi-candidate election, simple plurality rule throws away too much data. The voter's first choice is a poor summary statistic of preferences. Information regarding second and later choices is valuable in helping aggregate preferences. At the other extreme, we cannot reasonably ask people to vote in all possible pairwise elections. Even if there were only seven dwarfs running in a primary, this would require a voter to make 21 choices. Fortunately, we can easily infer pairwise preferences from ordinal voter rankings. For example, if a voter ranks the candidates $a > b > c$, we infer that a is preferable to b and c and that b is preferable to c. (Of course, making these inferred rankings imposes a consistency condition that voters might not obey, as discussed in Amartya Sen's companion paper.) With one exception (approval voting), all the methods we discuss use as their base data the voter's ranking of the individual candidates. In general, these rankings provide more information than we need to tally the election. For our purposes, we assume that voters rank all the candidates on their ballots, and do not score candidates as tied.[2]

Voting theorists from the Marquis de Condorcet to Kenneth Arrow have shared the conviction that we should judge candidates on the basis of their pairwise performance. A candidate who wins every head-to-head matchup is called a Condorcet winner, in honor of Condorcet's *Essay on the Application of Mathematics to the Theory of Decision-Making* (1785). A Condorcet winner will win an election under most of the rules we describe below (although in some instances a good argument exists for not choosing the Condorcet winner, as Peyton Young explains in this issue). Most of the difficult issues in vote counting arise when no Condorcet winner exists; instead there is a voting cycle, i.e., three candidates a, b, c such that a beats b, b beats c, and c beats a.[3] Each method treats cycles differently leading to discrepancies in how they rank the candidates.

Once we translate the voter rankings into paired comparisons, we often organize the information into a "paired-comparisons matrix". In this matrix, the ijth entry is the number of votes for i over j. The entries on the diagonal are all 0. Writing down this matrix actually loses information contained on individual ballots. That is, the matrix might show that candidate i received 45 votes over j, but it does not reveal whether those voters placed i first on their ballots and j last, or i sixth and j seventh. We may make an informed guess, but we cannot recover individual rankings from the paired-comparisons matrix.

Some voting rules further distill this information by only distinguishing the winner of each head-to-head comparison. They utilise a "win-loss matrix," where the ijth entry is 1 if more voters prefer candidate i to j and -1 if more voters prefer j to i. If there is a tie between candidates i and j, we enter a 0. Once again, all entries on the diagonal are 0 by definition.

The first five voting rules discussed are categorized as "rank-scoring" rules because they score directly from the rankings. The following six rules are "paired-comparisons" rules because they rely on that matrix. The final set of rules use a variety of different approaches.

RANK-SCORING RULES

Plurality voting

Plurality voting is the most common method of ranking candidates in an election and is used in almost every political election in the United States. Under plurality election rules, each voter picks a single most preferred candidate. The candidate with the most votes wins. In an election with more than two candidates, a candidate does not necessarily need a majority vote to win. Bill Clinton won the 1992 presidential election with less than 50 percent of the vote.

When there are only two candidates in an election, plurality voting is the natural choice as an election rule: it is simply the rule of the majority. With three or more candidates, however, plurality voting can lead to disturbing results. Suppose there is an election with three candidates, two of whom have closely related views, while the third candidate has a radically different platform. Even if a large majority would choose either of the two related candidates over the third candidate, the third candidate might win if the majority split its votes between the two similar candidates.

In an indirect way, this coordination failure may have even changed the presidency of the United States. As told by Lowell Anderson (1990), the story starts with the 1966 Democratic primary for the governor of Maryland:

> George P. Mahoney received about 40 percent of the vote while his two opponents, Thomas Finan and Carlton Sickles, each received about 30 percent. Both Finan and Sickles are relatively liberal, and Maryland is a relatively liberal state. Mahoney is an unabashed ultraconservative, and it is extremely unlikely that he could have beaten either Finan or Sickles in a one-on-one contest. Maryland is a heavily Democrat state. However, in the main election, many Democrats could not support the ultraconservative Mahoney, and sufficiently many crossed over to vote Republican that the Republican candidate won. It is widely believed that had either Finan or Sickles won the Democrat primary, then he would have beaten the (at that time) relatively obscure Spiro T. Agnew, in the main race. Agnew won, was later elected vice-president, and then resigned under pressure. Richard Nixon nominated Gerald Ford in Agnew's place and, when Nixon resigned, Ford became president.

The rest, as they say, is history.

While most presidential elections involve only two serious candidates, redistributing the votes that went to serious third-party candidates (Wallace, Anderson, Perot) would have had the potential to swing an election. The coordination failures of plurality rule tend to be most glaring in a primary, where one often finds more than two serious candidates.

However, we should emphasize that the number of candidates in an election is not exogenous. It is partly determined by the type of electoral system in use. One of the consequences of using plurality rule is that it leads the outcome towards a two-party system. This empirical result is known as Duverger's law. When there are more than two parties, people tend to abandon the third party so as not to waste their votes.[4] This may not be a bad thing; an electoral voting rule that did a better job of representing preferences over more than two candidates might result in a proliferation of candidates, and the resulting factionalization could be worse for the democracy in the long run (as Douglas Rae explores in this issue). Since the job of winnowing a large

number of candidates in a primary is quite different from the job of choosing between
a smaller number in the general election, society might consider using a different
voting rule for primaries and for the general election.

Multiple-winner extensions

If an election is to produce multiple winners, there are several extensions of plurality
rule. One option, used to elect the legislature in Japan, is the "single nontransferable
vote". Everyone gets one vote, and we simply pick the top several candidates based on
the plurality voting. Under cumulative voting, voters are given a number of votes equal
to the number of winners desired.[5] Depending on the rules, voters may or may not
assign more than one of their votes to a single candidate. The candidates with the
highest vote totals win the election.

In theory, cumulative voting is designed to foster minority representation. In an
election with ten positions to fill, any group that controls 10 percent of the vote has the
opportunity to elect one candidate. How these coalitions might form is less clear, and
failure to coordinate could result in a loss of electoral power. In this regard, the single
transferable vote electoral system (discussed below) is a more satisfactory method,
although it is more complicated.

Approval voting

Approval voting was invented in the 1970s. It is the only method we consider that does
not require voters to rank the candidates. Instead, voters approve or disapprove each
candidate on the ballot—that is, they select some subset of candidates. Candidates are
ranked by the number of voters who approve them, and the highest ranked candidate
(or candidates if more than one winner is required) wins. Thus with three candidates
A, B and C, a voter has the opportunity either to vote for A or against A (by approving
both B and C). Approving all three candidates is equivalent to not voting since it has
no differential impact. Approval voting is the most frequently adopted alternative to
plurality rule and is now used by several professional associations to elect their officers
(Brams and Nagel, 1991). Robert Weber's companion article focuses on this voting
method.

A variant of approval voting can be used if we do not require a fixed number of
winners, but rather a level of acceptance. We can set a quota and declare as winners
any candidates reaching that quota. The election of baseball players to the Hall of
Fame employs this form of approval voting. Sportswriters vote up or down on each
candidate, and candidates who receive a certain (previously specified) number of votes
head for Cooperstown.[6]

Runoff voting

In runoff voting, or a "double election," voters rank the candidates, and voters are
tabulated just as in a plurality election. If one candidate commands a majority vote,

that candidate wins the election. If no candidate receives more than half the votes, we have a runoff election between the two candidates. The winner of the head-to-head runoff wins the election. Again, variations exist to runoff voting. In New York City primaries, the top two candidates engage in a runoff if the top candidate receives less than 40 percent of the vote in the primary. In France, candidates must also garner a certain minimum vote in order to participate in the runoff election. This has sometimes led to the peculiar result of a runoff election with only one candidate on the ballot, which then leads to imaginative and colorful voter responses (Rosenthal and Sen, 1980)!

In a multi-candidate election, runoff voting can prevent some of the potentially skewed results generated by a plurality count. Suppose we have four candidates, three similar candidates who evenly divide 70 percent of the vote, and a radically different candidate who commands a 30 percent minority. The 30 percent candidate would win outright under plurality, but would suffer a sound defeat in a runoff against any one of the other three candidates.

Single transferable vote

The single transferable vote, also known as "Cincinnati Rules" or "Hare voting", extends the logic of runoff voting by eliminating no more than one candidate at a time. A single transferable vote election with only one winner is sometimes called the "alternative vote". We consider this case first. Voters begin by ranking the candidates. If any candidate is ranked first by a majority, that candidate wins immediately. If no winner exists, we eliminate the candidate with the fewest first place votes and tabulate the ballots again as if that candidate never existed. This means votes for the losing candidate get redistributed to one of the remaining candidates. If still no candidate controls a majority, we again delete the candidate with the fewest votes and repeat the process. Eventually, barring a tie, a winner must emerge.

When there are many candidates and multiple winners, the algorithm for a single transferable vote becomes considerably more complex. However, it still works quite well in theory and in practice, finding use in New York City school board and Cambridge city council elections. With multiple winners, each one cannot control a majority, but rather should control some dominant share. Following the logic of the majority winner, we want this share (or quota) to be as small as possible, yet big enough to allow no more than the desired number of winners. For example, with two winners, we would require a winning candidate to control at least 34 percent of the vote. This is the smallest percentage that could be gained by no more than two candidates.[7]

Now suppose there are w winners and a corresponding quota q. The election runs as above until we find the first winner. When a candidate exceeds the vote quota, single transferable vote rules specify that the winner's surplus—that is, the number of votes the candidate receives over the quota—be redistributed to the voters' second-place choices. We call the surplus s, where $s = $ *total votes received* $- q$, and divide it up using the following method: the winner receives a score of q and is then deleted from the ballots. Next, we tabulate who receives the transferred votes, but count them not as one full point, but as $s/(s + q)$. This weighting ensures that the sum of all candidate's scores remains equal to the number of votes originally cast, which in turn guarantees that we do not exceed w winners (recall that we chose the quota big enough so that not more than w candidates could control a share q). If the transferred votes result in another winner, we repeat the surplus distribution process for the new winner. The election ends when w candidates reach the quota.[8]

One attractive feature of single transferable vote in a multi-winner election stems from the fact that it theoretically leads to proportional representation. A united minority can elect candidates in proportion to the size of the minority, ensuring diverse representation and avoiding tyranny of the majority. Suppose a region can elect six representatives. Any candidate who can control 17 percent of the vote will win, so that of course a dominant majority candidate will win, but beyond that, a candidate ranked second or third by a majority may or may not defeat a candidate with a small but loyal minority base. Also, unlike cumulative voting, there is no need to coordinate. If two candidates appeal to the same group, some voters can rank them 1 and 2 and the others 2 and 1, and the group will not lose its voice. In particular, single transferable vote avoids gerrymandering district lines to ensure minority representation (as discussed in Pildes and Niemi, 1993). If congressional elections were done on a statewide basis using single transferable vote, there would by no need to engage in the time-consuming and controversial act of redistricting following each census.

Coombs voting

Clyde Coombs (1964) suggests a variant of the alternative vote. In successive rounds, instead of deleting the candidate with the fewest first-place votes, we eliminate the candidate with the most last-place votes. The election ends when only the desired number of winners remains. Unlike Hare voting, where candidates may qualify as winners in early rounds, Coombs voting always requires the full number of rounds. Duncan Black (1958, p. 69) describes an identical scheme called "exhaustive voting", which requires voters to approve all but one of the remaining candidates in each round. After each round of voting, the candidate with the fewest votes is eliminated. Again, the election ends when we reach the desired number of winners.[9]

Coombs voting loses some of its appeal in the light of analysis by Myerson (1993) and Cox (1990). Under Coombs voting, a candidate who takes a stance favored by a majority of voters may lose if all the other candidates take the opposite position. For example, suppose 75 percent of the electorate favors a certain proposition, but only one of five candidates supports it. The views of the candidates are identical on all other issues. Then 25 percent of the voters will rank the differing candidate last, while the majority, the 75 percent, if they split their last votes equally, give each of the other four candidates less than 20 percent of the last place votes. Even though 75 percent of the electorate agreed with the proposition, the candidate in favor will be the first eliminated.

PAIRED-COMPARISONS RULES

Borda voting

Jean-Charles de Borda, in a paper that marks the beginning of serious study in voting theory, proposed this elementary rule to the French Academy of Sciences in 1770. Suppose there are k candidates. Voters submit their rankings, and candidates receive $k-1$ points for every first place vote, $k-2$ points for every second place vote, and so on. We rank the candidates by their total points. Borda voting is a familiar scheme and is widely used to rank candidates or teams—the AP football poll is one example. Since every point a candidate receives may be considered a head-to-head vote against some other candidate, Borda scores are equal to the total number of head-to-head votes a candidate receives. This means we can count Borda scores by writing a paired-comparisons matrix and summing the rows to generate the candidates' scores.[10]

Interestingly, a Condorcet winner will not necessarily win a Borda election. We show a very simple example of this phenomenon with the pairwise-comparisons matrix and three candidates:

	a	b	c	Borda	a	b	c
a	0	51	51	Scores	102	114	84
b	49	0	65	a is a Condorcet winner but			
c	49	35	0	b wins under Borda rules.			

Here, the Condorcet winner a defeats b and c by a minimal margin, 51–49, while b beats c, 65–35. This election raises the question of whether one winner is intrinsically better than the other. As b beats c so decisively, we can be fairly sure that b is preferable to c, but less sure about the contests involving a. On a different day, with slightly different voter turnout, b or c might well beat a, but it is unlikely that c would beat b. In such cases, the Borda winner may have a better claim on the election (as Peyton Young discusses in this issue).

We should note that there are a infinite number of possible variations to the basic Borda scheme.[11] For example, the choice of a linear point system is somewhat arbitrary; there is no reason to suppose that ordinal rankings should translate neatly into linear preferences. By manipulating the point values, we could arrive at dozens of alternative schemes.

Additional variations to Borda can be created by coupling it with other systems such as Coombs voting. E. J. Nanson, an Australian mathematician, worked on voting theory between 1875 and 1922. He proposed a variation of Borda voting that applies the Borda score in successive rounds. Under the Nanson rule, any candidate with a below-average Borda score is eliminated.[12] We then recompute Borda scores and repeat the elimination procedure. The last remaining candidate wins the election. This resembles Coombs voting as described earlier, except that low Borda scores substitute for last-place votes.

Copeland voting

A. H. Copeland (1951) proposed the obvious paired-comparisons scheme where candidates are scored by their win–loss record across all head-to-head competitions. Employing the win–loss matrix, we sum the rows to determine each candidate's Copeland score. The sum of row i is equal to the number of pairwise wins candidate i has minus the number of losses. Equivalently, we might rank candidates by their winning percentages.

An example of Copeland scoring in sports occurs when competitors play a round-robin, and the teams or individuals are ranked by their number of victories. The first rounds of the Olympic hockey competition and the World Cup finals use this method.[13] When we use a Copeland system, we must also adopt a contingency plan for ties, since they may occur in the case of a cycle. Both the Olympic and the World Cup use total goals as a tiebreaker.

We might say intuitively that since professional sports leagues rank teams by winning percentages, they are using Copeland rules; but, if we consider each game between two teams as equivalent to the decision of a single voter, they are actually using Borda scoring. That is, teams are ranked by their total number of victories (or votes) over all head-to-head contests. In baseball, for example, teams in the same league play each other either 12 or 13 times each season, and 12 or 13 decisions are scored—under Copeland scoring, the winner of the season series would get one point. Of course in sports, rather than having ballots with rankings, we are truly interested in observing the $n(n-1)/2$ pairwise contests separately.

A Copeland winner must defeat all other candidates if a Condorcet winner exists. Even when there is no Condorcet winner, the Copeland winner dominates every other candidate in the sense that he either defeats him directly or defeats a third candidate who defeats him (Maurer, 1978; Miller, 1980). We say he can defeat any other candidate through a chain of length one or two.[14] However, just as several candidates might tie for first in a Copeland election, more than one candidate could dominate each of the others through a chain of length one or two.

Minimum violations

Minimum violations is the first computationally difficult method we cover. After voters rank the candidates, we tabulate the head-to-head votes to determine the winner of each matchup. We then consider each permutation of the candidates a, b, c, and so on, as a potential ranking. The best ranking, according to the minimum violations criteria, is the permutation that has the fewest "contradictions," where by contradiction we mean that a candidate with lower rank defeats a candidate with higher rank.

One method to compute a minimum violations ranking is to use the win–loss matrix and maximize the sum of the entries above the diagonal by permuting the rows and columns. From this algorithm, we can see that the winning list of candidates will never display the feature that a candidate is ranked *immediately* above another who defeated her head-to-head. If this were the case, the list that switches only these two candidates would result in one less violation and no other changes.

If there are no cycles, the minimum violations results will be identical to the Copeland ranking, and this order will be a zero violations ranking. Problems can arise if there are voting cycles, because in this instance a zero violations ranking does not exist, the best ranking is not necessarily unique, and the minimum violations criterion provides no particular way of resolving these ambiguities.

Ranked pairs

Condorcet's (1785) seminal paper expresses the idea that a candidate who would defeat each of the others head-to-head should win the election. If no such candidate exists, then large majorities should take precedence over small majorities in breaking cycles. In his own words, the general rule was "to take successively all the propositions that have a majority, beginning with those possessing the largest. As soon as these first decisions produce a result, it should be taken as a decision, without regard for the less probable decisions that follow". How is this idea implemented? Consider all the possible lists that order the candidates from top to bottom. Find the largest margin of victory in any pairwise match—and then eliminate all potential rankings that contradict this preference. For example, if the largest victory is for candidate a over candidate b, eliminate all potential rankings which place b above a. Next, consider the second largest margin of victory, and eliminate all potential rankings that disagree. Continue this process until only one ranking remains.

With only three candidates, this method is well defined and is equivalent to ignoring the election with the smallest margin of victory. The problem is that in elections with four or more candidates, considering the largest unconsidered margin of victory may, at some point, force us to eliminate all remaining potential rankings (by locking in a cycle). Condorcet does not discuss this possibility, an omission which has led to criticism and some confusion.

T. N. Tideman suggests one solution to the dilemma of cycles: simply skip over a head-to-head result that will lock in a cycle. Tideman further notes that if ties exist, there may be more than one potential ranking left even after we have considered all victories. In this case, we declare a tie among the candidates who have first-place ranks in the remaining potential rankings. Tideman calls this scheme "ranked pairs."

In the pairwise-comparisons matrix below, we first lock in $a > b$, then $b > c$. This implies that $a > c$. The next largest victory is $c > a$, but this locks in a cycle, so we ignore that head-to-head result. We then lock in $a > d$, $b > d$, $c > d$, which leaves us with a final ranking $a > b > c > d$.

	a	b	c	d
a	0	61	41	51
b	39	0	60	51
c	59	40	0	51
d	49	49	49	0

We further discuss this example in the Kemeny–Young section.

Simpson–Kramer min–max rule

The Simpson–Kramer min–max rule adheres to the principles offered by Condorcet in that it emphasizes large majorities over small majorities. A candidate's "max" score is the largest number of votes against that candidate across all head-to-head matchups. The rule selects the candidates with the minimum max score. A Condorcet winner will always be a min–max winner. When there is a cycle, we can think of the min–max winner as being the "least-objectionable" candidate. It is the person whose biggest defeat is the closest to 50:50. Large majorities take precedence over small majorities in that we are willing to ignore defeats if they are close enough to 50:50.

While the min–max rule works well for choosing the winner of an election, it may be less effective as a ranking technique, especially when a dominant Condorcet winner exists. In the election below, candidate a defeats all others by a large margin. As a result, the other candidates are ranked solely by their performances against a, while their head-to-head matchups are disregarded. Despite beating b and c head-to-head, candidate d places last in the election by virtue of having the poorest score against a.

	a	b	c	d
a	0	61	63	64
b	39	0	49	45
c	37	51	0	44
d	36	55	56	0

Min–Max	a	b	c	d
Scores	39	61	63	64

Kemeny–Young method

H. Peyton Young (1988) concluded that Condorcet intended to rank candidates in the order with which the most voters agree. In other words, we should maximize the number of head-to-head votes that agree with the ranking (or minimize the number of votes that disagree). As it turns out, Kemeny (1959) had suggested a method identical to the Young interpretation.

Kemeny–Young voting is very similar to the minimum violations method, except that it emphasizes decisive wins over smaller majority margins. Again, begin by considering all possible rankings of the candidates. However, instead of maximizing the sum of the entries in the upper diagonal of the win–loss matrix, Kemeny–Young voting uses the paired-comparisons matrix. The example nearby demonstrates this process. The left-hand pairwise-comparisons matrix shows the original rankings. The sum of entries in the upper right half is $51 + 45 + 58 + 53 + 44 + 49 = 300$. Note that a cycle exists in these rankings: $c > a$, $d > c$, and $a > d$. Kemeny–Young resolves this cycle by placing $c > a$, $a > d$ and $c > d$. In the right-hand matrix, the sum of the upper diagonal is $55 + 49 + 47 + 58 + 51 + 56 = 316$.

	a	b	c	d			c	a	d	b
a	0	51	45	58		c	0	55	49	47
b	49	0	53	44	$\Rightarrow$	a	45	0	58	51
c	55	47	0	49		d	51	42	0	56
d	42	56	51	0		b	53	49	44	0

How do these rankings make c end up first? After all, although c beats a decisively, it loses to both b and d. Well, c must beat a, because the largest majorities must be respected. However, c cannot be *immediately* ahead of either b or d. Just as in the minimum violations ranking, a candidate cannot be ranked directly above another candidate who defeated her head-to-head. If c must be ahead of a, but cannot be one place ahead of either b or d, then the one possible position for c is first. Because a defeats d decisively, we place a ahead of d, and the rest follows. If b or d complain that they "should" have won the election, based on pairwise results with c, the Kemeny–Young answer is that both b and d clearly deserve to be defeated by a, and thus have a weak claim to victory.

When there is a Condorcet winner, Kemeny–Young and minimum violations both rank that winner first. Differences appears when there are cycles. The minimum violations winner in the above election is not c, but a. Minimum violations actually ranks c last.

It is also interesting to compare the min–max and Kemeny–Young methods. Again both will rank a Condorcet winner first. But if there is a cycle, the Kemeny–Young and the min–max rule may not agree on the winner: and even if a Condorcet winner exists, they may not rank the lower candidates in the same order. In the example above, the min–max ranking is *cabd*; the Kemeny–Young rank is *cadb*. Examples can readily be created where the two methods pick dramatically different winners. In the example in the ranked-pairs section, candidate d, who receives 49 votes in each pairwise competition, is the min–max winner, and yet places last under Kemeny–Young rules. This disparity makes sense in that a, b, and c are locked in a cycle. It would be hard to make an argument that candidate d should be inserted into the middle of the cycle rather than placed above or below it. Interestingly, Caplin and Nalebuff (1988) prove that in a spatial voting model—where voters each have a most preferred point and each candidate occupies a position in Euclidean space—this outcome could not occur. In particular, the ranked-pairs winner will agree with the min–max winner because no cycle can occur if we restrict attention to majorities larger than the biggest margin involving the min–max winner.

METHODS DERIVED FROM SPORTS TOURNAMENTS

Kendall–Wei/power rank method

Kendall–Wei extends the Copeland method by attempting to account not only for a candidate's head-to-head wins but for the strength of the candidates beaten. To find the Kendall–Wei scores, we begin by giving each candidate a score equal to that candidate's number of pairwise wins. We then give each candidate a second score equal to the number of wins earned by candidates she defeated. In the third iteration, each candidate's score equals the sum of the second round scores of the candidates she defeated. The process continues; at each stage, the candidate's score is equal to the sum of the previous round scores of the candidates she defeated. This results in each candidate having an infinite sequence of scores. As it turns out, these sequences converge, and we call the convergent limits Kendall–Wei scores.

It would be impossible to carry these calculations ad infinitum. Fortunately, we can find the limits of these sequences through an elegant shortcut. Writing the win–loss matrix and counting 1 point for wins and 0 for losses (instead of -1), we find the eigenvector v associated with the largest positive eigenvalue of the matrix. If W is the win–loss matrix, and l is the largest possible eigenvector, we find a vector v, where $Wv = lv$. This vector is the candidates' Kendall–Wei scores.

This method only works if there is a cycle, otherwise the matrix W will have no nonzero eigenvalues. We present an example with a cycle below:

$$W = \begin{array}{c|cccc} & a & b & c & d \\ \hline a & 0 & 1 & 1 & 1 \\ b & 0 & 0 & 1 & 0 \\ c & 0 & 0 & 0 & 1 \\ d & 0 & 1 & 0 & 0 \end{array} \qquad l = 1 \qquad v = \begin{array}{c|c} a & 3 \\ b & 1 \\ c & 1 \\ d & 1 \end{array}$$

Because the Kendall–Wei method does not resolve cycles, we offer an extension called the power rank method. This compares to Kendall–Wei except that it uses the paired-comparisons matrix rather than the win–loss matrix, and does not require a voting cycle. Given the paired-comparisons matrix A, power rank scores are defined by the eigenvector belonging to the matrix's largest positive eigenvalue. We present an example below:

$$W = \begin{array}{c|cccc} & a & b & c & d \\ \hline a & 0 & 7 & 6 & 9 \\ b & 3 & 0 & 7 & 4 \\ c & 4 & 3 & 0 & 8 \\ d & 1 & 6 & 2 & 0 \end{array} \qquad l \sim 13.9 \qquad v \sim \begin{array}{c|c} a & 34 \\ b & 24 \\ c & 25 \\ d & 17 \end{array}$$

In this election, candidate a dominated the other candidates, and receives by far the highest power ranking. Although b beats c convincingly, 7–3, c earns the highest power score by virtue of stronger performances against a and d. As a comparison, the Borda method would agree with the power rank method, while the Kemeny–Young and ranked-pairs rules would rank b above c. The min–max rule, the Copeland rule, and the minimum violations method would place them in a tie.

Jech method (maximum likelihood estimation)

The Jech method, also proposed by Zermelo (1929), Bradley and Terry (1952), and Ford (1957), is a probabilistic ranking method. Jech's (1983) goal is to provide an ordering of the candidates that not only demonstrates whether i is superior to j, but also by how much. Each candidate i is given a strength T_i. Given these strengths, Jech defines a probability matrix p where the probability that i defeats j in a pairwise election (or game) is $pij = T_i/(T_i + T_j)$. Jech makes two assumptions: first, that odds multiply and second, that expected wins equal actual wins. Jech proves that only one matrix exists that satisfies this criteria. Candidates (or teams) receive a score equal to their expected winning percentage. In an election, this ranking is equivalent to the Copeland method. This can be viewed as an independent argument for using the Jech method. For sports teams, Jech's method works even if not all teams play one another. In this case, Jech's method predicts the number of wins a team might have in a full round-robin tournament (essentially an expected Copeland score).

CHOOSING AN APPROPRIATE VOTING SYSTEM

In the examples we looked at, there was surprisingly little difference between the winners under the various election methods. We tested nine of the methods—plurality, single transferable vote, Borda, Copeland, min–max, Kendall-Wei, power ranking, minimum violations, and Kemeny–Young—using voting data from British union elections. All elections were multi-candidate elections where voters ranked their preferences. With the exception of plurality rule, all the other methods obtained similar results. Plurality rule frequently resulted in a different winner than the other methods, and single transferable vote occasionally led to a different outcome. The other methods essentially differed only when there was a voting cycle, and even then, it did not affect the winner. While rankings were not identical, a Condorcet winner typically emerged, and this winner tended to be the Borda winner as well.

Given the variety of election formats, and that their results do not differ so dramatically, it is natural to ask how to choose among them. The answer may depend on which features of a voting rule are most important in a particular situation. We consider five aspects that distinguish the various methods.

Level of complexity

A voting method should be relatively simple and transparent, both for voters and for those calculating the winner. The tolerable level of complexity depends on how many voters and candidates there are, who the voters are, and what purpose the election serves.

Simplicity helps explain why plurality voting is so widespread and why approval voting and Borda voting are the two most frequently used alternatives. The US presidential election is something of an anomaly to this principle of simplicity—hence the periodic calls for a direct (plurality) election to replace the electoral college. In some cases, we accept greater complexity to gain accuracy. For example, the professional tennis rankings and *The New York Times* college football rankings (forms of power ranking) both require a computer for calculation. They can account for a great deal of information, much more than if we ranked tennis players simply by total matches won or tournaments won.

Voting in a single transferable vote election is straightforward: the main hurdle would be explaining the vote-counting procedure to voters and establishing the legitimacy of the system. Here, charts can be extremely useful. Edwin Newman and Miles Rogers (1952), in their analysis of the 1951 Cambridge city election, compare cumulative voting outcomes where the voters are given between 1 and 9 votes (there were nine city council seats). In their chart, presented as Table 1, we see how the candidates move up and down the rankings as voters are allowed more choices. The graph clearly demonstrates the importance of second, third and lower-place choices in capturing voter preferences. Note how candidate 20 rises from seventh to second place, candidate 06 rises from eighteenth to eighth position, and candidate 14 drops from fifth to twelfth.

This issue of how voters express preferences on a ballot is separate from how the preferences are combined. When a corporate board votes on a set of well-defined proposals, it would be reasonable to ask the board members to rank their preferences. A board member would presumably be well informed and interested, so we could use a more involved paired-comparisons technique to determine the winning choice. On the other hand, in an election for student government, with many candidates and mostly disinterested voters, ranking candidates could be capricious. Instead, we might ask voters to approve or disapprove each candidate, or approve a set number, or just pick their favorite. Simplicity is a relative term.

Voter strategies

In an election, the possibility always exists for voters to cast their ballots strategically, rather than in accordance with their true preferences. All voting systems are susceptible to strategizing. For example, in a three-candidate plurality election, a voter might vote for her second choice if her preferred candidate lags far behind in preelection polls. An honest vote might be considered "wasted." Another person might vote for the lagging candidate as a protest vote, even if she did not prefer that candidate over the others. Or suppose two of the three candidates—the ones with relatively similar views—are running neck and neck. Supporters of the first might rank their candidate first and the other last, even if in truth they would have chosen the other as their second choice. In recognition of this danger of strategizing, Borda wrote that his method was appropriate only for honest voters. For this reason, Borda counting works well when there is little incentive to strategize—for example, in the AP sports poll where writers, in general, have no vested interest in the outcome of the poll.

Voter strategizing provides a counterargument to the benefit of simplicity; the more complex schemes are harder to strategize and by their very complexity may help promote honest behavior.

Table 1. Plurality count with each number of choices

Rank	PR count	1	2	3	4	5	6	7	8	9
1	03	03	03	03	03	03	03	03	03	03
2	25	25	25	20	20	20	20	20	20	20
3	05	23	20	25	05	05	05	05	05	05
4	20	05	05	05	25	25	25	25	11	11
5	23	14	23	23	23	23	11	11	25	25
6	11	26	26	26	26	11	23	23	23	23
7	14	20	14	07	11	26	26	26	26	26
8	07	11	11	11	07	07	07	07	07	06
9	26	17	07	14	14	14	14	14	06	07
10	17	27	17	17	17	17	17	08	08	08
11	27	08	27	27	08	08	08	17	14	18
12	08	07	15	08	27	02	06	06	18	14
13	15	15	08	15	02	27	02	18	17	17
14	01	01	01	02	15	06	18	02	02	16
15	02	02	02	01	06	18	27	27	16	02
16	18	19	19	18	18	15	15	15	27	27
17	19	18	18	06	01	19	19	16	15	15
18	06	06	06	19	19	01	16	19	19	19
19	12	12	12	12	16	16	01	01	01	01
20	16	16	16	16	12	12	12	12	12	12
21	13	13	13	13	13	13	13	04	04	04
22	21	21	09	09	09	09	04	13	13	13
23	24	09	21	21	24	04	09	09	09	24
24	09	24	24	24	21	24	24	24	24	09
25	04	04	04	04	04	21	21	21	21	10
26	10	10	10	10	10	10	10	10	10	21
27	22	22	22	22	22	22	22	22	22	22

Chart showing rank of candidates under assumption of vote by varying number of choices. Numbers in the table refer to candidates.

Candidate strategies

Electoral systems may influence candidate strategies as well. In plurality voting, a minority candidate could win if two similar candidates split the majority vote. Because of this, some candidates would do better to generate strong minority support instead of trying to attract a majority vote. Cox (1987, 1990) confirms this suspicion, finding that candidates do best by solidifying minority support rather than taking centrist positions. Myerson (1993) shows that in a two-candidate plurality election, candidates fare best when exactly half the electorate are promised benefits above the average. As the number of candidates increases, Myerson demonstrates that the optimum strategy shifts: candidates do better by promising the bulk of the resources to a smaller and smaller minority, seeking to cultivate a small bloc of strong support rather than widespread appeal.

When there are only two candidates, the approval voting and plurality rule lead to the same incentives. As the number of candidates increases, the incentives are different under approval voting. Here, to win broad approval, the optimum campaign strategy is to spread the bulk of the resources over a larger and larger segment of the electorate.

For single transferable vote elections, more than one possible equilibrium exists. Candidates might opt to seek majority support, but they might also choose to cultivate minority support at the expense of the majority. Suppose all but one candidate offer a distribution of benefits to voters that equals the distribution that each of these candidates would have granted in a plurality election with four candidates. The final candidate offers a uniform distribution of benefits, seeking majority support. She will be the very first candidate eliminated, even though head-to-head she would defeat any of the others. If the final candidate chooses the optimum strategy for a five-candidate plurality election, she will rank first in each stage until only four candidates remain, but will face elimination at this stage, as all the other candidates have taken the optimum four-candidate strategy.

All paired-comparisons methods, including the Borda rule, offer candidates precisely the same incentives. Rather than encouraging candidates to seek minority support, candidates in a paired-comparisons election do best to appeal to a majority.[15] We see this intuitively if we look at the head-to-head comparisons as simultaneous two-candidate plurality elections, all of which are symmetric. A candidate wants to do well in each of these individual head-to-head contests, hence the two-candidate plurality strategy.

Ranking vs. picking a winner

In an election to fill an office, we care solely about determining one winner. In other elections, we need to elect several candidates. In a weekly football poll, the number one team matters, but we also want to know the rankings of the other teams as well. These different goals suggest different voting rules. Methods that use a good deal of the information available on the ballots, such as Kendall–Wei, power rank, Jech, Borda, Copeland, and Kemeny–Young work particularly well for ranking all the candidates. Each of these takes into account a candidate's or a team's head-to-head performance against each of the other teams. Kendall–Wei and Copeland count only wins and losses; the more complex of these ranking techniques, Jech, power rank, and Kemeny–Young, consider the margins of victory as well. Single transferable vote works well only when the quota is adjusted based on the number of candidates we seek to rank.

Plurality, approval voting, and min–max are better suited for choosing the winner of the election than ranking the candidates. Plurality works poorly for ranking mainly because it also takes into account only first-place rankings, and thus discards much of the available information. For example, a candidate who ranks second on every ballot, but first on none, probably deserves a relatively high rank, yet plurality gives that candidate zero votes. Min–max works poorly on the lower rankings when one candidate wins by an enormous margin. All the remaining candidates are then ranked solely by their performance against the strong candidate—because that will be their minimum vote—regardless of how they fare against each of the others. A candidate with only one head-to-head loss might wind up last with a bad enough defeat against the winner.

Minority support and the safe choice

Suppose a business wants to introduce a new brand of cereal. They do not want to market a cereal that everyone picks as the second or third best but no one picks first. Consumers will buy the cereal they like best. It doesn't matter whether they like a cereal second best or fifth best; they won't buy it. The company should market a cereal that generates strong preferences, even if some tasters rank it very low. Counting systems such as plurality or weighted Condorcet, which emphasize strong preferences, work better for product testing than methods such as min–max or Borda, which reward consensus and wide approval.

Elections are different from product testing. The usual goal is a candidate who appeals to a large portion of the electorate, rather than one who draws forceful support from a strong minority. When the objective is to pick a "safe" choice, systems like approval voting or min–max will favor the least objectionable over more controversial candidates. Similarly, Borda rewards strong preferences to an extent, but a winning Borda candidate will probably not have alienated a large minority. A candidate who places second or third on each ballot stands a strong chance in a Borda, approval or min–max election, even though such a candidate has little hope of winning a weighted Condorcet or plurality election.

CONCLUSION

If the multitude of available vote-counting systems leaves you overwhelmed, you are not alone. Several of the relatively simple schemes—such as single transferable vote,

Borda counting, min–max, Kemeny–Young, power ranking, and approval voting—possess qualities that are often desirable. Others, such as Copeland, minimum violations, or Jech may be useful for specific purposes. The diversity of questions we might ask about vote-counting procedures, their biases and their outcomes, is enormous. Many researchers, following Arrow's (1951) lead, have concerned themselves with stating various desirable or undesirable criteria and attempting to classify systems by these means. In contrast, there are far fewer papers written concerning the application of alternative systems in practice.

Despite the wealth of alternative voting mechanisms documented here, plurality rule remains the overwhelming favorite choice. Why do alternatives to plurality rule have such a difficult time being adopted?

Part of the answer is probably that when voter preferences are sufficiently similar, a variety of voting systems will lead to similar choices, and these choices will have desirable properties. In this case, the choice between voting systems will seem to make little difference. In many other cases, society does not have a consensus about what the goals of an electoral system should be. One is to establish legitimacy of the victor. A second is to encourage participation. A third may be to discourage the formation of a large number of political parties. A fourth is to assure a representative political system although the very definition of "representativeness" is part of the problem. For participants in the system, a fifth goal is often that "their side" improve its chances of winning.

No voting system will satisfy everyone on all of these dimensions; the choice is always between flawed alternatives. Between the entrenched power of the status quo, and with conflicting theoretical guidance to help select a second-best alternative, it is not surprising that electoral reform is difficult to implement. Most of the variety in electoral schemes comes from the choice of different metrics for measuring the distance between one ranking and another.

The Marquis de Condorcet (1785) believed that in an election, there exists some underlying truth to be discovered—that one candidate should be the "true" winner. We suggest a more modest conclusion, but one that might stop us from looking for some perfect Holy Grail of a voting method that meets all needs: a voting system can't find a consensus when none exists.

APPENDIX: ADDITIONAL VOTING RULES

Young method

Peyton Young, whose interpretation of Condorcet's work we have already described, proposed a separate method. Under the Young method, if there is no Condorcet winner, each candidate receives a score equal to the largest subset of voters for which that candidate is a Condorcet winner. The Young winner is the candidate with the highest score. In the example below, b is the Young as well as min–max winner.

Voters	Ballot
2	$a > b > c$
3	$b > c > a$
2	$b > a > c$
4	$c > a > b$

Young	a	b	c		a	b	c
				a	0	6	4
Scores	3	9	7	b	5	0	7
				c	7	4	0

Here, a defeats the others if we count the two ballots that rank a first and any one other ballot. To compute b's score, we count the 5 first-place ballots and any 4 of the others, for a score of 9. Finally, for c we count the 4 first-place ballots and any three of the others, for final scores of 3, 9, and 7. The final ranking is *bca*. This method is similar to the min–max rule and will produce the same winner so long as the number of last-place votes each candidate receives is at least as large as that candidate's largest loss margin in a head-to-head match (Tideman, 1993, ch. 13).

Dodgson rule

Charles Dodgson, mathematician and author of *Alice in Wonderland* (under the pen name Lewis Carroll) studied elections and lawn tennis tournaments at Oxford in the late 19th century. He agreed with Condorcet that a candidate who is undefeated head-to-head should win an election, but felt that if a Condorcet winner did not exist, the election should be called off. In discussing this opinion, he proposed this method of scoring candidates: if there is no Condorcet winner, the Dodgson rule holds that a candidate's score should be defined to be the total number of inversions on individual ballots necessary to make that candidate a Condorcet winner. More than one inversion may be needed on some ballots to make a candidate a Condorcet winner. This sounds difficult to compute, and it is.

A simplified Dodgson rule can be calculated directly from the paired-comparisons matrix. To compute the simplified Dodgson scores, we write the paired-comparisons matrix and for each candidate sum the vote difference in each of that candidate's head-to-head losses. The simplified Dodgson winner is the candidate who has the smallest total differential over all losses. The simplified Dodgson method bears a close similarity to the Borda rule, in that if we were to tabulate total differential over wins and losses, that is to sum the differential over all wins and subtract the simplified Dodgson scores, we would arrive at the Borda rankings.

Estimated centrality

Discussed by T. N. Tideman and I. G. Good in 1976 (Tideman, 1993), estimated centrality assumes that each candidate occupies some spatial position, and that voters likewise have some ideal preferred point in space. Under estimated centrality, the candidate who occupies that point in space closest to the "median," or zero moment, of the voters' ideal points wins the election. (We might, in fact, take any moment of the voter's ideal points—here we take the zero moment). Good and Tideman have proven that it is possible to use the fraction of voters who place the candidates in each of the possible orders to compute the estimated centrality winner, but the actual computation is still quite difficult.

NOTES

1. To give just the most simple example, if the population is uniformly distributed between positions 0 and 1, and we are to choose three representatives, should they be equally spaced [0.25, 0.5, and 0.75], or should they be selected so as to minimize the average distance traveled to the nearest legislator [0.16, 0.5, and 0.83]?
2. Many theorists have addressed the issue of how to deal with voters who either fail to rank some candidates, or rank two or more candidates as tied. Because of the immediate complications these issues generate, we try to avoid raising them in the general discussion. In a paired comparisons approach, there are basically two options when a voter ranks two or more candidates as tied. When we compare the candidates head-to-head, we can either ignore that voter, or give each candidate 1/2 point. If we do not count the voter, some head-to-head matches will have fewer total points than others. Since this leads to problems later, we could normalize all head-to-head scores so that a candidate's score is the percentage of the electorate won against the opponent. This method differs from giving each candidate 1/2 point in a tie. For example, if the score is 60 to 30 among 90 of the voters, with 10 ties, normalizing the scores results in a 66.6 to 33.3 election, while adding 1/2 point makes the score 65 to 35. What if a voter fails to rank some candidates? In our empirical work computing various schemes, we assume a ranked candidate is preferable to an unranked candidate. This means a single unranked candidate losses every head-to-head comparison and is effectively ranked last. If two or more candidates are unranked, we may place them in a tie for last place on the ballot and then treat the tie vote in one of the two ways described above.
3. If there is no Condorcet Winner, there must be a voting cycle, but not vice versa. An example of an election with a Condorcet winner and a cycle is $a > b$, $a > c$, $a > d$, $b > c$, $c > d$, $d > b$. Here a beats the other three candidates, who are in a cycle.
4. This argument is a bit specious, since nearly all votes are wasted in the sense that they do not determine the outcome of an election. And votes are equally well wasted on a party with a large lead. Evidence from the '94 elections suggests that Duverger's Law may be breaking down.
5. Endorsement of cumulative voting was one of the "radical" positions taken by Lani Guinier. For a popular discussion, see *The New York Times Magazine*, Feb. 27, 1994.
6. Actually, there is an upper bound on the number of players a sportswriter may list on his or her ballot. The limit is ten players, which is high enough that except in extraordinary years, the vote ceiling is rarely a factor.
7. In general, we define a quota $q = [n/(w + 1)] + 1$, where n is the number of voters, w is the desired number of winners, and the bracket notation $[x]$ means "greatest integer less than x". This choice achieves the goal of having the smallest possible quota such that no more than w candidates may exceed it.
8. In the Cambridge and New York elections, votes are hand counted, a practice fixed by law. Because of this, rather than assign transferred votes a weight of $s/(s + q)$, $s/(s + q)$ ballots are randomly selected as transferred votes, and count as one full vote. Clearly, this is less preferable, because it adds an element of randomness to the election. Even with this time-saving procedure, Cambridge city council elections have taken as long as a week to be counted.
9. It is easy to imagine other reverse elimination schemes. For example, the Nanson rule, which eliminates candidates based on their Borda scores, appears in the Appendix.

10. Obviously, from its original description, Borda voting could also be thought of as a rank-scoring rule.
11. Duncan Black (1958) proposed a compromise between Borda and Condorcet. Under the Black rule, we compare candidates based on their head-to-head performances. If a Condorcet winner exists, that candidate wins the election. Otherwise, the candidate with the highest Borda score wins.
12. If there are n voters and k candidates, the "average" score is $n(k/2)$.
13. In order to encourage aggressive offensive play, the World Cup now treats ties in a novel manner, awarding both teams one point. When one team wins a game, they receive three points to the loser's zero. Devaluing a tie is meant to provide both teams with incentives to play more exciting soccer.
14. However, Niemi and Riker (1976) note that under certain conditions, the Copeland method can choose as the winner a candidate who loses by near unanimity to the Borda winner.
15. Similarly, following Cox (1987), candidates have an incentive to adopt positions close to the political center. Cox uses a spatial model of voter preferences and shows that there is an equilibrium of candidate strategies when candidates adopt the position of the median voter.

REFERENCES

Ali, I., Cook, W. D. and Kress, M., On the minimum violations ranking of a tournament. *Management Science*, June 1986, **32**: 660–672.
Anderson, Lowell. Voting and paired comparisons. Extracted from Grotte, J., Anderson, I., and Robinson, M., Selected Judgmental Methods in Defense Analyses. Institute for Defense Analyses paper p. 2387, 1990.
Anderson, Lowell. How to Take Votes: New Ideas on Better Ways to Determine Winners, research draft, Institute for Defense Analyses, 1994.
Arrow, Kenneth J. *Social Choice and Individual Values,* New Haven: Yale University Press, 1951.
Black, Duncan. *The Theory of Committees and Elections.* London: Cambridge University Press, 1953.
Board of Elections, Cincinnati, Ohio. *Proportional Representation Count: Rules and Instructions to Employees,* 1955.
Bradley, R. A., and Terry, M. E. The rank analysis of incomplete block designs. I. The method of paired comparisons, *Biometrika*, 1952, **39**: 324–335.
Brams, Steven, and Nagel, Jack. Approval voting in practice, *Public Choice*, August 1991, **71**: 1–17.
Caplin, Andrew, and Nalebuff, Barry. On 64%-Majority Rule, *Econometrica*, July 1988, **56**: 787–814.
Caplin, Andrew, and Nalebuff, Barry. Aggregation and social choice: A mean voter theorem, *Econometrica*, January 1991, **59**, 1–24.
Condorcet, Marquis de. Essay on the application of mathematics to the theory of decision making, 1785. In Baker K., ed. *Condorcet: Selected Writings.* Indianapolis: Bobbs-Merrill, 1976.
Coombs, Clyde. *A Theory of Data.* New York: Wiley, 1964.
Copeland, A. H. *A 'Reasonable' Social Welfare Function,* mimeo, University of Michigan Seminar on Applications of Mathematics to the Social Sciences, 1951.
Cox, Gary W. Electoral equilibrium under alternative voting institutions, *American Journal of Political Science*, February 1987, **31**: 82–108.
Cox, Gary W. Centripetal and centrifugal incentives in electoral systems, *American Journal of Political Science*, November 1990, **34**: 903–935.
David, H. A. Ranking the players in a round robin tournament, *Review of the International Statistical Institute*, 1971, **39**(2): 137–147.
Ford, I. R. Solution of a ranking problem from binary comparisons," *American Mathematical Monthly*, 1957, **64**: 28–33.

Goddard, Steven T. Ranking in tournaments and group decision-making, *Management Science*, December 1983, **29**: 1384–1392.

Jech, Thomas. The ranking of incomplete tournaments: A mathematician's guide to popular sports, *American Mathematical Monthly*, 1983, **90**: 246–266.

Kemeny, John. Mathematics without numbers, *Daedalus*, Fall 1959, **88**: 571–591.

Maurer, Stephen B. *The King Chicken Theorems*, working paper, Princeton University Mathematics Department, 1978.

Miller, N. A new solution set for tournaments and majority voting, *American Journal of Political Science*, February 1980, **24**: 68–96.

Myerson, Roger. Incentives on cultivate favored minorities under alternative electoral systems, *American Political Science Review*, December 1993, **87**: 856–869.

Newman, Edwin B., and Rogers, Miles. *PR voting: An analysis of the 1951 Cambridge City election*, unpublished (available from Barry Nalebuff), 1952.

Neimi, Richard, and Riker, William. The choice of voting systems, *Scientific American*, 1976, **234**(6): 21–27.

Pildes, Richard, and Niemi, Richard. *Expressive Harms, 'Bizarre Districts,' and Voting Rights: Evaluating Election-District Appearances after Shaw*, working paper, University of Michigan Law School, 1993.

Rosenthal, Howard, and Sen, Subrata. Electoral participation in the French Fifth Republic, *American Political Science Review*, March 1973, **67**: 29–54.

Stob, Michael. A supplement to 'A Mathematician's Guide to Popular Sports,' *American Mathematical Monthly*, May 1984, **91**: 277–282.

Tideman, Nicolaus. *Collective Decisions and Voting*, draft, March 1993.

Young, H. Peyton. Condorcet's Theory of Voting, *American Political Science Review*, December 1988, **82**: 1231–1244.

Zermelo, E. Die berechnung der Turnier-Ergebnisse als ein maximumproblem der wahrscheinlichkeitsrechnung, *Math. Z.*, 1929, **29**: 436–460.

Subject Index

Name Index

Abraham, Katharine, 363n
Abreu, D., 73–74, 405
Adams, William James, xx, 244
Addison, J.T., 85
Admati, A.R., 84
Agathon, 439
Agnew, Spiro T., 470
Aigner, Dennis, 325
Aivazian, V.A., 52n
Aizerman, Mark, 457n
Akerlof, George A., xxi, 90, 133, 191n, 285, 297, 300n, 301, 307, 311, 317– 318, 330, 337, 342, 344, 347–348, 355n, 358n, 362n
Alcaly, Roger, 355n
Alchian, Armen, xii–xiv, xxiv n, xxv n, 3, 122, 136
Aleskerov, Fuad, 457n
Allais, Maurice, 171–172
Allen, Beth, 178, 383
Allen, Franklin, 335, 337, 350, 358n
Anand, Sudhir, 458n
Anderson, Lowell, 468, 470
Anderson, O.W., 294n
Angell, F.J., 295n
Annable, James E., 337
Archibald, G.C., 280
Aristotle, 439
Arkes, Hal R., 188
Arneson, Richard, 457n
Arnott, Richard, 331, 346, 357n, 361n
Arrow, Kenneth, xxiii–xxiv, 118, 125, 127, 134, 137, 142, 145, 148, 156, 167, 188, 190, 191n, 294n, 360n, 434, 438n, 439, 441–442, 447, 453, 455, 456n, 458n, 467, 469, 485
Ashenfelter, O., 84–85, 92n
Atkinson, Anthony, 446, 456n, 458n
Aumann, Robert, 52n
Auster, Richard, 20n
Azeridis, Costas, 361n

Bailey, Martin J., 137, 261n
Baldwin, R., 260n
Barberà, Salvador, 456n
Bar-Hillel, Maya, 187–188
Barro, Robert, 362n
Barzel, Yoram, 148
Basu, Kaushik, 457n, 459n
Battalio, Raymond C., 173
Baumol, William J., 122, 136, 412, 447
Bayard, Thomas F., 355
Becker, Gary S., 129, 133
Becker, Gordon M., 178, 192n
Becker, Selwyn W., 188
Bell, David E., 180, 191n
Benassy, J.P., 409n
Benoit, J.-P., 75
Berg, Joyce E., 179
Bergson, Abram, 441
Bergstrom, Theodore, 137
Bernheim, B.D., 63
Bernoulli, Daniel, 166
Bernoulli, Nicholas, 166
Bertrand, J., xxii–xxiii, xxv n, 379, 381, 384
Bertrand, P.V., 85
Besanko, David, 343
Bester, Helmut, 343
Bhattacharya, Sudipto, 360n
Binmore, Kenneth, xxv n, 63, 82, 91n, 456n
Black, Duncan, 447, 473, 488n
Blackorby, Charles, 456n, 458n
Blair, Douglas, 457n
Blau, Julian, 457n
Blinder, Alan, 350
Bliss, Christopher, 355n
Blyth, Colin R., 180
Bond, Eric W., xxi, 301, 307, 309n, 311
Borch, Karl H., xviii, xxv n, 118
Borda, Jean-Charles de, xxiv, 448, 474
Bordes, Georges, 457n
Boudreau, Bryan, 110
Bowles, Samuel, 335, 357n, 363n